THE ROUTLEDGE HANDBOOK OF THE COLD WAR

This new Handbook offers a wide-ranging overview of current scholarship on the Cold War, with chapters from many leading scholars.

The field of Cold War history has consistently been one of the most vibrant in the field of international studies. Recent scholarship has added to our understanding of familiar Cold War events, such as the Korean War, the Vietnam War, the Cuban Missile Crisis and superpower détente, and shed new light on the importance of ideology, race, modernization, and transnational movements.

The Routledge Handbook of the Cold War draws on the wealth of new Cold War scholarship, bringing together chapters on a diverse range of topics such as geopolitics, military power and technology and strategy. The chapters also address the importance of non-state actors, such as scientists, human rights activists and the Catholic Church, and examine the importance of development, foreign aid and overseas assistance.

The volume is organized into nine parts:

- **Part I:** The Early Cold War
- **Part II:** Cracks in the Bloc
- **Part III:** Decolonization and its Consequences
- **Part IV:** The Cold War in the Third World
- **Part V:** From Confrontation to Negotiation
- **Part VI:** Human Rights and Non-State Actors
- **Part VII:** Nuclear Weapons, Technology, and Intelligence
- **Part VIII:** Psychological Warfare, Propaganda, and Cold War Culture
- **Part IX:** The End of the Cold War

This new Handbook will be of great interest to all students of Cold War history, international history, foreign policy, security studies and IR in general.

Artemy M. Kalinovsky is Assistant Professor of East European Studies at the University of Amsterdam, the Netherlands, and is author of *A Long Goodbye: The Soviet Withdrawal from Afghanistan* (2011) and co-editor of *The End of the Cold War in The Third World* (Routledge, 2011).

Craig Daigle is Associate Professor of History at the City College of New York, CUNY, USA, and is author of *The Limits of Détente: The United States, the Soviet Union, and the Arab–Israeli Conflict, 1969–1973* (2012).

THE ROUTLEDGE HANDBOOK OF THE COLD WAR

Edited by Artemy M. Kalinovsky and Craig Daigle

LONDON AND NEW YORK

First published 2014
by Routledge
2 Park Square, Milton Park, Abingdon, Oxon, OX14 4RN

and by Routledge
711 Third Avenue, New York, NY 10017

Routledge is an imprint of the Taylor & Francis Group, an informa business

© 2014 selection and editorial material, Artemy M. Kalinovsky and Craig Daigle; individual chapters, the contributors

The right of the editor to be identified as the author of the editorial material, and of the authors for their individual chapters, has been asserted in accordance with sections 77 and 78 of the Copyright, Designs and Patents Act 1988.

All rights reserved. No part of this book may be reprinted or reproduced or utilised in any form or by any electronic, mechanical, or other means, now known or hereafter invented, including photocopying and recording, or in any information storage or retrieval system, without permission in writing from the publishers.

Trademark notice: Product or corporate names may be trademarks or registered trademarks, and are used only for identification and explanation without intent to infringe.

British Library Cataloguing in Publication Data
A catalogue record for this book is available from the British Library

Library of Congress Cataloging in Publication Data
The Routledge handbook of the Cold War /
edited by Artemy Kalinovsky, Craig A. Daigle.
pages cm
Includes bibliographical references and index.
1. Cold War--Handbooks, manuals, etc. 2. Military history, Modern--20th century--Handbooks, manuals, etc. 3. World politics--1989---Handbooks, manuals, etc. I. Kalinovsky, Artemy M., editor. II. Daigle, Craig, editor.
D843.R675 2014
909.82'5--dc23
2013041409

ISBN: 978-0-415-67701-1 (hbk)
ISBN: 978-1-315-88228-4 (ebk)

Typeset in Bembo
by Saxon Graphics Ltd, Derby

Printed and bound by CPI Group (UK) Ltd, Croydon, CR0 4YY

CONTENTS

Notes on contributors   ix
List of abbreviations   xiii
Introduction – Craig Daigle and Artemy M. Kalinovsky   xvii

PART I
The Early Cold War   1

1 Incompatible Universalisms: The United States, the Soviet Union, and the Beginning of the Cold War   3
Mario Del Pero

2 Fear, Want, and the Internationalism of the Early Cold War   17
Amanda Kay McVety

3 The Early Cold War and its Legacies   32
Vojtech Mastny

PART II
Cracks in the Bloc   43

4 Polish Communism, the Hungarian Revolution, and the Soviet Union   45
Anita J. Prażmowska

5 Berlin and the Cold War Struggle over Germany   56
Hope M. Harrison

6 The Sino-Soviet Split and its Consequences   74
Lorenz M. Lüthi

PART III
Decolonization and its Consequences — 89

7 Decolonization and the Cold War — 91
   Ryan M. Irwin

8 Vietnam and the Global Cold War — 105
   Jessica M. Chapman

9 Modernization and Development — 118
   Nathan J. Citino

PART IV
The Cold War in the Third World — 131

10 The Cold War in Latin America — 133
    Tanya Harmer

11 The Cold War in Africa — 149
    Jeffrey James Byrne

12 The Cold War in the Middle East — 163
    Paul Thomas Chamberlin

13 The Cold War in South and Central Asia — 178
    Artemy M. Kalinovsky

PART V
From Confrontation to Negotiation — 193

14 The Era of Détente — 195
    Craig Daigle

15 Zhou Enlai and the Sino-American Rapprochement, 1969–1972 — 209
    Yafeng Xia

16 The Conference on Security and Cooperation in Europe: A Reappraisal — 223
    Angela Romano

PART VI
Human Rights and Non-State Actors — 235

17 Human Rights and the Cold War — 237
    Sarah B. Snyder

18 U.S. Scientists and the Cold War — 249
    Paul Rubinson

19 The Catholic Church and the Cold War — 259
    Piotr H. Kosicki

PART VII
Nuclear Weapons, Technology, and Intelligence — 273

20 Nuclear Weapons and the Cold War — 275
    Ruud van Dijk

21 Technology and the Cold War — 292
    Elidor Mëhilli

22 Intelligence and the Cold War — 305
    Ben de Jong

PART VIII
Psychological Warfare, Propaganda, and Cold War Culture — 321

23 Propaganda and the Cold War — 323
    Nicholas J. Cull and B. Theo Mazumdar

24 The Cold War and Film — 340
    Andrei Kozovoi

25 Soviet Studies and Cultural Consumption — 351
    Sergei I. Zhuk

PART IX
The End of the Cold War — 369

26 Explanations for the End of the Cold War — 371
    Artemy M. Kalinovsky and Craig Daigle

27 Humanitarian Aid, Soft Power, and the End of the Cold War in Poland 388
    Gregory F. Domber

28 Neoliberalism, Consumerism and the End of the Cold War 401
    David Priestland

Bibliography *416*
Index *425*

CONTRIBUTORS

Jeffrey James Byrne is Assistant Professor of History at the University of British Columbia. He works on modern international history, particularly as it concerns Africa, the Middle East, and the developing world. His book, *Mecca of Revolution: Algeria, Decolonization, and the Third World's Cold War*, is forthcoming from Oxford University Press.

Paul Thomas Chamberlin is Associate Professor of History at the University of Kentucky. He is author of *The Global Offensive: The United States, the Palestine Liberation Organization and the Making of the Post-Cold War Order* (Oxford University Press, 2012). He is now working on a history of the Cold War in the Third World.

Jessica M. Chapman is Assistant Professor of History at Williams College. She is author of *Cauldron of Resistance: Ngo Dinh Diem, the United States, and 1950s Southern Vietnam* (Cornell University Press, 2013). Her current project explores the commodification of Kenyan runners in Europe, the United States, and the Middle East.

Nathan J. Citino is Associate Professor of History at Colorado State University and the Associate Editor of *Diplomatic History*. He is the author of *From Arab Nationalism to OPEC: Eisenhower, King Sa'ud, and the Making of U.S.-Saudi Relations* (Indiana University Press, second edition 2010). His current book project is entitled "Envisioning the Arab Future: Modernization in U.S.-Arab Relations, 1945–1967."

Nicholas J. Cull is Professor of Public Diplomacy at the University of Southern California's Annenberg School for Communication. His works include *The Decline and Fall of the United States Information Agency: American Public Diplomacy, 1989–2001* (Palgrave, 2012) and *The Cold War and the United States Information Agency: American Propaganda and Public Diplomacy, 1945–1989* (Cambridge University Press, 2008). He is currently editor of *The Journal of Place Branding and Public Diplomacy* and president of the International Association for Media and History.

Craig Daigle is Associate Professor of History at the City College of New York. He is author of *The Limits of Détente: The United States, the Soviet Union and the Arab-Israeli Conflict,*

1969–1973 (Yale University Press, 2012). He is currently working on a textbook on the Cold War, forthcoming from Yale University Press.

Mario Del Pero is Professor of International History at the Institut d'Études politiques de Paris-Sciences Po. Among his recent works are *Libertà e Impero: Gli Stati Uniti e il Mondo, 1776–2011* [*Empire and Liberty: The United States and the World, 1776–2011*] (Rome-Bari, Laterza, 2011), and *The Eccentric Realist: Henry Kissinger and the Shaping of American Foreign Policy*, (Cornell University Press, 2010). He is currently working on a study of transnational anti-nuclear activism in the late 1970s/early 1980s.

Ruud van Dijk is Assistant Professor of History at the University of Amsterdam. He is the senior editor of the *Encyclopedia of the Cold War* (Routledge, 2008), and co-editor of *The Long 1968: Revisions and New Perspectives* (Indiana University Press, 2013). In 2013, he was a visiting fellow at the Woodrow Wilson International Center for Scholars, working on his project on the Euromissile Crisis of the late 1970s and early 1980s.

Gregory F. Domber is Assistant Professor of History at the University of North Florida. He was a Hewlett Post-doctoral Fellow at Stanford University's Center on Democracy, Development, and the Rule of Law, and is the author of *Empowering Revolution: America, Poland, and the End of the Cold War* (University of North Carolina Press, 2014).

Tanya Harmer is Lecturer in International History at the London School of Economics specializing in the history of the Cold War in Latin America. She is the author of *Allende's Chile and the Inter-American Cold War* (University of North Carolina Press, 2011), which won the Latin American Studies Association Luciano Tomassini book award.

Hope M. Harrison is Associate Professor of History and International Affairs at George Washington University. She is the author of *Driving the Soviets Up the Wall: Soviet–East German Relations, 1953–1961* (Princeton University Press, 2003), which won the 2004 Marshall Shulman Book prize from the American Association for the Advancement of Slavic Studies. Her current book project examines how Germans are dealing with the East German past.

Ryan M. Irwin is Assistant Professor at the University at Albany, SUNY and writes about decolonization, global governance, and American foreign relations. He is the author of *Gordian Knot: Apartheid and the Unmaking of the Liberal World Order* (Oxford University Press, 2012). Currently, he is working on a comparative biography of the mid-1970s and an intellectual history of the nation-state in the twentieth century.

Ben de Jong is a retired lecturer from the University of Amsterdam, where he specialized in the history and politics of the Soviet Union and Russia. He also developed a special interest in intelligence history and was one of the founding members of the Netherlands Intelligence Studies Association (NISA) in 1991. He is co-editor of *The Future of Intelligence* (forthcoming).

Artemy M. Kalinovsky is Assistant Professor of East European Studies at the University of Amsterdam. He is the author of *A Long Goodbye: The Soviet Withdrawal from Afghanistan* (Harvard University Press, 2011), and co-editor, with Sergey Radchenko, of *The End of the Cold War and the Third World: New Perspectives of Regional Conflict* (Routledge, 2011).

Contributors

Piotr H. Kosicki is Assistant Professor of History at the University of Maryland at College Park. He is co-editor, with Justyna Beinek, of *Re-mapping Polish–German Historical Memory: Physical, Political, and Literary Spaces since World War II* (Slavica, 2011), and is currently finishing a manuscript entitled *Between Christ and Lenin: A European History of Poland, Catholicism, and the Social Question, 1891–1991*.

Andrei Kozovoi is Associate Professor in Russian history at the Lille 3 University (France). His publications include *Beyond the Wall: The Soviet Cold War Culture Between Two Détentes* (2009), *Russian Secret Services from the Tsars to Putin* (2010), and *The Fall of the Soviet Union, 1982–1991* (Tallendier, 2011). He is currently working on a comparative history of Cold War cinema, including US–Soviet film trade and various aspects related to film distribution and exhibition.

Lorenz M. Lüthi is Associate Professor of History at McGill University. He is the author of *The Sino-Soviet Split: Cold War in the Communist World* (Princeton University Press, 2008). He is currently working on a second book project which examines the regional Cold Wars in Europe, East Asia, and the Middle East.

Amanda Kay McVety is Associate Professor of History at Miami University. She is the author of *Enlightened Aid: U.S. Development as Foreign Policy in Ethiopia* (Oxford University Press, 2012). Her current research project examines the opening decades of the international effort to eradicate rinderpest.

Vojtech Mastny has been professor of history and international relations at Columbia University, Boston University, and the Johns Hopkins School of Advanced International Studies as well as coordinator of the Parallel History Project on NATO and the Warsaw Pact. His books include *Russia's Road to the Cold War* (Columbia University Press, 1979), and *The Cold War and Soviet Insecurity: The Stalin Years* (Oxford University Press, 1996).

B. Theo Mazumdar is completing his PhD at the University of Southern California's Annenberg School for Communication. His research interests include public diplomacy, media and foreign policy, journalism studies and U.S. domestic politics.

Elidor Mëhilli is Assistant Professor of History at Hunter College of the City University of New York. He has held fellowships at Columbia University and the University of Pennsylvania. He is currently writing a book on socialist globalization through the angle of Albania under Yugoslav, Soviet, Eastern bloc, and Chinese patronage.

Anita J. Prażmowska is Professor of International History at the London School of Economics. Her recent publications include *Civil War in Poland: 1943–1948* (Palgrave, 2004) and *Poland: A Modern History* (I.B. Tauris, 2010). A biography of Władysław Gomułka is forthcoming from I.B. Tauris.

David Priestland is University Lecturer in History at Oxford University and a Fellow of St Edmund Hall. He is author of *Stalinism and the Politics of Mobilization: Ideas, Power and Terror in Inter-war Russia* (Oxford University Press, 2007); *The Red Flag: Communism and the Making of the Modern World* (Allen Lane, 2009); and *Merchant, Soldier, Sage: A New History of Power* (Allen Lane, 2012).

Contributors

Angela Romano is Honorary Research Fellow in the School of Social and Political Sciences, University of Glasgow. Her main research interests include the Cold War, integration processes in Europe, East–West economic relations, and the Conference on Security and Cooperation in Europe (CSCE) process. She is the author of *From Détente in Europe to European Détente: How the West Shaped the Helsinki CSCE* (Peter Lang, 2009). Her second monograph, *The European Community and Eastern Europe in the Cold War*, will be published as part of Routledge's Cold War Series in late 2014.

Paul Rubinson is Assistant Professor of History at Bridgewater State University. His publications include "Crucified on a Cross of Atoms: Scientists, Politics, and the Test Ban Treaty," in *Diplomatic History*, April 2011, and "The Global Effects of Nuclear Winter: Science and Antinuclear Protest in the United States and the Soviet Union during the 1980s," forthcoming in *Cold War History*.

Sarah B. Snyder is a Lecturer in International History at University College London. Her first book, *Human Rights Activism and the End of the Cold War: A Transnational History of the Helsinki Network* (Cambridge University Press, 2011), won the 2012 Stuart L. Bernath Prize and the 2012 Myrna F. Bernath Book Award from the Society for Historians of American Foreign Relations.

Yafeng Xia is a guest professor at the Center for Cold War International History Studies, East China Normal University in Shanghai and Professor of History at Long Island University in New York. He is the author of *Negotiating with the Enemy: U.S.–China Talks during the Cold War, 1949–72* (2006) and many articles on Cold War history. He is at work on a book with Zhihua Shen, tentatively titled, "Friendship in Name Only: Mao Zedong, Kim Il Sung, and the Myth of Sino-North Korean Relations, 1949–1976."

Sergei I. Zhuk is Associate Professor of Russian and East European History at Ball State University. He is the author of *Russia's Lost Reformation: Peasants, Millennialism and Radical Sects in Southern Russia and Ukraine, 1830–1917* (Woodrow Wilson Center Press, 2004) and *Rock and Roll in the Rocket City: The West, Identity, and Ideology in Soviet Dniepropetrovsk, 1960–1985* (Johns Hopkins University Press and Woodrow Wilson Center Press, 2010). He is now writing a book about social and cultural history of American studies in the USSR.

ABBREVIATIONS

ABM	Anti Ballistic Missile system
AEC	Atomic Energy Commission
ANC	African National Congress
ANZUS	The Australia, New Zealand, United States Security Treaty
APRA	American Revolutionary Popular Alliance (Peru)
ARVN	Army of the Republic of Vietnam
ASA	Army Security Agency (US, predecessor of the NSA)
ASEAN	Association of Southeast Asian Nations
CARE	Cooperative for American Remittances to Europe
CBM	Confidence Building Measures
CCP	Chinese Communist Party
CDU	Christian Democratic Union
CELAM	Latin American Episcopal Conference
CENTCOM	United States Central Command
CENTO	Central Treaty Organization
CIA	Central Intelligence Agency (US)
CMEA	Council for Mutual Economic Aid (also known as Comecon)
CoCom	Coordinating Committee for Multilateral Export Controls
COMINFORM	Communist Information Bureau
COMINTERN	Communist International
CPE	Communist Party of Egypt
CPSU	Communist Party of the Soviet Union
CRS	Catholic Relief Services
CSCE	Conference on Security and Cooperation in Europe
DEFCON	Defense Readiness Condition
DRV	Democratic Republic of Vietnam
EC	European Community
ECOSOC	United Nations Economic and Social Council
EEC	European Economic Community
FAO	Food and Agriculture Organization
FBI	Federal Bureau of Investigation (US)

Abbreviations

FLN	Front de Libération Nationale (Algeria)
FMLN	Farabundo Martí National Liberation Front
FNLA	National Front for the Liberation of Angola
FRG	Federal Republic of Germany (West Germany)
FRUS	*Foreign Relations of the United States*
FSLN	Sandinista National Liberation Front
GATT	General Agreement on Tariffs and Trade
GDP	Gross Domestic Product
GDR	German Democratic Republic (East Germany)
GRU	Chief Intelligence Directorate (military intelligence, USSR)
HRW	Human Rights Watch
HUAC	House Committee on Un-American Activities (US)
Humint	Intelligence from Human Sources
IAEA	International Atomic Energy Agency
ICBM	Intercontinental Ballistic Missile
ICC	International Cancer Congress
IDF	Israel Defense Forces
IMF	International Monetary Fund
KCEP	Charitable Commission of the Polish Episcopate
KGB	Committee for State Security (USSR)
KMT	Chinese Nationalist Party
KPD	Communist Party of Germany
KPP	Polish Communist Party
MAD	Mutually Assured Destruction
MBFR	Mutual and Balanced Force Reduction
MBP	Ministry for Public Safety (Poland)
MI5	Military Intelligence, Section 5 (UK)
MIRV	multiple independently targetable reentry vehicles
MLF	Multilateral Force
MPLA	Popular Movement for the Liberation of Angola
MPT	Multilateral Preparatory Talks
NAACP	National Association for the Advancement of Colored People
NAS	National Academy of Sciences (US)
NATO	North Atlantic Treaty Organization
NGO	non-governmental organization
NKVD	People's Commissariat for State Security (KGB predecessor, USSR)
NLF	Front for the National Liberation of South Vietnam
NPG	Nuclear Planning Group (NATO)
NPT	Non-Proliferation Treaty
NSA	National Security Agency (US)
NSDD	National Security Decision Directive (US)
NWICO	New World International Communication Order
OAPEC	Organization of Arab Petroleum Exporting Countries
OAS	Organization of American States
OAU	Organization of African Unity
OPEC	Organization of the Petroleum Exporting Countries
OSCE	Organization for Security and Cooperation in Europe
OSS	Office of Strategic Services (CIA predecessor, US)

PACCF	Polish American Congress Charitable Foundation
PAIGC	African Party of Independence of Guinea and Cape Verde
PCF	French Communist Party
PCI	Italian Communist Party
PCP	Peruvian Communist Party
PGT	Guatemalan Workers' Party
PLA	People's Liberation Army (People's Republic of China)
PLO	Palestine Liberation Organization
PRC	People's Republic of China
PRM	Presidential Review Memorandum (US)
PSAC	President's Science Advisory Committee (US)
PSP	Popular Socialist Party (Cuba)
PTBT	Partial Test Ban Treaty
PUWP	Polish United Workers' Party
PZPR	See PUWP
RDF	Rapid Deployment Force
RFE	Radio Free Europe
RVN	Republic of Vietnam
SALT	Strategic Arms Limitation Treaty
SAM	surface-to-air missile
SDI	Strategic Defense Initiative
SEATO	Southeast Asia Treaty Organization
SED	Socialist Unity Party of Germany
Sigint	signals intelligence
SIS	Secret Intelligence Service, UK (also known as MI6)
SPD	Social Democratic Party of Germany
SRAC	Short-Range Agent Communication Device
START	Strategic Arms Reduction Treaty
SVN	State of Vietnam
SWA	Southwest Africa
TVA	Tennessee Valley Authority
UAR	United Arab Republic
UDHR	Universal Declaration of Human Rights
UDI	Unilateral Declaration of Independence (Rhodesia)
UN	United Nations
UNESCO	United Nations Educational Scientific and Cultural Organization
UNITA	The National Union for the Total Independence of Angola
UNRRA	United Nations Relief and Rehabilitation Agency
USAID	United States Agency for International Development
USIA	Untied States Information Agency
VOA	Voice of America
VWP	Vietnam Workers' Party
ZANU	Zimbabwe African National Union
ZMP	Association of Polish Youth
ZSL	Association of Polish Writers

INTRODUCTION

Craig Daigle and Artemy M. Kalinovsky

For nearly fifty years, the Cold War was the dominant paradigm in international relations. What began as primarily an ideological confrontation between the Soviet Union and the United States over the shape of post-war Europe ultimately had deep and lasting effects on the political, military, and economic institutions around the globe. The Cold War shaped developments as varied as decolonization, European integration, domestic politics, science and technology, and mass culture. It exacerbated civil wars in Vietnam, Angola, and Afghanistan. It brought about coups in Iran, Guatemala, and the Congo. And it led to nuclear standoffs in Cuba, the Middle East, and Eastern Europe. Indeed no part of the world was unaffected – from North Korea to Argentina, from Alaska to Cape Town.

As the Cold War raged, historians and political scientists sought answers to how and why the two superpowers went from alliance during World War II to confrontation so soon after. Early "orthodox" accounts tended to lay the blame with the Soviet side, accusing Stalin for violating war-time agreements on Eastern Europe and forcing Washington to respond.[1] During the 1960s and early 1970s, a second wave of historians, inspired in part by their critique of the American military involvement in Vietnam, argued that the United States was chiefly responsible for the breakdown of the alliance, and that US capitalist greed had made it an aggressive and even imperialist power overseas. These "revisionists" challenged accounts not just of the breakdown in US–Soviet relations, but US claims of a benign and anti-imperialist foreign policy and President Truman's decision to use the atomic bomb in August 1945.[2] Eventually, a kind of "post-revisionist" synthesis emerged that explained the Cold War as the result of a dynamic of relation between the US and the Soviet Union whereby both superpowers sought strategic defense through political, economic, and military expansion.[3]

While many of these studies were then, and remain now, instrumental in how we understand Cold War developments, they were often incomplete and provided only partial explanations. They relied almost exclusively on US archives, or selected memoirs and interviews from participants who were willing or able to speak openly and freely. And they focused primarily on decision-making between the superpowers, at the highest levels of government, without paying enough attention to the peoples and societies that were affected by their decisions, the role of non-state actors, and the importance of transnational groups in shaping the Cold War. Historians in Europe began to challenge this framework in the late 1980s by examining the story from the view of Paris, London, and Berlin, but even these studies, while important and useful, left much about the Cold War, particularly in the global South, unexplored.[4]

With the ending of the Cold War in Europe and the collapse of the Soviet Union in 1991, the study of Cold War history went through a dramatic transformation. Prompted by the opening of Eastern European and former Soviet archives, as well as access to new material from the People's Republic of China, Cuba, Latin America, the Middle East, and Africa, historians were compelled to rethink much of what they first knew about the Cold War and to place American and Soviet decision making in its broader international and domestic context. Historians of the "new" Cold War history have offered important studies that focus attention on ideology, culture and race, and provide much-needed agency to leaders in the Third World who were often viewed as Soviet or American "puppets."

New scholarship on the international history of the Cold War has not only added to our understanding of familiar Cold War events, such as the Korean War, the Cuban Missile Crisis, and superpower détente,[5] but it has shed new light on the importance of ideology during the Cold War, on the role of personality, and on development and modernization policies, including President Truman's Point Four program and John F. Kennedy's Alliance for Progress.[6] This new scholarship has deepened our understanding of the rise and demise of the Sino-Soviet alliance.[7] It has demonstrated how events in the Third World, such as the outbreak of the Angolan Civil War, in which Cuba's Fidel Castro played a major role,[8] or in Latin America, where the United States often cultivated relationships with right-wing military dictatorships in the Southern Cone, shaped Cold War policies.[9] And it has provided needed attention to the role of human rights advocacy and the development of transnational networks that significantly contributed to the end of the Cold War.[10]

Simultaneously with developments in the field of the international history of the Cold War, social and cultural studies have vastly added to our understanding of the impact of the domestic side of the Cold War. Scholars trained in American studies, law, communication, sociology, and anthropology, as well as historians of race, ethnicity, culture, and gender have examined the ways in which domestic policy influenced the direction of Cold War policy and vice versa. In the last decade or so, for example, scholarship on the subject of race and the Cold War has flourished.[11] Where once the history of the Civil Rights movement and the struggle for Black equality were treated almost entirely in a domestic American history context, or as part of African-American studies, these subjects have now been integrated into the broader Cold War narrative. The "cultural turn" in Cold War studies has also highlighted the role of public diplomacy and propaganda during the Cold War, of the uses of psychological warfare programs, such as the United States Information Agency and President Eisenhower's Atoms for Peace program, and the important contributions of science and technology, education, cinema, and music to Cold War culture.[12]

The rapid expansion of the international, social, and cultural history of the Cold War has also had a dramatic impact on the study of Cold War history around the world. As George Washington University historian Hope M. Harrison detailed in a recent article, most colleges and universities have courses that cover the Cold War specifically or as part of a broader course on US foreign relations, the Soviet Union, or international conflict and cooperation.[13] Six universities – the University of California at Santa Barbara; George Washington University; Harvard University; New York University; London School of Economics; and East China Normal University (Shanghai) – have established centers specifically dedicated to studying the Cold War. Two journals – *Cold War History* and the *Journal of Cold War Studies* – were created to deal with the wealth of new scholarship outside of the traditional venues of *Diplomatic History* and *Diplomacy and Statecraft*. And the Cold War International History Project, established in

1991 by the Woodrow Wilson Center for Scholars, has become one of the leading centers for Cold War studies around the world.

The present volume takes advantage of the growth of Cold War history and draws on the wealth of new Cold War scholarship across the globe since the early 1990s. It is primarily aimed at upper-level undergraduate and graduate students, although even more advanced scholars will find many of these chapters useful references. The volume brings together chapters on more familiar topics like geopolitics, military power and threat perception, but also ones that highlight new scholarship on technology and strategy, ideology and patterns of international trade. The chapters explore the importance of non-state actors, such as scientists, human rights activists, and the Catholic Church. They examine the importance of development, foreign aid, and overseas assistance. And they look at how film, technology, and propaganda shaped our understanding of peoples, societies, and cultures on both sides of the Iron Curtain as well as in the Third World.

The book is not meant to be an encyclopedia and is in no way exhaustive of existing Cold War scholarship. Rather, our aim was to assemble a volume that would give the reader a sense of how the field has evolved and where it is heading. To that end, we asked our contributors to combine a narrative approach with a discussion of their sub-field's historiography, as well as their assessment of where related research is headed. Some of the contributors will focus on the recent developments in more traditional Cold War topics, such as Germany, nuclear weapons, and détente, while most of the chapters examine the developments that we associate with the new Cold War history. In this way, we hope to highlight how the field has changed since the early 1990s and offer students and scholars new directions for potential research and study.

Although we have tried to make the chapters as consistent as possible, not all chapters are identical. Some, like Gregory F. Domber's chapter on the end of the Cold War in Poland, where the literature is not as extensive and is only beginning to be written, rely more on primary documentation. Others, like Nathan J. Citino's chapter on modernization, take a more historiographical approach. This was a conscious decision on the part of the editors and the author to introduce students to a large, growing literature that does not recognize a single definition of "modernization" or "development." The range of approaches employed by scholars forced Citino to conclude that it is not yet possible to provide a coherent, unitary narrative on this theme in Cold War history. His aim, therefore, is to criticize, rather than just describe, the literature and to explain why this set of topics is significant for Cold War studies as a whole.

The contributors for this volume have been selected because they are doing some of the most exciting work in the field. They represent many of the leading academic institutions that have concentrations on the international history of the Cold War and have been deeply grounded in the methodological changes and historiographical developments in the field of Cold War history since the early 1990s. Most contributors have either studied or taught the Cold War at institutions in the United States, Europe, China, Canada, and Russia. They have conducted research in European archives, on both sides of the Iron Curtain, as well as in the Middle East, Latin America, Asia, and Africa. And most have deep language backgrounds that allow them to examine new literature and historiographical developments in non-English-language sources, which will allow students and scholars who utilize this volume to get a comprehensive view of how the Cold War is being studied around the world.

The volume consists of twenty-eight chapters and is divided into nine parts. Part I examines the origins of the Cold War and its legacies. All three chapters in this part engage with the issue of universalism and the way specific concerns and paradigmatic aspects of US and Soviet foreign policy shaped the post-war order. They do so from different perspectives, however. Mario Del Pero's chapter examines the way the inter-war experience of the two superpowers shaped their behavior after 1945, while Amanda Kay McVety turns to the broader ambitions of political and social leaders and technocrats in the post-war period. She argues that they were guided by four faiths: "the centrality of the state, the wonder-working ability of human ingenuity to bring progress, the growth of a properly managed global economy, and the dictates of a higher power – shaped the internationalism of the 1940s and animated the quest for 'freedom.'" This idealism rubbed up against the realities of the Cold War, they became a part of its arsenal but also shaped the struggle. Foreshadowing the chapters on decolonization and the Cold War, she concludes that the Cold War "muted some internationalist principles, but it gave a greater voice to others as the United States and the Soviet Union used them to try to win more power and the rest of the world used them to try to reduce it."

Part II focuses on the intra-bloc crises of the early Cold War and how they came to reshape the conflict. Anita J. Prażmowska, Hope M. Harrison, and Lorenz Lüthi highlight the fractures inside the communist bloc during the 1950s, which had worldwide consequences. In looking at the rise and demise of the Sino-Soviet alliance, one of the most examined topics of the new Cold War history, Lüthi demonstrates how the "estrangement" that grew between the Soviet Union and the People's Republic of China was felt in the non-Socialist Third World, South Asia, in particular, and the Afro-Asian Movement, in general.

Part III includes chapters on the impact of decolonization and Part IV on the Cold War in the Third World. This is arguably where some of the most exciting research in Cold War history has taken place since the early 1990s. Ryan M. Irwin explores the complicated ways that decolonization interacted with the Cold War. Like a number of chapters in this volume, Irwin's begins not in 1945 but at the end of World War I, setting the stage for a discussion of empire, colonialism, and the nation-state. In the chapter that follows, Jessica M. Chapman takes up the theme of colonization and the Cold War in her overview of the wars in Vietnam. Like Irwin, Chapman begins the story in the aftermath of World War I, tracing the emergence of Vietnam's anti-colonial struggle and the way that struggle ultimately became part of the Cold War. Finally, Nathan J. Citino reviews the sub-field of development studies within Cold War history. As he writes, "Reinterpreting the Cold War as a struggle for development means understanding postwar history as a series of conflicts over resources, power, and ideology within a global consensus about the need for rapid material and technological progress." His meta-analysis of the literature on the Cold War and development shows how the field has evolved from a critique of the liberal American project to appreciation of the global and transnational aspects of the subject.

Citino ends his chapter by emphasizing the importance of investigating "regional" histories along with the "international" histories of the Cold War. The following part offers chapters on the Cold War in the Middle East, Latin America, Africa, and South and Central Asia. All of the chapters take broad chronological boundaries and engage with the themes raised in the previous part. They are also united in looking at the "cold wars" within the Cold War – that is, the regional struggles that took place in the larger international context.

Part V shows the important work being done on the era of détente. Yafeng Xia's chapter picks up where Lüthi's chapter left off, demonstrating that the Soviet invasion of Czechoslovakia and the Brezhnev Doctrine compelled Chinese officials to change their relationship with the United States. Xia gives added attention to the role of personality, especially that of Zhou En-lai, as he concludes, based on new evidence from Chinese archives, that Zhou – not Mao – was the chief "promoter" of the policy of rapprochement with the United States. Craig Daigle's chapter argues that détente was not a monolithic policy; its application and effect varied depending on the context. Thus, while détente found success at the global strategic level, at the regional level, particularly in the Third World, continued superpower competition would bring an end to détente. Angela Romano, meanwhile, moves beyond traditional interpretations which view the Conference on Security and Cooperation in Europe and the Helsinki Final Act as a "seal" on détente and argues instead that they "constituted a step in the process of setting relations in Europe to a new pattern beyond the Cold War."

Parts VI through VIII move away from the regional aspects of the Cold War and focus on thematic and transnational developments. One could say that these chapters examine the "tools" with which the Cold War was fought, including intelligence, nuclear weapons, and propaganda. Some of the chapters examine the way non-state and transnational actors engaged with and contested the Cold War paradigm. Paul Rubinson's chapter, for example, shows how US scientists engaged in developing military technology for Cold War purposes came to see themselves playing a special role in trying to end the conflict, even if their efforts to "transcend" the Cold War met with only limited success. In a similar vein, Andrei Kozovoi's chapter on cinema shows how the production of many post-World War II films which sought to play a part in the Cold War struggle, whether by Hollywood and by Soviet studios, was a complex process involving the needs of the respective governments and relevant agencies, the commercial ambitions of the film industry, and the artistic ambitions of the artists involved.

Turning to another aspect of the "cultural Cold War," Elidor Mëhilli looks at the way Washington and Moscow competed on the level of "high" technology and scientific achievement like space exploration, and consumer technology like kitchen appliances. Mëhilli finds not only plenty of similarities in how the two sides approached this competition, but also interaction and mutual learning. Mëhilli's Cold War "was a race between capitalism and socialism over consumption: everyday conveniences like televisions, washing machines, and modern kitchens. But underlying this race in mundane consumer artifacts were aspirations for a better life, shared by millions across the world, and the pursuit of international prestige and modernization." Finally, rounding out this part, Sergei Zhuk provides a meta-analysis of how "cultural" studies of the former Soviet Union by scholars in the UK and US have been transformed over the previous two decades.

The final part examines how and why the Cold War came to an end in the late 1980s. Without question, this is one of the mostly hotly contested topics among Cold War historians. Thus far, scholars have offered numerous explanations for the end of the Cold War, including the importance of Soviet economic stagnation, the personalities of President Ronald Reagan and Soviet General Secretary Mikhail Gorbachev, human rights activism, Eastern European agency, and overextension abroad. The editors of this volume seek to give an overview of some of these views, while Gregory Domber's chapter, like Piotr Kosicki's chapter in Part VI takes us back to the link between transnational, regional, and national histories in their studies of the Catholic Church and humanitarian aid at the end of the Cold War.

As stated earlier, this book takes a rather expansive definition of the Cold War. This was, in part, a deliberate choice made when we started to plan the volume, but it also reflects the way the field has developed since the early 1990s. The idea that the Cold War was a binary contest between two great superpowers has been largely abandoned. Some might complain that the study of the Cold War has acquired imperialist dimensions of its own, colonizing subjects and approaches that are far outside of its legitimate purview. Yet, if the essays in this volume show anything, it is that the Cold War paradigm has only enriched our understanding of the international history of the twentieth century, and the regional and local histories which were a part of it. We agree with Odd Arne Westad's recent observation that "The Cold War was one of many developments that shaped the world of today, and probably the predominant feature of the international system in the latter half of the twentieth century. We may dislike the Cold War, both as a concept and as a system, and we may want to decenter it, but we cannot dissolve it."[14]

Notes

1. Some of the best-known orthodox accounts are, William Hardy McNeill, *America, Britain, and Russia: Their Cooperation and Conflict, 1941–1946* (New York: Oxford University Press, 1953); Herbert Feis, *Churchill–Roosevelt–Stalin: The War They Waged and the Peace They Sought* (Princeton, NJ: Princeton University Press, 1957); Feis, *From Trust to Terror: The Onset of the Cold War* (New York: Norton, 1970); Arthur Schlesinger, Jr., "Origins of the Cold War," *Foreign Affairs*, 46 (October 1967): 22–52.
2. See William Appleman Williams, *The Tragedy of American Diplomacy* (Cleveland: World Pub Co., 1959); Williams, *The Roots of the Modern American Empire* (New York: Random House, 1969); Gabriel Kolko and Joyce Kolko, *The Limits of Power: The World and United States Foreign Policy 1945–1954* (New York: Harper and Rowe, 1972); Thomas G. Paterson, *Soviet–American Confrontation: Postwar Reconstruction and the Origins of the Cold War* (Baltimore, MD: Johns Hopkins University Press, 1973); Gar Alperovitz, *Atomic Diplomacy: Hiroshima and Potsdam: The Use of the Atomic Bomb and the American Confrontation with Soviet Power* (New York: Vintage Books, 1965); Lloyd C. Gardner, *Architects of Illusion: Men and Ideas in American Foreign Policy* (Chicago, IL: Quadrangle Books, 1970).
3. See John Lewis Gaddis, "The Emerging Post-Revisionist Synthesis on the Origins of the Cold War," *Diplomatic History*, Vol. 7:3 (1983): 171–190.
4. See, for example, Geir Lundestad, "The United States and Western Europe, 1945–1952," *Journal of Peace Research*, Vol. 23:3 (September 1986): 263–277; Anne Deighton, *Britain and the First Cold War* (London: Palgrave Macmillan, 1990).
5. On the Korean War see, Chen Jian, *China's Road to the Korean War* (New York: Columbia University Press, 1999); William W. Stueck, *Rethinking the Korean War* (Princeton, NJ: Princeton University Press, 2002). On the Cuban Missile Crisis see, Timothy Naftali and Aleksandr Fursenko, *'One Hell of a Gamble': Khrushchev, Castro, and Kennedy, 1958–1964* (New York: W.W. Norton, 1997). On détente see, Jeremi Suri, *Power and Protest: Global Revolution and the Rise of Détente* (Cambridge, MA: Harvard University Press, 2003); Vladislav Zubok, *A Failed Empire: The Soviet Union in the Cold War from Stalin to Gorbachev* (Chapel Hill, NC: University of North Carolina Press, 2007); Craig Daigle, *The Limits of Détente: The United States, the Soviet Union and the Arab-Israeli Conflict, 1969–1973* (New Haven, CT: Yale University Press, 2012).
6. Geoffrey Roberts, *Stalin's Wars: From World War to Cold War, 1939–1953* (New Haven, CT: Yale University Press, 2008); Vladislav Zubok and Constantine Pleshakov, *Inside the Kremlin's Cold War: From Stalin to Khrushchev* (Cambridge, MA: Harvard, 1996). On modernization and development, see Michael E. Latham, *Modernization as Ideology: American Social Science and "Nation Building" in the Kennedy Era* (Chapel Hill, NC: University of North Carolina Press, 2000); Nils Gilman, *Mandarins of the Future: Modernization Theory in Cold War America* (Baltimore, MD: Johns Hopkins University Press, 2003); David Ekbladh, *The Great American Mission: Modernization and the Construction of an American World Order* (Princeton, NJ: Princeton University Press, 2010); Jeremy Kuzmarov, *Modernizing Repression: Police Training and Nation-Building in the American Century* (Amherst, MA: University of Massachusetts Press, 2012); Gregg Brazinsky, *Nation Building in South Korea: Koreans, Americans, and the Making of a Democracy* (Chapel Hill, NC: University of North Carolina Press, 2007); and Amanda Kay McVety, *Enlightened Aid: U.S. Development as Foreign Policy in Ethiopia* (New York: Oxford University Press, 2012).
7. On the Sino-Soviet Alliance see, Odd Arne Westad, *Brothers in Arms: The Rise and Fall of the Sino-Soviet Alliance* (Stanford, CA: Stanford University Press, 1998); Chen Jian, *Mao's China and the Cold War* (Chapel Hill, NC: University of North Carolina Press, 2001); Lorenz Lüthi, *The Sino-Soviet Split: Cold War in the Communist World* (Princeton, NJ: Princeton University Press, 2008).
8. Piero Gleijeses, *Conflicting Missions: Havana, Washington, and Africa* (Chapel Hill, NC: University of North Carolina Press, 2002).
9. Hal Brands, *Latin America's Cold War* (Cambridge, MA: Harvard University Press, 2010); Tanya Harmer, *Allende's Chile and the Inter-American Cold War* (Chapel Hill, NC: University of North Carolina Press, 2011); Stephen Rabe, *The Killing Zone: The United States Wages Cold War in Latin America* (New York: Oxford University Press, 2012).
10. Sarah B. Snyder, *Human Rights Activism and the End of the Cold War: A Transnational History of the Helsinki Network* (Cambridge: Cambridge University Press, 2011); Daniel C. Thomas, *The Helsinki Effect: International Norms, Human Rights, and the Demise of Communism* (Princeton, NJ: Princeton University Press, 2001); Matthew Evangelista, *Unarmed Forces: The Transnational Movement to End the Cold War* (Ithaca, NY: Cornell University Press, 1999).

Introduction

11 Influential works on how race and ethnicity influenced the Cold War include: Carol Anderson, *Eyes Off the Prize: The United Nations and African American Struggle for Human Rights 1944–1955* (Cambridge: Cambridge University Press, 2003); Thomas Borstelmann, *The Cold War and the Color Line: American Race Relations in the Global Arena* (Cambridge, MA: Harvard University Press, 2003); Mary Dudziak, *Cold War Civil Rights* (Princeton, NJ: Princeton University Press, 2000); Philip E. Muehlenbeck, ed., *Race, Ethnicity and the Cold War* (Nashville, TN: Vanderbilt University Press, 2012).

12 On psychological warfare programs see, Kenneth Osgood, *Total Cold War: Eisenhower Secret Propaganda Battle at Home and Abroad* (Lawrence, KS: Kansas University Press, 2006); Laura A. Belmonte, *Selling the American Way: U.S. Propaganda and the Cold War* (Philadelphia, PA: University of Pennsylvania Press, 2008); and Nicholas Cull, *The Cold War and the United States Information Agency: American Propaganda and Public Diplomacy 1945–1989* (Cambridge: Cambridge University Press, 2008). On education, see Andrew Hartman, *Education and the Cold War: The Battle for the American School* (New York and London: Palgrave Macmillan, 2008). On "musical diplomacy" during the Cold War, see Penny Von Eschen, *Satchmo Blows Up the World: Jazz Ambassadors Play the Cold War* (Cambridge, MA: Harvard University Press, 2004).

13 Hope M. Harrison, "Teaching and Scholarship on the Cold War in the United States," *Cold War History*, 8:2 (May 2008): 259–284.

14 Odd Arne Westad, "Epilogue: The Cold War and the Third World," in Robert J. McMahon, ed., *The Cold War in the Third World* (New York: Oxford University Press, 2013), 217.

PART I

The Early Cold War

1
INCOMPATIBLE UNIVERSALISMS

The United States, the Soviet Union, and the Beginning of the Cold War

Mario Del Pero

At the end of World War II vast parts of Europe, Russia, and Asia lay in ruins. Between 60 and 70 million people, a majority of them civilians, had lost their lives in the worst carnage in human history. Millions of displaced people wandered around Europe. For the first and only time in history, nuclear weapons had been used in a war and against civilians. "No other conflict in recorded history," wrote historian Tony Judt, "killed so many people in so short a time."[1]

Two powers stood above the others: the United States and the Soviet Union. Their troops occupied most of Europe and portions of East Asia; their military and national security apparatuses were fully mobilized; their confidence had been bolstered by the war successes and the final, absolute defeat of their formidable enemies, Japan and Germany. There was also a third member in the anti-Fascist coalition that had won the war: Great Britain. Prostrated by the costs of war, and lacking the necessary resources, Britain was far inferior to the countries that would soon be labeled as the two "superpowers." The post-World War II system was thus bipolar: there were two power poles, theoretically capable of balancing each other and acting as magnets to attract lesser allies in need of help, protection and patronage. This new bipolarism was nevertheless highly asymmetrical. One pole, the United States, was incommensurably more powerful than the other.

At the end of the war, the Soviet Union possessed a gigantic military apparatus, retaining a standing army of approximately 10 million men. In its westward advance, it had occupied most of Central–Eastern Europe, where it established friendly or at least non-hostile regimes. It controlled part of Germany and hoped to extract from the former enemy reparations and resources necessary for its reconstruction. The heroic struggle against the Nazi enemy had bolstered the myth of the Soviet Union and of its leader, Iosif Stalin. The USSR had been able to transform itself into a major industrial power and defeat Hitler's Germany; it thereby saved Europe from Nazi dominance and gained international legitimacy, prestige and recognition.

But the costs had been immense. The country was devastated; according to most estimates, it had lost between 20 and 25 million people in the war, and a vast portion of its industrial potential. Seventy thousand villages and 1,700 Soviet towns had been destroyed. In 1945, women exceeded men by about 20 million: an imbalance that would affect demographic trends for many years to come.[2]

In the bipolar frame, the contrast between the weakness of the Soviet Union and the augmented strength of the United States was therefore remarkable. The U.S. was the only country to emerge from the war richer and more powerful. Thanks to the stimulus provided by defense spending, its GDP had increased by 60 percent during the war and its economy had finally overcome the dramatic post-1929 recession; at the end of the war, the U.S. possessed 65 percent of the world's gold reserves and 50 percent of its manufacturing capacity; the dollar was soon to become the dominant currency. The United States had lost 400,000 men in the conflict: significant as this was as a national sacrifice, it paled in comparison to what the USSR and all the other participants in the war had experienced. Furthermore, its national territory had been left unscathed – the U.S. suffered no attacks on its soil – while the projection of its power had been reinforced by the acquisition of a vast network of bases around the world and the monopolistic possession of the atomic bomb.[3] The contrast was thus between a real global power, the United States, and one that was such only in ambition and *in potentia*, the Soviet Union.

Soviet and American Plans

Despite these differences, Moscow and Washington shared some common geopolitical assumptions and each thought it possible and necessary to continue their collaboration. Both assumed that some sort of bipolar, possibly British–Soviet, equilibrium would emerge in Europe; both hoped for a period of peace and stability; each believed that time was on its side and that its universal model of modernity would in the end prevail; neither wanted a new war or the collapse of the wartime alliance.

But a war, fortunately cold, they in the end got. Structural factors, misperceptions, fears, opportunism and strategic mistakes converged in nourishing a vicious spiral that rapidly ended the collaboration of the previous years. In a brief span of time, the two allies of the anti-Fascist war became total and irreconcilable enemies, intent on mobilizing their military apparatuses and alliances against each other and waging a full-fledged ideological war.

To understand why and how this happened, it is necessary to, first, compare the U.S. and Soviet plans, ideas and visions for the postwar period and understand why they proved to be incompatible; and second, focus on some of the key turning points of the period 1945–50, when a novel situation of no peace/no war – of a "peace impossible, war unlikely," in the words of Raymond Aron – gradually emerged. A novel situation required a specific, and itself ambiguous, metaphor – the "Cold War" – to describe its unique and highly contradictory character.[4]

Between 1944 and 1946, the United States redefined and clarified its goals and visions for the postwar international order. The U.S. had three basic objectives, which stemmed not just from an assessment of the radical changes in the international system which the war had brought, but also by what were considered to be the "lessons of history" and the need to avoid repeating the mistakes that had led to World War II.

The first American goal was to preserve, and possibly expand and consolidate, the condition of clear and unchallengeable superiority *enjoyed* by the United States at the end of the war. The global correlation of forces should work to the advantage of the U.S.; its 1945 preponderant power had to be rendered structural and permanent. This meant keeping and extending a capillary network of bases around the world and maintaining an advantageous balance of power, where the United States could control, directly or indirectly, the main economic and geopolitical pivots, in Asia and Europe, and have access to crucial resources and raw materials, particularly in the Middle East.

The second objective was to restore, and update, the capitalist and liberal international order that had collapsed after the 1929 crisis. Compromises were needed, and a form of "embedded" and partial liberalism, whereby international economic multilateralism coexisted with national interventionism, was finally instituted.⁵ Nevertheless, ideological assumptions and economic imperatives pushed in the direction of promoting free trade and removing the obstacles to profitable opportunities for investment. The assumption was that greater economic interdependence would stimulate growth, guarantee political stability and foster peace among nations.

The third and last goal was to avoid a return of isolationism in the United States. Postwar geopolitical globalism required a costly, proactive and interventionist foreign policy that many in the U.S. still opposed. It meant making permanent, and even expanding, the military and national security apparatuses established during the war; accepting high defense expenditures and a very intrusive state; and projecting power globally, by keeping troops and forces in occupied areas much longer than originally planned. The presence of an external, existential threat – part real, part perceived, part invented and exaggerated – served this function well: it offered a powerful catalyst to generate the necessary, and somehow missing, domestic consensus on what was soon to become Washington's Cold War policy and strategy.⁶

When implemented, however, these goals and visions proved to be incompatible with those of the Soviet Union. The USSR had to face the immense task of its economic and physical reconstruction. It needed aid from the U.S. and reparations from the German territory it now co-occupied with the United States, Great Britain and France. A deterioration of the relationship with its wartime ally was not in its interest.

Like the United States, Moscow had three main objectives in 1945. The first originated from a conception of security that maximized the importance of controlling space: in Asia and particularly in Central–Eastern Europe. The main pillar of the postwar Soviet security strategy was the establishment of a sphere of influence in the countries which the Soviet armed forces had occupied in their drive West during the last phase of the war: Czechoslovakia, Poland, Hungary, Romania, Bulgaria. Relying on local pro-Soviet communist parties, the USSR sought friendly regimes in the area that were willing to accept both limitations of their national sovereignty and subservience of their foreign and security policies to Moscow. There was an element of geopolitical orthodoxy in such a vision: the assumption was that Germany still constituted the main security threat and that a buffer zone must be established between the Soviet and the German territories. And there was also a degree of uncertainty on how this objective – creating a Soviet sphere of influence in Central–Eastern Europe – could be pursued and achieved. Conditions varied from country to country; plans had not been defined; and the military operated often in a chaotic as well as brutal and uncoordinated way. That the Soviets should somehow control half of Europe was not, however, up for discussion and the legitimacy of such a request was recognized also by the United States and Great Britain.⁷

Strengthening its security via the creation of a buffer zone on its Western borders, while simultaneously focusing on the domestic reconstruction, was a vital precondition for achieving the second Soviet goal: buying time. Stalin and the Soviet leadership believed that history was on their side and that sooner or later the inevitable contradictions of capitalism would explode once again. The Soviet Union aimed at projecting a counter-universalism to the U.S.–liberal one. The ultimate, messianic goal was to expand socialism globally. To do so, it was necessary to reinforce the socialist motherland, the USSR itself, and prepare for a recrudescence of tensions among capitalist states and work to render the period of U.S. unquestioned superiority transient and historically contingent.

The final objective of the Soviet Union was to punish, divide and exploit Germany, which had invaded Russia and the USSR twice in the previous thirty years. Just as with Central and Eastern Europe, Stalin's plans were initially flexible, if not inconsistent, although the brutal behavior of the Soviet army shocked many observers and made more difficult the collaboration with the other occupying powers in Germany. The rest of Europe fell under what was soon to become the U.S. sphere of influence. Moscow recognized this geopolitical partition of the Continent and the hegemony of the United States in its Western half. It hoped, however, that postwar Western European governments would not be hostile to the USSR and that existing pro-Soviet parties could play a role in their national polities.

From Collaboration to Confrontation

There was, therefore, a flexibility that bordered on incoherence in the Soviet approach. What were not flexible or negotiable, however, were the Soviet reparation requirements from defeated Germany: an issue that immediately created a rift between Moscow and the other occupying powers. Germany was the first and primary theatre where the transition from the U.S.–Soviet wartime collaboration to Cold War antagonism became patent. The other two areas were the Near and Middle East and East Asia. In all these theatres the incompatibility between the plans of the "superpowers," along with their numerous inconsistencies and omissions, emerged very quickly.

In typical liberal fashion, the Truman administration believed that political radicalism – and communism was considered one of its quintessential manifestations – prospered in conditions of economic poverty and distress. The rapid economic recovery of postwar Europe was therefore deemed necessary for both political and economic reasons: to create the liberal economic space the U.S. wanted, but also to foster the political stability needed to consolidate the postwar order and prevent radical groups from influencing it. It was soon realized that these goals could be achieved only through the involvement and participation of Germany, or at least of its Western zones occupied and administered by the United States, Great Britain and France. Despite the devastation of the war, Germany remained the main economic power in Europe, thanks to its industries, technological know-how and coal. If adequately managed and reintegrated into the European sphere, Germany could act as the economic locomotive the rest of the Continent badly needed. Punishing the old enemy and curtailing its industrial potential – as the Soviets and, initially, the Americans wanted to do – became irreconcilable with the U.S. objective of promoting a rapid economic recovery of at least that part of Europe that fell under its domain.[8]

Furthermore, accepting the punitive Soviet position risked provoking the resentment of the German population, which itself needed to re-establish manufacturing infrastructure and the export of industrial commodities to pay for foodstuff and raw materials. In the months after the end of the war, the German population was living or, indeed, starving, on little more than 1,000 daily calories per capita. This state of affairs could not last indefinitely, for it heightened the fears of the British and the Americans that the country could fall into the hands of the Soviet Union and its German communist allies.

Notwithstanding public declarations to the contrary, the Truman administration and U.S. officials began very early to consider a division of Germany both inevitable and desirable.[9] The plans to punish the former enemy were abandoned; in January 1947, the U.S. and Britain united their zones of occupation, creating the so-called Bizone. It was the first step of the process that would eventually lead to the creation of a new West German state, although France did not initially join the other two Western countries.

This fueled the fears and concerns of the Soviet Union that, just a few months after the end of the war, the German state could be resurgent, integrated economically and, in perspective, even militarily into the U.S. sphere of influence. As often in these early phases of the Cold War, the actions of the Soviet Union proved counterproductive for Moscow, exacerbating fears and anxieties in the West and thus strengthening the position of those hardliners in the United States who believed that no collaboration with the former ally was possible.

In northern Iran, Stalin delayed the previously agreed withdrawal of the Soviet troops deployed there during the war, only to backpedal after the harsh reaction from London and Washington. With regard to Turkey, Moscow vainly tried to secure control of the Straits, exerting pressures on the Turkish government and even concentrating troops on the border. Again, the Soviet leader faced the reaction of Britain and the U.S., which backed Turkey.

These two cases proved the persistence of traditional Russian imperialist ambitions (in the case of Turkey) and the increasing geopolitical relevance of the Middle East and its resources (in the case of Iran). They also exposed Stalin's opportunism and weakness. Historians have long debated both the matrices and the objectives of Stalin's foreign policy in the early Cold War years. Traditional imperial ambitions matched with socialist messianism in nourishing what historians Vladislav Zubok and Constantine Pleshakov, in a path-breaking study published in 1996, called an "imperial-revolutionary paradigm." These factors combined with the search for an absolute security that was impossible to attain and a deep mistrust of the wartime allies. They did not signal, however, Moscow's intention to launch an all-out offensive and, on the contrary, revealed the cautiousness of Stalin, his awareness of U.S. superiority and the inconsistency of many of his policies and plans.[10]

However, in the United States, the crises were interpreted as part of a more general Soviet offensive, and connected to what was happening in Europe. The main danger was considered to be a power vacuum in the heart of the Continent. This offensive – it was now believed – had to be met with firmness and resolution to avoid the risk that the Soviets, bolstered by success, could test America's resolve in other theatres.

The hardening of the positions of the two sides was sanctified theoretically and strategically. In an influential and widely read analysis, the U.S. Chargé d'Affaires at the Moscow Embassy, George Kennan, described the behavior of the Soviet Union as being informed by a mix of traditional Russian insecurity, Socialist messianism and the necessity for Stalin and the Soviet leadership to have an external enemy in order to justify their authoritarian rule, and the permanent mobilization of the Soviet society. An imperial-revolutionary logic – Kennan in his own way argued – informed Soviet actions and strategies. "At bottom of Kremlin's neurotic view of world affairs," Kennan wrote, "is traditional and instinctive Russian sense of insecurity ... Thus Soviet leaders are driven [by] necessities of their own past and present" to present "the outside world as evil, hostile and menacing, but as bearing within itself germs of creeping disease and destined to be wracked with growing internal convulsions until it is given final *coup de grace* by rising power of socialism and yields to new and better world."[11]

In later assessments, Kennan called for "a long-term, patient but firm and vigilant containment of Russian expansive tendencies." "Soviet pressure against the free institutions of the Western world," Kennan wrote, "is something that can be contained by the adroit and vigilant application of counterforce at a series of constantly shifting geographical and political points, corresponding to the shifts and maneuvers of Soviet policy, but which cannot be charmed or talked out of existence."[12] The Soviet Union ceased to be a legitimate, and even normal, interlocutor; its positions, whatever their merit and causes, were *ipso facto* presented as illegitimate. Dialectical rejection of the counterpart in the name of firmness justified the suspension for the time being of any diplomatic interaction with the former Soviet ally.[13]

On the Soviet side, a similar analysis was produced by the Soviet Ambassador to the United States, Nikolai Novikov. The foreign policy of the United States, Novikov argued, reflected "the imperialist tendencies of American monopolistic capital," and was "characterized ... by a striving for world supremacy." This was "the real meaning of the many statements by President

Truman and other representatives of American ruling circles: that the United States has the right to lead the world," the Ambassador wrote. "The preparation by the United States for a future" was thus "being conducted with the prospect of war against the Soviet Union, which in the eyes of the American imperialists is the main obstacle in the path of the United States to world domination."[14]

More moderate voices still existed, on both sides. However, the move from collaboration to confrontation, from the wartime alliance to the Cold War antagonism, was irresistible. Between 1947 and 1949 the residual forms of cooperation between the United States and the Soviet Union, over Germany and in the regular summits of the foreign ministers of the three winners of the war, came to an end and the rigid partition of the Cold War took a clearly defined shape. As highlighted by Melvin Leffler, both sides believed they were acting defensively and pursuing their legitimate security interests. Their actions, however, nourished the fears and reaction of the counterpart, which frequently perceived them as threatening and offensive. This "security dilemma" produced a vicious spiral that, according to Leffler, rendered the Cold War antagonism almost inevitable.[15]

Prostrated by the war, Great Britain could not act as a "balancer" of the USSR in the Eastern Mediterranean, as was initially assumed by the U.S. and Britain itself. In early 1947, London made clear its inability to finance and support the governments of Greece and Turkey, facing respectively strong domestic communist forces (which received little support from Moscow) and the above-mentioned Soviet pressures. Applying deforming binary lenses to what were peculiar and specific national and regional cases, the Truman administration read the two crises in strict Cold War terms: as a test of its newly defined strategy of containment of the Soviet Union and international communism. Vivid metaphors were deployed, then and retrospectively, to highlight what was considered to be the inherent interconnectedness of events and crises that in reality were loosely tied one to the other. The "Soviet pressure on the Straits, on Iran, and on northern Greece had brought the Balkans to the point where a highly possible Soviet breakthrough might open three continents to Soviet penetration," the then Undersecretary of State, Dean Acheson, later wrote. "Like apples in a barrel infected by one rotten one, the corruption of Greece would infect Iran and all to the east. It would also carry infection to Africa through Asia Minor and Egypt, and to Europe through Italy and France, already threatened by the strongest domestic Communist parties in Western Europe. The Soviet Union was playing one of the greatest gambles in history at minimal cost."[16]

This apocalyptic view informed the reaction of the United States. The Truman administration deemed it necessary to intervene, replace the British ally and provide the necessary aid to Greece and Turkey. It had, however, to convince a very reluctant country. Presenting the case to Congress and the American public, Truman resorted to a Manichean language that juxtaposed two "alternative ways of life": one "based upon the will of the majority" and "distinguished by free institutions, representative government, free elections, guarantees of individual liberty, freedom of speech and religion, and freedom from political oppression," and the other founded "upon the will of a minority forcibly imposed upon the majority" and relying "upon terror and oppression, a controlled press and radio; fixed elections, and the suppression of personal freedoms." The United States, the President maintained, had "to support free peoples who" were "resisting attempted subjugation by armed minorities or by outside pressures."[17]

The Greek and Turkish governments hardly fell within the category of freedom-loving democracies. Unstable as it was, the Greek government had been involved since 1945 in a civil war against communist forces and deployed violence against civilians and communist sympathizers. In Turkey, some modest liberal reforms had been introduced after the war and the one-party system had ended in 1946. The transition to a more democratic system was nevertheless gradual, and controlled by those holding power in the old autocratic regime. Nevertheless, the "Truman Doctrine," as it became known, fixed the public representation of the Cold War in the United States and defined the semantic perimeter in which post-World War II international relations and U.S. foreign policy could be presented, narrated and justified.

Reconstructing Europe

Meanwhile, the lack of hard currency (i.e. dollars) needed to purchase raw materials and foodstuffs threatened to stall the surprisingly rapid recovery of most Western European countries. This dollar shortage preoccupied the United States, which feared its economic and, even more, political implications.

In June 1947, Secretary of State George Marshall announced a broad plan for the economic resurgence of Europe. The plan aimed at stimulating growth, integrating the economies of European states and providing the much-needed dollars. The plan was also offered to the Soviet Union, which, after careful consideration, rejected it. It was a calculated bet. Congress would never have approved a plan that included the new Cold War enemy. The U.S. could not, however, afford to appear as the side causing the rift and knew that Moscow would not accept the forms of economic integration, co-management and interference in its internal affairs that the plan envisioned. The Marshall Plan, as it came to be known, highlighted the change in the U.S. approach to European matters and put the Soviet Union on the defensive. It did not start the Cold War, but "surely marked a point of no return,"[18] based as it was on the assumption of both a division of Europe and a permanent U.S. commitment in its Western half. The plan also relied on the idea that Germany, or at least its Western part, had to be at the center of any European economic recovery: that its resources and industrial potential could not be restrained anymore. The plan aimed at fostering coordination and integration among the beneficiaries of U.S. aid. It also provided for forms of participation and involvement of U.S. officials and experts that represented, inevitably, a form of interference in the domestic affairs of the recipient countries. Such integration was only loosely attained: national governments used American aid according to their policies, economic philosophies and goals; clashes between local and U.S. officials were frequent; Washington repeatedly expressed its frustration over how U.S. funds were used and sometimes mismanaged.

Contrary to a consolidated mythology, the Marshall Plan was not decisive in restarting the shattered Western European economies. Furthermore, its impact, and the ways in which American aid was used, varied from country to country. But the plan was crucial, and successful, in filling the dollar gap, allowing the continuation of the postwar economic recovery and strengthening transatlantic cooperation and interdependence. Finally, it represented a major political success for the United States and its European partners, bolstering domestic pro-U.S. political forces and contributing to the formation of a strong network of Atlantic elites.[19]

The Soviets reacted with a typical mix of ideological rigidity and political short-sightedness. They intensified the consolidation and control of their sphere of influence, imposing greater discipline on its members and in the coordination of their policies. This was achieved through the creation of the Cominform, an organization that included the Central–Eastern European communist parties, as well as those of Italy (PCI) and France (PCF). The two Western European communist parties were severely denounced for their collaboration with what had become pro-U.S. national governments, and pressured to mobilize against the Marshall Plan. Political dissent and pluralism were harshly repressed. Many communist leaders fell from favor with Moscow; a wave of purges removed dissidents and independent political figures; a generation of loyal "little Stalins" ascended to power, ready to deploy in their domestic sphere the same methods of the

Soviet dictator. Pro-Moscow parties achieved power by eliminating other political groups and establishing communist one-party systems. The February 1948 coup in Czechoslovakia led to the collapse of the last non-communist and multi-party government in the Soviet bloc.

As was often the case in the early Cold War years, Soviet actions backfired. Following the Czech coup, the U.S. Congress approved the Marshall Plan (although the final appropriation of $5.3 billion was far lower than the sum required by the Europeans and requested by the Truman administration). The hard line of the PCI and PCF, and their opposition to the very popular Marshall Plan, was electorally counterproductive and self-defeating. In the crucial Italian elections of April 1948, the leftist alliance of the pro-Soviet forces – the Fronte Popolare – suffered a crushing defeat, receiving just 31 percent of the vote. The centrist Christian Democrats and their minor allies easily formed a pro-U.S. government, whose main goal was to anchor Italy to the Western security sphere. Most recent studies have showed how domestic factors were paramount in determining the electoral outcome.[20] Often interpreted as a clear (and successful) example of American interference in the domestic affairs of another country, the Italian elections proved instead the popularity of U.S. economic aid and the desire of Western European elites to "keep" the United States in Europe and obtain from it political support, military protection and financial assistance. Norwegian historian Geil Lundestad has defined this process with the formula "empire by invitation": in the immediate postwar years the United States, Lundestad argued, built its own empire in Western Europe, but such imperial presence was invited by the European partners of Washington themselves, more than imposed by the U.S. Immensely successful, the "empire by invitation" formula tends to simplify the much more complex and ambiguous relationship between the United States and its allies in Europe: the invitation came from specific non-communist and anti-communist groups, and it was from the beginning partial and qualified. Nevertheless, Western European pressures and initiatives played a role in convincing the United States, and its public opinion, to commit itself to the protection and economic reconstruction of Western Europe.[21]

Within the Soviet bloc, Stalin's desire to exercise a more direct control over its allies clashed instead with the autonomy and independence of Josif Tito's Yugoslavia, the only socialist country in Europe that had liberated itself from the Nazi occupier without relying on the Soviet army. Unwilling to subordinate its foreign and domestic policies to the Soviet diktats and turnarounds, Tito clashed with Moscow and in June 1948 Yugoslavia was formally expelled from the Cominform. The Soviet–Yugoslav rift offered Moscow the justification for a further hardening of its policies in Central–Eastern Europe: a new wave of purges ensued and various allegedly "Titoist" national leaders – such as former Hungarian Minister of the Interior, László Rajk – were arrested and, in some cases, executed.

The Yugoslav defection revealed the intrinsic fragility of the Soviet bloc. Furthermore, it made manifest this additional asymmetry between the American and the Soviet European empires. The former was based both on a series of compromises between the senior partner, the United States, and its lesser allies, and on the emergence of specific Atlantic anti-communist elites, whose choices and leadership were legitimated through the electoral process. In contrast to the "consensual hegemony"[22] built by the U.S. in Western Europe, a high level of coercion characterized the Soviet dominance in the East, somehow reflecting the improvisation and inconsistency of Stalin's foreign policy. The two terms, "Americanization" and "Sovietization," came thus to symbolize and represent different ways of projecting power and exerting influence in international politics.

This difference, and the ability of U.S. propaganda to exploit it very effectively, was exemplified by another Cold War crisis: the Berlin Blockade, which lasted from June 1948 to May 1949. Berlin, the former capital of the Nazi empire, fell within the Soviet zone of occupation in the

Eastern part of Germany. The city, however, had itself been divided into four sectors, administered by the four occupying powers. A limited number of air, road, rail and river routes could be used to access Berlin from the Western parts of Germany, and later the Bizone.

In June 1948, Moscow decided to block the access to the city. Only three air corridors remained open. By hijacking Berlin, Stalin hoped to stop the process that was inexorably leading to the creation of a new German state in the West. In the highly asymmetrical bipolarism of the Cold War, "owning" Berlin was one of the few assets the Soviets had: primarily for symbolic reasons, Washington deemed it vital to preserve control of the Western sector and its access to the Bizone. The Soviet blockade was a gamble and proved to be a significant political mistake. The United States, Great Britain and France broke the blockade through a massive airlift, which delivered to the Western sectors the goods necessary for their daily needs. The Cold War was also a propaganda competition: a struggle for the hearts, minds and, ultimately, allegiance of people; a conflict whose final jury would be represented by world opinion. On this, the Berlin blockade represented a major victory for the United States and the West. The Soviet Union was perceived as a brutal and unscrupulous power, willing, if necessary, to starve the innocent people of Berlin in order to achieve its goals.

The Soviet defeat over Berlin accelerated the division of Germany in two separate states: the exact outcome Moscow wanted to avoid. France had finally accepted to merge its zone with the Anglo-American one. In June 1948, a new currency – the Deutsche mark – had been introduced in the Western occupation zones, thus facilitating their economic integration and triggering the Soviet reaction that led to the ill-thought-out Berlin blockade. Marshall aid began pouring into the West German economy, stimulating its industrial recovery and, with it, that of Western Europe as a whole. In May 1949, the Federal Republic of Germany (FRG), which comprised the three Western zones of occupation, was created. A few months later, the German Democratic Republic (GDR) was established in the Soviet zone. The division of Germany – and that of Berlin, later epitomized by the Wall built to separate the two parts of the city – came to symbolize the geopolitical partition of Europe imposed by the Cold War. Unjust as it certainly was, splitting Germany in two states solved a potentially irresoluble issue and therefore guaranteed a measure of stability in the European postwar settlement.[23]

A U.S.-led political and economic sphere was thus taking a definite shape in the Western part of Europe. Often in a reactive way, the Soviets were themselves consolidating their sphere of influence in the other half of the Continent.

To complete the process, a new security architecture had to be imagined. Only U.S. technological superiority and nuclear potential could balance the huge Soviet conventional military superiority, or so believed most Western European leaders, led by British Foreign Secretary Ernest Bevin. But U.S. public opinion was wary of permanent military entanglements, yearned for a reduction of American defense expenditures and global commitments and was convinced that the Europeans should do more to help themselves. Any initiative leading to a new, transatlantic defensive system – the Truman administration explained to its European partners – had to start in Europe.

Britain took the lead. In March 1947 it signed with France the Treaty of Dunkirk: an alliance that still had an anti-German character, but that provided for forms of security cooperation that were lacking. One year later, France, Britain, Belgium, the Netherlands and Luxembourg signed the Treaty of Brussels, which created a new military alliance: the Western European Union. According to article IV of the treaty: "if any of the High Contracting Parties should be the object of an armed attack in Europe, the other High Contracting Parties will, in accordance with the provisions of Article 51 of the Charter of the United Nations, afford the Party so attacked all the military and other aid and assistance in their power."[24]

The Treaty of Brussels was the model for a broader and more ambitious initiative: the British initiative was in many ways instrumental in inviting, again, the United States into Europe. In July 1948, preliminary talks began in Washington concerning the creation of a military alliance that included also the United States. A U.S. commitment would mean extending the American "nuclear umbrella" to protect Western Europe and match Soviet conventional preponderance. After months of discussions, the North Atlantic Treaty was signed in April 1949. Article V summarized the nature and philosophy of the alliance: "the Parties agree that an armed attack against one or more of them in Europe or North America shall be considered an attack against them all and consequently they agree that, if such an armed attack occurs, each of them, in exercise of the right of individual or collective self-defence recognised by Article 51 of the Charter of the United Nations, will assist the Party or Parties so attacked by taking forthwith, individually and in concert with the other Parties."[25] The treaty was signed by the United States, Canada and ten European states. Among them were countries like Italy that could not properly qualify as "Atlantic" and others, like Portugal, that were authoritarian and quasi-fascist. In 1952, Greece and Turkey also joined the alliance, while Franco's Spain was anchored to the Western security system via a bilateral agreement with the United States, signed in 1953. Cold War choices and imperatives seemed to justify relevant political, and even ethical, compromises.

The North Atlantic Treaty and the subsequent organization it created, NATO, had primarily a political and psychological function. They complemented the Marshall Plan and were meant to reassure pro-U.S. European governments and elites of Washington's commitment to protect and support them. The main consequence was a further consolidation and crystallization of the bipolar partition of Europe. A few years later, in 1955, the FRG would also join the Atlantic alliance, while in 1956 the Soviet Union and its allies formed a carbon-copy defense organization, the Warsaw Pact.

In mid-1949 the United States seemed to be on the winning side of the Cold War competition. The economic recovery of Western Europe was underway; the largest and richest part of Germany was solidly tied to the U.S.-led bloc, the USSR had already suffered the defection of Yugoslavia; and Moscow's hold on the countries falling within its sphere of influence – brutal and authoritarian as it was – appeared weaker and more tenuous.

The Globalization of the Cold War

In the second half of 1949, two events seemed to alter this state of affairs and the global balance of power, or at least its perception in the United States. In August of 1949 the Soviet Union conducted its first atomic test, much earlier than U.S. intelligence agencies had predicted. At least virtually, the U.S. nuclear monopoly had come to an end (Washington, however, preserved an undisputed nuclear superiority until the mid-1960s). A few weeks later, the Chinese civil war ended with the victory of the Communist Party led by Mao Zedong. With the birth of the People's Republic of China, the most populous country in the world joined the communist front, radically altering the power equilibria in Asia.

Washington reacted with alarm, while a domestic controversy erupted in the United States, with the Right denouncing the Truman administration for its alleged "loss of China." Washington pressured its allies to increase their contribution to the common defense effort, and accept the rearmament of the FRG and its speedy integration into the Atlantic security system. U.S. aid to Western Europe was reoriented to the production of military items. With regard to the People's Republic of China, the United States adopted an intransigent posture, refusing any diplomatic interaction and backing instead the Chinese nationalist and anti-communist regime established on the island of Taiwan.

Ideological doctrinarism was not the exclusive property of the Soviet Union. The idea that communism was a monolith, led and directed by the Muscovite center, blinded the U.S. for years to come, preventing it from understanding (and exploiting) the intra-communist tensions that were to find in the Sino-Soviet rift its quintessential, and geopolitically more relevant, expression.[26] The end of the Chinese civil war accelerated the transfer of the bipolar competition from its original European core to Asia. Historian Tsuyoshi Hasegawa has shown how the last phase of World War II, the Soviet decision to enter the war against Japan in August 1945 and the US choice to resort to the atomic bomb, hinted already at the future bipolar antagonism in the Far East.[27] But the inception of the Korean War represented the crucial turning point. Annexed by Japan in 1910, Korea had been liberated during World War II only to see its territory occupied by the two superpowers, the Soviet Union in the North and the United States in the South. Divided along the 38th parallel, the two parts were separated into two formally sovereign states, the pro-Soviet Democratic People's Republic of Korea in the North and the pro-U.S. Republic of Korea in the South.

In June 1950, North Korea launched an attack against its Southern counterpart. The goal was to reunify the peninsula under the communist banner. Albeit reluctantly, Stalin and Mao approved the North Korean action. They believed that the U.S. would not react, and had been bolstered by the recent success in China. But they were also competing between themselves for the allegiance of a lesser ally, North Korea, anticipating a Cold War dynamic that would return in later years.

Almost no-one in the U.S. doubted that Moscow was behind the North Korean attack. The Truman administration, and the vast majority of U.S. experts and commentators, interpreted it as the first salvo of a more general communist offensive, which could rapidly extend to Europe. That was not the case, and local dynamics were playing a crucial role in what was in many regards a civil war.[28] The homologating nature of the Cold War, and of its simple and binary partition, was revealing its strength and pervasiveness. The symbolic relevance of the Korean crisis informed the reaction of the United States. The Truman administration did not consider the Korean peninsula to be strategically vital. Nevertheless, it acted promptly to block and reverse the North Korean offensive. What was at stake, Truman and his advisors believed, was the credibility of the United States and its commitment to contain communism globally. It was necessary to give a clear and unequivocal message to enemies and friends alike. The price of inaction, it was thought, would have been a more aggressive Soviet Union and less loyal and firm partners: Germany could easily follow Korea.

The UN Security Council passed two resolutions that authorized support for the Republic of Korea to repel the armed attack. The USSR did not veto the resolutions: the Soviet delegate in the council was not attending the session in protest against Taiwan's membership in the organization. A UN contingent led by General Douglas MacArthur, the Commander of U.S. Forces in the Far East, was dispatched to Korea. American forces represented almost 90 percent of the contingent. North Korean troops had penetrated deeply into South Korean territory. However, a popular uprising failed to materialize and UN forces launched a counterattack that pushed back the North Korean army. Having reached the original dividing line, on the 38th parallel, UN troops continued to move northwards. The original objective to restore the border between the two Koreas was replaced by that of uniting the peninsula militarily. This decision triggered the reaction of Communist China, which not only feared the possibility of facing U.S. troops on its border but also saw the opportunity to defend and export the revolution successfully achieved at home. The Chinese intervention again altered the course of events and pushed the front back south. The internationalization of the war threatened to cause an escalation of the conflict, as shown by Truman's decision to remove MacArthur, who wanted to expand the war to the Chinese territory. The front then stabilized and, after a long stalemate, an armistice was finally signed in 1953. Korea remained divided along a line not dissimilar to that of June 1950; a situation that has lasted until today and that offers a powerful reminder of the persistent legacy of the Cold War.

With the Korean conflict, the Cold War definitely exited its original European perimeter. The former Japanese enemy was finally transformed into a crucial ally in the containment of communism in Asia, offering the United States bases and loyalty in exchange for economic aid and the abandonment of U.S. punitive plans. Japan was thus assigned the role of the Far East's geopolitical pivot in Washington's global strategy. In moving to Asia, the Cold War began a process of globalization that would only intensify in the following years.[29]

Oppressive as it was, the European Cold War order produced a stability that helped to guarantee a "long peace" in the Continent.[30] This "long peace" was founded on the nuclear balance of terror, the acceptance of an often brutal Soviet rule in Central–Eastern Europe and a less draconian curtailment of political rights and national sovereignty in the U.S. bloc. Outside Europe, however, the Cold War could not, in any way, be characterized as an era of peace. There, it often lost its frosty nature and, interacting with other dynamics and processes, served to amplify local wars and conflicts, whose human and material costs proved to be immense. Korea is a case in point. The Korean casualties of the war were approximately 3 million, one tenth of the entire population; the refugees numbered 5 million, while millions of families were permanently separated by the conflict. The impact on the industrial plant and the infrastructures of the two sides was devastating, just as it was on the environment, another of the many victims of the global Cold War that began and ended in Europe, but had its most dramatic impact on the rest of the world.[31]

Notes

1 Tony Judt, *Postwar: A History of Europe since 1945* (New York: Penguin, 2005), 18.
2 Judt, *Postwar*, 16–19.
3 Melvyn P. Leffler, "The Emergence of an American Grand Strategy," in Melvyn P. Leffler and Odd Arne Westad, eds., *The Cambridge History of the Cold War. Volume I: Origins* (Cambridge: Cambridge University Press, 2010), 67–69.
4 R. Aron, *Paix et guerre entre le nations* (Paris: Calmann-Lévy, 1962); Anders Stephanson, "Fourteen Notes on the Very Concept of the Cold War," in Gearóid Ó Tuathail and Simon Dalby, eds., *Rethinking Geopolitics* (London: Routledge, 1998), 62–85.
5 J. Ruggie, "International Regimes, Transactions, and Change: Embedded Liberalism in the Postwar International Order," *International Organization* 2 (Spring 1982): 379–415; Robert Latham, *The Liberal Moment: Modernity, Security and the Making of the Postwar International Order* (New York: Columbia University Press, 1997).
6 Michael Hogan, *A Cross of Iron: Harry S. Truman and the Origins of the National Security State, 1945–1954* (Cambridge: Cambridge University Press, 1998).
7 S. Pons, *L'impossibile egemonia. L'URSS, il PCI e le origini della Guerra Fredda* (Roma: Carocci, 1999); Warren Kimball, *The Juggler: Franklin Roosevelt as Wartime Statesman* (Princeton: Princeton University Press, 1994).
8 A. Milward, *The Reconstruction of Western Europe* (London: Methuen, 1984). More generally see Federico Romero, *Storia della Guerra Fredda. L'ultimo conflitto per l'Europa* [History of the Cold War. The Last Conflict Over Europe] (Torino: Einaudi, 2009).
9 Carolyn Eisenberg, *Drawing the Line: the American Decision to Divide Germany, 1944–1949* (Cambridge: Cambridge University Press, 1996).
10 Vladislav M. Zubok and Constantine Pleshakov, *Inside the Kremlin's Cold War: From Stalin to Khrushchev* (Cambridge, MA: Harvard University Press, 1996). Stalin's search for absolute security – and the inconsistency of his policies – is discussed in Vojtech Mastny, *The Cold War and Soviet Insecurity: The Stalin Years* (New York: Oxford University Press, 1996). A different interpretation that stresses the

ideological matrices of Stalin's foreign policies and presents the Soviet dictator as a "romantic revolutionary" is in John Lewis Gaddis, *We Now Know: Re-Thinking Cold War History* (Oxford: Oxford University Press, 1997).

11 *The Chargé in the Soviet Union (Kennan) to the Secretary of State*, Moscow, February 22, 1946, National Security Archive, Washington, D.C.

12 "X" (George Kennan), "The Sources of Soviet Conduct," *Foreign Affairs* 4 (July 1947): 575.

13 Anders Stephanson, "The Cold War Considered as US Project," in S. Pons and F. Romero eds., *Reinterpreting the Cold War: Issues, Interpretations, Periodizations* (London: Routledge, 2004), 52–67; John Lewis Gaddis, *George Kennan: An American Life* (New York: Penguin, 2011).

14 Telegram from N. Novikov, Soviet Ambassador to the US, to the Soviet Leadership, September 27, 1946, (http://legacy.wilsoncenter.org/va2/index.cfm?topic_id=1409&fuseaction=HOME.document&identifier=952E8C7F-423B-763D-D5662C42501C9BEA&sort=Subject&item=UN, last accessed January 23, 2013).

15 Melvin P. Leffler, *A Preponderance of Power: National Security, the Truman Administration and the Cold War* (Stanford: Stanford University Press, 1992) and ibid., *For the Soul of the Mankind: the United States, the Soviet Union and the Cold War* (New York: Hill & Wang, 2007), 11–83. The idea of the Cold War as a "security dilemma" is discussed also in Robert Jervis, "Was the Cold War a Security Dilemma?," *Journal of Cold War Studies* 1 (Winter 2001), 36–60.

16 Dean Acheson, *Present at the Creation: My Years at the State Department* (New York: Norton, 1969), 197.

17 Address of the President to Congress, Recommending Assistance to Greece and Turkey, 12 March 1947, *Public Papers of the President of the United States: Harry S. Truman*.

18 William I. Hitchcock, "The Marshall Plan and the Creation of the West," Melvyn P. Leffler and Odd Arne Westad, eds., *The Cambridge History of the Cold War. Volume I: Origins* (Cambridge: Cambridge University Press, 2010), 167.

19 David Ellwood, *The Shock of America: Europe and the Challenge of the Century* (Oxford: Oxford University Press, 2012), 340–386.

20 See for example, Kaeten Mistry, *The United States, Italy, and the Origins of Cold War: Waging Political Warfare, 1945–50* (Cambridge: Cambridge University Press, forthcoming 2014).

21 Lundestad first formulated his "empire by invitation" thesis in Geir Lundestad, "Empire by Invitation? The United States and Western Europe, 1945–52," *Journal of Peace Research* 3 (September 1986): 263–277. A similar approach can be found in the now classic John L. Gaddis, "The Emerging Post-Revisionist Synthesis on the Origins of the Cold War, *Diplomatic History* 7 (Summer 1983): 171–190. For an application to the Italian case see Alessandro Brogi, *L'Italia e l'egemonia Americana nel Mediterraneo* [Italy and the American Hegemony in the Mediterranean] (Firenze: La Nuova Italia, 1996).

22 C. Maier, "Alliance and Autonomy: European Identity and US Foreign Policy in the Truman Years," in M.J. Lacey, ed., *The Truman Presidency* (Cambridge: Cambridge University Press, 1989), 273–298.

23 Marc Trachtenberg, *A Constructed Peace: The Making of the European Settlement, 1945–1963* (Princeton: Princeton University Press, 1999).

24 *The Treaty of Economic, Social and Cultural Collaboration and Collective Self-Defence*, March 17, 1948 (http://www.cvce.eu/obj/the_brussels_treaty_17_march_1948-en-3467de5e-9802-4b65-8076-778bc7d164d3.html, last accessed January 27, 2013).

25 *The North Atlantic Treaty*, April 4, 1949 (http://www.nato.int/cps/en/natolive/official_texts_17120.htm, last accessed January 27, 2013).

26 Lorenz M. Lüthi, *The Sino-Soviet Split: Cold War in the Communist World* (Princeton: Princeton University Press, 2008).

27 Tsuyoshi Hasegawa, *Racing the Enemy: Stalin, Truman and the Surrender of Japan* (Cambridge, MA: Harvard University Press, 2005). See also Sayuri Guthrie-Shimizu, "Japan, the United States and the Cold War," in Melvyn P. Leffler and Odd Arne Westad, eds., *The Cambridge History of the Cold War. Volume I: Origins* (Cambridge: Cambridge University Press, 2010), 245–265.

28 On this see the different interpretations of Bruce Cumings, *The Origins of the Korean War* (Princeton: Princeton University Press, 1981 and 1990), and William Stueck, *The Korean War: an International History* (Princeton: Princeton University Press, 1995).

29 Odd Arne Westad, *The Global Cold War: Third World Interventions and the Making of Our Times* (Cambridge: Cambridge University Press, 2005).

30 John Lewis Gaddis, "The Long Peace. Elements of Stability in the Postwar International System," *International Security* 4 (Spring 1986): 99–142.

31 H. Kwon, *The Other Cold War* (New York: Columbia University Press, 2010). On the environmental costs of the Cold War see the masterful J.R. McNeill, *Something New Under the Sun: an Environmental History of the Twentieth Century World* (New York: Norton, 2000). For a detailed and original reflection on the historiography of the Cold War see Holger Nehrig, "What Was the Cold War?" *English Historical Review* 527 (2013): 920–949.

2
FEAR, WANT, AND THE INTERNATIONALISM OF THE EARLY COLD WAR

Amanda Kay McVety[1]

In his 1941 State of the Union address, Franklin D. Roosevelt announced that he "unhappily" found it "necessary to report that the future and the safety of our country and of our democracy are overwhelmingly involved in events far beyond our borders." Freedom was under siege around the globe, he continued, and the United States was not going to be able to remain neutral in that struggle. Nor should it want to, because winning the fight would allow for a restructuring of the international state system. "In the future days, which we seek to make secure, we look forward to a world founded upon four essential human freedoms," he told his listeners, and, notably, the readers of his speech (an audience that reached far beyond the United States): "freedom of speech and expression," "freedom of every person to worship God in his own way," "freedom from want," and "freedom from fear."[2] It was just a speech, but it was a speech that changed the way people thought about the war. Its language framed the Allied struggle for victory and for "a different world order," both during and after the war.

The Allied pursuit of a postwar peace opened the door to new assessments of the purposes and possibilities of international cooperation. Four core beliefs animated the discussion. First and foremost, policymakers maintained their confidence that the state should remain the center of authority, although they agreed that they needed to combine forces on some key issues. Second, policymakers bolstered this confidence in the state as a force for good with a faith in human technological ingenuity and large-scale planning, both of which helped lead the Allies to victory. Third, changes in the discipline of economics and the introduction of the idea of "an economy" that could be manipulated into the production of greater wealth (and the prevention of a serious recession) put economic planning at the forefront of postwar planning. Finally, policymakers in Europe and the United States turned to religion for answers for a way forward to a brighter future for all. For some, this was no doubt merely a language that would better sell their policies to a believing public. But, for others, religion (or a social conscience) was a powerful guiding force that demanded action to relieve suffering and fight injustice. These four faiths – the centrality of the state, the wonder-working ability of human ingenuity to bring progress, the growth of a properly managed global economy, and the dictates of a higher power – shaped the internationalism of the 1940s and animated the quest for "freedom."

Fear

The drive for freedom from fear began with alliances. "It is no exaggeration to say that the future of the whole world and the hopes of a broadening civilization founded upon Christian ethics depend upon the relations between the British Empire or Commonwealth of Nations and the U.S.A.," Churchill insisted in response to Roosevelt's 1941 State of the Union address.[3] That August, the two met secretly off the coast of Newfoundland. The American president was not prepared to declare war, but he was prepared to do everything short of it, even offering to issue a declaration of Anglo-American aims for war and peace. Negotiations about what those aims were quickly ensued, with the text of Roosevelt's Four Freedoms the guiding vision.[4] Some of his freedoms made it directly into the text: "after the final destruction of the Nazi tyranny, they hope to see established a peace which will afford to all nations the means of dwelling in safety within their own boundaries, and which will afford assurance that all the men in all lands may live out their lives in freedom from fear and want." The freedoms of speech and religion, Roosevelt later explained, were there in principle, if not in fact. The absence of the latter was meant as a nod to Stalin, whom Roosevelt and Churchill already decided had to be supported in his struggle against Hitler. In addition to declaring their hopes for postwar freedom, the two disavowed any territorial aims, promised support for self-determination, freer trade (to American insistence and British dismay), and a reduction in armaments, and expressed hope for "the establishment of a wider and permanent system of general security."[5] The Atlantic Charter – as the agreement was dubbed – was a statement, not a treaty, but it shaped both the subsequent Anglo-American alliance and the international conversation about the purpose of the war. As Elizabeth Borgwardt has argued, "Early planning documents for subsequent, detailed blueprints such as the charters of the United Nations, Nuremberg, and Bretton Woods all drew their inspiration, and in many cases their specific provisions, explicitly from the Atlantic Charter."[6]

Britain and the United States had announced that this was a war for a better world – one dedicated to the pursuit of freedom from fear and want for "all the men in all lands." Neither Churchill nor Roosevelt knew precisely what that meant, but each had a generally conservative notion that it would be something similar to the way the world had operated before the rise of fascism. Others disagreed. "Inspired by the Atlantic Charter and the fight of the Allies against tyranny and oppression," Nelson Mandela later wrote, "the ANC created its own Charter … [to show] that the principles they were fighting for in Europe were the same ones we were advocating at home."[7] This was a decidedly unwelcome development for Churchill, and it symbolized the problem of uniting the world in a war against tyranny while sanctioning it at home. The charter's repeated use of "all" proved a source of both strength and weakness, from the perspective of its authors. It helped to rally people around the world to the cause, but it also opened a conversation about self-determination that proved impossible to contain.[8] But, for the moment, it did what needed most to be done: it reassured the British people that the United States was with them. In the aftermath of Pearl Harbor, it provided the foundation of the most powerful alliance in history: the United Nations.

On January 1, 1942, representatives of twenty-six countries pledged themselves "to employ [their] full resources, military or economic, against those members of the Tripartite Pact and its adherents with which such government is at war." They did so, they explained, because they "subscribed to a common program of purposes and principles embodied in … the Atlantic Charter," because they were "convinced that complete victory over their enemies is essential to defend life, liberty, independence and religious freedom, and to preserve human rights and justice in their own lands as well as in other lands, and that they are now engaged in a common struggle against savage and brutal forces seeking to subjugate the world."⁹ This was the alliance that Winston Churchill and Joseph Stalin had been waiting for but, by invoking the Atlantic Charter, it reiterated the problem of the charter itself: it promised to be more than its authors intended. Then again, the most powerful of the signatories were well aware that once their enemies had been defeated, they would be in a position to organize the world as they saw fit. They already knew what they wanted: security and prosperity.

The Allies spent 1942 and the first half of 1943 working desperately to change the tide of the war and they were successful. By the fall of 1943, eventual victory seemed certain, though distant. This shift in fortune opened the door for more serious conversation about what peace should look like. Roosevelt had already insisted that it be based on collective security, with the United States, Great Britain, the USSR, and China serving as the Four Policemen. He recognized that this did not fit with the ideals of the Atlantic Charter, telling a British representative, "You can't invoke high moral principles where high moral principles do not exist. In international politics they don't always apply, unfortunately, and our job is to win the war." He was not ready to throw out the charter, however, recognizing its international cachet, so he tried to keep its vision alive at the same time as he worked to create his Four Policemen.¹⁰ At a meeting in Moscow that October, Secretary of State Cordell Hull, Foreign Secretary Anthony Eden, and Minister of Foreign Affairs Vyacheslav Molotov drafted a Joint Four-Nation Declaration that recognized "the necessity of establishing at the earliest practicable date a general international organization, based on the principle of the sovereign equality of all peace-loving states, and open to membership by all such states, large and small, for the maintenance of international peace and security."¹¹ Four nations (really only three, since China was not present) were making the declaration, but they were insisting on the equality of all nations. It was a delicate balancing act.

While Roosevelt focused his attention on collective security, policymakers in the State Department and in Whitehall pursued plans for this "general international organization" reminiscent of the League of Nations. In the fall of 1944, these plans became the foundation of a conference at Dumbarton Oaks, where delegates from the United States, Great Britain, the USSR, and China (although the Soviets refused to meet with the Chinese) outlined the essential framework of a postwar United Nations.¹² The devised organization attempted to blend the Four Policemen with the Atlantic Charter. The permanent members of the Security Council were granted enormous power, but the organization itself promised both to maintain peace and, after intense pressure from the Americans, to "promote respect for human rights and fundamental freedoms."¹³ This language would return in the United Nations Charter, which was drafted at a meeting in San Francisco in April of 1945 that included forty-five, rather than four, nations. South African Prime Minister Jan Smuts drafted a preamble to the new charter that called on the organization to "re-establish faith in fundamental human rights, in the sanctity and ultimate value of human personality, in the equal rights of men and women, and nations large and small." The irony of the father of apartheid talking about "fundamental human rights" symbolized the limitations of the new organization, which was far *less* equal than the League of Nations had been.¹⁴ Whether or not the United Nations was a step forward for international relations or a step backward was open to debate.

What was not open to debate was the reality that the United Nations was a decidedly nationalistic international organization. It relied primarily upon the military strength of the five permanent members of the Security Council to keep the peace and it backed away from limitations on their sovereignty. Article 2 of the Charter insisted that "Nothing contained in the present Charter shall authorize the United Nations to intervene in matters which are essentially within the domestic jurisdiction of any state."¹⁵ While General Assembly resolutions were not binding, every nation that signed the Charter agreed to recognize all Security Council resolutions as binding. To further enhance the national power of the five permanent members – at Soviet insistence – they were granted veto power over "substantive" decisions, even if they involved their own countries.[16] By the time the San Francisco conference ended, there was no doubt about which nations controlled the international state system.

Despite their frustrations, there were still reasons for small states to remain hopeful that this new organization could do more for them than help prevent another world war. The United Nations contained an Economic and Social Council (ECOSOC) that could "make or initiate studies and reports with respect to international economic, social, cultural, educational, health, and related matters" and "make recommendations for the purpose of promoting respect for, and observance of, human rights and fundamental freedoms for all."[17] ECOSOC tried to make the most of its limited powers, establishing the Commission on Human Rights and the Commission on the Status of Women in 1946, and appointing experts to a committee to draft an agenda for the upcoming International Health Conference. The Commission of Human Rights was immediately charged with creating an international bill of rights.[18] It would be a daunting task, because cracks in the alliance were already showing. They began in a debate over how to ensure postwar prosperity.

Memories of the Great Depression overshadowed conversations about the possibilities of the postwar world and shaped Allied war planning from the beginning. Lend-Lease aid to Britain included a clause that attacked imperial preference and trade controls. In the end, the British were able to maneuver some wiggle room, adding "within the limits of their governing economic conditions" and "with due respect for their existing obligations" clauses promising to promote freer trade.[19] But the point had been made that the United States was not going to allow the economics of the postwar world to look the same as the economics of the prewar world.

It was not just a question of trade (although that was a critical part[20]); it was a fundamental shift in economic understanding. Dean Acheson later explained, "We were embracing the Keynesian ideas of an expanding economy."[21] What he meant was that the United States government had come to accept the idea that something called "an economy" existed and that it could be manipulated into growth. The idea was only a decade old, but it was transforming international relations. Conversations about national economies soon gave way to conversations about *an* international economy, which would require regulation and manipulation on an entirely different level.[22] Here, the quest for prosperity collided head-on with the quest for security, since another global depression could seemingly easily give way to another global war. American and British representatives began tentatively discussing the subject during the Lend-Lease talks of 1941 and started passing drafts of a plan for a new international economic organization back and forth across the Atlantic. The changing fortunes of the war in 1943 opened the door to the possibility of a formal conference on the matter, just as they did for a conference on international security.[23]

In July of 1944, before the gathering at Dumbarton Oaks, representatives of forty-four nations met in Bretton Woods, New Hampshire, "for the purpose of formulating proposals of a definite character for an international monetary fund and possibly a bank for reconstruction and development."[24] Of course, the foundational proposals had already been discussed by the British and the Americans, but the conference was a nod to their sincere belief that these needed to be truly international organizations – even if they were ultimately going to be dominated by only a few powers. U.S. Secretary of the Treasury Henry Morgenthau worked to ensure cooperation from the Soviet delegation, fearful of the consequences of a Soviet refusal to join. The conference ended on a positive note with an agreement to create the

International Bank for Reconstruction and Development (soon to be known as the World Bank) and the International Monetary Fund (IMF). Keynes remarked, "We have shown that a concourse of 44 nations are actually able to work together at a constructive task in amity and unbroken accord." If we can keep it up, he continued, "The brotherhood of man will have become more than a phrase."[25] It was a noble sentiment, but it breezed over underlying concerns. It was unclear whether the Soviets would join.[26] Voting rights in both of the new organizations were distributed according to financial contributions, which necessarily ensured that control rested with the wealthiest nations. In addition, in the name of financial stability, the conference set the U.S. dollar as the benchmark against which all other currencies were valued, giving the United States an enormous amount of international economic control.[27]

In the end, although it marked an important step forward in global cooperation, Bretton Woods also highlighted the unwillingness of the British and American governments to surrender much power in the pursuit of prosperity and Moscow's unwillingness to surrender any at all (it would refuse to ratify the agreements). But the story does not end there, because Bretton Woods was not the only place where the Allies discussed freedom from want, and the outcomes of those other conversations had just as lasting repercussions for the postwar world. While the World Bank and the IMF were clearly created in such a way as to benefit London and Washington most of all, other wartime organizations were not. Here, where the question of prosperity was seen to be further removed from security, policymakers drew greater inspiration from a sense of responsibility for fellow human beings.

This sense came from two primary sources. First were religious traditions that emphasized the value of each person and placed a responsibility on believers to relieve the suffering of those in need when they could do so. Second was the secular discourse of an "international community" linked "by a common humanity."[28] Although scholars often highlight the influence of the latter over the former, Samuel Moyn cautions that such an approach is more representative of modern secularism than mid-century reality. "Kantians were few and far between in the 1940s," he writes.[29] Most of the policymakers at the center of this history (the Soviets aside) seem to have been motivated in part by the dictates of their religion and a vague sense of a common humanity, both of which had already gained expression in the Atlantic Charter. They had been taught that they should do something in the face of human suffering. Memories of the last war and its aftermath reinforced the urge to act, and recent advances in science and technology offered new tools for the task. They had will, ways, and a seemingly unlimited supply of people who needed help. It was, after all, the middle of the most devastating war in human history, and there was a great deal of want.[30]

Want

In the fall of 1942, Roosevelt received a memo from an Australian official, titled "United Nations Programme for Freedom from Want of Food," which called for the creation of a permanent international organization to address hunger. Roosevelt was intrigued, but cautious, about the "permanent" part. Continued pressure from interest groups to "do something" led him to order the State and Agriculture Departments to organize an international conference on the subject, which was held in Hot Springs, Virginia, in May–June of 1943.[31] It was not the same kind of conference as those that would soon be taking place in Bretton Woods and Dumbarton Oaks. "Hot Springs," Amy L. Sayward wrote, "differed from most previous international conferences in that the focus was on technical questions handled by experts rather than on traditional topics of diplomacy."[32] The initiative for Hot Springs came from the sense of a need to address suffering. The overriding faith that guided the conference itself, however, was confidence in human scientific and technological ingenuity.

By the 1940s, the Western world was enamored with "scientism", the idea that scientific knowledge could be mobilized to solve social problems. Engineers, scientists, and technicians eagerly pursued large-scale projects in the pursuit of large-scale progress.[33] "Hunger" was on their hit list. It had been since journalists began publishing photographs of skinny, malnourished colonial children in British newspapers in the late nineteenth century. Hunger rose to prominence again from reports of suffering in Belgium during World War I. But the transformation of hunger from a humanitarian to a technical problem required that it be defined in a scientific way.[34] As Nick Cullather has shown, it was the turn-of-the-century discovery of the calorie that "made the abstract idea of food supply tangible, taking a hypothetical limit on human potential and distilling it into a political problem that had scientific and organizational solutions." The United States government embraced the idea of political organization for this scientific problem in 1917, when Woodrow Wilson appointed Herbert Hoover, who had already become famous for running the Commission for Relief in Belgium, as U.S. Food Administrator. In 1919, Hoover founded the American Relief Administration (ARA) to attack hunger in postwar Europe. He deemed it too dangerous to leave alone: "famine breeds anarchy," he warned, and anarchy spreads.[35]

Hoover was not the only one concerned. Throughout the 1920s and 1930s, citizens became less tolerant of hunger and demanded greater action from their governments.[36] While often viewed from a national perspective, it was clear that it was also an international problem. In 1935, the League of Nations organized the Mixed Committee on the Problem of Nutrition in response to "a growing recognition of the importance of taking active measures to improve nutrition." The committee's 1937 report compiled consumption and production statistics from around the globe and encouraged greater international cooperation to defeat hunger. The outbreak of war in Europe put a temporary halt to these efforts, but they came back to life at Hot Springs.[37]

Food distribution played a role in Allied planning from the beginning of the war, both as a critical military supply and as an important part of Lend-Lease aid. Shortages throughout the United Nations, however, soon caused Washington and London to rethink their approach. A 1945 report looking back on the spring of 1942 explained, "Some means had to be found for the interchange of information and the development of international plans to make the best use of the free world's diminishing resources of manpower, machinery, fertilizers, and other material on the food front." That "means" was the June 1942 creation of the Combined Food Board to organize the production and distribution of food in over seventy countries.[38] Many of the agricultural experts involved in the 1943 conference at Hot Springs argued that this kind of planning and coordination would need to extend past the war itself, but many of the politicians at the conference disagreed – preferring to see a reincarnation of League of Nations initiatives. The debate continued for two years, as an interim commission of representatives from fifteen countries struggled to define the parameters of what would become the Food and Agriculture Organization (FAO). The final product was too conservative for many, burdened by the sovereignty claims of its most powerful members.[39]

At its first meeting in 1945, the FAO's new director-general, Sir John Boyd Orr, was dismayed, because "the hungry people of the world wanted bread, and they were to be given statistics. The food deficient countries were to be told by Western experts how to modernize their agriculture, but there were no means of enabling them to get the industrial equipment needed to do this."[40] Although the FAO demonstrated far more sensitivity to the needs of the world's poorer nations than did the organizations recently established at Bretton Woods, its ability to seriously tackle the problem of international hunger was severely restricted by limited funds and authorizations. But the machinery was in place for it to become a more interventionist organization when international focus shifted, as, indeed, it soon did. The first shift centered on relief; the second, on development.[41]

The official Allied relief effort began in November 1943 with the creation of the United Nations Relief and Rehabilitation Agency (UNRRA) to provide aid to areas liberated from Axis control. There was a bit of uncertainty about what the "rehabilitation" part might mean, but the "relief" part seemed obvious, because people were already doing it.[42] British citizens had created Oxfam in 1942 to send food to Greeks dying of starvation. Catholic Relief Services began operations in 1943 and was soon joined by Lutheran World Relief. Veterans of World War I's American Relief Administration formed the nonprofit Cooperative for American Remittances to Europe (CARE) in 1945.[43] Humanitarianism united the sacred and the secular in the cause of freedom from want.

By the fall of 1945, it had become clear that relief and rehabilitation were going to take far longer than the Allies had hoped. Much of the world was physically and morally devastated by years of brutal fighting. Global food supply had fallen 12 percent per person from 1939 levels; fields and animals were destroyed; cities were leveled; tens of millions of people were homeless; and tens of millions were far from home, victims of forced deportations and migrations. Most were hungry. Many were ill. As Tony Judt wryly noted, "Surviving the war was one thing, surviving the peace another." The UNRRA stepped in to help, but it was not enough.[44] New intergovernmental agencies were created to join the fight – the United Nations International Children's Emergency Fund; the International Refugee Organization; the United Nations Educational, Scientific, and Cultural Organization; and the World Health Organization – and dozens of nongovernmental organizations, but the situation still felt desperate.[45] Europe turned to the unscathed United States for more help.

Prime Minister Clement Attlee cabled the White House in early January of 1946, explaining that "the maximum quantities that could be spared" needed to be exported from all producing countries so as to avoid widespread famine in Europe and Asia. Truman recalled in his memoirs that Attlee "emphasized, too, that the effects of this would spread far beyond the national boundaries of the countries concerned and would undoubtedly make infinitely more difficult the work of building a sound peace through the United Nations."[46] The sentiment was similar to that which Herbert Hoover had expressed in the aftermath of World War I. Truman asked the American people to ramp up production and cut back on consumption, and then asked Hoover to chair a Famine Emergency Committee that would investigate the situation on the ground.

Both Truman and Hoover stressed that the United States had a moral responsibility to act. The night before he left on his round-the-world tour, Hoover told the American people that "this is an issue of religious faith and morals which affects our country as a whole and each individual. ... These starving women and children are in foreign countries, yet they are hungry human beings – and they are also your neighbors. ... I know that the heart of the American people will respond with kindliness to suffering."[47] Hoover and his team traveled through thirty-eight countries that spring, primarily evaluating the food situation in each, but also taking keen note of their political situation. His diary entries record ominous meetings with distraught leaders who feared that they were losing control of their countries. During his visit to Italy, President of the Council, Alcide de Gasperi, "said the situation was very precarious. ... the [Communists] were spending several hundred millions per month on propaganda" and "whenever they were able to seize local governments, they misused UNRRA supplies for their purposes." He warned Hoover "that if Italy and France went Communist, western civilization had collapsed in western Europe."[48] Conditions were worse elsewhere. The American ambassador to Poland told Hoover that the country "was a terrorist police state" and that the Soviets "in no way are complying with Teheran, Yalta or Potsdam."[49] The American ambassador to Czechoslovakia told him that "up to a short time ago all food trains came into Czechoslovakia with a picture of Stalin on the locomotives and red flags on the cars; that at every station where a car was put off for distribution, it was met by a Communist Committee with ceremonies of thanks to Uncle Joe. All these trains were, of course, American and Canadian food – a gift paid for 80 percent by the U.S. and not a dime of money or a grain of wheat contributed by Russia."[50] Food had become a tool of political manipulation, and the United States wanted its flag on those trains.

Hoover's observations recorded a growing divide between former allies over the future of Europe in particular, but also the world in general. Pinpointing the origins of the Cold War is beyond the scope of this chapter, but as 1946 gave way to 1947, the language used by American policymakers to describe their relief efforts changed. "We have dedicated ourselves to the task of securing a just and lasting peace," Truman announced in a radio address in October of 1947. "We cannot turn aside from that goal." The countries of Western Europe, he continued, must be maintained as "free self-supporting democracies" and "they cannot do it if thousands of their people starve." More aid was the only option; "peace" could not "be lost because Americans failed to share their food with hungry people."[51] Relief was no longer sold as a primarily humanitarian act, but as a security act. The shift represented a genuine fear that communism was gaining ground over democracy because rehabilitation had not yet followed relief. "There is no choice between becoming a Communist on 1,500 calories a day and a believer in democracy on 1,000," U.S. military commander Lucius Clay reported from Germany.[52] Freedom from want seemed even more important in 1947 than it had in 1941.

"The year 1947 was to prove crucial," Tony Judt concluded, "the hinge on which was suspended the fate of the continent." Europe endured another bitter winter and then entered one of the hottest summers on record. American Hamilton Fish wrote of the Continent that summer, "there is too little of everything."[53] Requests for aid continued to pour in to Washington. U.S. policymakers recognized that real rehabilitation depended upon the creation of a comprehensive recovery program that would have to include Germany. Secretary of State George C. Marshall announced the plan at a commencement address at Harvard that summer. "It is logical that the United States should do whatever it is able to do to assist in the return of normal economic health in the world, without which there can be no political stability and no assured peace," he told his audience, notably appealing to their sense of self-preservation, not their sense of a common humanity. "Our policy is directed not against any country or doctrine but against hunger, poverty, desperation and chaos. Its purpose should be the revival of a working economy in the world so as to permit the emergence of political and social conditions in which free institutions can exist."[54] Of course, the policy *was* directed against a specific country and a specific doctrine. Melvyn Leffler has persuasively shown that "the United States launched the Marshall Plan to arrest an impending shift in the correlation of power between the United States and the Soviet Union."[55]

Washington feared that Moscow was gaining the upper hand in Europe, which threatened the strength of the global economic system constructed at Bretton Woods. American policymakers insisted that global prosperity depended upon a *capitalist* European recovery. They opened the aid to all the countries of Europe, but Moscow decided that the money was not worth the potential cost to national sovereignty. Stalin forbade nations under Soviet influence to participate, consolidating his own power in his own orbit.[56] He had his own vision of postwar rehabilitation: "during the very years when the Marshall Plan injected some $14 billion *into* Western Europe's recovery economy, Stalin – through reparations, forced deliveries and the imposition of grossly disadvantageous trading distortions – extracted approximately the same amount *from* Eastern Europe."[57] The quest for international security and prosperity became a quest for regional security and prosperity. Both sides would invoke "freedom" in the struggle, but so too would nations who wanted to stay out of their fight.

Limitations

In 1949, reflecting on the displaced person crisis in Europe, Hannah Arendt wrote that "the problem of statelessness on so large a scale had the effect of confronting the nations of the world with an inescapable and perplexing question: whether or not there really exist such 'human rights' independent of all specific political status and deriving solely from the fact of being human?" Could "the Rights of Man" exist without citizenship, she wondered.[58] Recent events raised doubts. The UN was a decidedly nation-centered organization designed to protect national sovereignty. At Nuremberg, the Allied powers had limited their prosecution to crimes committed outside of Germany proper, leaving unresolved the question of who could hold leaders responsible for what happened within their borders.[59] This had not gone unnoticed.

The postwar period was marked by a sharp rise in self-determinism, in large part because people recognized nationhood as essential to security in the UN system. Freedom from fear and freedom from want appeared to depend first and foremost on the freedom to be a nation. Displaced Jewish survivors in Europe were more cognizant of this than anyone, but they were not alone. Subjugated peoples around the globe called on their colonial overlords to honor the Atlantic Charter's promise of self-determination and grant them their freedom.[60] Arendt's question, meanwhile, represented a central preoccupation of ECOSOC's Commission on Human Rights, which had released its Universal Declaration of Human Rights to the General Assembly of the UN the year before.

The Universal Declaration of Human Rights answered the question of where rights came from by proclaiming that people gained them at birth. They were not, then, tied to citizenship, but to being human, which involved both rights and duties, because people were "endowed with reason and conscience and should act towards one another in a spirit of brotherhood."[61] The Declaration called for the international community to allow the dictates of conscience to prevail over self-interest. It seems, in retrospect, a high point of postwar internationalism, but that might demand a second look. In her history of its creation, Mary Ann Glendon argued that the Declaration "charted a bold new course for human rights by presenting a vision of freedom as linked to social security, balanced by responsibilities, grounded in respect for equal human dignity, and guarded by the rule of law."[62] Samuel Moyn countered (in a chapter notably titled "Death from Birth") that "the Universal Declaration and associated developments like the European Convention on Human Rights (1950) were minor byproducts of this era, not main features. Human rights were already on the edge of the stage in the postwar moment, even before they were pushed off entirely by Cold War politics."[63] Mark Mazower took a middle path, highlighting the Declaration's limitations: "Behind the smokescreen of the rights of the individual, in other words, the corpse of the League's minority policy could be safely buried," but also acknowledging that "sufficient ambiguity was built into the UN's approach to allow a new emphasis on human rights to emerge during the Cold War."[64] The Declaration's authors were, for the most part, driven by a genuine concern for suffering and a genuine desire to promote human rights, but they had to operate within an international system that permitted them little room for action.

Many people were strongly committed to the pursuit of human rights, but their plans were hijacked by, first, the Big Three's insistence upon states' rights, and, second, the Cold War.

This struggle is particularly evident in the history of the African American response to the Declaration, which had placed "race" first in its list of reasons for which people could not be denied "all the rights and freedoms" they deserved as human beings. Racism was, in their minds, first and foremost a human rights issue. But, as Carol Anderson deftly demonstrated in her history of the National Association for the Advancement of Colored People (NAACP) during this period, efforts by the organization to frame its struggle in that way were quickly quashed by the United States government, which began labeling their calls for equal access to housing, education, and medical care evidence of Communist sympathies.[65] Anderson's point is that while it is important to acknowledge, as other historians have done, that the Cold War encouraged the United States government to make some concessions to the NAACP in order to bolster its global image,[66] the government also used the Cold War to limit the kind of rights for which African Americans could publically lobby. They could fight for political and legal rights, but not social and economic ones. Anti-Communist "witch-hunts," Anderson argued, "twisted the definition of human rights into the hammer and sickle, and forced the NAACP to take its eyes off the prize of human rights." The Civil Rights Movement, then, "was, in the end, only a *civil rights*, not a human rights, movement."[67] The United States government had its own definition of the kinds of rights to which people were entitled and it did not sanction challenges to that definition, either at home or abroad.

The language of human rights did not disappear in the aftermath of the Declaration, but it was co-opted by, first, Washington and, second, Moscow in their struggle to win hearts and minds (and resources and UN votes).[68] In his 1949 inaugural address, Truman defined the struggle between democracy and "the false philosophy" of communism as a fight about "material well-being, human dignity, and the right to believe in and worship God." Since the end of the war, he continued, "the United States has invested its substance and its energy in a great constructive effort to restore peace, stability, and freedom to the world." And it was ready to invest more. In the future, Truman promised, we will "continue to give unfaltering support to the United Nations and related agencies," "continue our programs for world economic recovery," "strengthen freedom-loving nations against the dangers of aggression," and "embark on a bold new program for making the benefits of our scientific advances and industrial progress available for the improvement and growth of underdeveloped areas."[69] The United States had, of course, excellent reasons for continuing to support the United Nations and global economic recovery, since both enhanced its power. Truman's third point referenced discussions for an Atlantic defense treaty that had been going on throughout 1948. NATO was more about soothing European fears than reorienting US foreign policy, but it highlighted the regionalization of Europe.[70] The fourth point made it clear that the United States was planning to expand such regionalization beyond the North Atlantic.

Truman's fourth point promised development – the path to freedom from want – as the cure for underdevelopment and the vaccine against communism. A State Department article that spring explained that what was now being called Point Four "reflects a belief that visible progress toward the elimination of poverty can alone sustain the hope necessary to keep alive faith in political democracy."[71] The political message echoed the ones that had gone out about European suffering in 1947. Point Four moved from an idea to a program in 1950, with the establishment of the Technical Cooperation Administration. The American urge to utilize development as a tool of foreign policy drew – in differing degrees – on all four of the animating faiths of the 1940s highlighted in this chapter: confidence in human technological ingenuity and large-scale planning, a sense of moral obligation to relieve human suffering, hope that a managed global economy would keep expanding, and the centrality of the state in the international system.[72] The goal was to develop *nations*, not individuals, although the language used to sell the program often emphasized the latter. Point Four aid went to governments – members of the United Nations. Political leaders around the world embraced the idea, because they saw national development as a way to ensure not only their people's freedom from fear and want, but their own domestic security. Colonial leaders added "development" to the top of the list of possibilities that could follow self-determination, adding greater urgency to the cause.[73]

Point Four did not just change U.S. foreign policy, it oriented the entire international state system toward development. Immediately following Truman's speech, Moscow announced the creation of the Council for Mutual Economic Assistance to develop "basic types of production that would allow us [the Soviet bloc] to get rid of essential equipment and raw materials imported from capitalist countries."[74] A State Department staffer wrote "that the USSR has taken the President's pronouncement as a challenge to prove whether communism or democracy can actually provide the greatest benefits for the people."[75] The idea transformed the UN. A 1965 history of the organization explained that "in 1950 came the beginning of change. Powerful world currents and events disclosed critical urgent needs for development help in three underdeveloped continents, and led by the United States ... the United Nations and its family of organizations stepped up its response to the need." The change was readily apparent. While the FAO had previously been confined to collecting statistics and writing reports, it was now called upon to *act* on those findings, which was exactly what Orr had wanted in 1946.[76] ECOSOC gathered a panel of economists to investigate under-employment in underdeveloped countries; their final report, which was published in 1951, ended up doing a great deal more. *Measures for the Economic Development of Under-Developed Countries* was essentially a guidebook for development – a primer on contemporary theory with explanations for how countries could turn those theories into practice. The expert panel tried to draw on the best of each side of the Cold War divide, praising both five-year plans and freer markets.[77] Most of their readers did the same in practice, taking knowledge and assistance where they could get it. The United States and the Soviet Union would prove eager to oblige, because both linked the legitimacy of their systems to their ability to deliver on their promises of development. As Odd Arne Westad noted, they "needed to change the world in order to prove the universal applicability of their ideologies."[78] Development assistance became one of the most powerful forms of internationalism throughout the Cold War.[79]

"When we strike against the enemies of mankind – poverty, illiteracy, hunger, and disease – we work for freedom," Truman wrote in 1952.[80] In some cases that was true. UN-led campaigns against malaria and rinderpest (cattle plague) in the 1950s were motivated by a desire to utilize human ingenuity to relieve suffering, as were others like them. The catch to Truman's quote, however, is that it comes from the introduction to a report to Congress on the Mutual Security Program, which had recently gained authority over Point Four – vastly expanding its budget, but also tying all aid to military priorities. One of the ironies of the Cold War is that at the same time as it rallied the international community to invest expansive amounts of money and manpower in the quest for freedom from want, it forsook freedom from fear, particularly for those nations who most desperately needed both. Postwar internationalism gave, but it also took. The Third World recognized the danger and drew on one of the central principles of the Big Three for protection: national sovereignty. At the 1955 Bandung Conference, a representative from Lebanon insisted that "if human rights are sacred," then "the rights of nations themselves, no matter how small, to the respect of the greater nations is at least just as sacred."[81]

The faiths that had animated the internationalism of the 1940s – the centrality of the state, the wonder-working ability of human ingenuity to bring progress, the growth of a properly managed global economy, and the dictates of a higher power – lived on in the 1950s. Internationalism's advertised end product – Roosevelt's "world order" based on "the cooperation of free countries, working together in a friendly, civilized society" – remained elusive, but it was closer than it had been in 1941. The Cold War muted some internationalist principles, but it gave a greater voice to others as the United States and the Soviet Union used them to try to win more power and the rest of the world used them to try to reduce it.[82]

Notes

1 I want to thank Steve Norris for his helpful comments on this chapter.
2 Franklin D. Roosevelt, State of the Union (6 January 1941), available at http://www.fdrlibrary.marist.edu/fourfreedoms.
3 Andrew Preston, *Sword of the Spirit, Shield of Faith* (New York: Alfred A. Knopf, 2012), 319–324, 346–348.
4 Elizabeth Borgwardt, *A New Deal for the World: America's Vision for Human Rights* (Cambridge, MA: Harvard University Press, 2005), 20–23.
5 Atlantic Charter (14 August 1941), available at http://avalon.law.yale.edu/wwii/atlantic.asp.
6 Borgwardt, *A New Deal for the World*, 44.
7 Quoted in ibid., 29.
8 Ibid., 28–30; Mark Mazower, *No Enchanted Palace: The End of Empire and the Ideological Origins of the United Nations* (Princeton, NJ: Princeton University Press, 2009), 55–57; Samuel Moyn, "Imperialism, Self-Determination, and the Rise of Human Rights," in *The Human Rights Revolution: An International History*, ed. Akira Iriye, Petra Goedde, and William I. Hitchcock (New York: Oxford University Press, 2012), 162–163.
9 Declaration by the United Nations (1 January 1942), available at http://avalon.law.yale.edu/20th_century/decade03.asp. Elizabeth Borgwardt wrote that it was likely "human rights," which was not in early drafts, got included because of a memo from Roosevelt's key diplomatic advisor, Harry Hopkins, "who wrote that 'another sentence should be added including a restatement of our aims for human freedom, justice, security, not only for the people in our own lands but for all the people of the world'" (Borgwardt, *A New Deal for the World*, 55).
10 Frank Costigliola, *Roosevelt's Lost Alliances* (Princeton, NJ: Princeton University Press, 2012), 169–170, 191–192.
11 Joint Four-Nation Declaration (October 1943), available at http://avalon.law.yale.edu/wwii/moscow.asp.
12 David L. Bosco, *Five to Rule Them All: The U.N. Security Council and the Making of the Modern World* (New York: Oxford University Press, 2009), 14–24; S. M. Plokhy, *Yalta: The Price of Peace* (New York: Penguin, 2011), 117–121.
13 Borgwardt, *A New Deal for the World*, 167.
14 Mazower, *No Enchanted Palace*, 55–65, 149; Paul Kennedy, *The Parliament of Man: The Past, Present, and Future of the United Nations* (New York: Vintage, 2006), 26–27.
15 Chapter 1, Charter of the United Nations, available at http://www.un.org/en/documents/charter/chapter1.shtml.
16 Kennedy, *The Parliament of Man*, 29–45; Plokhy, *Yalta*, 117–127; Bosco, *Five to Rule Them All*, 29–31.
17 Chapter 10, Charter of the United Nations, available at http://www.un.org/en/documents/charter/chapter10.shtml; Akira Iriye, *Cultural Internationalism and World Order* (Baltimore: The Johns Hopkins University Press, 1997), 140–141.
18 Mary Anne Glendon, *A World Made New: Eleanor Roosevelt and the Universal Declaration of Human Rights* (New York: Random House, 2001), 30–32; Amy L. S. Staples, *The Birth of Development: How the World Bank, Food and Agriculture Organization, and World Health Organization Changed the World, 1945–1965* (Kent, OH: The Kent State University Press, 2006), 132.
19 Dean Acheson, *Present at the Creation* (New York: W.W. Norton & Company, 1969), 31; The Atlantic Charter, available at http://avalon.law.yale.edu/wwii/atlantic.asp.
20 Thomas W. Zeiler, *Free Trade Free World: The Advent of GATT* (Chapel Hill, NC: The University of North Carolina Press, 1999).
21 Acheson, *Present at the Creation*, 32.

22 Timothy Mitchell, *Rule of Experts* (Berkeley, CA: University of California Press, 2002), 4, 81–84; Amanda Kay McVety, *Enlightened Aid: U.S. Development as Foreign Policy in Ethiopia* (New York: Oxford University Press, 2012), 38–61.
23 Acheson, *Present at the Creation*, 81.
24 Quoted in ibid.
25 Staples, *The Birth of Development*, 12–21.
26 Vladislav Zubok has argued that it was unclear in Moscow as well, as the Soviet bureaucracy was divided over the issue. Some officials stressed the useful role American loans and technology could play in Soviet recovery while others "argued that foreign debts would undermine Soviet economic independence." By the winter of 1946, the latter had won out, and Stalin "announced an unabashedly unilateralist postwar course" in his famous 9 February speech (*A Failed Empire: The Soviet Union in the Cold War from Stalin to Gorbachev* [Chapel Hill, NC: University of North Carolina Press, 2007], 51–52).
27 Kennedy, *The Parliament of Man*, 30; Michael A. Bernstein, *A Perilous Progress: Economists and Public Purpose in Twentieth-Century America* (Princeton, NJ: Princeton University Press, 2001), 92.
28 Michael Barnett, *Empire of Humanity: A History of Humanitarianism* (Ithaca, NY: Cornell University Press, 2011), 102–103.
29 Samuel Moyn, "Personalism, Community, and the Origins of Human Rights," in *Human Rights in the Twentieth Century*, ed. Stefan-Ludwig Hoffman (Cambridge: Cambridge University Press, 2011), 86, 105. The debate is central to the historiography of human rights. For two excellent introductions to the literature, see Stefan-Ludwig Hoffmann, "Genealogies of Human Rights," in *Human Rights in the Twentieth Century* and Kenneth Cmiel, "The Recent History of Human Rights," *American Historical Review* 109:1 (2004): 117–135.
30 For a detailed look at the worldwide struggle with food management during the war, see Lizzie Collingham, *The Taste of War: World War II and the Battle for Food* (New York: Penguin, 2012).
31 Borgwardt, *A New Deal for the World*, 114–115.
32 Staples, *The Birth of Development*, 76.
33 Michael Adas, *Dominance by Design: Technological Imperatives and America's Civilizing Mission* (Cambridge, MA: Harvard University Press, 2006), 185–216.
34 James Vernon, *Hunger: A Modern History* (Cambridge, MA: Harvard University Press, 2007), 17–40, 83.
35 Nick Cullather, *The Hungry World: America's Civil War Battle against Poverty in Asia* (Cambridge, MA: Harvard University Press, 2010), 13–25. See also, Nick Cullather, "The Foreign Policy of the Calorie," *American Historical Review* 112:2 (April 2007): 336–364. For more on the ARA, see Bertrand M. Patenaude, *The Big Show in Bololand: The American Relief Expedition to Soviet Russia in the Famine of 1929* (Stanford, CA: Stanford University Press, 2002).
36 Vernon, *Hunger*, 104–117.
37 Staples, *The Birth of Development*, 71–74; Cullather, *The Hungry World*, 32–34; Food and Agriculture Organization of the United Nations, *So Bold an Aim: Ten Years of International Co-operation Toward Freedom From Want* (Rome: FAO, 1955), 25–52; The Mixed Committee on the Problem of Nutrition of the League of Nations, *The Relation of Nutrition to Health, Agriculture and Economic Policy* (14 August 1937), available at http://ia600305.us.archive.org/35/items/finalreportofmix00leaguoft/finalreportofmix00leaguoft.pdf.
38 United States Department of Agriculture War Food Administration, *Report of the Combined Food Board* (April 1945); General Documentation, Combined Food Board (2CFB17); Food and Agriculture Organization Archives.
39 Staples, *The Birth of Development*, 78–81;
40 Lord Boyd Orr, *As I Recall* (Garden City, NY: Doubleday and Company, Inc., 1967), 162–163.
41 Food and Agriculture Organization of the United Nations, *So Bold an Aim*, 73–74.
42 Acheson, *Present at the Creation*, 64–80; Borgwardt, *A New Deal for the World*, 118–121.
43 Barnett, *Empire of Humanity*, 112–118. See also Michael Barnett and Janice Gross Stein, eds. *Sacred Aid: Faith and Humanitarianism* (New York: Oxford University Press, 2012).
44 Tony Judt, *Postwar: A History of Europe since 1945* (New York: Penguin, 2005), 13–27; Collingham, *The Taste of War*, 467–476.
45 Barnett, *Empire of Humanity*, 111–115; Akira Iriye, *Global Community: The Role of International Organizations in the Making of the Contemporary World* (Berkeley, CA: University of California Press, 2002), 37–59.

46 Harry S. Truman, *Memoirs by Harry S. Truman*, Vol. 1: Year of Decisions (Garden City, NY: Doubleday and Company, Inc., 1955), 467–468.
47 "Address by Herbert Hoover on World Famine," (16 March 1946); HH Diaries, Round World Trip; PPS – Famine Emergency Committee; Herbert Hoover Presidential Library.
48 Hoover, "My Impressions of Italy" (22–24 March 1946), 2–3; in ibid.
49 Hoover, "Political Impressions of Poland" (28–30 March 1946), 2; in ibid.
50 Hoover, "My Impressions of Czechoslovakia" (27–28 March 1946), 4; in ibid.
51 Address by Truman on the President's Citizens Food Committee Program (5 October 1947), Cabinet Food Committee – Box 1; Papers of Dennis A. Fitzgerald, 1945–1969; Dwight D. Eisenhower Presidential Library.
52 Clay quoted in Greg Behrman, *The Most Noble Adventure* (New York: Free Press, 2007), 29. For more on hunger in postwar Germany, see Alice Weinreb, "'For the Hungry Have No Past nor Do They Belong to a Political Party': Debates over German Hunger after World War II," *Central European History* 45 (2012): 50–78.
53 Judt, *Postwar*, 86–87.
54 George C. Marshall, Address at Harvard (5 June 1947), available at http://www.marshallfoundation.org/library/index_documents.html.
55 Melvyn P. Leffler, *A Preponderance of Power: National Security, the Truman Administration, and the Cold War* (Stanford, CA: Stanford University Press, 1992), 163.
56 Ibid., 184–186; Robert Service, *Stalin: A Biography* (Cambridge, MA: Harvard University Press, 2005), 500–504.
57 Judt, *Postwar*, 195. For more on Soviet rehabilitation, see Karl D. Qualls, *From Ruins to Reconstruction: Urban Identity in Soviet Sevastopol after World War II* (Ithaca, NY: Cornell University Press, 2009) and Elena Zubkova, *Russia after the War: Hopes, Illusions, Disappointments, 1945–1957*, trans. Hugh Ragsdale (Armonk, NY: M.E. Sharpe, 1998).
58 Arendt quoted in G. Daniel Cohen, "The 'Human Rights Revolution' at Work," in *Human Rights in the Twentieth Century*, ed. Stefan-Ludwig Hoffman (Cambridge: Cambridge University Press, 2011), 47–48.
59 For more on Nuremberg and its role in the origins of the Cold War, see Francine Hirsch, "The Soviets at Nuremberg: International Law, Propaganda, and the Making of the Postwar Order," *American Historical Review* 113:3 (2008): 701–730.
60 Moyn, "Imperialism, Self-Determination, and the Rise of Human Rights," 161–164; Andreas Eckert, "African Nationalism and Human Rights," in *Human Rights in the Twentieth Century*, ed. Stefan-Ludwig Hoffman (Cambridge: Cambridge University Press, 2011), 290–294; Mazower, *No Enchanted Palace*, 55–56. See also, Brad Simpson, "The United States and the Curious History of Self-Determination," *Diplomatic History* 36:4 (September 2012): 675–694.
61 The Universal Declaration of Human Rights, available at http://www.un.org/en/documents/udhr/index.shtml#a1.
62 Glendon, *A World Made New*, 235.
63 Samuel Moyn, *The Last Utopia: Human Rights in History* (Cambridge, MA: Harvard University Press, 2010), 7, 46. G. Daniel Cohen argues that the European Convention of Human Rights needs to be considered as an entirely separate case from the Declaration as it was, in fact, a reaction against the latter's unenforceability ("The Holocaust and the 'Human Rights Revoluion,'" in *The Human Rights Revolution: An International History*, ed. Akira Iriye, Petra Goedde, and William I. Hitchcock [New York: Oxford University Press, 2012], 63).
64 Mark Mazower, "The Strange Triumph of Human Rights," *The Historical Journal* 47:2 (2004): 389, 397. Margaret E. McGuinness writes about the lasting influence of the Declaration in "Peace v. Justice: The Universal Declaration of Human Rights and the Modern Origins of the Debate," *Diplomatic History* 35:5 (November 2011): 749–768.
65 Carol Anderson, *Eyes Off the Prize: The United Nations and the African American Struggle for Human Rights, 1944–1955* (Cambridge, MA: Cambridge University Press, 2003).
66 "U.S. government officials realized that their ability to sell democracy to the Third World was seriously hampered by continuing racial injustice at home. Accordingly, efforts to promote civil rights within the United States were consistent with, and important to, the more central U.S. mission of fighting world communism" (Mary L. Dudziak, "Desegregation as a Cold War Imperative," *Stanford Law Review* 41:1 [November 1988]: 62–63). See also Brenda Plummer, *Rising Wind: Black Americans and U.S. Foreign Affairs, 1935–1960* (Chapel Hill, NC: University of North Carolina Press, 1996);

Thomas Borstelmann, *The Cold War and the Color Line: American Race Relations in the Global Arena* (Cambridge, MA: Harvard University Press, 2001); and Jonathan Rosenberg, *How Far the Promised Land?: World Affairs and the American Civil Rights Movement from the First World War to Vietnam* (Princeton, NJ: Princeton University Press, 2006).

67 Anderson, *Eyes Off the Prize*, 5, 269.
68 For more on Moscow's use of human rights language during the 1950s, see Jennifer Amos, "Embracing and Contesting: The Soviet Union and the Universal Declaration of Human Rights, 1948–1958," in *Human Rights in the Twentieth Century*, ed. Stefan-Ludwig Hoffman (Cambridge: Cambridge University Press, 2011), 147–165.
69 Harry S. Truman, Inaugural Address (20 January 1949), available at http://www.trumanlibrary.org/whistlestop/50yr_archive/inagural20jan1949.htm.
70 Judt, *Postwar*, 149–151.
71 State Department, "Building the Peace," *Foreign Affairs Outlines* 21 (Spring 1949): 1; Near Eastern and African Staff subject files 1951–1953; Technical Cooperation Administration; General Records of the Agency for International Development and its Predecessor Agencies, Record Group 469; National Archives at College Park.
72 For more information on this, see McVety, *Enlightened Aid*; Cullather, *The Hungry World*; David Ekbladh, *The Great American Mission: Modernization and the Construction of an American World Order* (Princeton, NJ: Princeton University Press, 2010); Michael E. Latham, *The Right Kind of Revolution: Modernization, Development, and U.S. Foreign Policy from the Cold War to the Present* (Ithaca, NY: Cornell University Press, 2011); David Engerman, Nils Gilman, Mark H. Haefele, and Michael E. Latham, eds. *Staging Growth: Modernization, Development, and the Global Cold War* (Amherst, MA: University of Massachusetts Press, 2003); Nick Cullather, "Development? It's History," *Diplomatic History* 24:4 (Fall 2000): 641–653; Gilbert Rist, *The History of Development: from Western Origins to Global Faith*, New Edition, trans. Patrick Camiller (London: Zed Books, 2002).
73 Eckert, "African Nationalists and Human Rights,", 294–300. The British had in fact created a Colonial Development and Welfare Programme in 1940, which was copied by France in 1946 and Belgium in 1947, but these were rightly perceived as old wine in new wineskins.
74 Quoted in Zubok, *A Failed Empire*, 78.
75 Benjamin Hardy to Mr. Russell, "Significance of the Soviet-sponsored 'ECMA,'" (27 January 1949), Point IV File; Hardy Papers; Harry S. Truman Presidential Library.
76 Joseph M. Jones, *The United Nations at Work: Developing Land, Forests, Oceans … and People* (Oxford: Pergamon Press, 1965), 109.
77 *Measures for the Economic Development of Under-Developed Countries* (New York: The United Nations Department of Economic Affairs, May 1951).
78 Odd Arne Westad, *The Global Cold War: Third World Interventions and the Making of Our Times* (Cambridge: Cambridge University Press, 2005), 4.
79 For a fascinating example, see Erez Manela, "A Pox on Your Narrative: Writing Disease Control into Cold War History," *Diplomatic History* 34:2 (April 2010): 299–323.
80 "Third Report to Congress on the Mutual Security Program" (31 December 1952), X; Near Eastern and African Subject Files 1951–1953; Technical Cooperation Administration; General Records of the Agency for International Development and Predecessor Agencies, 1948–1961; National Archives at College Park.
81 Quoted in Roland Burke, *Decolonization and the Evolution of International Human Rights* (Philadelphia, PA: University of Pennsylvania Press, 2010), 25.
82 For an example, see Charles Dorn and Kristen Ghodsee, "The Cold War Politicization of Literacy: Communism, UNESCO, and the World Bank," *Diplomatic History* 36:2 (April 2012): 373–398.

3

THE EARLY COLD WAR AND ITS LEGACIES

Vojtech Mastny

From the perspective of half a century, the early Cold War is distant history. As long as the seemingly interminable conflict lasted, contemporaries were mainly preoccupied with its origins. Its unexpected termination changed the perspective, bringing to the fore the Cold War's legacy. Trying to understand a legacy of history means focusing not so much on what was important at the time as on what counts as important in retrospect. This includes institutions that have survived, events that resulted in developments with lasting consequences, as well as ideas that continue to inspire. Outstanding legacies of the first half of the Cold War are international structures established at its beginning, the long-term consequences of the Korean War of 1950–53, and the nuclear weapons that had started accumulating by the end of the period as a result of policies pursued during the preceding twenty-five years.

Enduring International Institutions

The world that has emerged from the Cold War is markedly different from that which followed World War II. Yet the incipient East–West confrontation left behind an array of international institutions of mainly American origin, lending support to the observation that "the world the United States and its allies created after World War II remained intact," regardless of the Cold War interlude, after which it was "simply consolidated and expanded."[1] In fact, the relevant institutions did not remain intact, but proved resilient as well as adaptable all the same.

Foremost among the new American creations, the United Nations (UN) has since been criticized as ineffective or worse, ironically, more in the United States than in any other country. Its core Security Council of five veto-wielding permanent members was poorly designed, reflecting the distribution of power in 1945, including not only the victorious United States, Great Britain, and the Soviet Union, but also Nationalist China and France as their clients. It has become anachronistic, yet not dispensable. After the UN went into decline during the Cold War, the Council reaffirmed its authority in the absence of a competitor, making the main issue its reform rather than abolition. The problem could have been avoided if Washington's original proposal to establish a mechanism that would allow for enlargement of the select group by bringing in newly rising powers, citing particularly Brazil, had not failed on British opposition.

The UN has been described as a replica of the nineteenth-century Concert of Europe, "fundamentally a traditional alliance" of the great powers of the day that would enable them to orchestrate the world while balancing each other. To the American architects of the project, however, alliances were an Old World abomination, and balance of power a prescription for war rather than for peace. President Franklin D. Roosevelt conceived of the position of the original "four policemen" on the Security Council not as one of privilege but of responsibility. So, too, did his successor Harry S. Truman, praised by UN Secretary General Kofi Annan for having understood that "the responsibility of the great states is to serve and not dominate the peoples of the world." In any case, for the world's majority of developing nations, which soon became the majority of UN members, the organization became the main forum for asserting their growing international influence.[2]

The UN project sought to apply the principles of Roosevelt's New Deal to promote the rule of international law as the "common law of mankind."[3] Despite appearances to the contrary, the Cold War did not bring about a decline of international law but its maturation. Before the conflict escalated, the UN General Assembly had managed in 1948 to pass unanimously the Universal Declaration of Human Rights, thanks to abstention by the Soviet Union and its allies, joined by the duo of Saudi Arabia and South Africa. Although not legally binding, the declaration led to the adoption of covenants that, ratified by 1976 by the requisite number of countries, assumed the force of law, inducing a growing, if grudging, respect for human rights.

After the experience of two world wars, the UN understandably focused on security in the military sense. It promised "collective security," which presupposed collective will to face down aggressors if necessary with the force of arms, but delivered only "selective security" on occasions when the permanent members of the Security Council did not see their important interests being at stake. Peacekeeping, not originally envisaged in the UN Charter, was invented as a modest substitute and, typically entrusted to personnel from developing nations, subsequently expanded to become the biggest item in the UN budget.[4]

Some of the UN's specialized agencies, initially included in it as something of an afterthought, became more important than its core because of their agenda concerning the increasingly relevant non-military aspects of security. The World Health Organization, for example, assumed the role of global provider of health security, the Food and Agriculture Organization of food security. The controversial agencies for economic development indirectly linked with the UN system – the World Bank and the International Monetary Fund – were likewise able to start operating thanks to Soviet boycott, and gradually established themselves as developing nations gained influence in the management of these institutions. The General Agreement on Tariffs and Trade (GATT) languished during the Cold War, but provided the foundation for the establishment of the World Trade Organization afterward.

Regionalization and Militarization

Even before the East–West conflict escalated, the adequacy of the world organization had already been questioned in Latin America. After the Roosevelt administration repudiated the Monroe Doctrine by adhering to the 1945 Act of Chapultepec, which committed the United States to upholding hemispheric security collectively rather than enforcing it unilaterally, Latin American governments insisted on including in the UN Charter the right to regional self-defense, exempt from the veto power of the Security Council. Supported by Soviet leader Iosif V. Stalin for his own reasons to help him legitimize Moscow's bilateral treaties with its Eastern European dependencies, the exemption not only allowed for the subsequent formation of regional military alliances but also facilitated the later growth of their regional substitutes.

The American internationalists' concept of economic security reflected their belief that economic interdependence fostered both national and international security. The belief underlay the strategy of containment, inaugurated in 1947 with the Marshall Plan for the economic recovery of Western Europe as its key component, as originally conceived by the far-sighted U.S. diplomat George F. Kennan. While the policy soon became controversial, not least with Kennan himself, and was in any case limited by the life-span of the Soviet Union, the Marshall Plan has continued to live on as one of the Cold War's least controversial legacies. Having fulfilled its original purpose, it not only provided the administrative structure for the Western nations' Organization for Economic Cooperation and Development, but has also been repeatedly invoked in crises for its "institutional architecture in which governments, international organizations, and markets interact so as to create the best possible environment" for the economic and political recovery of ravaged regions.[5]

The Marshall Plan's reputation has been in contrast with that of America's "national security state," which emerged at the same time. Its iconic National Security Council, National Security Agency, Department of Defense, and Central Intelligence Agency have been frequent targets because of their practices, from inflating expenditures for alleged defense needs to indulging in abuses in the name of security. But the dreaded "garrison state" never came about and the permanence of the institutions, regardless of changes of administration and a changing security environment has proved their functionality in a political system sufficiently capable of correcting its excesses and blunders.[6]

In the fall of 1947, the insulation of the Soviet-controlled part of Europe from the Marshall Plan resulted in the division of the Continent that would last for over forty years. The immediate effect was the conclusion in Rio de Janeiro of a treaty to defend Latin American countries against the advance of communism by military means, followed the year after by the establishment of the Organization of American States (OAS). While the defense was never needed and the treaty would unravel even before the Cold War ended, the OAS has managed to survive because its "genius, or individuality" has been "mainly in the field of economic and social development."[7] Even so, the subsequent rise of Latin America's own regional structures independently of the United States put the organization's future in doubt, suggesting the need for different institutional arrangements for interaction between the north and the south of the hemisphere.

The Rio treaty provided the model for the establishment in 1949 of the North Atlantic Treaty Organization (NATO), history's longest-lasting, as well as atypical, military alliance. A European rather than American initiative, it was originally meant for reassurance rather than for defense, with the intent not to plan for military action but to avoid having to plan for such. Even after the United States sponsored the alliance, it initially envisaged its own contribution to be mainly political and economic, anticipating an "indefinite period free of any military emergency."[8] Washington's contingency plans, kept hidden from its allies, though not so hidden from proficient Soviet spies, envisaged a retreat from Europe before trying to liberate it from overseas, as in World War II. The Soviet Union did not find it necessary to respond to the creation of NATO by creating an alliance of its own in addition to the already existing network of bilateral treaties with its Eastern European dependencies.

The launching of NATO accelerated but did not start the militarization of the Cold War, which had started the year before because of Stalin's attempt to compel a settlement in Germany on his terms by imposing the Berlin blockade at the risk of a military confrontation with the Western occupation powers. Challenging them to force the blockade, the possible confrontation was avoided, thanks to the improbable success of the airlift they organized to keep supplying the population of the city. Although the blockade was subsequently lifted, Stalin's apparent readiness to take the risk gave the Cold War a military dimension it never lost. The Soviet Union, in conformity with its Marxist ideology, continued to regard the conflict as an essentially political one, but the United States, as the main guarantor of Western security, came to conceive of it primarily in military terms. Consequently, as philosopher Reinhold Niebuhr observed, "the American nation has become strangely enamored with military might."[9]

Among the casualties of the militarization was the Council of Europe, which had been promoted by Britain as a political complement of NATO in the hope of bringing together additional Western European states and, eventually, all of Europe. "Passed over in contemptuous silence" by the Soviet Union, "as a contemporary British observer noted, "because of its remoteness from military affairs,"[10] the Council remained out of the limelight during the Cold War, but afterward it did bring in all European states, with the sole exception of Belarus, with remarkable effect. Having adopted the European Convention of Human Rights in the Cold War's darkest years, it proceeded to establish in 1959 the European Court of Human Rights in Strasbourg, where citizens of any member state can now find redress by suing their sovereign governments, the largest caseload coming from Russia.

The main features of the settlement in Europe that would later end the Cold War where it had started had already emerged by 1950, although they were not visible to contemporaries. The Continent had been divided and Germany split in two, but the manner of the division prefigured how they would be reunited and the conflict resolved. The Marshall Plan laid the foundations of Western Europe's unprecedented prosperity under a reformed capitalist system, just as the Sovietization of Eastern Europe under communist rule imposed there a political and economic system bound to fail. At the same time, NATO brought West Europeans together in a lasting security arrangement with the United States just as the unity of international communism, in which Stalin had invested Soviet security, started cracking in Eastern Europe following his split with Yugoslavia. If the Cold War nevertheless continued, this was as a result of its extension to Asia after the unsuccessful attempt by North Korea's communist regime to forcibly reunify the peninsula by invading its southern part in July 1950.

The Consequences of the Korean War

The Korean War, still not formally concluded after its end in armistice in 1953, was replete with far-reaching consequences. Having provoked American and then Chinese intervention, it delayed rapprochement between the two countries for twenty years. In Europe, its outbreak accelerated movement toward Western European integration, which, in its final effects, would make the Continent the most peaceful part of the world. The extension of the superpower competition beyond Europe prompted the rise and decline of the nonaligned movement in what was then called the Third World and would eventually emerge as the most dynamic part of the world.

"It was the Korean war and not World War II," reminisced American diplomat Charles Bohlen, "that made us a world military-political power." The resulting worldwide network of U.S. military bases, however, was conducive to "imperial overstretch" of what Norwegian historian Geir Lundestad termed America's European "empire by invitation," bearing the seeds of its own later relative decline.[11] Stimulated by the war, U.S. defense spending increased by a margin not seen since World War II and, although never to be seen again, would eventually climb to reach nearly the level of all other nations combined, regardless of the dividend that was expected to accrue from the peaceful termination of the Cold War.

Misperceived as a prelude to a Soviet attack in Europe, the shock of the aggression in East Asia instilled NATO with the military substance it had been lacking before. Since, however, it was never tested in battle as long as the Cold War lasted, the efficacy of the alliance in fighting its main adversary remains a matter of conjecture. In the absence of the test, its indisputable achievements have been political. NATO accommodated the diverse security interests of its unequal members, respected by the United States to a degree not common for a great power. It co-opted former enemies to reconcile them, induced nations with different military traditions to implement civilian control of their militaries, and acculturated their high-ranking officers in habits of multilateral day-to-day cooperation.

NATO's first enlargement, in 1954, which brought in Greece and Turkey – the second largest contributor of troops fighting alongside the United States on the Korean front – was far more consequential than could be foreseen. It not only helped mitigate the two nations' traditional enmity but also set Turkey on course toward democracy. Moreover, it opened the door to Turkish immigration to Western Europe, starting to change Europe's demography and cultural interaction, reorienting its security interests toward the Mediterranean, and ensuring Turkey's indispensable future role as a bridge between the West and the Moslem world.

The project of European Defense Community, initiated in response to the outbreak of the Korean War so as to bolster NATO by bringing a rearmed West Germany into the Western defense system under French tutelage, has been retrospectively touted as the forerunner of today's common European Security and Defense Policy. Voted down by the French National Assembly after the war scare had passed, however, it was little more than an expedient, superseded by the substitute solution whereby West Germany entered NATO as a full-fledged member in 1955. Its entry was a milestone in the transformation of Europe's former serial aggressor into the bulwark of its stability.

The imminent expansion of the Western alliance prompted the proclamation of the Warsaw Pact as a belated imitation of NATO, intended by Soviet leader Nikita S. Khrushchev to prod the West to negotiate away both alliances in the hope of reversing the correlation of forces in favor of the Soviet Union. The failure of the scheme left the proclaimed alliance in search of a purpose. Although Khrushchev's successors later built it up and equipped it with military attributes, the Warsaw Pact never found a purpose other than being used by the Soviet Union against its own members. A military expression of Europe's political and ideological division, the alliance disintegrated as soon as that division had ended.

The hardening of the division after the Soviet suppression of the 1956 uprising in Hungary boosted the movement for European integration in the West, leading the year after to the establishment of the Common Market as the nucleus of the European Community (EC). The movement followed the prophecy of its spiritual father, French businessman, economist, and diplomat, Jean Monnet, that "there will be no peace in Europe if the states rebuild themselves on the basis of national sovereignty" and unless they "form a federation or a European entity that would make them into a common economic unit."[12]

The EC built on the success of the Schuman Plan for the European Coal and Steel Community, started as a complement to the Marshall Plan. The project implemented the ingenious idea of enmeshing the economies of Western European states so as to make it impossible for them to mobilize the resources necessary for waging war against each other. Intended to change "the destinies of those regions which have long been devoted to the manufacture of munitions of war," it set into motion developments that would change the destiny of all of Europe once it had been reunited, ending its history of internecine wars. In this sense, Europe began to diverge from those parts of the world whose historical experiences had been different.

If Europe's formative experience was that of World War II, followed by the impact of the Cold War division, for most countries in the Third World the formative experience was that of decolonization, coincidental with the rise of the Cold War rivalry and aggravated by it. Attempts to imitate NATO outside Europe, such as was the British-sponsored CENTO in the Middle East or American-made SEATO in southern Asia, failed because of their association with former colonial powers, as well as the lack of common interests and common values. Washington was drawn into Asia on the perception that "European integration is connected with our policy in Asia, for Soviet success in the East would make the Allied position in Europe untenable."[13] The original American intention was to create a Pacific NATO, but under the impact of Korean War the United States constructed a "hub-and-spokes" system of bilateral rather than multilateral alliances.

The construction started in 1951 with the conclusion of a defense treaty with the Philippines and the ANZUS pact with Australia and New Zealand, followed by different kinds of treaties with Japan, South Korea, Thailand, and the Chinese Nationalist government in Taiwan. Although the original reason for rallying for defense against another communist aggression supported by the Soviet Union and China subsequently lost its rationale, the system continued to defy predictions of its demise. Despite ups and downs, its flexible security arrangements, unencumbered by rigid command structures, satisfied the different needs of America's partners while adapting to changing circumstances. In the long term, the United States' demographic and economic shift from Europe and the Atlantic to Asia-Pacific favored the preservation of the system, regardless of the demise of the Soviet Union and the rise of China.

The Rise and Decline of Nonalignment

The persisting military rivalry between the superpowers and their respective alliances after the Korean War gave rise to the nonaligned movement (NAM) as an anti-alliance of the Third World's newly independent nations. At their 1955 conference in Bandung in Indonesia, they pledged to abstain from "any arrangements of collective defense to serve the particular interests of any of the big powers,"[14] and six years later organized themselves as NAM. In fact, the movement tilted toward the Soviet Union, whose economic model developing nations initially found more congenial than the Western capitalist one. Emblematic of these nations' common debut on the international scene, the organization still nominally exists, claiming no fewer than 120 member states and struggling to remain relevant after the rivalry it originally proposed to overcome has ceased and the notion of Third World has become meaningless. In 2005, the Declaration of a New Asian African Strategic Partnership, adopted by heads of states from the two continents on the fiftieth anniversary of Bandung, invoked its legacy in a largely symbolic attempt at forging common policy.

The NAM never coalesced to develop a coherent policy before starting to disintegrate because of divisions among its members. The "Panchsheel" principles of peaceful coexistence, proclaimed in 1954 by India and China as the ideological foundation of nonalignment, did not prevent the two countries from going to war in 1962 over their common border, leaving a lasting legacy of mutual enmity and the border still unsettled. Two years later, the NAM peaked at its second summit in Cairo, but in 1965 received a fatal blow because of the ouster of nonalignment's leading protagonist, Indonesia's President Sukarno, by the country's generals. Later in the decade, further ascendancy of nationalist military regimes in the Third World underlined its disunity. The incidence of military conflicts there increased as the superpowers' control over their local clients diminished. The 1965 Indian–Pakistani and 1967 Arab–Israeli wars left unresolved two major conflicts that have outlasted the Cold War.

The disintegration of the NAM paralleled the unraveling of the Sino-Soviet alliance, originating in the unequal treaty of 1950 between the two communist countries that had been a historical anomaly to start with. For China, it amounted to a reversed "tributary" relationship of a state that used to be considered the "Middle Kingdom" with a neighboring "barbarian" power. The treaty enabled Stalin, as the supreme leader of international communism, to shift onto China the main risk of supporting the North Korean aggression. The Chinese supreme leader, Mao Zedong, accepted the risk on common ideological grounds, with detrimental consequences for his country's interests.

The outbreak of the war delayed indefinitely the planned seizure of Taiwan by the Chinese communists and, after Mao's unsuccessful attempts to achieve its surrender by means of demonstrative artillery bombardment of Nationalist-held offshore islands in 1954–58, left open the threat, however diminishing, of Taiwan's forcible unification with the mainland. The Chinese intervention in the war, which saved the North Korean regime from extinction, also resulted in the emergence of nuclear-armed North Korea as another threat. Making matters worse, in 1961 Mao contracted for China to maintain North Korea's unpredictable regime by concluding with it a mutual defense treaty, unusual not only in providing for automatic military assistance against any third party, but also in requiring mutual consent to any changes.

After Mao had asserted China's independence following Stalin's death and the conclusion of the Korean War, his erratic policies climaxed in the 1960s as he competed with the Soviet Union in both his domestic and his foreign policies. His "Great Leap Forward" resulted in history's worst human-made famine; his commitment to support revolutionary movements in the Third World in a common struggle against both Soviet "revisionists" and Western "imperialists" drove China into international isolation, leaving it by the end of the decade with remote Albania as its only ally. Most damaging, the advent in 1967 of Mao's self-destructive Cultural Revolution, which traumatized China's society and its ruling party, left a collective memory that endangered the accomplishments of his successors after they reversed his course and set the country on the trajectory of regaining its historic place as a pre-eminent world power.

By contrast, the Indonesian military regime, otherwise complicit in atrocities and mired in corruption, in 1967 performed a constructive role after having terminated its predecessor's confrontational campaign against neighboring Malaysia, waged by Sukarno to destabilize the country he loathed as a remnant of British imperialism. Indonesia brokered the establishment of the Association of Southeast Asian Nations (ASEAN), bringing together, besides the two former adversaries, countries as different as Thailand, Singapore, and the Philippines, which had also been quarrelling with one another. As a new kind of regional organization, ASEAN has been regarded as a breakthrough in creating a nascent "security community."[15]

One of the officials present at its creation, Singapore's foreign minister S. Rajaratnam, has testified that ASEAN was born "out of fear rather than idealistic convictions about regionalism." The fear was that of communist subversion of the unstable states because of repercussions of the Vietnam War, which made the grouping tilt to the West and rely, as Rajaratnam quipped, on "Adam Smith's Invisible Hand" in order to become resilient by developing market economies.[16] In the spirit of nonalignment, the ASEAN members preferred to avoid military arrangements with other countries as well as with each other, but were ready to reach outside by inviting additional countries as "dialogue partners."

Opinions differ about whether ASEAN's allegedly distinctive "Asian way," with its reliance on consensus among the elites, preference for shelving rather than resolving problems, and aversion to institutionalization, has been conducive to results or to setting their limitations. As long as the Cold War lasted, ASEAN was largely ignored, but once the conflict subsided and the world's center of gravity started shifting to Asia-Pacific, it became a desirable partner. It not only incorporated its former Vietnamese enemy and all other countries of Southeast Asia, but also became the pivot of a growing network of overlapping structures of multilateral cooperation,

The Nuclear Revolution

Concurrent with the Sino–Indian War, the 1962 Cuban missile crisis was the climactic moment of the Cold War, being the time when the world may have come closest to nuclear war, but otherwise it passed with few enduring consequences. One of these has been the survival of communist Cuba as a Cold War relic, with Fidel Castro, its leader until 2008, being remembered for having urged Khrushchev at the height of the crisis to employ Soviet nuclear weapons against the United States, offering to sacrifice his own people. Another consequence is Mexico's initiative, in response to Cuba's attempted introduction of the Soviet missiles into the neighborhood, which resulted five years later in the establishment of the Latin American nuclear-free zone, the prototype of more such zones to come.

The brush with disaster underlined the perils of the nuclear revolution, which had started at the end of World War II and before the start of the Cold War, but predetermined its course once the use of atomic bombs to defeat Japan left no doubt about their extraordinary destructiveness. Whether the war remained cold as a result, or the standoff that it created prolonged it at the risk of the weapons being used again, has been much debated and will never be certain. What is certain is that the demonstration, at the cost of sacrificing several hundred thousand people in Japan, created the "nuclear taboo" against the weapons' use, which has held ever since.[17] In the early years of the East–West confrontation, however, both the United States and the Soviet Union were ready to tolerate their being used, and the resulting arms race left behind useless stockpiles of the weapons as the Cold War's most deplorable legacy.

At the critical stages of the race, which was fueled not so much by action and reaction as by "anticipatory reaction," the United States was first to act, whereas its weaker adversary reacted. After the Soviet Union broke the American atomic monopoly by testing its first bomb in 1949, Washington's decision the year after to up the ante by building the vastly more powerful hydrogen bomb preceded the outbreak of the Korean War. The qualitative jump, followed by a quantitative jump to "overkill" once the United States decided in 1952 to deploy thousands of tactical nuclear weapons in Europe before the Soviet Union responded in kind, resulted in "vertical" proliferation, as each superpower started building up its stockpiles.[18]

In the same year, Great Britain set a precedent for "horizontal" proliferation – the acquisition of the weapons by additional countries. According to the official historian of the United Kingdom Atomic Energy Authority, Margaret Gowing, Britain decided to acquire nuclear weapons not in "response to an immediate military threat but rather [as] something fundamentalist and almost instinctive, ... feeling that atomic weapons were a manifestation of the scientific and technological superiority on which Britain's strength ... must depend."[19] The same kind of feeling has since driven the nuclear programs of developing nations, promoted by their nuclear scientists for professional reasons.

Mutual lack of trust made disarmament negotiations an exercise in futility, but resulted in 1955 in the creation within the UN of the International Atomic Energy Agency (IAEA), assigned to deal with peaceful uses of nuclear energy. Though toothless at first, the agency would evolve into the global watchdog guarding against the diversion of nuclear energy for military purposes, while Euratom, established two years later as part of the EC, developed an exemplary system of safeguards and controls. The arms race between the superpowers nevertheless continued, each preparing to employ what Kennan aptly called "a sterile and hopeless weapon, ... which cannot in any way serve the purposes of a constructive and hopeful foreign policy," and drawing up contingency plans of growing absurdity.[20]

The plans, which remained in effect despite the Cuban experience, give the flavor of the era. The American plans, for example, called for the dispatch of at least 2,500 nuclear warheads at a moment's notice. The 1964 Warsaw Pact plan envisaged the detonation of several hundreds of warheads over the European battlefield, whereupon the Soviet-led armies would supposedly march through the wasteland to victory. "It was like in the fairytale," recalled a Polish participant in the alliance's exercises. "At the time of the battle, clouds burst, and the downpour made the enemy troops soaking wet while our own became pleasantly refreshed."[21]

The twin challenge of the nuclear revolution and Cold War influenced the theory of international relations, creating security studies as its special field, with nuclear weapons as the main point of reference, and the sub-field of strategic studies intended to apply theory to policy but increasingly divorcing it from reality. American defense intellectuals, beholden to the realist school of thought, converged with Soviet military planners in imagining "realistic" scenarios that would allow war to be fought without crossing the nuclear threshold. The theory of deterrence that "proposed to defend the state by a strategy which threatens to destroy it," presumed "an adversary with a compelling urge to take the action being deterred" and "enemy intentions ... as a given rather than a subject for analysis." It presupposed, as Australian scholar Hedley Bull commented, the "'rational action' of a kind of 'strategic man,' a man who on further acquaintance reveals himself as a university professor of unusual intellectual subtlety."[22]

In the aftermath of Cuba, the unworkable concept of disarmament was superseded by that of arms control. Rather than reverse the arms race, however, the new concept legitimized its continuation for the rest of the Cold War. Of the two landmark treaties of the period that have remained both valid and relevant after its end, the 1963 Limited Test Ban Treaty is so named because a fleeting opportunity to make it comprehensive was lost at that time. The comprehensive treaty was later signed, but is yet to be ratified to become operative. To the extent that it has been observed, the observance is suggestive of its diminishing value after testing became technologically dispensable.

Containing Proliferation

The more pertinent issue of containing the spread of nuclear weapons accounts for the abiding relevance of the 1968 Non-Proliferation Treaty (NPT). The treaty was a product of six years of negotiations, which got underway after France became the fourth nuclear power, China was about to become the fifth, and no fewer than ten other states were expected to follow soon. The negotiations centered in the Eighteen-Nation Disarmament Committee, the successor of which still meets regularly in Geneva under UN auspices. Originally created by the two superpowers, which found it desirable to include in it not only members of their own alliances but also countries broadly representative of the Third World, the committee evolved into a unique forum of multilateral diplomacy.

The committee's agenda addressed issues that have remained topical ever since. The main decisions for or against going nuclear that determined the subsequent pattern of proliferation were made during the run-up to the treaty. India, driven by its ambitious nuclear scientists, secretly embarked upon its program to achieve the capability to produce nuclear weapons, subsequently reciprocated by Pakistan in a competition that made South Asia the most vulnerable to becoming a nuclear battlefield. At the same time, not only did Latin America become a nuclear-free zone, but also all of the states in Western Europe that had intended to acquire nuclear arsenals abandoned the intention for political or economic reasons. So did Japan, as a matter of principle, under the influence of its pacifist public opinion.

From the perspective of the ongoing Cold War, the security guarantees that the NPT offered could be fairly described as "pretended" and "misbegotten."[23] In return for the superpowers' empty promise to reverse their arms race and proceed toward "nuclear zero," the developing nations accepted restrictions so as to prevent the diversion of their own nuclear programs for military purposes. With the end of the U.S.–Soviet rivalry, vertical proliferation ceased once the United States and Russia started to dismantle their oversized arsenals. In the meantime, except in South Asia, horizontal proliferation had not increased, as those states that had intended to go nuclear had either discontinued their programs – Brazil, Argentina, South Africa – or failed to come closer to implementing them – Libya, Iraq, North Korea.

While the future prospect of proliferation remained open, the outcome does not justify the conclusion that the NPT worked well enough during the Cold War but was bound to fail afterward because "during the Cold War states learned that there are legitimate reasons, as outlined in classical deterrence theory, for acquiring nuclear weapons."[24] The "rogue" states that have persisted in trying to acquire weapons did so for no legitimate reasons but in defiance of international norms. Established by the NPT and enforced by the International Atomic Energy Agency, the norms led to the establishment of "the largest multilateral security regime in existence,"[25] which has made violations politically costly and technically more difficult. In this sense, the treaty succeeded in containing the spread of the nuclear revolution, which had run its course by 1968.

That year was the Cold War's watershed year. The political and social upheaval that shook both the Western and the communist worlds heralded the ascendancy of a new generation, for which the origins of the conflict were no longer a living memory. If the legacies of the first half of the East–West confrontation had been decisively shaped by the recent experience of World War II, those of the second half would point to the future, prefiguring in different ways the shape of the post-Cold War age of globalization.

The early period of the Cold War has defined the thrust of the historiography of the Cold War in general. The primary role of the superpowers in its origin, and their primacy during the next twenty years, have made the study of the Cold War largely a subject in U.S. foreign policy – a bias that is accentuated by the lack of primary sources other than American ones as long as the conflict lasted. America-centrism nevertheless remained a common feature of writings of the traditional, revisionist, and post-revisionist varieties even after archives "on the other side" had started to open up. But the new sources that became available have altered the previous picture in at least two important ways. They have shown that Western perceptions of the Soviet threat were greatly exaggerated, as initial Soviet military plans were defensive rather than offensive. And they have shown the Soviet–Chinese interaction that led to the Korean War to have been much more complex than was previously suspected. The complexity of the whole picture increased further during the second half of the Cold War, when the superpowers' preeminence began to erode.

Notes

1 G. John Ikenberry, "The Restructuring of the International System after the Cold War," in *The Cambridge History of the Cold War*, ed. Melvyn P. Leffler and Odd Arne Westad, vol. 3 (Cambridge: Cambridge University Press, 2010), 535–556, at p. 535.
2 Michael Howard, "Introduction," in *The Quest for Stability: Problems of West European Security, 1918–1957*, ed. Rolf Ahmann, A.M. Birke, and Michael Howard (Oxford: Oxford University Press, 1993), pp. 1–17, at p. 12. Truman cited by UN Secretary General Kofi A. Annan in speech at Truman Library, 11 December 2006, http://www.un.org/News/ossg/sg/ stories/statments_full.asp?statID=40.

3 Anne-Marie Burley, "Regulating the World: Multilateralism, International Law, and the Projection of the New Deal Regulatory State," in *Multilateralism Matters: The Theory and Practice of an Institutional Form*, ed. John G. Ruggie (New York: Columbia University Press, 1993), 125–56.
4 Adam Roberts and Dominik Zaum, *Selective Security: War and the United Nations Security Council since 1945*, Adelphi Paper no. 395 (London: Routledge, 2008).
5 Pier Carlo Padoan, "A 21st Century OECD Vision for Europe and the World," in *The Marshall Plan: Lessons Learned for the 21st Century*, ed. Eliot Sorel and Pier Carlo Padoan (Paris: OECD Publishing, 2008), 97–103, at p. 103.
6 Michael J. Hogan, *A Cross of Iron: Harry S. Truman and the Origins of the National Security State, 1945–1954* (Cambridge: Cambridge University Press, 1998); Aaron L. Friedberg, *In the Shadow of the Garrison State: America's Anti-statism and Its Cold War Grand Strategy* (Princeton, NJ: Princeton University Press, 2000).
7 Alan K. Henrikson, "The Growth of Regional Organizations and the Role of the United Nations," in *Regionalism in World Politics*, ed. Louise Fawcett and Andrew Hurrell (New York: Oxford University Press, 1996), 122–168, at p. 142.
8 Ernest R. May, "The Impact of Nuclear Weapons on European Security 1945–1967," in *The Quest for Stability: Problems of West European Security, 1918–1957*, ed. Rolf Ahmann, A.M. Birke, and Michael Howard (Oxford: Oxford University Press, 1993), 513–32, at p. 519.
9 Reinhold Niebuhr, *The World Crisis and American Responsibility: Nine Essays* (New York: Association Press, 1958), 116.
10 Max Beloff, "The Russian View of European Integration," in his *The Great Powers: Essays in Twentieth-Century Politics* (London: Allen & Unwin, 1959), 129.
11 Charles Bohlen, *Witness to History, 1929–1962* (New York: Norton, 1973), 303. Geir Lundestad, "Empire by Invitation? The United States and Western Europe, 1945–1952," *Journal of Peace Research* 23, no. 3 (August 1986): 263–77.
12 Jean Monnet on 5 August 1943, http://www.ena.lu/jean_monnets_thoughts_future_algiers_august_1943–020000404.html.
13 Memorandum by John W. Auchincloss, 9 February 1950, *Foreign Relations of the United States*, 1950, vol. 4 (Washington: U.S. Government Printing Office, 1980), 591–596, at p. 591.
14 Quoted in Odd Arne Westad, *The Global Cold War: Third World Interventions and the Making of Our Times* (Cambridge: Cambridge University Press, 2005), 102.
15 Amitav Acharya, *Constructing a Security Community in Southeast Asia: ASEAN and the Problem of Regional Order* (New York: Routledge, 2001).
16 S. Rajaratnam, "ASEAN: The Way Ahead," in *The ASEAN Reader*, ed. Kernial Singh Sandhu (Singapore: Institute of Southeast Asian Studies, 1992), xxiii–xxvi, at p. xxvi.
17 Nina Tannenwald, *The Nuclear Taboo: The United States and the Non-use of Nuclear Weapons since 1945* (Cambridge: Cambridge University Press, 2007).
18 Barry Buzan, *Introduction to Strategic Studies: Military Technology and International Relations* (London: Palgrave, 1987), pp. 87–88. David Alan Rosenberg, "The Origins of Overkill: Nuclear Weapons and American Strategy, 1945–1960," *International Security* 7, no. 4 (Spring 1983): 3–71.
19 Margaret Gowing, *Independence and Deterrence: Britain and Atomic Energy, 1945–1952*, vol. 1 (London: Macmillan, 1974), 184–185.
20 George F. Kennan, *Russia, the Atom, and the West* (New York: Oxford University Press, 1958), 55.
21 Tadeusz Pióro, *Armja ze skazą: W Wojsku Polskim 1945–1968 (wspomnienia i refleksje)* [The Defective Army: In the Polish Army, 1945–1968 (Memories and Reflections)] (Warsaw: Czytelnik, 1994), 191.
22 Barry Buzan, *People, States and Fear: An Agenda for International Security Studies in the Post-Cold War Era* (Boulder, CO: Lynne Rienner, 1991), 275; Hedley Bull, *The Control of the Arms Race: Disarmament and Arms Control in the Missile Age* (London: Weidenfeld & Nicolson, 1961), 48.
23 Alva Myrdal, *The Game of Disarmament: How the United States and Russia Run the Arms Race* (Manchester: Manchester University Press, 1977), 171.
24 William C. Martel, "Proliferation and Pragmatism: Nonproliferation Policy for the Twenty-First Century," in *Deterrence and Nuclear Proliferation in the Twenty-First Century*, ed. Stephen J. Cimbala (Westport, CT: Praeger, 2001), 103–118, at 114.
25 Ken Booth and Nicholas J. Wheeler, *The Security Dilemma: Fear, Cooperation and Trust in World Politics* (New York: Palgrave, 2008), 124.

PART II

Cracks in the Bloc

4
POLISH COMMUNISM, THE HUNGARIAN REVOLUTION, AND THE SOVIET UNION

Anita J. Prażmowska

In the history of the Cold War Soviet policies were of critical importance in determining what happened in the East European areas which were within the Soviet sphere of influence. This was because, since 1945, the Soviet Union had absolute military, political and economic control over the whole of Eastern Europe. Nevertheless, in each of the so-called satellite states, the Soviet-sponsored governments retained a minimal degree of freedom to implement Soviet policies as appropriate.

After the onset of the Cold War in 1947 the Communist regimes of Eastern Europe were expected, more than in previous years, to fully and unquestioningly implement Soviet instructions. Following Stalin's death in March of 1953, the degree of Soviet control weakened, allowing for variations in the way de-Stalinization took place. In 1956, when the Stalinist model was openly criticized in Moscow by Nikita Khrushchev, the Communist regimes in the satellite states reformed or altered the way they governed. In two cases when Soviet control was loosened, this process was accompanied by violence. In Poland, the Communists nevertheless retained control and thus prevented direct Soviet intervention. In Hungary, the anti-Communist opposition took control and this led to a Soviet invasion which reinstated a Communist government.

Developments in Poland and Hungary were affected by Yugoslavia's split from Moscow in 1948. The Yugoslav Communists had their own vision of how Yugoslavia would be transformed and their determination to implement their own model inspired some Communists in the other satellite states to think of the possibility of a "national road to socialism." In 1956, during the debate in Poland and Hungary on whether and in what form Communists could rule, Yugoslavia acted as an example for local Communists. All this would suggest that our understanding of the Cold War can be enhanced by examining how each of the satellite states interacted, first, with the Soviet Union, and second, with the other satellite states. Our study of the Cold War cannot be confined to the understanding of the way the Soviet Union functioned but calls for an equal engagement with the question of how Soviet control over the satellite states functioned, and consequently how it altered. This, in turn, requires us to accept that while the Soviet Union dominated all decision making in the East European states, local Communists were active in building Communism in their states and, as a result, relations between the Soviet Union and those states changed over time.

This chapter will seek to show how, in 1956, far from being entirely subservient to Soviet instruction, Polish Communists sought to secure some degree of freedom to resolve problems which confronted them. Poland avoided Hungary's fate during that same year. Unlike Hungary, Poland did not face an invasion of Soviet troops, and Polish Communists were left to deal with the process of de-Stalinization and to implement economic reforms. During the 1960s the Communists ruled in Poland without further challenges. In the history of the Cold War Poland is an example of a Communist state which did not challenge the authority of the Soviet Union but which was allowed to pursue its own "national road to socialism."

The Establishment of Communism after the Second World War

The study of the history of Communism in Poland after the Second World War was made difficult by the simple fact that the party was never open about its own origins. The ruling Polish United Workers' Party (Polska Zjednoczona Partia Robotnicza – PZPR) always denied that it had ideological or organizational roots within the Polish Communist Party (Polska Partia Komunistyczna – KPP) which existed during the inter-war period. The latter's dissolution in 1938, on Soviet instructions, and the ensuing demise of the Polish revolutionary cadre in the Soviet Union, has not been well researched.[1] Recent publications suggest that in the history of Communism in Poland the events of 1956 are seen as a seminal point.[2]

Initially, the Allies collaborated with the Polish government in exile which was established in France after Poland's defeat in September 1939. When the French fell to Nazi forces in 1940, the government moved to London, where it resided throughout the war. This government attempted to influence all allied discussions concerning the Polish question after Germany's defeat. The Soviet Union, however, refused to agree to Poland's restoration to its pre-war borders. Stalin made it clear that after the war the Soviet Union would retain Poland's territories east of the Curzon Line, which represented Poland's ethnic boundary. Neither Churchill nor Roosevelt (FDR) wanted to agree to these concessions but both were dependent on the Soviet contribution to the war and ultimately accepted Stalin's demands. At the meeting of the allied leaders held in Teheran from 28 October to 1 November 1943, FDR and Churchill agreed that Poland's post-war borders would be shifted west through the acquisition of German territories and the loss of the eastern regions to the Soviet Union. The final stages of the international negotiations over Poland were completed during the Yalta Conference from 4 to 11 February 1945. At that stage the Red Army controlled most of Polish territory, including Warsaw, where it had installed a provisional government which, despite claims that it was a coalition, was in reality a Communist-dominated grouping which included minority sections of pre-war parties.

At Yalta, Stalin made a commitment that free elections would be held in Poland, but when these took place in January 1947 there was no disguising the fact that they had been anything but free. The Peasant Party, which assumed the role of a legal opposition and which hoped to win the elections, was attacked by the Communists. Peasant Party leaders were arrested and electoral officials were intimidated. British and US officials in Poland reported widespread electoral fraud. The official result was that the Communist Party, in coalition with a number of allies, had won an outright majority, but everyone knew these were rigged results. Soon after the elections the Peasant Party was disbanded and the Socialist Party was absorbed into the Communist Party, forming the PZPR which ruled until 1989.[3]

The Tito–Stalin Split and Soviet Domination in Eastern Europe

In September 1947 the Comintern was founded. Ostensibly its role was to coordinate the policies of the Communist parties; in reality it was an organization that the Soviet Union would use to control the activities of the East European Communist parties. When Yugoslavia refused to accept this situation conflicts between the Soviet Union and Yugoslavia became open and resulted in Yugoslavia's expulsion from the Comintern. This coincided with the onset of the Cold War. The Soviet Union imposed strict control over states within its sphere of influence and Soviet intervention in the internal affairs of the satellite states became absolute. Soviet advisors were deployed in state, civil and military organizations, and all internal matters, from economic to social policies, were dictated from Moscow.

Between 1951 and 1953, Poland witnessed a wide-ranging purge, implemented by a small but influential Stalinist group, which led to a change in the composition of the Party membership. In 1945 the Party had consisted of old and new members, including men and women who had rebuilt the Party in the occupied territories as well as those who had spent the entire war in the Soviet Union. Some had belonged to the pre-war KPP. By 1950 these groups were in open conflict on the extent of subordination to Soviet instructions. Those who belonged to the so-called nationalist group, namely those who believed that the Soviet model of economic development was not appropriate to Poland, were expelled from the Party and its leaders arrested. Władysław Gomułka, who had been secretary of the Party in occupied Poland, objected to Poland following the Soviet model of development, based on heavy industry and collectivization of agriculture. He and a number of his colleagues were arrested.[4] These purges were coordinated from Moscow but the arrests and torture of those accused of "nationalist deviation" were conducted by Polish Communists who firmly believed in the correctness of Soviet policies.

As a result of censorship, the full implications of these processes were not known to Poles, though many suspected that arrests were taking place. Party members also did not know who was arrested, as they were not allowed to discuss the events. Even after Stalin's death in March 1953 the situation did not change. On the contrary, party members and non-members, variously accused of being in the capitalists' pay, of ideological deviation, of having collaborated with the Gestapo during the war and finally of supporting the Yugoslav leader, continued to be arrested by the secret service. The Soviet role in these purges was at that time difficult to discern because instructions were conveyed only to Jakub Berman, the head of the State Security Service.

Stalin's death and the ensuing battle within the Soviet leadership created a new situation which had implications for all of the satellite states and for the ruling Communist regimes. In each of the states the situation evolved differently. During the initial stage of uncertainty the full implications of the changes taking place in Moscow were absorbed slowly, with the ruling Stalinist groups in the satellite states trying to retain an absolute grip on power. The main challenge to their monopoly of power came not from any organized opposition, as this had been destroyed earlier, but from within the ranks of the Communist Party. Once the mold was broken, wider sections of the intellectual, student and workers' communities extended the debate. The Cold War paradigm was thus being renegotiated. By the beginning of 1956, in Poland, in common with other satellite states, the debate on crimes committed during the Stalinist period and on the way forward was not confined to the closed ranks of the Party Central Committee but involved wider sections of the population. The implications of these events were that the Communist parties everywhere split into factions.

Poles found out about the full extent of arrests and executions when, on 28 September 1954, Western radio broadcast a series of interviews with Józef Światło, the deputy director of the X Department (Central Committee for Party Control) of the PZPR, who had recently defected to the West.[5] In these broadcasts he revealed that the Ministry for Public Safety (Ministerstwo Bezpieczeństwa Publicznego – MBP) had been systematically arresting, torturing and executing Polish citizens. It quickly transpired that a high proportion of the victims were Party members who had been condemned for "ideological deviation." The Politburo of the PZPR was not entirely sure how to proceed. Stalin's death gradually gave the Poles the freedom to review their position, but just what that meant was not clear. The Party leadership knew that it had to address accusations made by Światło. Its preference would have been to treat this as an internal Party issue, though it quickly became apparent that Poles in all walks of life had started talking about the crimes committed during the recent years. They also cautiously asked questions about who was responsible.

The II Party Congress of the PZPR, which took place between 10 and 17 March, witnessed the first changes. Nikita Khrushchev's attendance at the meetings, soon after he had consolidated his position within the Soviet leadership, indicated to the Poles that they were expected to instigate reforms in line with those implemented in Moscow. On 7 December, the Politburo agreed to release Gomułka from arrest and allowed him to receive medical treatment to help him overcome the consequences of imprisonment and maltreatment.[6] Until then Gomułka epitomized the worst case of "nationalist deviation" in the Party, to the extent that the phrase "*gomułkowszczyzna*" was used as an accusation of all that had been wrong with those who looked back to the pre-war KPP and who in 1947 opposed the adoption of the Soviet model of industrialization and agricultural reform. The gradual reassessment of the role of the Party and a debate on the purges also proceeded in tandem with the opening of talks with Yugoslavia.[7] One of the problems created by Yugoslavia's estrangement from the Soviet Union was that some sections within the satellite Communist parties would have wanted their own parties to show a similar degree of independence.

As relations with the Soviet Union were becoming the subject of open debate in Poland, it was inevitable that Yugoslavia's case would be reconsidered and questions would be asked as to whether Poland could not find its own path to socialism, allied to the Soviet Union but not subordinated to it. This particular point was addressed during the III Plenary meeting of the Central Committee, which took place in January 1955. Bierut, the Party Secretary, realized that even though efforts were being made to maintain the ideological framework, relations with Yugoslavia had to be reviewed. The nationalist section of the PZPR, which had disagreed with the Comintern's criticism of Yugoslavia, hoped that Poles would be able to discuss in what form socialism could be built in Poland.[8] In 1955, the new Soviet leadership wanted to find ways of repairing relations with Yugoslavia but neither side would admit to having been wrong. The Polish Communists watched these developments very carefully, as the most important conflicts in the leadership during the Stalinist period related to the very same question, namely the degree of freedom that Poland would have while remaining within the Communist bloc.

In 1955, in the absence of clear Soviet instructions, the PZPR Central Committee and the Politburo discussed subjects which could not be aired previously. In due course admissions were made to past mistakes, but that only highlighted the painful dilemmas over what was to be made of the new freedom and, in particular, the question of what was to be the Polish road to socialism. The debates focused on a number of dilemmas. One such subject was the fate of Communists who had been the victims of the Stalinist period. Another was the failures of the Six-Year Plan, which had been introduced in 1948. The Soviet model of economic development had been inappropriate for Poland. The rapid pace of industrialization and the collectivization of agriculture had caused economic problems and led to discontent. Another subject widely discussed in 1956 was Soviet treatment of Poland as a de facto colony. The Poles were required to supply the Soviet Union with resources which were needed in Poland. For a brief period, intellectuals, writers, workers and Party members freely debated hitherto forbidden subjects in the streets and in newspapers. They also considered what changes should take place and the basis of Poland's future relations with the Soviet Union.

During the months that followed, the Politburo fought to maintain a grip on the pace of events. The literary community, until then kept firmly in place by strict censorship regulations, requested permission to hold an annual congress. Already during the IV Congress of the Association of Polish Writers (Związek Literatów Polskich – ZSL) in June 1954 a reference was made by a writer to "the new wind," a phrase which would worry members of the Politburo.[9] No better phrase illustrates the way Soviet control over Eastern Europe changed during this period. While the ruling parties were immobilized by lack of instructions from Moscow, the rank and file of the Party and the intellectual communities assumed the initiative in opening up the debate and in discussing what was to happen in the circumstances where the Soviet Union was clearly willing to loosen its control over all aspects of life in the satellite states. Literary journals published articles about daily hardships faced by workers under Communism. This had been a taboo subject, and by opening the debate it was inevitable that the next question would relate to the Party's responsibilities for these failings. Adam Ważyk's *Poem for Adults*, a coruscating condemnation of the social consequences of industrialization and neglect of standards of living, appeared in August 1955. The openness of his criticism and the fact that the censors agreed to the journal publishing his poem marked an important stage in the widening of the debate.[10]

The Twentieth Congress of the Soviet Communist Party, which opened in Moscow on 14 February 1956, marks a critical stage in Poland's Cold War. Most assessments of the Congress are dominated by one key event, namely Khrushchev's "secret speech" in which he condemned Stalinism. Often overlooked in the same speech was his assurance that the Kremlin would not intervene in the internal affairs of other Communist countries. It remained unclear to East European Communist Party leaders whether this would mean that countries of the socialist bloc would be allowed to develop their own road to socialism. For the Poles, the confusing situation was compounded by the fact that when the Polish delegation returned to Warsaw, Bierut stayed behind, as he had become too ill to travel. He died on 12 March in a Russian hospital. The leadership contest could not have come at a more difficult time for the Polish Communists.

Khrushchev attended the VI Plenary meeting of the Central Committee of the PZPR on 20 March 1956, the first since Bierut's death. In line with what he had said in Moscow, Khrushchev reiterated to the Polish Communist leadership the need to reform the Party and to broaden the membership of the Politburo and the Central Committee.[11] He made no direct reference to his earlier condemnation of Stalin. Nevertheless, it has been suggested that during informal meetings with the Polish Party leadership he urged it to abandon the case against Gomułka and others accused of "national deviation."[12] If indeed he did make these points the Politburo was resolutely determined not to follow his advice.[13] Thus, once more, those studying the Cold War are confronted with a puzzling scenario of Soviet leaders urging reforms and advising the local Communists to develop policies appropriate to their countries, whereas the local Communist leaders, in most cases unreformed Stalinists, refused to take advantage of the freedom to renegotiate the rigid and oppressive political system over which they had presided until then.

The result was that the process of de-Stalinization in Poland was that of the Party confronting the increasingly mobilized nation. The debate rapidly went beyond the narrow confines of the Politburo and the Central Committee. On 7 April, *Trybuna Ludu*, the Party daily newspaper, announced that the Communist Party cleared Gomułka of all accusations. By then the matter had become the subject of public discussion. The debates taking place in *Nowe Drogi*, the Party journal, were followed by similar ones in the journal *Po Prostu* published by the young activists of the Association of Polish Youth (Zrzeszenie Młodzieży Polskiej – ZMP). From March 1956 the openness with which contentious issues were aired in the Party and in the media broke all previous boundaries. While each publication clearly voiced its readership's concerns, the debate went well beyond what could be considered to be subjects of interest to that readership. The public debate continued, apparently without either instruction from above or attempts to limit it.

On 28 June 1956 a strike took place in the town of Poznań which resulted in a confrontation between the workers and the security services. The causes of the Poznań strike were manifold but related mainly to changes in wage structures and the lowering of take-home pay for skilled workers.[14] The aim of the Six-Year Plan had been to rapidly build up heavy industry in Poland, but by 1954 it was widely known that this plan had failed. The managers of state enterprises responded by increasing productivity rates and lowering pay. In June 1956 the workers of Poznań transformed a dispute over wages and rates of pay into a political protest against the Communist regime and Soviet domination of Poland. Belatedly, the Party leaders admitted that they should have paid attention to clearly articulated disaffection among the workers. As the demonstration turned into an attack on institutions like the prison, the headquarters of the police and the secret service, the authorities called in regular army units to quell the unrest. The deployment of regular army units finally enabled the regime to regain control. Subsequent investigations clearly stated that what had started as a strike became a mass demonstration. By the end of the day 73 people were dead and 239 were wounded. Even now historians disagree as to whether this was a failed revolution or only a city-wide strike.[15]

On hearing of events unfolding in Poznań, the Party leadership reacted predictably, namely by defining what was happening as "hostile provocation." The town was surrounded by troops until the authorities regained the initiative. During the following days the authorities conducted mass arrests of those suspected of having participated in the events, ensuring that the demonstrations did not spread to other towns. Nevertheless the Politburo requested a thorough investigation of the causes of the strikes.[16] The leadership's discomfort was compounded by the fact that information about what had happened in Poznań was conveyed to the Western media by businessmen attending the International Trade Fair. The CIA-funded Radio Free Europe transmitted details of the Poznań events during the evening of 18 June.[17] This led to worldwide speculation as to whether the Soviets would loosen their control over Poland. Some Western politicians indicated that this would be the right moment to challenge the Soviet Union and thus to weaken if not destroy the Communist system outright.[18] But it did not happen.

The full extent of what occurred in Poznań was addressed by the VII Plenary meeting of the Central Committee in July 1956. Although Edward Ochab, Bierut's successor, tried to control the debate by admitting that the Party had made some mistakes, this was no longer acceptable to the members of the Central Committee. The Politburo's stubbornness can be explained only by a sense of panic which overwhelmed the leaders after the Poznań strikes.[19] In the meantime the public had assumed that Gomułka would be released and that this would automatically lead to further reforms. This expectation put pressure on the Party leaders to respond in a positive way. On 4 August an announcement was made that Gomułka's Party membership had been restored.

People Power

During the summer months the Party leadership seemed to be paralyzed with indecision, whereas the people voiced demands for change and started organizing.[20] In factories, workers who no longer trusted the Party and the official trade unions formed councils which spoke openly about mismanagement, economic mistakes and the economic consequences of the

Six-Year Plan. The expectation that with Gomułka's return to the Party leadership de-Stalinization would continue at a rapid pace was voiced within the Party ranks and openly in the streets. On 13 October Gomułka participated in the Politburo meeting, during which he made cutting comments about Poland's uneven relations with the Soviet Union, in particular in the pricing of coal exported to the Soviet Union and the financial burden of stationing Soviet troops on Polish soil. The phrase that Gomułka used to describe Soviet relations with Poland was "inappropriate" (*niewłaściwe*). Displaying a remarkable command of detail, he launched an attack on the Six-Year Plan and its economic shortcomings. Finally he reminded Politburo members that he had objected to the creation of collective farms when the subject was originally discussed in 1947.[21] His criticism of policies which had been imposed by the Soviet Union on Poland since 1947 contained an outline of his vision of the Polish road to socialism.

By the time of the VIII Plenary meeting of the Central Committee, which met on 19 October, the Party landscape changed again. Ochab resigned and Gomułka became the First Party Secretary. The remarkable point about these changes was the fact that the Soviet leaders had made it quite clear that they wanted to see the Polish Party reformed, and that meant replacing Stalin's puppets with new men. With the Soviet Party fully preoccupied with changes taking place in Moscow, East European parties responded to these instructions in their own way. As has been shown, the leadership of the PZPR did so only after it faced mass protests and criticism from its own ranks.

During a meeting with Soviet leaders on 19 October, Polish leaders defied the Soviets by dismissing Marshall Konstantin Rokossovky, the Soviet-appointed Polish Minister of Defense. When he departed, Soviet military advisors who had been in Poland since the end of war were also withdrawn, at the Poles' request. In the end, notwithstanding their anxieties, the Soviet leaders let the Polish comrades conduct the VIII Plenary meeting without interference.

The result of the discussions which took place in Warsaw and the subsequent reassessment of the situation conducted in Moscow was that the Soviet leaders decided that Gomułka should guide Poland's reforms, though they did not discount the possibility of military intervention. An important element in the Soviet compromise was the decisiveness with which the Chinese leadership indicated that it would not tolerate Soviet intervention in Polish affairs. What had mattered to the Chinese was not Poland's fate but the lack of consultation between Moscow and Beijing.[22] At the same time the responses of the West European governments would have been analyzed in Moscow. US Secretary of State John Foster Dulles' statement expressing glee that events in Poland weakened the cohesiveness of the Communist bloc and a similar analysis by the British Foreign Office underlined the need for caution.[23] Neither of these governments warned the Soviet Union against taking military action against Poland, but the Soviet Union had no way of knowing whether or not the Western democracies would view Soviet intervention in Poland as a threat which warranted some form of response.

On 20 October Gomułka reaffirmed his authority when, in a public address, he assured Poles that Soviet troops in Poland, which had earlier been put on alert, would return to their bases. He concluded by asking people to go back to work. At that time, writers, workers and Party members who supported him still thought that this was only the beginning of a longer process of reform which would follow. For that reason the demonstrations ended peacefully, with the hope that the dialogue between the Party and the people had only just begun.

The Hungarian Revolution

In the meantime, events in Poland had an impact on those unfolding in Hungary. There, too, Stalin's death had led to infighting in the Party leadership. Khrushchev's admission that crimes had been committed during the Stalinist period and revelations that many of the Hungarian Communists who sought political sanctuary in the Soviet Union had been executed caused anger and led to calls for openness about what had been happening in Hungary since the end of the war. As in Poland's case, writers and university students took up the debate on the Stalinist period. The Hungarian Communist Party, led by the staunchly Stalinist Mátyás Rákosi, tried to stall on reforms which the new Soviet leadership had expected it to introduce after Khrushchev's speech. On hearing of the Poznań riots in Poland, Rákosi attempted to mount a counter-offensive against the reformers by warning that similar disturbances could engulf Hungary. He was unsuccessful, as the Party reformers, with Krushchev's support, pushed on with demands for changes.[24] In July Rákosi was forced to resign, giving many Hungarians hope that a review of policies would follow.

There was a clear link between what had been happening in Poland and the pace of change in Hungary. Hungarians looked to Poland and hoped that they too would be allowed to openly discuss Stalinist crimes, economic problems and the consequences of Soviet domination. On 23 October students in Budapest organized a demonstration to express their solidarity with the Poles. This took a violent turn when troops were called to control the gathering. Troops started shooting at the demonstrators. The Party moved quickly to deal with the mounting crisis. On the following day Imre Nagy became the Prime Minister, while János Kádár was appointed First Party Secretary.

Both appointments had great political significance. Nagy had been appointed as Prime Minister in July 1953, a position he occupied until November 1955, when the Stalinists in the Hungarian Communist Party managed to expel him. In the public mind Nagy was associated with the first wave of liberalization, instigated with Soviet approval after Stalin's death. Kádár had been in the resistance movement during the war, unlike his arch-rival Rakosi, who was seen as Moscow's agent. The Hungarian people believed Kádár was a nationalist. When both men returned to public life Hungary looked to be set on a course for major reforms. Nagy promised to hold free elections, a point which struck a chord with all Hungarians angry at Soviet intervention in the country's internal affairs. Hungarians were assured that Soviet troops stationed in Hungary since 1945 would be withdrawn. In spite of popular support for these reforms, many within the Party leadership disagreed with both the character and the pace of de-Stalinization. In Budapest, Hungarians emboldened by the new sense of freedom destroyed Communist symbols and called for Hungary to be freed from Soviet tutelage. Fighting erupted in the capital and there was a genuine fear that Hungary would be engulfed by civil war. This in turn created conflicts within the ruling group.[25] Kádár fled to the Soviet Union, where he was appointed head of a new Hungarian government, which in turn legitimized the Soviet invasion.[26]

In Poland, Gomułka and the Party leadership knew only too well the precariousness of their position during the Hungarian revolution. One fact nevertheless militated against a call for the removal of Soviet troops from Polish soil, namely continuing anxiety about the unresolved German question. The issue of Germany's future after World War II divided the world powers. The Soviet Union would have wanted Germany united under the supervision of the war-time allies. Britain, France and the United States instead consolidated their zones of occupation. In 1949 these became the Federal Republic of Germany. Poland, which had acquired German territories in East and West Prussia as well as areas up to the river Oder after the war, was very anxious about the lack of international agreement to ensure that Germany would not become an aggressor again. Gomułka's suspicion of the Western powers' long-term objectives was shared by the Polish community as a whole. In the circumstances, Soviet commitment to Poland's post-war borders and to the maintenance of troops on Poland's western border was very important.[27]

On 30 October the Soviet Union issued a declaration committing to resolve all problems with Poland through "friendly talks which would be based on absolute equality, respect for territorial integrity, national independence and sovereignty and mutual non integration in internal matters of each country." In a personal note made on a copy of the draft of this declaration Gomułka added: "both parties accept the correctness of these arguments and will act in accordance with these principles."[28] Thus the PZPR, unlike the Hungarian comrades, won the right to define Poland's internal policies. Poles generally believed that the new Party Secretary had successfully defended Polish interests, and in that he secured public support.

As fighting in Budapest escalated, the Polish leadership did not attempt to reduce the scale of public expressions of sympathy for the Hungarians. On 22 November Nagy was kidnapped from outside the Yugoslav embassy, where he and his family had sought asylum when the Soviet troops invaded. On hearing of this, Gomułka and other leaders expressed strong disapproval of Soviet actions. The Polish Communist leadership nevertheless did not actively support the Hungarian revolutionaries; they were themselves very uneasy about the strength of anti-Communist and anti-Soviet expressions in Budapest. Nagy's earlier declaration that Hungary was withdrawing from the Warsaw Pact had caused Gomułka anxiety, and this in turn prevented him from openly declaring his support for the Hungarians. Subsequently, during the Soviet invasion, Gomułka tried to act as a mediator to limit the consequences of the breakdown between Nagy and the Soviet leadership. All this would suggest that he remained firmly committed to the idea of a Soviet bloc but did not want to see the clock set back to the Stalinist years when that meant subordination to the Soviet Union.[29]

After 1956

Within the next two years Gomułka turned against the intellectuals who had been his and the Central Committee's allies in the critical months of 1956. Working-class mobilization, which was the most visible element of popular responses to de-Stalinization, was stifled. In the years to come Gomułka admitted that after October 1956 he had most of all feared that the radical sections of the Party and working class would continue to push for reforms and for a larger degree of freedom from the Soviet Union. This, he knew, on the basis of the Hungarian example, the Soviet Union would not tolerate. He personally also believed that the there was no need to introduce further changes. The limits of reforms which he considered necessary had been reached. Poland was to remain a Communist state, closely allied to the Soviet Union through the Warsaw Pact. Gomułka intended Poland to remain within the Soviet economic sphere.

Within the Party the rehabilitation process took the form of amnesties and admission of judicial failures. In economic terms this meant the abandonment of the program for rapid industrial development and the dissolution of the peasant cooperatives. The pace of industrialization slowed down. At the same time investments were made into light industries and into the production of consumer goods. The public approved of these changes and credited Gomułka with steering them through. Supply of goods to the market was guaranteed by a tacit agreement that small-scale retail could coexist with state control of industry and production. Gomułka personally renegotiated earlier economic treaties which had been disadvantageous to Poland, in particular those relating to the export of coal and sulfur to the Soviet Union. He was also angry that Poland had to pay for the upkeep of Soviet troops on Polish territories. During the coming years the Polish Communist leadership felt bold enough to negotiate the precise conditions on which Soviet bases would be maintained in Poland. The Poles argued that Moscow had to share the costs.

After 1956 the Polish Party leadership remained profoundly aware of its precarious domestic and international position. The PZPR knew only too well that, were the economic situation to deteriorate, the working class could take to the streets once more. The Poznań riots acted as a warning of what might happen again. But the leaders of the Party were Communists and they remained committed to the Soviet political model. This meant that although Gomułka disagreed with official statements that suggested that the Soviet Union was the undisputed leader of the Socialist bloc, he was in equal measure aware of Poland's need for Soviet economic and military support. Unlike in the other countries of the Socialist bloc, the defense of Poland's borders, and in particular the Western border, would require Soviet military assistance. In that context the still unresolved German issue haunted the Poles and led them to reaffirm their commitment to the Warsaw Pact.[30]

At the same time Poland's relations with the Western democracies were unique among the countries of the Socialist bloc. The Gomułka leadership readily embraced the Soviet principle of peaceful coexistence with the capitalist states, reintroduced under Khrushchev, which allowed Poland to develop diplomatic and economic ties with the West. After 1956 the Eisenhower administration and the British government recognized Poland as a special case, one where there was a likelihood of an evolution away from dependence on the Soviet Union. This allowed Gomułka to develop close trading links with capitalist economies. Whereas otherwise there would have been political barriers to economic relations between the capitalist and socialist countries, in Poland's case these were lowered, which meant that Poland could purchase grain and food-stuffs on the world markets and benefit from Western technology.[31]

In the formulation of foreign policy as well as in any commercial contact Gomułka decided what was right for Poland. Poland remained a staunch member of the Warsaw Pact, but this did not prevent the Party leadership from exercising a degree of independence in its dealings with the Soviet Union and the Western powers. During the Sino-Soviet crisis after 1961, Poland was critical of the Chinese, but at the same time the Chinese embassy in Warsaw was a center through which talks between both sides were maintained by indirect means. Gomułka wanted Poland to play the role of a mediator, and indeed in 1964 he was approached by the US to find out if North Vietnamese leaders would be willing to open talks on the withdrawal of US troops from Vietnam. This initiative ultimately failed, though the Poles tried their best in discussing the matter with North Vietnamese and Chinese leaders. During the mid 1960s Poland put forward a plan for the creation of a nuclear-free zone in Central Europe, known as the Rapacki Plan, though it is still not clear whether this was a purely Polish idea or one which the Soviet government wanted the Poles to put forward. In 1968 Poland condemned changes taking place in Czechoslovakia, and when the Warsaw Pact troops invaded, Polish troops were part of the force which entered Prague. This was not because the Polish leadership was compelled to do so, but because Gomułka genuinely disapproved of the introduction of capitalist methods into the economy, which the Czechs wanted to do. He also did not agree with their suggestions that the Communist Party should relinquish the monopoly of power.

Notes

1. M.K. Dziewanowski, *The Communist Party of Poland. An Outline of History* (Cambridge, MA: Harvard University Press, 1959); Jan B de Weydenthal, *The Communists of Poland: An Historical Outline* (Stanford, CA: Hoover Institution Press, 1986); Jan Alfred Reguła, *Historia Komunistycznej Partii Polski w świetlica faktów i dokumentów* (Toruń: Portal, 1994).
2. Pawel Machcewicz, *Rebellious Satellite: Poland 1956* (Palo Alto, CA: Stanford University Press, 2009).
3. Marcin Zaremba, *Komunism, legitymizacja, nacjonalizm* (Warszawa: Wydawnicto TRIO, 2005), 135–174.

4. Andrzej Skrzypek, *Mechanizmy uzależnienia, stosunki polsko-radzieckie 1944–1957* (Pułtusk: Oficyna Wydawnicza ASPRA-JR, 2002), 207–208.
5. Andrzej Paczkowski, *Trzy twarze Józefa Światły* (Warszawa: Prószyński I S-ka, 2009), 197–198.
6. Archiwum Akt Nowych, Warsaw (henceforth AAN), PZPR V/27, 7 December 1954.
7. AAN, PZPR V/27, 15 October 1954.
8. AAN, PZPR III/12, 21–24 January 1955.
9. Archiwa Związeku Literatów Polskich, Warszawa, Vol. 1. 1954. 9 June 1954.
10. Ann Sobór-Świderska, *Jakub Berman. Biografia komunisty* (Warszawa: Instytut Pamięci Narodowej, 2009), 429–431.
11. AAN, PZPR III/15, 20 March 1956.
12. Skrzypek, *Mechanizmy uzależnienia, stosunki polsko-radzieckie 1944–1957*, 361
13. AAN, PZPR III/15, 20 March 1956.
14. Machcewicz, *Rebellious Satellite*, 91–93.
15. Marek Leszek Wojciechowski, "Poznański Czerwiec 1956: insurekcja, rewolta czy 'wypadki'?" in Stanisław Jankowiak i Agnieszka Rogulska (eds.), *Poznański Czerwiec 1956* (Warszawa: IPN, 2002), 91–94.
16. Edmund Makowski, *Poznański Czerwiec 1956 pierwszy bunt społeczeństwa w PRL* (Poznań: Wydawnictwo Poznańskie, 2006), 176–180.
17. Filip Leśniak, "Reakcja prasy zachodniej na poznański Czerwiec 1956," in Stanisław Jankowiak i Agnieszka Rogulska (eds.), *Poznański Czerwiec 1956* (Warszawa: IPN, 2002), 56–60.
18. Makowski, *Poznański Czerwiec 1956*, 209–214.
19. Peter Raina, *Władysław Gomułka: Życiorys polityczny* (London: Polonia Book Fund, 1969), 77.
20. Joanna Granville, "Satellites or prime movers? Polish and Hungarian reactions to the 1956 events: new archival evidence," *East European Quarterly*, No. 34/4 (Winter 2001).
21. AAN, KC PZPR V/41 Biuro Politiczne, 12 October 1956.
22. Machcewicz, *Rebellious Statellite*, 168–169.
23. Jacek Tebinka, *Uzależnienie czy suwerenność. Odwilż październikowa w dyplomacji Polskiej Rzeczpospolitej Ludowej 1956–1961* (Warszawa: Neriton, 2010), 35.
24. Granville, "Satellites or prime movers?"
25. János M. Rainer, *Imre Nagy: a biography* (London: I.B. Tauris, 2009), 114.
26. Roger Gough, *A Good Comrade: János Kádár. Communism and Hungary* (London: I.B. Tauris, 2006), 97–99.
27. Tebinka, *Uzależnienie czy suwerenność*, 58–63.
28. AAN, KC PZPR XIA/71I, 8 November 1956.
29. Janusz Karwat and János Tischler, *1956. Poznań – Budapeszt* (Poznań: Media Rodzina, 2006), 197–198.
30. Tebinka, *Uzależnienie czy suwerenność*, 284–285.
31. Ibid., 283–284.

5

BERLIN AND THE COLD WAR STRUGGLE OVER GERMANY

Hope M. Harrison

The Cold War began and ended in Germany. Superpower disagreements over how to treat the ruins of Nazi Germany reflected and fueled the developing Cold War. The results were a divided Germany and Berlin. They occupied the front line of the Cold War conflict between NATO and the Warsaw Pact, between democracy and capitalism, on the one hand, and oppressive communist rule on the other. The East German regime even solidified the divide with a concrete wall. After forty years of German division and a world split into two camps, the surprise toppling of the Berlin Wall in 1989 symbolized and further propelled the end of the Cold War. Understanding the respective roles of the two German states and their superpower patrons is central to comprehending the dynamics of the Cold War. This chapter will examine key developments at the front line of the Cold War in Germany, adopting a "pericentric" framework that takes into account not only the superpowers but also their German allies.[1]

With the creation of the two German states in 1949, each of the German leaders sought two things: to gain greater sovereignty from their Great Power overseers and to be accepted by their own citizens and the rest of the world as the sole legitimate German regime. One of the fascinating developments of the Cold War was the way the two Germanys went from being part of the defeated and despised Nazi regime that needed to be kept weak and ostracized to becoming the central ally of the two superpowers at the core of their political, military, and economic strategy. Each German state did all it could to fuel its rise from pariah to partner of the superpowers in the Cold War. Yet partnership was not enough; the Germans also sought to get back control over their own fates from their postwar occupiers, the US, Soviet Union, Great Britain and France.

Inevitably there were moments when the Germans saw their interests as diverging from those of their Great Power patrons, moments which added a component of intra-bloc tension in the broader context of inter-bloc tensions in the Cold War. For example, separate German interests at times dictated greater tensions between the blocs than their superpower patrons favored and at times dictated more cooperation between the blocs than Moscow and Washington supported. From the start, the two German leaders, Konrad Adenauer in the West and Walter Ulbricht in the East, sought to use Cold War tensions to gain more power, and they generally feared that with a lessening of Cold War tensions the Four Powers led by Washington and Moscow would come to an agreement on Germany over their heads. During the Berlin Crisis of 1958–61, the two German leaders were less inclined toward compromise than the US and Soviet leaders were. The roles were reversed in the early 1980s, when the two Germanys sought to shield their relations from renewed East–West tensions in the "second Cold War." Examining Cold War dynamics in Germany sheds broader light on important aspects of the Cold War concerning the role of alliance politics, nationalism, ideology, economics, and military security in the global struggle that lasted over forty years.

The Early Years

The first two leaders of divided Germany, Adenauer and Ulbricht, had impeccable credentials as far as their Great Power backers were concerned. Both had resisted the Nazis and suffered accordingly and both were strong adherents of the type of system – democratic and capitalist vs. communist – their superpower backers supported. Adenauer had been trained as a lawyer and was the mayor of Cologne until he was ousted by the Nazis in 1933. He was imprisoned for short periods in 1934 and in 1944. After the war he helped found what would be one of West Germany's two key political parties, the Christian Democratic Union (CDU). Equally important, he was chairman of the 1948–49 constitutional convention of the Parliamentary Council formed under American, British, and French tutelage in the three western zones of Germany to draft a constitution (the Basic Law) for a new West German state. After the formation of the West German state, the Federal Republic of Germany (FRG), in May 1949, he was elected leader as chancellor in September and would remain in power until 1963.

Walter Ulbricht joined the Communist Party of Germany (KPD) in 1920, was trained in Moscow in 1924–25, and became Communist Party leader in Berlin in 1929. He was a KPD member of the German parliament, the Reichstag, until the Nazis banned the KPD in 1933. Ulbricht then fled the country to avoid imprisonment, living in exile in Paris and Prague before moving to the Soviet Union in 1937, where he remained for eight years, being trained as a future German communist leader. In April 1945, he returned to Berlin, where he began laying the groundwork for a communist Germany. He oversaw the creation of the Soviet-style Socialist Unity Party (SED) in 1946 from a forced merger of the KPD and the Social Democratic Party (SPD). Ulbricht became the leader of the German Democratic Republic (GDR), the East German state, in October 1949, five months after the creation of the FRG, and stayed in power until 1971.

Although Adenauer and Ulbricht were the leaders of the two German states created in 1949, neither of them had full control over domestic or foreign policies. The Four Powers together retained the rights to oversee policy on German unification and a German peace treaty, which had not been signed at the end of the war, due to disagreements over terms among the four. They also remained very involved in domestic policies in their respective parts of Germany. Both German leaders thus sought full autonomy as soon as possible. This arguably was more important to Adenauer and Ulbricht than was German reunification. They each felt that they could lose their leadership role in a united Germany. They also were both rather skeptical about the advisability of German unification after the aggression perpetrated by the Nazi regime which was not stopped by the Germans themselves but only by the Allied victory in World War II. Publicly, however, they both pledged to do all they could to bring about unification and blamed division on the other.

The launching of the Korean War in June 1950 with the communist North Korean attack on South Korea offered Adenauer the chance to achieve greater independence from the US, British and French High Commissioners in Germany and their roles as laid out in the Occupation Statute of 1949. The communist attack in Korea helped to pivot the attention of skeptics of a strong, independent West German state only five years after the defeat of Nazi

Germany toward the clear and present dangers of the communist bloc led by the Soviet Union. Many in the West felt that they needed to be prepared to ward off a similar communist attack by Soviet-backed East Germany on West Germany. The Occupation Statute stipulated Allied control over continued German disarmament and demilitarization,[2] but now many in the West, including Adenauer, argued that West German armed forces were necessary for defense against the communist threat just across the border. As NATO countries debated how best to integrate West German forces into the Western alliance so that Germany's recent enemies in the West, particularly France and Britain, would not feel threatened by a new German military, Adenauer saw that he could tie the West's need for a German contribution to military defense to his desire for greater FRG autonomy and an end to the Occupation Statute.[3]

In the Paris Agreements of 1954, which took effect on May 8, 1955, Adenauer was able to trade an end to the Occupation Statute for the creation of West German armed forces and the FRG's accession to NATO. These forces were limited to a maximum of 500,000 troops (which was not achieved until the 1970s) and completely subsumed into NATO integrated command structures (so as not to threaten France, Britain, or anyone else with an independent West German military).[4] With the end of the Occupation Statute, Adenauer could now assume control over foreign policy, foreign trade, industrial production, and domestic legislation. The Allies retained rights only in Berlin (which remained under Four Power control) and with regard to questions on German unification and a peace treaty, as well as in the event of an emergency. Allied troops stationed in West Germany would remain there as part of joint defense, not as occupiers. Adenauer also secured Western agreement that the FRG should be seen as the sole legitimate representative of the German people in global affairs until the signing of a peace treaty. He proved adept at using broader Cold War tensions, as evidenced in the Korean War, to attain near-complete sovereignty in domestic and foreign policy just six years after the creation of the FRG.

Ulbricht also sought more control in the GDR but faced greater problems than Adenauer did in West Germany. The Western Allies changed tack much faster than the Soviets did from policies aimed at keeping Germany weak, extracting reparations, and exacting revenge on the Germans to policies directed toward rebuilding Germany and making it into a strong ally.[5] It was much harder for Ulbricht to gain support and legitimacy, to say nothing of building a stable East German state, when the Soviets continued to dismantle and remove entire factories to the Soviet Union, Red Army troops raped countless German women and girls, and the Soviets generally did whatever they wanted in the GDR.[6] Ulbricht's Stalinist proclivities in his style of rule did not help matters either.

The devastation of the western part of the Soviet Union by the Wehrmacht in World War II drove Soviet anger toward the Germans as well as the Soviets' need for all the help they could get from their zone of Germany to aid recovery at home. The fact that the more productive and potentially military-related industrial areas were located in western Germany also meant that the Soviets strove for unification longer than the Western Powers did. Soviet leader Josef Stalin held out hope that he could gain access to the key resources and larger population of western Germany with German unification. After the 27 million Soviet lives lost in World War II, the future of Germany was of intense importance to the Soviets. Stalin did not want to give up on the chance for communist influence in the West, and he certainly did not want to see a remilitarized West Germany integrated into NATO. Thus, to Ulbricht's chagrin, in March 1952, Stalin proposed to the Western Powers a united, neutral Germany that would have its own limited military forces for self-defense. The Soviet leader clearly hoped that he could wield influence in such a Germany and have good relations with this united, neutral Germany. Yet the West had seen enough of Stalin's hard-line policies in the GDR and elsewhere to mistrust letting go of the FRG and halting the talks on remilitarizing West Germany after the start of the Korean War. The Western Powers were skeptical that there was anything behind Stalin's initiative except an effort to lure West Germany away from the West and did not seriously engage the offer.[7]

In the wake of this rebuff, Stalin finally gave up on efforts to expand communist influence in a united Germany and focused on shoring up communist East Germany. Accordingly, in the summer of 1952 he authorized the militarization of the border between East Germany and West Germany (although not between East and West Berlin). Beginning in May 1952, the East Germans cleared a broad strip of land along the entire 865-mile border between East and West Germany, forcing people out and demolishing homes, forests, and anything else in the way. Multiple layers of fencing, guards, guard towers, trip wires, anti-tank barriers, and dogs were then installed (mines were added later) to prevent any unauthorized movement across the border. This meant that after May 1952, the only place in all of Germany where there was free movement between East and West was in Berlin. Berlin became the front line of the Cold War, a status fully on display in a crisis that was to come six years later.

In the summer of 1952, Stalin also gave Ulbricht the go-ahead for the "Construction of Socialism" program launched in July in the GDR. Stalin had held off on this when he was hoping for an agreement with the West on a united Germany, but after the West's rejection of his March note and in light of Ulbricht's desire to move ahead with socialist policies, Stalin agreed. The Construction of Socialism program entailed intensifying Soviet-style policies in East Germany, including an acceleration of industrialization, forcing more farmers into collective farms run by the state, squeezing out free enterprise, as well as pressure on the intelligentsia, the clergy, and anyone else who did not conform to the image of a workers' and peasants' communist state. Introducing these policies when the GDR was still recovering from the destruction of World War II and still forced to pay reparations to the Soviet Union was a recipe for disaster. The Construction of Socialism program led to serious shortages of food and goods and prompted many East Germans to flee to better conditions in the West, where the beginnings of the West German "Economic Miracle" due to Western investment (including with the Marshall Plan) and free market practices was beginning.

The 1953 Uprising in the GDR

By the spring of 1953 and in the wake of Stalin's death on March 5, 1953, the new Soviet leaders decided that Stalin's policies at home and in Eastern Europe had been too harsh and needed to be moderated with a "New Course."[8] In late May, Stalin's successors formulated a series of "Measures to Improve the Health of the Political Situation in the GDR," and summoned the East German leaders to Moscow to give them these new guidelines. Telling Ulbricht and his colleagues that the Construction of Socialism program was "mistaken under current conditions" and had "led to the mass exodus of East Germans to West Germany," the Soviet leaders insisted that the East Germans should relax their policies in all spheres of the economy and social life. When Ulbricht balked at an admission of mistakes and setting a New Course, the Soviets forced him to publish their "Measures to Improve the Health of the Political Situation in the GDR" on June 11.[9] The East German leader did this, but did not rescind a new regulation that insisted the East German workers should produce 10 percent more for the same wages. The combination of this pressure on the workers with a public admission of mistakes and change of course sparked workers to take to the streets of East Berlin on June 16, believing that they could force the government to rescind the changed work norms. When the GDR regime did not respond, on June 17 strikes and protests spread throughout the country into a full-blown uprising calling not only for better working conditions, but also free elections and the ouster of Ulbricht.

The uprising took the East German and Soviet leaders by surprise. While the East German leaders were sequestered, for their safety, at Soviet military headquarters in Karlshorst-Berlin, Soviet troops and tanks put down the uprising, killing tens of protesters and arresting thousands. Publicly, the Soviets and East Germans blamed the uprising on Western provocateurs sponsored by the US and West Germany, but internally they were aware of the problems within the GDR and now knew how close the GDR was to collapse without Soviet military backing. What to do next was the subject of debate and disagreement. Some in Moscow and East Berlin wanted to oust Ulbricht and replace him with a leader who would improve relations with the East German people based on more moderate policies. Others, including Ulbricht of course, argued that getting rid of him would only make them all look weak and would make "reactionaries" in East Germany and the "imperialist adversaries" believe they had won. The tables were turned in Ulbricht's favor after the Soviet leaders ousted secret police chief Lavrenty Beria, who had ironically supported a more moderate course in the GDR and who was accused by his Kremlin adversaries of wanting to give up the GDR and allow German unification so as to reduce tensions with the West.[10] Ulbricht in turn ousted his own adversaries at home and backed away from the New Course.

In August 1953, the Kremlin leaders invited Ulbricht to Moscow to show their firm support for him and the GDR and announced they would stop taking reparations, cancel GDR debt to the Soviet Union, and give the GDR more aid in terms of food, consumer goods, and economic credit. They upgraded relations with the GDR by exchanging ambassadors and turning over more sovereignty to Ulbricht. Thus, Ulbricht saw that the weakness of his regime, reflected in its near collapse in the face of the popular uprising, had led to greater Soviet support. He would learn from this experience and in the future use the threat of collapse in urging Moscow to give increasing amounts of economic, political, and military aid.[11] Two years later, in September 1955, at another summit meeting in Moscow (just a week after the Soviet leaders had hosted Adenauer in Moscow for the establishment of diplomatic relations), the Soviets gave the GDR permission to create a defensive National People's Army and to join the Warsaw Pact military alliance the following year. The Soviets also announced "full sovereignty" for the GDR by allowing the East Germans to defend their own borders and to oversee the civilian transit routes between West Germany and West Berlin, although the Soviets would retain control over supervising Western military access between West Germany and West Berlin.

Military Developments

By the mid–late 1950s, it was clear that Germany's place in the Cold War was central on at least two distinct levels: the strategic, military level; and what could be called the ideological–reputational level. Located at the front line of the two military alliances, each Germany and its allies sought to do whatever was necessary to defend itself from an enemy attack. The West felt at a disadvantage due to the superiority of Soviet conventional forces in Europe and the geographic distance of the US from the European continent, leading some to question the US commitment to extended deterrence. Accordingly, with Dwight D. Eisenhower's presidency, starting in 1953 the US adopted a "New Look" policy that placed more emphasis on nuclear weapons in deterring a Soviet attack and involved the stationing of tactical nuclear weapons with US forces in West Germany and elsewhere to bolster a NATO "forward defense" that would stop a Soviet attack.

Rapid Soviet technological advancements in 1957 made this even more urgent. In August 1957, the Soviets successfully tested their first intercontinental ballistic missile (ICBM). Two months later, they launched the first-ever satellite into outer space and followed this up in November with another one. This demonstrated that the Soviets now had the capacity to send nuclear weapons great distances on missiles, and that the security of the US homeland from Soviet nuclear weapons was no longer guaranteed. Thus, in December 1957, NATO decided to augment Western military forces in Europe with stockpiles of nuclear weapons (which were also cheaper than conventional forces), although who would be in control of the weapons – the US or the allies – when the time came to mate them to the warheads, was unclear. In March 1958, the Bundestag voted to agree to the Bundeswehr receiving nuclear warheads as well. Fearful of the growing threat from Soviet nuclear weapons and wanting equality in US nuclear sharing rather than being "singularized" as untrustworthy Germans, Adenauer and Defense Minister Franz Josef Strauss spoke publicly in 1957 and 1958 of the possibility of the FRG having access to the control of US tactical nuclear weapons on its territory, rather than settling for their total US control.[12] All of this made the East Germans and Soviets quite nervous.

The Berlin Crisis

Equally or even more important than the military aspect of the place of Germany in the Cold War was the ideological–reputational aspect. Located at the front line of the Cold War, each Germany stood as the representative of its side in the Cold War: communism and a planned economy in the East and democracy and capitalism in the West. These battle lines between the two ways of life were very important to the superpowers and each wanted to ensure the victory of its system in Germany over the other. The divided city of Berlin was ground zero of this competition, and the West was winning.

The geography of Berlin is central to understanding why it was so important in the Cold War. At the end of World War II, the Four Powers had decided to each maintain an occupation sector in the capital of the former Nazi Reich. Divided Berlin was located far to the east in what remained of postwar Germany, 110 miles inside of the Soviet occupation zone, which became the GDR. With West Berlin deep inside of the GDR, the Western Powers benefited from the chance to create an outpost of their democratic, capitalist system in West Berlin and of course to use West Berlin as a key espionage base against the Soviet bloc. But, since the details of Western access from West Germany across 110 miles to West Berlin were left unspecified by the Four Powers, Western access to West Berlin was vulnerable to Soviet and/or East German pressure. Stalin had blockaded land access for the Western Powers to West Berlin for a year, from 1948–49, in a failed effort to get the West to stop plans for the creation of a West German state. The Western airlift saved the day for the West Berliners, but the West always feared another blockade.

Accordingly, in the 1950s, Eisenhower believed strongly "that we have at stake 2.2 million free Germans who trust us and upon whom we may not turn our back."[13] The West also sought to make West Berlin into a magnet to lure East Germans westward and a showcase of all the advantages of life in the West. Tax breaks and exemption from the draft helped to keep stores well stocked and city life humming. The bright life, freedoms, and goods in West Berlin[14] and West Germany attracted 10,000–30,000 East Germans to move to the West each month.[15]

The militarization of the inner-German border in the summer of 1952, followed by a 1957 East German passport law requiring East Germans to have a visa in order to leave the country for travel abroad and designating West Germany and West Berlin as foreign territory, reduced but did not stop the exodus of refugees. By 1958 over 90 percent of people leaving the GDR did so through West Berlin by simply walking across the border or taking a subway, bus, tram, or car. In addition, over 50,000 East Germans commuted daily for work in West Berlin, where they were paid higher salaries, had more freedom than workers in the GDR, and could make daily comparisons of life in the two halves of the city, comparisons which, as the Soviet ambassador to the GDR noted, "did not always turn out in favor of [East] Berlin."[16]

Throughout the 1950s, Ulbricht urged the Soviets to turn over control of the access routes to him so that he could "exercise sovereign control over East German territory" and stop East German citizens from fleeing to the West. Due to the fact that the West did not control the access routes it relied on to reach West Berlin, Khrushchev called West Berlin "the Achilles' heel," the "sore blister," and "the testicles" of the West, a place to put pressure on the West to accede to his wishes.[17]

In November 1958, Khrushchev dramatically stepped up this pressure by launching the Berlin Crisis with an ultimatum to the US, Great Britain, and France.[18] He demanded that a peace treaty with a united Germany or the two Germanys finally be signed and that West Berlin be turned into a demilitarized "free city" with the withdrawal of the 12,000 Western troops stationed there. If the Western Powers did not comply with his two demands within six months, Khrushchev asserted that he would sign a separate peace treaty with the GDR and turn over control of the access routes to Ulbricht. The West would then have to negotiate with Ulbricht about the use of the access routes. Given that the Western Powers (and the FRG) did not recognize the GDR regime, due to its lack of free elections, this was essentially an effort by Khrushchev to force the West to recognize East Germany. While the US, UK, and France were not inclined to recognize the GDR or to withdraw their troops from West Berlin, there were differences among them, and with Adenauer, on how flexible or inflexible to be in responding to Khrushchev's threats, as the Soviet leader knew there would be.

The Berlin Crisis witnessed great tensions in Berlin and beyond, exacerbated by Khrushchev's regular threats about the small number of Soviet nuclear weapons it would take to wipe out the FRG, the UK, France, or the olive groves of Italy.[19] Multiple factors led Khrushchev to launch the Berlin Crisis. He was fond of dramatic moves that could solve several problems at once.[20] Khrushchev was eager to shore up East Germany as a key communist ally and frustrated that the West had not recognized the GDR. He was concerned about NATO's deployment of nuclear weapons in the FRG and the chance that West German leaders could get control of them.[21] Khrushchev worried about the weakness of the GDR as evidenced by the flow of refugees westwards. He raged over the Western use of West Berlin for espionage and "subversion" against the Soviet bloc and as a "show window" of capitalism and democracy. The brash Soviet leader was also hoping to translate Soviet military-technological progress on nuclear weapons and ballistic missiles into political gains for himself and his country on the world stage.

With so many factors in mind, Khrushchev's attention wandered at times during the crisis, which lasted more than three years. Ulbricht's attention, on the other hand, increasingly narrowed to closing the border in Berlin to stop the outflow of refugees. This resulted in tensions between Khrushchev and Ulbricht during the crisis, and these were mirrored by tensions among the American, British, French, and West German leaders over how to respond to Khrushchev's threats. Both German leaders were afraid that their Great Power allies might give in too much to the other side and thus, throughout the crisis, they acted to hinder any new East–West agreement on Germany or Berlin.

Khrushchev's ultimatum led to a scurry of deliberations among the Western Powers about how to respond. President Eisenhower and British Prime Minister Harold Macmillan were more willing to engage in talks with the Soviets than French President Charles de Gaulle and Adenauer were. Eisenhower complained vociferously to his advisors about being caught between Macmillan's weak-kneed desire to do anything possible to avoid war and Adenauer's rigid insistence that any negotiations involving the GDR would be the start of a "slippery slope" leading to the recognition of this illegitimate regime. The Berlin Crisis seriously exacerbated tensions between the US leaders, Presidents Eisenhower and Kennedy, and Chancellor Adenauer. Neither side fully trusted the other. Adenauer feared that any compromises on dealing with the GDR over West Berlin or anything else would help his opposition at home, the SPD, which was critical of Adenauer's close ties with the Western Allies at the price of, as the SPD saw it, better relations with the East and progress toward unification. Adenauer and the US feared that if he lost power, the SPD might indeed take West Germany down a path toward neutrality and closer ties with the communists. Eisenhower and Kennedy nonetheless felt that Adenauer was too insecure and too rigid and that his uncompromising position seriously constrained US options in the Berlin Crisis, essentially giving Adenauer veto power over Allied policy.[22]

Ultimately the West did agree to meet with the Soviets in talks on Germany and Berlin within the six months' deadline. There were Four Power talks over the next two years, but without any agreement on a peace treaty or a new status for West Berlin, with each side playing for time.

Meanwhile, the Western Powers met to formulate contingency plans, codenamed LIVE OAK, in case Khrushchev or Ulbricht shut down the access routes or tried to take over West Berlin. These top-secret plans desperately tried to find some satisfactory way to deal with the fact that, with 12,000 troops in West Berlin and over 200,000 Soviet troops surrounding them in the GDR, short of a nuclear option, it was going to be hard to defend West Berlin.[23]

Ulbricht's Pressure on Khrushchev to Close the Border

As the crisis went on without resolution and Khrushchev delayed carrying out his threats, Ulbricht's patience with his ally's delaying tactics and with his own lack of control over all of Berlin and the access routes between West Berlin and West Germany wore thin. In the final year of the crisis leading up to the Berlin Wall, Ulbricht grew more aggressive and unilateral in steps aimed to stop free movement in and out of West Berlin. With the crisis attracting world headlines, more East Germans fled to the West. In 1959, 120,230 people fled to West Berlin, and in 1960, 182, 278 fled, a 66 percent increase.[24] Young people, skilled labor, and the intelligentsia were leaving in droves, seeking a better, freer life. Top East German officials emphasized that "[t]he open border with West Berlin facilitates the crossing."[25]

In the fall and winter of 1960–61, Khrushchev told Ulbricht not to make any changes at the border in Berlin[26] while he waited first for the results of the American elections and then gave President Kennedy time to acclimatize to office and schedule a summit meeting. Yet, on multiple occasions between October 1960 and May 1961, Soviet diplomats in East Berlin sent worried reports to Moscow that Ulbricht was not waiting and was indeed behaving unilaterally on the border in Berlin. In October 1960, the Soviet second secretary at the embassy in East Berlin, A. Kazennov, reported to Moscow: "[O]ur friends are studying the possibility of taking measures directed toward forbidding and making it more difficult for GDR citizens to work in West Berlin and also toward stopping the exodus of the population of the GDR through West Berlin. One of such measures by our friends could be the cessation of free movement through the sectoral border …"[27] In January 1961, Ulbricht established a top-level East German working group to formulate options for stopping "Republikflucht," flight from the Republic.[28]

In the spring, Kennedy agreed to meet with Khrushchev in Vienna in early June. Khrushchev emphasized to Ulbricht that before this Vienna summit, the GDR leader was not to change anything at the border in Berlin. However, on May 19, Ambassador Pervukhin urgently notified Soviet Foreign Minister Gromyko that the East Germans wanted to "… close the 'door to the West' and reduce the exodus of the population from the Republic … [O]ur German friends sometimes exercise impatience and a somewhat unilateral approach to this problem, not always studying the interests of the entire socialist camp or the international situation at the given moment. Evidence of this, for example, is their effort to stop free movement between the GDR and West Berlin as soon as possible by any means …"[29]

Ulbricht did not believe that the US would give in to Soviet pressure on Berlin, and no doubt wanted to ensure that he could stop the refugee exodus regardless of the outcome of the Vienna summit. As was often the case with a small ally and a superpower in the Cold War, the interests of the small ally were more intense and more narrowly focused than the interests of the superpower. Khrushchev was eager for the US to see him and the Soviet Union as on a par with the US. Thus, he kept waiting to meet with the new American president. Ulbricht just wanted to stop the refugee exodus.

Superpower Stalemate on Berlin

Khrushchev and Kennedy met at Vienna from June 2 to 4. Their interactions and statements on Germany and Berlin both then and in the surrounding period are indicative of the essential role that the two Germanys and the two parts of Berlin played in the Cold War. At the Vienna summit, Khrushchev continued to insist that the West must leave West Berlin and that a German peace treaty must be signed. Kennedy declared that any Soviet or East German move to interfere with Western access to West Berlin (including turning over control of the access routes to the GDR), the Western troops in West Berlin, or life in West Berlin (the so-called "three essentials") would be seen as a cause for war. Kennedy made clear that the US was definitely not leaving West Berlin: "If the US were driven out of West Berlin by unilateral action, and if we were deprived of our contractual rights by East Germany, then no one would believe the US now or in the future. US commitments would be regarded as a mere scrap of paper."[30] Eisenhower's ambassador in West Germany, David Bruce, had argued similarly: "The abandonment by [the] US of [the] Berliners would destroy confidence in our engagements everywhere."[31] The US's reputation as an ally was on the line. Before the Lyndon B. Johnson administration would apply the domino theory to Southeast Asia a few years later, both Kennedy and Eisenhower believed that West Berlin was essentially a "super-domino": giving it up could cause many other dominoes to fall, starting with West Germany and going on to other countries.[32]

While Kennedy emphasized these "three essentials," he was quiet on the rights of East Berliners and on free movement across the sectoral border between East and West Berlin. This stance has led Frederick Kempe to argue that Kennedy essentially gave Khrushchev a green light to close off the East Germans' route to West Berlin, since this would not interfere with Kennedy's three essentials.[33] Wanting to help his increasingly desperate East Germany ally to stabilize the situation by stopping the flow of refugees, yet also wanting to avoid a war with the West, Khrushchev no doubt paid close attention to what Kennedy did and did not say. The summit ended in a tense stand-off, with Khrushchev renewing his Berlin ultimatum and Kennedy standing firm on not leaving West Berlin.[34]

Just as Kennedy felt the US's reputation as an ally was on the line in defending West Berlin, Khrushchev felt his reputation as an ally and the leader of the socialist bloc was on the line in shoring up the GDR. On multiple occasions during the crisis, Khrushchev and other Soviet leaders told Ulbricht, "your needs are our needs."[35] For many people from the West, East Berlin and East Germany were the only examples of communism they had the chance to see, and

Khrushchev wanted them to thrive and not be overshadowed by the economic prosperity and political freedom of West Berlin. As Khrushchev's closest colleague, Anastas Mikoian, told the East German leaders in June 1961 after the Vienna summit: "The GDR, Germany, is the country in which it must be decided that Marxism-Leninism is correct, that communism is also the higher, better, social order for industrial states. ... You cannot do this alone. ... We cannot and must not lose out to West Germany. If socialism does not win in the GDR, if communism does not prove itself as superior and vital here, then we have not won. The issue is this fundamental to us."[36]

As the Berlin Crisis reached its peak in the summer of 1961, 17,791 East Germans fled in May, and 19,198 fled in June. This *Torschlusspanik* (fear of the door closing) caused over 1,000 East Germans to leave each day in July and early August.[37] Ulbricht told the Soviet ambassador to make it clear to Khrushchev that "if the present situation of open borders remains, collapse is inevitable."[38]

The Berlin Wall

In order to save his key ally in the face of this population drain, Khrushchev finally agreed in mid-July to close the border around West Berlin. East German and Soviet officials then worked in great secrecy on preparations for Operation "Rose"[39] to seal off the escape route for any more East Germans.[40] In the middle of the night on the weekend of August 12–13, East German troops used barbed wire to close off the border around West Berlin. East Berliners and East Germans awoke on Sunday, August 13 to find that they could no longer freely travel to West Berlin. Overnight, families, friends, schoolmates, and work colleagues were cut off from each other. Buses, subways, and trams stopped going to the West and streets and waterways that led to the West were closed off.

The Western Powers made no move to stop the border closure, issuing only written protests. Privately, many of them were relieved that the East German refugee crisis had not led to war in the heart of Europe. They were also relieved that the Soviets and East Germans did not block Western access to West Berlin. Indeed, President Kennedy told his aides that although it was "not a very nice solution ... a wall is a hell of a lot better than a war."[41] Once the communists saw that the West was not interfering with sealing the border, the East Germans replaced the barbed wire with a concrete wall. In the months and twenty-eight years ahead, the East German regime would make the Berlin Wall more impenetrable, turning it into a "death strip" manned by armed guards with a shoot-to-kill order and comprised of a forward and rear wall with anti-tank barriers, trip wires, guard towers, guard dogs, sand zones to show any footprints, and bright lights deployed between the two walls.[42]

The Berlin Wall would come to symbolize the Cold War stalemate between East and West. The outcome of the Berlin Crisis demonstrated that the superpowers recognized each other's spheres of influence in Germany and Berlin and preferred sticking with the status quo rather than risking war to meddle in the other side's sphere of influence. Kennedy did not interfere with the crackdown on the East Germans' freedom of movement; and Khrushchev did not interfere with Western access to West Berlin or life in West Berlin. This mutual recognition of the US and Soviet spheres of influence was a fundamental reality of the Cold War, and it did not always make the German people happy.

Two months after the Berlin border was closed, Ulbricht tried to usurp Soviet control over access by the Western Powers to East Berlin. He allowed East German border guards at the crossing point for the Western Powers between West and East Berlin, Checkpoint Charlie, to demand to see the identification papers of the US Deputy Chief of Mission in Berlin, Allan Lightner, in order to enter East Berlin on October 22. Lightner refused and was escorted through by US military vehicles. He called for reinforcements to make clear the US right to enter East Berlin as one of the Four Powers. US Military Commander General Clay then brought up four tanks to emphasize the point. In response, the Soviets brought four tanks to the other side of the checkpoint. By the height of the Checkpoint Charlie Crisis on October 27, the Americans and Soviets each had ten tanks facing off against each other, the only time in the entire Cold War that US and Soviet tanks confronted each other directly. Secret US–Soviet talks resolved the crisis, with first the Soviets and then the Americans slowly backing up their tanks and then removing them on October 28. Khrushchev decided thereafter not to turn over control of the access routes to Ulbricht.

Lessons from the Berlin Crisis

Khrushchev learned that he did not want to entrust the power to risk war over the access routes to his aggressive East German ally. He also learned that when faced with a fait accompli at the border in Berlin, the West did not stop him. This would embolden him to try again the following year by deploying missiles in Cuba. Khrushchev made two major miscalculations the second time: he thought he could have the missiles operational before the US discovered them; and he thought the US would allow him to keep the missiles in Cuba. As he found out during the Cuban Missile Crisis, he was wrong on both counts.

Scholars who have studied the Cuban Missile Crisis based on US sources have tended to believe that Khrushchev deployed the missiles in Cuba primarily to gain leverage against the US on Berlin and force the West out of West Berlin. Kennedy's frequently expressed belief to this effect during the crisis, as evidenced in documents and tapes, has deflected scholars from the far more important Soviet sources on Khrushchev's motivations.[43] The Soviet sources make it clear that the Kremlin leader sought to protect Cuba from the very real threat of a US attack and also sought to "give the US a dose of its own medicine" and balance out the nuclear stand-off by having missiles off the coast of Florida, just as the Soviets faced NATO missiles across their border with Turkey.[44]

There were also repercussions from the Berlin Crisis in the Western bloc. Already before the Berlin border was closed, the crisis had strained US–FRG relations, but when the US barely responded to the Wall, it pushed US and West German leaders even farther apart and led to closer West German–French ties with the signing of the Élysée Friendship Treaty in 1963.[45] De Gaulle's decisions to develop France's own nuclear arsenal and to take France out of NATO's integrated military command also stemmed from his lesson from the Berlin Crisis that the US clearly placed its own interests above those of its Western Allies. West Berlin Mayor Willy Brandt, of the SPD, was so appalled by the fact that the Western Allies, as he put it, had allowed "Ulbricht to take a swipe at the Western superpower" by building the Berlin Wall that he "lost certain illusions" about relying on the US to help achieve German unification and resolved to seek a change of course in FRG policy toward the East.[46] He was able to do just this when he became foreign minister from 1966–69, and then chancellor from 1969–74.

Ostpolitik

As far as Brandt was concerned, Adenauer's uncompromising policy toward the GDR and the West German policy of relying on the Western Allies to support the FRG's national interests had both reached dead ends with the building of the Berlin Wall. A new approach was needed.

Brandt's new approach had a very straightforward name: *Ostpolitik*, policy toward the East. Adenauer's focus had been *Westpolitik*, and it had succeeded in making the FRG a democracy, a capitalist state, and enmeshed in Western institutions safe from Soviet aggression. His eastern policy was framed around isolating the GDR by relying on the Hallstein Doctrine of non-recognition.[47] But this policy had not achieved any progress regarding unification or helping his fellow countrymen in the GDR, now imprisoned behind the Berlin Wall.

Brandt and his closest colleague, Egon Bahr, realized that if they wanted to try to expand ties across the Wall and attempt "change through rapprochement" in the GDR, they would first need to improve relations with the East Germans' big brother, the Soviets, especially after the Soviets emphasized their power in Eastern Europe with their invasion of Czechoslovakia in 1968 to crush the Prague Spring reforms. Brandt's overtures to Moscow threatened the West Germans' superpower patron, the US. The new US administration of Richard Nixon and national security advisor Henry Kissinger was concerned that closer West German–Soviet ties would come at the expense of West Germany's postwar focus on integration with the West. As Kissinger later wrote, he and Nixon "were determined to spare no effort to mute the latent incompatibility between Germany's national aims and its Atlantic and European ties."[48] Fearful of an independent West German bridge to the Soviets, Nixon and Kissinger "sought to preempt Germany by conducting an active détente policy on [their] own. In this sense, *Ostpolitik* ... contributed to a race to Moscow,"[49] as Kissinger has described in his memoirs.

Once again, developments in Germany were deeply interconnected with the broader Cold War. The West German–Soviet Treaty of Non-Aggression in August 1970 and the West German–East German Basic Treaty finally establishing relations between the two states in December 1972 became part of a broader détente as the two superpowers signed their own political and military agreements in Moscow in May 1972. An important part of these détente agreements was the September 1971 Quadripartite Agreement on Berlin, which at long last codified Western access rights to West Berlin and included a renunciation of force clause regarding Berlin. Brandt received the Nobel Peace Prize in 1971 for his *Ostpolitik*.

When Ulbricht tried to insist on taking the lead instead of the Soviets in the response to Brandt's *Ostpolitik*, including in the Quadripartite talks on Berlin, his heretofore deputy, Erich Honecker, plotted against him with the Soviets and succeeded in ousting Ulbricht in May 1971. Honecker promised to be more compliant with Soviet wishes and not compete with them for the lead in talks with West Germany.[50]

The Basic Treaty and détente led to a vast expansion of East–West German ties, which were in turn enmeshed in expanded ties between Eastern and Western Europe with the signing of the Helsinki Final Act of the Conference on Security and Cooperation in Europe in 1975. The East German government attempted to limit the effect on its citizens of burgeoning relations with West Germany, for fear of "contagion" from the West German system of democracy and capitalism. Yet, as the 1970s progressed, and into the 1980s, more and more East Germans were exposed to the West indirectly via television, radio, the phone, mail, visitors, and, if they were lucky (or so old that the GDR did not care if they returned), directly with trips to the FRG. The FRG gave increasing amounts of economic aid and credits to the GDR in return for a loosening of restrictions on movement back and forth between the two countries. The East and West German leaders developed greater and greater stakes in the relationship.

The 1980s

Thus, for both Germanys there was much to lose in the early 1980s, when the "second Cold War" flared up in US–Soviet relations in the wake of the Soviet invasion of Afghanistan in 1979 and Ronald Reagan's assumption of the presidency in 1981. The downward turn in East–West relations was highlighted in 1983, when US–Soviet nuclear arms talks collapsed and

NATO went ahead with new nuclear missile deployments in Western Europe, including West Germany, where Pershing II and cruise missiles were deployed. The Soviets responded by deploying more modern nuclear missiles in the GDR. Honecker and West German Chancellor Helmut Kohl (CDU) tried to "limit the damage" and work together in a "coalition of reason" to protect inter-German relations from the new Cold War "in the shadow of the missiles."[51] They planned to meet at a summit in West Germany's capital, Bonn, in September 1984, but the Soviet leaders forced Honecker to cancel this visit. This impulse of the German leaders to protect their relations from broader Cold War tensions had been visible already in December 1981, when West German Chancellor Helmut Schmidt (SPD) was visiting Erich Honecker for talks outside of East Berlin as the Poles declared martial law just across the border. Schmidt stayed and finished the talks instead of storming out in protest over the events in neighboring Poland. The US had not appreciated this, nor was it happy with growing West German imports of gas from the Soviet Union and export of pipes and technology to the Soviet Union in the 1970s and 1980s.[52]

Only with the advent of Mikhail Gorbachev to power in the Kremlin in 1985 and his *perestroika* and *glasnost* reforms, coupled with a policy of non-interference in East European affairs, was Honecker able to make his long-awaited visit to Bonn in 1987. No one could have imagined then, when it seemed that both German states were firmly entrenched, that in two years' time the Wall would fall, and with it the East German communist regime. Gorbachev's reforms and Honecker's resistance to them (combined with the Polish example of throwing off communist rule in the summer of 1989) increasingly led in the fall of 1989 to East Germans expressing their frustration with the SED by either fleeing to West German embassies in allied communist countries or taking to the streets in the GDR to demand change, including the right to travel.

On the evening of November 9, 1989, SED Politburo member and spokesman Günter Schabowski addressed a press conference about planned changes in the East German travel laws. He had not taken the time to carefully read over the new travel regulations and astonishingly and mistakenly announced that the borders of East Germany, including with West Berlin, were open immediately. Thousands of East Germans then massed at the crossing points in the Berlin Wall demanding to be let through to visit West Berlin. Border guards, who could not get clear directives from their superiors about how to handle this unforeseen situation, finally gave up and let the people through the checkpoints into West Berlin.[53] The East German regime never recovered from this.

German Unification

In the first and last free elections in the GDR, in March 1990, the people voted for rapid unification with the FRG, as promised by the CDU candidate Lothar de Maizière. Quick thinking and careful policy making by Chancellor Helmut Kohl, backed by President George H.W. Bush, in the winter, spring and summer of 1990 persuaded the initially worried (due to German behavior when it was last united under the Nazis) British, French, and Soviets to support the absorption of the GDR by the FRG and the membership of united Germany in NATO.[54] On August 31, 1990, the two German leaders signed a treaty on unification, and on September 12, the Four Powers relinquished their rights in East and West Germany in the 2 + 4 treaty with the two Germanys (which also served as a World War II peace treaty). On October 3, less than a year after the unexpected opening of the Berlin Wall, Germany united.

The Berlin Wall had bought the SED regime twenty-eight more years in power but, in the end, the desires of the East German people for the freedom and opportunities offered in the West were stronger than the capacity of the East German regime to suppress them. The economic strength of West Germany, so visible after the "economic miracle" of the 1950s, also helped to attract East Germans eager for the quantity and quality of consumer goods and foodstuffs available in the West. As Ulbricht told Khrushchev after sealing the border in Berlin, "The experiences of the last years have proven that it is not possible that a socialist country such as the GDR can carry out a peaceful competition with an imperialist country such as West Germany with open borders. Such opportunities will first appear when the socialist world system has surpassed the capitalist countries in per-capita production."[55] This never happened, as the mobs of East Germans in supermarkets and stores in West Berlin after the opening of the Wall in November 1989 made very clear. West German economic power was also used via trade deals, loans, and credits, to help persuade Gorbachev to give up the GDR.[56]

It was not just the stronger West German economy that won the Cold War battle in Germany; it was also the democratic system more generally. People in East Germany and throughout Eastern Europe and the Soviet Union were tired of the oppressive regime of the Communist Party backed by the secret police and voted with their feet or at the ballot boxes for change. For forty years, the leaders of East and West Germany had sought greater power and legitimacy than they had in 1949. Both German states ended up gaining autonomy from their occupiers, but the East German regime found that it did not have the legitimacy among its people to survive in the end without explicit Soviet backing. The result was the absorption of the GDR into the FRG, with unification on October 3, 1990.

Conclusion

To this day, there is much debate within Germany over the role played by the FRG in the downfall of the GDR. This debate is not just of interest to historians; South Koreans have studied the development of the two Germanys very closely to see if there are any relevant lessons for their own relations with North Korea.[57] The debate in Germany is highly politicized. Social Democrats argue that Brandt's *Ostpolitik* based on "change through rapprochement" played the crucial role in bringing the two Germanys closer together by enmeshing the SED leadership in a series of links that involved West German financing in exchange for more movement across the border. This in turn exposed more East Germans to life in the FRG and showed the East Germans that the kind of life they wanted was possible under the West German system and not the East German system.[58]

Christian Democrats, on the other hand, argue that when they were in power in the 1980s, the SPD became too accommodationist with the GDR, bordering on appeasement, and was not in favor of rapid and certain unification in 1990 by means of the East German state's becoming part of the FRG. The CDU focuses on the strong start of West Germany under Adenauer and how the open political and economic system he established, combined with the essential partnership (including military) with the Western Allies, served as a magnet for East Germans. Although the CDU emphasizes West Germany's *Westpolitik*, as started by Adenauer and continued through Kohl, as opposed to *Ostpolitik*, even under Kohl, the FRG continued intensive contacts with the GDR leaders, climaxing with Honecker's trip to Bonn in 1987, and expanded on the economic ties and major credits to the GDR that were begun earlier. The reality is that for an East German populace who wanted freedom and prosperity, both West Germany's rootedness in the Western alliance (which could protect it from a possibly resurgent Moscow if Gorbachev were ousted) and its policy of reaching out to the East were attractive.

The two German states had been created as a result of the Cold War and merged into one again with the end of the Cold War. For most of the forty years of division, each superpower saw its German ally as a "super-domino" to be preserved and protected at all costs. The German people grew accustomed to the division and tried to live with it as best as possible. In the wake of the Wall, Brandt reached across the divide to at least create more contacts even if unification seemed far off. In the process, he and his successors created deeper ties with Moscow that in the end helped Soviet leader Gorbachev to trust the FRG enough (as well as relying on it for economic aid) that he agreed to give up the GDR and let it merge with West Germany. The fall of the Wall, the collapse of the GDR regime, and the unification of Germany in 1989–90 reflected and encouraged the broader winding down of the East–West Cold War conflict that had been centered in Germany. These world-changing events were also indicative of widespread recognition of the greater legitimacy of the Western system as compared with the communist system.

Notes

1 Tony Smith, "New Bottles for New Wine: A Pericentric Framework for the Study of the Cold War," *Diplomatic History* 24, no. 4 (Fall 2000), 567–91.
2 The text of the Occupation Statute of April 8, 1949 is accessible at http://images.library.wisc.edu/History/EFacs/GerRecon/omg1949n161/reference/history.omg1949n161.i0021.pdf
3 Thomas Alan Schwartz, *America's Germany: John J. McCloy and the Federal Republic of Germany* (Cambridge, Mass.: Harvard University Press, 1991), 148–50.
4 The first Secretary General of NATO, Lord Ismay, is said to have said something to the effect that NATO's mission was "to keep the Russians out, the Americans in and the Germans down."
5 John Farquharson, "The 'Essential Division': Britain and the Partition of Germany, 1945–49," *German History*, IX (Feb. 1991), 23–45; Carolyn Eisenberg, *Drawing the Line: The American Decision to Divide Germany, 1944–1949* (Cambridge: Cambridge University Press, 1996).
6 Norman Naimark, *The Russians in Germany: A History of the Soviet Zone of Occupation, 1945–1949* (Cambridge, Mass.: Belnap Press of Harvard University Press, 1997).
7 For the debate on whether the Stalin Note was serious or not, see Ruud van Dijk, "The 1952 Stalin Note: Myth or Missed Opportunity for German Unification?" Cold War International History Project (CWIHP), Working Paper No. 14 (1996); and Peter Ruggenthaler, ed., *Stalins grosser Bluff. Die Geschichte der Stalin-Note in Dokumenten der sowjetischen Führung* (Munich: Oldenbourg, 2007).
8 Accordingly, the Soviets rejected Ulbricht's appeal in March 1953 to close the border between East and West Berlin as the border between East and West Germany had been closed in 1952. Stalin's successors called Ulbricht's proposal "politically unacceptable and grossly simplistic." So soon after Stalin's death, they did not want to risk interfering in Four Power rights in Berlin and alienating the Western Powers. That calculation would change five years later. March 18, 1953, Arkhiv Vneshnei Politiki Russkoi Federatsii (AVPRF), Fond (F.) 06, Opis (Op.) 12, Papka (Pap.) 18, Portfel' (Por.) 283. This document and many others related to this chapter are available in the Digital Archive of the Wilson Center: http://digitalarchive.wilsoncenter.org/
9 For an English translation of this document and many others connected to the June 1953 East German popular uprising, as well as analytical essays, see Christian F. Ostermann, ed., *Uprising in East Germany, 1953: The Cold War, the German Question, and the First Major Upheaval Behind the Iron Curtain* (New York: Central European University Press, 2001). The two main works in German on the uprising are volumes by Roger Engelmann and Ilko-Sascha Kowalczuk, eds., *Volkserhebung gegen den SED-Staat. Eine Bestandsaufnahme zum 17. Juni 1953. Analysen und Dokumente* (Göttingen: Vandenhoeck und Ruprecht, 2005); and Bernd Eisenfeld, Ilko-Sascha Kowalczuk, and Ehrhart Neubert, *Die verdrängte Revolution. Der Platz des 17. Juni 1953 in der deutschen Geschichte* (Bremen: Edition Temmen, 2004).
10 Mark Kramer, "The Early Post-Stalin Succession Struggle and Upheavals in East–Central Europe: Internal–External Linkages in Soviet Policy Making," parts 1–3, *Journal of Cold War Studies* I, nos. 1–3 (Winter, Spring, Fall 1999).
11 For more on the Soviet–East German relationship, see Hope M. Harrison, *Driving the Soviets up the Wall: Soviet–East German Relations, 1953–1961* (Princeton, N.J.: Princeton University Press, 2003).
12 Wolfram F. Hanrieder, *Germany, America, Europe: Forty Years of German Foreign Policy* (New Haven, Ct.: Yale University Press, 1989), 42–3; Marc Trachtenberg, *A Constructed Peace: The Making of the European Settlement, 1945–1963* (Princeton, N.J.: Princeton University Press, 1999), 193–200, 219, 231–6.

13 "Memorandum of Conference With President Eisenhower [and Congressional Leaders]," Washington, March 5, 1959, 10:30 a.m., *Foreign Relations of the United States, 1958–1960, Vol. VIII, Berlin Crisis, 1958–1959*, 432.
14 Wilfried Rott, *Die Insel. Eine Geschichte West-Berlins 1948–1990* (Munich: Beck, 2009).
15 For refugee numbers, see Helge Heidemeyer, *Flucht und Zuwanderung aus der SBZ/DDR, 1945/1949–1961: Die Flüchtungspolitik der Bundesrepublik Detuschland bis zum Bau der Berliner Mauer* (Dusseldorf: Droste Verlag, 1994); and Patrick Major, *Behind the Berlin Wall: East Germany and the Frontiers of Power* (New York: Cambridge University Press, 2010), 56–108.
16 Mikhail Pervukhin, "O nekotorykh voprosakh ekonomicheskogo i politicheskogo polozheniia v demokraticheskom Berline (politicheskoe pis'mo)," AVPRF, Referentur po GDR, Op. 4, Por. 3, Pap. 27.
17 Nikita S. Khrushchev, *Khrushchev Remembers: The Last Testament*, trans. and ed., Strobe Talbott (Boston, Mass.: Little, Brown, 1974), 501, 504; Oleg Troyanovsky, *Cherez Gody i Rasstoianiia: Istoriia Odnoi Sem'i* (Moscow: Vagrius, 1997), 212–13.
18 This author has written extensively on the Berlin Crisis in *Driving the Soviets up the Wall* and the updated German version, *Ulbrichts Mauer. Wie die SED Moskaus Widerstand gegen den Mauerbau brach* (Berlin: Proplyläen, 2011). Other major works which focus on the Berlin Crisis and rely on archival evidence available since the end of the Cold War include Gerhard Wettig, *Chruschtschows Berlin-Krise 1958 bis 1963. Drohpolitik und Mauerbau* (Munich: Oldenbourg, 2006); Michael Lemke, *Die Berlinkrise 1958 bis 1963: Interessen und Handlundsspielräume im Ost-West-Konflikt* (Berlin: Akademie Verlag, 1995); Rolf Steininger, *Die Berlin-Krise und Mauerbau 1958 bis 1963* (Munich: Olzog, 2009); Manfred Wilker, *Der Weg zur Mauer. Stationen der Teilungsgeschichte* (Berlin: Christoph Links, 2011); Jens Schöne, *Ende einer Utopie: Der Mauerbau in Berlin 1961* (Berlin: Berlin Story Verlag, 2011); Frederick Taylor, *The Berlin Wall: A World Divided, 1961–1989* (New York: Harper Collins, 2006); Frederick Kempe, *Berlin 1961: Kennedy, Khrushchev and the Most Dangerous Place on Earth* (New York: Putnam, 2011); and John P.S. Gearson and Kori Schake, eds., *The Berlin Wall Crisis: Perspectives on Cold War Alliances* (New York: Palgrave/Macmillan Cold War History Series, 2002). Documentary collections on the Berlin Crisis include four volumes from the US State Department's *Foreign Relations of the United States* series (*1958–1960, Vol. VIII, Berlin Crisis, 1958–1959; 1958–1960, Vol. IX. Berlin Crisis, 1959–1960; 1961–1963, Berlin Crisis, 1961–1962* as well as the volume on *1961–1963, Vol. VI, Kennedy–Khrushchev Exchanges*, available in hard copy from the US Government Printing Office; the first two are available online, http://uwdc.library.wisc.edu/collections/FRUS); Gerhard Wettig, ed., *Chruschtschows Westpolitik 1955 bis 1964. Gespräche, Aufzeichnungen und Stellungnahmen. Band 3: Die Kulmination der Berlin-Krise* (Munich: Oldenbourg, 2011); Matthias Uhl and Armin Wagner, eds., *Ulbricht, Chruschtschow und die Mauer: Eine Dokumentation* (Munich: Oldenbourg, 2003); and the appendices of Harrison, "Ulbricht and the Concrete 'Rose': New Archival Evidence on the Dynamics of Soviet–East German Relations and the Berlin Crisis, 1958–1961," CWIHP, Working Paper No. 5 (Washington, D.C.: May 1993). This Working Paper and the appended documents and many other related documents are available from CWIHP online at http://www.wilsoncenter.org/program/cold-war-international-history-project. In addition, the German Bundesarchiv has now made available online all of the documents from Ulbricht's office (including those related to the Berlin Crisis, but also many that are not) at http://startext.net-build.de:8080/barch/MidosaSEARCH/dy30bul/index.htm.
19 For Khrushchev's nuclear threats during the crisis, see Arnold L. Horelick and Myron Rush, *Strategic Power and Soviet Foreign Policy* (Chicago, Ill.: University of Chicago Press, 1965, 1966).
20 On Khrushchev's personality and its impact on his policies, see William Taubman, *Khrushchev: The Man and His Era* (New York: W.W. Norton & Company, 2003).
21 Marc Trachtenberg emphasizes this motivation in *A Constructed Peace*, 251–6.
22 William Burr, "Avoiding the Slippery Slope: The Eisenhower Administration and the Berlin Crisis, November 1958–January 1959," *Diplomatic History*, Vol. 18, no. 2 (Spring 1994): 177–205; and Kara Stibora Fulcher, "A Sustainable Position? The United States, the Federal Republic, and the Ossification of Allied Policy on Germany, 1958–1962," *Diplomatic History*, Vol. 26, no. 2 (Spring 2003): 283–307.
23 On LIVE OAK, see Gregory R. Pedlow, "Allied Crisis Management for Berlin: The LIVE OAK Organization, 1959–1963," in William W. Epley, ed., *International Cold War Military Records and History: Proceedings of the International Conference on Cold War Military Records and History Held in Washington, D.C., 21–26 March 1994* (Washington, D.C.: Office of the Secretary of Defense, 1996): 87–116.
24 Helge Heidemeyer, *Flucht und Zuwanderung aus der SBZ/DDR, 1945/1949–1961: Die Flüchtungspolitik der Bundesrepublik Detuschland bis zum Bau der Berliner Mauer* (Düsseldorf: Droste Verlag, 1994).

25 December 1, 1960 letter from Tzschorn to Willi Stoph, "Analyse der Abwandung vom 1.1. bis 30.9.1960," Stiftung Archive der Parteien und Massenorganisationen im Bundesarchiv (SAPMO-BArch), NY4090/448; January 4, 1961 Politburo meeting, "Stichwort-Protokoll der Beratung des Politbüros am 4. Januar 1961 über *Die gegenwärtige Lage und die Hauptaufgaben 1961*," in Politbüro "Reinschriftenprotokoll Nr. 1 vom 4.1.1961," SAPMO-BArch, DY 30/J IV 2/2/743; and January 10, 1961 Politburo meeting, "Reinschriftenprotokoll Nr. 2 vom 10.1.1961," "Anlage Nr. 1 zum Protokoll Nr. 2 vom 10.1.1961," ibid.
26 Khrushchev letter to Ulbricht, October 24, 1960, SAPMO-BArch, DY 30/3682.
27 "Zapis' besedy s sekretarem Berlinskogo okruzhkoma SEPG G. Daneliisom," October 17, 1960, from the diary of A.P. Kazennov, October 24, 1960, Rossiiskii Gosudarstvennyi Arkhiv Noveishei Istorii (RGANI), Rolik (R.) 8948, Fond (F.) 5, Op. 49, Delo (D.) 288.
28 "Schlussbemerkungen des Genossen Ulbricht," Politburo, (Fortsetzung der Sitzung vom 4. Januar)," SAPMO-BArch, DY/30 J IV 2/2/743; and "Reinschriftenprotokoll Nr. 2 vom 10.1.1961," Politburo, "Anlage Nr. 1 zum Protokoll Nr. 2 vom 10.1.1961," ibid.
29 Report from Ambassador Pervukhin to Foreign Minister Gromyko, May 19, 1961, AVPRF, F.: Referentura po GDR, op. 6, Por. 34, Pap. 46.
30 "Memorandum of Conversation, Meeting Between the President and Chairman Khrushchev in Vienna," June 4, 1961, 10:15 a.m., *FRUS, 1961–63, Vol. XIV: The Berlin Crisis, 1961–1962*, 91.
31 "Telegram from the Embassy in Germany to the Department of State," Bonn, March 2, 1959, 1 p.m., ibid., 180.
32 On West Berlin as a super-domino, see Burr, "Avoiding the Slippery Slope," 180.
33 Frederick Kempe, *Berlin 1961: Kennedy, Khrushchev and the Most Dangerous Place on Earth* (New York: Putnam & Sons, 2011), 486, 488–9.
34 "Memorandum of Conversation, Meeting Between the President and Chairman Khrushchev in Vienna," June 4, 1961, 3:15 p.m., *FRUS, 1961–63, Vol. VIX: The Berlin Crisis, 1961–1962*, 97–8; and Richard Reeves, *President Kennedy: Profile of Power* (New York: Simon & Schuster, 1993), 171.
35 See, for example, Khrushchev's speech of August 4, 1961 at the Warsaw Pact meeting in Moscow that sanctioned the closing of the border. Bernd Bonwetsch and A.M. Filitov, intro. and annot., "Iz stenogrammy soveshchaniia pervykh sekretarei TsK kommunisticheskikh i rabochikh partii stranychastnits Varshavskogo Dogovora po voprosam, sviazannym s podgotovkoi k zakliucheniiu Germanskogo mirnogo dogovora," Moskva, 4 avgusta 1961 g, Utrennee zasedanie, Vystuplenie tov N.S. Khrushcheva, in "Kak prinimalos' reschenie o vozvedeni Berlinskoi steny," *Novaia i noveishaia Istoriia* 2 (March–Apr. 1999), 72.
36 Politbüroprotokoll Nr. 24 vom 6. Juni 1961, Anlage 2: "Niederschrift über die wichtigsten Gedanken, die Genosse Mikojan in einem Gespräch in kleinstem Kreis … äusserte," SAPMO-BArch, DY 30/J IV 2/2/766.
37 Ann Tusa, *The Last Division: A History of Berlin, 1945–1989* (Reading, Mass.: Addison-Wesley Publishing Company, 1997), 252; Norman Gelb, *The Berlin Wall: Kennedy, Khrushchev, and a Showdown in the Heart of Europe* (New York: Dorset Press, 1986), 121–2; Heidemeyer, *Flucht und Zuwanderung*, 339; and Patrik Major, "Toschlusspanik und Mauerbau. 'Republikflucht' als Symptom der zweiten Berlinkrise," in Burghard Ciesla, Michael Lemke, and Thomas Lindenberger, eds., *Sterben für Berlin? Die Berliner Krisen 1948:1958* (Berlin: Metropol, 2000), 221–43. See also the Soviet analysis of the refugee exodus, Iu. Ruibakov, "O politicheskikh nastroeniiakh srednikh sloev naseleniia GDR (spravka)," June 30, 1961, sent by Pervukhin to the Central Committee, RGANI, R. 8979, F. 5, Op. 49, D. 381.
38 Julij Kwizinskij, *Vor dem Sturm. Erinnerungen eines Diplomaten* (Berlin: Siedler Verlag, 1993), 179, 175.
39 "Protokoll über die Dienstbesprechung am 11.8.1961," top secret, Zentrale Auswertungs- und Informationsgruppe (ZAIG) 4900, Bundesbeauftragte für die Unterlagen des Staatssicherheitsdienstes der ehemaligen Deutschen Demokratische Republik (BStU), 1, 3, 6.
40 "Notes on the Conversation of N.S. Khrushchev with W. Ulbricht on 1 August 1961," CWIHP e-dossier No. 23, http://www.wilsoncenter.org/publication/e-dossier-no-23-new-evidence-the-building-the-berlin-wall.
41 Kennedy quote cited in Michael Beschloss, *The Crisis Years: Kennedy and Khrushchev 1960–1963* (New York: Harper-Collins, 1991), 278.
42 Leo Schmidt, "The Architecture and Message of the 'Wall': 1961–1989," in *German Politics and Society, Special Issue: The Berlin Wall after Fifty Years, 1961–2011*, Issue 99, Vol. 29, no. 2 (Summer 2011), 57–77.

43 Ernest R. May and Philip D. Zelikow, eds., *The Kennedy Tapes: Inside the White House during the Cuban Missile Crisis* (Cambridge, Mass.: Belnap Press, 1997). Recordings are accessible at the website of the Miller Center of the University of Virginia, http://millercenter.org/scripps/archive/presidential recordings/kennedy. For misleading accounts of Khrushchev's motivation in Cuba stemming from Berlin, see Graham Allison and Philip Zelikow, *Essence of Decision: Explaining the Cuban Missile Crisis, 2nd Edition* (New York: Longman, 1999); and Aleksandr Fursenko and Timothy Naftali, *Khrushchev's Cold War: The Inside Story of an American Adversary* (New York: W.W. Norton & Company, 2006).

44 For the latest archival evidence and analysis on the Cuban Missile Crisis, including Soviet motivations, see James G. Hershberg and Christian F. Ostermann, eds., *Global Cuban Missile Crisis at 50: New Evidence from behind the Iron, Bamboo and Sugarcane Curtains, and Beyond*, CWIHP *Bulletin*, Issue 17/18 (Washington, D.C.: The Wilson Center, Fall 2012), http://www.wilsoncenter.org/publication/bulletin-no-17-18.

45 Jill Kastner, "The Berlin Crisis and the FRG, 1958–62," in John Gearson and Kori Schake, eds., *The Berlin Wall Crisis: Perspectives on Cold War Alliances* (New York: Palgrave Macmillan, 2002), 125–46.

46 Willy Brandt, *People and Politics: The Years 1960–1975*, trans. J. Maxwell Brownjohn (Boston, Mass.: Little, Brown, & Co., 1987), 20.

47 On Adenauer's campaign to keep the GDR isolated and without diplomatic relations with other countries, see William Glenn Gray, *Germany's Cold War: The Global Campaign to Isolate East Germany, 1949–1969* (Chapel Hill, N.C.: University of North Carolina Press, 2003).

48 Henry Kissinger, *White House Years* (Boston, Mass.: Little, Brown, & Co., 1979), 408–10.

49 Henry Kissinger, *Years of Upheaval* (Boston, Mass.: Little, Brown, & Co., 1982), 146.

50 Mary Elise Sarotte, *Dealing with the Devil: East Germany, Détente and Ostpolitik, 1969–1973* (Chapel Hill, N.C.: University of North Carolina Press, 2001), 109–11; and W.R. Smyser, *From Yalta to Berlin: The Cold War Struggle over Germany* (New York: St. Martin's Press, 1999), 248–55.

51 Michael J. Sodaro, *Moscow, Germany, and the West from Khrushchev to Gorbachev* (Ithaca, N.Y.: Cornell University Press, 1990), 292–316; and A. James McAdams, *Germany Divided: From the Wall to Reunification* (Princeton, N.J.: Princeton University Press, 1993), 158–74.

52 Jonathan Stern, "Gas Pipe-line Cooperation between Political Adversaries: Examples from Europe," Chatham House Paper (London: Royal Institute of International Affairs, Jan. 2005), 1–3, http://www.chathamhouse.org/sites/default/files/public/Research/Energy,%20Environment%20and%20Development/jsjan05.pdf.

53 Hans-Hermann Hertle, *Chronik des Mauerfalls. Die dramatischen Ereignisse um den 9. November 1989, 12th edition* (Berlin: Ch. Links, 2012); Hertle, "The Fall of the Wall: The Unintended Self-Dissolution of the East German Ruling Regime," in CWIHP *Bulletin*, 12/13, *The End of the Cold War* (Fall/Winter 2001), 131–64, accessible at http://www.wilsoncenter.org/publication/bulletin-no-1213-fallwinter-2001. See also the documentary film on the fall of the Wall, *When the Wall Came Tumbling Down: 50 Hours that Changed the World*, directed by Gunter Scholz and Hertle, VHS release in English, 2000.

54 Mary Elise Sarotte, *1989: The Struggle to Create Post-Cold War Europe* (Princeton, N.J.: Princeton University Press, 2009).

55 Ulbricht's letter to Khrushchev, September 15, 1961, SAPMO-BArch, DY 30/3509.

56 Sarotte, *1989*, 158–9, 178, 182, 186–93.

57 The South Korean Ministry of Unification has been closely examining the lessons from German unification. For recent thinking on the comparisons, see Harriet Torry, "Lessons from German Reunification," on the *Wall Street Journal*'s "Korea Realtime" blog, January 10, 2012, http://blogs.wsj.com/korearealtime/2012/01/10/lessons-from-german-reunification/; and Jochen-Martin Gutsch, "Germans Give pep Talks on Korean Unification," *Spiegel Online*, January 6, 2012, http://www.spiegel.de/international/world/seoul-searching-germans-give-pep-talks-on-korean-unification-a-807123.html.

58 Timothy Garton Ash is very critical of West German aid to East Germany, arguing that it actually prolonged the life of the regime rather than cutting it short; *In Europe's Name: Germany and the Divided Continent* (New York: Random House, 1993), 141–85.

6

THE SINO-SOVIET SPLIT AND ITS CONSEQUENCES

Lorenz M. Lüthi

On February 14, 1950, the Soviet Union and the People's Republic of China (PRC) signed a friendship and alliance treaty which provided New China with economic aid and instant military security. It formally went into force on April 11 and was supposed to last for thirty years. Ten years later, in early February 1960, the unnecessarily ideological and provocative speech of the Chinese observer delegate Kang Sheng to the Consultative Meeting of the Warsaw Pact Political Committee triggered an éclat, in which the Soviet leader Nikita S. Khrushchev insulted his Chinese counterpart, Mao Zedong.[1] After another nine years, in early March 1969, the two sides went to war over their un-demarcated border. Within one more decade, in February 1979, Mao's successor, Deng Xiaoping, visited the United States after the two sides had formally established diplomatic relations in the wake of the Soviet–Vietnamese alliance. And ten years later, in May 1989, the reformist Soviet leader Mikhail Gorbachev visited Beijing in search of normalization.

The Sino-Soviet split not only affected the two countries' mutual relationship during the Cold War. The sheer size of the two allies-turned-enemies insured that their actions had an impact beyond themselves. The following pages address first the course and the reasons for the falling-out and then progress to its consequences on a worldwide scale. The estrangement had of course an immediate bearing on the socialist world. However, as this chapter tries to sketch out, it probably had a larger impact on the non-socialist Third World – South Asia, in particular, and the Afro-Asian Movement, in general – before leading to the much-remembered Sino-American rapprochement. Thus, the Sino-Soviet split was an event with international repercussions hardly remembered today.

Observers and academics wrote on the Sino-Soviet split as early as it became visible to the outside world, in the early 1960s. Four distinctive explanations for the split have since emerged. Some authors have argued that national interests split the alliance apart.[2] Others perceived relative changes in military and political power within the Sino-Soviet-American power triangle as the sources for the split and the subsequent Sino-American rapprochement.[3] A third group of scholars has tried to connect the split to domestic politics.[4] And finally, several academics, including the author of this chapter, believed the source of the split lay in ideology.[5] Almost no document-based literature has emerged on the international consequences of the split, however, apart from the vast historiography on Sino-American rapprochement.[6]

The opening of archives in Russia, Eastern Europe, India and the PRC itself has provided much new evidence for the split and its consequences. Yet, documents concerning top decision-making procedures in Beijing and Moscow still are almost inaccessible. The following pages sketch the events from mid-1955 to the late 1980s as clearly as it is possible at the moment. New evidence, particularly with regard to the late 1960s and the 1970s, hopefully, will in the future confirm much of the following account.

The Course of the Sino-Soviet Split

The collapse of the Sino-Soviet alliance roughly spans the ten-year period from 1956 to 1966.[7] Nikita Khrushchev's famous secret speech in the early-morning hours of February 25, 1956 triggered the disagreements between Beijing and Moscow. While Khrushchev's attack on Stalin's personality cult, disrespect for collective leadership, and unlawful rule was rooted in the domestic need of the Communist Party of the Soviet Union (CPSU) to restore credibility at home, the bombshell nature of the speech threatened to undermine Communist Party rule in many of the socialist states. Although Khrushchev's call for de-Stalinization created, for the first time, a limited pluralistic debate within the socialist world, most Communist parties in power feared political liberalization as a threat to their own dominance. In the PRC, it was particularly the Chairman of the Chinese Communist Party (CCP), Mao Zedong, who worried that the Secret Speech raised issues of political responsibility that his fellow leaders could also use against him. Although he was able to quell a party-wide debate over the spring of 1956, the Party congress in the fall did limit some of his prerogatives.

Poland and Hungary were the only socialist states in which de-Stalinization after the Secret Speech led to major political changes. The Polish October, in which that country's Communist Party established autonomy from Soviet political interventionism, and the concurrent Hungarian uprising, which outright threatened Communist Party rule and which eventually was suppressed by a Soviet military intervention, revealed to Mao both the need for and limits of reform of the socialist system. In an attempt to prevent a political explosion like the one in Hungary, Mao allowed a strongly controlled liberalization of the political debate at home in the spring of 1957, only to reap political demands similar to those raised in that East European country six months earlier. The failed experiment convinced the Chairman not only that liberalization was dangerous but that the socialist system had not yet been firmly established in China. Given the developments abroad and at home in 1956 and 1957, Mao concluded that the Secret Speech was a grave political error that had created political confusion within the socialist world.

The Great Leap Forward, 1958–60, was in many respects a great flight away from the political problems of 1957. In its very essence, however, it was an implicit challenge to the Soviet economic development model and to Soviet leadership of the socialist world. The resulting famines in 1959–61, which cost the lives of tens of millions of Chinese citizens, revealed the utter economic illiteracy of Mao and the leaders around him. The unnecessary ideological claims that Beijing raised against Moscow during this period undermined the alliance. By late 1959, Mao had also decided that the partnership had run its course in economic and military terms; thus, he subsequently micromanaged the collapse of the alliance for his domestic needs. Thereby, the Sino-Soviet split became a function of Mao's struggle against real and mostly perceived enemies at home. However, Soviet actions exacerbated the emerging rift in 1960, when Khrushchev decided at short notice to withdraw all economic specialists. While the economic impact of this sudden withdrawal on the broken Chinese economy was minor, the decision symbolically marked the advanced breakdown of the Sino-Soviet relationship.

From early 1961 to mid-1962, the partnership between Beijing and Moscow went through a period of uncertainty. Both sides had reasons not to let the relationship deteriorate further. The collapse of the Great Leap Forward had discredited Chinese ideological claims in building socialism; the country had to focus on the economic recovery, above all. The Soviet Union itself, after a mini-détente with the United States had floundered in May 1960, concentrated on finding an understanding with the PRC. However, the warmth and the depth of the earlier years of the relationship did not return. Economic relations continued to crumble, particularly after the PRC opened its trade to the non-socialist world in order to reduce its economic dependency on the Soviet Union.

Fearing the restoration of capitalism in China, Mao turned sharply against the economic recovery policies in the summer of 1962. Using his personal charisma and accusing his fellow leaders of political empiricism and thereby of revolutionary heresy, the Chairman managed to seize supreme decision-making power that August. Subsequently, he tried to inject revolutionary élan into China's foreign policy towards the United States, the Soviet Union, and the Third World. The double crisis in the Himalayas and the Caribbean – the second Sino-Indian border war and the Cuban Missile Crisis, respectively – in the fall of 1962 was a God-sent gift for the Chairman, as it offered him the opportunity both to portray the PRC as a revolutionary power fighting bourgeois India and to accuse the Soviet Union of buckling in the face of imperialist pressure. Subsequently, Mao pushed the worsening of the Sino-Soviet alliance while painting his internal leadership rivals as ideologically less reliable than even Khrushchev.

In this context, an ideological reconciliation on the basis of mutual compromise was no longer possible. The bilateral party talks that convened in Moscow in the summer of 1963 for that purpose resembled a mutual lecturing by two deaf preachers. When Mao, in subsequent years, realized that he was unable to outmaneuver his internal leadership rivals, he decided to bypass them by appealing to the revolutionary yearnings of students. For what was to become the Cultural Revolution (1966–76), however, he needed the prior destruction of the remnants of the Sino-Soviet alliance so that he could portray the PRC as a socialist model society that had broken with both the capitalism of the past and the false socialism of the Soviet Union.

The Vietnam War should have been the test case for the unified defensive capabilities of the socialist world against U.S. imperialist aggression. But Beijing eyed Moscow's military commitment to Hanoi with ideological suspicion. The sharp debates on the correct nature of the military, economic, political, and diplomatic assistance to the North Vietnamese comrades in their hour of greatest distress symbolized the total collapse of the Sino-Soviet alliance.

The border clashes in March 1969 were the consequence, not the source of the Sino-Soviet split. Despite the lack of demarcation of the joint border, territorial disagreements did not ravage the partnership in the 1950s, during the period of close cooperation. Only by the 1960s did quarrels on the border start to flare up. The 1969 clashes on a godforsaken stretch of the Ussuri River reflected the strained relationship between the two former alliance partners. In their wake, the two sides tried – unsuccessfully – to come to an agreement on some form of cohabitation, while the PRC also attempted – with more success – to seek rapprochement with the United States.

The Sources of the Sino-Soviet Split

The sources of the split are manifold. From the very beginning, the Chinese side seemed to have perceived the partnership as a temporary venture. The military security and the economic aid which the Soviet Union provided were supposed to help restore China to it former greatness and glory after a century of imperialist humiliation. Yet, even if Beijing looked at the alliance in such instrumental terms, this does not explain why the partnership ended in such bitterness. Historically, many alliances have dissolved without their former partners engaging in hostile propaganda or even going to war with each other.

Chinese witnesses and scholars have in retrospect stressed the unequal nature of the alliance. In their view, the Soviet comrades had treated their Chinese counterparts with arrogance and lack of respect, and thus triggered the disagreements that ultimately led to the split. Many of these claims are made with hindsight. But it is true that the partnership was lop-sided. For much of what Moscow supplied in terms of military hardware, economic aid, and other forms of assistance, Beijing had little to offer in return, apart from debt repayment-in-kind with strategic and semi-finished products. And while the Soviet Union provided military security to the new member of the socialist world system, China was far from being capable of matching this through reciprocal means.

Most importantly, the alliance had different meanings for each partner. For the PRC, it was the *defining* moment by which New China established itself as a socialist state in international relations. For the Soviet Union, the alliance was just *another* asset in its pursuit of world revolution – an asset it had obtained rather unexpectedly after suffering major setbacks in Europe. The different role which the establishment of the alliance played for each of the two partners also explains their respective behavior when the partnership broke up. As Mao's China had to redefine its own identity once fissures in the alliance occurred, it expended much time and energy to divest itself of it through public attacks on the Soviet Union. For Moscow, however, the partnership with Beijing was less central to its own self-understanding, and thus it tended to neglect maintaining it.

Yet, these inherent characteristics of the alliance cannot conclusively explain the course and the bitterness of the break-up. Marxism-Leninism – the ideology to which the two sides professed to adhere – formed the basis of the partnership and simultaneously was its greatest affliction. Victory in the Chinese civil war of 1949 had predetermined China's alliance choice. A *triumphant Guomindang* government would hardly have entered a strategic partnership with the Soviet Union, but the victorious CCP actively sought it. Yet the specific nature of the shared ideology also supplied the seeds of the split. On the one hand, Marxism-Leninism is sufficiently ambivalent about some of its core visions; the classical texts reveal little about how exactly the socialist revolution should progress towards the communist paradise. On the other hand, Marxism-Leninism makes claims in principle about the nature of politics. Thus the combination of theoretical ambivalences and claims in principle tends to lead to disagreements in principle on theory. Much of the Sino-Soviet split was a *substantive struggle* over the correct interpretation of Marxism-Leninism, and not just a rhetorical battle about theoretical minutiae.

The ideological disagreements between Beijing and Moscow occurred in three realms of theory. From 1955, Beijing disputed the validity of the Soviet economic development model that it had inherited from Moscow in previous years. Given the differences in the make-up and characteristics of the Soviet and Chinese economies, that Soviet model was an ill fit for the PRC, in any case. Yet, Mao's push for the use of a Soviet development strategy from the 1930s not only betrayed the ideological nature of his choice – he did not even consider non-Soviet models at all – but also provided the source of the ideological disagreements with the Soviet comrades who just were trying to overcome the difficult economic legacies of the Stalinist period.

The second cause for disagreements revolved around the question of how to handle U.S. imperialism. Mao had established the PRC in 1949 as a utopian, anti-imperialist country. New China was supposed to struggle against imperialism on a worldwide scale and against its remnants at home. Moreover, the Chinese revolution was to be the model for other decolonizing countries to follow. PRC foreign policy in the early decades, thus, was often one dimensional. The Soviet Union, historically, was not any less anti-imperialist, but as a superpower it operated in different waters. With an increasing set of commitments around the world, Moscow followed a multidimensional foreign policy that, as a result, bore the danger of pursuing conflicting goals. Furthermore, as a nuclear power, it found itself in a community of interest with the United States. Faced with the danger of a nuclear war that could annihilate mankind, by the late 1950s both Moscow and Washington reluctantly engaged in negotiations to prevent the possibility of such a conflict breaking out. Thus, China's one-dimensional, revolutionary, and anti-imperialist foreign policy clashed with both the Soviet Union's multidimensional commitments across the world and the necessary cooperation with the imperialist arch-enemy.

Finally, the two sides clashed over the course of world revolution in general. As the first, most advanced, and militarily most powerful socialist state, the Soviet Union naturally claimed leadership of the socialist world. Dissatisfied with Moscow's ideological revisionism in the construction of socialism and in handling imperialism, however, Beijing asserted the revolutionary purity of the PRC and its supreme leader. By the early 1960s, in Mao's eyes, New China was holding the banner of world revolution high, whereas the Soviet Union just left an ideologically bleached flag fluttering in the wind. As Mao's PRC was unable to convince the majority of the socialist world to follow its course, it decided to break off relations and instead to lead the Third World in its struggle against imperialism. Yet, even here, its revolutionary appeal was less convincing than Soviet economic aid, and thus, by the second half of the 1960s, Mao's China found itself as an isolated socialist model society charting its path through a hostile world.

Apart from these ideological disagreements, a series of other factors influenced the course of the Sino-Soviet split. As mentioned above, Mao had painted his internal rivals as Soviet revisionists since 1959. Consequently, the Sino-Soviet split increasingly assumed a central function in Chinese domestic politics. Mao's decision to move against his internal rivals in 1966, at the start of the Cultural Revolution, required the prior destruction of the last vestiges of the alliance. However, this domestic conflict did not cause but only accelerated the split.

Personality conflicts, particularly between Khrushchev and Mao, did not make managing the alliance any easier. While the Soviet leader could be volatile and impulsive, his Chinese colleague tended to be petty and vindictive. After Stalin's death, and particularly after the events in Poland and Hungary in 1956, Mao considered Khrushchev to be both immature and no equal of the late Stalin. Implicitly, as the paramount leader of the Chinese revolution, he perceived himself as the elder statesman of world revolution. But this clash of difficult personal characteristics was not sufficient to cause the split, although it clearly did not lubricate the smooth working of the alliance.

While the assumed imperialist nature of the United States played a major role in the ideological debates between the two alliance partners, the actual policies of the American superpower had little effect until the early 1960s. The wedge strategy, as implemented by presidents Harry S. Truman and Dwight D. Eisenhower, was a misguided and uninformed attempt to split an alliance that eventually faltered by the late 1950s for unrelated reasons. Yet, the U.S. offer to the Soviet Union in the summer of 1962 to negotiate a Nuclear Test Ban Treaty greatly helped to accelerate the emerging split. While it was not the main cause, the U.S. desire to hinder Beijing in its acquisition of nuclear know-how was an important impetus to Washington's pursuit of the treaty. Furthermore, the United States hoped that the almost universal endorsement of the treaty by the world's nations would help to isolate the PRC even further. In the end, Mao's hard-line stance during the Party reconciliation talks in Moscow in mid-1963 made the ideological split irrevocable and thereby drove the Soviet comrades into agreeing to the Test Ban Treaty with the American imperialists. In its wake, the PRC called for universal nuclear disarmament while accelerating its own A-bomb program. As a result, in mid-October 1964, China tested its first nuclear device.

In sum, the Sino-Soviet split was a combination of long-term and short-term factors. While the nature of the alliance and the instrumental purposes of the Chinese in entering into it did not presage a long-lasting partnership, these two traits also did not predetermine the course and the bitterness of the break-up as it unfolded in the 1960s. The Sino-Soviet split occurred as the result of genuine ideological disagreements, coupled with Mao's abuse of the faltering alliance for domestic purposes, and additional secondary factors, such as personality conflicts and outside influence.

The Sino-Soviet Split and the Socialist World

The Sino-Soviet split not only was one of the major events in the Cold War but also loomed large in the socialist world. Khrushchev's speech in early 1956 had sanctioned a certain degree of ideological pluralism within the socialist world. As each socialist state tried to deal with the economic and political legacies of Stalinism, it naturally was looking toward alternative models as they emerged within the socialist world.

Even if the Great Leap Forward turned out to be a lethal disaster in the PRC, China's apparent march toward communism initially found admirers in East Germany, Poland, Hungary, and Bulgaria.[8] The Balkan country even launched its own Great Leap Forward in October of 1958; that endeavor collapsed around the same time the Chinese version did.[9] East Germany lauded the Great Leap Forward in its propaganda from 1958 to 1960 because it was trying to increase its own rural and industrial production, with the aim of stemming an increasing refugee stream to West Germany. In mid-1960, when Sino-Soviet ideological problems were mounting, East Berlin ceased its propaganda, on Moscow's order.[10]

Albania, however, was the first country to confront the fall-out of the emerging Sino-Soviet split. Following Yugoslavia's expulsion from the socialist camp in 1948, both China and Albania had decided to lean closely towards the Soviet Union in order to escape possible charges of Titoism.[11] Yet Beijing and Tirana each reacted differently to Khrushchev's attempts to mend fences with Iosip Broz Tito in 1955 and to his censure, in early 1956, of Stalin's responsibility for the events of 1948. While Mao greeted the rapprochement and agreed with Khrushchev's assessment of Stalin's liability,[12] Albania's leader, Enver Hoxha, criticized Khrushchev for adopting revisionist positions with regard to his neighbour.[13] The failure of the Soviet-Yugoslav rapprochement in 1957 and the adoption of a "liberal" party constitution by the League of Yugoslav Communists in the spring of 1958 found Moscow, Beijing, and Tirana again on the same side of the issue.[14] In the emerging Sino-Soviet split in the summer of 1960 and with renewed Soviet-Yugoslav rapprochement two years later, Albania and the PRC found themselves opposed to Yugoslav and Soviet revisionism.[15] As a consequence of the Soviet end of economic assistance in the early 1960s, Albania received one sixth of China's foreign aid by the middle of the decade.[16] However, with Sino-Yugoslav rapprochement in 1977, following Mao's death the year before, Albania found itself abandoned.[17]

Unlike Albania, Romania never went as far as splitting from the Soviet-dominated rump-socialist camp. The Soviet attempt in the summer of 1963 to reorient the Warsaw Pact away from Europe and against the PRC appalled the Romanians. In the fall of 1963, Bucharest indicated not only to Beijing its unwillingness to support Soviet policies directed against the PRC, but also to Washington that it did not consider itself to be bound to its Warsaw Pact obligations in the event of a Soviet-American conflict.[18] For the remainder of the Cold War, Romania followed a policy of entertaining good relations with the PRC and with Israel, particularly after 1967, when the socialist camp decided to side unequivocally with the Arab states. This enabled the country's leader, Nicolae Ceaușescu, to play a minor role in the Sino-American rapprochement in 1969 and a major role in the Egyptian–Israeli rapprochement in 1977.[19]

Among all socialist countries, North Vietnam bore the brunt of the fall-out from the Sino-Soviet split. Once Hanoi had decided to find a military solution to the division of the country in 1959, it tried to mediate between Moscow and Beijing in the fall of the following year. Its attempts eventually helped to achieve a truce in the ideological debates at the meeting of the world's Communist parties in the Soviet capital late in 1960.[20] As Khrushchev decided to disengage from the conflict in Indochina by early 1963, the Vietnamese communists took sides with the Chinese comrades in the Sino-Soviet split.[21] Following Khrushchev's fall from power in mid-October 1964, his successors, Leonid Brezhnev and Aleksei Kosygin, did not reverse any of his foreign policies – except the one on Southeast Asia. The sudden Soviet willingness to support the North Vietnamese struggle against the mounting U.S. intervention was a double-edged sword. On the one hand, Hanoi welcomed additional military and economic support, but on the other, the Vietnam War thereby turned into one of the main battlefields of the Sino-Soviet conflict. In a mixture of justified security concerns and ideological hyperbole, Beijing refused cooperation with Moscow regarding military, economic, political, and diplomatic support for Hanoi.[22] In the long term, however, Soviet material aid and sensible advice in the war against the United States convinced North Vietnam to embrace closer cooperation with the Soviet Union than with the PRC. Sino-American rapprochement after 1969 further undermined the relationship between Hanoi and Beijing. Even if the PRC remained a loyal ally to the DRV until the end of American involvement in the war in 1973, North Vietnam was convinced that its northern neighbour had betrayed the anti-imperialist brotherhood.[23] Even the Soviet-Vietnamese alliance in late 1978, immediately before the Vietnamese assault on Pol Pot's Cambodia, and the resulting Sino-Vietnamese border war early the following year, echoed the Sino-Soviet split.

The Sino-Soviet Split and South Asia

As the largest non-socialist Third World state, India naturally attracted Chinese and Soviet interest. The end of the Korean War helped the PRC to break out of its isolation from the non-socialist world. In 1954, prime ministers Zhou Enlai and Jawarlahal Nehru established, with the five principles of peaceful coexistence, a working basis between socialist China and non-socialist India.[24] On Delhi's proposal, the emerging Afro-Asian Movement also invited the PRC to its first meeting in Bandung in April of 1955.[25] Similarly, Khrushchev ended Stalin's political neglect of South Asia by receiving Nehru as a guest in the summer of 1955 and visiting India the following autumn.[26]

Despite the appearance of friendship, the Sino-Indian relationship suffered early on from Indian unease about Chinese policies. While Nehru had little sympathy for the feudal and theocratic government of Tibet, he distrusted Chinese intentions for a nation that had close cultural and historical links to India.[27] Indeed, it was Chinese actions in Tibet and the non-demarcated nature of the borders that would break Sino-Indian friendship in 1959. Caught between the Chinese ally and the Indian friend, the Soviet Union decided to be neutral during the first border war, which the PRC in turn regarded as tacit support for India.[28] Beijing was willing to come to a compromise deal over the open border issues during Zhou's visit to Delhi in April of 1960, but Nehru refused any settlement.[29] After Mao had injected ideology and the emphasis on Chinese leadership of the Third World into Chinese foreign relations in the late summer of 1962, the PRC went to war with India, its rival for leadership in the decolonizing world, in October.[30] During the second border war in the Himalayas, which preceded the Cuban Missile Crisis by a few days, Moscow dithered in its support for Beijing, only to harvest later an ideological Chinese attack on the supposed Soviet weakness in the Caribbean in the face of imperialist pressure.[31] Most importantly, the Soviet Union also lost influence in India, as Delhi turned to Washington and London for military aid.[32]

The Sino-Indian conflict triggered a rapprochement between the PRC and Pakistan, at that time a Cold War ally of the United States. After the first border war with India in 1959, China had approached its southern neighbours with proposals to settle the Himalayan border by way of compromise.[33] The Second Sino-Indian border war, and the subsequent U.S. delivery of arms to Pakistan's arch-enemy in South Asia, revived the slow and tedious Sino-Pakistani border negotiations and eventually opened the path to a closer relationship. While Beijing in the first years of the relationship tried to wean Islamabad away from the partnership with Washington, in the end it was Pakistan, following the Sino-Soviet border war in 1969 and after ping-pong diplomacy in 1971, which facilitated Sino-American rapprochement and Kissinger's famous visit to the PRC, respectively.[34]

Pakistan's dance between the two Cold War enemies-turned-friends in the 1969–71 period was related to its need to prevent the breakaway of its eastern half, today's Bangladesh. The territorial division of the country, with one half situated on either side of India, and the misrule of Eastern Pakistan by Western Pakistani elites led to a civil war by 1971. While Islamabad relied on its good relationship with Washington and Beijing for political and military support, India tried to mobilize Western European capitals in support of Bangladeshi national aspirations.[35] The Sino-Soviet split and the Sino-American rapprochement also helped Delhi to forge an alliance with Moscow – and with that, to obtain political backing – before it intervened in the Pakistani civil war against the government in Islamabad, in early December.[36] Despite the call by the majority of United Nations members for a ceasefire in the Indian–Pakistani war, India continued its massive military intervention, thereby both weakening its arch-enemy and forcing the birth of Bangladesh.[37] The creation of new realities in South Asia, despite the earlier condemnation of India by the United Nations General Assembly, also led to the rapid and almost universal recognition of the newly emerged state, including by the United States and the PRC.[38] In the end, however, many of the events in South Asia were unrelated to developments in Sino-Soviet relations, but the split and its international consequences helped to line up international forces in support of Bangladeshi nationhood.

The Sino-Soviet Split and the Afro-Asian World

China's participation in the Bandung conference in 1955 primarily helped the country to increase its standing in international relations. However, membership in the Afro-Asian Movement did not lead to a greater engagement with the decolonizing world until the mid-1960s. This seeming Chinese failure was largely due to the movement's inability to keep up momentum after the mid-1950s, but due also to Beijing's increasing involvement in the ideological debates within the socialist world. In any case, the PRC had little to offer apart from being a self-appointed model; the PRC's ability to provide economic aid was limited, especially after the Great Leap Forward had turned out to be a disaster. No wonder that the PRC garnered diplomatic recognition only from roughly half of the African countries that obtained independence in the late 1950s and early 1960s.

In the second half of 1962, China's policy towards the Third World changed, as mentioned above. On the one hand, Mao's ideological call for the PRC to lead the newly decolonized states marked a shift in Chinese foreign policy which, however, did not immediately lead to any concrete policy changes. On the other hand, India gambled away its position as the natural leader of the decolonized when it turned to the United States and the United Kingdom, a former imperial power, in the wake of the second border war in late 1962. As a consequence, India gave up on the slumbering Afro-Asian Movement and decided to engage with the emerging Non-Aligned Movement.[39]

At the first Non-Aligned Conference, in Belgrade in September 1961, the Indonesian leader, Sukarno, had called for another Bandung conference of the Afro-Asian Movement, which the PRC, due to its lack of membership in the Non-Aligned Movement, welcomed.[40] In the first half of 1963, the PRC remained diplomatic by stressing its willingness to attend a second Afro-Asian conference even if it was convened in Delhi.[41] But as Sino-Soviet party talks floundered over the summer and the PRC found itself almost universally isolated in its rejection of the Nuclear Test Ban Treaty, the Chinese leadership launched a new Afro-Asian policy initiative which had distinct anti-Indian and anti-Soviet tones. This involved two trips by Zhou Enlai through several African and Asian countries around the turn of 1963–64, with the purpose of drumming up support both for a new conference and for China's positions. The diplomacy of China's Premier, however, met with only limited success.[42] And when the Soviet Union declared itself an Afro-Asian country in April 1964, the cards were stacked for a showdown.[43]

The Chinese position in the race for control of the agenda of the Afro-Asian Movement improved after the first successful Chinese nuclear test in mid-October 1964. Many Afro-Asian countries welcomed that one from their midst had broken the monopoly of nuclear weapons by "white" powers, and rejoiced over the prospects of an "Afro-Asian bomb."[44] In the wake of the test, the Afro-Asian Movement decided to convene the second Bandung conference in Algiers in 1965.[45] With a date in sight, and buttressed by its increased standing, the PRC promoted its revolutionary ideology in general, and its anti-Soviet and anti-Indian stances in particular, within the Afro-Asian Movement.[46] Even among its supporters, the PRC did not always find much sympathy; Algeria's Ben Bella, for example, was irritated by China's hard-line ideological positions.[47] And Egypt's Gamal Abdel Nasser, one of the original founders of the Afro-Asian Movement, bluntly informed the Chinese leaders that the PRC could not impose its own views, such as the exclusion of India and the Soviet Union, on the movement.[48] The second Chinese nuclear bomb test, in mid-May of 1965, which fell during a period of intense preparations for the second conference in Algiers, also did not receive as positive an echo as the first one had.[49]

That China had overplayed its hand in pressuring the Afro-Asian Movement into accepting its own ideological positions became obvious in the summer of 1965. On June 5, 1965, in Tanzania, Zhou Enlai called Africa and Asia "ripe for revolution."[50] While such a statement made sense at home within the context of the increasingly revolutionary discourse before the Cultural Revolution, it alienated many recently decolonized countries, whose post-colonial elites concluded that they were the target of Zhou's call. Over the turn of 1965–66, a great number of those sub-Saharan African countries that had recognized the PRC some years before broke off relations.[51]

Then, on June 19, Ben Bella's sudden overthrow forced the delay of the second Bandung conference until November. In talks with Zhou Enlai, who happened to be in Egypt in the subsequent week, Nasser gleefully rejoiced over the fall of a man whom he had considered to be a competitor for Pan-Arab leadership and who also happened to have been close to the PRC.[52] Nasser drove the defeat home two months later. On the day of Ben Bella's fall, the PRC had submitted a memorandum to Egypt on Chinese opposition to Soviet participation in the second Bandung conference.[53] In late August, during a visit to Moscow, Nasser invited China's arch-nemesis to the postponed conference.[54] Given Zhou Enlai's call for revolution earlier that summer, Nasser had judged the mood in the Afro-Asian Movement correctly; over the course of the fall, the majority of the members agreed with the invitation of the USSR to the postponed conference.[55]

Once Beijing heard by late September about Moscow's probable attendance at the conference, it decided first to boycott and then to sabotage the conference for which it had worked so hard.[56] On October 9, Premier Zhou predicted to a Pakistani delegation that the meeting would not occur at all, since Soviet participation would turn it into a "battlefront of Sino-Soviet Split."[57] After the attempted coup against the Indonesian President Sukarno by a small group of dissident army officers on September 30, which the army first suppressed and then used as pretext to persecute the Communist Party in Indonesia, the PRC lost another revolutionary friend. On October 15, Zhou accused U.S. imperialism and Soviet revisionism of destroying the world's revolutionary movement.[58] Five days later, he informed an Egyptian delegation that the PRC would not participate in the conference.[59] To Chinese claims of victory, the Afro-Asian countries decided in early November to cancel the conference for good.[60] With that, the movement died.

The Sino-Soviet Split and the Western World

While revolutionary fervour had ruined China's standing in the Afro-Asian world, the country's economic needs helped to improve relations with the Western world. In the wake of the sudden withdrawal of the Soviet specialists in mid-1960, the Chinese leaders rethought their foreign economic policy. Drawing a lesson from its past dependence on Moscow for trade and technology imports, Beijing decided to spread its foreign economic relations more evenly. Within five years, China's trade with the Soviet Union shrank from roughly 50 percent to a low level, accompanied by similar developments in the country's goods exchange with most of the other East European socialist countries.[61] Moreover, the PRC jettisoned ideology in its trade policy. In urgent need of food aid and technological assistance, the PRC was willing to set aside political and ideological obstacles, such as the Taiwan issue or the supposed imperialist nature of capitalist countries, and to engage in trade with Japan, Australia, Western Europe, Canada, and even the United States (i.e., U.S. grain was laundered through France).[62] By 1965, China's largest trading partner – Japan – had increased its share from zero five years earlier to roughly 10 percent, with West Germany and the United Kingdom closely following.[63]

In parallel to the initiative towards the Afro-Asian world in the second half of 1963, the PRC also engaged with France. Both states were among the few nations that did not sign the Nuclear Test Ban Treaty. As nuclear pariahs, they gravitated not only away from their respective superpower allies but also towards each other. It was France that took the first step, contacting the PRC embassy in Berne, Switzerland, via its own, less than one month after the conclusion of the treaty.[64] Beijing instantly responded by inviting former Prime Minister Edgar Faure,[65] who visited the Chinese capital in late October bringing a hand-written letter from French President Charles de Gaulle.[66] Subsequently, on his tour through the Middle East and Africa at the turn of 1963–64, Zhou Enlai conducted from afar the negotiations on Sino-French recognition between the two embassies in Berne.[67] The establishment of diplomatic relations in late January 1964 had more symbolic than real purpose; Paris grew quickly frustrated with the lack of further development in the partnership.[68] In 1965, when the Afro-Asian Movement collapsed, Japan realized that the PRC wanted to draw close only for instrumental reasons; China did not even reduce its negative propaganda on the Sato government.[69]

Sino-American rapprochement in 1969–72 was not the result of the Sino-Soviet split, although the falling-out between the two communist allies was a necessary precondition for the alignment of the two Cold War enemies in East Asia. For some time in the late 1960s, Washington had tried to find an opening with Beijing, but the opportunity occurred only after the Sino-Soviet border clashes in March 1969 and the Soviet intervention in Czechoslovakia in August the year before. The fragile rapprochement floundered quickly over American support for the coup against Prince Sihanouk in Cambodia in March 1970. Yet, given the major changes in China's foreign relations later that year, including the opening of relations with Canada, Beijing signalled to Washington its willingness to resume rapprochement in early 1971. Ping-pong diplomacy, the Pakistani backchannel, and Islamabad's logistical assistance set in motion Kissinger's famous secret visit to Beijing in July. President Richard M. Nixon's tour to China eight months later, however, was more symbolic than substantive. Only on January 1, 1979 did the two sides establish full diplomatic relations, partially pushed by the Soviet–Vietnamese alliance and Vietnam's assault on Cambodia in late 1978. Yet, the changes in China's attitude towards the outside world in 1970 and the Sino-American rapprochement in 1971 had broken the political dam that had kept the PRC out of the United Nations and had allowed the country to establish relations with a vast array of nations within a short period of time. The turn to the West thus ended China's isolation from the world, which had started when the young PRC joined the socialist camp in 1950.[70]

Conclusion

Following the Soviet–Vietnamese alliance and Vietnam's assault on Cambodia in late 1978, and after Deng Xiaoping's famous visit to President Jimmy Carter's White House and the Sino-Vietnamese border war in early 1979, Beijing informed Moscow that it would not renew the alliance of thirty years. Technically, neither side had ever decided to abrogate the pact before it was contractually obligated to do so, a year before its expiration. In reality, the alliance had lost its original meaning roughly at the half-way point of its thirty-year duration.[71] With China's notification, the alliance legally expired on April 11, 1980.[72]

Sino-Soviet quarrels, however, did not end with the formal dissolution of the once most-powerful socialist alliance. The Soviet intervention in Afghanistan, at the western edge of the PRC, in late 1979 created in China a feeling of encirclement: Soviet troops to the north, a Soviet alliance to the south, and Soviet aggression to the west. Moscow quickly understood the monumental blunder it had committed by intervening in the fractured country in the Western Himalayas.[73] In order to avoid international pressure, the aging Brezhnev offered an improvement of relations with the PRC in March 1982, reversing his own past derogatory language about the Soviet neighbour by calling China a socialist state.[74] In the summer, Deng responded that the Soviet presence around China had established "three barriers" to full normalization. Still, by October, the two sides held their first high-level talks in over a decade.[75]

In the context of ongoing trade talks, Sino-Soviet relations started to improve in the last week of 1984, less than three months before Mikhail Gorbachev's ascent to power. After decades of rhetoric denying the ideological credentials of the Soviet Union, the PRC affirmed that its northern neighbour was a "socialist state" and the Soviet leaders "were communists."[76] Ten months later, Deng offered an improvement of relations if Gorbachev removed only one of the barriers – the Vietnamese presence in Cambodia.[77] But the path to normalization, accomplished during Gorbachev's visit to Beijing in May 1989, remained long and stony.

The Sino-Soviet split will continue to fascinate historians, as it is one of the most important turning points in the Cold War. Much original research waits to be conducted once the relevant archives in Moscow and Beijing, particularly with records pertaining to decision making, become open. Apart from the Sino-American rapprochement, much of the literature on the consequences of the split is still in its infancy as well. This chapter could only sketch some of them; future historians will have to flesh out, revise, confirm, or reject much of this chapter on the basis of original research not only in Russia or China but also in the archives of those world regions affected by the falling-out between Moscow and Beijing during the Cold War.

Notes

1. "Speech of Comrade Kang Sheng on the Meeting of the Political Consultative Committee of the Members of the Warsaw Pact," [February 4, 1960], *Stiftung Archiv der Parteien und Massenorganisationen der DDR im Bundesarchiv* [Foundation Archive of Parties and Mass Organizations of the GDR in the Federal Archive, Berlin; hereafter: *SAPMO-BArch*], DY 30/3386, 87–99. Wu Xiuquan, *Huiyi yu huainian* [*Recollections and Memories*] (Beijing: Zhonggong zhongyang dangxiao, 1991), 333–335.
2. Richard Lowenthal, "National Interests and the Orthodox Faith," Clement Zablocki, ed., *Sino-Soviet Rivalry* (New York: Praeger, 1966), 27–32; Richard Lowenthal, "The Degeneration of an Ideological Dispute," Douglas Stuart *et al.*, eds., *China, the Soviet Union, and the West* (Boulder, CO: Westview, 1982), 59–71; Klaus Mehnert, *Peking and Moscow* (New York: Putnam, 1963).
3. Donald Zagoria, "A Strange Triangle," Clement Zablocki, ed., *Sino-Soviet Rivalry* (New York: Praeger, 1966), 43–52; Michel Tatu, *The Great Power Triangle* (Paris: Atlantic Institute, 1970); Robert Scalapino, "The American-Soviet-Chinese Triangle," William Kintner *et al.*, eds., *SALT* (Pittsburgh, PA: Pittsburgh, 1973), 141–166; Harry Schwartz, "The Moscow-Peking-Washington Triangle," *Annals of the American Academy of Political and Social Sciences* 414, 41–54; William Griffith, "The World and the Great-Power Triangles," Griffith, ed., *The World and the Great-Power Triangles* (Cambridge, MA: MIT, 1975), 1–33; Banning Garrett, "China Policy and the Strategic Triangle," Kenneth Oye *et al.*, eds., *Eagle Entangled* (New York: Longman, 1979), 228–263.
4. Richard Thornton, *The Bear and the Dragon* (New York: American Asian Educational Exchange, 1971); Kenneth Lieberthal, "The Background in Chinese Politics," Herbert Ellison, *The Sino-Soviet Conflict* (Seattle, WA: University of Washington, 1982), 3–28; Jürgen Domes, "Domestic Sources of PRC Policy," Douglas Stuart *et al.*, eds., *China, the Soviet Union, and the West* (Boulder, CO: Westview, 1982), 39–58; Vernon Aspaturian, "The Domestic Sources of Soviet Policy Toward China," Stuart, *China*, 59–72.
5. Donald Zagoria, *The Sino-Soviet Conflict, 1956–1961* (Princeton, NJ: Princeton University Press, 1962); Jean Baby, *La Grande Controverse Sino-Soviétique (1956–1966)* [*The Great Sino-Soviet dispute*] (Paris: Bernard Grasset, 1966); François Fejtö, *Chine–USSR: De l'alliance au conflit, 1950–1972* [*China–USSR: from alliance to conflict*] (Paris: Seuil, 1973); Franz Michael, "Common Purpose and Double Strategy," Clement Zablocki, ed., *Sino-Soviet Rivalry* (New York: Praeger, 1966), 15–16; Melvin Gurtov *et al.*, *China under Threat* (Baltimore, MD: Johns Hopkins University Press, 1980); Richard Lowenthal, *World Communism* (New York: Oxford University Press, 1964); Hans Morgenthau, *A New Foreign Policy for the United States* (New York: Praeger, 1969), 32–42; Lorenz M. Lüthi, *The Sino-Soviet Split: Cold War in the Communist World* (Princeton, NJ: Princeton University Press, 2008)
6. The most detailed and research-based is: Xia Yafeng, *Negotiating with the Enemy: U.S.–China Talks during the Cold War, 1949–1972* (Bloomington, IN: Indiana University Press, 2006).
7. This section and the following section on the causes of the split are a digest from my own book: Lorenz M. Lüthi, *The Sino-Soviet Split: Cold War in the Communist World* (Princeton, NJ: Princeton University Press, 2008).
8. Roderick MacFarquhar, *The Origins of the Cultural Revolution*, vol. 2 (New York: Columbia University Press, 1983), 262; Nikita S. Khrushchev, *Khrushchev Remembers: Last Testament* (Boston: Little, Brown, 1974), 276–277; Werner Meissner and Anja Feege, eds., *Die DDR und China 1949 bis 1990: Politik, Wirtschaft, Kultur: eine Quellensammlung* [*The GDR and China, 1949 to 1990: Politics, Economy, Culture: a Collection of Sources*] (Berlin: Akademie, 1995), 102.
9. John D. Bell, *The Bulgarian Communist Party from Blagoev to Zhivkov* (Stanford, CA: Stanford University Press, 1986), 118–119.

10 Meissner and Feege, *Die DDR*, 116, 122; André Steiner, *Von Plan zu Plan: eine Wirtschaftsgeschichte der DDR* [*From plan to plan: an economic history of the GDR*] (Berlin: Aufbau, 2007), 124–138.
11 Bo Yibo, "The Making of the 'Lean-to-One Side' Decision," *Chinese Historians* 5/1 (1992), 57–62; James S. O'Donnell, *A Coming of Age: Albania under Enver Hoxha* (Boulder, CO: East European Monographs, 1999), 27–32.
12 Mao Zedong, "History and Current Reality Demand that We Unite and Cooperate," June 30, 1955, Mao Zedong, *On Diplomacy* (Beijing: Foreign Languages Press, 1998), 165–166; "Record of Conversation, Soviet Beijing Ambassador Pavel Iudin and Mao Zedong, March 31, 1956," Odd Arne Westad, ed., *Brothers in Arms: The Rise and Fall of the Sino-Soviet Alliance, 1945–1963* (Washington, D.C.: Woodrow Wilson Center, 1998), 341.
13 O'Donnell, *A Coming of Age*, 40–44.
14 Lüthi, *Sino-Soviet Split*, 74–78, 82.
15 William E. Griffith, *Albania and the Sino-Soviet Rift* (Cambridge, MA: MIT Press, 1963); Lüthi, *Sino-Soviet Split*, 169–174, 201–205, 221–223, 230–231.
16 Wang Taiping, *Zhonghua renmin gongheguo waijiaoshi* [*A diplomatic history of the People's Republic of China*], vol. 2, *1957–1969* (Beijing: Shijie zhishi, 1998), 344.
17 F. Stephen Larrabee, "Whither Albania?" *The World Today* 34/2 (1978), 61–69.
18 Lüthi, *Sino-Soviet Split*, 269, 278; Raymond L. Garthoff, "When and Why Romania Distanced Itself from the Warsaw Pact," *Cold War International History Project Bulletin* 5, 111.
19 In 1969, Pakistan played a more important role than Romania, see: Lorenz M. Lüthi, "Restoring Chaos to History: Sino-Soviet-American Relations, 1969," *The China Quarterly* 210 (2012), 378–97. In 1977, Israel used Romania's good offices, see: "Rumanian Good Offices Are Accepted to Begin," *New York Times* [hereafter: *NYT*], August 27, 1977, 37; "Rumania Was Go-Between," *NYT*, November 17, 1977, 4.
20 Lüthi, *Sino-Soviet Split*, 183–191.
21 Lüthi, *Sino-Soviet Split*, 303–305.
22 Lüthi, *Sino-Soviet Split*, 302–339. Lorenz M. Lüthi, "The Vietnam War and China's Third-Line Defense Planning before the Cultural Revolution, 1964–1966," *Journal of Cold War Studies* 10/1 (2008), 26–51.
23 Lorenz M. Lüthi, "Beyond Betrayal: Beijing, Moscow, and the Paris Negotiations, 1971–1973," *Journal of Cold War Studies* 11/1 (2009), 57–107.
24 "Text of Statement by Chou and Nehru," *NYT*, June 29, 1954, 4.
25 "Red China Invited to Talks of Asian-African Powers," *NYT*, December 30, 1954, 1.
26 On Nehru's 1955 visit, see: Two notes by Nehru in *Nehru Memorial Museum and Library* [Delhi; hereafter: *NMML*], T.N. Kaul Papers, I to III Installment, Subject Files, File #15, 348–375. On the Khrushchev–Bulganin visit to India, see for Soviet and Indian documentation: "Information," January 11, 1956, *SAPMO-BArch*, DY 30/3634, 1–10; "Note by the Prime Minister on the visit of the Soviet leaders to India in November–December 1955," December, 1955, *NMML*, Subimal Dutt Papers, Subject Files, File #17, 1–9.
27 "Prime Minister Secretariat," June 18, 1954, *NMML*, Subimal Dutt Papers, Subject Files, File #6, 4–7.
28 Lüthi, *Sino-Soviet Split*, 138–146.
29 Lorenz M. Lüthi, "Sino-Indian Relations, 1954–1960," *Eurasia Border Review* 3, Special Issue (2012), 112–18.
30 For the ideological dimension of the war, see conversation between the PRC ambassador with an East German representative in mid-November: "Report," November 21, 1962, *Der Bundesbeauftragte für die Unterlagen des Staatssicherheitsdienstes der ehemaligen Deutschen Demokratischen Republik* [*The Federal Commissioner for the Documents of the State Security Service of the former German Democratic Republic*, Berlin; hereafter: *BStU*], MfS – HA XX 17469, 3–11.
31 Lüthi, *Sino-Soviet Split*, 224–228.
32 Srinath Raghavan, *War and Peace in Modern India: a Strategic History of the Nehru Years* (Ranukhet: Permanent Black, 2010), 304–308.
33 Lüthi, "Sino-Indian Relations, 1954–1960."
34 Christopher Tang, "Trust Exercises: Sino-Pakistani Relations before the Backchannel, 1962–1971," unpublished M.A. research paper, McGill University, 2010.
35 Kalyani Shankar, *Nixon, Indira, and India: Politics and beyond* (Delhi: Macmillan, 2010), 222.

36 "Talks between P.M. and Gromyko on 10.8.71 – 11.20 A.M. New Delhi," no date, *NMML*, T.N. Kaul Papers, I to III Installment, Subject Files, File #19, 365–371.
37 After vetoing a Security Council resolution, the Soviet Union and its East European client states supported India in opposing the call for a ceasefire, see: "U.N. Assembly, 104-11, urges Truce," *NYT*, December 8, 1971, 1, 19.
38 In 1972, ninety-seven countries, more than half of the world, recognized Bangladesh, see: Rounaq Jahan, "Bangladesh in 1972: Nation Building in a New State," *Asian Survey* 13/2 (1973), 199–210.
39 "Information," February 6, 1963, *Politisches Archiv des Auswärtigen Amtes, Bestand: Ministerium für Auswärtige Angelegenheiten* [*Political Archive of the Office for Foreign Affairs, Files: Ministry for Foreign Affairs [of the former GDR]*, Berlin; hereafter *PAAA-MfAA*], Abteilung Süd-Südostasien/Sektion Indien, Microfiche C 1738/76, 22–33.
40 Mentioned in: "Information," August 7, 1964, *PAAA-MfAA*, Botschaft Belgrad – Politische Abteilung, Microfiche C 1572/72, 76–81
41 Zhonggong zhongyang wenxian yanjiushi bian [CCP, Central Documents Research Office], ed., *Zhou Enlai nianpu, 1949–1976* [*A chronicle of Zhou Enlai's life*], vol. 2 [hereafter: *ZELNP2*], 549.
42 For China's ideological stand during Zhou's visit to Egypt in December of 1963, see the following East German analysis: "Information," no date, SAPMO-BArch, DY 30/IV A 2/20/890, 1–13. According to this report, China demanded of Egypt to cut relations with the Soviet Union, Yugoslavia, and India. For a similar Chinese memorandum of conversation, see: "The Record of the Fourth Political Talk of Premier Zhou Enlai with President Ben Bella," December 26, 1963, *Waijiaobu Dang'anguan* [*Foreign Ministry Archive*, Beijing; hereafter: *WJBDAG*], 203-00614-06, 39–54.
43 *ZELNP2*, 641.
44 See for example: "Assessment," January 11, 1965, *PAAA-MfAA*, Abteilung Ferner Osten – Sektor China, C 911/76, 1–27. "On the Reactions of our Nuclear Test," October 17, 1964, *WJBDAG*, 113-00396-09, 8–9; "The Reactions of All Sides On the Nuclear Explosion," October 24, 1964, *WJBDAG*, 113-00397-15, 84–86; "Brief Report on Nyerere's Talk," November 1, 1964, *WJBDAG*, 113-00397-15, 88–90.
45 "Dear comrade Böttger," December 1, 1964, *PAAA-MfAA*, 2. AEA Sektor India, Microfiche A 14038, 1–2.
46 "Conc.: 2nd Afro-Asian conference in Algiers," January 3, 1965, *PAAA-MfAA*, Abteilung Arabische Staaten – Gesamtarabische Fragen, A 13344, 1–5.
47 "The Matter of the Talks of the Algerian Ambassador in Syria talking about the Second Afro-Asian Conference," March 21, 1965, *WJBDAG*, 107-00636-04, 43–46.
48 "Resubmitting the Circumstances of the Talks of Ambassador Hui with Political Department Head of the Egyptian Foreign Ministry," March 27, 1965, *WJBDAG*, 107-00636-04, 55–58.
49 "Reactions by the Algerian Military towards the Explosion of Our Atomic Bomb," May 19, 1965, *WJBDAG*, 107-00943-01, 6–7; "Information," June 9, 1965, *PAAA-MfAA*, Abteilung Ferner Osten – Sektor China, C 923/76, 1.
50 Mentioned in: "Chou, in Tanzania, calls U.S. a Bully," *NYT*, June 6, 1965, 1.
51 George T. Yu, "China's Role in Africa," *Annals of the American Academy of Political and Social Science* 432 (1977), 98.
52 "Record of third conversation by Zhou Enlai with Nasser," June 21, 1965, *WJBDAG*, 107-01081-09, 30–34.
53 "The Issue of Sending a Memorandum to the Egyptian Foreign Ministry," June 19, 1965, *WJBDAG*, 107-00613-01, 33–34.
54 "Report on the Talks of Nasser in Moscow," September 28, 1965, SAPMO-BArch, DY 30/J IV 2/2J/1512, 1–7.
55 "Africa-Asia Talk Off Indefinitely," *NYT*, November 2, 1965, 6.
56 *ZELNP2*, 757–758.
57 *ZELNP2*, 758–759.
58 "Statement by Zhou Enlai: informal meeting on October 15 [1965]," *JSSDAG*, 3011, zhang 1162, 96–100.
59 *ZELNP2*, 759–760. Wang, *Zhonghua renmin gongheguo waijiaoshi*, 122–123.
60 "Afro-Asia Talk Off Indefinitely," *NYT*, November 2, 1965, 1, 6.
61 *Dangdai Zhongguo congshi* [*Contemporary China Collection*], *Dangdai Zhongguo duiwai maoyi* [*Contemporary China Trade*], vol. 1 (Beijing: Dangdai Zhongguo chubanshe, 1992), 371–388.

62 Lüthi, "Chinese Foreign Policy," 157; Roderick MacFarquhar, *The Origins of the Cultural Revolution*, vol. 3 (New York: Columbia University, 1997), 27.
63 *Dangdai Zhongguo duiwai maoyi*, vol. 1, 31, 371–388.
64 "The Matter of Faure Visiting China," August 20, 1963, *WJBDAG*, 110-01982-01, 157–158.
65 "Again on the Matter of Faure Visiting China," August 20, 1963, *WJBDAG*, 110-01982-01, 159.
66 "Dear Mister President," October 9, 1963, *WJBDAG*, 110-01982-07, 146–147.
67 Among the abundant documentation in the Chinese foreign ministry archive, see especially files in *WJBDAG*, 110-01997-02, 110-01997-03, 110-01997-04, 110-01997-05 and 110-01997-06.
68 "Political Report no. 20," August 4, 1964, *Bundesarchiv Bern* [*Federal Archive Berne*; hereafter: *BA Bern*], E 2300, Aksession 1000/716, 361, "Politische Berichte, 1964," 1–2. "Copy," December 11, 1965, *PAAA-MfAA*, Ministerbüro Winzer, Microfiche G-A 408, 327.
69 "Political Report no. 17," May 4, 1965, *BA Bern*, E 2300, Aksession 1000/716, 361, "Politische Berichte, 1965." "Political Report no. 34," September 6, 1965, *BA Bern*, E 2300, Aksession 1000/716, 361, "Politische Berichte, 1965."
70 Chen Jian, *Mao's China and the Cold War* (Chapel Hill, NC: University of North Carolina Press, 2001), 238–276; Lüthi, "Restoring Chaos to History"; Lorenz M. Lüthi and Chen Jian, "East Asia 1962–1972," forthcoming.
71 "[No title]," June 5, 1979, *SAPMO-BArch*, DY 30/IV 2/2.035/64, 17–20.
72 "On the annulment," April 4 [?], 1979, *PAAA-MfAA*, Abteilung Ferner Osten, C 6560, 71–73.
73 Artemy M. Kalinovsky, *A Long Goodbye: The Soviet Withdrawal from Afghanistan* (Cambridge, MA: Harvard University Press, 2011), 55–63.
74 "Brezhnev Presses Overtures to the Chinese Leaders," *NYT*, March 25, 1982, A8.
75 Zhonggong zhongyang wenxian yanjiushi [Chinese Communist Party, Central Committee, Research Office of Government Documents], ed., *Deng Xiaoping nian pu (1975–1997)* [*Chronicle of life of Deng Xiaoping (1975–1979)*], vol. 1 [hereafter: *DXPNP*] (Beijing: Zhongyang wenxian chubanshe, 2004), 835.
76 "More Information," January 9, 1985, *SAPMO-BArch*, DY 30/11608, 1.
77 *DXPNP*, 1085–1086.

PART III

Decolonization and its Consequences

7

DECOLONIZATION AND THE COLD WAR

Ryan M. Irwin

This chapter is organized around the claim that decolonization and the Cold War were component parts of a larger story: the rise of the twentieth-century nation-state. The emergence of the nation-state beyond its geographies of origin – Europe and the United States – occurred alongside the creation of internationalist institutions that regulated interstate behaviour. These two processes shaped each other; it is impossible to understand one without the other. In substantiating this thesis, the chapter first places self-determination within a global conversation about the national state. Even as consensus deepened after World War I that government planning could manage globalization and make modernity universal, disagreement spread over the benefit (and possibility) of international interdependence. The United States was an important but ambiguous prism for this contest, shaped in equal measure by progressive advocacy and racial discrimination. Washington's embrace of the United Nations frames the chapter's second section and provides a window to reflect on the mid-century intersections of decolonization and the Cold War. The liberal order fused development thinking with international interdependence in a way that addressed the tensions of the interwar years and facilitated the creation of several large national states in Asia. Within this "One World," tensions over capitalism and empire culminated in the mid-1950s and the chapter's final section turns to the exigencies that accompanied second-wave decolonization. The number of nation-states doubled in the decade after 1955. By exploring the subtle differences between pan-Asianism and pan-Africanism, the chapter sheds light on the significance of the Black Atlantic's independence during the Cold War. Even as black states successfully challenged racism and universalized development, they raised difficult questions about the U.N.'s political purpose and the economic capacity of small postcolonial polities with limited resources. Although the nation-state was everywhere by the late 1960s, its ubiquity masked new divisions over the meaning of sovereignty, autonomy, and U.N. membership.

Peace without Meaning

The nation-state's meteoric rise was hardly preordained. For many of the Europeans who came of age in the late nineteenth century, intellectual debate revolved instead around the relationship between colonialism, imperialism, and empire. Widely seen as synonymous with European migration, colonialism was associated with enlightened self-governance in places like the

United States, Canada, Australia, Argentina, and Chile. Bound by a culture of "whiteness," John Hobson captured the rhetorical tendencies of the time when he wrote that colonialism was "a natural overflow of nationality" that "transplant[ed] civilisation … to [a] new natural and social environment."[1] Empire, in contradistinction, was viewed as a cosmopolitan project defined by the classic and timeless struggle to balance universal civilization with geopolitical security. As late as World War I, Jefferson's empire of liberty seemed wholly consonant with London's move toward a commonwealth of settler nations. Imperialism existed in an entirely different milieu. Emerging on the heels of Europe's small wars, this neologism marked the supposed discontinuity from preindustrial great power politics; imperialism was a violent, crass, and unstable form of what scholars have learned to call industrial or modern globalization. As historian Adam Tooze explains,

> If we accept this three-way distinction – between colonialism, empire and imperialism – much about the politics of the early twentieth century becomes clearer. … [Woodrow Wilson] had virtually nothing to say about colonialism [because] the civilizing mission per se was not in question. … He could express guarded admiration for recent British policy within its Empire, which he understood, on a good day, as a vehicle for the spread of liberal values. At the same time he could be an open and aggressive opponent of imperialistic tendencies both within the United States and in the wider global system.[2]

The tone was different outside the pan-European world, but these distinctions maintained their basic form. Early advocates of pan-Asianism and pan-Islamism worked assiduously to disconnect the civilizing mission from the apparatus of European imperialism. Living in the aftermath of Europe's industrial divergence from East Asia, politicized intellectuals lamented neither the West's universalist rhetoric nor the decline of some preindustrial life. "Their main thesis," historian Cemil Aydin argues, "was that European imperialism was hampering, not fostering, pro-European style reform, and thus there was a need for anti-imperial solidarity to achieve the desired civilizational progress."[3] Empire was fine but imperialism was not. Codified initially in Meji Japan and the Tanzimat era of the Ottoman Empire, this mindset delegitimized Eurocentric imperialism even as it preserved and recreated many of the ideas associated with colonialism. By untangling modernity from Orientalist discourse and European militarism, universal civilization was reformulated in terms of racial and religious pluralism, thereby transforming Hobsonian colonialism into a nonwhite enterprise. Writing in the immediate aftermath of Japan's 1905 military victory over the Russian Empire, W.E.B. Du Bois could revel in the idea that the "Color Line in civilization [had] been crossed in modern times as it was in the great past," yet call for something more ambiguous than empire's end: "Shall the awakening of these sleepy millions [in Asia] be in accordance with, and aided by, the great ideals of white civilization, or in spite of them and against them?"[4]

World War I provided an answer. By tethering the civilizing mission to the League of Nations, Europe's peacemakers hoped to promote cooperation between the great powers – thereby reducing the instability that stemmed from industrialized imperialism – and codify colonialism through a Mandate system that formalized European rule in Africa and parts of Ottoman Asia. A unified legal structure would clarify any ambiguity about the meaning of pan-European power. The subsequent pushback, embodied in the so-called Wilsonian moment, underscored the national state's awkward conceptual place in this rhetorical stew. As historian Eric D. Weitz shows, a subtle transformation was underway: the British Reform Act, German and Italian unification, the Austro-Hungarian *Ausgleich*, the U.S. Civil War and reconstruction, and peasant reforms in Russia, among other events, all pointed toward a reassessment of the relationship of agrarian territoriality and dynastic sovereignty to racialized nationhood and representative government. Faced with the exigencies of industrialized urbanism at home and unbridled militarism abroad, elites on both sides of the imperial divide were coming to embrace "population politics."[5] The 1919 debate over self-determination stemmed from this wider confluence. For many of the activists who converged on Paris, the question was not whether the national state would end empire but how civilizational progress – wrapped now within this process and embodied by the League – would square with Europe's tendency to employ racial discrimination in Eurasia and Africa. Was empire making, in other words, possible beyond Europe?

The watershed came with Japan's request to make racial equality one of the League's founding principles. In response, many pan-European thinkers came to treat self-determination as a discursive vehicle that invigorated imperialism through colonialism. The phrase hinted at what Frederick Lugard called the dual-mandate empire, which paradoxically embraced civilizational uplift as the *raison d'être* of European power even as it made racial difference an insurmountable barrier to universal civilization. Codified by the Mandate system, this argument tacitly extended the logic of separate but equal, marrying self-government to racial homogeneity in a way that made autonomy – especially in the Black Atlantic – contingent on the whims of European racists. Indeed, the mandate idea was an intellectual project with distinctly African origins. Having grown from the antislavery movement of the nineteenth century, it reflected the deeper sense that sub-Saharan Africans possessed distinct cultural traits that required a system of rule distinct from the one that governed former Ottoman subjects and East Asians. Self-determination – framed as the endpoint of trusteeship – promised not independence but calibrated membership in a multi-national system defined by white privilege.

Confronted by such an elaborate defense of the status quo, many critics turned to Vladimir Lenin. Popularized during the Bolshevik Revolution, Lenin's writings highlighted the economic dimensions of European power. If contemporaries wanted to truly "grasp the meaning of self-determination," they needed to reject European law and other abstractions, he argued in 1914. "Examining the historico-economic conditions of the national movements" made it clear "that the self-determination of nations [required] the political separation of these nations from alien national bodies, and the formation of an independent national state."[6] This mindset, which recast colonialism, empire, and imperialism as linear reflections of capitalist development, cultivated a binary that pitted capitalism/imperialism against anti-capitalism/imperialism, with agricultural collectivization and industrial expropriation serving as two sides of a common political and intellectual project. In this formulation, politics and economics trumped the significance of race and civilization.

The disjuncture between these distinct visions – with self-determination invoked both to signify membership within a European superstructure and detachment from this superstructure – reinforced a push to disaggregate the national state from empire even as it infused both terms with irreconcilable meanings. Although the language of population politics increasingly framed the national state's meaning, disagreement proliferated over whether the nation-state grew from within the existing order or in revolution against it. This schism gave the interwar years a Janus-faced quality. On the one side, consensus deepened in favor of economic anti-imperialism, or import-substituting industrialization. Confronted by the exigencies of imperialism/globalization, governing elites in and beyond Europe drifted toward a mindset that used public funds for heavy industrialization; created tariffs, trade quotas, and quantitative trade restrictions; and deployed agricultural surpluses to invest in industry. The proper role (if any) of direct foreign investment remained contested, as did the nature of the indigenous private sector and the extent and sectoral distribution of public ownership – but this framework increasingly rendered older (mostly British) discourses of free trade obsolete. Sun Yat-sen's claim that China would "proceed along the path pointed out" by Lenin was not a sign of his revolutionary Marxism; it was evidence that even non-communists saw state-led anti-imperialist economics as an effective way to achieve modernity after World War I. The choice facing leaders in China, Turkey, and Iran, among other polities, was not whether to take control of local economic exchange but on what terms and to what degree.

On the other side, however, this consensus masked deep disagreements over the meaning and future of the League of Nations. Import-substituting industrialization existed awkwardly alongside the ideal of institutional interdependence. After flirtations with the Comintern, which provided an institutional platform for Lenin's anti-capitalist/imperialist revolution, many non-Western intellectuals came to see inclusive internationalism as a viable pathway toward universal civilization. Formed in 1927, the League Against Imperialism, for instance, took its name to mock Lugard's dual mandate of empire. The group lobbied Geneva, in part, to extend membership to more Asian countries. "Get your national ownership, get your national control, that is right and proper, but do not stop there," one member argued in the late 1920s. "Nationalism is to be blended with internationalism, because until it is, until the world is built on the foundation of international comradeship … all our labour is in vain."[7] Others saw the League as the problem. In Germany, Carl Schmitt, a legal scholar who became active in the Nazi Party, lamented universal civilization – especially as constituted by the League of Nations – as a hollow rhetorical device and embraced Washington's hegemony over the Western hemisphere as a model for the future; "America for the Americans, Europe for the Europeans," in Adolf Hitler's infamous words.[8] The thesis echoed in East Asia, where Japanese intellectuals employed the Monroe Doctrine to justify their Chinese conquests. Even within Josef Stalin's Soviet Union, where urban planning and political terror were remaking social life in fundamental ways, the United States lingered in the background. The "Soviet cult of America … took many forms," historian Stephen Kotkin explains,[9] but it stemmed from a common desire to build a polity that balanced economic autonomy and modernized industrialism with geographic hegemony and cultural relativism. League membership – and all that it entailed – was unimportant.

One World, Everywhere

The United States was an ambiguous prism for this debate. Born from the cauldron of anticolonial war, the country had carved a sphere of influence in the Americas by taking advantage of Europe's preoccupation with Eurasia during the nineteenth century. Within this zone, Washington's experiments seemed to support the presupposition that nation-states could thrive only in fully autonomous zones of influence. The Civil War, which wrenched America's cotton industry from Europe's global economy, unfolded just after a Mexican conflict that remade the nation's southern border in terms of racialized peoplehood, as well as a sustained border war that forced assimilation or extermination upon Native Americans. The resulting vision, codified by the rise of Jim Crow and wrapped in a language of exceptionalism, equated nationhood with race, statehood with industrial planning, and citizenship with capitalist output, and appeared to point toward a Schmittian conclusion: the United States was free to do what it wanted within its national space. This formula was hardly uncontested. Labor unrest, anarchism, and internal migration dramatized the plight of those left behind in this "nation of nations" and hinted at the inherent problems of hegemony based on racialized citizenship. Yet even the progressive movement, spearheaded by Anglo Saxon reformers and dedicated to rehabilitating universal civilization, never transcended the logic of Lugard's dual mandate –

especially toward the African American community – and by the 1930s, the United States had become the archetype of import-substituting industrialization, with New Dealers from Hugh Johnson to Marriner Eccles employing novel state interventions to bind and invigorate American society. The country evinced the claim that economic and political independence were mutually constitutive and seemed to prove (by extension) that interstate interdependence was the aberration. The future belonged to national states that could marshal natural resources, provide for their citizens, and promote economic development.

In the face of Hitler's *Lebensraum*, Washington reformulated this narrative. "When we talk of freedom and opportunity for all nations, the mocking paradoxes of our own society become so clear they can no longer be ignored," politician Wendell Willkie admitted in 1943. Going forward, the United States had to "choose one of three courses: narrow nationalism, which inevitably means the ultimate loss of our own liberty; international imperialism, which means the sacrifice of some other nation's liberty; or the creation of a world in which there will be an equality of opportunity for every race and every nation."[10] Willkie's three-part formulation pointed toward a middle space between Schmitt and Lugard, and offered a new answer to Du Bois's old question. At Dumbarton Oaks, Bretton Woods, and San Francisco, U.S. planners rehabilitated a style of institutional interdependence based on freer trade, population politics, and import-substituting industrialization. National states would be bound together in an economic and political network that recognized the unique authority of great powers, especially in the realm of security, but encouraged small states to influence norms and achieve development with the help of the United Nations and American economic aid.

If the United States could coax the Soviet Union into embracing this system, the resulting "One World" would ostensibly chart a middle way between hegemonic nationalism and industrialized imperialism. Instead of promoting a universalism laced with Lugardian hypocrisy, this order promised a combination of stability and modernity based on power politics, institutional cooperation, and economic prosperity. Historian Paul Kramer has labeled this governance strategy "international empire" – suggesting that Washington saw nation-states as tools to manage global exchange and extend American hegemony – but such an interpretation downplays the discursive impact of mid-century social science.[11] Although self-determination once again promised calibrated membership in a multi-national system, this time technocratic development supplanted the rhetoric of racial difference, especially in East and South Asia. By extending Security Council status to China and encouraging India's membership in the United Nations, U.S. planners subtly reformulated the nation-state/empire dichotomy in a way that consolidated territoriality, good neighborliness, and social progress under a single institutional umbrella. Decolonization could now be contextualized as United Nations membership.

Europeans bristled immediately at this formulation. Before the ink had dried on the 1941 Atlantic Charter, Winston Churchill publicly rejected the view that self-determination extended to the British Raj, and Dutch leaders – despite being exiled from the East Indies by Japan – embraced colonialism as the only legitimate conduit for the civilizing mission. "[A] new doctrine is being put forward, whereby colonial responsibilities [will] be assumed ... by some international organization," France's colonial secretary summarized in 1945. "Neither the interests nor the wishes of the colonial populations would be served by a reform which would transfer to a caretaker organization, acting under a collective name, the continuation of the colonizing work which is liberating the primitive societies from the great calamities which are ravaging them and which are called: disease, ignorance, superstition, tyranny."[12] The problem, once again, was not the principle of universal civilization but its institutional form beyond Europe. In subsequent debates over the U.N.'s trusteeship system, British officials tried to distinguish self-determination, which now implied statehood within the United Nations, from self-government in a commonwealth dedicated to democracy and development. But Washington refused to abandon the One World idea. The great powers "administering dependent peoples shall be held responsible by the public opinion of the world," Sumner Welles explained in 1945.

> If the United Nations ... fails to deal with this great problem in the same spirit in which this war for freedom was waged, Gandhi's prophesy that unless the peoples of the East obtain their fundamental liberties, another and a bloodier war will be inevitable, will ... be realized.[13]

This equation – where interconnected nation-states bequeathed fundamental liberty to non-European populations – produced three distinct political trajectories after the war. On the one hand, Europeans tried to recast empires as power-sharing modernization projects. Under Jean Monnet's postwar recovery plan, France's Fourth Republic attempted to break down the barrier that separated the metropole from the periphery by articulating a vision of a French Union based on shared development and citizenship. Several bureaucracies were actually redesigned to promote African welfare through *équipement sociale*, with forced labor schemes giving way to education, health, and welfare services and foreign investment. As historian Frederick Cooper explains, French officials "thought that extending citizenship to all, while limiting representation to a small number of elected deputies, would channel the energies of the 'évolués' into the [empire] without upsetting the life of the 'paysans.'"[14] Britain's Labour Party focused energy on the working class at home and advanced a revised version of Lugard's dual mandate in these years, introducing power-sharing constitutions in the Gold Coast (Ghana), among other locales. Yet Whitehall similarly relinquished the logic of racialized tribalism and worked to balance relations among traditional collaborators and urban elites who wanted better wages, fairer trade policies, and greater autonomy. Fifty years earlier few Europeans differentiated indigenous people in this manner, especially in Africa; the shift hinted at a style of empire based on universal development and cultural pluralism. "Imperialism is dead," a British brochure summarized succinctly after the war. But the "colonial system was a practical illustration of democracy under tuition."[15]

On the other hand was decolonization. Washington set a precedent by making the Philippines a member of the United Nations in 1946. As the Raj crumbled in India, Jawaharlal Nehru articulated his response to empire's revived logic, arguing that "true internationalism would [never] triumph" if his country remained a "junior partner in the British Empire or Commonwealth."[16] But he called for something short of Schmittian autonomy: the era of "the small national state [was] doomed," and destined to be replaced by diverse "supra-national polities" bound together by a single world organization. Even if world security was centralized among the great powers, the General Assembly promised U.N. members the chance to "mobilize incalculable moral opinion" and "form the conventions of world self-rule."[17] For many Asian nationalists, this seemed like a reasonable trade-off. The United Nations clarified decolonization's form in a way that conferred legitimacy to new leaders as they wrestled with the ambiguities of nationhood and statehood, phrases that cloaked the ugly realities that accompanied political coalition building in postcolonial settings. The organization also provided a conduit to deal with the legacy of industrialized globalization. During the "past one hundred years, four million Indians have been transplanted to various parts of the world under the aegis of the colonial governments concerned," an Indian delegate explained to her U.N. colleagues in 1947.[18] By the late 1940s, South Asians could be found in the Caribbean, South America, South and East Africa, Mauritius, Ceylon (Sri Lanka),

Southeast Asia, Burma, the Persian Gulf, and the Pacific Islands. Within this context, what was a country to do if its nation was bigger than its state? Although the United Nations did not provide an answer, it gave nation-states the means to negotiate collaborative solutions – and bolster the international minority rights regime.

No less important was the place of capitalism in this One World. The Cold War between Washington and Moscow grew, in part, from their disagreement over the fate of postwar Germany. But Lenin's assertions about pan-European power – specifically about the mutually constitutive nature of universal civilization and imperial exploitation – held deep implications after World War II. The duality of this moment was noteworthy. The early postwar years saw the phenomenal and unprecedented economic integration of the United States, Western Europe, and Japan, which remade the geography of global capitalism and supplanted Europe's imperial economies with a zone of industrialized economic exchange anchored by the American marketplace. But at almost the same moment, China, which many U.S. thinkers assumed would be the Asian linch-pin of this system, became communist. And Mao was not just communist, but a revolutionary Leninist. Events in China prompted Moscow and Washington to reassess their respective spheres of influence, as well as the compatibility of their development models.

In 1950, as Stalin quietly authorized Pyongyang's invasion of South Korea, Harry Truman mobilized the United Nations into action. The resulting conflict was a turning point that launched a debate over self-determination's relationship to the United Nations. Pitted against U.N. forces and convinced that the organization was synonymous with Western imperialism, Mao embraced a series of modernizing initiatives – often with disastrous results – that reified his country's autonomy from the international community. Because "political incursion, economic exploitation, and military aggression" by Europeans "had undermined the historical glory of the Chinese civilization," Mao, historian Chen Jian explains, embraced "revolutionary programs aimed at reviving China's central position in the world."[19] His approach created tensions with the Soviet Union, now an influential status quo power and United Nations member, but it inspired revolutionary thinkers from Frantz Fanon to Ho Chi Minh, as well as the now elderly W.E.B. Du Bois. "I have seen the world," Du Bois wrote in the 1950s. "But never so vast and glorious a miracle as China," a country that seemed to have achieved genuine autonomy from the capitalist world. "America makes or can make no article that China is not either making or can make better and cheaper."[20] For the equally aged Schmitt, Mao stood in "opposition of the *One World*, of a political unity of earth and its humanity," and showed that "Großräumen [large spatial areas]" remained relevant in the ascendant Cold War.[21]

These three political trajectories – modernizing empire, decolonization, and the Cold War – converged during the mid-1950s. At the 1955 Asian–African conference in Bandung, Indian and Chinese leaders attempted to square their competing approaches toward self-determination. Negotiating alongside dozens of postcolonial leaders from across Eurasia, Nehru and China's Zhou Enlai elaborated ideas they'd developed in earlier meetings about the Tibetan border, diaspora minority rights, and regional coexistence. The conference denounced "colonialism in all its manifestations" and underscored equality's intellectual centrality to interracial and international affairs. By explicitly tying sovereignty to territoriality and reproving the principle of cross-border interference, the agreement seemed to buttress the national state as a wholly autonomous unit in foreign affairs. However, unlike in the 1954 Panchsheel Treaty, human rights were linked explicitly to the purposes and principles of the United Nations. Even more, the U.N. charter was invoked as the framework to settle interstate conflicts. Nonalignment infused this seemingly contradictory stance with discursive coherence. Interconnected by a common superstructure, national states would steer a "third way" through the Cold War, rehabilitating the U.N.'s peacemaking credentials – damaged by Korea – while dramatizing the decolonized world's separateness from pan-European empire. This formula tacitly disconnected anti-capitalism from anti-imperialism and harmonized self-determination's contested meaning by making it possible to see the national state simultaneously in terms of membership in and separation from the international community. New national states, in theory, could be part of the United Nations order and independent from Western hegemony.

Nation-state Triumphant?

Egypt's nationalization of the Suez Canal the following year grew directly from this synthesis. It also put the United States in a difficult position. In the decade after World War II, Washington had used its voting support among Latin American and West European delegates to shape the agenda of the General Assembly and bolster the authority of the United Nations, especially during the Korean War. There "is no longer any alternative to peace," President Dwight Eisenhower said in 1954. "[T]here is no alternative" to being "loyal to the spirit of the United Nations and dedicated to the principles of the Charter."[22] Nonalignment dovetailed with this sentiment yet challenged Washington's intellectual preponderance in New York – and it unfolded within an altered superpower landscape. As Nikita Khrushchev emerged as the face of Soviet statecraft after Stalin's death, Moscow began establishing economic and security relationships with independent states throughout Eurasia. U.S. aid still dwarfed Soviet assistance, but Mao's shadow loomed large in American thinking, and Gamal Abdel Nasser's seizure of the Suez Canal in 1956 – an emblem, he argued, of Egypt's imperial bondage – seemed to embody both the challenge of nonalignment and the dangers of this newly global Cold War. For Nasser, Egypt's future turned on its strategic resources and economic relations with Moscow. The joint Anglo-French-Israeli invasion forced a stark choice on the United States: Was ending European empire – as a conceptual premise and political reality – the only realistic way to convince people that the nation-state could grow organically from (and thrive within) the United Nations order?

Eisenhower's rebuke of his European allies provided an answer. "The wind of change is blowing," British Prime Minister Harold Macmillan reflected as his government picked up the pieces from its failed intervention in Egypt. "[W]hether we like it or not, this growth of national consciousness is a political fact." His calibrated and deliberate words captured the essence of America's mindset:

> As I see it the great issue in this second half of the twentieth century is whether the uncommitted peoples of Asia and Africa will swing to the East or to the West. Will they be drawn into the Communist camp? Or will the great experiments in self-government that are now being made in Asia and Africa ... prove so successful ... that the balance will come down in favour of freedom and order?[23]

Macmillan was in South Africa when he spoke these words, and he was presiding over the dissolution of the British Empire in the Black Atlantic. On the surface, the creation of forty-plus nation-states – forty new United Nations members – between 1957 and 1963 reified the arguments articulated at the 1955 Asian-African gathering. Indeed, African and Asian delegates moved decisively to pass a resolution on the meaning of self-determination when they took control of the General Assembly in 1960. "All people have an inalienable right to complete freedom, the exercise of their sovereignty and the integrity of their national territory," the declaration read. The "subjection of peoples to alien subjugation" was not just a denial of human rights; it was contrary to the United Nations charter and the principal cause of international and interracial conflict. Political independence and U.N. membership were the only viable routes to a durable and lasting world peace.[24] By making statehood the prerequisite of the civilizing mission, the declaration moved to frame U.N. membership in revolutionary terms. The resulting formulation rejected the essence of classic Leninism – treating the liberal order as an agent of empowerment rather than a vehicle of capitalist/imperialist exploitation – even as it reproduced the rhetoric of Lenin's claims about autonomy and self-sufficiency. "I look upon the United Nations as the only organization that holds out any hope for the future of mankind," Ghana's Kwame Nkrumah said to the 1960 General Assembly. "In this twentieth century of enlightenment, some nations still extol the vain glories of colonialism and imperialism … [but] in my view possession of colonies is now quite incompatible with membership of the United Nations."[25] Nation-states were to be interconnected in a pluralistic superstructure, as Washington had wanted in the 1940s. But the organization's discursive agenda belonged to the Third World rather than liberal internationalists.

Two problems came into focus almost immediately. The first related to pan-Africanism, which formed the prism through which many new U.N. members articulated their claims after 1956. Nehru's push for South Asian decolonization in the 1940s had hinged on the "Rediscovery of India," a project that flowed from the presupposition that India's nationhood claims were authentic and rooted in tangible historical experience. By fixing the country's "collective identities in place and refashioning local and regional solidarities in accord with a larger national whole," Nehru, historian Manu Goswami suggests, created a basis to modernize the Indian "nation" through state-led engineering, machine-based industry, scientific research, and electric power. (With the United Nations both legitimizing this process and helping Delhi promote universal rights for its diaspora beyond the Indian state.) Although mid-century African thinkers reproduced aspects of this framework, they staked out a more fluid understanding of nationhood. Nationalism was not the reclamation of Africa's pre-imperial past but "a complex and positive reaction to – indeed, a recreation of – that past," Ghana's foreign minister explained in the early 1960s.[26] This recreation process unfolded "as colonial states and African labor movements struggled with and influenced each other" during the final phases of European empire, Cooper explains,[27] and it sat atop an older discursive architecture about Africa's place in the Atlantic world. Having been brought into the modern international system by the slave trade, the continent was cast as a uniquely backwards place in the nineteenth and twentieth centuries – a region supposedly devoid of the heritage that marked the Levant and East and South Asia. This legacy created a conceptual gap between pan-Asianism and pan-Africanism. Whereas the former discourse evolved from an anti-Orientalist conversation about empire making and became a conversation about the terms and meaning of internationalism, the latter emerged from an effort to rehabilitate the inherent virtues of blackness. The task for African nationalists was not only to prove that the nation-state could deliver the civilizing mission in Africa; at stake was the meaning of blackness in the international community.

Going into the 1960s, subtle tensions separated nonalignment from this campaign to rehabilitate blackness. Nonalignment was a rhetorical device that harmonized self-determination's meaning, making it possible to see the national state simultaneously in terms of membership in and separation from the international community. Anti-racism was a pan-African nation-building project that articulated and reified the African personality. This project took form, on the one hand, in an array of postcolonial federations. Fragmented into dozens of microstates by the decolonization process, black elites worked against historical precedent (and with little success) to organize new sorts of polities in Africa and the Caribbean. On the other hand, this project took shape at the United Nations. The campaign against South Africa, for instance, was not merely a fight between good and evil; it was an attempt to use apartheid – an ideology premised on the incompatibility of blackness and economic development – to bolster the habits of political unity and remake the United Nations in Africa's image. While Asian nationalists saw article 2(7) of the U.N. charter as the sacrosanct principle of international affairs (and enshrined its importance at Bandung), African diplomats purposefully recalibrated territoriality's relationship to slavery. Because slavery was not under "the domestic jurisdiction of any State" – and any state that practiced anti-black discrimination was a slave state – it followed that the United Nations had a responsibility to take punitive action against any country with racially discriminatory laws, Nigeria's U.N. delegate explained in 1963. Such claims put many Asian states in a difficult position and forced a crucial question on the Third World: Was racism a greater threat to international peace than the Cold War? The answer revealed the different genealogies of pan-Africanism and pan-Asianism, as well as the political imperatives masked by the Bandung moniker. Beyond abstractions and generalized rhetoric, true unity across the postcolonial world was a chimera.

A second problem exposed in this moment was capacity. For American planners, the national state was always a political unit designed to weave material interconnection with cultural pluralism. "Through alliances and aid programs, we have done what no leading power in history has done – shared our power with others, [and] tried to build up other nations and international agencies," American official Harlan Cleveland reflected in the 1970s. This approach stemmed not from American "generosity" but from "enlightened selfishness: we didn't want all those foreigners on our back."[28] Asia's centrality to this schema was often muddled by the mid-century's universalist rhetoric. Powered by the American economy – and underwritten by an expansive network of military bases – Washington's One World theoretically achieved broad-based material growth through aid, planning, and shared technological expertise. In historian Nick Cullather's words, "How and on what terms Asia's population would be integrated into the [postwar] world economy, whether fragile postcolonial states could extend mechanisms of taxation and authority over vast ungoverned hinterlands, and whether poverty on this scale could be ameliorated were all questions that lay outside of the customary conventions of international relations." But they were crucial to the future of international peace.[29] Washington's arrogance in promoting development (and its willingness to covertly topple unfriendly nationalists) has been well documented; occasionally forgotten is that the United States wanted this system to work. From 1953 to 1961, to take one of dozens of examples, the United States subsidized the foreign-exchange costs of India's five-year plans to the extent of two and a half billion dollars.[30] American aid dwarfed the corresponding support of the Soviet Union in these years and many saw the superpower contest as a sideshow to the Asian development drama.

Was the scale of this support possible in an arena with twice as many members? Or, phrased differently, was import-substituting industrialization – bolstered by the United Nations and subsidized by American money – a sustainable political project? Going into the mid-1950s, there were sixty nation-states within the United Nations community; in the ten years after Suez that number more than doubled. The flaw in Washington's logic was foreshadowed by Nehru's own mid-century conclusion that "the era of the small national state was over." Beyond platitudes, Africa – as a place and an idea – was an abstraction in his writing, and an empty canvas for most of the U.N.'s original intellectual architects. "After seeing a bit of it and its people, one is apt to become more puzzled than ever as to what is to become of it, or even what should become of it," African American policymaker Ralph Bunche wrote shortly before designing the U.N.'s trusteeship system at San Francisco.[31] Yet the Black Atlantic arrived at the United Nations in the 1960s and forced policymakers to confront a pair of questions: First, how could the United States – a country where slavery's legacy continued to shape daily life – lead an international community where the members were now mostly black? And second, would the logic of the United Nations order – where interconnected nation-states delivered economic progress through development planning (and bolstered by U.S. aid) – survive as the polities themselves became smaller and smaller and smaller? "No one can deny that we are facing a very critical period," a U.S. official admitted in 1961. One that turned on whether "the United States and the smaller states [would] rise to the occasion and help make the United Nations a truly effective organization."[32]

One side of this story is well known: it's not a mistake that the United States embraced civil rights and voting rights legislation in the midst of this global transformation. But the capacity side of this story remains riddled with ambiguity. Consider the example of Ghana: Kwame Nkrumah was an ardent believer in state-led modernization and worked assiduously to foster Ghana's economic diversity during the 1960s. He pushed his country's cocoa farmers toward horticulture to promote self-sufficiency and took out a series of loans to begin construction on a dam on the Volta River. His hope was that this dam would provide Accra with a durable source of energy, which would facilitate the growth of heavy industry in southern Ghana and help the country achieve what Walt Rostow once called "liftoff." In theory, Ghana would stand shoulder to shoulder with Great Britain within the decade. In reality, Nkrumah's regime collapsed in less than decade.

Nkrumah found himself pinched on three levels in the early 1960s. First, even as Ghana's overall agricultural production rose dramatically on his watch, the price of cocoa plummeted after the British Empire dissolved, as more and more countries turned to cash crops like cocoa to balance their trade ledgers. The country simply ran headlong into the rules of supply and demand in the post-mercantile (post-sterling bloc) capitalist economy. Second, as cocoa profits flat-lined in the face of increased production, cocoa planters – longtime powerbrokers in Ghanaian society – turned against Nkrumah and began criticizing his plans to diversify the economy (and thus weaken the authority of northern farmers). All of which unfolded, third, against rising public sector debt that eroded Nkrumah's ability to pay unionized workers in Accra. The result was a slow-moving catastrophe, which in different ways faced nearly every leader in the Black Atlantic in the years after independence. Something was wrong. Perhaps the development guidebook had crashed up against the realities of geography and politics. Or perhaps enthusiasm for the national state – as a delivery system for the civilizing mission – had been outstripped by the ease with which elites could claim, create, and legitimize new polities through the United Nations. Regardless, the resulting gatekeeper states married sovereignty to external organizations and flattened the heterogeneity of real African societies.

End of Something

Ironically, the Vietnam War gave everyone from Nkrumah to Herbert Marcuse a much simpler explanation. The United States – the architect of the liberal order and its principal backer after World War II – was imperialist. Washington's military involvement in Southeast Asia unfolded just as smaller national states confronted these ambiguities, and the war revived the anti-capitalist/imperialist framework that had been sublimated at Bandung. "As late as the 1950s and early 1960s, it was felt that so long as you could industrialize it was great, because the old colonial division of labor [had] stopped us from industrializing," Caribbean activist Walter Rodney wrote in 1974. But such optimism ended with Nkrumah's fall, and events now demanded "new and searching questions about the character of industrialization: what is it all about, who owns, who controls, what do you actually produce? When you produce this, does it help the development of our economy? Does it make us more independent?"[33] In both Africa and Latin America, intellectuals found answers in dependency theory and neocolonialism, arguing that the petite bourgeoisie's supposed cooptation of the nation-state – which ostensibly extended American hegemony – guaranteed that genuine freedom could come only through revolutionary violence. Lenin had been right all along. "Liberalism did not disappear," theorist Immanuel Wallerstein explained. "[I]t did, however, lose its role as the defining ideology of geoculture."[34] OPEC's oil embargoes extended both the logic and ambiguity of this moment – invigorating economic nationalism as oil prices combined with high interest rates to devastate African economies – and New International Economic Order merely dramatized the toothless nature of the Third World at the United Nations. Although small nation-states shaped the discourse of development at the United Nations, their actions merely underscored the growing gap between rhetoric and power in the polycentric Cold War. By the mid-1970s, many nongovernmental organizations were openly repudiating nationalism and investigating new ways to conceptualize human rights, equality, and liberation.

For very different reasons, the United States also moved away from the United Nations order in these years. Popularized by Richard Nixon, the policy of détente worked explicitly to deal with what Henry Kissinger called "multi-polarity," a condition that supposedly stemmed from the proliferation of black "micro-states" during the 1960s. "For the two decades after 1945, our international activities were based on the assumption that technology plus managerial skills gave us the ability to reshape the international system and to bring about domestic transformations in 'emerging countries,'" Kissinger wrote in 1969. Yet "political multipolarity [had made] it impossible to impose an American design."[35] Washington's subsequent pivot toward Beijing hinted at an emerging landscape shaped not by the nation-state/empire dichotomy – with political discourse organized by the contest to define self-determination's political contours – but by the differences between large and small polities in the decolonized world. Not only had America's nation-building prowess been sullied in South Vietnam, but the Sino-Indian border war had buckled the original Bandung spirit in South and East Asia. Small states, in short, were reviving Leninist arguments just as larger states were experimenting with new security pacts and political assumptions. "Because we live in a new world, many of the old institutions are obsolete and inadequate," Nixon declared in the midst of these changes. "The UN, NATO, foreign aid, USIA were set up to deal with a world of twenty years ago."[36] Going forward, Washington tightened one-to-one relations with strategically critical states such as China and the Soviet Union, as well as Saudi Arabia, Egypt, and the Congo, among many others, and developed alternative modes of global governance – most obviously the G-7 – to bring together highly industrialized governments to manage economic stability in this cacophonous environment. The notion of universal civilization was not dead. But it shifted definitively from technocratic development and U.N. membership toward individual human rights and humanitarian intervention.

By the mid-1970s, decolonization had fulfilled a particular vision of postimperialism and carried forward the systemic contradictions of self-determination and American hegemony. These contradictions – always present – were on full display, and raised the inevitable question: What now? Historicizing decolonization and the Cold War in this manner does not provide an answer so much as put the question in a productive context. Commentators have often read the nation-state's proliferation backwards, using contemporary debates and issues to either celebrate the nation-state's ongoing relevance or castigate its many shortcomings. Looking at the nation-state as an entity in time – one that changed fundamentally as decolonization evolved from an intellectual premise to a political reality – provides a point of leverage to explain more precisely the nature and the scope of the changes that unfolded during the middle decades of the twentieth century. For a brief moment, arguably from the 1940s through the 1960s, the United Nations functioned as a powerful and contested platform for this debate, normalizing certain ideas and framing the politically possible, as well as critiques against the politically possible. It would be a mistake to view the national state's growth as a linear consequence of Western history. The West – as a narrative – was appropriated and the form of this appropriation was always contested. Decolonization fulfilled the logic of mid-century liberal internationalism even as it carried forward certain contradictions that culminated in the Black Atlantic's complex remaking of the international system. The effects were deeply felt and by the mid-1970s politicized intellectuals everywhere were lamenting the United Nations as either a sanitarium of the Third World or a tool of U.S. imperialism.

Notes

1 J.A. Hobson, *Imperialism* (London: George Allen and Unwin Ltd., 1902), 2–3.
2 Adam Tooze, "Empire, Imperialism and American Power in the 20th Century," September 2011, unpublished discussion paper.
3 Cemil Aydin, "Beyond Civilization: Pan-Islamism, Pan-Asianism and the Revolt against the West," *Journal of Modern European History* 4:2 (Fall 2006): 205.
4 Quoted in Bill V. Mullen and Cathryn Watson, eds., *W.E.B. Du Bois on Asia: Crossing the World Color Line* (Jackson: University Press of Mississippi, 2005), vii.
5 Eric D. Weitz, "From the Vienna to the Paris System: International Politics and the Entangled Histories of Human Rights, Forced Deportations, and Civilizing Missions," *American Historical Review* 113:5 (2008): 1313.
6 Lenin, *Collected Works*, vol. 20 (Moscow: Progress Publishers, 1972), 393–454.
7 Quoted in Michele Luoro, "Comrades against Imperialism: Nehru, India and the Interwar Origins of Bandung," unpublished essay, 5.
8 Quoted in Mark Mazower, *Governing the World* (New York: Penguin, 2012).
9 Stephen Kotkin, *Magnetic Mountain: Stalinism as Civilization* (Berkeley, CA: The University of California Press, 1995), p. 363.
10 Wendell Winkie, *Prefaces to Peace: A Symposium* (New York: Simon and Schuster, 1943).
11 Paul Kramer, "Power and Connection: Imperial Histories of the United States in the World," *American Historical Review* 116:5 (December 2011): 1348–91.
12 Quoted in Mazower, *Governing*, 250–51.
13 Quoted in Wm. Roger Louis, *Imperialism at Bay* (Oxford: Oxford University Press, 1977), 499.
14 Frederick Cooper, *Decolonization and African Society* (Cambridge: Cambridge University Press, 1996), 18.
15 Mazower, *Governing*, 251.
16 Nehru, *The Discovery of India* (Calcutta: Oxford University Press, 1946) 41–2.
17 K.M. Munshi, *Our Greatest Need and Other Addresses* (Bombay: Hindustani Cellulose and Paper Co., 1958), 214–16.
18 Quoted in Manu Bhagavan, "A New Hope: India, the United Nations, and the Making of the Universal Declaration of Human Rights," *Modern Asian Studies*, 44:2 (2010), 341–2.
19 Chen Jian, *Mao's China and the Cold War* (Chapel Hill, NC: University of North Carolina Press, 2001), 12.
20 Quoted in Mullen and Watson, eds., *W.E.B. Du Bois on Asia,* 190–5.
21 Carl Schmitt, *The Theory of the Partisan: A Commentary/Remark on the Concept of the Political* (Berlin: Duncker & Humblot, 1963), 41.
22 Francis Wilcox and Carl Marcy, *Proposals for Changes in the United Nations* (Washington, DC, 1955), 455.
23 See Nicholas Mansergh, ed., *Documents and Speeches on Commonwealth Affairs, 1952–1962* (London, 1963), 347–51.
24 "Declaration on the Granting of Independence to Colonial Countries and Peoples," adopted by U.N. General Assembly as resolution 1514 (XV) of 14 December 1960.
25 "Osagyefo at the United Nations," September 23, 1960, available at: http://www.nkrumah.net/un-1960/kn-at-un-1960-02.html, accessed October 28, 2012.
26 Alex Quaison-Sackey, *African Unbound: Reflections of an African Statesman* (New York: Praeger, 1963), 37.

27 Frederick Cooper, "Nationalism and Labor Movements in Postwar French Africa," in Frederick Cooper and Ann Stoler, *Tensions of Empire: Colonial Cultures in a Bourgeois World* (Berkeley, CA: The University of California Press, 1997), 428.
28 Harlan Cleveland, *The Third Try at World Order* (New York: University Press of America, 1977), 5.
29 Nick Cullather, *The Hungry World: America's Cold War Battle against Poverty in Asia* (Cambridge, MA: Harvard University Press, 2010), 4.
30 Cited in Wm. Roger Louis, "The Imperialism of Decolonization," *The Journal of Imperial and Commonwealth History* 22:3 (1994), 473.
31 Quoted in Charles Henry, *Ralph Bunche: Model Negro or American Other?* (New York: NYU Press, 1999), 68.
32 Francis Wilcox, "United States Policy in the United Nations," Wilcox and H. Field Haviland, Jr., eds., *United States and United Nations* (Baltimore, MD: Johns Hopkins University Press, 1961), 178.
33 Walter Rodney, *Walter Rodney Speaks: The Making of an African Intellectual* (Trenton, NJ: Africa Press, 1990), 68–9.
34 Immanuel Wallerstein, *Essential Wallerstein* (New York: New Press, 2000), 466.
35 Essays by Henry Kissinger, *Foreign Relations of the United States, 1969–1972: Volume 1* (Washington, DC, 2003), document 4.
36 Quoted in Jussi Hanhimaki, "An Elusive Grand Design," Frederik Logevall and Andrew Preston, eds., *Nixon in the World* (New York: Oxford University Press, 2008).

8
VIETNAM AND THE GLOBAL COLD WAR

Jessica M. Chapman

Nowhere did the concurrent phenomena of decolonization and the Cold War converge more fully than in Vietnam. The country's thirty-year struggle for independence, marked by wars with France (1945–54) and the United States (1965–73), was the culmination of a longer quest for liberation from French colonial rule that began decades earlier. Vietnam's anti-colonial leaders shared a common goal, but differed widely in how they aimed to achieve independence and how they envisioned post-colonial Vietnam. As they sought ideological inspiration and international support for their movements, what started as a debate between radicals and reformers in the 1910s morphed into a competition between communists and anti-communists by the 1950s. Spurned by American proponents of self-determination at Versailles in 1919, the revolutionary icon Ho Chi Minh turned to communists in China and the Soviet Union for support. His opponents, strongest in the southern part of the country, first looked to Japan for anti-colonial solidarity, then attempted to negotiate gradual independence from France, and ultimately turned to the United States for help resisting a communist take-over.

Following World War II, and especially after 1950, the struggle for Vietnam's 330,000 square miles of land along the South China Sea captured the attention of the United States, China, and the Soviet Union. Each of those Cold War superpowers perceived at one time or another that the success of their domestic and international programs hinged on their support for Vietnamese allies. Yet all three powers grossly overestimated their ability to influence those allies, and found their own foreign policy agendas altered radically by their involvement in a conflict over which their massive aid programs bought them little control. Thus the collision that took place in Vietnam between two historical processes that largely defined the second half of the twentieth century – decolonization and the Cold War – altered the course of both, not just in Vietnam but around the globe. The Vietnam War contributed significantly to the Sino-Soviet Split, dramatically altered both Soviet and American policies towards the decolonizing world, and inspired revolutionaries the world over to follow the Vietnamese model for national liberation.

Recent scholarship on the Vietnam Wars has internationalized, enabling us to better understand it as both a national conflict and a crucible of the global Cold War. A small but growing number of historians have delved into Vietnamese archives, generating more nuanced views of the Vietnamese political milieu in which the French, Americans, Chinese, and Soviets intervened. Others have taken advantage of post-Cold War archival openings around the world to develop a fuller, more complex understanding of the international context in which Vietnam's wars unfolded. This chapter will discuss Vietnam's thirty-year struggle for independence and unification, and the legacies that struggle produced, in light of these new historiographical trends.

Historians and the Vietnam Wars

During America's war in Vietnam and in the decades immediately thereafter, historians divided roughly into two camps. The majority of scholars, who are often labeled orthodox, condemn the war as illegal, immoral, and so misguided that the United States was more or less destined to lose. So-called revisionists defend the moral purpose of the war, which they tend to describe as a noble and necessary battle to resist communist aggression, to stand by an ally, and to preserve geopolitical order. Many revisionists claim that the war was winnable, but that some combination of flawed strategy and a breakdown of support from the media and the American public led to a tragic defeat. As this interpretive divide emerged in the 1960s, 1970s, and 1980s, scholarship on the Vietnam War was based overwhelmingly on American sources and focused on questions pertaining to American policies and Americans' experiences.[1]

In the early 1990s, as the Cold War ended, archives across the communist and non-communist worlds began to open their doors and allow researchers access to documents that shed light on the international context of Vietnam's wars for independence. Historians made pilgrimages to the archives of key players like China, the Soviet Union, Poland, France, and Vietnam. Their efforts have produced a new wave of international histories that have begun to explain critical elements of the conflict that, until recently, were shrouded in mystery or simply unexplored. These new works take up such questions as the process by which the United States was persuaded that the First Indochina War was a critical Cold War conflict; the complex nature of Washington's relationship with Ngo Dinh Diem of South Vietnam; the centrality of concerns about international credibility to Lyndon Johnson's decision to Americanize the war in 1965; and the effects of the Sino-Soviet Split and Richard Nixon's "triangular diplomacy" on the Paris peace negotiations and the resulting accords signed in January 1973. While traces of orthodoxy and revisionism are not entirely absent from this new literature, the questions that animate it tend to be less narrowly focused on how the United States lost the war and more broadly devoted to understanding the forces that shaped the conflict from all sides.

The French War

A number of themes have emerged from recent studies of Vietnamese anti-colonial movements and the broader international system that surrounded World War II, Vietnam's August Revolution of 1945, and the French War that followed. The first of these themes is that Vietnamese anti-colonialists, far from being united behind Ho Chi Minh and the Viet Minh, hotly contested Vietnam's post-colonial future. Non-communist nationalists in the southern part of the country, where communism had never taken firm hold, resisted Viet Minh efforts to consolidate power in the two years after the August Revolution. That resistance developed into a low-grade civil war, upon which French forces capitalized to entrench themselves in the southern half of the country. A second theme addresses the process by which France, with some help from Britain, worked to convince the United States to aid its battle against the Viet Minh by casting it as a critical Cold War struggle against communist expansion. The third theme is that from the earliest days of their alliance, China and the Soviet Union exhibited very different, and often conflicting, attitudes towards revolution in the Third World. Nowhere was this more evident than in Vietnam, conflict over which would come to play a central role in the development of the Sino-Soviet Split.

World War II was a critical turning point for Vietnam's anti-colonial movements. Following Germany's devastating invasion of France in May 1940, Japanese troops took advantage of the severely weakened position of French colonial forces to occupy all of Indochina by the end of 1941. They allowed French authorities to retain control over quotidian affairs until March 1945, when Japan finally staged a coup to install Japanese troops in their stead. Some – especially non-communist nationalists in the south – sought to collaborate with the Japanese in an effort to liberate Asia from European imperialist control.[2] Others perceived that both France and Japan's days in Indochina were numbered, especially once the United States entered the war, and began preparations to seize the revolutionary moment.

By the war's end, the Viet Minh claimed a prime position to capitalize on the power vacuum left by retreating Japanese forces. In May 1941, buoyed by Franklin Roosevelt's pronouncements against colonialism and in support of self-determination, revolutionary leader Ho Chi Minh gathered the Central Committee of the Indochinese Communist Party in a cave near the Chinese border to create the new broad patriotic front.[3] The Viet Minh organization downplayed its communist affiliation in hopes of appealing to moderate and radical Vietnamese nationalists as well as Americans. In the wake of Japan's surrender, General Vo Nguyen Giap led Viet Minh forces in what would become known as the August Revolution.

On September 2, 1945, Ho declared independence for the newly established Democratic Republic of Vietnam (DRV), headquartered in Hanoi. Hoping to secure Washington's support, he quoted liberally from the U.S. Declaration of Independence. In the months that followed, the new government boasted of a smooth seizure of power and widespread, spontaneous support for Viet Minh leadership. However, those claims overlooked the disjointed, decentralized manner in which the Viet Minh attempted to capture control of much of the country. The new government exerted only tenuous authority in many locales. This was especially true in the south, where communism had never really taken root, due to a combination of heterodox regional characteristics and French crackdowns on revolutionary activity in the 1930s and early 1940s.[4]

From the outset, Ho's new government faced external challenges that compounded domestic obstacles to political consolidation. At the end of World War II, following an agreement among the allied powers, the British entered southern Vietnam and the Chinese marched into the north to disarm Japanese troops. Britain facilitated the quick return of the French army, thereby exacerbating Viet Minh troubles in the south, where the leaders faced dogged resistance from entrenched anti-colonial organizations including the Cao Dai, Hoa Hao, and Binh Xuyen.[5] Negotiations between France and the DRV over the future of southern Vietnam stalled by spring 1946. By the end of the year the two powers had descended into a war that would last nearly eight years.

Despite Washington's history of anti-colonial rhetoric, especially under Franklin D. Roosevelt, Harry Truman made it clear that the United States would not stand in the way of France's efforts to restore colonial rule. The U.S. remained officially neutral, neither sanctioning nor condemning France's actions, in the hope that it might earn French support for its European recovery programs without unduly alienating Asian nationalists. As the war ground to a stalemate by 1948, French leaders realized that they needed to draw support away from the DRV and court international backing, especially from Washington. Recent multinational research has shed light on the two-pronged strategy Paris pursued to achieve those ends.[6] First, French officials announced that they would no longer negotiate with Ho. Instead they installed the former emperor Bao Dai at the head of an alternative nationalist government in Saigon, the

State of Vietnam (SVN). By granting a modicum of independence to this new government, and promising to improve upon it down the line, France hoped to convince some non-communist Vietnamese nationalists to support the new government and, equally important, to persuade the United States to assist its ongoing war effort. Second, French officials recast the war not as a colonial conflict but as a Cold War struggle in which the battle against Ho and the Viet Minh was essential to the larger goal of preventing Soviet and Chinese communist expansion.

American officials resisted French entreaties until 1950, when a series of geopolitical events convinced them to abandon their officially neutral stance. Following on the heels of Mao Zedong and the Chinese Communist Party's victory in 1949, first China and then the Soviet Union recognized the DRV in January 1950. Truman's administration thus perceived that it had no choice but to recognize the SVN. The outbreak of war in Korea in June 1950 heightened American anxieties about communism in Asia and helped France to persuade Washington that its war against the Viet Minh was a crucial battle against Sino-Soviet expansion.[7] Ironically, Washington reached the conclusion that Indochina was critical to its Cold War strategy of containment just as France was growing war weary. Over the next four years, as Paris concluded that the conflict was not worth its financial or political cost, Washington increased economic support to France and pressured it to continue the fight.[8]

Just as French and American perspectives regarding the SVN differed, the Chinese and the Soviets also held divergent attitudes towards their Vietnamese allies. China eagerly supported the Viet Minh with aid, supplies, training, and diplomatic support, while the Soviet Union provided only reluctant diplomatic backing. Mao considered support for Ho a critical component of his larger effort to curb American influence in Southeast Asia and roll back Washington's containment of China. Thus, Beijing's support for Vietnam's revolution was intended to help secure China's role as the great promoter of anti-imperialist revolution in the Third World.[9] The Soviet Union, on the other hand, oriented its policy much more to the West, which made its leaders reluctant to support Vietnam's revolution. After Joseph Stalin's death in 1953 and Nikita Khrushchev's subsequent rise to power, the Soviets adopted a more conciliatory policy towards the West, further dampening Moscow's enthusiasm for the revolution in Vietnam.[10]

In spring 1954, Viet Minh forces overwhelmed the French at the Battle of Dien Bien Phu on the eve of an international conference in Geneva. In the ensuing negotiations, both Moscow and Beijing encouraged DRV leaders to accept a settlement that privileged Cold War geopolitics over Viet Minh success on the battlefield.

Vietnam Divided

The Geneva Accords, signed on July 21, 1954, divided Vietnam at the seventeenth parallel, leaving Ho and the DRV in control of the North and newly appointed SVN Prime Minister Ngo Dinh Diem at the helm in the South. The ceasefire agreement also established a demilitarized zone and provided a window of time for French-led forces to regroup to the South and Viet Minh forces to withdraw to the North. Countrywide reunification elections were to be held two years thence.

The terms of the ceasefire represented a compromise that deprived the DRV of the full fruits of its military victories. China and the Soviet Union pressed North Vietnam to accept national division in order to avoid confrontation with the United States. The exhausted, war-weary DRV accepted the advice of its patrons, neither of which was willing to fund an indefinite continuation of armed struggle. Rather than regarding division as a defeat, Vietnam

Workers' Party (VWP) leaders viewed it as another step along the path to revolution. Indeed, multi-archival studies published in the last two decades point to strong efforts by both the SVN and the DRV in the aftermath of Geneva to discredit each other and establish themselves as the legitimate government of Vietnam in its entirety. The United States proved a reliable partner for Diem's anti-communist project while China and, to a much lesser extent, the Soviet Union backed Ho's patient bid to unify Vietnam under socialism.

Recent research reveals that VWP leaders in Hanoi initially accepted the Geneva agreement and expected that abiding by its provisions would facilitate peaceful reunification and promote the development of socialism in Vietnam.[11] From the outset, however, "stay behind" revolutionary forces in the South suspected that the American-backed Diem administration was determined to flout the agreement. Over the next few years, Hanoi focused on socialist development in the North while encouraging southern cadres to restrict themselves to peaceful political activity. This would soon lead to disquiet amongst southern revolutionaries, who suffered under an ever more oppressive and terroristic Saigon government.[12]

Southern revolutionaries' suspicions were correct. Washington had joined Diem in refusing to sign the Geneva agreement. By the end of the French War, Eisenhower's administration believed that a non-communist government in South Vietnam was critical to American national security. U.S. officials viewed Ho's government as an extension of Chinese and Soviet power, and feared that South Vietnam's collapse would subject the neighboring states of Laos, Cambodia, and more importantly Malaya, Thailand, and Indonesia, to revolutionary forces that could topple them all into the communist camp like a row of dominoes.[13] Such an eventuality would isolate Japan and leave it without viable regional trading partners. These fears continued to drive American policy towards Vietnam throughout the Eisenhower and Kennedy administrations.

Thus, despite serious misgivings about Diem's leadership abilities, the United States supported him as the best – in Washington's view the only – nationalist figure capable of keeping South Vietnam non-communist. Some have suggested that Americans' preconceptions about religion and race factored heavily into Washington's dogged support for Diem, a Westernized Catholic with whom many powerful religious and political leaders in the United States had grown comfortable during his sojourn to the American northeast in the early 1950s.[14] During his first year, Diem faced challenges from three powerful organizations – the Cao Dai, Hoa Hao, and Binh Xuyen – which controlled roughly one-third of the territory and population of the South. Those groups found support from national army General Nguyen Van Hinh, chief-of-state Bao Dai, and the French, who expressed serious misgivings about Diem's ability to lead even before he was appointed.

Diem remained committed to leading South Vietnam in an anti-communist "national revolution" based in the arcane philosophy of Personalism – a middle way between democratic capitalism and communism that has been a topic of much discussion in recent literature on South Vietnam's First Republic.[15] His vision of a Personalist state included uncontested authority concentrated in the hands of a moral sovereign. To that end, he appointed cabinet members from among his family and closest associates. He displayed favoritism towards Catholics, many of whom fled from North to South after the ceasefire, leading many Buddhist southerners to regard them as outsiders.[16] Rather than follow American advice that he include representatives from powerful non-communist opposition groups, he set out to divide and conquer his challengers.

Diem faced the first threat of a coup in September 1954, when the "big three" politico-religious organizations joined with Nguyen Van Hinh to demand that he broaden his cabinet. That coup attempt quickly dissolved, but many of the same entities came together in March 1955 to pose a much more serious threat to the Saigon government. The ensuing two-month standoff, known as the "sect crisis," nearly convinced the United States to give in to French pleas that it declare the "Diem experiment" a failure and replace the prime minister with a more viable coalition government. However, government forces surprised everyone by rallying to Diem's side, soundly defeating rebel troops. This reaffirmed Eisenhower's support for Diem, whom many Americans would thenceforth regard as a "Miracle Man" for consolidating control in South Vietnam against such stark odds.[17]

Americans emerged from the sect crisis wedded to a policy of support for Diem as the greatest hope for spreading democracy and blocking communism in South Vietnam. Thereafter, the U.S. committed itself to working with Diem on a nation-building program. Between 1955 and 1961, Washington funneled over $1.5 billion in economic and $500 million in military aid into the South.[18] Yet, even as Diem accepted this massive infusion of aid and advisory support, he pursued his own nation-building vision that often conflicted with that of his American advisors. Moreover, he was determined to pursue independent policies – both domestic and foreign – to counter the perception that his government was a puppet of the United States.[19]

Diem consolidated his power rapidly following the sect crisis. By summer 1956 he had staged an election to depose Bao Dai as chief of state and to promote himself to president of a new, more permanent Republic of Vietnam (RVN). He used this as a pretext for evading reunification elections, a decision that the U.S. tacitly supported. He went on to draft a constitution and elect a national assembly, while his brother Ngo Dinh Nhu implemented programs designed to eliminate opposition to the government via intimidation, violence, and imprisonment.

For a time, these measures generated an illusion of control. Armed opposition to the RVN never disappeared, but the Ngo brothers created the appearance of order. In doing so they alienated much of the southern population and paved the way for renewed anti-government activity that would emerge by the decade's end. In 1959, the VWP finally responded to the pleas of embattled southern cadres and authorized the resumption of armed struggle in the South. And in December 1960 Hanoi oversaw the formation of the broad-based Front for the National Liberation of South Vietnam (NLF).

Saigon's early efforts to suppress the anti-government insurgency backfired to generate even greater, more widespread disaffection. In 1959 the Ngo brothers began relocating rural southerners to "Agrovilles," fortified villages designed to isolate villagers from Viet Cong infiltrators. In the process, however, they forcibly removed people from their ancestral homes and subjected them to harsh working conditions while failing to identify and exclude communist cadres, who took advantage of the situation to recruit for the NLF. At the same time, the Ngos passed Decree 10/59, which intensified their anti-terror program, subjecting anyone suspected of anti-government activity to arrest, imprisonment, torture, and sometimes death. In April 1960, to protest these unpopular measures, a group of non-communist politicians gathered in Saigon to issue the "Caravelle Manifesto," which harshly criticized the government and demanded reform.[20]

When John F. Kennedy (JFK) assumed the presidency in January 1961, he inherited the job of bolstering an increasingly precarious South Vietnam. As the crisis intensified, Kennedy authorized a huge expansion of support for Saigon. In spring 1961 he presided over an enlargement of the Army of the Republic of Vietnam (ARVN) and sent additional American advisors. American assistance to Saigon doubled between 1961 and 1962. Although JFK resisted sending American combat troops to aid the embattled ARVN, he increased the number of American advisors, many of whom found themselves in informal combat roles.

In 1962, it seemed as though this increase in American support was working to suppress the communist insurgency. Kennedy was so encouraged by news of progress in South Vietnam by July 1962 that he considered plans for a gradual withdrawal of American advisors, beginning in late 1963. Yet Kennedy's optimism was short lived.

The political and military situation in South Vietnam deteriorated as Hanoi stepped up its support for the insurgency. In January 1963, a stunning NLF victory over lackluster ARVN forces at Ap Bac revealed both South Vietnamese incompetence and communist determination to fight in the face of superior U.S. firepower. Shortly thereafter, a series of anti-government protests initiated by Buddhist leaders spread throughout the South. In mid-July, a Buddhist monk doused himself in gasoline and set himself on fire in protest of government repression – an act that several of his coreligionists followed in the coming days. The foreign press corps criticized the Ngos as out-of-touch tyrants. Nhu's wife compounded that negative perception immeasurably by flippantly referring to the self-immolations as "barbeques" and noting that she hoped to see more. Kennedy's administration implored Diem to fire his brother and soften his response to Buddhist protestors, to no avail. By the end of the summer, Washington's relationship with Saigon was damaged irreparably.

On November 1, 1963, with tacit support from the U.S., a cabal of ARVN generals launched a coup. The Ngo brothers escaped from the palace through underground tunnels and sought sanctuary in a church in Cholon, but were found several hours later in the back of an armored vehicle, dead from shots to the head. Many point to Washington's decision to sanction the coup, and to continue support for the succession of short-lived military governments that followed, as the point of no return that guaranteed American involvement in a larger war. Key decisions about how to respond to the growing crisis in South Vietnam would fall not to Kennedy, who himself succumbed to an assassin's bullet just three weeks later, but to his successor, Lyndon Johnson (LBJ).

In 1964 LBJ campaigned for re-election on the promise that he was "not about to send American boys 9 or 10,000 miles away from home to do what Asian boys ought to be doing for themselves."[21] Yet he would not let communism advance under his watch. Following an incident in the Tonkin Gulf in which two American naval ships were reportedly fired on by North Vietnamese torpedoes, LBJ secured from Congress the "Gulf of Tonkin Resolution" with a 98–2 vote in the Senate and a unanimous vote in the House. The resolution, which effectively stood as a substitute for the constitutionally mandated declaration of war, served as the platform for a massive escalation of war in the coming year.

Americanization and War

Johnson's decision to Americanize the war in early 1965 is often regarded as nearly inevitable. Many scholars have insisted that the logic of the Cold War locked him into escalating the conflict to make good on American commitments initiated by Eisenhower in 1954 and deepened under Kennedy. Some argue that war in Vietnam was in fact critical to American national security – a "necessary war" – while most insist that Vietnam was of little strategic importance, but that the U.S. public and its government were largely blinded to that fact by a pervasive "Cold War Consensus."[22] According to this view, LBJ perceived that Washington was morally bound to defend South Vietnam, and needed to do so in order to prevent a loss of credibility amongst allies. American officials feared that the implications of inaction in Vietnam could extend far beyond falling dominoes in Southeast Asia, to cripple Washington's entire Cold War alliance structure. At the very least, many claim, LBJ believed that he could not withdraw without provoking a domestic political backlash that would hand Republicans the tools to defeat his beloved Great Society legislation.

Fredrik Logevall has advanced a compelling case that no "Cold War Consensus" existed amongst the American public. Instead, domestic politics in the year prior to Johnson's decision for war was fluid, with many influential members of government and the press arguing against escalation, and very few eager for a fight. Moreover, the United States was largely isolated in the international community by 1964. American credibility was hardly contingent upon its willingness to fight a war that almost all of its allies warned against. Instead, LBJ and his coterie of advisors inherited from JFK – most notably Secretary of State Dean Rusk, Secretary of Defense Robert McNamara, and National Security Advisor McGeorge Bundy – chose war due to a rigid way of thinking that prevented them from planning for negotiation and withdrawal. In the end, Logevall argues, Johnson and his advisors escalated the war to preserve the credibility of the United States, the Democratic Party, and, most importantly, themselves.[23]

Whatever LBJ's motivations were for escalating the war, his moves put pressure on China and the Soviet Union to step up and defend their embattled North Vietnamese ally. The imperative to wade into the Vietnam War exacerbated existing ideological divisions between the two communist powers, straining their fragile alliance.[24] Those ideological divisions revolved around China's determination to promote wars of national liberation throughout the Third World, which conflicted with the Soviets' desire to pursue peaceful coexistence with the West. Moscow was loath to sacrifice improved relations with the United States, but neither was it willing to relinquish its position as the leader of the communist world. China had long been Hanoi's staunchest ally, providing the DRV with military aid and advisory support dating back to 1949, and even as Beijing withheld direct military assistance to Hanoi between 1954 and 1960, it continued to send massive amounts of aid. By 1964, in anticipation of a major war involving the United States, China renewed its commitment to provide Hanoi with military aid and advisors. Throughout the 1950s and 1960s, the Soviet Union was much more circumspect, offering smaller amounts of economic aid and "political support" to Ho's government. Moscow only reluctantly waded into the Vietnam conflict to prevent Beijing from seizing the revolutionary vanguard.

Despite its frustrations with Moscow, the DRV continued efforts to bridge the ideological Sino-Soviet dispute. Hanoi's three-pronged strategy of military, political, and diplomatic struggle prioritized efforts to secure support from China, the Soviet Union, and a host of smaller socialist countries. The Sino-Vietnamese alliance was clearly paramount in the early years of the American war, but the Soviet Union kept its hand in the game, especially following Khrushchev's fall from power in 1964. Thereafter, Moscow began significantly increasing military and political aid to Hanoi.[25]

Recent studies based on Vietnamese and Western sources have added a great deal to our understanding of Hanoi's diplomatic strategy. In the early years of its war with the United States, the DRV refused to negotiate lest it appear weak. The "war politburo" won out over a "peace faction" – a group within Hanoi's leadership that was skeptical of prospects for victory over the U.S. – and embraced Mao's thinking about the centrality of armed struggle to national liberation movements.[26] Rather than negotiate, DRV leaders resolved to fight for victory and focused their diplomatic energies on obtaining maximum assistance from communist allies and on influencing world opinion to gain support and isolate the United States internationally. Hanoi's leaders even sought to sway American public opinion, which they perceived to be especially malleable.[27] North Vietnamese officials hoped that by defeating the U.S. they could establish Vietnam as a model for revolutions across the Third World.

North Vietnam's reluctance to meet the United States at the negotiating table conflicted sharply with Moscow's determination to pursue peaceful coexistence with the West. While China sent significant aid and materiel to help North Vietnam liberate the South by force, the Soviet Union refused to endorse that quest. Moscow did send aid and equipment for Hanoi for the defense of the North, knowing that it would be used for the war in the South, but encouraged DRV leaders to open negotiations. Hanoi found Moscow's policy wishy-washy and two faced, but did not abandon its efforts to bridge the Sino-Soviet ideological divide.

As the war ground to a stalemate, Hanoi reconsidered all aspects of its strategy. Whereas the DRV had previously made the complete withdrawal of American forces a precondition for negotiations – a condition that it knew Washington would not meet – it indicated in early 1967 that it would negotiate if the U.S. unconditionally ceased bombing the North. That overture yielded no breakthrough and by the end of the year Hanoi decided it was necessary to win a quick and decisive victory to force the Americans to admit defeat. The result of that decision was the Tet Offensive, launched on January 30, 1968. Communist forces violated a holiday ceasefire agreement to strike a number of cities and towns across the South, overwhelming ARVN and U.S. defense capacity. They made short-term gains, but were quickly driven back and dealt a decisive defeat. The general uprising that DRV leaders hoped would sweep across the southern countryside never materialized. However, the offensive did serve the communists' political goal of widening the credibility gap between Washington's narrative of progress and what the American people were coming to perceive as a hopeless quagmire.

Negotiating a Peace

The aftermath of Tet occasioned strategic reconsiderations by all of the sides and led them to the conference table. Hanoi, Saigon, and Washington, no longer able to pursue total military victories, each had to devise approaches that took into account the military, political, and diplomatic aspects of fighting.[28] In the face of staggering military setbacks, VWP leaders perceived that the decisive victory they sought would be difficult to attain anytime soon. This was compounded by strains in North Vietnam's relations with China, occasioned by a combination of the waning status of the Cultural Revolution, the rapid deterioration of Sino-Soviet relations, and the resulting thaw in Beijing's approach to Washington.[29] Some historians point to the DRV's decision to open negotiations with the U.S. in May 1968 as a shift away from China and towards the Soviet Union. Indeed, such an alliance shift was in the offing, but Vietnamese leaders insisted that they pursued their own autonomous line and continued efforts to balance relations with Beijing and Moscow.

In the U.S., the hawkish Republican Richard Nixon replaced LBJ as president in 1969, amidst a public outcry against the war. He campaigned on promises of a secret plan to end the war, which appears to have involved increasing military and diplomatic pressure on Hanoi while generating the appearance of drawing down the American commitment. When he took office, he implemented a program of Vietnamization, by which he reduced American troop levels while turning over greater responsibility for fighting to the ARVN. He simultaneously stepped up pressure on the enemy by illegally widening the war to Cambodia and Laos, where he hoped that massive bombing campaigns and covert incursions would interrupt Hanoi's ability to send personnel and equipment to the South via the Ho Chi Minh trail.

On the diplomatic plane, Nixon set out to exploit Sino-Soviet discord in order to advance Washington's objectives in Vietnam through a program of "triangular diplomacy." In the late 1960s and early 1970s, Mao came to perceive a greater threat to China's security from its former Soviet ally than from its traditional foe in Washington. Nixon and his National Security Advisor, Henry Kissinger, hoped that by pursuing rapprochement with China and détente with the Soviet Union they could drive a deeper wedge between the two communist powers and compel them to pressure the DRV to accept American terms. Beijing's relationship with Hanoi rapidly deteriorated, which led to stronger ties between Moscow and Hanoi. Yet North Vietnamese officials doggedly resisted Soviet manipulation.

After Nixon assumed the presidency, it quickly became obvious to South Vietnamese president Nguyen Van Thieu that America's days in Vietnam were numbered. As the United

States improved its relations with China, its relationship with the government of South Vietnam deteriorated rapidly and Thieu became ever more fearful that American negotiators would stab him in the back by striking a secret deal with Hanoi. Given North Vietnam's resistance to Moscow and Beijing's pressure to meet American terms, it took Nixon's entire first term to reach an agreement with Hanoi. The Paris Agreement on Ending the War and Restoring Peace came only after one last series of devastating military escalations and diplomatic scuttling. North Vietnam launched a major offensive in spring 1972, which provoked an American reprisal in the form of sustained bombing of Hanoi and mining of North Vietnamese ports. Nixon and Kissinger thought they would be able to negotiate a peace settlement before the elections in November, but were thwarted by Thieu, who played the last card in his hand by refusing to comply with their demands. This was enough to cause a breakdown in peace talks, leading Washington to rain down one last barrage of bombs on the North in an attempt to secure the best possible terms in the next round of negotiations.

The Paris peace agreement, finally signed on January 27, 1973, ended American involvement in the war but did not bring peace to Vietnam.[30] The war would continue two more years, until Saigon fell. Even then, southern Vietnam operated under a reign of terror as the Hanoi government pursued policies designed to punish and "reeducate" those who had collaborated with the Saigon regime and to collectivize southern agriculture and enterprise. Furthermore, as Edwin Martini argues, the United States continued to wage a form of diplomatic and economic warfare on Vietnam for another quarter century, thereby impeding its postwar recovery efforts.[31]

Legacies

The Vietnam War generated profound and lasting legacies for much of the world. The unified Socialist Republic of Vietnam, established in 1976, struggled to make the transition from prosecuting war to establishing peace. Almost as soon as its own war ended, Hanoi found itself embroiled in a conflict with its Cambodian neighbor. Its intervention to remove the genocidal Khmer Rouge regime, which had been provoking Vietnam with a series of cross-border raids, inspired the pro-Khmer Rouge Chinese to invade Vietnam in 1979, avowedly to teach Hanoi a lesson. However, the lesson backfired, as Hanoi's forces quickly overwhelmed the invaders from the north. Over the next two decades, the United States and China both worked to isolate and ostracize Vietnam among the international community. Until the end of the Cold War, Vietnam was forced to operate in a restricted diplomatic universe, inclusive of only the Soviet Union and a handful of allies in the revolutionary Third World.

Vietnam's triumph over the United States and South Vietnam served as a great motivation for communist and leftist movements throughout the Third World. Hanoi's example demonstrated not only that it was possible to stand up to the U.S. military behemoth, but that smaller revolutionary movements could maneuver between China and the Soviet Union to do so on their own terms. Although Vietnamese revolutionaries tended to inspire, rather than directly support foreign movements, their victory led to an immediate upsurge of like-minded revolutionary activity in Malaysia, Thailand, and the Philippines. And as the main stage of decolonization moved to Africa in the 1970s, many African revolutionaries claimed to follow the example set by their Vietnamese comrades. Even in Europe and the United States, Vietnam's revolutionary triumph helped to shape the influential New Left movement, which set out to redress the domestic and international inequities embodied by the European colonial order.[32]

The outcome of the Vietnam War also exerted profound influence over both Washington and Moscow's strategies towards the Third World. The United States emerged from the conflict beset with what some call the "Vietnam Syndrome," having taken from its defeat at the hands of Vietnamese guerillas the lesson that it should avoid direct military interventions for fear of another quagmire. Instead, Washington placed a higher priority on influencing global affairs through economic aid, modernization programs, and a new emphasis on human rights.

The Soviet Union, on the other hand, read the Vietnamese communist victory as a sign that the triumph of socialist revolution was nigh the world over. It stepped up its efforts to assist revolutionary movements in Africa and the Middle East. While Moscow continued to pursue détente, it was determined to do whatever was in its power to protect and advance socialist revolutions abroad.[33] Moscow was determined to prove that the Soviet model was superior not only to American-style democratic capitalism, but also to the Chinese brand of communism. Some argue that the lessons of the Vietnam War, and subsequent victories in Ethiopia and Angola, led Moscow to war in Afghanistan and kept it embroiled there for a decade (1979–89). Its determination to aid Third World revolutionaries as a means of establishing legitimacy as a superpower ultimately contributed to the demise of the Soviet Union and the end of the Cold War.[34]

Notes

1. For more on the orthodox-revisionist divide, see Gary R. Hess, *Vietnam: Explaining America's Lost War* (Malden, MA: Blackwell Publishing, 2009).
2. Tran My-Van, "Japan and Vietnam's Caodaists: A Wartime Relationship (1939–45)," *Journal of Southeast Asian Studies* 27:1 (March 1996), 179–193; Vu Ngu Chieu, "The Other Side of the 1945 Vietnamese Revolution: The Empire of Viet-Nam (March–August 1945)," *The Journal of Asian Studies* 45:2 (February 1986), pp. 293–328; Ralph Smith, "The Japanese Period in Indochina and the Coup of 9 March 1945," *Journal of Southeast Asian Studies* 9:2 (September 1978), 268–301.
3. Mark Philip Bradley, *Imagining Vietnam and America: The Making of Postcolonial Vietnam, 1919–1950* (Chapel Hill, NC: The University of North Carolina Press, 2000). For more on Ho Chi Minh, see Pierre Brocheux and Claire Duiker, *Ho Chi Minh: A Biography* (Cambridge: Cambridge University Press, 2007); William J. Duiker, *Ho Chi Minh: A Life* (New York: Hyperion, 2001); Sophie Quinn-Judge, *Ho Chi Minh: The Missing Years 1919–1941* (Berkeley, CA: The University of California Press, 2003).
4. David Marr, *Vietnam 1945: The Quest for Power* (Berkeley, CA: The University of California Press, 1997), 402–471.
5. Shawn McHale, "Understanding the Fanatic Mind? The Việt Minh and Race Hatred in the First Indochina War (1945–1954)," *Journal of Vietnamese Studies* 4:3 (Fall 2009), 98–138; François Guillemot, "Autopsy of a Massacre: On a Political Purge in the Early Days of the Indochina War (Nam Bo 1947)," *European Journal of East Asian Studies* 9:2 (2010), 225–265; Christopher E. Goscha, "A 'Popular' Side of the Vietnamese Army: General Nguyen Binh and War in the South," in Christopher E. Goscha and Benoît de Tréglodé, eds., *Naissance d'un État-Parti: Le Viêt Nam depuis 1945* (Paris: Les Indes Savantes, 2004), 325–353.
6. See Mark Atwood Lawrence, *Assuming the Burden: Europe and the American Commitment to War in Vietnam* (Berkeley, CA: The University of California Press, 2005); Kathryn C. Statler, *Replacing France: The Origins of American Intervention in Vietnam* (Lexington, KY: University Press of Kentucky, 2007).
7. Marilyn B. Young, "'The Same Struggle for Liberty': Korea and Vietnam," in Mark Atwood Lawrence and Fredrik Logevall, eds., *The First Vietnam War: Colonial Conflict and Cold War Crisis* (Cambridge, MA: Harvard University Press, 2007), 196–214.
8. Laurent Cesari, "The Declining Value of Indochina: France and the Economics of Empire, 1950–1955," in Lawrence and Logevall, eds., *The First Indochina War*, 175–195.
9. Qiang Zhai, *China and the Vietnam Wars, 1950–1975* (Chapel Hill, NC: University of North Carolina Press, 2000), 3–4.
10. Ilya V. Gaiduk, *Confronting Vietnam: Soviet Policy Toward the Indochina Conflict, 1954–1963* (Stanford, CA: Stanford University Press, 2003), 11.

11 Pierre Asselin, "Choosing Peace: Hanoi and the Geneva Agreement on Vietnam, 1954–1955," *Journal of Cold War Studies* 9:2 (Spring 2007), 95–126.
12 See Robert K. Brigham, *Guerrilla Diplomacy: The NLF's Foreign Relations and the Viet Nam War* (Ithaca, NY: Cornell University Press, 1999); *War by Other Means: National Liberation and Revolution in VietNam 1954–60* (Sydney: Allen & Unwin, 1989). Le Duan, "The Path of the Revolution in the South" (Duong Loi Cach Mang Mien Nam) was a document of guiding principle for southern revolutionaries between 1956 and 1959. A copy of it was captured in 1957 and deposited with the Center for Research Libraries by Jeffrey Race as Race Document 1002.
13 "Sino-Soviet Direction and Nature of the Indochina Conflict", nd. White House Office, National Security Council Staff: Papers, 1948–1961, Box 37, OCB 091.Indo-China (File #1) (1) (November 1953–July 1954), DDEL.
14 Seth Jacobs, *America's Miracle Man in Vietnam: Ngo Dinh Diem, Religion, Race, and U.S. Intervention in Southeast Asia* (Durham, NC: Duke University Press, 2004).
15 Philip Catton, *Diem's Final Failure: Prelude to America's War in Vietnam* (Lawrence, KS: University Press of Kansas, 2002); Edward Garvey Miller, "Grand Designs: Vision, Power, and Nation Building in America's Alliance with Ngo Dinh Diem," Ph.D. dissertation, Harvard University, 2004; Edward Miller, "Vision, Power, and Agency: The Ascent of Ngo Dinh Diem, 1945–1954," *Journal of Southeast Asian Studies* 3:35 (October 2004), 433–458; Matthew B. Masur, "Hearts and Minds: Cultural Nation Building in South Vietnam, 1954–1963," Ph.D. dissertation, Ohio State University, 2004; Jessica M. Chapman, *Cauldron of Resistance: Ngo Dinh Diem, The United States, and 1950s Southern Vietnam* (Ithaca, NY: Cornell University Press, 2013).
16 For a nuanced reappraisal of Catholic refugees see Peter Hansen, "Bac Di Cu: Catholic refugees from the North of Vietnam, and Their Role in the Southern Republic, 1954–1959," *Journal of Vietnamese Studies* 4:3 (2009), 173–211.
17 Kathryn Statler, "The Diem Experiment: Franco-American Conflict over South Vietnam, July 1954–May 1955," *The Journal of American–East Asian Relations* 6:2–3 (Summer–Fall 1997), 145–173; Jessica M. Chapman, "The Sect Crisis of 1955 and the American Commitment to Ngo Dinh Diem," *Journal of Vietnamese Studies* 5:1 (Winter 2010), 37–85.
18 John Prados, *Vietnam: The History of an Unwinnable War, 1945–1975* (Lawrence, KS: the University Press of Kansas, 2009), 58.
19 Catton, *Diem's Final Failure*; Miller, "Grand Designs"; Miller, "Vision, Power, and Agency"; Masur, "Hearts and Minds." Some still insist that Diem was nothing more than a puppet of the U.S. See James M. Carter, *Inventing Vietnam: The United States and State Building, 1954–1968* (Cambridge: Cambridge University Press, 2008).
20 See "Report of the Office of the Secretary of Defense Vietnam Task Force," January 15, 1969, Part IV.A.5 Evolution of the War. Origins of the Insurgency, 19–20.
21 Lyndon B. Johnson, "Remarks in Memorial Hall, Akron University," October 21, 1964. Online by Gerhard Peters and John T. Woolley, *The American Presidency Project*. http://www.presidency.ucsb.edu/ws/?pid=26635.
22 Michael Lind, *Vietnam: The Necessary War: A Reinterpretation of America's Most Disastrous Military Conflict* (New York: Free Press, 1999); Mark Moyar, *Triumph Forsaken: The Vietnam War, 1954–1965* (New York: Cambridge University Press, 2006).
23 Fredrik Logevall, *Choosing War: The Lost Chance for Peace and the Escalation of War in Vietnam* (Berkeley, CA: The University of California Press, 1999); see also David Kaiser, *American Tragedy: Kennedy, Johnson, and the Origins of the Vietnam War* (Cambridge, MA: The Belknap Press of Harvard University Press, 2000); Howard Jones, *Death of a Generation: How the Assassinations of Diem and JFK Prolonged the Vietnam War* (Oxford: Oxford University Press, 2003).
24 Lorenz M. Lüthi, *The Sino-Soviet Split: Cold War in the Communist World* (Princeton, NJ: Princeton University Press, 2008).
25 Qiang Zhai, *China and the Vietnam Wars, 1950–1975* (Chapel Hill, NC: University of North Carolina Press, 2000).
26 Lien-Hang T. Nguyen, "The War Politburo: North Vietnam's Diplomatic and Political Road to the Tet Offensive" *The Journal of Vietnamese Studies* 1:1–2 (February–August 2006), 4–58.
27 Pierre Asselin, "'We Don't Want a Munich': Hanoi's Diplomatic Strategy, 1965–1968," *Diplomatic History* 36:3 (June 2012), 547–581
28 Lien-Hang T. Nguyen, "Cold War Contradictions: Toward an International History of the Second Indochina War, 1969–1973," in Mark Philip Bradley and Marilyn B. Young, eds., *Making Sense of t*

he Vietnam Wars: Local, National, and Transnational Perspectives (Oxford: Oxford University Press, 2008), 220.
29 Chen Jian, "China, the Vietnam War, and the Sino-American Rapprochement, 1968–1973," in Odd Arne Westad and Sophie Quinn Judge, eds., *The Third Indochina War: Conflict between China, Vietnam, and Cambodia, 1972–1979* (New York: Routledge, 2006), 33–64.
30 Lien-Hang T. Nguyen, *Hanoi's War: An International History of the War for Peace in Vietnam* (Chapel Hill, NC: University of North Carolina Press, 2012); Pierre Asselin, *A Bitter Peace: Washington, Hanoi, and the Making of the Paris Agreement* (Chapel Hill, NC: University of North Carolina Press, 2012).
31 Edwin A. Martini, *Invisible Enemies: The American War on Vietnam, 1975–2000* (Amherst, MA: University of Massachusetts Press, 2007).
32 Odd Arne Westad, *The Global Cold War: Third World Interventions and the Making of Our Times* (Cambridge: Cambridge University Press, 2007), 191.
33 Westad, *The Global Cold War*, 204.
34 Artemy M. Kalinovsky, *A Long Goodbye: The Soviet Withdrawal from Afghanistan* (Cambridge, MA: Harvard University Press, 2011).

9

MODERNIZATION AND DEVELOPMENT

Nathan J. Citino

In July 1962, delegates from more than thirty nations met in Cairo to attend the Conference on Questions of Economic Development. The participating countries included not only allies of the United States such as Saudi Arabia, but also communist Cuba, whose leader Fidel Castro had agreed only weeks earlier to install Soviet missiles on Cuban soil. The conference was led, however, by the non-aligned states India, Indonesia, Yugoslavia, and the host country of the United Arab Republic (UAR). In addressing the assembled delegates, UAR president Gamal 'Abd al-Nasser cited the desire of poor peoples around the world for economic development. "These peoples," Nasser declared, "are now firmly determined to compensate for the past and catch up with the future under circumstances of rapid progress."[1] Nasser's words evoke the universal concern with economic development during the Cold War, particularly in the decolonizing states of the "third world." His speech and its setting also point to some of the critical issues that historians have addressed in studying postwar development. By portraying development as "catch[ing] up with the future," the Egyptian leader proclaimed his faith in linear historical progress, a shibboleth among postwar officials and intellectuals who otherwise disagreed over how best to promote development. Indeed, members of Nasser's audience were sharply divided over how best to achieve the "rapid progress" of which he spoke. They differed over whether to pursue the liberal development model offered by the United States, to adopt one of the rival communist models promoted by the Soviet Union and the People's Republic of China, or to devise another, "third way" approach. Their decisions about which path to follow carried heavy implications in terms of securing their countries' economic futures and political independence. Given the global interest in the problem articulated by Nasser, historians have therefore focused on the ideas and conflicts surrounding development in an international system dominated by the superpower struggle.

Several factors helped to account for the global turn toward economic development after World War Two. Such a commitment was central to postwar internationalism and embedded within the institutions of the United Nations, including the World Bank, the World Health Organization, and the Food and Agriculture Organization.[2] In 1951, a group of UN-appointed experts published *Measures for the Economic Development of Under-Developed Countries*, establishing universal standards at a time when the focus of development efforts was shifting from rebuilding war-torn Europe to addressing poverty in Latin America, Asia, and Africa.[3] New techniques in economics concerned with measuring and growing national economies helped to create a shared conception of the underdevelopment problem internationally, just as the circulation of other forms of expertise would promote similar approaches on the issues of agricultural reform, public health, and population control. Most important, however, was the conjunction between the Cold War and decolonization, which created dozens of new countries across Asia and Africa by the 1960s. As historian Odd Arne Westad explains, in a conflict between two versions of western modernity, the superpowers battled "to prove the universal applicability of their ideologies, and the elites of the newly independent states proved fertile ground for their competition."[4] This competition led the United States, building on its experiences of reconstructing Western Europe and Japan, to increase its commitment to development. It began in 1949 with Harry Truman's Point Four program of technical assistance and over the next decade shifted away from an emphasis on trade and private investment and toward greater direct aid with "Food for Peace" and the Development Loan Fund. It climaxed in John F. Kennedy's proclamation of the 1960s as the "Development Decade," marked by the establishment of the Peace Corps and Agency for International Development. Drawing on the domestic precedents of the New Deal era, the U.S. promoted agrarian reform and commercial agriculture overseas.[5] In countries as varied as Turkey, the Philippines, and Argentina, the U.S. also encouraged import-substitution industrialization.[6] For its part, the Soviet Union held out to poor countries the potential for rapid industrialization under Marxism-Leninism. Even non-aligned nations such as India responded by accepting assistance to build steel works and other industrial projects. Moscow expanded its influence in the "third world" particularly after Soviet premier Nikita Khrushchev dispensed with Stalinist doctrine and pledged support for non-communist revolutionary movements.[7] By the 1960s, the Soviets were assisting not only communist allies outside of Eastern Europe, such as Cuba, but also non-communist states including Nasser's Egypt.

While the superpowers advanced competing claims about whose economic model was superior and represented the culmination of history, postcolonial elites such as Nasser, Ghanaian president Kwame Nkrumah, and Indian prime minister Jawaharlal Nehru based their political legitimacy on promises that they could lead their societies out of poverty and into a prosperous future. Attempting to make good on this claim, Nehru initiated India's first five-year plan in 1951 and set an example for other developing states.[8] In search of Cold War allies, the superpowers were driven to promote "third world" progress, while postcolonial leaders were compelled out of concern for their own authority to seek aid from one or both superpowers. This mutual dependence, however unequal were the relationships that resulted, ultimately accounts for the importance of development after World War Two. Reinterpreting the Cold War as a struggle for development means understanding postwar history as a series of conflicts over resources, power, and ideology within a global consensus about the need for rapid material and technological progress. "Widespread desire for higher levels of economic production, as well as conflicts over the path to higher production," writes historian David C. Engerman, "defined the shape of international relations in the Cold War as well as the experiences of those who lived through it."[9]

This chapter offers students of the Cold War a framework for approaching the growing body of scholarship about development, which has reached the sort of critical mass that permits debates over the nature of this subfield. Rather than provide a comprehensive survey, my aim is to identify major issues in that scholarship and to provide a critical perspective on its meaning for interpretations of the Cold War. I borrow my framework from historians' own critiques of the postwar development literature and of the set of ideas that U.S. officials in particular used to justify interventions in the "third world." Historians' critiques have focused on modernization theory, the Cold War social-science orthodoxy that they have associated with U.S. foreign policy disasters, including Kennedy's in Vietnam and Latin America. As distinguished from a general concern with development, modernization envisioned a linear process by which poor countries advanced along a universal path previously traveled by developed countries exemplified by the United States. The belief that U.S. aid could hasten this process and guide it in an anticommunist direction gave a self-serving rationale to American interventions. As part of this rationale, explains historian Michael Latham, Cold War intellectuals assumed that "'traditional' and 'modern' societies are separated by a sharp dichotomy."[10] In the way that historians have featured this dichotomy as the basis for their criticisms of modernization, my chapter explores the linked series of dichotomies that characterizes their work and that of other scholars who study development as an aspect of the Cold War. Just as historians themselves have done with respect to writings produced by Cold War intellectuals and policy makers, I consider the ideas and approaches inherent in the historical scholarship. While far more positive in my assessment of these historians than they are of Cold War modernizers, my conclusions nevertheless indicate how a focus on development can serve to challenge the prevailing globalist perspective that currently dominates the field of Cold War studies.

America or the World

Among the best analyses of Cold War development ideas are those that criticize modernization theory as a product of American liberalism. Nils Gilman has traced the genealogy of ideas about "third world" development to postwar claims about the "end of ideology," the elite theory of democracy, and consensus history. He describes the juncture of ideas and institutions personified by economist Walt Rostow, author of *The Stages of Economic Growth*, who led MIT's Center for International Studies before becoming a presidential advisor. Gilman ascribes anti-populism to modernization theorists and a determination to eliminate the social question from discussions of industrialization. These cold warriors projected an idealized account of the American past onto underdeveloped regions as an alternative to communism's formula for rapid development: "a high-concept version of Americanism" promising "materialism without class conflict" and "democracy without disobedience."[11] Other historians situate development within the American liberal tradition but employ a wider chronological frame than Gilman. Latham has described modernization in Kennedy's policies toward Vietnam and Latin America as evoking older American ideals of Manifest Destiny, while David Ekbladh emphasizes how the New Deal confronted rival fascist and communist development models overseas during the 1930s. For Ekbladh, the Tennessee Valley Authority (TVA) came to serve as a "grand synecdoche" during and after World War Two for an American approach that combined massive infrastructure projects, electrification, and agricultural reform while supposedly preserving grass-roots democracy. The TVA's regional planning inspired similar initiatives along the Jordan, Indus, and Mekong.[12] Jeremy Kuzmarov identifies the Progressive era as a different kind of "watershed" when the professionalization of law enforcement intersected with U.S. imperialism in the Philippines and elsewhere to establish police training as the basis for projecting American power.[13] Although they differ over whether modernization policies inherently prioritized stability over democracy or became anti-democratic in their implementation, historians acknowledge the authoritarian and counter-revolutionary effects of such policies in various "third world" settings.[14]

Historians' success in relating modernization to American liberalism means that they necessarily devote less attention to non-U.S. contexts and overestimate American influences on "third world" development. In particular, these perspectives neglect the continuities between western colonialism and postcolonial development, as well as the ways in which elites from underdeveloped countries appropriated the superpowers' economic strategies and formulated their own in order to achieve political ends. This neglect is relative and a question of emphasis. Historians of U.S. modernization initiatives acknowledge that those policies were rooted in Enlightenment values, as Soviet communism was. Latham also notes that postcolonial leaders such as Nkrumah and Nehru incorporated American aid into their political and economic agendas.[15] The historians' critique rests, however, on the contrast that they draw between U.S. support for authoritarian regimes on the one hand, and American democratic values on the other. In doing so, they follow the example of New Left scholars such as William Appleman Williams and Walter LaFeber, whose influence some acknowledge explicitly.[16] By featuring the American context, their approach is susceptible to the more general criticism that historians of U.S. foreign relations place their subject matter outside of global history and as a result portray the United States as playing a singular and exceptional role unlike that of the European powers.

The other half of the "America or the World" dichotomy comes from scholars who criticize development as a global discourse. Written mostly by non-historians, this literature subordinates the influence of both superpowers to an adaptable set of ideas and practices that governed relations between rich and poor countries during the twentieth century. Anthropologist Arturo Escobar opens his critical study with Truman's 1949 inaugural address announcing the Point Four program, which Truman envisioned as helping to achieve the "American dream of peace and abundance." But this dream "was not solely the creation of the United States," Escobar insists, and would be "universally embraced by those in power." Nor was development mainly a product of U.S. liberalism, as the period 1920–50 reflected an "overlap of colonial and developmentalist regimes of representation" with respect to the poor in Asia, Africa, and Latin America. Development shared with colonialism the "teleology" that "the 'natives' will sooner or later be reformed." For Escobar, the discourse served to empower "development professionals" such as administrators at the World Bank, an institution that "should be seen as an agent of economic and cultural imperialism at the service of the global elite."[17] Anthropologist James Ferguson's influential study of Lesotho similarly identifies a global cadre of specialists for whom development is a "machine for reinforcing and expanding the exercise of bureaucratic state power, which incidentally takes 'poverty' as its point of entry." Ultimately, Ferguson argues, by "reducing poverty to a technical problem," the machine has the effect of depoliticizing it.[18] The longest view is taken by Swiss scholar Gilbert Rist, who criticizes development not only as a "global phenomenon" but as one with deep roots in the western tradition extending back to Aristotle. Rist rejects the distinction between tradition and modernity, because "'development' is part of our modern religion" and "*modernity itself lies within a certain tradition.*" He traces development from Aristotle and Augustine through Darwin, Comte, and Marx. By the time of Truman's Point Four and the publication of Rostow's *Stages*, progress itself had for the West become an object of worship. Like Escobar, Rist sees continuities between the Cold War and the late colonial period, noting that it was Article 22 of the League of Nations Covenant that "*introduced the concept of 'stage of development'*" into international governance and justified supervision of underdeveloped states by developed ones.[19]

Such accounts are open to opposite criticisms from those faced by historians of modernization in U.S. Cold War strategy. They shift responsibility for the human outcomes of development policies from individuals to a disembodied discourse. They also have difficulty in drawing distinctions among the alternative development policies that competed for influence in the "third world." Rist unwittingly reinforces two of modernization theorists' principal claims, by equating development with westernization and by consecrating the United States as the culmination of western history. James C. Scott's *Seeing Like a State*, widely cited by historians of modernization, similarly illustrates the advantages and pitfalls of writing a global history of development. As his subject, Scott takes projects of "state-initiated social engineering," and particularly those he associates with "authoritarian high modernism." In instances when a powerful state succeeded in eliminating "local monopolies of information" and rendering society "legible," it could impose large-scale, utopian projects. These failed because, while possessing a schematic rationality, they were devoid of the practical, local knowledge by which societies actually function. Scott's ingenious argument allows him to combine a wide range of development initiatives in a single critique. Industrial-scale agricultural schemes including the Thomas Campbell farm in Montana, the late-colonial Gezira project in Sudan, and Khrushchev's "Virgin Lands" program all fall under this analysis. But Scott is also indiscriminate enough to include in his "Hall of Fame of Authoritarian High Modernism" the architect Le Corbusier, U.S. defense secretary Robert McNamara, the Shah of Iran, TVA administrator David Lilienthal, Bolshevik leader Vladimir Lenin, and Tanzanian president Julius Nyerere.[20] The dilemma between whether to focus on superpower policies toward "third world" development – and especially on Washington's policies – or on the protean idea of development itself reflects the challenge faced by historians in identifying the object of inquiry.

National or Transnational

A second dichotomy takes the form not of two distinct literatures but of a dialectic between the consolidation of national states and the transnational circulation of values and technologies. A number of historians have portrayed decolonization and the proliferation of nation-states as distinguishing the post-1945 international system from what came before. Mark T. Berger notes that the "key shift in the period" was "not just the growing significance of the idea of development *per se*, but the way in which it was consolidated and naturalised as specifically national development in the context of the establishment of the United Nations and the universalisation of the nation-state system in Asia, Africa and Oceania."[21] Matthew Connelly's *A Diplomatic Revolution* provides the best illustration of how the intersection between national states and international norms remade global politics. In the sense that colonial rulers understood the term, "modernization had become muddled in Algeria." Universal norms of rights and development, and the emergence of the United Nations as a supranational forum for defending these norms, delegitimized France's claims of sovereignty over Algeria and protests that its colonial war was an internal matter. Algeria's Front de Libération Nationale (FLN) won the "battle of New York" for global opinion, which proved more important to achieving national independence than the military struggle to control territory. This shift in the international system occurred in the context of the Cold War but ultimately transcended the superpower conflict.[22]

Some of the most original scholarship has examined the intersection of national state building and transnational development. This approach has overcome many of the disadvantages of focusing either on U.S. modernization theory or on development as a discourse. As Erez Manela has shown in his work about superpower cooperation within the World Health Organization, development was an aspect of the Cold War but was not subservient to it.[23] In his global history of population control, Connelly explains how a "transnational network of population experts took up where empires left off," even though it was Americans who "played a leading role in institutionalizing both the science of demography and the political strategy of family planning." He shows how population control scrambled conventional political alignments such that "communist and Catholic countries were arrayed opposite socialist and capitalist states."[24] Nick Cullather similarly examines Americans' role in agricultural development and the Green Revolution in Asia but notes that Asian leaders such as Nehru took up economic planning before Truman announced Point Four. Cullather also describes how "developmental politics pitted transnational coalitions of experts against each other."[25] Rather than criticize it as an amorphous discourse, these scholars assign direct responsibility for the ultimate consequences of development. Both Connelly and Cullather feature the leading role of the U.S. philanthropic organizations, the Rockefeller and Ford foundations, in defining development objectives and funding global campaigns. They describe respectively the effects of coercive sterilization programs, and the economic inequalities and environmental degradation that resulted from the Green Revolution. Such outcomes were the result of a convergence between the global activism of development experts and the political agendas of national leaders such as Indian prime minister Indira Gandhi and Philippine president Ferdinand Marcos. These authors indicate development's potential for destruction when the resources of non-governmental organizations were aligned with ambitions for rapid change on the part of postcolonial rulers.[26]

Although these scholars justifiably criticize their subjects' faith in technological progress regardless of the human costs, their emphasis on the concomitant universalization of the nation-state model and development expertise is not altogether novel. The significance of this convergence was well understood by postwar officials and intellectuals. In 1967, political scientist Dankwart A. Rustow explained in *A World of Nations* that "in Latin America, Asia, and Africa, nationhood and modernity have appeared as two facets of a single transformation."[27] As early as 1951, the U.S. State Department and other agencies sponsored a global conference on land reform that was described as "an experiment in international intellectual co-operation" that could "smooth the way for constructive programs of both the individual countries and by international agencies."[28] A more important criticism is that this literature frames development in a way that is geographically broad – indeed, global – but that is focused chronologically on the postwar period. Despite the pre-1945 historical background that Connelly offers on eugenics and that Cullather provides about the calorie, their analysis compares contemporary development initiatives and explores the transnational links between them. This approach minimizes the differences between states and the historical circumstances that shaped their struggles for independence. It cuts development programs off from their colonial antecedents in particular places and lends a self-fulfilling quality to the argument that the postwar international system represented something new.

Universalism or Essentialism

A third dichotomy concerns the nature of the academic expertise cultivated as part of the Cold War. This dichotomy corresponds to the distinction between international and area studies, which were focused respectively on the global processes of development and their unfolding within particular regional and cultural settings.[29] On the one hand, as Engerman has written about Russian studies, a "turn toward universalism" distinguished the postwar social sciences, whose "first step was to abandon history in favor of ideology" and next step was "to throw over ideology in favor of social structure." The structuralism of sociologist Talcott Parsons downplayed culture, and social scientists widely adopted Parsons' insights in portraying modernization as a singular, integrated process experienced by "third world" societies irrespective of their cultural differences.[30] On the other hand, older forms of expertise about particular civilizations, including familiarity with their languages and high culture, persisted into the Cold War period. In *Orientalism*, Edward Said traced the genealogy of the scholarly tradition of studying Islamic cultures to European imperialism. Orientalism took for granted that the West stood atop the civilizational hierarchy and ascribed inferior, essential characteristics to the Orient. After World War Two, Said argues, European Orientalism was inherited by the university social scientist based in the U.S., in whose hands that tradition "became scarcely recognizable."[31] The question of how fully postwar modernizers relinquished a belief in cultural essentialism is therefore linked to debates about how significant the continuities were between the era of European empires and that of the superpowers' struggle for the "third world."

Various scholars have observed how postwar area studies combined regional expertise with the new insights in social science while embracing the latter's universalism. In a book that anticipated much of the later scholarship on Cold War social science, Irene Gendzier wrote that "dominant interpretations of Middle East studies in the years since World War II in the United States" have adopted "the prevailing paradigms associated with Modernization and Development studies."[32] Berger makes a similar point about Asian studies: "The dominant narratives within Asian Studies between the 1940s and the 1970s emphasised the need for the various nation-states of Asia to develop gradually toward a relatively universal form of capitalist modernity." Berger relates Lucien Pye's scholarship on Southeast Asia, which de-emphasized distinct historical contexts, to Pye's involvement with the Social Science Research Council's Committee on Comparative Politics.[33] Anthropologist Heonik Kwan describes Orientalism as "an invented tradition" during the Cold War and notes how "bipolar politics" between the superpowers "transformed the old orientalist, essentialist differentiation between the Western and the non-Western world into a largely technical issue that could be resolved by political and economic interventions."[34] The Cold War made it imperative politically for the superpowers to portray their ideologies as universal. It was only in the aftermath of the Soviet Union's collapse that prevailing accounts of international politics could again invoke a "clash of civilizations."[35]

At the same time, however, the influence of older, philological scholarship persisted in postwar Middle East studies in a way that both contested and contributed to new approaches in the social sciences. "Orientalism and modernization theory divided up the world in different ways," Zachary Lockman explains, but the two disciplines shared assumptions about western superiority over non-western peoples. Although Orientalist scholars could portray "social scientists as undereducated dabblers overly inclined to grandiose theories" and social scientists could skewer "Orientalists as ivory-tower scholars preoccupied with their moldering texts," their collaboration on policy-relevant scholarship combined universalism with cultural essentialism.[36] Matthew F. Jacobs has described a network of Middle East experts in the U.S. that resorted to cultural arguments to explain Arab behavior. It came to include the philologists H.A.R. Gibb and Gustave von Grunebaum, as well as social scientists such as Daniel Lerner and Manfred Halpern. According to Jacobs, Halpern identified a spectrum of political alternatives in the Middle East and North Africa that complicated the modernizers' simple binary between tradition and modernity.[37] My work has argued that philologists such as Gibb gave social scientists textual access to the ideas of nineteenth-century Ottoman reformers, thereby introducing non-western influences into American ideas about modernization.[38] On the Soviet side, the universal doctrine of Marxism-Leninism co-existed with a strong Orientalist tradition cultivated at the U.S.S.R. Academy of Sciences. Alexei Vassiliev and Yevgeny Primakov embody the links within the Soviet system among journalism, Middle East studies, and policy making.[39] Scholars are therefore not only studying the relationship between knowledge and power in Cold War relations with the "third world" but are also debating the significance and provenance of area studies expertise.

Racism imposed a major qualification on U.S. promises to develop "third world" peoples according to a universal model.[40] Through their study of American popular culture, historians have criticized the cultural essentialism inherent in postwar depictions of East Asian societies. Seth Jacobs has shown how racist portrayals of Asians served to justify U.S. support for the authoritarian Catholic Ngo Dinh Diem as America's non-communist client in South Vietnam. Jacobs analyzes Henry Luce's *Life* magazine, James Mitchener's novels, William J. Lederer and Eugene Burdick's *The Ugly American*, and the doctor-priest Tom Dooley's dispatches to illustrate the racist logic inherent in America's modernizing vision for Asia. Citing Senator Mike Mansfield, one of Diem's early supporters who was touted as an East Asian expert, Jacobs indicates just how much overlap existed between racist depictions of Asians in popular culture and what passed for area expertise early in the Cold War.[41] Christina Klein's interpretation of the musical and film *The King and I* similarly focuses on the childlike depiction of the King of Siam, who required instruction from the white governess Anna in the same way that Asian peoples presumably required tutelage from Americans in the ways of modernity. *The King and I* was an example of the "narratives of anti-conquest" embraced by middlebrow intellectuals, according to Klein. Such narratives "repudiated imperialism as an acceptable model for East–West relations" and "legitimated U.S. expansion while denying its coercive or imperial nature."[42] Crucially, however, Klein's reading stresses that the play "had its roots in European imperial and American missionary history."[43] The real Anna Leonowens, on whom Rodgers and Hammerstein based the character, was an English woman who came from British India and who served as a tutor at the Siamese court in the 1860s. Klein addresses Americans' racism in their relations with the "third world" and argues that the U.S. adopted the colonial role of the European powers together with the attitude of cultural superiority used to justify that role. As in the debate over the relationship between international and area studies, scholars of Cold War culture have identified contradictions between universalism and essentialism in the ways that Americans perceived non-western peoples. These contradictions arose not only out of America's own history of Manifest Destiny and "uplifting" non-whites but also from the European colonial legacy that the U.S. inherited as it sought to develop Asia, Africa, and Latin America.

Global or Regional

A fourth dichotomy, one that arguably encompasses the three already discussed, involves the contrast between a global perspective on development as part of the Cold War and a regional perspective that analyzes continuities with various colonial pasts. Development takes on different historical meanings based on the temporal and spatial boundaries that scholars employ to frame it. Recent studies of development in a regional context have revealed the limits of the "global cold war" as an analytical framework and called into question the idea that the Cold War constituted a coherent global event. As Kwan writes, focusing on "locally specific historical realities and variant human experiences" undermines "the dominant image of the cold war as a single, encompassing geopolitical order."[44]

One strategy of regional analysis has been to examine how successive development regimes attempted over a century or more to remake a particular landscape or topography. In *Rule of Experts*, Timothy Mitchell studies policies for developing the Nile valley in a history that spans "the apex of British colonial power in the later decades of the nineteenth century, to the structural adjustment and financial stabilization programs of the [International Monetary Fund] at the close of the twentieth." Coercive programs to transform Egypt's people and territory were based on modern types of knowledge that assumed a "separation of the real world from its representations." While cadastral surveys and irrigation schemes may have served this purpose when Britain dominated the Nile valley, it was the concept of the "national economy" that did so during the mid-twentieth century. Mitchell provides a longer chronological and narrower spatial context than the global Cold War for Egypt's main postwar development project, the Aswan High Dam. He also pre-empts the Cold War narrative that associates development with the universalization of the nation-state system by pointing out that "the modern state that emerged in the lower Nile valley in the eighteenth and nineteenth centuries was not yet a national state" and was officially ruled by the Ottoman empire, even during the British occupation.[45] Unlike most literature on the Vietnam War, David Biggs' environmental study of the Mekong delta is "one of the first to consider continuities and overlaps between precolonial, colonial, and postcolonial eras of nation-building." Whereas Cullather focuses on the postwar American land-reform expert Wolf Ladejinsky, who worked in Japan, Korea, India, and Vietnam, Biggs argues that "American advisors such as Ladejinsky played more of a supporting role as enablers rather than as architects." Instead of adopting American ideas, South Vietnam's policies "borrowed heavily from older, colonial plans" attempted by the French "in the same troubled areas" of the Mekong. These were influenced by "former employees of government and colonial services" who "joined private consulting firms to undertake projects in postcolonial countries."[46]

Another strategy has examined how "third world" elites appropriated Cold War development formulas based on their societies' particular experiences with colonialism and anti-colonialism. Although Westad identifies the interaction between the superpowers and postcolonial elites as a universal theme, other scholarship analyzes development as a feature of distinct anti-colonial struggles. An example is Gregg Brazinsky's study of U.S.–South Korean relations in postwar state building. This episode was only the latest example of Koreans' "experience adapting foreign philosophies to their own needs and values." In particular, Koreans understood postwar development through the history of Japanese colonialism, and their "capacity to draw on their colonial experience meshed well with U.S. tolerance for autocracy" during the Cold War. By incorporating Confucian and Buddhist values, Korean intellectuals also hoped that these "traditions could infuse South Korea's modernization process with a moral dimension that was absent from Euro-American versions."[47] My work on the Arab world has examined how the competition among anti-colonial movements from early in the twentieth century, involving nationalists, communists, and Islamists, translated into multisided struggles over modernization in different Arab states after 1945.[48] Michael Mahoney describes a battle to define modernity between the Portuguese colonial state and the FRELIMO resistance in Mozambique: "in a context in which 'modernity' was such a widely shared value," the two "had to compete to become, so to speak, 'More modern than thou'."[49] Often, regional leaders' debates over adopting particular development models occurred *in extremis* while they were embroiled in wars of decolonization. Jesse Ferris has described how Egypt's policy of accepting aid from both the Soviets and the U.S. became subordinated to Nasser's disastrous intervention in Yemen.[50] Lien-Hang T. Nguyen portrays the North Vietnamese as facing the zero-sum question of whether to pursue national economic development or armed struggle in the South, at the same time that opting for an industrial or agricultural route to modernity meant alienating either China or the U.S.S.R.[51] Writing about the FLN's combined struggle against the French and for economic development, Jeffrey James Byrne concludes: "Algeria sought out its own path to modernity."[52]

Ironically, Cold War historians' recent shift in focus to "third world" development threatens to undermine the basic premise of Cold War studies: that global politics after 1945 constituted an international *system*. Despite the superpower competition among emerging countries, the patchwork of pre-colonial, colonial, and anti-colonial legacies amounted to an unsystematic historical diversity across the new nations of Asia, Africa, and Latin America. In this sense, global Cold War studies are subject to the very criticisms recently leveled against postwar modernization theory that "questions of culture and history tended to disappear" into an approach that "flattens history, elevating messy histories into a consistent project."[53] As Bradley Simpson notes, the modernization discourse had the effect of "wiping out the vastly different colonial experiences" in East Asia, such as those of Korea under the Japanese and Indonesia under the Dutch.[54] A similar fallacy characterizes accounts of the global Cold War that analyze assistance to "third world" countries mainly as aspects of the superpowers' grand strategies or in terms of the transnational circulation of expertise. Kwan rightly concludes that from the perspective of postcolonial societies "it is misleading to think of the cold war as a unitary historical reality."[55]

Yet, just as "tradition" and "modernity" represented a false dichotomy in describing such societies, so too are global and regional frames of reference complementary in analyzing development. With respect to the Cairo conference that began this chapter, Nasser sought to use his prestige within the Non-Aligned Movement to promote Arab Socialism, an economic program that was based partly on Josip Broz Tito's in Yugoslavia and that depended for its success on aid from both the U.S. and U.S.S.R. At the same time, Nasser's program must be understood in terms of the long competition within Egypt among Arab nationalism, communism, and Islamism as anti-colonial movements against British rule. In the postcolonial era, Nasser sought to win the contest for domestic legitimacy against the Muslim Brotherhood at a time when its most radical leader portrayed "Islam as a corporate entity in competition with other ideologies," reflecting "the sharply polarized categories of the Cold War."[56] So far, historians who study development have emphasized U.S. foreign policy and the superpowers' global strategic rivalry. The key to constructing richer accounts is to re-engage with the regional historiographies that were marginalized by international studies after 1945 and that have since been criticized as steeped in cultural essentialism and Orientalism. Though Cullather observes how research on modernization "puts the framework inside the frame" and "treats development *as* history," the latest trends seek to historicize development more fully and to explore the radically different meanings of the Cold War in particular places.[57]

A final dichotomy concerns whether development is past or present, whether humanity's faith in its ability to create the future is over. Development has "suffered the same fate as that of other messianisms," argues Rist. "End of sequence. End of game," he writes; "The lights that made the hope glow have gone out."[58] If development and modernization belonged to the era of nation building, the Cold War, and the universalization of the state system, then that era came to an end with the rise of neo-liberalism, the collapse of the Soviet Union, and the triumph of globalization. Yet those who study modernization theory hear echoes of Cold War ideology in America's twenty-first-century nation-building campaigns in Iraq and Afghanistan.[59] Studying modernization and development poses a series of dilemmas not only because these topics raise difficult questions about how to relate the Cold War to decolonization and even about the nature of progress itself. Doing so also requires that historians impose temporal and spatial boundaries on the most recent period of global history as a way of attempting to understand the world in which we live.

Notes

1 Nasser's speech attached to Brubeck to Bundy, 11 July 1962, UAR General 7/62–8/62, Box 168A, National Security File, John F. Kennedy Library, Boston, MA.
2 See Amy Sayward, *The Birth of Development: How the World Bank, Food and Agriculture Organization, and World Health Organization Changed the World, 1945–1965* (Kent, OH: Kent State University Press, 2006).

3 United Nations Department of Economic Affairs, *Measures for the Economic Development of Under-Developed Countries* (New York: UN Department of Economic Affairs, 1951).
4 Odd Arne Westad, *The Global Cold War: Third World Interventions and the Making of Our Times* (New York: Cambridge University Press, 2005), 4.
5 See Sarah T. Phillips, *This Land, This Nation: Conservation, Rural America, and the New Deal* (New York: Cambridge University Press, 2007), 242–283.
6 See Sylvia Maxfield and James H. Nolt, "Protectionism and the Internationalization of Capital: U.S. Sponsorship of Import Substitution Industrialization in the Philippines, Turkey and Argentina," *International Studies Quarterly* 34 (March 1990): 49–81.
7 See Christopher Andrew and Vasili Mitrokhin, *The World Was Going Our Way: The KGB and the Battle for the Third World* (New York: Basic Books, 2005), 5–9.
8 See Dennis Merrill, *Bread and the Ballot: The United States and India's Economic Development, 1947–1963* (Chapel Hill, NC: University of North Carolina Press, 1990), 81–84.
9 David C. Engerman, "The Romance of Economic Development and New Histories of the Cold War," *Diplomatic History* 28 (January 2004): 24.
10 Michael E. Latham, *Modernization as Ideology: American Social Science and 'Nation Building' in the Kennedy Era* (Chapel Hill, NC: University of North Carolina Press, 2000), 4. See also Michael Adas, *Dominance by Design: Technological Imperatives and America's Civilizing Mission* (Cambridge, MA: Harvard University Press, 2006), 242–46.
11 Nils Gilman, *Mandarins of the Future: Modernization Theory in Cold War America* (Baltimore, MD: Johns Hopkins University Press, 2004), 13. See W.W. Rostow, *The Stages of Economic Growth: A Non-Communist Manifesto* (Cambridge, England: Cambridge University Press, 1960).
12 David Ekbladh, *The Great American Mission: Modernization and the Construction of an American World Order* (Princeton, NJ: Princeton University Press, 2010), 8.
13 Jeremy Kuzmarov, *Modernizing Repression: Police Training and Nation-Building in the American Century* (Amherst, MA: University of Massachusetts Press, 2012).
14 Contrast Mark T. Berger, "Decolonisation, Modernisation and Nation-Building: Political Development Theory and the Appeal of Communism in Southeast Asia, 1945–1975," *Journal of Southeast Asian Studies* 34 (October 2003): 426, and Thomas C. Field, Jr., "Ideology as Strategy: Military-Led Modernization and the Origins of the Alliance for Progress in Bolivia," *Diplomatic History* 36 (January 2012): 153, with Gilman, *Mandarins of the Future*, 11, and Bradley R. Simpson, *Economists with Guns: Authoritarian Development and U.S.–Indonesian Relations, 1960–1968* (Stanford, CA: Stanford University Press, 2008), 31.
15 Michael E. Latham, *The Right Kind of Revolution: Modernization, Development, and U.S. Foreign Policy from the Cold War to the Present* (Ithaca, NY: Cornell University Press, 2011), 65–92.
16 See Latham, *Modernization as Ideology*, 14.
17 Arturo Escobar, *Encountering Development: The Making and Unmaking of the Third World* (Princeton, NJ: Princeton University Press, 1995), 4, 27, 53–54, 167.
18 James Ferguson, *The Anti-Politics Machine: 'Development', Depoliticization, and Bureaucratic Power in Lesotho* (New York: Cambridge University Press, 1990), 255, 256.
19 Gilbert Rist, *The History of Development: From Western Origins to Global Faith*, rev. ed., trans. Patrick Camiller (New York: Zed Books, 2002), 4, 21, 61 (original italics).
20 James C. Scott, *Seeing Like a State: How Certain Schemes to Improve the Human Condition Have Failed* (New Haven, CT: Yale University Press, 1998), 4, 78, 88.
21 Berger, "Decolonisation, Modernisation and Nation-Building," 422.
22 Matthew Connelly, *A Diplomatic Revolution: Algeria's Fight for Independence and the Origins of the Post-Cold War Era* (New York: Oxford University Press, 2002), 32.
23 Erez Manela, "A Pox on Your Narrative: Writing Disease Control into Cold War History," *Diplomatic History* 34 (April 2010): 299–323.
24 Matthew Connelly, *Fatal Misconception: The Struggle to Control World Population* (Cambridge, MA: Harvard University Press, 2008), 9, 10, 11.
25 Nick Cullather, *The Hungry World: America's Cold War Battle against Poverty in Asia* (Cambridge, MA: Harvard University Press, 2010), 6.
26 See Inderjeet Parmar, *Foundations of the American Century: The Ford, Carnegie, and Rockefeller Foundations in the Rise of American Power* (New York: Columbia University Press, 2012).
27 Dankwart A. Rustow, *A World of Nations: Problems of Political Modernization* (Washington, D.C.: The Brookings Institution, 1967), 2.

28 *Land Tenure*, ed. Kenneth Parsons, *et al.* (Madison, WI: University of Wisconsin Press, 1956), vi.
29 See Bruce Cumings, "Boundary Displacement: Area Studies and International Studies During and After the Cold War," in *Universities and Empire: Money and Politics in the Social Sciences during the Cold War*, ed. Christopher Simpson (New York: The New Press, 1998), 159–188.
30 David C. Engerman, *Modernization from the Other Shore: American Intellectuals and the Romance of Russian Development* (Cambridge, MA: Harvard University Press, 2003), 280.
31 Edward Said, *Orientalism* (New York: Vintage Books, 1978), 290.
32 Irene Gendzier, *Managing Political Change: Social Scientists and the Third World* (Boulder, CO: Westview, 1985), xi.
33 Berger, "Decolonisation, Modernisation and Nation-Building," 422.
34 Heonik Kwoan, *The Other Cold War* (New York: Columbia University Press, 2010), 79.
35 See Latham, *Right Kind of Revolution*, 192.
36 Zachary Lockman, *Contending Visions of the Middle East: The History and Politics of Orientalism* (New York: Cambridge University Press, 2004), 139.
37 Matthew F. Jacobs, *Imagining the Middle East: The Building of an American Foreign Policy, 1918–1967* (Chapel Hill, NC: University of North Carolina Press, 2011), 169–72.
38 Nathan J. Citino, "The Ottoman Legacy in Cold War Modernization," *International Journal of Middle East Studies*, 40 (November 2008): 579–597.
39 See Yevgeny Primakov, *Russia and the Arabs: Behind the Scenes in the Middle East from the Cold War to the Present*, trans. Paul Gould (New York: Basic Books, 2009), 39.
40 See Thomas Borstelmann, *The Cold War and the Color Line: American Race Relations in the Global Arena* (Cambridge, MA: Harvard University Press, 2001).
41 Seth Jacobs, *America's Miracle Man in Vietnam: Ngo Dinh Diem, Religion, Race, and U.S. Intervention in Southeast Asia* (Durham, NC: Duke University Press, 2004).
42 Christina Klein, *Cold War Orientalism: Asia in the Middlebrow Imagination, 1945–1961* (Berkeley, CA: University of California Press, 2003), 13.
43 Christina Klein, "Musicals and Modernization: Rodgers and Hammerstein's *The King and I*," in *Staging Growth: Modernization, Development, and the Global Cold War*, ed. David C. Engerman, *et al.* (Amherst, MA: University of Massachusetts Press, 2003), 133.
44 Kwan, *The Other Cold War*, 7.
45 Timothy Mitchell, *Rule of Experts: Egypt, Techno-Politics, Modernity* (Berkeley, CA: University of California Press, 2002), 6, 8, 12.
46 David Biggs, *Quagmire: Nation-Building and Nature in the Mekong Delta* (Seattle, WA: University of Washington Press, 2010), 10, 162, 170–171.
47 Gregg Brazinsky, *Nation Building in South Korea: Koreans, Americans, and the Making of a Democracy* (Chapel Hill, NC: University of North Carolina Press, 2007), 6, 7, 174.
48 Nathan J. Citino, "The 'Crush' of Ideologies: The United States, the Arab World, and Cold War Modernization," *Cold War History* 12 (February 2012): 89–110.
49 Michael Mahoney, "*Estado Novo, Homem Novo* (New State, New Man): Colonial and Anti-Colonial Development Ideologies in Mozambique, 1930–1977," in *Staging Growth*, 188. See also Daniel Speich, "The Kenyan Style of 'African Socialism': Developmental Knowledge Claims and the Explanatory Limits of the Cold War," *Diplomatic History*, 33 (June 2009): 449–466.
50 Jesse Ferris, *Nasser's Gamble: How Intervention in Yemen Caused the Six-Day War and the Decline of Egyptian Power* (Princeton, NJ: Princeton University Press, 2013).
51 Lien-Hang T. Nguyen, *Hanoi's War: An International History of the War for Peace in Vietnam* (Chapel Hill, NC: University of North Carolina Press, 2012).
52 Jeffrey James Byrne, "Our Own Special Brand of Socialism: Algeria and the Contest of Modernities in the 1960s," *Diplomatic History*, 33 (June 2009): 429.
53 Michael Latham, "Introduction: Modernization, International History, and the Cold War," in *Staging Growth*, 13; and Frederick Cooper, *Colonialism in Question: Theory, Knowledge, History* (Berkeley, CA: University of California Press, 2005), 117.
54 Simpson, *Economists with Guns*, 7.
55 Kwan, *The Other Cold War*, 121.
56 John Calvert, *Sayyid Qutb and the Origins of Radical Islamism* (New York: Columbia University Press, 2010), 162.

57 Nick Cullather, "Modernization Theory," in *Explaining the History of American Foreign Relations*, ed. Michael J. Hogan and Thomas G. Paterson, 2nd ed. (New York: Cambridge University Press, 2004), 214 (original italics).
58 Rist, *The History of Development*, 220.
59 See Latham, *Right Kind of Revolution*, 186–219.

PART IV

The Cold War in the Third World

10
THE COLD WAR IN LATIN AMERICA

Tanya Harmer

The history of the Cold War in Latin America is waiting to be written. Recent scholarship has led to new conceptualizations of it and generational distance has allowed for more measured analysis. Yet what the Cold War meant in a Latin American context or to Latin Americans is still relatively unclear. Scholarship is largely fragmented between different countries and time periods. There is little agreement about when the Cold War in the region began and ended, whether it was imposed or imported and precisely how it evolved over time. Some argue that the very concept of the Cold War is irrelevant in a Latin American context.[1] Others contend that the region's Cold War set something of a precedent for what happened elsewhere.[2] In short, we still have a lot to learn.

There are several reasons for this. Until recently, access to Cold War-related archives was scarce in Latin America. Scholars relied on US documents to narrate the hemisphere's twentieth-century history. This in turn led to US-focused histories that treated Latin Americans as passive victims or "puppets."[3] The United States' interventions in Guatemala (1954), Chile (1973) and Nicaragua (1980s) were the headlines but few examined what happened between crises. It was also unclear what was especially 'Cold War' about them, when compared to US interventionism in the nineteenth or twenty-first centuries.[4]

Latin America's distance from the Soviet Union is the second reason why historians have not written more about the Cold War in the region. True, Latin American communist parties followed the Comintern, maintained close relations with Moscow and sought the Soviet Union's support (we also have more to learn about these relationships). Yet, ties were limited by the lack of Soviet regional expertise until at least the mid-1950s and the fragmentation of left-wing parties as some diverged from Moscow's line.[5] When it came to supporting revolutionary processes, Soviet policy tended to be hesitant and cautious; Moscow's leaders were reactively supportive of revolutions that had already triumphed, not proactive promoters of revolution itself in Latin America.[6] As in the Third World overall, but more so, the asymmetry of power between the Soviet Union and the United States was therefore heavily weighted in the latter's favour.[7] Beyond the Cuban Missile Crisis in 1962, Latin America did not become a direct theatre of superpower conflict or tension in the same way as Europe or Korea. Until the Central American conflicts of the 1980s, there were also no major international wars in Latin America during the latter half of the twentieth century, like the Vietnam War, despite high levels of internal state-led repression.

Latin America is also often chronologically out of step with Cold War chronology. The region was not a priority for Washington or Moscow in the immediate post-war years. The most violent and ideological years of the Cold War in South America occurred precisely during détente in the late 1960s and 1970s. And although Central American crises coincided with the re-escalation of Cold War tensions in the late 1970s and 1980s, the decade of the 1980s was otherwise a period of gradual democratization and the rise of free market capitalism. By this point, South America's Marxist Left had mostly been defeated and marginalized for at least a decade.[8] Although it had a dramatic impact on Fidel Castro's Cuba and some in Latin America worried about the implications of unchecked US global power, the fall of the Berlin Wall was therefore rather irrelevant.[9]

Instead of trying to understand Latin America in terms of what was happening in other parts of the world, scholars are today focusing on determining what the Cold War meant to people across Latin America, how they experienced it and to what extent it changed their lives. As Leslie Bethell and Ian Roxborough have argued, historians need to find a "framework helpful in understanding the indigenous origins of Latin America's Cold War."[10]

The declassification of documents since the early 1990s has greatly helped in this regard. Thanks to human rights activists, investigative journalists, truth commissions and the search for justice by relatives of those killed or disappeared during the Southern Cone's "Dirty Wars", as well as accidental discoveries of police archives in Paraguay and Guatemala, historians now have a wealth of documents to work with.[11] Thirtieth anniversaries of the region's military coups at the beginning of the twenty-first century also fostered new academic interest in the recent past and led to associated funding for research, conferences and publications.[12] Moreover, new declassification procedures and access to Latin American diplomatic archives have opened up the parameters for research. True, in Brazil there was, until very recently, a reluctance to declassify top-level records, Argentina's diplomatic archives remain only partially open and Cuba's are firmly sealed. Still, historians interested in Latin American foreign relations overall now have many more sources to work with than they once did. Researchers also have growing access to party archives, institutional records, intelligence sources and private papers that enable them to examine local, transnational, social and cultural dynamics. For example, they are examining the experience of exiles and looking at party networks.[13] We also know more about autonomous intelligence agencies and regional cooperation – separate from CIA-initiated schemes – between them.[14] Finally, oral history projects, memoirs, testimonies and document collections have provided new sources for scholars to work with.[15] At one level, this has involved elite interviews such as those conducted by the Centro de Pesquisa e Documentação de História Contemporânea do Brasil at the Funação Getulio Vargas in Rio de Janeiro.[16] At another level, emphasis on oral history and published testimonies has centred on recovering memories "from below."[17]

Altogether, these developments have opened up the history of the Cold War in Latin America to unprecedented degrees. Scholars have been *able* to examine internal, regional and local levels of the conflict. And in doing so, they have found that Latin Americans were more often participants and protagonists of the Cold War than pawns or puppets. In some cases, regional leaders even fought ideological battles *more* forcefully than their superpower sponsors.[18] Many more Latin Americans had their lives changed as a direct result of struggles to determine the region's future.[19] This is not to say that external powers were not important. Integrating Latin American perspectives is also not to say that Latin American actors had overarching power. Instead, understanding the indigenous dynamics of the Cold War is about looking at what it amounted to *in* the region. It also means assessing the relevance of the "Cold War" as a useful term for historical analysis.

Definitions

In order to assess the relevance of the Cold War for Latin America, we need to agree what it was. In this respect, new Latin American-focused histories have pointed to four defining characteristics. First, the Cold War in Latin America was not cold.[20] It left hundreds of thousands dead, tortured or disappeared, forced millions into exile and yet millions more to change their way of life.[21] Although there was violence on all sides, more often than not it was the state that carried out the majority of this violence (the Guatemalan state's responsibility for 93 percent of deaths in over three decades of violence is an extreme, but by no means anomalous, example).[22]

Second, revolution and counter-revolution characterized the Cold War in Latin America. As Greg Grandin has put it, the region experienced "an epochal cycle of revolutionary upheavals and insurgencies" in the twentieth century.[23] Most revolutions were unsuccessful. They also had varying goals, means and outcomes. But in responding to particularities of capitalist modernity, unequal social and political structures and US intervention in Latin America, their efforts to transform or overturn the existing status quo shaped the twentieth century.

Third, scholars now studying the history of the Cold War in Latin America point to the international, multidimensional and transnational characteristics of the conflict. We have learned that crises and events in one country had an impact across the region, the overthrow of Jacobo Arbenz in 1954 and the Bay of Pigs being obvious examples.[24]

Fourth, the Cold War in Latin America is understood as having been underpinned by the United States' intervention in the region.[25] At the very least, its intervention in the region and hegemonic power is seen as a common denominator. As Grandin writes, "what most joined Latin America's insurgencies, revolutions, and counterrevolutions into an amalgamated and definable historical event was the shared structural position of subordination each nation in the region had to the United States."[26]

While these four features are undisputable characteristics of Latin America's twentieth-century history, the question here is whether they amount to a definition of the Cold War. Documenting the violence that plagued Latin America in the twentieth century is important, particularly for those involved. But does scholarship on violence, US interventionism or revolutionary upheavals relate to what the Cold War was and why or what it amounted to? Similarly, emphasizing multidimensional and transnational dynamics does not necessarily distinguish the Cold War from other periods of Latin American history either, with nineteenth-century independence wars springing to mind as the most obvious example of previous regional interconnectedness.

Indeed, recent histories of the Cold War in Latin America are still relatively ambiguous on definitions. In *Latin America's Cold War*, Hal Brands examines the foco theory, the National Security Doctrine *as well as* Latin American economic nationalism, dependency theory, third worldism and diplomatic challenges to the United States in the 1970s without narrowing down precisely what the Cold War was.[27] The thought-provoking chapters in Greg Grandin and Gilbert Joseph's edited volume, *A Century of Revolution*, also sow confusion. Together, Joseph suggests that they offer a way to reframe the Cold War in a "rather bold fashion. Here it is not a fight among proxies or post-Second World War superpowers," he explains, "but an attempt by the United States (and its local clients) to contain insurgencies that challenged post- (or neo-) colonial social formations predicated on dependent economies and class, ethnic, and gender equality."[28] However, the more all-encompassing these definitions of the Cold War become, the more they lack specificity and meaning. One begins to wonder whether *all* Latin American revolutions and nationalism were part of the Cold War. Likewise, if the Cold War was all about resistance to the United States and/or capitalism, did it not begin before the twentieth century and continue past it?

The problem of defining the Cold War in a Latin American context is of course that the term itself – the 'Cold War' – is a foreign concept to the region. When George Orwell coined it in 1945, it was to describe the growing tensions between the United States and the Soviet Union that stopped short of war and that he foresaw as being determined by the atomic bomb.[29] When George Kennan wrote his Long Telegram and when the Truman Doctrine was announced, Latin America was ignored. Latin Americans also did not explicitly see *La Guerra Fría* as a local or regional phenomenon, but rather tended to talk about its impact *on* Latin America and the ebbing and flowing of it around the world in the decades after World War II. So does the concept of the Cold War have any meaning for the region at all?

In a narrow definition of the Cold War as a superpower conflict, one could argue that its meaning is peripheral to Latin America. And yet, particularly since the collapse of the Soviet Union, ideas about what the Cold War meant and how historians understand it have evolved.[30] Reflecting access to sources in the 1990s, New Cold War Historians found that ideas, ideology and culture mattered a great deal more to how the Cold War played out than had previously been thought. As Westad has argued, at its core, the Cold War was ultimately a struggle between two different ideas of modernity – socialism and capitalism – that came to shape international, domestic and local affairs around the world; "a clash of ideas and cultures as much as a military and strategic conflict."[31]

New Cold War Historians also acknowledged that this ideologically driven conflict was not a one-way street; communism and capitalism were propagated most obviously by the US and the Soviet Union but were not fought uniquely by them. The struggle between those who believed in capitalist modernity and those who relied on Marxist critiques of capitalism as a guide for proposing alternatives – and there were many as opposed to *one* Marxist alternative – was complex, international and multidimensional.[32]

Pivotally, this complex ideological conflict was fought intensely in Latin America during the twentieth century as well. It may not have been cold, it may not have abided by the same chronology as it did in other parts of the world and it did not necessarily involve the direct participation of the United States and/or the Soviet Union. But ideological divides centering on a *specific* struggle between capitalism and Marxist-inspired socialism, broadly defined, profoundly shaped politics throughout the region for the majority of the twentieth century (and in some countries beyond). If we focus on this story rather than US–Soviet competition or *all* revolutions and nationalist resistance to US hegemony in the region, then the Cold War as a historical term of analysis becomes meaningful. I say historical term of analysis here because the label itself – "the Cold War" – is being appropriated from its original context for the purposes of examining an ideological conflict that otherwise has no name. One alternative would be to call it a "Regional Civil War." But this, again, clouds definitions as opposed to describing the conflict between capitalists and Marxist-inspired socialists that very concretely took place in Latin America during the twentieth century. For want of a better term, then, and because of its relationship to the same ideological struggle that bore its name in other parts of the globe, the Cold War seems the most appropriate label for historians to use.

If we accept this definition, it also gives us a framework for examining what happened in Latin America during the twentieth century. The violence, the revolutionary and counter-revolutionary cycles and the role of the United States are highly pertinent to this ideological struggle. However, not *all* of it was necessarily part of the Cold War. Instead, the specific challenge to capitalism from the Marxist Left is what is important. True, in many cases this challenge was wildly exaggerated or imagined in the eyes of those of feared it. But the way in which this challenge arose, how it was conceptualized, imagined and feared, and why it failed, should underpin the region's Cold War story.

Chronology

The Cold War in Latin America was never neatly confined or static. What it entailed – or, to be more precise, how ideological struggles between capitalism and Marxist-inspired alternatives (real or imagined) played out – depended to a large extent on where you were. Any regional chronological overview is therefore a simplification. However, an interesting feature of recent scholarship has been the overarching patterns between different countries that historians have uncovered. At least in the latter part of the twentieth century, when and how the Cold War moved between different phases of intensity was also often determined by events *in* the region and an *internal* Latin American, intra-regional logic that makes a broad outline of the conflict possible.

So how, when and why did this ideological conflict begin? To date, different definitions of the Cold War in Latin America have produced diverging interpretations.[33] If we take the above definition of the Cold War in Latin America, however, the beginning of it probably lies somewhere between the Mexican Revolution and World War II. The Mexican Revolution was undoubtedly a major social upheaval but it was not Marxist inspired in either its origins or outcome. Although Bethell and Roxborough persuasively argue that the mid-1940s embodied the widespread consolidation and institutionalization of Cold War language, norms and political struggles, ideological divisions within Latin America *already* existed when Latin America's democratic spring and its demise occurred in the immediate post-war years. These disputes may have been asymmetrical, and they may have ebbed and flowed, but they were nevertheless present and important to political developments in Argentina, Chile, Uruguay, Mexico, Cuba, Peru, El Salvador and Brazil during the interwar years.

Indeed, perhaps the easiest way to chart the beginning of the Cold War in Latin America is to look at the arrival of Marxist thought and opposition to it in the region. This new ideological struggle did not shatter a peaceful uncontested landscape. It superseded the era of nineteenth- and early twentieth-century civil wars between conservatism and liberalism, and codified existing complaints with positivist development.[34] The arrival of Marxist thought was also not something that happened overnight or uniformly across Latin America. As Sheldon B. Liss has written, "Marxism came to Latin America not as a mature and practical native doctrine but in piecemeal fashion as an ideology absorbed slowly by young workers and intellectuals."[35] This absorption responded, in part, to industrialization and export-led capitalist growth, their impact on labor movements and working conditions, and unequal socio-economic conditions, particularly in the Southern Cone. The arrival of European immigrants in the late nineteenth and early twentieth centuries also quite literally brought new ideas to the region, which provided explanations and frameworks for intellectuals and workers to interpret their reality. Among these, Marxism and Marxism-Leninism gave many Latin American intellectuals and labor movements a way in which to interpret their own situation and to propose specific alternatives to it. These groups may have modified Marxist theory to suit their own circumstances but they nevertheless used it as a starting point.

It was ultimately as a result of the Russian Revolution of 1917 that Marxist ideas became embedded in Latin American intellectual, political and labor circles. Prior to this, Luis Recabarren had founded the United Socialist Workers' Party. However, as one of its members would later recall, "People came from all camps ... We were not really Marxists. Marxism came ... after study, after reading the books from Europe, from international contacts, from the travels of our comrades, from the contact with the Communist International."[36] It was in the 1920s that a more explicit ideological challenge to the existing capitalist order in Latin America began to develop.[37] Communist parties affiliated to the Communist International were established in Argentina, Bolivia, Brazil, Chile, Mexico and Uruguay by 1922.[38] Influential Latin American interpretations of Marxist thought also appeared. José Carlos Mariátegui, for example, used Marxist theory to interpret Latin American and Peruvian society. Having been introduced to Marxism and Leninism whilst in exile in Europe between 1919 and 1923, he returned to Peru a self-proclaimed Marxist and admirer of the Russian Revolution. In arguing that Marxist thought had to be adapted to local conditions, Mariátegui nevertheless insisted that peasants had a role to play in the revolution and that, because Latin America was *already* part of an imperial capitalist system, strict historical determinism that held that colonial and neo-colonial countries – as Latin America was defined – had to first pass through a bourgeois-democratic revolution before passing on to socialism did not apply. For him, Latin America's revolution would have to be socialist from the outset if it was to bring about significant revolutionary change.[39]

As Marxism-Leninism – and regional interpretations of Marxist thought – grew in Latin America in the 1920s and 1930s, so, too, did anti-communism. As Joseph has argued, the region was home to "a domestic anti-Communism ... ingrained in the military, the Catholic hierarchy, and segments of the middle class – *independent* of U.S. prompting."[40] In Peru, for example, Augusto B. Leguía staged a coup in 1919, claiming that he wanted to "detain the advance of communism."[41] In Chile, landed elites, armed police and conservative governments repressed the Communist Party, labor unions and rural communities, partly under what Thomas Klubock has called "hyperbolic anticommunist hysteria." There was nothing particularly new about the violence; as Klubock has written, it had "roots in the violent colonization of Chile's southern frontier" stretching back decades. What *was* new, however, was the explicit association – real and exaggerated – between these struggles and communism.[42]

Interestingly, the radicalization and framing of political struggles in Cold War terms did not only occur in conflicts between the Left and Right, but framed disputes among left-wing groups and workers. In Peru, Haya de la Torre, founder of Peru's Alianza Popular Revolucionaria Americana (American Revolutionary Popular Alliance or APRA), came out in direct opposition to communism and Mariátegui in the late 1920s, despite being a staunch anti-imperialist and having been previously inspired by Marxism.[43] Meanwhile, the Partido Comunista Peruana (Peruvian Communist Party or PCP) found it hard to gain control of Peru's working-class movement as a result of the latter's rejection of political interference and fears that identification with the Party would bring repression. "Creole anti-communism," Drinot argues, was the "product of the political context in which the PCP and APRA competed to control labor, and, perhaps more importantly, of the ways in which labor attempted to shape, from below, its relationship with the merging political parties of the Left."[44]

At the same time as these ideological divisions were evolving *within* Latin America in the 1920s and 1930s, foreigners began interpreting Latin American politics through the prism of the Russian Revolution. In Washington, policy makers mistakenly regarded Plutarco Elías Calles' government in Mexico in the 1920s as "Bolshevist." True, successive US presidential administrations had been skeptical of revolutionary nationalists before this. What changed was the way in which events in the region were now codified. US officials also now referred to Augusto César Sandino's insurgency in Nicaragua as a Mexican conspiracy to spread Bolshevism to Central America.[45] It does not matter that these interpretations were wrong.[46] What matters is that in the late 1920s and early 1930s this is, at least partly, how his insurgency was perceived.

Ideological disputes that had arisen in Latin America during the 1920s and early 1930s diminished in the decade that followed. One reason was the Marxist Left's declining strength. Repression had weakened communist parties and workers' movements. Meanwhile, tensions between the Comintern and local communists and the power struggle between Stalin and

Trotsky had played out within Latin America to adverse effect. Stalin's triumph and the Comintern's subsequent emphasis on armed insurgency then led to significant setbacks for affiliated parties in Mexico, El Salvador and Brazil.[47] Meanwhile, Brazil's populist and corporatist leader, Getulio Vargas, co-opted the country's labor movement and brought it under the control of the state in a pattern that mirrored politics in Mexico and Argentina.

Another reason for the ebbing of Cold War tensions in Latin America during the late 1930s and the early 1940s was the international context. The Good Neighbor Policy, the outbreak of World War II and then the Soviet Union's entry into the war on the side of the Allies fostered a more collaborative, pluralistic political environment in Latin America. From 1941 onwards, communist and socialist parties forged alliances with the national bourgeoisie against fascism in accordance with the Comintern's Popular Front strategy and reduced their criticisms of the United States. In Argentina, this weakened the Marxist Left even further as the Communist Party distanced itself from its working-class base and allied with conservative elites and the United States against Juan Domingo Perón. But in Cuba, it brought the Communist Party into government and allowed it to influence policy.[48]

This relative thaw ended after World War II, when ideological conflicts that had begun in the 1920s and 1930s resurfaced and hardened. As Bethell and Roxborough have argued, there are "striking similarities" between what happened across the region.[49] Democratic openings closed, communist parties were banned, left-wing infighting re-appeared and anti-communists prospered. The creation of a post-war inter-American institutional framework comprising the Organization of American States (OAS) also ingrained anti-communist ideals into the hemisphere by 1948 as a result both of US goals and of Latin American governments' concerns.[50] If the beginning of the Cold War can be traced to the interwar period, therefore, the late 1940s and 1950s – what you might call the long 1950s – were years of consolidation and intensification.

Of course, these developments intersected with the formalization of the Cold War on a global scale. For much of this period, ideological disputes in Latin America remained peripheral for US and Soviet policy makers, who were concerned with Europe and Asia. But the very fact that the region was peripheral also had consequences for Latin America. For governments that had come to power and prospered during the years of the Good Neighbor Policy, the sense of abandonment was palpable. Washington rescinded earlier wartime promises of economic assistance to compensate for low commodity prices. Support for democracy declined and authoritarian regimes were praised for hunting down communists (both real and imagined). In line with NSC-68 and in the shadow of the Korean War, the Truman and Eisenhower administrations also took on the mantel of policing the world from Soviet and communist encroachments. From the mid-1950s on, they also began incorporating Latin America into this effort.[51]

Again, this is not to say that the United States imposed a Cold War paradigm. Rather, it is to underline that Washington encouraged and rewarded anti-communism. The overriding dependence of Latin American economies on US trade and aid made its influence particularly powerful. Prior to World War II, Latin American countries had important European trading partners, but bilateral ties with the United States dwarfed these thereafter. US military influence in the region simultaneously grew; by 1940, Washington had military missions in all Latin American countries, compared to only five in 1938. US military equipment, training programs and inter-American wartime forums for discussion between militaries from across the hemisphere also provided the foundations for future collaboration.[52] US cultural diplomacy also helped foster a new Cold War consciousness. Compared to propaganda efforts before, this offensive was not merely about promoting US values and co-operation, but specifically about fighting communism.[53] Within this context, the majority of Latin American governments quickly understood that anti-communism was needed to win Washington's favor even if they had their own reasons for pursuing communists themselves.

As democratic options were circumscribed and non-Marxist reformers were either replaced by right-wing leaders or failed to deliver on promises of development and sovereignty, Marxism and revolution, ironically, became more attractive.[54] Succeeding Guatemala's moderate president José Arévalo in 1951, Jacobo Arbenz was one of those who used Marx to interpret his country's predicament. Arbenz was not a communist and did not seek to transform Guatemala into a communist state. The country's communist party, the Partido Guatemalteco del Trabajo (Guatemalan Workers' Party or PGT), was also small and had weak relations with the USSR. Like other orthodox pro-Soviet communist parties throughout Latin America it also still believed that a two-stage revolution – national-bourgeois and *then* socialist – was necessary for Guatemala, which, as a semi-feudal country, had yet to reach a capitalist stage of development. Even so, Arbenz had read Marx and chose leading figures in the PGT as his closest advisors.[55] To him, there was nothing wrong with this. As the US ambassador in Guatemala recorded him as having explained, "there were some Communists in his Government ... but they were 'local'... [They] followed Guatemalan not Soviet interests. They went to Moscow ... merely to study Marxism, not necessarily to get instructions."[56] Arbenz's enemies in Guatemala, neighboring Central American countries and the United States disagreed. At the very least, they used Arbenz's relationship with the PGT to persuade the Eisenhower administration to act against him.[57]

Subsequently, the fallout in Latin America from the CIA-sponsored coup and overthrow of Arbenz in June 1954 was immense.[58] Frustration and anger led a new generation to seek alternatives to Arbenz-like reformers and traditional left-wing electoral strategies. The young Marxist Ernesto 'Che' Guevara, who had been in Guatemala during the coup, was furious at what he saw happen. As Guevara wrote to his mother, "Arbenz did not know how to rise to the occasion" and should have armed the people. Indeed, Guevara would increasingly advocate armed struggle as an essential component for any revolution and the only way to defend a revolutionary process. Having joined Fidel Castro's insurrection against Fulgencio Batista, this is certainly the advice he gave his new revolutionary companions; Cuba would not be Guatemala.[59]

It was not. Castro's successful insurgency against Batista and then its evolution into an explicitly socialist revolution by 1961 also marked the end of the long, constrained 1950s. While not initially Marxist inspired, the revolution developed its ideological character in the three years after its triumph. It is difficult to know precisely when Fidel Castro decided he was a Marxist. He had first become acquainted with Marxism-Leninism in the 1940s and had then read Marx, Lenin and Mariátegui in prison in the early 1950s.[60] However, there was considerable animosity between his 26th July Movement and Cuba's pro-Soviet Partido Socialista Popular (Popular Socialist Party or PSP), which had previously collaborated with Batista. It was only *after* the revolution triumphed that the PSP and individuals Union in the 26th July Movement who were influenced by Marxism and admirers of the Soviet Union, such as Guevara and Raul Castro, became influential in defining the character of the revolution.[61] As Louis Pérez has suggested, they were also encouraged and legitimized by popular grassroots pressure to accelerate the momentum of revolutionary change.[62] Aggressive US opposition to the revolution, the new Cuban leadership's search for alternative trading relationships and assistance, the PSP's existing ties with the Soviet Union and Moscow's willingness to provide support, gave impetus to the growing ideological character of the revolution.[63] This process culminated with Castro proclaiming the revolution to be socialist in April 1961 and declaring that he was a Marxist-Leninist later that year.[64]

With an explicitly socialist government in the Western Hemisphere aligned to the Soviet Union, a new, radicalized and intense phase of the Cold War in Latin America began. No longer was it merely non-state actors that championed Marxism in the region, but a popular revolutionary government. Crucially, Cuba also offered *direct* support to revolutionary groups in the region, training guerrilla groups in Cuba, extending covert and logistical support to insurgencies across Latin America and the Caribbean. Vowing to defeat US imperialism and capitalism, Castro publicly called on revolutionaries to "make revolution." In 1967, Cuba also published Che Guevara's message to the Tricontinental organization of Latin American, African and Asian revolutionaries, extolling the virtues of violent struggle and inciting them to create "two, three or many Vietnams" as a means of bringing the United States to its knees.[65]

Beyond concrete support for revolutionary insurgencies, the Cuban Revolution changed the character of the Cold War ideological struggle in Latin America by adding to the theory of revolution. A key idea was that Latin America could accelerate the process of revolution without having to first pass through stages of capitalist development and could create the conditions for revolution through armed struggle. In this respect, Cuba's brand of Marxism fused the thinking of Mariátegui, Guevara and others into a particularly unique ideology which, in turn, influenced a range of Latin Americans from democratic Marxist senators to armed guerrilla groups.[66] For Chilean socialists like Salvador Allende and Heraldo Muñoz it offered a *Latin American* alternative to the Soviet Union's model for revolution and an answer to alternative non-Marxist models of transformative nationalism.[67]

One of the implications of this new model, however, was that it undermined pro-Soviet communist parties' attachment to a gradual, two-phase revolutionary strategy in Latin America. In short, the Cuban Revolution proved to be what Gilbert Joseph has called "an important fulcrum in Latin America's century of revolution: the frustration and anger engendered by Latin America's failed democratic spring … produced a radicalization of the Left's political agenda in one nation after another."[68] Yet not all of Latin America's left wing radicalized to the same extent or in the same direction. The Cuban Revolution's example prompted growing heterodoxy, debate and division among those on the Marxist Left in a manner reminiscent of the tensions of the 1920s and 1930s over interpretations of theory and strategy. Indeed, the Cold War in the 1960s and 1970s was as much about ideological struggles on the Left, and the weaknesses that this fragmentation created, as it was a battle between capitalists and Marxist-inspired alternatives.

To be fair, fears whipped up about Cuba and the revolutionary groups that associated themselves with Havana, on the Marxist Left, the Center and the Right, tended to be grossly exaggerated. Cuba's influence over the region and Havana's power to shape developments in the Americas derived just as much – if not more so – from its enemies' imagination as from its own actions and sympathetic followers. Whether it was John F. Kennedy, the Dominican Republic's Joaquín Balaguer or Southern Cone military dictators, Cuba's enemies made Cuba more important than it otherwise would have been to inter-American politics.

At one level, their fears altered the political space that was available for nationalist reformers. It encouraged centrist parties to advocate reform and appropriate the notion of revolution as a means of undermining the Marxist Left.[69] Venezuela's Rómulo Betancourt and Chile's Christian Democrat president, Eduardo Frei, were prime examples of this tendency. However, there were limitations to what these non-Marxist reformers could achieve. On the Left, they were criticized for not going far enough. Meanwhile, conservative elites, right-wing parties and the military viewed them as communists, fellow travelers or naïve stop-gaps until communists took over. Indeed, fear of 'another Cuba' led to gross distortions in the way in which Brazil's president João Goulart or the Dominican Republic's reformist leader, Juan

Bosch, were perceived. Conceptualized by their enemies as communists, they were defeated and overthrown despite having ultimately chosen capitalism and not Marxist-inspired socialism as the model for their own countries.

These counter-revolutionary attacks on nationalist reformers in turn encouraged those that might otherwise have been hesitant to go to Havana in search of alternatives. One such leader was the Dominican Republic's Francisco Caamaño, a leader of the island's 1965 uprising aimed at restoring constitutional democracy. After the United States' invasion of the Dominican Republic, and seeing hopes of democratic reform quashed, Caamaño went to Cuba to begin military training for an invasion of the Dominican Republic.[70] That he failed to ignite revolution – and died – is only part of the story of the Cold War in Latin America. Beyond it is the Cuban Revolution's significance in changing the options and room for maneuver for Latin American politics.

Meanwhile, for regional military leaders and anti-communist elites, resistance to Cuba's influence was a preeminent concern. To be sure, the scale and scope of these fears changed, depending on specific circumstances. But, increasingly, hardline counter-revolutionaries lumped reformers and insurgents together under the idea of the National Security Doctrine. Originating in the 1940s and 1950s, this Doctrine had come to dominate military thinking across the region by the 1960s. Its adherents believed that security, particularly in the wake of the Cuban Revolution, depended on the military being ready to seize control from what they saw as inept civilian politicians and fight a total war against "subversives." By very broadly defining what a "subversive" was, the National Security Doctrine also inevitably blurred the line between combatants and civilians.[71] As one of its intellectual authors argued, there was "no longer a clear distinction between where peace ends and war begins." Argentina's General Videla's description of his enemies underlined this: "A terrorist is not just someone with a gun or a bomb," he argued, "but also someone who spreads ideas that are contrary to Western and Christian civilization [*sic*]."[72] Indeed, to protect this so-called "civilization," which was increasingly conceptualized in terms of conservative Catholic morality, Latin America's repressive dictatorial regimes engaged in terror and murder as a means of eradicating *ideas*.[73] Guerrilla movements existed and very concretely launched insurgencies, but their strength was hardly enough to topple these powerful regimes. Similarly, the Soviet Union was evoked as the mastermind *behind* these ideas but was largely absent from events on the ground. Meanwhile, a client–patron relationship persisted when it came to the relationships between these dictatorships and the United States, which had instilled the National Security Doctrine through military training and support.[74] But the regional actors also had their own ideas and priorities rather than having been plucked out of thin air and put in place by Washington.[75]

The first major counter-revolutionary victory and "game changer" in this regard was the Brazilian coup in 1964.[76] Predominantly home-grown and executed, even if encouraged by Washington, its significance would be to serve as a model and inspiration for coup leaders around the Southern Cone. Amidst what Brands rightly has termed the "rampant *golpismo* of the 1960s" it was by no means the only model around.[77] However, Brazil (and not the United States) was the model that Southern Cone dictators aspired to.

In hindsight, the chain of dictatorships that seized power in Latin America in the two decades after 1964 spelled the beginning of the end of the Cold War in South America. While Washington engaged in détente with Moscow and Jimmy Carter promoted human rights, Latin American dictatorships essentially took ownership of the Cold War during the 1970s. As they did, it became more violent and deadly, with the Marxist Left in the region decimated as a result.[78] Military regimes also hunted down all left-wing and centrist opponents in brutal "Dirty Wars". Even Fidel Castro, the most ardent proponent of revolutionary change in Latin

America, recognized the significance of counter-revolutionary victories during these years. From 1973 onwards he reportedly advised South American armed revolutionaries to hold off their offensives and wait until better conditions emerged.[79] But these conditions did not arrive. The Left's defeat and the way in which democracy returned to countries in the Southern Cone precluded any return of the Marxist-inspired alternatives to the existing capitalist order. Intentionally marginalized from politics in managed democratization processes, the Marxist Left had also lost legitimacy, due to fragmentation, Gorbachev's reforms and then the collapse of the Soviet Union and a widespread embrace of neoliberal free market reforms in the wake of the region's debt crisis in the 1980s.[80]

The exception to this general trend of events was Central America, which in the late 1970s and 1980s experienced its own acute phase of the Cold War more akin to South America's 1960s and 1970s. In 1979, twenty years after the Cuban Revolution, the revolutionary Frente Sandinista de Liberación Nacional (Sandinista National Liberation Front or FSLN) triumphed in Nicaragua. This was a popular and pluralistic revolution, initially supported by neighboring governments, priests, businessmen and liberal politicians. However, the FSLN's leadership was Cuban influenced and Marxist. After 1979, Nicaragua also started receiving arms and assistance from the Soviet Union and the FSLN drew on direct support and assistance from Latin American revolutionary exiles.[81] Meanwhile, in neighboring El Salvador a revolutionary insurgency was launched in the name of Farabundo Martí, the founding member of the Communist Party, peasant leader and martyr from the 1930s. The retaliation to the FSLN's victory and the counter-insurgency against the Frente Farabundo Martí para la Liberación Nacional (Farabundo Martí National Liberation Front or FMLN) in El Salvador was horrific. Heavily supported by the Reagan administration, local forces wrought catastrophic violence in Nicaragua and El Salvador. Meanwhile, in Guatemala, US-supported military regimes carried out genocide in the name of fighting communism.[82]

All told, the Cold War battles of the 1980s in Central America were intensely asymmetrical and they proved costly for those who had hoped to bring about revolutionary change. In 1990, the FSLN was voted out of power despite having managed to ward off a US-funded insurgency for the majority of a decade. In 1992, the FMLN laid down its arms as part of an internationally supervised UN-brokered peace agreement. For the United States, which had played such a significant role in the unfolding Cold War in Central America, the rationale for intervention (and assistance) to these war-torn countries disappeared with the fall of the Berlin Wall and the collapse of the Soviet Union.[83] In short, Cold War ideological struggles between capitalism and Marxist-inspired alternatives, both real and imagined, no longer served as a guiding rationale or justification for regional politics.

Indeed, by the 1990s, the Cold War in Latin America was largely over. Like the conflict's beginning, there was no single date that spelled its demise. Instead, the ideological struggle that had lasted seven decades came to an end slowly and, in places, painfully. In Guatemala, military doctrines fashioned during the Cold War morphed into post-Cold War strategies for constitutional state control and repression, as opposed to disappearing altogether. As one Guatemalan General put it: "Our strategic goal has been to reverse Clausewitz's philosophy of war to state that in Guatemala, politics must be the continuation of war. Thus we are acting in such a way that peace will truly arrive by way of political activity and by way of imposing our will on our opponents by means of military victory."[84] Meanwhile, Cuba's revolutionary regime survived as a socialist state into the 1990s, an apparent relic of a bygone era. The proclamation by Hugo Chavez in 2006 that he stood for "twenty-first century socialism," and adherence to that concept by other Latin American leaders, nevertheless made Cuba's survival less anachronistic. Indeed, in the twenty-first century, Cold War ideological conflicts are far from dead and buried even if the Cold War in the region as a whole no longer shapes Latin American politics, economics and society as it once did.

The Future

The future of Latin America's twenty-first-century socialism and Cuba's revolutionary regime is difficult to predict. It is unlikely that the Marxist Left will return in any major way to shape the region's politics or the fears of its adversaries. However, the direction that Cold War scholarship is likely to take when it comes to Latin America is easier to foresee, and in this respect there are four areas requiring further research.

The first relates to mapping out an intra-regional and transnational history of the Cold War in Latin America. Conferences and edited volumes have shifted attention towards multidimensional and comparative frameworks.[85] However, intra-regional or transnational history is a relatively new phenomenon for historians of Latin America. Specialists on "Brazil and the Cold War" or "Mexico and the Cold War" will nevertheless miss out on the regional Cold War patterns. Left-wing revolutionaries and counter-revolutionary generals thought in regional terms when they pictured their struggles against each other and more often than not embarked on strategies that extended across frontiers.[86] In short, it is increasingly hard to argue that the Cold War in Latin America was fought between nation-states or inside neatly delineated national boundaries.

The second issue deserving of attention is that of where protagonists got their ideas from and how these evolved.[87] To date, we know far more about the Left than the Right, partly because right-wing actions have often been ascribed to the United States and partly because documents pertaining to right-wing sectors are relatively more closed. However, we need to avoid understanding anti-communist struggles in terms of the United States "(and its local clients)." There were many millions of Latin American anti-communists in the twentieth century, and differences between them.[88] Third, but related to this point, we need a careful re-evaluation of the United States' role. Quite simply, it needs to be put in context so as to better understand its influence, effectiveness, strengths, limitations and impact.

Finally, we need to shed history's very own version of the Monroe Doctrine when it comes to studying Latin America's international relations.[89] To some extent, historians are now looking at how Latin Americans interacted with others across the globe and at developments in other parts of the world.[90] Yet these relationships are begging to be investigated further. Soviet-bloc archives, in particular, are waiting to be mined for what they hold. Latin America's external relations do not clash with the concept of a regional or even an inter-American Cold War. Instead, it is important to understand how external actors fed into and intervened in the region's ideological Cold War struggle. Latin Americans also very often internationalized their struggles against each other, evoking examples and language beyond their borders. The point here is that the ideological struggle at the heart of international politics that came to define the global Cold War also permeated language, choices and battles that were fought in this region with particular regional characteristics, turning points and consequences during the twentieth century. Understanding why this was the case is the challenge for historians of the Cold War in Latin America.

Notes

1 See, for example, Anders Stephanson, "Fourteen Notes on the Very Concept of the Cold War", H-Diplo Essays, http://www.h-net.org/~diplo/essays/PDF/stephanson-14notes.pdf.
2 See, for example, Greg Grandin, *Empire's Workshop: Latin America, the United States, and the Rise of the New Imperialism* (New York: Metropolitan Books, 2006).

3 Max P. Friedman, "Retiring the Puppets, Bringing Latin America Back in: Recent Scholarship on United States–Latin American Relations," *Diplomatic History* 27:5 (2003). On Cold War historiography's "hegemonic problem," see Thomas Blanton, "Recovering the Memory of the Cold War: Forensic History and Latin America," in *In From the Cold: Latin America's New Encounter with the Cold War*, edited by Gilbert M. Joseph and Daniela Spenser (Durham, NC/London: Duke University Press, 2008), 47.
4 On this crisis-driven approach, see Greg Grandin, "Off the Beach: The United States, Latin America, and the Cold War," in *A Companion to Post-1945 America*, edited by Jean-Christophe Agnew and Roy Rosenzweig (Oxford: Blackwell Publishers, 2002). For the Cold War as the continuation of longer patterns, see Gaddis Smith, *The Last Years of the Monroe Doctrine* (New York: Hill & Wang, 1994).
5 Nicola Miller, *Soviet Relations with Latin America, 1959–1987* (Cambridge: Cambridge University Press, 1989), 2, 32–43.
6 See Ariel C. Armony, "Transnationalizing the Dirty War: Argentina in Central America," in *In From the Cold*, 138; Piero Gleijeses, *Shattered Hope: The Guatemalan Revolution and the United States, 1944–1954* (Princeton, NJ: Princeton University Press, 1995), 185–89; Tanya Harmer, *Allende's Chile and the Inter-American Cold War* (Chapel Hill, NC: University of North Carolina Press, 2011); and Odd Arne Westad, *The Global Cold War: Third World Interventions and the Making of Our Times* (Cambridge: Cambridge University Press, 2005), 343–44.
7 Odd Arne Westad, "The Cold War and the International History of the Twentieth Century," in *The Cambridge History of the Cold War*, edited by Melvyn P. Leffler and Odd Arne Westad (Cambridge: Cambridge University Press, 2010), 10–11.
8 Duccio Basosi, "The 'Missing Cold War': Reflections on the Latin American Debt Crisis, 1979–1989," in *The End of the Cold War and the Third World: New Perspectives on Regional Conflict*, edited by Artemy M. Kalinovsky and Sergey Radchenko (Abingdon/New York: Routledge, 2011), 221.
9 Matias Spektor, "Brazilian Assessments of the End of the Cold War," in *The End of the Cold War and the Third World*, 231–32. See also Daniela Spenser, "Standing Conventional Cold War History on its Head," in *In From the Cold*, 382.
10 Leslie Bethell and Ian Roxborough, "The Impact of the Cold War on Latin America" in *Origins of the Cold War: An International History*, edited by Melvyn P. Leffler and David S. Painter, second edition (New York: Routledge, 2005), 431. See also Grandin, "Off the Beach", 427; and Gilbert M. Joseph, "What We Know and Should Know: Bringing Latin America More Meaningfully into Cold War Studies", in *In From the Cold*, 19.
11 Blanton, "Recovering the Memory", 51–58, 62–63. See also, Paraguay's "Archive of Terror," known as the "Centro de documentación y archivo para la defense de los derechos humanos," http://www.unesco.org/webworld/paraguay/index.html; the Guatemalan National Police Historical Archive (AHPN), https://ahpn.lib.utexas.edu/; the Digital National Security Archive, http://nsarchive.chadwyck.com/marketing/index.jsp; and the US Department of State, Freedom of Information Act, Electronic Reading Room, http://foia.state.gov/SearchColls/Search.asp.
12 Aldo Marchesi and Vania Markarian, "Cinco décadas de estudios sobre la crisis, la democracia y el autoritarismo en Uruguay," *Revista Contemporánea*, 3, November 2012.
13 See, for example, James N. Green and Pablo Yankelevich (eds.), *Exile and the Politics of Exclusion in the Americas* (Portland, OR: Sussex Academic Press, 2012); Olga Ulianova (ed.), *Redes Políticas y Militancias: La historia política está de vuelta* (Santiago: Adriana/Universidad de Santiago de Chile, 2010); Victor R. Figueroa Clark, "Chilean Internationalism and the Sandinista Revolution, 1978–1988" PhD dissertation, LSE, 2011; and Alessandro Santoni, *El comunismo italiano y la vía chilena: Los orígenes de un mito político* (Santiago: Ril editores, 2011).
14 See John Dinges, *The Condor Years: How Pinochet and His Allies Brought Terrorism to Three Continents* (New York: The New Press, 2004); J. Patrice McSherry, *Predatory States: Operation Condor and Covert War in Latin America* (Oxford: Rowman & Littlefield, 2005); and Pio Penna Filho, "O Itamaraty nos anos de chumbo – O Centro de Informações do Exterior (CIEX) e a repressão no Cone Sul (1966–1979)", *Revista Brasileira de Política Internacional* 52:2 (2009).
15 See Cristian Pérez (ed.), "La Izquierda Chilena Vista por la Izquierda" *Estudios Publicos*, 81 (2001); Fabian Escalante, *Operación Calipso* (Mexico City: Ocean Sur, 2008); and Humberto Ortega Saavedra, *La epopeya de la insurrección* (Managua: Lea Editorial, 2004).
16 See "Entrevistas do Programa de História Oral," http://cpdoc.fgv.br/acervo/historiaoral; and Matias Spektor (ed.), *Azevedo da Silveira: un depoimento* (Rio de Janeiro: CPDOC/FGV, 2010). See also Jennifer Schirmer, *The Guatemalan Military Project: A Violence Called Democracy* (Philadelphia, PA: University of Pennsylvania Press, 1998).

17 Blanton, "Recovering the Memory", 64 and *Memoria Abierta*, http://www.memoriaabierta.org.ar/.
18 See, for example, Tanya Harmer, "Fractious Allies: Chile, the United States and the Cold War, 1973–1976," *Diplomatic History* 37:1 (2013): 109–143.
19 Joseph, "What We Know and Should Know", 4.
20 See Gilbert M. Joseph, "Latin America's Long Cold War: A Century of Revolutionary Process and U.S. Power," in *A Century of Revolution: Insurgent and Counterinsurgent Violence During Latin America's Long Cold War*, edited by Greg Grandin and Gilbert M. Joseph (Durham, NC/London: Duke University Press, 2011), 399; Stephen G. Rabe, *The Killing Zone: The United States Wages Cold War in Latin America* (Oxford: Oxford University Press, 2012); and Hal Brands, *Latin America's Cold War* (Cambridge, MA: Harvard University Press, 2010), 1.
21 Brands, *Latin America's Cold War*, 1.
22 Blanton, "Recovering the Memory", 54. On asymmetrical uses of violence, see also Peter Winn, "The Furies of the Andes: Violence and Terror in the Chilean Revolution and Counterrevolution," in *A Century of Revolution*.
23 Grandin, "Living in Revolutionary Time: Coming to Terms with the Violence in Latin America's Cold War," in *A Century of Revolution*, 1. See also Joseph, "Latin America's Long Cold War", 397–98.
24 See Roberto García Fereira, "'El Caso de Guatemala': Arévalo, Árbenz y la Izquierda Uruguay, 1950–1971," *Mesoamérica* 49 (Jan–Dec 2007); Mark. T. Hove, "The Arbenz Factor: Salvador Allende, U.S–Chilean Relations, and the 1954 U.S. Intervention in Guatemala," *Diplomatic History* 31:4 (2007); and Eric Zolov, "¡Cuba sí, Yanquis no! The Sacking of the Instituto Cultural México-Norteamericano in Morelia, Michoacán, 1961" in *In From the Cold*.
25 See Rabe, *The Killing Zone* and Brands, *Latin America's Cold War*.
26 Grandin, "Living in Revolutionary Time," 29.
27 Brands, *Latin America's Cold War*, 7, 128, 129–63.
28 Joseph, "Latin America's Long Cold War," 402.
29 Westad, "The Cold War," 3.
30 Ibid., 3–6.
31 Westad, *Global Cold War*, 4–5 and 397–98; and Westad, "The Cold War," 13.
32 See Westad, "The Cold War," 10. For an overview of the Left in Latin America, see also Alan Angell, "The Left in Latin America Since c. 1920," in *The Cambridge History of Latin America*, Vol. VI, Part 12: *Latin America since 1930: Economy, Society and Politics* (Cambridge University Press, 1994) and Barry Carr, *Marxism and Communism in Twentieth-Century Mexico* (Lincoln, NE: University of Nebraska Press, 1992).
33 For a range of different explanations, see Joseph, "Latin America's Long Cold War," 398–400, Brands, *Latin America's Cold War* and Leslie Bethell and Ian Roxborough (eds.), *Latin America Between the Second World War and the Cold War, 1944–1948* (Cambridge: Cambridge University Press, 1997).
34 Charles D. Ameringer, *The Socialist Impulse: Latin America in the Twentieth Century* (Gainsville, FL: University Press of Florida, 2009), 1.
35 Sheldon B. Liss, *Marxist Thought in Latin America* (Berkeley, CA: University of California Press, 1984), 31, 33.
36 Elías Lafertte (1961) as quoted in Miller, *Soviet Relations with Latin America*, 29.
37 Miller, *Soviet Relations with Latin America*, 30.
38 Ibid., 30–31 and Liss, *Marxist Thought*, 34–35. By the early 1930s, there were also communist parties in Colombia, Ecuador, El Salvador, Paraguay, Peru and Venezuela.
39 Liss, *Marxist Thought*, 129–37 and Harry E. Vanden and Marc Becker (eds.), *José Carlos Mariátegui: An Anthology* (New York: Monthly Review Press, 2011), 13, 15, 17.
40 Joseph, "What We Know and Should Know", 21–22.
41 Leguía, as quoted in Thomas E. Skidmore and Peter H. Smith, *Modern Latin America*, fifth edition (New York: Oxford University Press, 2001), 195.
42 Thomas Miller Klubock, "Ránquil: Violence and Peasant Politics on Chile's Southern Frontier," in *A Century of Revolution*, 1, 136, 137, 140, 143–45, 148–50, 152.
43 Ameringer, *Socialist Impulse,* 7 and Liss, *Marxist Thought*, 129.
44 Paulo Drinot, "Creole Anti-Communism: Labor, the Peruvian Communist Party and APRA, 1930–1934," *Hispanic American Historical Review* 93:4 (November 2012). See also, Mario Rappaport, "Argentina," in *Latin America between the Second World War and the Cold War*, edited by Leslie Bethell and Ian Roxborough (Cambridge: Cambridge University Press, 1997), and Joseph, "What We Know and Should Know," 21.

45 Mark T. Gilderhus, *The Second Century: U.S.–Latin American Relations Since 1889* (Wilmington, DE: Scholarly Resources, 2000), 62. See also, Joseph, "Latin America's Long Cold War," 404.
46 Miller, *Soviet Relations with Latin America*, 35.
47 Ibid., 31–41.
48 Antoni Kapcia, *Cuba in Revolution: A History since the Fifties* (London: Reaktion Books, 2008), 91 and Louis A. Pérez, Jr., *Cuba: Between Reform and Revolution* (Oxford/New York: Oxford University Press, 2006), 211–12, 219.
49 Bethell and Roxborough, *Latin America*, 1.
50 See Resolution 32, "The Preservation and Defense of Democracy in America" (1948) in *Latin America and the United States*, edited by Robert H. Holden and Eric Zolov (Oxford: Oxford University Press, 2000), 193–94.
51 Vanni Pettinà "The Shadows of Cold War over Latin America: The U.S. Reaction to Fidel Castro's Nationalism, 1956–59", in *Cold War History* 11:3 (2011).
52 Lester D. Langley, *America and the Americas: The United States in the Western Hemisphere*, second edition (Athens, GA/London: The University of Georgia Press, 2010), 157 and Gilderhus, *Second Century*, 101–3.
53 See, for example, Seth Fein, "Producing the Cold War in Mexico: The Public Limits of Covert Communications," in *In From the Cold: Latin America's New Encounter with the Cold War*, edited by Gilbert M. Joseph and Daniela Spenser (Durham, NC/London: Duke University Press, 2008).
54 Miller, *Soviet Relations with Latin America*, 50.
55 Gleijeses, *Shattered Hope*, 141–43, 145, 147–48.
56 Telegram, US Ambassador in Guatemala (Peurifoy) to Department of State, 17 December 1953, *Foreign Relations of the United States, 1952–1954. Volume IV: the American Republics*, 1091–92.
57 Gleijeses, *Shattered Hope*.
58 Ferreira, "'El Caso de Guatemala'", 33–37; and Hove, "The Arbenz Factor", 631, 659.
59 Jorge Castañeda, *Compañero: The Life and Death of Che Guevara*, (London: Bloomsbury Publishing, 1997), 69–70 and Alan McPherson, *Intimate Ties, Bitter Struggles: The United States and Latin America Since 1945* (Washington, D.C.: Potomac Books), 39, 41.
60 Liss, *Marxist Thought*, 265–66.
61 Antoni Kapcia, *Cuba in Revolution*, 93–95 and Pérez, *Reform and Revolution*, 245–46.
62 Pérez, *Reform and Revolution*, 238, 242–43.
63 Kapcia, *Cuba in Revolution*, 95–96 and Pérez, *Reform and Revolution*, 245–51.
64 Pérez, *Reform and Revolution*, 252.
65 Harmer, *Allende's Chile*, 24.
66 Kapcia, *Cuba in Revolution*, 96–98 and Harmer, *Allende's Chile*, 24, 34.
67 Heraldo Muñoz, "The International Policy of the Socialist Party and Foreign Relations of Chile" in *Latin American Nations in World Politics*, edited by H. Muñoz and Joseph S. Tulchin (Boulder, CO: Westview, 1984), 153.
68 Joseph, "Latin America's Long Cold War," 406–7.
69 Joseph, "What We Know and Should Know," 26 and Stephen G. Rabe, *The Most Dangerous Area in the World: John F. Kennedy Confronts Communist Revolution in Latin America* (Chapel Hill, NC: University of North Carolina Press, 1999), 23–24.
70 Fred Halliday, *Caamaño in London: The Exile of a Latin American Revolutionary* (London: Institute for the Study of the Americas, 2010).
71 Brands, *Latin America's Cold War*, 73–75.
72 Golbery do Couto e Silva and Jorge Rafael Videla as quoted in Brands, *Latin America's Cold War*, 73.
73 Brands, *Latin America's Cold War*, 75.
74 See McSherry, *Predatory States*, 49–51, 56–58 and Rabe, *The Killing Zone*, 137–43.
75 Harmer, "Fractious Allies" and Brands, *Latin America's Cold War*, 78–79.
76 Tanya Harmer, "Brazil's Cold War in the Southern Cone, 1970–1975," *Cold War History* 12:4 (2012): 659–681.
77 Brands, *Latin America's Cold War*, 72, 76–78.
78 Harmer, "Fractious Allies."
79 Dinges, *Condor Years*, 56 and Manuel Piñeiro, Speech to the General National Liberation Department at the Cuban Ministry of the Interior (DGLN), 5 August 1972, in *Manuel Piñeiro: Che Guevara and the Latin American Revolutionary Movements*, edited by Luis Suarez Salazar (Melbourne: Ocean Press, 2001), 98.

80 On managed democratic transitions, see William Robinson, *Promoting Polyarchy: Globalization, US Intervention and Hegemony* (Cambridge: Cambridge University Press, 1996).
81 Westad, *Global Cold War*, 341–44 and Figueroa Clark, "Chilean Internationalism."
82 Rabe, *Killing Zone*, 159–74.
83 John H. Coatsworth, *Central America and the United States: The Clients and the Colossus* (New York: Twayne Publishers, 1994), 208.
84 Schirmer, *The Guatemalan Military Project*, 236, 239–41, 258–59.
85 See, for example, Bethell and Roxborough, *Latin America*; Joseph and Spenser, *In From the Cold*; Grandin and Joseph, *Century of Revolution*; and Ulianova, *Redes Políticas*.
86 See, for example, Gustavo Rodríguez Ostria, *Sin tiempo para las palabras: Teoponte, la otra guerrilla guevarista en Bolivia* (Cochabamba, Bolivia: Group Editorial Kipus, 2006) and Armony, "Transnationalizing the Dirty War", 134–35.
87 A good example is Mathilde Zimmerman, *Sandinista: Carlos Fonseca and the Nicaraguan Revolution* (Durham, NC/London: Duke University Press, 2000).
88 On the need for more research on the Right, see Joseph, "Latin America's Long Cold War," 399–400.
89 Ibid., 400.
90 See, for example, Piero Gleijeses, *Conflicting Missions: Havana, Washington, and Africa, 1959–1976* (Chapel Hill, NC: University of North Carolina Press, 2002). On the Vietnam War's significance in Latin America, see also Brands, *Latin America's Cold War*, 82, 102, 105 and Cold War International History e-Dossier No. 28, "Vietnam Trained Commando Forces in Southeast Asia and Latin America," http://www.wilsoncenter.org/publication/e-dossier-no-27-vietnam-trained-commando-forces-southeast-asia-and-latin-america.

11

THE COLD WAR IN AFRICA

Jeffrey James Byrne

Although the continent was always peripheral to the central contentions of international politics in the late twentieth century, a very large number of the Cold War's casualties were Africans. For three decades black, white, or Arab Africans fought each other in a plethora of national liberation struggles, civil wars, and secessionist campaigns that the superpowers frequently exacerbated with injections of arms, cash, or dangerous politics. In the 1970s, countries such as Angola, Ethiopia, and Eritrea became notorious exemplars of the "proxy war," whereby Washington and Moscow channeled their rivalry into some of the world's poorest – and remotest – places. But, as scholars such as Odd Arne Westad and James Scott have shown, an even greater number of Africans might be considered casualties of the Cold War's ideological battles.[1] Hundreds of thousands, if not millions, of African peasants became collateral damage in colonial counter-insurgency campaigns masquerading as anti-communist crusades, or subjected to the postcolonial state's ruthless and misguided efforts at social and economic transformation (as had so many Ukrainian and Chinese peasants before them). Thus, while not all of the continent's miseries over the past half-century are attributable to the Cold War, it is certainly a central concern in the history of modern Africa.

From World Wars to the Cold War

While the Cold War is typically considered to have begun in late 1940s postwar Europe, its ideological roots lie in the conclusion of the First World War, and this ideological kernel of the global contest between liberal capitalism and communism is relevant to African history because of its impact on the continent's nascent nationalist currents. Woodrow Wilson's Fourteen Points made a substantial impression on numerous African political figures in the northern Arab region especially, while the vital role of African-American (or "negro," in the language of the time) intellectuals and American-educated Africans in the transnational pan-Africanist movement was also a vector for the transmission of American liberal ideology – albeit not an unproblematic one, on account of the United States' own pronounced racial tensions. On the other side of the equation, Vladimir Lenin's relatively sparse pronouncements on the nature of the European imperial system, most notably *Imperialism: The Highest Stage of Capitalism*, soon came to be fundamental to mainstream anticolonial thought in Africa and a great many other parts of the world, although there were no African communist converts as influential as, say,

Mao Zedong and Ho Chi Minh were in their own homelands. Communism's influence in African politics was intentionally diluted and heavily mediated, but the mentorship of certain settler and metropolitan-based communist parties as well as the centrality of trade unionism to anticolonial mobilization in many African territories eventually resulted in a fairly thick dusting of Marxist-Leninist concepts across the continent's fertile political terrains.

Even after the tumult of the Great War, Europe's domination of Africa seemed untroubled, with 90 percent of the continent already under direct white minority rule and little sign of the imperial contest abating. For example, Germany's possessions in present-day Namibia passed to South Africa as a League of Nations mandate, while Benito Mussolini aspired to consolidate and expand Italy's holdings on the continent.[2] Nevertheless, intangible systemic changes eroded the foundations of the colonial order throughout the interwar period, perhaps the most important being Africa's increasing integration into the global economy.[3] Despite early indications of destabilizing side-effects, colonial political and commercial interests drove the process of economic change by increasing agricultural production and natural resource output in order to sell these commodities on the global market. Agricultural consolidation and the expansion of mines and transportation infrastructure greatly expanded the size of the native wage-labor force in many African colonies.[4] Although still constituting a small share of the total population, this growing stratum of workers and laborers sparked numerous strikes in British colonies in the 1930s, and French ones in the 1940s, in which they frequently added political complaints to the economic grievances that had initially inspired their protests. Consequently, Africa's labor movements wielded disproportionate influence over anticolonial and nationalist politics after the Second World War, popularizing the cognitive fusion of political reform and social justice.

Meanwhile, the United States and the Soviet Union also began to undermine the imperial *status quo* through their revolutionary anticolonial ideologies long before the onset of the Cold War proper. That said, Woodrow Wilson's Fourteen Points, with their emphasis on the principle of national self-determination, made less of a lasting impression in Africa than did the European labor movement's example of organized protest, the Bolshevik example of seizing state power from below, and of course the United States' own intellectuals of African descent and civil rights activists, who played a leading role in the transnational Pan-African movement.[5] America's anticolonial reputation suffered firstly with Wilson's notorious (in certain colonial circles) shunning of Egyptian, Syrian, and Indochinese nationalists at the Versailles Peace Conference in 1919, and secondly when African-American intellectuals such as W.E.B. Du Bois used the Pan-African Conferences of the 1920s and 1930s to call attention to the serious problem of racism in their home country.[6] Nnamdi Azikiwe, a leading figure in Nigeria's independence movement, who studied in the United States in the 1930s, later attested that "the introduction of the 'New Deal' reinforced my faith in the ultimate emergence of the United States as a moral force in the twentieth century world" and expressed the hope that America's racial problems only reflected a passing phase in the country's ascent to greatness.[7] These sentiments offer a good example of a widespread ambivalence about America among Africa's emerging national elites: admiration qualified by suspicion of America's open racism and unapologetic anti-egalitarianism.

In contrast, Moscow and the international communist movement actively sought the friendship of anticolonialist figures from Africa and Asia. For example, in 1922 the newly formed Egyptian Socialist Party converted into the Communist Party of Egypt (CPE) under the aegis of the Soviet-directed Communist International (COMINTERN), though the authorities in Cairo soon suppressed it.[8] Under Moscow's guidance, the French Communist Party (PCF) was particularly active in the early 1920s in helping African expatriates to found their own organizations and master vital mobilization and propaganda skills, while their German comrades helped a small group of Cameroonians to found the Liga zur Verteidigung der Negerrass (Negro Defense League) in Berlin in 1929.[9] Then, in February 1927, the Comintern organized a conference in Brussels known as the League Against Imperialism, which brought together militants from across the Third World, including India's Jawaharlal Nehru, the Algerian Messali Hadj, and the African National Congress' (ANC) president, Josiah (J.T.) Gumede.

Though Africa's representation at the event was comparatively small, such contacts did encourage the transmission of socialist and communist sentiments. "Those in the mines – what do they get?" Gumede asked rhetorically in Brussels. "They get two shillings a day. They have to go down the bowels of the earth to bring up gold to enrich the capitalist."[10] Likewise the 1932 program of Messali's North African Star party called for the nationalization of banks and industry, in addition to Algeria's independence.[11] Of course, Algeria and South Africa both had atypically large white populations and their own local communist parties that pursued particularly active relations with anticolonial "natives" at this time.[12]

On the other hand, Jopesh Stalin's strategic decision to "deprioritize" the anticolonial agenda in the 1930s, in order to build an anti-fascist alliance with France, created a sense of betrayal comparable to that created by Wilson at Versailles. George Padmore, the Trinidadian Pan-Africanist activist who became a close advisor to Ghana's Kwame Nkrumah, and Algeria's Messali Hadj were just two influential figures with bitter memories of their former comrades in the international communist movement. Consequently, neither the Soviet Union nor the United States enjoyed a great deal of credibility with African nationalists after the Second World War. The new generation of politicians rising to the fore on the continent in the 1940s and 1950s had enough familiarity with recent history to know that neither superpower could be counted on to practice what it preached so far as the colonial world was concerned. They realized that they would have to play to Washington and Moscow's sense of pragmatic self-interest as much as to their principles.

Africa's Cold Warriors in the 1950s and 1960s

The Cold War proper arrived first on the continent's northern, Arab littoral. While Sa'd Zaghlul's *Wafd* (delegation) movement had appealed in vain to Wilsonian princples at the Paris Peace Conference, by 1952 Egypt's liberal experiment had deteriorated so much that Gamal Abdel Nasser's Free Officers' Movement easily replaced it with a more authoritarian, self-styled "revolutionary" regime.[13] Yet, if Nasser seemed to be moving towards the socialist bloc by banning political parties, proceeding with land redistribution, and accepting Czechoslovak arms, the resolution of the Suez Crisis demonstrated how the dexterous (or fortunate) manipulation of both superpowers could advance the anticolonial cause.[14] Heeding the lesson, three years later a leading Algerian nationalist informed his colleagues that "the USSR is the great hope for the colonised peoples in their struggle for independence. Without it the USA would be lined up, as in 1918, on the side of the colonialist nations and they would have abandoned the principles of the San Francisco Charter as readily as they abandoned Wilson's 14 Points in 1918."[15]

Nasser's famous victory at Suez coincided with an upsurge of radical anticolonialism elsewhere in the continent. Though he had been fortunate in the manner of the crisis' outcome, the spectacle of both superpowers emphatically supporting Egypt's sovereignty in the face of Franco-British-Israeli aggression demonstrated the potential rewards awaiting those African leaders with the courage to exploit the explosive dynamics at the heart of international politics. Over the course of the following decade or so, from Accra to Angola, Conakry to Congo, nationalist leaders plunged into the Cold War maelstrom with wildly varying different degrees of success: while the Algerian Front de Libération Nationale (FLN) executed an exemplary diplomatic campaign in the pursuit of independence from France, Patrice Lumumba's foolhardy manipulation of US–Soviet tensions doomed the formerly Belgian Congo to years of instability, and cost him his life. But even in the case of cautionary tales like Lumumba's, Africans possessed a substantial degree of control over their own fates, and at least initially had to overcome Moscow and Washington's ill-informed or indifferent attitudes toward their continent. Even after independence, moreover, Africa's new leaders relied on the opportunities provided by the Cold War to pursue their extremely ambitious goals for nation building and socio-economic transformation.

Ghana (formerly the Gold Coast) and Guinea, which achieved their independence peacefully in 1957 and 1958 respectively, were two other important early cases of the Cold War interacting with African decolonization. As with Egypt, where Washington's refusal to fund the Aswan hydroelectric dam project served as *cassus belli* for Nasser's nationalization of the Suez Canal, the Eisenhower administration alienated Ghana and Guinea by declining to provide development economic assistance, thereby providing an opportunity for the Soviet Union to step in with alternative offers. The decision to extend or deny economic aid was fundamental to any developed country's relations with the new African states, for the continent's postcolonial elites recognized that both the national idea and their own ascendency depended on successful development. As the Ghanaian president, Kwame Nkrumah, told an audience in New York in 1958, "We cannot tell our peoples that material benefits and growth and modern progress are not for them. If we do, they will throw us out and seek other leaders who promise more … Africa has to modernize."[16]

By 1958, American officials had already decided that the Guinean president, Ahmed Sékou Touré, was a communist on the basis of his lead role in the country's labor movement. Guinea was the only country in Francophone Africa to decline Charles de Gaulle's offer to maintain tight economic integration with the former metropole after independence, but when Paris vindictively pulled out its advisors and terminated all its development projects in the country, the American government peremptorily rebuffed Conakry's desperate requests for assistance. Instead, Touré returned from Washington indignant at his treatment there, and gratefully accepted Soviet offers for assistance.[17] In contrast, the American government responded positively at first to Nkrumah's desire to build a massive hydroelectric dam on the Volta River, and Eisenhower pointedly welcomed the Ghanaian finance minister to the White House after hearing of his experience of racial prejudice in a Delaware restaurant. As in Egypt, the dam was first proposed by ambitious colonial officials, then revived after independence as a spur to industrialization and diversification from a mono-crop economy. However, in 1960 Accra and Washington furiously disagreed which each other's positions on the former Belgian Congo, where the CIA plotted to assassinate Nkrumah's close friend and ally, Prime Minister Patrice Lumumba. When Nkrumah used Soviet aircraft to ferry troops to Leopoldville, the Eisenhower White House declared him a communist stooge and withdrew its support for the Volta River project. In short, Washington had alienated two of Africa's most influential countries, and the incoming Kennedy administration, blaming its predecessors for an excessively Manichean approach to the developing world, made a priority of restoring America's plummeting reputation on the continent.

The early 1960s were the high point of the first phase of the Cold War in Africa, with Kennedy and the Soviet premier, Nikita Khrushchev, both convinced that the decolonizing Southern Hemisphere was the new front line in the battle between communism and capitalism. Soviet attitudes had changed dramatically since Stalin's death in 1953. Whereas the latter had deprecated the importance of the "colonial question," and had even hoped to wrangle some positions in Africa out of his allies at the end of the Second World War, Khrushchev's 1956 speech to the Soviet Communist Party Congress described the end of Europe's empires as a development "of world-historical significance," and stressed the need to support progressive national liberation movements:

> A remarkable phenomenon of our time is the awakening of the peoples of Africa.... Communists are revolutionaries, and it would be unfortunate if they did not take advantage of new opportunities and did not look for new methods and forms that would best achieve the ends in view.[18]

The epicenter of the Cold War in Africa in the 1950s and 1960s was the former "Belgian" Congo, subsequently renamed Zaire by its ruthless autocrat, Mobutu Sese Seko, in 1971. The Belgian authorities' preparations for the independence of Congo – a country comparable in geographical extent to Western Europe had only a few thousand university-educated black inhabitants – were particularly inadequate, so that Congo became synonymous with disorderly decolonization within days of the formal transfer of power, on 30 June 1960. The crisis began when black soldiers mutinied in protest of poor pay and their overbearing white officers. Other workers went out on strike in solidarity with the soldiers, but the protests quickly turned violent and the Western press terrified their readers with tales of physical and sexual assault committed against the white settler population. But the real drivers of the Congo Crisis were, on the one hand, the American and Belgian governments' distrust of the unapologetically left-wing prime minister, Patrice Lumumba, and on the other, Brussels' willingness to abet secessionist provinces in order to secure Belgian firms' continued access to valuable natural resources. Thus, Brussels dispatched soldiers to Congo in early July under the pretext of protecting white settlers, but with the real goal of assisting the mineral-rich province of Katanga's declaration of secession, supported by the powerful mining concern, Union Minère. When the outraged Lumumba turned first to the United Nations and then to the Soviet Union for assistance in forcibly re-integrating Katanga, President Eisenhower authorized the CIA to orchestrate his overthrow and assassination. American intelligence threw its backing behind a successful coup by the Congolese military chief, Joseph Mobutu, in December. Then, although the CIA's precise involvement in Lumumba's murder is still murky, Washington had its wish fulfilled in January 1961, when the Katangan leaders caught and executed him as he attempted to flee to the eastern part of the country.

The Congo Crisis polarized African politics into "pro-Western" and "anti-neoimperialist" camps, while Lumumba's death turned him into a compelling martyr figure for generations of the continent's politicians and activists – the African equivalent, in some respects, to Ernesto 'Che' Guevara.[19] Moreover, Congo's troubles were just beginning. The country was plagued by civil war for several years between the Western-backed Leopoldville government and a "Lumumbist" rebel government based in the eastern city of Stanleyville, which had the support of the communist bloc and the more radical independent African countries. Having initially stepped aside to allow the continuance of a civilian government, Mobutu carried out a second coup at the end of 1965 to install himself firmly in power. A solid American ally for the next three decades, Mobutu's Congo/Zaire also epitomized the systemic state brutality and cult of personality that characterized so many African countries after independence.[20]

Meanwhile, throughout the Cold War, a shadowy world of revolutionary movements and secessionist groups existed alongside the normal proceedings of African affairs. Although not a unique phenomenon, Africa was distinctive firstly for the sheer number of different movements at large, oftentimes several hailing from the one country, and second for the degree to which the legitimate and underground dimensions of international relations converged there. In the 1960s, Immanuel Wallerstein observed at first hand how groups such as the Algerian FLN or the South African ANC frequently attended continental events with the same official status as sovereign states, creating a culture that subverted traditional inter-state relations.[21] At the formation of the Organisation of African Unity (OAU) in 1963, every independent country agreed to fully support the national liberation movements of Southern Africa and to contribute annually to the budget of a Liberation Committee that would advise, equip, and train them. In practice, however, this unanimous principle quickly fell victim to Africa's polarization. Numerous governments manipulated the liberation movements to serve their own ends or indirectly attack regional rivals, while others buckled to Western pressure to withhold their support in the name of stability. Additionally, given how small many of these groups were, it was easy even for lesser powers such as Cuba, Yugoslavia, China, or France to compete for influence with the US and the Soviet Union.

By prevailing in Algeria's long and bloody war of independence, 1954–62, the FLN was undoubtedly the most successful of the transnational liberation movements. As recent scholarship, most notably Matthew Connelly's *A Diplomatic Revolution*, has shown, the Algerians set an example to others of how to conduct an effective diplomatic campaign by exploiting the Cold War's tensions.[22] At first, they appealed to the United States on the basis of anticolonial principles, hoping that Washington would pressure France into withdrawing from the Maghreb. However, when the American government proved unwilling to do so, the FLN's leaders made deliberate overtures to China and the Soviet Union in order to "blackmail" the US. In time, the communist world's military assistance and diplomatic support became ends in themselves. As a result, although independent Algeria officially pursued a non-aligned foreign policy and desired substantial economic relations with the United States, in reality the government in Algiers retained a scarcely concealed hostility toward American influence in Africa.

Accordingly, small guerrilla movements and revolutionary groups proved to be some of Africa's most active Cold Warriors. From the early 1960s, Angola's nationalists were models of factionalism and international intrigue, culminating in years of civil conflict beginning in the late 1970s. In a March 1961 press conference, the leader of one faction, Holden Roberto, rendered a "vibrant homage to the new American administration and to its young and dynamic leader John Kennedy" and predicted that Angola "will have the pride of having contributed to the concretization of a sharp turn in American politics in respect to Africa and decolonization."[23] Indeed, his National Front for the Liberation of Angola (Frente Nacional de Libertação de Angola, FNLA) quickly secured CIA patronage and funding, giving it an advantage over its hated rivals, Agostinho Neto's Movimento Popular de Libertaçao de Angola (Popular Movement for the Liberation of Angola, MPLA). As the party of leftist urban intellectuals, the MPLA in turn found support in the more radical African capitals, such as Algiers, Accra, Conakry, and Cairo. Although these countries initially encouraged all Angolans to reconcile and combine their efforts, they leaned increasingly toward the more "progressive" MPLA, while pro-Western leaders like Congo's Mobutu Sese Seko unapologetically backed Holden's movement. In time, outside interests such as Cuba, Yugoslavia, and the USSR took their lead from their radical African friends and began supporting the MPLA. The situation became more complicated still when a third Angolan figure, Jonas Savimbi, encountered a Chinese intelligence agent in Tanganyika and traveled to Peking in 1964 as a prelude to founding his own guerrilla movement.[24] Thus, with independence still a decade away, the transnational netherworld of Angolan nationalism already replicated the complexities of the Cold War international system.[25]

Angola was far from unique. Operating out of offices and bases in sympathetic countries like Tanganyika, Congo, or Ghana, nationalist figures traveled between the capitals of the Northern Hemisphere in search of arms, money, and patronage. Generally speaking, however, the communist countries provided more material support than did the West. Washington wished to remain on good terms with potential future leaders of independent countries like Holden or the leader of the Mozambican nationalist movement, Dr. Eduardo Mondlane, but could hardly fuel insurgencies within the colonies of its NATO ally, Portugal. US officials fretted that the likes of Mondlane, whom one senior State Department figure found to be an "exceptionally well-balanced, dedicated, serious man," would be forced into the arms of communism, and could even sympathize that the Mozambican "had to embark on a program of violence which, although it is out of character, is essential if he expects to continue to lead the liberation movement."[26] Duly enough, the FRELIMO (Mozambique Liberation Front) leader became resentful of the negative press that came from his reliance on Soviet and Chinese arms. "What are we supposed to do," he asked in a 1967 interview, "if apart from the Africans, only the communists will train and arms us?"[27]

The Soviet Offensive of the 1970s

While the first acute phase of the Cold War in Africa had petered out by the close of the 1960s, the second phase that began in the mid-1970s proved to be more explosive, entailing much more direct forms of outside intervention. As a consequence of greater access to material from Western, Eastern, Cuban, and South African archives, recent years have seen a substantial amount of groundbreaking research on the international dimensions of the demise of the Portuguese Empire and the collapse of white minority rule in Southern Africa.[28] Indeed, as Angola and the Horn region, in particular, became sites of archetypal superpower proxy wars, Africa as a whole seemed to occupy a more central role in the progression of the Cold War. At the decade's end, President Jimmy Carter's combative National Security Advisor, Zbigniew Brzezinski, perceived an "arc of crisis" that extended from Afghanistan through to the southern tip of Africa, and famously concluded in his memoirs that détente lay "buried in the sands of the Ogaden" as a result of US–Soviet confrontation in the Horn of Africa.[29]

Yet détente, after all, was the crowning success of Soviet diplomacy, signaling that the gatekeepers of international society – the major Western states – had at last accepted the USSR as a superpower. That the politburo risked this hard-won accomplishment by pursuing opportunities in Africa, even though it felt entitled to do so, speaks to the Soviet Union's conflicted identity as a *status quo* power and self-appointed motor of world revolution. At the beginning of the decade, mired in Vietnam and disheartened by their waning economic and military superiority, American political circles had little appetite for new adventures in the tropics. In contrast, while chastened by the misfortunes of the radical African leaders embraced by Khrushchev ten years earlier, the Soviet leadership enjoyed a new sense of potency thanks to much-improved military force-projection capabilities and the Nixon administration's recognition of strategic parity. Even so, contrary to the impression among Western officials that the Soviet Union was going "on the offensive" in Africa, in reality the Kremlin first responded to signs of a revolutionary upsurge with great trepidation. Yet, almost as if they knew that Moscow had set a higher bar for its analysts following the disappointments of the "African socialist" generation of Touré and Nkrumah, a new wave of radical nationalists emerged proclaiming a much more faithful adherence to the tenets of Marxism-Leninism than their antecedents. Having faith in the concept of historical progression, the experts in Soviet think-tanks and the foreign policy apparatus dared to believe that "the world was going our way."

First, in October 1969, General Muhammad Siad Barre led a military coup against the civilian government of Somalia, expelling American advisers and reaching out for closer military and intelligence cooperation with the Soviet Union. Offering friendly harbors on the Indian Ocean and the Gulf of Aden, the country had real strategic value, but the Soviet government was also encouraged by the tenor of political life in the renamed Somali Democratic Republic. Though its leaders seemed to have a fairly limited familiarity with the details of Marxist-Leninist theory, which they professed to have fused with Islam in a coherent fashion, they blanketed public spaces with "orthodox" communist symbols and regalia, and Siad Barre gave speeches flanked by imposing portraits of Lenin and Marx. In 1974, Moscow and Mogadishu concluded a Treaty of Friendship and Cooperation, and Soviet engineers began construction of a missile and naval base at Berbera, near the mouth of the Red Sea. With hundreds of personnel in the country, Somalia had quickly become the Kremlin's most substantial investment in Africa to date.

Meanwhile, at the southern end of the continent, Neto's MPLA, Amilcar Cabral's Partido Africano de Independência da Guine e Cabo Verde (African Party of Independence of Guinea and Cape Verde, PAIGC), and Robert Mugabe's Zimbabwe African National Union (ZANU) also seemed to represent a more authentically Marxist brand of nationalism. Still, Moscow's aid had dwindled in recent years, and even with the Portuguese Empire finally on its last legs, the Brezhnev politburo was wary of jeopardizing détente with the United States. In that light, Westad argues convincingly that the Kremlin's decision to increase military support to these groups again owed a great deal, first, to the fact that the Africans' Cuban advocates had themselves recently shown much more deference to Soviet counsel on socio-economic matters, second to the support of trusted communists in the new Portuguese military regime that seized power in April 1974, and third to a desire to trump Beijing's backing of rival local actors such as Jonas Savimbi in southern Angola.[30] In a sense, then, the Soviet Union rallied to Africa's remaining liberation movements in order to regain the revolutionary reputation that it had sacrificed over the past decade or so spent in pursuit of "peaceful coexistence" with the West – a strategy that, from the radical Third Worldist perspective, looked an awful lot like the behavior of a cautious, establishment power heavily invested in the global *status quo*.

The fact that the Soviet government had only belatedly rediscovered its commitment to southern Africa's anticolonial struggle did not prevent a deep sense of satisfaction regarding the outcome of Angola's chaotic and bloody accession to independence in 1975. The new government in Lisbon wasted little time in withdrawing from Portugal's last imperial possessions, and, given the history of mutual antipathy and international intrigue between three Angolan nationalist parties, their descent into open conflict was unsurprising. As the date of formal independence approached, 11 November, the MPLA, the FNLA, and Savimbi's UNITA all enjoyed escalating support from the foreign backers. Under a secret CIA operation called IAFEATURE, Henry Kissinger and President Gerald Ford rushed $50 million-worth of materiel to Holden and Savimbi's troops. Neto's MPLA received Soviet arms deliveries and, by October, Cuban advisors too. In November, the real fight for Angola broke out: denied further funds by a skeptical Congress, Kissinger pinned his hopes instead on a 3,000-strong South African force advancing from the south in alliance with UNITA, while Castro committed himself to airlifting a comparable Cuban force into MPLA-held Luanda. Over the next two months, as Piero Gleijeses in particular has recounted in riveting detail, the Cubans achieved a glorious victory, soundly routing first Holden's FNLA, then the South Africans.[31] African capitals quickly recognized the MPLA government, and while Moscow basked in the collective glory, Washington suffered the frustrations of defeat and condemnations for associating with the pariah apartheid state.

With the Kremlin buoyed by this success, a Marxist-inspired revolution in Ethiopia in 1974 led to the Soviet Union's most important intervention in Africa throughout the Cold War. The emperor, Haile Selassie, had ruled one of the continent's most populous countries since 1930, managing to preserve its independence amid a sea of colonialism while undertaking a reasonably successful and stable modernization drive. It was a testament to his regional prestige that Addis-Ababa had hosted the OAU's opening conference in 1963, but by the early 1970s the elderly emperor was losing his grip on Ethiopia's society and economy. Finally, in September 1974 a committee, or "Derg," of junior officers and NCOs seized control, and demonstrated their ruthless intent to break with the past by strangling the decrepit monarch and burying his corpse in an especially degrading fashion.[32] In time a Major Mengistu Haile Mariam emerged as the Derg's leader, and by vowing to transform Ethiopia in accordance with the tenets of "scientific socialism," he and his comrades seemed to epitomize the ascendancy of a more consciously Marxist generation of African nationalists. They also represented a stinging rejection of US-directed development, on which the *ancien régime* had become very dependent. Addis Ababa University had benefited from American largesse since its founding in 1950 – the main library was named after John F. Kennedy – but by the early 1970s the campus had become an intensely radical place and the intellectual wellspring of the Derg revolution. "In those days," one former student recalled, "not to be a Marxist was considered heretical."[33]

On account of its size and importance, and the enthusiasm of the Derg's revolutionary pronouncements, Ethiopia constituted the strongest validation yet of Marxist-Leninist ideology in Africa for an aging Soviet leadership.[34] Relations between the two countries developed quickly. As a Soviet foreign ministry report summarized, the Derg regime "emphasized the fact that it saw the Soviet Union as the main source of their support internationally ... [and] it was announced by our side that the Soviet Union regarded sympathetically the measures taken by the [Derg] for building a new society on progressive principles."[35] Reflecting their concern for the regime's survival, Soviet officials seemed to approve when Mengistu unleashed a bloody "Red Terror" in 1977 to eliminate those he perceived as his enemies within the elite and Ethiopian society.[36] Moscow invested heavily in Ethiopia's socialist transformation in the expectation of a sustained contest against the West.

Moreover, by then the Kremlin had been forced to choose between its two allies in the Horn of Africa, Ethiopia and Somalia. Somalia laid claim to the Ogaden desert, where it had set up a secessionist force, the Western Somali Liberation Front, to undermine Addis-Ababa's control. Seeing his neighbor caught in the throes of revolution, however, in the summer of 1977 Barre threw his own forces into battle, advancing them towards the Ethiopian capital. From the Soviet perspective, the Somali government had failed to live up to its initial Marxist rhetoric and had been pursuing a fairly conservative internal program and non-aligned foreign policy for several years, yet Mogadishu was still a cooperative ally and a useful strategic asset. In contrast, Ethiopia genuinely excited many leading figures within the socialist bloc: Fidel Castro and an East German delegation each visited the two countries and came away with the same clear preference for backing Mengistu over Barre.[37]

In the end, ideology decisively trumped pragmatism, and Moscow undertook its largest overseas military operation since the Korean War in order to save the Addis-Ababa regime. From late 1977 to the summer of 1978, the Soviet Union delivered $1 billion-worth of armaments and more than 11,000 Cuban troops, which swiftly turned the tide of battle. As Brzezinski subsequently attested, this massive military intervention in the Horn of Africa dealt a fatal blow to détente, and augured a new period of determined American counter-offensive in Africa and elsewhere in the Third World.

That said, the Carter administration also instigated a less Manichean approach to the problem of white minority rule in southern Africa. First, while the Nixon–Ford administrations had pursued very close relations with the apartheid regime in Johannesburg on the basis of staunch mutual anti-communism, Carter signaled that he would not continue to deprioritize moral and human rights issues to the same degree by ceasing cooperation with the South African nuclear program. Second, his administration made substantial effort to resolve the Rhodesian (Zimbabwe) and South West African (Namibia) crisis, reaching out to black nationalists from both territories in spite of their relations with Cuba and the Soviet Union. But although British–American diplomacy did help bring about a peaceful end to Ian Smith's white regime in 1980, the South West African conflict continued to escalate into the new decade.[38]

There Is No Alternative: The End of the Cold War in Africa

Ronald Reagan captured the White House in 1980 in part by accusing the Carter administration of timidity in the face of economic recession and a Soviet offensive in the Third World, and the new president's solutions for both problems would have serious consequences for Africa. The most significant (and best-known) cases of the Reagan administration's counter-offensive in the developing world were in Central America and Afghanistan, where the US funneled arms and other forms of support to guerrilla movements battling Soviet-allied leftist regimes, but a similar policy also applied to southern Africa. Quite unlike Carter, Reagan seemed to believe that without Soviet interference and scheming, there would not even be any local crises such as those in Namibia and Mozambique. "If [the Soviets] weren't involved in this game of dominoes," he said in 1982, "there wouldn't be any hotspots in the world."[39] Washington now re-intensified its cooperation with the pariah government in Pretoria – which had developed several nuclear weapons by the early 1980s – and offered Savimbi's UNITA rebels battling the MPLA regime in Luanda similar equipment to that provided to the Afghan *mujahideen*, including *Stinger* shoulder-mounted anti-aircraft missiles.[40]

Yet the Reagan administration's greatest impact in Africa – and many would argue a more damaging one than exacerbating civil wars – lay in the economic sphere. In ways both intended and unintended, the United States led the way in accelerating the demise of Africa's state-centric economic models, completely reversing the trend of both Western and socialist development assistance over the past three decades. Agreeing with Margaret Thatcher's mantra that "There Is No Alternative" for curing the West's malaise, Reagan and his team declared Keynesian economics dead and pressed a determined neo-liberal agenda that loosened capital controls, restricted the dollar supply, raised interest rates, and lowered corporate taxation. Though conceived with America's own needs in mind, these policies had significant consequences for the developing world.

First, the US went into a recession that helped depress the market value of Third World countries' export commodities. Secondly, rich and poor countries alike had borrowed heavily during the advantageous circumstances of the 1970s, when interest rates were lower than the dollar's rate of inflation, but now the US and other Western economies continued to depend on the global capital markets to cover widening budget deficits. The cost of capital rose sharply, with developing countries forced to compete for credit with the United States, which became the world's largest debtor practically overnight. Thus squeezed between plummeting export revenues and the skyrocketing cost of debt, many Third World economies began to collapse, and while some regions fared better than others, Africa was hit the worst. During the 1980s, income per capita in sub-Saharan Africa declined by 30 percent relative to the advanced Western economies.[41]

These structural forces had a leveling effect on the continent's economies. Their fortunes had already begun diverging in the late 1960s, with Côte d'Ivoire and Kenya performing relatively well by focusing on cocoa and coffee production, respectively, while Ghana's program of socialist-oriented industrialization made little headway. In the early 1970s, the surging price of oil and natural gas killed off Africa's few promising pockets of industrial growth, but was also a bonanza for countries like Algeria, Libya, and Nigeria. It was no coincidence that the high point of the Third Worldist dream of restructuring the global terms of trade, the New International Economic Order, occurred at this time, nor that energy-rich Algeria was one of the most dynamic African participants. Yet OPEC's oil embargo in 1973 proved to be the only successful instance of commodity exporters flexing their collective muscle, and even the petro-states could not repeat the trick. Instead, when the price of oil bottomed out in the early 1980s, these countries found themselves in the same dire straits as everyone else, due to their overdependence on a single capricious export. Thus, although the GNP per capita of Africa as a whole had grown by about 20 percent between 1960 and 1980, in the subsequent decade even high fliers like Côte d'Ivoire saw their achievements erased.[42]

With the Soviet leadership confronting their own grave economic dilemmas, African governments had little alternative to the new development agenda being pushed by Western governments and international institutions, in particular the US and the International Monetary Fund (IMF). In marked contrast to previous years, when foreign donors were broadly supportive of expensive large-scale projects and a state-centric approach, Africans were effectively prescribed Washington and London's own preference for severe reductions in state expenditures, including social provisions and subsidized industrialization efforts. Naturally, the resultant pain was far more severe than that inflicted by neo-liberal reforms in the West, but it also opened up many avenues for conspicuous enrichment for those in advantageous positions.

Furthermore, perhaps as a consequence of Africa's relative insignificance in economic terms, the American agenda there had been distinctly "anti-communist" rather than "pro-capitalist" until the 1980s. Under the Kennedy, Johnson, and Nixon administrations, it was quite common even for Africa's more determinedly socialist economies to enjoy more significant trading and development relationships with the US than with the communist bloc. For the most part, successive American governments prior to the Reagan years tended to leverage these economic ties to influence African states' diplomatic and international policies rather than their internal politics (the Johnson administration was particularly fond of wielding American food aid deliveries as a cudgel against developing countries that seemed to cooperate with Soviet foreign policy, such as Egypt, Algeria, and India).[43] It is in this respect that the Reagan era appears to differ, with both the American government and the international institutions under its influence taking an extremely interventionist approach to the inner workings of Africa's economies. While there is no doubt that the officials concerned believed that they were working in Africans' best interests, a worthy question for future study may be whether Reagan's White House saw the destruction of the Third World's socialist economies as a desirable goal in itself.[44]

On the whole, it is difficult to discern a single clear narrative for the Cold War in Africa. Clearly, as occurred in other areas of the developing world, numerous local African crises attracted the attention of the superpowers, with disastrous results. Whether in Congo in the early 1960s, the Horn of Africa in the late 1970s, or much of southern Africa throughout the 1980s, American and Soviet competition tended to escalate, deepen, and prolong political conflict on the continent. At the same time, however, perhaps the more systemic effect of the Cold War on Africa resulted from the combination of, on the one hand, the intense ideological rivalry between liberal capitalism and socialism/communism, and on the other, the intense search for pragmatic solutions and inspiring aspirations that accompanied independence. Because of decolonization, Africa arguably experienced a more profound process of reinvention than any other region in the second half of the twentieth century, so even without the emergence of emphatically capitalist- or communist-oriented regimes such as those found in East Asia, the Cold War environment did embolden Africa's nation- and state-building projects in a generalized, yet subtle fashion.[45] Consequently, American and Soviet policy makers (as well as those from Cuba, China, France, and so on) certainly deserve some of the blame for those that died in "proxy wars" in Mozambique, Angola, Ethiopia, or Congo. But representatives of Africa's new nationalist elites also bear responsibility for the Cold War's other victims: those that died at the hands of single-party police states and misguided, overly ambitious modernization projects.[46]

Notes

1 Odd Arne Westad, *The Global Cold War: Third World Interventions and the Making of Our Times* (Cambridge: Cambridge University Press, 2007); James C. Scott, *Seeing Like a State: How Certain Schemes to Improve the Human Condition Have Failed* (New Haven, CT: Yale University Press, 1999).
2 For a good overview, see David B. Abernethy, *The Dynamics of Global Dominance: European Overseas Empires, 1415–1980* (New Haven, CT: Yale University Press, 2002), 81–103.
3 Abernethy, *Dynamics of Global Dominance*, 104–32 again provides an excellent overview of the interwar period. On the global economy more generally, see Jeffry A. Frieden, *Global Capitalism: Its Fall and Rise in the Twentieth Century* (New York: W. W. Norton & Company, 2007), 127–54.
4 For example, see the relevant chapters in John Ruedy, *Modern Algeria: The Origins and Development of a Nation* (Indianapolis: Indiana University Press, 2005) and Mahfoud Bennoune, *The Making of Contemporary Algeria, 1830–1987: Colonial Upheavals and Post-Independence Development* (Cambridge: Cambridge University Press, 1988). On the Gezira irrigation scheme in Sudan, see Mohammed Hashim Awad, "The Evolution of Land Ownership in the Sudan," *Middle East Journal* 25:2 (1971): 212–228 and Victoria Bernal, "Colonial Moral Economy and the Discipline of Development: The Gezira Scheme and 'Modern' Sudan," *Cultural Anthropology* 12:4 (1997): 447–479.
5 Erez Manela, *The Wilsonian Moment: Self-Determination and the International Origins of Anticolonial Nationalism* (New York: Oxford University Press, 2009).
6 Imanuel Geiss, *The Pan-African Movement* (London: Methuen, 1974); Penny M. Von Eschen, *Race Against Empire: Black Americans and Anticolonialism, 1937–1957* (Ithaca, NY: Cornell University Press, 1997).
7 Nnamdi Azikiwe, *My Odyssey: An Autobiography* (London: Hurst, 1970), 194–7.
8 Joel Beinin and Zachary Lockman, *Workers on the Nile: Nationalism, Communism, Islam, and the Egyptian Working Class, 1882–1954* (Princeton, NJ: Princeton University Press, 1987), 140–9.
9 Robbie Aitken, "From Cameroon to Germany and Back via Moscow and Paris: The Political Career of Joseph Bilé (1892–1959), Performer, 'Negerarbeiter' and Comintern Activist," *Journal of Contemporary History* 43(4): 597–616.
10 Speech of J.T. Gumede, President of the African National Congress, at the International Congress Against Imperialism, Brussels, 10–15 February 1927, available at the official ANC website, http://www.anc.org.za/ancdocs/speeches/1920s/gumedesp.htm.
11 "Programme de l'Etoile Nord-Africaine Assemblée générale tenue à Paris, mai 1933," in Jacques Simon ed., *Messali Hadj par les textes* (Paris: Editions Bouchène, 2000), p. 22. See also Abderrahim Taled Bendiab, "La Pénétration Des Idées Et L'implantation Communiste En Algérie Dans Les Années 1920," in *Mouvement Ouvrier, Communisme Et Nationalismes Dans Le Monde Arabe*, ed. René Gallissot (Paris: Editions Ouvrières, 1978), 127–46.
12 On the role of communism in South Africa, see Peter Delius, "Sebatakgomo and the Zoutpansberg Balemi Association: The ANC, the Communist Party and Rural Organization, 1939–55," *The Journal of African History* 34 (1993): 293–313.
13 Joel Gordon, *Nasser's Blessed Movement: Egypt's Free Officers and the July Revolution* (New York: Oxford University Press, 1992).

14 Salim Yaqub, *Containing Arab Nationalism: The Eisenhower Doctrine and the Middle East* (Chapel Hill, NC: University of North Carolina Press, 2004); and Nigel John Ashton, *Eisenhower, Macmillan and the Problem of Nasser: Anglo-American Relations and Arab Nationalism, 1955–59* (Basingstoke and New York: Palgrave Macmillan, 1996).

15 "Rapport de politique générale," by Ferhat Abbas, 20 June 1959, from the archives of the Front de Libération Nationale's Provisional Government of the Algerian Republic (GPRA), dossier 5.8, Algerian National Archives, Algiers.

16 Quoted in Michael E. Latham, "The Cold War in the Third World, 1963–1975," *The Cambridge History of the Cold War* (Cambridge: Cambridge University Press, 2010), vol. 1, 480.

17 Elizabeth Schmidt, *Cold War and Decolonization in Guinea, 1946–1958* (Athens, OH: Ohio University Press, 2007); Sergey Mazov, Politika *SSSR v zapadnoi Afrike, 1956–1964: Neizvestnye stranitsy istorii kholodnoi voiny* (Moscow: Nauka, 2008), 60, 79, 152; Philip E. Muehlenbeck, "Kennedy and Touré: A Success in Personal Diplomacy," *Diplomacy & Statecraft* 19:1 (2008): 69–95.

18 Nikita Khrushchev, "Speech to a Closed Session of the CPSU Twentieth Party Congress, 25 February 1956," in *Khrushchev Speaks!*, edited by Thomas P. Whitney (Ann Arbor, MI: University of Michigan Press), 259–65.

19 See, for example, the excellent film on Lumumba's brief time in power and murder, directed by the Haitian filmmaker, Raoul Peck, *Lumumba*, 2002.

20 On the Congo Crisis in the early 1960s, see Madelaine Kalb, *The Congo Cables: The Cold War in Africa from Eisenhower to Kennedy* (New York: Macmillan, 1982) and Crawford Young, *Politics in the Congo: Decolonization and Independence* (Princeton, NJ: Princeton University Press, 1965). See also Sean Kelly, *America's Tyrant: The CIA and Mobutu and Zaire* (Washington, DC: American University Press, 1993).

21 See Immanuel Wallerstein, *Africa: The Politics of Unity* (Lincoln, NE: University of Nebraska Press, 2005).

22 Matthew Connelly, *A Diplomatic Revolution: Algeria's Fight for Independence and the Origins of the Post-Cold War Era* (New York: Oxford University Press, 2003); Irwin M. Wall, *France, the United States, and the Algerian War* (Berkeley, CA: University of California Press, 2001).

23 Holden Roberto press conference in Leopoldville, Congo, 24 March 1961, *Africa Liberation Reader*, edited by Immanuel Wallerstein and Aquino de Bragança (London: Zed Press, 1982), vol. 2, 48.

24 Yves Loiseau and Pierre-guillaume de Roux, *Portrait d'un révolutionnaire en général: Jonas Savimbi* (Paris: La Table Ronde, 1987), 106–7.

25 See John Marcum, *The Angolan Revolution* (Cambridge, MA: MIT Press, 1969–1978).

26 Quoted from Harriman to Rusk, 1 July 1964, in *Foreign Relations of the United States, 1964–1968*, vol. XXIV, 742, and Wright to Williams, 14 December 1964, *ibid.*, 747.

27 Quoted in Alan Hutchinson, *China's African Revolution* (London: Hutchinson & Co., 1975), 229.

28 For example, Westad, *Global Cold War*, 207–49; Westad, "Moscow and the Angolan Crisis, 1974–1976: A New Pattern of Intervention," *Cold War International History Project Bulletin*, no. 8 (1996): 21–32; Piero Gleijeses, *Conflicting Missions: Havana, Washington, and Africa, 1959–1976* (Chapel Hill, NC: University of North Carolina Press, 2002); Gleijeses, "Moscow's Proxy? Cuba and Africa, 1975–1988," *Journal of Cold War Studies* 8(4): 98–146; Gleijeses, "Cuba and the Independence of Namibia," *Cold War History* 7(2) (2007): 285–303; Sue Onslow, "Research Report: Republic of South Africa Archives," *Cold War History* 5(3) (2005): 369–75; Onslow, "A Question of Timing: South Africa and Rhodesia's Unilateral Declaration of Independence, 1964–65," *Cold War History* 5(2): 129–59; Chris Saunders, "Namibian Solidarity: British Support for Namibian Independence," *Journal of Southern African Studies* 35(2) (2009): 437–54.

29 Brzezinski coined the term "arc of crisis" in a December 1978 speech; see Raymond Garthoff, *Détente and Confrontation: American–Soviet Relations from Nixon to Reagan* (Washington, DC: The Brookings Institution, 1994), 728. On the "sands of the Oagaden," see Zbigniew Brzezinski, *Power and Principle: Memoirs of the National Security Adviser, 1977–1981* (New York: Farrar, Straus & Giroux, 1983), 189.

30 Westad, *Global Cold War*, 208–18.

31 Gleijeses, *Conflicting Missions*, chapters 12–15.

32 Selassie's remains were found buried under a toilet in the grounds of his palace in February 1992, see "Ethiopians Celebrate a Mass for Exhumed Haile Selassie," *New York Times*, 1 March 1992.

33 Forrest D. Colburn, *The Vogue of Revolution in Poor Countries* (Princeton, NJ: Princeton University Press, 1994), 20–2. For the internal dynamics of the Ethiopian Revolution, see also Donald L. Donham, *Marxist Modern: An Ethnographic History of the Ethiopian Revolution* (Berkeley, CA: University of California Press, 1999), and Andargachew Tiruneh, *The Ethiopian Revolution 1974–1987:*

A Transformation from an Aristocratic to a Totalitarian Autocracy (Cambridge: Cambridge University Press, 2009).

34 Mengistu's predecessor as Derg Chairman, General Tafari Bante, declared that the Ethiopian revolution "is an integral part of a global process of economic and social change which has a historical continuity," *Africa in Russia, Russia in Africa: Three Centuries of Encounters*, edited by Maxim Matusevich (Trenton, NJ: Africa World Press, 2006), 230.

35 Soviet Foreign Ministry, Background Report on Soviet–Ethiopian Relations, 3 April 1978, from the *Cold War International History Project* online archive, www.cwihp.org.

36 Westad, *Global Cold War*, 274.

37 For a detailed history of the Ethiopian–Somalian conflict, see Gebru Tareke, *The Ethiopian Revolution: War in the Horn of Africa* (New Haven, CT: Yale University Press, 2009).

38 Chris Saunders and Sue Onslow, "The Cold War and Southern Africa," *Cambridge History of the Cold War* (Cambridge: Cambridge University Press, 2012), vol. 3, 222–43.

39 Thomas Bortelsmann, *The Cold War and the Color Line: American Race Relations in the Global Arena* (Cambridge, MA: Harvard University Press, 2001), 261.

40 On US–South African nuclear relations, see Martha van Wyck, "Sunset over Atomic Apartheid: United States–South African Nuclear Relations, 1981–93," *Cold War History* 10(1) (2010): 51–79. For general histories of Reagan's approach to Africa, see Pauline Baker, *The United States and South Africa: The Reagan Years* (New York: Ford Foundation, 1989) and Alex Thompson, *Incomplete Engagement: United States Foreign Policy towards the Republic of South Africa, 1981–1988* (Aldershot: Avebury, 1996).

41 Giovanni Arrighi, *The Long Twentieth Century: Money, Power and the Origins of Our Times* (London: Verso, 2010); Frieden, *Global Capitalism*, 363–91.

42 IMF figures reproduced in Frederick Cooper, *Africa since 1940: The Past of the Present* (London, New York: Cambridge University Press, 2002), 93–7; Frieden, *Global Capitalism*, 435–56.

43 Kristin L. Ahlberg offers a study of the Johnson administration doing so in India, but the documentary record indicates that the same policy was applied with Algeria and Egypt; see "'Machiavelli with a Heart': The Johnson Administration's Food for Peace Program in India, 1965–1966," *Diplomatic History* 31:4 (2007): 665–701.

44 For the connection between IMF neo-liberalism and the near-collapse of the Algerian state, see J.N.C. Hill, "Challenging the Failed State Thesis: IMF and World Bank intervention and the Algerian Civil War," *Civil Wars*, 11(1) (2009): 39–56. Conversely, Timothy Mitchell explores how neo-liberalism created a sense of exuberance and possibility in Egypt during roughly the same period, "No Factories, No Problems: The Logic of Neo-Liberalism in Egypt," *Review of African Political Economy* 26(82) (1999): 455–68.

45 For example, see Tanja R. Müller, "'Memories of paradise' – Legacies of socialist education in Mozambique," *African Affairs*, 109 (2010): 436, 451–70.

46 On post-independence disillusionment, see Giacomo Macola, "'It Means as if We Are Excluded from the Good Freedom': Thwarted Expectations of Independence in the Luapula Province of Zambia, 1964–6," *Journal of African History*, 47 (2006): 43–56.

12

THE COLD WAR IN THE MIDDLE EAST

Paul Thomas Chamberlin

Between 1945 and 1991, the Middle East became one of the most hotly contested theaters in the Cold War between the United States and the Soviet Union. It can be argued that no other region would witness such a constant stream of warfare, crises, and strategic realignments over such a sustained period of time. No other theater of the Cold War contained such a volatile mix of crumbling empires, strategic commodities, revolutionary nationalism, ethnic and religious diversity, and potential proxy armies. No other Cold War frontier would be so unstable and subject to such dramatic change over the entire course of the Cold War: between 1945 and 1955, the Middle East would lean toward the West; from 1955 to 1975, it would lean toward Moscow; from 1975 onward, it would again shift toward Washington. All of these factors would combine in the decades following the end of World War II to generate an almost constant stream of diplomatic and military conflicts in the Middle East – fueled by massive arms shipments from the superpowers – many of which would ultimately outlive the Cold War itself.

In recent years, historians of foreign relations have begun to pay increasing attention to the region. Driven by an overall turn toward the Third World and the contemporary political-military developments in the Middle East, larger numbers of scholars have come to focus on the area. They can be divided, roughly, into four groups. The first, and largest, consists of scholars whose focus rests on the formation of U.S. policy in the Middle East. These historians have traced the struggle between various organs of the American state and across different presidential administrations to craft a policy toward the region. The most fully developed subset, their works include traditional diplomatic and political history as well as cultural and social analyses of U.S.–Middle East relations.[1] The second group of scholars focuses on Israeli foreign policy, most often on the Arab–Israeli dispute. Historians of Israel have used a blend of archival research and journalistic techniques to craft a deep body of scholarship on the topic that stretches across a variety of interpretations.[2] The third set of historians consists of Soviet specialists who have studied Moscow's extensive involvement in the region. A significant new strain in this scholarship has examined the ways that Moscow sought to employ Islam as a tool of cultural diplomacy.[3] The fourth and final group has worked to incorporate the perspectives of Arab, Iranian, and Turkish peoples and states, blending area studies scholarship with foreign relations history. These multi-archival, multi-lingual studies have sought to present local players as dynamic agents in the making of the region's history.[4]

Beginning of the Cold War

Hints of the Cold War competition in the Middle East were visible even before the end of World War II. The region was important to the Allied powers for a variety of reasons. As had been the case before the war, the British saw Southwest Asia as a key component of their worldwide empire and the site of the most direct approaches to India. France, suffering from the stigma of defeat and Nazi occupation, hoped to regain some of its prestige and economic influence by resurrecting its power in its former mandates, Syria and Lebanon. Meanwhile, Soviet leaders hoped to extend their influence into the region both to secure access to warm-water ports – the Bosporus was of particular interest – and to maintain a buffer zone of friendly states surrounding the Soviet Union's southern flank. The United States also understood the geostrategic significance of the region and hoped to ensure access to markets and airfields there. Like Moscow, Washington hoped to keep the Middle East from falling under the influence of any hostile power. Perhaps most significantly, all of the parties involved recognized the importance of the Middle Eastern oilfields for postwar reconstruction, particularly in Western Europe.[5]

One of the first major crises of the Cold War took place at the eastern end of the Middle East, in Iran. Soviet and British troops had occupied Iran in 1941 in order to prevent its leader, Reza Shah, from bringing Iran into alignment with the Axis powers. The Allied powers installed Reza's son, Mohammed Reza Pahlavi, on the throne and established a line of military supplies through Iran to the Soviet Union. As the war against Germany began to wind down, however, signs appeared that the Soviet Union did not intend to liquidate its occupation of the north of the country. Soviet troops restricted the movements of Iranian security forces in the north at the same time that the Kremlin supported Azeri separatists in their bid to establish a breakaway socialist republic in northern Iran. Stalin hoped that this Soviet puppet state, created in November 1945, would function as a buffer to protect vital oil facilities at Baku. British and U.S. protests over Soviet actions continued through 1945 and 1946, illustrating the widening schism among the Allies and drawing the attention of the newly established United Nations to Stalin's provocations. Though London and Washington could do little to contest the consolidation of Soviet power in Eastern Europe, Western diplomacy in Iran proved more effective. By early 1946, Stalin recognized that his brinksmanship had backfired, galvanizing Western resistance to Soviet power in other parts of the world. Rather than perpetuate the crisis, the Kremlin chose to concede to diplomatic pressure and pulled its troops out of Iran. The episode was a harbinger of rising U.S.–Soviet tensions and the importance of the Middle East and Iran in the coming Cold War struggle.[6]

The Iran Crisis also illuminated the importance of the Anglo-American relationship in the Middle East. In the early years of the Cold War, U.S. policymakers hoped to use the remnants of the British Empire in the Middle East to support American interests in the region. While Washington had been active during World War II in pressuring London to retreat from its imperial possessions, U.S. leaders were forced to balance their competing priorities of decolonization against the desire to keep Soviet influence out of regions like the Middle East. Thus, Washington looked to Great Britain to police the region on behalf of the Western powers. London, for its part, hoped to maintain Britain's status as a great power by maintaining a sort of benevolent imperialism in the Middle East. As time would show, however, local nationalists saw little benefit in maintaining this sort of relationship with their former imperial overlords. Nothing short of full independence would satisfy the peoples that actually lived in the region.[7]

The British found it difficult to sustain the financial burden of maintaining their position in the Middle East at the same time that they were seeking to rebuild in the wake of the war. One area of acute concern was Greece, which was in the midst of a civil war between the recognized government and Greek Communists. The British had been working to prop up the pro-Western government, recognizing that its collapse would have ramifications for the balance of power in the Eastern Mediterranean and place added strain on Turkey – which faced strong Soviet pressure to grant open navigation through the Bosporus. In late 1946, London informed Washington that it could no longer support the Greek government and asked the United States to accept the burden. Viewing the situation in Greece and Turkey alongside the earlier crisis in Iran and George Kennan's "Long Telegram," President Harry Truman concluded that the United States must step into Britain's role in the region. In March 1947, the President delivered an address to Congress calling for aid to Greece and Turkey for the purpose of contesting Soviet advances in the region. What became known as the Truman Doctrine provided the basic blueprint for U.S. containment strategy toward the Soviet Union during the rest of the Cold War and helped to secure Turkey's place in the Western alliance. For the time being, Washington's containment strategy along the Northern Tier – Turkey, Iraq, Iran, and Pakistan – appeared to be working.[8]

For the indigenous peoples of the Middle East, two linked issues overshadowed the emerging U.S.–Soviet rivalry: the struggle for independence and the mounting crisis in Palestine. Inherent in the struggle for independence was the question of what form it should take as various forces in the Arab world – bourgeois, royalist, revolutionary, and religious – vied for leadership. More radical plans called for Pan-Arab unity that would link states like Transjordan, Iraq, Syria, Lebanon, Palestine, and Egypt. Within states, contests for power between monarchists, constitutionalists, and progressive parties would become more pronounced in the years following the end of the war. The British Mandate of Palestine would play a decisive role in determining the outcome of these internal struggles. In the earlier decades of the twentieth century, Palestine became the principal site of interest for Jewish colonists from Europe, or Zionists, who hoped to create a Jewish state in their ancient homeland. The Zionists received encouragement from London's Balfour Declaration of 1917, which became the foundational document of the British imperial mandate in Palestine following World War I. Over the next thirty years, the Jewish population in Palestine increased – mainly through immigration from Europe – from less than 10 percent of a total to around 33 percent. Arabs throughout the Middle East saw this stream of settlers and the Balfour Declaration as a threat to Arab aspirations to sovereignty in Palestine.[9]

British attempts to restrict Jewish immigration to Palestine – most notably the 1939 White Paper that would effectively trap many Jews in Europe as the Nazis took control – sparked a Zionist rebellion in 1944. By late 1946, London had had enough and began calling for the liquidation of the Palestine mandate. As the British made plans to leave, civil war between the Arabs and Zionists loomed. Two basic plans for Palestine emerged: a one-state solution where Jews would be a minority, and a two-state solution that would partition the mandated territory into a Jewish and an Arab state. The official American position was conflicted. Although American diplomats and Arab leaders warned the White House that support for the Zionists would jeopardize U.S. standing in the region, President Truman faced strong pressure from pro-Zionist groups to back plans for a partition. Against the counsel of his advisors, Truman came down on the side of the Zionists and partition. Truman's support would prove instrumental in the coming months, most notably in the passage of the 1947 UN Partition Plan, which gave over 56 percent of the land to the Jewish minority, leaving the Arab majority with less than 44 percent. The Soviet Union, which at this time supported the Zionist project, would also back this partition plan. While the Zionists accepted the plan, the Arabs rejected it and a state of civil war between the two communities began.[10]

The British terminated their mandate in May 1948, whereupon Zionist leaders proclaimed the creation of the state of Israel. While both Washington and Moscow hurried to recognize the new state, Arab armies entered Palestine. The Arab invasion has been a subject of controversy: while some scholars describe this as an attack on Israel, others see it as a defense of the Arab population. Regardless, the war went badly for the Arabs, who were outgunned, outnumbered, and outgeneraled for most of the conflict. By the time an armistice was signed in 1949, Israel had expanded its borders to comprise 78 percent of Palestine and over 700,000 Palestinians had become refugees. The 1948 war would have long-lasting repercussions for the region and the Cold War in the coming decades.[11]

Years of Revolution

The first major consequence of the 1948 war would be to discredit the Arab regimes that had fought in it. As the scope of their defeat became clear, the regimes in Syria, Egypt, Iraq, and Jordan suffered major blows to their prestige and support mounted for their opponents. Meanwhile, serious cracks began to appear in the Anglo-American alliance's dominant position in the Middle East. In Egypt in 1952, a group of young officers untainted by the humiliation of 1948 launched a successful coup against the regime in Cairo and proclaimed a revolutionary republic. In the following months the Free Officers Movement consolidated power in Egypt and passed a series of major reforms. By 1954, Gamal abd al-Nasser had emerged as the most powerful member of the group.[12]

Even as the revolution swept through Egypt, high drama was unfolding in Iran. There, nationalist leaders were calling for the renegotiation of the Anglo-Iranian Oil Company's 1933 petroleum concession, which channeled the majority of the profits from Iran's oil to Britain. In 1951, the Iranian parliament nationalized the oil industry and elected Mohammad Mossadegh as Prime Minister. Britain refused to renegotiate the terms of the petroleum concession and approached Washington for assistance in overthrowing the democratically elected regime, arguing that Mossadegh would not effectively restrict the growth of communist power in Iran. Truman declined London's approaches but his successor, Dwight Eisenhower, was more receptive. Afraid of the potential for Iran to slip into the Soviet sphere, the Eisenhower administration authorized the Central Intelligence Agency to cooperate with British intelligence to overthrow Mossadegh. In August 1953, American and British intelligence services managed to topple the Mossadegh government, returning the Shah to absolute control of Iran and eliminating the constitutional regime. The Shah would remain in power for the next twenty-six years, during which time he would become a pro-Western strongman in the region.[13]

The Western powers would have more trouble dealing with the regime in Egypt, however. Still following the rubric of containment, the Eisenhower hoped to construct an alliance system in the Middle East starting with the Northern Tier states – Turkey, Iraq, Iran, and Pakistan – and Great Britain that would function as a bulwark against Soviet expansion. The Baghdad Pact, as it became known, was signed into existence in February 1955. President Nasser fiercely rejected any notion of participating in the organization and launched a concerted propaganda campaign against it. Syria, Saudi Arabia, and Egypt formed a rival organization, dramatically undermining the Baghdad Pact's appeal. In addition to his international efforts, Nasser faced the challenge of modernizing Egypt's economy and military forces and claiming the mantle of leadership of the Arab world. To do this, he would need two principal things: financial aid to construct the enormous hydroelectric dam at Aswan and military assistance to strengthen the Egyptian army. Eisenhower, who initially viewed Nasser as a potential anticommunist ally, was at first inclined to support the Egyptian President. Nasser's opposition to the Baghdad Pact and a flare-up in border tensions with Israel prompted Washington to reconsider, however. In particular, concerns about sending weapons to Egypt that might be used against Israel weighed heavily on the administration.[14]

Refusing to accept the strings attached to U.S. aid, Nasser turned to the USSR. Stalin's death in 1953 had opened the door to a new leadership in Moscow that was interested in expanding Soviet influence in the developing world. Thus, Soviet Premier Nikita Khrushchev seized this opportunity to expand his relations with Egypt. In September 1955, Nasser concluded a deal with Czechoslovakia – a Warsaw Pact intermediary – for some $200 million in arms. In effect, the Czech Arms Deal circumvented the Baghdad Pact and provided a new entry point for Soviet influence in the Middle East. Hoping to counterbalance the Soviets in Egypt, Washington and London proposed a plan to finance the Aswan Dam project in December. The final terms of the agreement were held up in the following months, however, and Washington's relationship with Nasser began to deteriorate as the latter sent hints that he would be willing to entertain Soviet offers to fund the project. The last straw came in 1956, however, when Nasser recognized Communist China. Furious, the Eisenhower administration withdrew its offer to fund the dam. In response, Nasser authorized Egyptian forces to seize control of the Suez Canal, bringing the strategic waterway under the control of the Egyptian government at the end of July.[15]

Nasser's move touched off a crisis between Egypt, France, and Great Britain. While the Eisenhower administration sought to resolve the situation through diplomatic means, France, Great Britain, and Israel developed a plan to invade Egypt and seize the canal. London and Paris were driven by strategic and financial motivations; Israeli leaders feared that Nasser was becoming too much of a threat to their security. At a secret meeting at Sèvres in October 1956, French, British, and Israeli officials concluded an agreement for joint military action against Egypt. This plan was activated on 29 October, when Israel launched an attack on Egyptian forces in the Sinai. London and Paris then pointed to the hostilities as a pretext for their intervention in order to protect the canal and British warplanes began bombing military targets near the canal. On 5–6 November, British and French paratroops dropped over Port Said and an invasion force began moving toward Suez City. This three-way conspiracy fooled no one; both Moscow and Washington were incensed. While Moscow feared the loss of a potential ally and issued threats to attack London and Paris, President Dwight Eisenhower denounced an invasion that smacked of nineteenth-century colonialism and risked a Cold War conflagration. The American president feared that such actions were likely to drive the whole of the Arab world – and perhaps other postcolonial nations – into the arms of the Soviet Union. To make matters worse, the Suez Crisis coincided with the Soviet army's bloody crackdown in Hungary, robbing NATO of the opportunity to focus world attention on the Kremlin's brutality. Eisenhower thus made the controversial decision to side with Moscow and Nasser and demand the withdrawal of British, French, and Israeli forces from Egypt.[16]

The Nasser Era

The Suez Crisis propelled Nasser to regional superstardom and provided inroads for Moscow to expand its influence in the Arab world. The Egyptian leader had withstood the assault of Europe's imperial forces – and their Israeli allies – despite embarrassing setbacks on the battlefield. On the basis of this growing prestige, Nasser pushed a regional program of secular Pan-Arabism and Arab Socialism with the aim of spreading the fervor of the Egyptian Revolution across the Arab world. The international impact of the crisis was also pivotal: Moscow received a boost for its diplomatic defense of Cairo while Washington remained suspect; Britain and France were humiliated and the Western alliance was divided; and the debacle at Suez would signal the beginning of the end of the British Empire in the Middle East. Eisenhower was well aware of these implications and began moves to shore up Western interests in the region, principally through an effort to limit Nasser's influence, limit Soviet advances, and compensate for the decline of British power in the region. These goals were articulated in the Eisenhower Doctrine – announced in January 1957 – which promised U.S. economic and military support for any state under threat from "international communism." It amounted, in the words of one historian, to an effort to contain Nasser's Arab Nationalism.[17]

It would be only a matter of months before the Eisenhower Doctrine was activated during the climactic year of 1958, in which three of the pro-Western regimes in the Arab world were threatened by revolution. In February, the Ba'athist government in Syria announced the creation of the United Arab Republic (UAR) with Nasser's Egypt. For many, the birth of the UAR was seen as the first step toward the creation of a Pan-Arab state and the realization of decades-old aspirations of Arab Nationalism. Western anxieties received another jolt on 14 July when a Free Officers group deposed the Hashemite monarchy in Iraq, killing King Faisal II and longtime Prime Minister Nuri al-Said and destroying the cornerstone of the Baghdad Pact. The reverberations from the events in Syria and Iraq hit Lebanon next. Through the month of July, the pro-Western nation remained on the brink of civil war between Maronite Christians struggling to hold on to power and Sunni groups, many of which had Pan-Arab sympathies. When Christian President Camille Chamoun heard news of the coup in Iraq, he requested U.S. intervention. Eisenhower – who worried that the pro-Soviet Nasser was on the brink of gaining power over the majority of the Arab world – decided to send U.S. forces into Lebanon. The 14,000 troops that landed in Beirut managed to stabilize the immediate tensions, but they did nothing to resolve the deep sectarian divisions in the fragile republic. The specter of revolution also threatened the pro-Western Hashemite regime in Jordan. Fearing that the revolution in neighboring Iraq would spread to his country, King Hussein requested Western support and received it in the form of British troops. Thus, at the end of July 1958, both Washington and London had military deployments in the region.[18]

While the U.S. and British interventions had saved the pro-Western governments in Lebanon and Jordan, political tides in the region seemed to favor Nasser and the Soviet Union at the end of the 1950s. The Cold War in the Middle East was not a zero-sum game, however. The Kremlin was alarmed by the formation of the UAR, fearing that it might undermine good relations with Syria and recognizing that the merger would strengthen Nasser, thus allowing him to become more independent. Hence, the revolution in Iraq appeared to Moscow as an opportunity to counterbalance Nasser's rising power by strengthening the pro-Soviet regime in Baghdad. Soviet leaders would be somewhat disappointed, however, as the regime in Iraq – like Egypt before it – would ruthlessly suppress local communist parties. Moreover, Cairo, Damascus, and Baghdad would all compete for leadership of the Arab Nationalist cause, especially after the dissolution of the UAR in 1961. Nevertheless, a rough alignment emerged during the period in what one scholar has called the Arab Cold War between the progressive Arab republics of Egypt, Syria, and Iraq, which leaned toward the Soviet Union, and the pro-Western conservative monarchies of Saudi Arabia and Jordan. The most dramatic manifestation of this regional cold war would take place in North Yemen, where royalist forces backed by Saudi Arabia and Jordan sought to undermine the republican regime, which received support from Egypt and the USSR. The war, which would last from 1962 until 1970 and see the involvement of between 60,000 and 70,000 Egyptian troops, would be remembered as a disaster for Egypt, sapping the regime's strength and drawing comparison as "Nasser's Vietnam."[19]

The Arab–Israeli Wars

The Nasser era came to a dramatic end on the morning of 5 June 1967 when Israeli jets destroyed the Egyptian air force as it sat on the ground, marking the start of the 1967 Arab–Israeli War. The war had been precipitated by a series of crises in the region. Nasser's prestige was suffering as a result of stagnant economic conditions in Egypt and the stalemated conflict in Yemen. In the midst of this, Soviet intelligence relayed a false report that Israel was planning to invade Syria in retaliation for recent Palestinian guerilla attacks in May. It appears that Soviet leaders were using the threat of an Israeli attack to frighten their Arab allies into a closer alignment with the Soviet bloc. The Kremlin's gambit quickly spun out of control, however. Hoping to restore a measure of his Pan-Arab credibility, Nasser initiated a bout of saber rattling, mobilizing the Egyptian army in the Sinai and calling for the evacuation of UN peacekeepers stationed there since 1956. He then made the fateful decision in late May to close the Straits of Tiran to Israeli shipping, a move seen by Israel as an act of war. As Washington and Moscow worked to defuse rising tensions, Israeli military leaders – wary of a prolonged military mobilization – pushed for a preemptive strike. On 4 June, Israeli officials agreed and the Jewish state struck Egyptian and Syrian airfields the following day.[20]

The 1967 war quickly turned into a regional conflict as the Jordanian army joined the fight and a number of the Arab states sent expeditionary forces. Israeli forces, which had secured virtual control of the air following their preemptive attack, proved devastatingly effective against the Egyptian, Syrian, and Jordanian armies. By 10 June, when an armistice was finally brokered, Israel had conquered the Sinai Peninsula and Gaza Strip, the Golan Heights, and the West Bank, bringing an area nearly twice the size of Israel under the control of the Israel Defense Forces (IDF). The war also created approximately 300,000 additional Palestinian refugees and placed around one million Palestinians in the West Bank and Gaza under Israeli military occupation. Many observers were convinced that the long-sought formula for a regional peace had been achieved. Israel could use these territories as bargaining chips to secure diplomatic recognition and peace treaties from its Arab neighbors, bringing the Arab–Israeli conflict to an end. This land-for-peace formula was the spirit behind what would become the central document of the post-1967 peace process, UN Security Council Resolution 242, endorsed by both Cold War superpowers.[21]

Once conquered, however, these new territories proved difficult for the Israeli government to relinquish. While the IDF lauded the dramatic increase in Israel's strategic depth, large segments of the Israeli population celebrated the conquest of Jerusalem and Judea and Samaria (the West Bank). The Arab states' rejection of any diplomatic negotiations – under duress brought on by what they considered an illegal occupation of their territory – at the Khartoum Conference made matters worse. By late 1967, it appeared as if the hopes for a postwar peace settlement were little more than fantasies. Further complicating matters, the war had energized Palestinian guerilla groups, who began launching attacks in the occupied territories and from neighboring Arab states. In 1968, these groups gained control over the Palestine Liberation Organization (PLO), which became a central player in regional diplomacy. The PLO linked Palestinian nationalism to the global causes of decolonization and national liberation. Taking a page from guerilla revolutions in China, Vietnam, Algeria, and Cuba, the PLO refashioned itself as an Arab Viet Cong, quickly becoming a cause célèbre among left-wing states and progressive groups around the world. At the same time, Palestinian fighters gained the patronage of the People's Republic of China and the Soviet Union. Through a combination of armed operations and an international diplomatic campaign, the PLO managed to put the Palestinians on the global map of Third World revolutionaries and return the Palestinian question to the center of the Arab–Israeli conflict. In doing so, they emerged as one of the most dynamic players in Arab politics and a revolutionary new force in the Cold War international system. If nothing else, the guerillas had guaranteed that the Palestinians could never again be ignored – there would be no peace in the Middle East until their grievances had been addressed.[22]

With the diplomatic process stalled and the PLO gaining international accolades as the new face of the revolution in the Arab world, in 1969 Nasser launched a "War of Attrition" against the IDF along the Suez Canal, which consisted of artillery exchanges, aerial combat, and commando raids between the two sides. Cairo could no longer afford to accept the humiliating status quo that left the IDF in occupation of the Sinai with a defensive line deep inside Egyptian territory along the Suez Canal. Egyptian artillery attacks, however, sparked punishing reprisals in the form of deep penetration raids from the Israeli air force. To defend against these reprisals – and to aid in resisting the Israeli occupation of the Sinai – Nasser called upon Moscow for aid. Thus, Egyptian forces were bolstered by a large contingent of Soviet military advisers that Moscow had sent to the country to assist in the reconstruction of Cairo's armed forces in the wake of the 1967 disaster. At its height, the Soviet mission comprised some 20,000 advisers, including Soviet pilots in MiGs bearing Egyptian markings and Russian crews manning anti-aircraft missile batteries. While the Kremlin had qualms about becoming directly embroiled in the regional conflict, leaders in Moscow had to provide for the defense of their most important ally in the Middle East or risk suffering a major blow to their credibility in the region. Although Secretary of State William Rogers was eventually able to negotiate a ceasefire, underlying tensions remained.[23]

Meanwhile, the growing power of the PLO threatened to upset an already volatile situation. In September 1970, a civil war broke out in Jordan between King Hussein and Palestinian fighters, sparked by the hijacking of four jetliners. After bloody fighting in refugee camps that left thousands of Palestinians dead, the King's forces gained the upper hand and forced the PLO to relocate its headquarters to Beirut. The conflict had profound regional consequences, nearly resulting in another general war as Syrian forces crossed into the northern part of the country only to be stared down by the threat of Israeli intervention at the request of the United States. In the aftermath of the war, Hafiz al-Assad would consolidate power in Damascus and set up a powerful regime in Syria. Nasser had worked exhaustively to bring an end to the fighting. After securing a ceasefire on 27 September, the Egyptian president suffered a fatal heart attack. In the coming months, splinter factions of the PLO began launching a series of spectacular armed operations throughout the international system that would help to catapult the Palestinians to global prominence. Attacks like the 1972 Munich Olympics Massacre and the 1973 Khartoum killings would earn the Palestinians alternately acclaim as "freedom fighters" and infamy as "terrorists." By 1974, the PLO would wield diplomatic influence in forums like the United Nations that was drastically greater than its conventional forces on the ground. The problems of converting political victories in the international sphere into concrete progress toward the creation of a Palestinian state remained, however, as the United States moved into a position of blocking pro-Palestinian initiatives in the UN Security Council.[24]

While Palestinian fighters made headlines, the new leaders in Cairo and Damascus were working to regain control of those territories lost in 1967. Anwar Sadat, Nasser's unlikely successor, made a series of gestures attempting to restart the stalled peace process. The most dramatic of these came in July 1972 with the expulsion of nearly 20,000 Soviet military advisors from Egypt. The move, which gutted Moscow's largest deployment in the developing world, was designed to gain Washington's attention and to give Cairo a free hand in subsequent developments. This second issue would prove more salient as Sadat and Syrian President Hafiz al-Assad made plans to launch a fourth Arab–Israeli war. On 6 October 1973 – Yom Kippur on the Jewish calendar, the tenth day of Ramadan on the Muslim calendar – Egyptian and Syrian forces launched a coordinated attack on IDF units across the Suez Canal and the Golan Heights. The surprise assault drove Israeli forces back in a series of initial successes that gave Egypt a beachhead on the east side of the Suez Canal and threatened to drive the IDF out of the Golan. Sadat's goal was to force a new round of diplomacy, however, and he made the fateful decision to halt his offensive and keep his troops under the cover of surface-to-air missiles on the west bank of the canal. This pause aided IDF efforts to regroup and launch a counterattack against Syrian positions in the Golan. As Israeli forces gained ground, Assad pleaded with Sadat to renew his offensive in the Sinai. Sadat relented and moved his forces out from under their protective missile umbrella, giving the IDF the opportunity to begin a counterattack in the Sinai on 14 October, which marked the turning of the war's tide in favor of the Israelis. That same day, the United States began a massive resupply of weapons to Israel.[25]

The Egyptian–Syrian attack had also come as a surprise to Moscow and Washington. Both superpowers feared that another Arab–Israeli war could initiate a wider crisis and sought to limit hostilities in the region. Once the war began, however, both the United States and USSR sought to gain diplomatic advantage. While the Kremlin pushed for an early ceasefire that would secure Egyptian and Syrian advances, the White House delayed, hoping to buy the IDF time to counterattack and strengthen Israel's postwar negotiating position. This diplomatic struggle reached an alarming crescendo on the night of 24–25 October when Soviet Premier Leonid Brezhnev informed U.S. President Richard Nixon of Moscow's willingness to intervene in order to force the IDF to accept a ceasefire. Rather than taking the matter to the President – who was deeply depressed over the Watergate scandal – Secretary of State Henry Kissinger chose to meet the Soviet threat head on, declaring a nuclear alert and moving the U.S. military to DEFCON 3 for the first time since the Cuban Missile Crisis. Shocked, Moscow backed down, but the threat of nuclear war had a sobering effect on both superpowers. Though no one knew it at the time, the 1973 war would be the last general war in the Arab–Israeli conflict. The two major wars of 1967 and 1973 would also provide a definitive demonstration of the superiority of Western weapons systems over their Soviet counterparts and expose Moscow's inability to secure a settlement in the Arab–Israeli conflict that would satisfy its allies in Cairo and Damascus. As such, the Arab–Israeli wars would become a sort of testing ground for a hypothetical Soviet–American military confrontation.[26]

The Peace Process

The 1973 war and the postwar peace process would transform the diplomatic landscape of the Middle East, marking a period of Cold War realignment in the region. Its first major impact, however, was to bring a new power into play in the form of the Arab oil weapon. On 17 October, in response to the news that Washington was rearming the IDF, the Organization of Arab Petroleum Exporting Countries (OAPEC) elected to cut oil production by 5 percent, a number to be increased as long as U.S. support for Israel in the conflict continued. The boycott threw global oil markets into disarray and sparked a sharp increase in the price of oil over the 1970s as petroleum-producing states in the Middle East gained greater control over the sale of their natural resources. Combined with the nuclear alert, it helped to pull the United States into closer diplomatic engagement on the Arab–Israeli peace process. The key American figure in that story was Nixon and Ford's Secretary of State, Henry Kissinger.[27]

Earlier in 1969–70, the Nixon administration had launched an abortive attempt to achieve a comprehensive peace settlement based on UN Resolution 242 in the form of the Rogers Plan – named for Nixon's first Secretary of State, William Rogers. Both Nixon and Kissinger had undermined this plan – with the help of Israeli Prime Minister Golda Meir – because they favored a stalemate in the conflict that might wear down Soviet influence in the region. The post-1973 diplomatic situation allowed Kissinger to launch a new set of initiatives in the peace process known as "shuttle diplomacy." In contrast to earlier attempts to create a comprehensive peace on UN Resolution 242's formula, Kissinger began a step-by-step approach in which Israel would forge agreements with individual Arab states. Kissinger's shuttle diplomacy had the effect of strengthening Israel's negotiating position and pushing the USSR to the periphery of the peace process while placing Washington at its center. This approach achieved dramatic success on the Egyptian front with the signing of the Sinai II agreement in 1975, which helped to pave the way for an eventual peace between Israel and Egypt. While it removed the principal Arab belligerent in the Arab-Israeli conflict – ensuring that no more general wars would take place in the Middle East during the Cold War – Kissinger's shuttle diplomacy also removed pressure on Israel to come to a lasting peace with Syria and, more notably, the PLO. In pulling Sadat's Egypt out of the conflict, Kissinger's diplomacy made the prospect of a comprehensive peace in the region less likely. The Secretary of State did succeed, however, in wooing Egypt away from the Soviet sphere, accomplishing perhaps the most important Cold War realignment of the 1970s. In 1978, Sadat, Israeli Prime Minister Menachem Begin, and President Jimmy Carter would hammer out a plan for peace between Egypt and Israel at Camp David in Maryland. Henceforth, Cairo would lean toward NATO and the United States while Moscow's key allies in the region would be Syria, Iraq, and the PLO. Sadat's defection proved to be a pivotal event in the superpower contest in the Middle East and one of the most important strategic transformations of the decade.[28]

Although Washington was gaining ground in the Cold War struggle for the Middle East in the 1970s, the region was by no means a more peaceful place. Signs of deep troubles appeared first in the pro-Western republic of Lebanon in the spring of 1975. The presence of left-wing Palestinian guerillas – most of whom were Sunni – in Lebanon had upset the fragile sectarian balance between Maronite Christians, Sunni, Shi'a, and Druze. Combined with military reprisals against the PLO, these tensions pushed the nation into a fifteen-year civil war in 1975. The nation would effectively become the first failed state in the Middle East as state control collapsed and Beirut's downtown was turned into a warzone. Lebanon became a microcosm for many of the changes that would take place in the region and around the developing world in the coming decades; religious nationalism, heavily armed private militias, sectarian strife, massacres of civilians, and urban guerilla war would all touch the small Mediterranean nation. At the same time, Lebanon became the principal battleground in the post-1973 Arab–Israeli conflict as Syrian and Israeli forces joined the conflict.[29]

Meanwhile, dramatic new political, social, and economic forces were rising throughout the region. Sadat's bold diplomatic moves were accompanied by the *Infitahi*, a series of economic initiatives designed to replace Nasser's Arab socialism with a more capitalistic system open to foreign investment. Egyptian power in the Arab world was in a state of decline, however, which opened the door to the rising influence of Saudi Arabia. Propelled by spectacular oil revenues, Saudi leaders stepped into the power vacuum left by Nasser's departure and Sadat's decision to pull Cairo out of the Arab–Israeli conflict. Saudi influence spread throughout the region in the form of financial aid and development packages. The Saudi state – created in 1932 – had always consisted of a sort of partnership between the Saudi royal family and Wahhabi religious leaders, a bond that dated back to the eighteenth century. Thus, along with petrodollars, this development network spread Wahhabi religious doctrine through the Arab world. Some scholars have identified the 1970s and the rise of Saudi power as a key factor in the resurgence of political Islam in the Middle East.[30]

Revolution and War

Concerns over the rising power of Islamic forces would first surface in the United States and Soviet Union at the end of the 1970s. While U.S. leaders had initially seen Islam as a potential bulwark against communism – an ostensibly atheist ideology – many Soviet leaders assumed that religious faith would fade away as the irresistible march of history spread Marxist-Leninism around the globe. However, Moscow recognized that the nearly fifty million Muslims inside the Soviet Union and the Muslim countries that lay on its southern borders represented a potential source of unrest. Both superpowers would receive a rude awakening in 1978 as a revolution in Iran shook the Middle East and the world and signaled the beginning of a new era in the region.

Since the 1953 Anglo-American coup had returned him to power, Shah Mohammad Reza Pahlavi had ruled Iran with an iron fist. With the help of his secret police – trained by the CIA and Israeli Mossad – the Shah had systematically crushed all organized opposition in Iran except for the Shi'a religious authorities in Qom. After a quarter-century, however, the Shah's power had begun to slip. Severe economic dislocation brought on by soaring inflation – the result of skyrocketing oil prices – generated a broad coalition of anti-Shah forces in Iran. As this movement grew, it became clear that the Shah's security forces could not regain control. The Shah was thus forced to flee the country with his family in January 1979 and a new revolutionary leadership took power. While the new government was initially composed of a broad set of opposition leaders – middle-class intellectuals, left-wing activists, and liberals – Shi'a clerics, as the best-organized group, were able to consolidate power in the following months and give the revolution a theocratic character. This left Ayatollah Ruhollah Khomeini as Supreme leader of the new Islamic Republic of Iran. In the midst of this reconsolidation of power, student supporters of Khomeini stormed the U.S. Embassy in Tehran and took its occupants hostage in November 1979. In what became a national humiliation broadcast on the nightly television news, the fifty-two American hostages remained in Iranian hands for 444 days as the Carter administration negotiated for their release. Making matters worse, a botched rescue attempt – codenamed Operation Eagle Claw – resulted in the deaths of eight U.S. servicemen in April 1980.[31]

The resurgence of political Islam created problems for both superpowers, which feared a Cold War power shift in the Middle East and broader Islamic world. While Washington scrambled to recover from the overthrow of the pro-Western regime in Tehran, Soviet leaders – who were still reeling from Egypt's defection – feared that Iran's example could foment uprisings among the Muslim populations living inside the Soviet Union and along its borders. Indeed, the pro-Soviet regime in Afghanistan had been engaged in ongoing skirmishes with Muslim rebels that intensified over the course of 1978 and 1979. In March 1979, the embattled Afghan government requested Soviet military assistance, which rose to the level of a full-scale Soviet military intervention in December to change the regime. The Carter administration viewed the Soviet move into Afghanistan as a thrust toward the oilfields of the Persian Gulf states designed to take advantage of the unstable situation in Iran. In response, the president increased aid to the Afghan rebels, issued the Carter Doctrine – which pledged to defend the Persian Gulf with military force – and redoubled his efforts to create the new Rapid Deployment Joint Task Force (RDF), which would become U.S. Central Command (CENTCOM) in 1983. The Middle East was becoming a center of late-Cold War militarization.[32]

The Iranian Revolution also piqued the interest of Saddam Hussein's Ba'thist regime in neighboring Iraq. The two countries had long been rivals for preeminence in the Persian Gulf and Baghdad viewed the revolution next door as both an opportunity and a danger if

Tehran was able to radicalize Iraq's Shi'a majority. Hoping to seize the oil-rich province of Khuzestan – which contained a significant Arab population – and undermine his regional rival, Saddam Hussein launched a surprise invasion of Iran in September 1980. The initial assault made some advances but the quick victory that Saddam Hussein hoped for was out of reach. Rather, the Iran–Iraq War would become a drawn-out war of attrition complete with trench fighting reminiscent of World War I. Iranian forces weathered the initial onslaught and slowly managed to reverse the tide as much of the nation rallied around Khomeini. By 1982, Iran had taken the offensive with the help of human-wave attacks consisting of thousands of volunteers seeking religious martyrdom. On the defensive, Baghdad deployed chemical weapons and missile attacks against Iranian cities as both sides continued to suffer massive casualties. In 1984, the conflict spread into the Persian Gulf as Iraq began attacking Iranian oil tankers. During the course of the war, both the USSR and the United States backed Baghdad, sending financial and military aid as well as intelligence to Saddam's regime. By the time the war came to an end in 1988, an estimated 1.5 million people had been killed and nearly $1.2 trillion had been spent, making it one of the bloodiest and most destructive conflicts of the Cold War era. Aside from this destruction, the war's main results were to strengthen the theocratic regime in Iran and plunge Iraq into debt. As the specter of a wider Islamic resurgence came into view, both Washington and Moscow considered strategies aimed at manipulating this new political force for their Cold War strategic aims. Neither superpower would find the means to do so, however.

The other major conflict of the 1980s came with Israel's intervention in the ongoing civil war in Lebanon. Even before the war began, Israeli leaders had tried to force Lebanese authorities to strengthen their southern border, which was the launching site for Palestinian guerilla attacks against the Jewish state. In 1978, Israel launched a limited invasion of southern Lebanon in an attempt to push the PLO out of the area, create a more secure frontier, and guard against Syrian attempts to assert influence in Lebanon. The 1978 invasion failed to dislodge the PLO and led Israeli leaders to conclude that the elimination of Palestinian influence would require more drastic measures. Following a series of PLO attacks on Galilee in the summer of 1982, the IDF launched a full-scale invasion of Lebanon. The invasion was designed to destroy the PLO's presence in Lebanon and install a pro-Israeli Christian regime in Beirut led by Bashir Gemayel. With little regard for civilian casualties, the IDF smashed through south Lebanon and then laid siege to Beirut. As civilian casualties mounted, the international community grew increasingly critical of Israel's attack. In August 1982, the United States helped to negotiate an agreement that provided for the evacuation of the PLO from Beirut, the IDF's withdrawal back to southern Lebanon, and the stationing of U.S. and French peacekeepers in the country. In September, however, recently elected President Gemayal was assassinated. Enraged by the assassination, Christian militias entered the Palestinian refugee camps of Sabra and Shatila in Beirut and massacred between 1,000 and 2,000 civilians as the IDF – which had surrounded the camps and allowed the militia to enter – stood by. The violence in Beirut underlined the degree to which the Cold War was beginning to fade as a dominant international relations paradigm in the Middle East.[33]

In response to the massacres, U.S. President Ronald Reagan sent peacekeepers back into Beirut in the hope of restoring stability and supporting a new government led by Amine Gemayel – Bashir's brother. Though designated as peacekeepers, U.S. forces were tasked with supporting the Christian regime in Lebanon, embroiling them in the civil war. In April 1983, a suicide bomber from the Shi'a militant group Islamic Jihad detonated a van full of explosives beneath U.S. Embassy in Beirut, killing sixty-three people, including most of the CIA's station in Lebanon. In October, two more suicide attacks against U.S. and French peacekeepers killed a total of 241 American and 58 French troops. In the next several months, American forces engaged in a number of skirmishes with local forces and it appeared as if the United States was being pulled into the civil war. In February 1984, under pressure from Congress and the American public, Reagan announced the withdrawal of U.S. troops from Lebanon. The Iranian Revolution, Iran–Iraq War, and the Lebanese Civil War demonstrated that, although the United States had gained the upper hand in the Cold War struggle for the Middle East, the region was still fraught with tension. Indeed, the Middle East of the 1980s was in many respects a more dangerous place than it had been in previous decades, despite or perhaps even because of the declining influence of the Soviet Union.

The End of the Cold War

Thus, as the Cold War in the Middle East came to an end, dynamics like political Islam, regional power struggles, and the specter of the failed state – all of which had been held back by the superpower conflict – reemerged in places like Saudi Arabia, Iran, Iraq, and Lebanon. Two final events in the last years of the Cold War would forecast the key issues of the post-Cold War era. In late 1987, the West Bank and Gaza exploded in a series of popular Palestinian uprisings. Frustration with twenty years of military occupation, combined with anger at the failures of the PLO – which had been exiled to Tunisia after Israel's 1982 invasion of Lebanon – erupted in the first *Intifada*. Though Israeli Prime Minister Yitzhak Rabin ordered the IDF to crush the uprising, the demonstrations continued as thousands of Palestinian youths took to the streets, throwing rocks and Molotov cocktails. The *Intifada* prompted dramatic changes in the Israel–Palestine dispute as PLO leaders in Tunisia scrambled to gain a measure of control over the spontaneous uprising. The biggest beneficiary of the *Intifada* was Hamas – an offshoot of the Palestinian Muslim Brotherhood – an organization that had remained in the Occupied Territories and established a substantial social welfare network. Hamas leaders endorsed extreme violence against the Israeli occupation and represented a rival center of power to the PLO. Recognizing the erosion of their authority, PLO leaders scrambled to jumpstart the stalled peace process, renouncing "terrorism" and accepting Israel's right to exist. The United States responded by establishing a dialogue with the PLO and renewing efforts to reach a settlement in the regional dispute. These efforts helped to lead to the Madrid and Oslo Meetings in 1991 and 1993 in which leaders from Israel and the PLO met face to face for the first time. The high hopes of the 1990s would not be realized, however, as the peace process fell apart in the coming years.

Meanwhile, another conflict was brewing in the Persian Gulf. In August 1990, Iraqi forces invaded neighboring Kuwait, quickly seizing control of the small emirate and its vast oil reserves. Saddam Hussein justified the move by claiming that Kuwait was stealing Iraqi oil, driving down petroleum prices, and refusing to forgive Baghdad's debts from the Iran–Iraq War. U.S. President George H.W. Bush rejected this rationale, began massing troops in Saudi Arabia, and, with UN backing, demanded the evacuation of Iraqi forces by 15 January 1991. With the Soviet empire crumbling as the USSR entered its final months, U.S. power was now virtually unrivaled in the world. CENTCOM, the successor to Jimmy Carter's RDF, now took center stage as another war in Mesopotamia approached. Following the expiration of the deadline for evacuation, U.S. forces launched Operation Desert Storm, the massive invasion of Kuwait and Iraq. The full weight of U.S. power – which utilized new military technologies like laser-guided bombs, cruise missiles, and stealth bombers – overwhelmed Iraqi forces. The war ended on 28 February 1991, a dramatic success for the United States and a signal of the ascendancy of U.S. global power.[34]

Conclusion

Perhaps more than any other part of the world, the Middle East showcased the volatile combination of regional rivalries, ethnic and religious conflicts, and superpower competition during the second half of the twentieth century. While the underlying tensions in the Middle East predated the Cold War, the superpower rivalry amplified the scale, destructiveness, and duration of many of the conflicts in the region by providing huge shipments of weapons to various belligerents and preventing decisive victories that might have laid a number of regional tensions to rest. Instead, both Washington and Moscow chose to prop up a series of regimes with dubious claims to popular representation and questionable human rights records. Stepping back, it can be said that the region played a critical role in the larger superpower struggle: from the crises in Iran and Turkey that signaled the onset of the Cold War to the Czech Arms Deal and the Suez Crisis that demonstrated the rising power of the Soviet Union in the developing world; from the Arab–Israeli wars of 1967 and 1973 that showcased the superiority of western military technology to the debacles in Iran, Afghanistan, and Lebanon that foreshadowed the end of an era dominated by the superpowers; and finally, culminating in the U.S. invasion of Iraq that announced the emergence of the United States as a hyperpower in the post-Cold War international order.

The superpower struggle would leave behind a region ravaged by war and still simmering with tensions. Both Washington and Moscow had channeled large amounts of military hardware to their allies in the Middle East, allowing regimes throughout the region to build large armed forces without mobilizing wide domestic support and without establishing democratic accountability. As the superpower struggle entered its twilight years, an array of heavily armed states, guerrilla groups, and militias emerged as contestants for regional power in the post-Cold War order. At the same time, the surging new power of political Islam – which transformed religious zeal into a potent mix of nationalism and ideology – came forward to fill the political vacuum left by the decline of the Cold War rivalry. The legacies of the superpower struggle would thus serve as a prologue to a string of conflicts that would erupt throughout the Middle East in the post-Cold War era.

Notes

1 See, for instance, Douglas Little, *American Orientalism: The United States and the Middle East since 1945* (Chapel Hill, NC: University of North Carolina Press, 2002), William Stivers, *America's Confrontation with Revolutionary Change in the Middle East* (New York: St. Martin's Press, 1986), Peter Hahn, *Crisis and Crossfire: The United States and the Middle East since 1945* (Washington, DC: Potomac Books, 2005), and Melani McAlister, *Epic Encounters: Culture, Media and U.S. Interests in the Middle East since 1945* (Berkeley, CA: University of California Press, 2005).

2 See, for example, Benny Morris, *Righteous Victims: A History of the Zionist–Arab Conflict, 1881–1999* (New York: Vintage, 2001) and Avi Shlaim, *The Iron Wall* (New York: W.W. Norton, 2001).

3 See Galia Golan, *Soviet Policies in the Middle East: From World War II to Gorbachev* (New York: Cambridge University Press, 1990), Robert O. Freedman, *Soviet Policy toward the Middle East since 1970* (Westport, CT: Greenwood Publishing, 1979), Alvin Z. Rubinstein, *Red Star on the Nile* (Princeton, NJ: Princeton University Press, 1992), and Masha Kirasirova, "Sons of Muslims in Moscow," *Ab Imperio* (2011) 4: 106–132.

4 See Rashid Khalidi, *Sowing Crisis: The Cold War and American Dominance in the Middle East* (Boston, MA: Beacon Press, 2010), Salim Yaqub, *Containing Arab Nationalism: The Eisenhower Doctrine and the Middle East* (Chapel Hill, NC: University of North Carolina Press, 2006), Ussama Makdisi, *Faith Misplaced: The Broken Promise of U.S.–Arab Relations, 1820–2001* (New York: Public Affairs, 2010), and Paul Thomas Chamberlin, *The Global Offensive: The United States, The Palestinian Liberation Organization, and the Making of the Post-Cold War Order* (New York: Oxford University Press, 2012). For focused accounts of the region itself, see William Cleveland, *A History of the Modern Middle East*

(Boulder, CO: Westview Press, 2002) and Roger Owen, *State, Power, and the Making of the Modern Middle East* (London: Routledge, 2004).

5   See Daniel Yergin, *The Prize: The Epic Quest for Oil, Money, and Power* (New York: Touchstone, 1993) and David Painter, *Oil and the American Century* (Baltimore: Johns Hopkins University Press, 1986).
6   See Bruce Kuniholm, *Origins of the Cold War in the Near East* (Princeton, NJ: Princeton University Press, 1980).
7   Ibid., and William Roger Louis, *The British Empire in the Middle East, 1945–51* (New York: Oxford University Press, 1984).
8   Louis, *The British Empire in the Middle East*.
9   See Morris, *Righteous Victims*, Shlaim, *The Iron Wall*, and David Fromkin, *A Peace to End All Peace: The Fall of the Ottoman Empire and the Making of the Modern Middle East* (New York: Henry Holt, 2001).
10 See Peter Hahn, *Caught in the Middle East: U.S. Policy toward the Arab–Israeli Conflict, 1945–61* (Chapel Hill, NC: University of North Carolina Press, 2004).
11 See Hahn, *Caught in the Middle East*, Morris, *Righteous Victims*, and Shlaim, *Iron Wall*.
12 See Peter Hahn, *The United States, Great Britain, and Egypt, 1945–56* (Chapel Hill, NC: University of North Carolina Press, 1991).
13 See James F. Goode, *The United States and Iran* (New York: St. Martin's Press, 1997).
14 See Hahn, *The United States, Great Britain, and Egypt*.
15 Ibid.
16 See Keith Kyle, *Suez* (London: I.B. Tauris, 2003), William Roger Louis, *Suez 1956* (New York: Oxford University Press, 1989), and Donald Neff, *Warriors at Suez* (New York: Simon and Schuster, 1981).
17 See Salim Yaqub, *Containing Arab Nationalism*.
18 Ibid.
19 See Golan, *Soviet Policies in the Middle East*, and Malcolm Kerr, *The Arab Cold War, 1958–70* (London: Oxford University Press, 1971).
20 See *The Soviet Union and the June 1967 Six Day War*, Yaacov Ro'i, et al., eds., (Palo Alto, CA: Stanford University Press, 2008); Michael B. Oren, *Six Days of War: June 1967 and the Making of the Modern Middle East* (New York: Oxford University Press, 2002) and Donald Neff, *Warriors for Jerusalem* (New York: Simon & Schuster, 1984).
21 See William B. Quandt, *Peace Process: American Diplomacy and the Arab–Israeli Conflict since 1967* (Washington, DC: Brookings Institution Press, 2005).
22 See Chamberlin, *The Global Offensive*.
23 See Craig Daigle, *The Limits of Détente: The United States, the Soviet Union and the Arab–Israeli Conflict, 1969–1973* (New Haven, CT: Yale University Press, 2012) and David A. Korn, *Stalemate: The War of Attrition and Great Power Diplomacy in the Middle East, 1967–1970* (Boulder, CO: Westview Press, 1992).
24 Chamberlin, *Global Offensive*; Nigel Ashton, *King Hussein of Jordan* (New Haven, CT: Yale University Press, 2008); Avi Shlaim, *Iron Wall*.
25 See Daigle, *The Limits of Détente* and Patrick Seale, *Asad* (Berkeley, CA: University of California Press, 2008).
26 See Quandt, *Peace Process*.
27 Ibid.
28 Ibid.; Chamberlin, *The Global Offensive*.
29 See David Hirst, *Beware of Small States: Lebanon, Battleground of the Middle East* (New York: Perseus, 2010), Robert Fisk, *Pity the Nation* (New York: Nation Books, 2001), and James Stocker, "Diplomacy as Counter-Revolution: The 'Moderate States', the Fedayeen and State Department Initiatives towards the Arab-Israeli Conflict (1969–1970)," *Cold War History*, 12:3 (2012): 407–428
30 See Gilles Kepel, *Jihad: The Trail of Political Islam* (Cambridge, MA: Belknap Press, 2002) and Victor McFarland, "The United States, Saudi Arabia, and Oil in the 1970s," Dissertation in progress, Yale University.
31 James Bill, *The Eagle and the Lion: The Tragedy of American–Iranian Relations* (New Haven, CT: Yale University Press, 1988).
32 Artemy M. Kalinovsky, *A Long Goodbye: The Soviet Withdrawal from Afghanistan* (Cambridge, MA: Harvard University Press, 2011).
33 See Hirst, *Beware of Small States,* and Fisk, *Pity the Nation*.
34 See Michael R. Gordon and Bernard E. Trainor, *The General's War: The Inside Story of the War in the Gulf* (New York: Back Bay Books, 1995) and Rick Atkinson, *Crusade* (New York: Mariner Books, 1994).

13

THE COLD WAR IN SOUTH AND CENTRAL ASIA

Artemy M. Kalinovsky[1]

The Cold War in South and Central Asia can be divided into three periods. The first, lasting from the early 1950s until the mid-1960s, saw an independent India and Pakistan, as well as Afghanistan and Soviet Central Asia, take advantage of the Cold War competition to advance their own economic and development programs, while the superpowers tried to prove that their respective systems had the best tools to reach those goals. Strategic interests and competition, both between the states in the region and between the superpowers competing there, were important but secondary. In the second phase, lasting from the mid-1960s to the late 1970s, economic development took a backseat as the idealistic projects of the 1950s failed to deliver broad prosperity, and both the US and the USSR focused increasingly on military aid. The period also saw the politicization of religious movements as a response to the failure of secular alternatives. The final phase, lasting from the Soviet intervention in Afghanistan in 1979 to the end of the Cold War, saw the region's full militarization, with consequences that lasted beyond the Cold War itself.

The legacies of colonialism, whether in the border issues between Pakistan and Afghanistan, or in the conflict over Kashmir between India and Pakistan, conditioned the countries' interactions with the superpowers. The leaders of the countries under discussion were agents in their own right, at some points trying to chart a course that sought to avoid Cold War dynamics, at others deliberately drawing in the rival superpowers to advance their domestic or regional aims, and often pursuing these aims simultaneously. Finally, the Sino-Soviet split made itself felt in the region; China was a Soviet ally in the 1950s and helped defend the USSR against charges of imperialism by non-aligned nations, but by 1959 it was on its way to becoming an enemy of both the Soviet Union and India and a friend of Pakistan, playing a role in a number of the sub-continent's conflicts, including the nuclear arms race.

Diplomatic historians traditionally looked at the region's Cold War history from the point of view of strategic imperatives, whether of the superpowers or of local actors.[2] They highlighted the importance of these countries as part of a "northern tier" that US officials from the Eisenhower administration onward believed needed to be mobilized to resist communist expansion. More recently, some historians have followed the "Cultural Turn" and drawn attention to the way that mutual perceptions shaped these Cold War interactions,[3] while others have argued that it was the prerogative of demonstrating superiority in economic and development practices that shaped the Cold War competition in the region.[4] While all these studies are heavily grounded in US and British archives, several scholars have begun to take advantage of Soviet, Eastern-bloc, and Indian sources to re-center our reading of this history.[5] Memoirs and document collections published in the region have further enriched our understanding of the Cold War in South Asia, although scholarship on the Cold War emerging from the region has thus far been scant.

The End of Empire, the Cold War, and Modernization

Historians generally date the beginning of the Cold War in South Asia to Stalin's death and the power struggles that followed in its wake. Despite ties with Indian communists that went back to the inter-war period, Stalin was skeptical of the party's role in Indian politics, and the USSR's engagement with India and Pakistan was limited. A year after his death, however, the Indian embassy in Moscow was noting an "extremely favorable" situation developing; new Soviet interest in the subcontinent and the post-colonial world in general could bring with it factories, expertise, and goods that India needed. The embassy's assessment proved correct; Nikita Khrushchev criticized Stalin for failing to take advantage of anti-imperialist sentiment on the subcontinent and the potential for partnership with the USSR.[6] In 1955, Indian leader Jawaharlal Nehru made an official state visit to Moscow, while Khrushchev undertook a multi-state tour that brought him to India, Afghanistan, and Burma, promising aid at each stop.

Khrushchev sensed that the growth of Soviet influence in Europe had stalled, and that newly independent states would be looking for allies that were not tainted by a history of colonialism but could provide the economic and military aid necessary to overcome that legacy and preserve independence. The immediate benefits of such alliances for the USSR in the immediate term were unclear, however, and Khrushchev had to face down resistance from colleagues who thought he was throwing Soviet resources to the wind. Indeed, while the USSR had some sympathetic supporters among the Indian public and elites (especially foreign minister V.K. Krishna Menon), the Soviet partnership with India provided Moscow with few tangible benefits in its early years.[7] As David Engerman has shown, however, early intellectual exchanges helped shape not only Indian ideas about planning but also Soviet ones.[8]

The US foreign policy establishment of the late 1940s was almost as dismissive of India as Stalin had been. Truman could not believe that "anyone thought [India] was important," while his National Security Council concluded that an alliance with that country would be a burden on the US. It also advised against the US providing significant economic aid.[9] India and Pakistan were both considered "remote from the USSR and not subject to Soviet aggression," according to a 1947 CIA report.[10] With the war in Korea, however, India began to take on new strategic importance for US officials.

At the same time, as Nick Cullather has recently argued, it was the possibility of demonstrating America's power to tackle issues like hunger that really put India front and center for US officials and public opinion. India's approach to development, which borrowed elements of socialist planning for its industrial policy but avoided Soviet- or Chinese-style collectivization, could be used to differentiate "free-market," and thus US-friendly, economic policies from communist-oriented ones. After several years of self-sufficiency, Indian planners from the mid-1950s turned to US food aid as a way to keep prices down while pursuing industrialization. Food aid, encouraged by a US domestic farm lobby eager to off-load its own surplus, grew. But it was one part of a broader aid and development program to tackle agricultural poverty and help put India on the path of self-sustaining, non-Soviet and non-Chinese oriented growth that began in the early 1950s and expanded massively under John F. Kennedy.[11]

Afghanistan likewise became a recipient of aid from the US and USSR in this period. The ruling Musahiban dynasty was looking for ways to jump-start its own country's modernization and began courting support from the great superpowers as well as other donors for irrigation, hydroelectric, infrastructure, and other projects. US loans provided for an engineering firm, Morrisson-Knudsen Associates, to develop a large dam and irrigation system in the Helmand Valley, in a project inspired directly by the Tennessee Valley Authority. The Soviets built a road network connecting Afghanistan's major cities, as well as military bases and factories, and helped Afghanistan develop its natural gas fields. The World Bank, the World Health Organization, and smaller donors from both camps were all working on various projects during this time. Typical of the Cold War logic of some of these development projects, however, was that even when their viability was in doubt the need to maintain the goodwill of the local government and prove superiority over the competitor's system made pulling out almost impossible. The Helmand Valley project was recognized as a failure as early as 1954, but the US government was still pouring money into it as late as 1979.[12]

The Afghan government was also playing a dangerous game with its next-door neighbor, Pakistan. The border between the two countries had been drawn by a British colonial official in 1893 to demarcate the limits of British India and (semi) independent Afghanistan, and divided the Pushtun tribes between two polities. Talk of "reuniting the Pushtun tribes" under Kabul put US officials on edge, and they would refrain from providing significant support to the Afghan military. That role would be taken up by the Soviets, who would assume increasing responsibility for training Afghan officers and supplying military hardware over the following decades. Nevertheless, both sides expected Afghanistan to remain a neutral state, friendly to both the US and USSR, maintaining good relations with China, India, and Iran. And until the late 1970s, it was.[13]

Khrushchev's opening to the Third World also affected Soviet Central Asia. The five republics (Tajikistan, Uzbekistan, Turkmenistan, Kyrgyzstan, and Kazakhstan) had already been assigned the role of inspiring the "foreign East" in the 1920s, when their borders were first drawn. But in the Cold War and post-colonial context their role grew in importance, especially after delegates at the Bandung Conference of Asian–African Countries criticized the USSR for its policies in Eastern Europe and Central Asia. The need to demonstrate that the Soviets were not a colonial power required the promotion of cadres from the region to diplomatic posts as well as giving them a more prominent role in Moscow. Nuritdin Mukhitdinov, an Uzbek Party leader, became the first Central Asian member of the Politburo, the Communist Party's top decision-making body. As Khrushchev explained to him, the new international situation meant that Moscow needed someone at the center who knew how to reach out to the world's Muslims.[14]

Central Asian party leaders, meanwhile, used their new-found importance to negotiate for more investment in their own republic's industrialization, education, and cultural heritage. With the exception of Kazakhstan, all were primarily agricultural; now people like Tursun Uldzhabaev, first secretary of Tajikistan from 1956 to 1961, successfully used the rhetoric of anti-colonialism to argue that producing raw materials and agricultural goods for industry in the European part of the USSR was inconsistent with Soviet ideals. Sharof Rashidov, a rising star in the Uzbek party organization who travelled to India and other countries on Khrushchev's itinerary, likewise lobbied for more investment in the restoration of mosques and other architectural sites by pointing out that they could be used to counter western propaganda aimed at Muslim countries that portrayed the USSR as oppressing religion.[15]

Nonalignment and the Blocs

New Delhi may have been happy to take advantage of aid being offered by the US and Soviets, but in the 1950s it became a leading critic of the Cold War confrontation, a position that would culminate in Nehru's leading role as organizer of the Asian–African Conference at Bandung in 1955 and, ultimately, the Non-Aligned Movement, formally launched at the Belgrade Conference in 1961. Nehru's critique of the Cold War paradigm stemmed from a moral revulsion at the possibility of mankind-annihilating nuclear war. He believed that India had to play a role in lessening tensions between the blocs; under the doctrine of "positive neutrality," New Delhi would attempt to play a role in the resolution of the Korean and Vietnamese conflicts. But for US officials, not least Eisenhower's Secretary of State John Foster Dulles, Nehru's neutralism really meant a tacit pro-Soviet line, particularly dangerous for a large, important country like India that was destined to play a leading role among newly decolonized states.[16]

Pakistan's leaders, while also involved in the nascent Non-Aligned Movement, were nevertheless eager to declare themselves for the US camp in the Cold War. India had inherited a disproportionate amount of military hardware and installations from the British Raj, while Pakistan was in many ways starting from scratch. (The two countries fought a war right after independence over the Hindu-ruled but Muslim-majority state of Kashmir, and would fight a number of wars in the ensuing decades.) As Washington and London worked to extend their military alliances that began with NATO and that were meant to protect European democracies from Soviet threats, to the Middle East and Pacific, Pakistan became a founding member of both the Central Treaty Organization (CENTO, founded with the Baghdad Pact of 1955) and the Southeast Asian Treaty Organization (SEATO, founded with the signing of the Manilla Pact in the same year). Neither organization developed into a military alliance of the sort that their model, NATO, was, but they did cement Pakistan as a Cold War ally and recipient of US arms.

If US officials were vexed by India's positive neutrality, in Pakistan they found an ally that seemed to have no doubt about with whom its allegiances should lie. Pakistan's first Prime Minister, Liaquat Ali Khan, was assassinated in 1951, the increasingly influential military and civil service elite were eager for US support to develop Pakistan's military capabilities against India. Taking advantage of Dulles' emerging "Northern Tier" concept, General Ayub Khan (Army Chief of Staff from 1951, Minister of Defence from 1954, and President following a military coup in 1958) lobbied US policymakers and congressmen, presenting his country as a crucial and determined ally in the resistance to communism. He found a willing audience, especially in Secretary of State Dulles, who on an earlier trip had reported that "Pakistan is one country that has moral courage to do its part in resisting communism." Indian protests did little to sway the Eisenhower administration, which argued that India's military superiority made it unlikely that US aid to Pakistan would pose a threat, and that the dangers of communism meant that the US could not refrain from an alliance just because relations between New Delhi and Islamabad were tense. The agreement, concluded in 1954, had the predictable result of evoking anger from Indian officials and pushed New Delhi closer to Moscow; it may also have stimulated Nehru to play a more active role in the emerging Non-Aligned Movement.[17] Throughout the Cold War, India's status as a democracy earned it sympathy in US public opinion; its neutralism, and seeming unwillingness to "fight" the Cold War vexed American administrations. By contrast, US officials admired the "martial qualities" they found in Pakistan's elite, but Pakistan's oscillation between democratic governments and military rule made it a difficult partner for the US.

Nehru cultivated like-minded leaders, and his diplomacy led to the Afro-Asian conference at Bandung in 1955. The themes of the conference included economic independence and cooperation, sovereignty and territorial integrity, and resistance to colonialism. Denouncing the formation of blocs and the deadly power of nuclear weapons, Nehru told the conference: "I belong to neither and I propose to belong to neither whatever happens in the world. If we have to stand alone, we will stand by ourselves, whatever happens (and India has stood alone without any aid against a mighty Empire, the British Empire) and we propose to face all consequences."[18] Eisenhower and Dulles worried that the message of neutralism might catch on, and that Nehru's neutralism might make their quest for development funds a harder sell in Congress. Nevertheless, the administration felt that the best way to respond was to highlight America's own support for self-determination and willingness to provide economic aid.[19] (The Soviets, who were heavily criticized at the conference, at least had China, represented by Foreign Minister Zhou Enlai, to defend them.) But the show of solidarity belied underlying tensions: between states leaning to different modes of development, and leaders who calculated that their country's defense could not be secured without the aid of one of the great powers. Although the conference would be followed by a meeting in Cairo in 1957 and at Belgrade in 1961, the latter formally establishing the Non-Aligned Movement, the solidarity of these states was already waning, and the movement's practical significance for the Cold War was limited. Indeed, the Eisenhower administration believed that Bandung itself had largely been a failure for Nehru, even if the issue of neutralism was not going to go away.[20]

Indeed, the Sino-Indian friendship barely outlasted the decade. A conflict over the countries' border near Tibet (another colonial legacy, the so-called McMahon line), broke into open warfare in October 1962, and the Chinese "wiped the floor with the Indians," in the words of a staffer on the US National Security Council.[21] Moscow, neutral at first, leaned towards the Chinese position – even though its relationship with Beijing was already fraying, it was the middle of the Cuban missile crisis, and Khrushchev needed Chinese support; the non-aligned countries, with the exception of Egypt and Yugoslavia, also refused to back India. Nehru turned to the US and other western countries for aid. Though the Kennedy administration reacted sympathetically, it now had to contend with Pakistani anger. But the US was suddenly popular even among the left-wing press in India. This turnabout, too, was short lived, as the continued deterioration of Sino-Soviet relations meant that India and the USSR now shared a "main enemy," an assessment reflected in growing arms sales and defense cooperation.[22]

India and Pakistan would fight two more conflicts during the Cold War, one over Kashmir, and one over East Pakistan. The first, in 1965, was the result of General Ayub Khan's ill-conceived intervention in Kashmir, Operation Gibraltar. Having performed well in a small confrontation earlier in the year, and wanting to strike before India's post-1962 rearmament swung the military balance further in India's favor, Khan hoped that Pakistani forces with Kashmiri irregulars could finally bring Pakistan a victory. Instead, a tank battle ensued. Both Washington and Moscow tried to work through the UN to secure a ceasefire. The US tried to take an even-handed approach, but ended up angering both sides. Once a ceasefire came into effect, however, the USSR took the lead in negotiating a peace deal, bringing Indian leader Lal Bahadur Shastri (in office from Nehru's death in 1964 until his own in 1966) and Ayub Khan to Tashkent and brokering an agreement in January 1966.[23] This was a small but significant victory for the USSR, marking the beginning of a special Soviet–Indian relationship.

The Cold War in South Asia During the Long 1970s

One result of the 1965 war was that the US began to play a more limited role in South Asian affairs. Neither India nor Pakistan was happy with the US response to the crisis, while in the US both policymakers and congressional leaders were frustrated that aid provided by the US was mostly used by the two countries to fight each other. (Pakistan's growing friendship with

China, which was evident during the war, made aid to that country even trickier politically.) Even food aid was becoming difficult to justify politically – disappointment over Indian economic performance, the demands of the war in Vietnam, and Johnson's domestic program all made Congress balk at the growing cost of aid to India, the largest recipient.[24]

By contrast, Indian relations with the USSR grew closer. In 1968, India refrained from publicly criticizing the invasion of Czechoslovakia, as it had after the 1956 invasion of Hungary and would do again when the USSR invaded Afghanistan in 1979. In 1971, India and the USSR signed a Treaty of Friendship which bound them to come to each other's defense in the event of a conflict with a third party. The treaty provided security that both wanted against China, but it also gave New Delhi the confidence, in 1971, to once again risk war by supporting separatists in East Pakistan. Although Soviet leaders tried to convince Indira Gandhi that a military conflict was to be avoided at all costs, she reportedly told them "we are going to do it and you have to decide whether you are our friends or not."[25] The Soviets decided that they were indeed friends, and provided additional military aid. Once the fighting got underway, they also blocked any action in the UN Security Council that could have put pressure on India.

The US response to the growing crisis in 1971 was formulated in the context of the Nixon administration's opening to China (in which Pakistan was to play a key role), and Richard Nixon's conviction, dating back to the Eisenhower administration, that the US needed to stop favoring India and move closer to Pakistan. Nixon ignored his own consulate staff in Dakka when it warned of a genocide and criticized the administration's policy of strict non-intervention. The President and his National Security Adviser, Henry Kissinger, came away from their own efforts to convince Gandhi to avoid war even more distrustful of the Indian leader.[26] In the aftermath of the war, US relations with Pakistan grew still closer, as Islamabad played a crucial role in facilitating US–Chinese rapprochement that year, and the Chinese, in turn, made it clear that they expected Washington to contain Indian ambitions.[27]

The Soviets may have had dreams of making India "the socialist countries' bridgehead in Asia," both in economic and in strategic terms, but in reality New Delhi used Soviet and East German aid to reinforce its own regional power. In a period when the US mood was turning increasingly against development aid, and turmoil caused by the war in Vietnam led Washington to scale back aid and military cooperation, the Soviet Union stepped in with ever-increasing military supplies. The Sino-Soviet split had escalated into a small border war in 1969, and with the US–Chinese rapprochement in the 1970s, Moscow needed India more than ever. But Indian officials made their strategic calculations on the basis not of what Moscow wanted, but of what their own reading of the regional situation told them. When Indian officials decided to test a nuclear weapon in 1974 (motivated by fear of a nuclear-armed China), Moscow was powerless to stop them.[28]

If the 1970s were a decade when the Cold War in the Third World was at its peak, local and regional dynamics were the cause of instability in South Asia. The early part of the decade saw a short-lived but hopeful moment with India, Pakistan, and newly independent Bangladesh all led by progressive regimes that sought to channel mass support into programs to abolish poverty. But all three projects were damaged by the oil shock that followed the 1973 Arab–Israeli war.[29] In India, strikes and political unrest led Indira Gandhi to push for a State of Emergency which lasted from 1975 to 1977. (Soviet officials, worried about the consequences of political unrest in their main regional ally, apparently welcomed the move[30]). In Pakistan, the military humiliation of 1971 helped bring the Pakistan People's Party to power. But by 1977 Zulfikar Ali Bhutto, the party's populist leader, had made enemies on the left and right. Despite a strong showing in the March 1977 elections, he soon faced street protests, and later that year his government was ousted in a coup led by army General Zia ul Haq, a devout Muslim who moved the country away from

Bhutto's secularizing policies and economic program.[31] India's nuclear explosion in 1974, meanwhile, brought the arms race to the subcontinent. Each country continued to struggle with separatist movements that the other tried to take advantage of: India by supporting Baluch rebels in Pakistan; Pakistan by supporting Sikh separatists in India.

Afghanistan in the 1970s was a peaceful but increasingly politicized country feeling the effects of two decades'-worth of aid programs large and local. Even a seemingly innocuous project like Kabul University proved to be problematic. On the one hand, its campus became a breeding ground for radical politics, whether leftist or Islamist. On the other, it produced more educated personnel than the economy required, leaving the government no option than to absorb these graduates into an increasingly bloated and useless bureaucracy or risk further disaffection.[32]

In 1973, Mohammed Daoud, a modernizer impatient with the pace of political and economic reforms, overthrew his cousin, King Zahir Shah, and proclaimed a republic. As Prime Minister in the 1950s, Daoud had championed the unification of Pushtun lands on the Pakistani side of the border with those on the Afghan side, and he returned to that rhetoric in the 1970s. He may also have set up training camps for Baloch rebels. For a Pakistani leadership wary of unrest in its tribal areas, the meddling of a neighboring power was unwelcome. When a number of young Islamists, many of whom were affiliated with Kabul University, fled to Pakistan to escape persecution, Bhutto authorized the Inter Service Intelligence (ISI) to train them for infiltration into Afghanistan. These were half-hearted attempts that were never intended to do anything more than demonstrate to Daoud the folly of his Pushtun policy, but they worked. In 1976 Bhutto and Daoud exchanged visits, and Daoud waxed lyrical about Afghan–Pakistani friendship.[33]

Bhutto's support of the Afghan Islamists was not the only reason Daoud was trying to reorient his foreign policy at the end of the 1970s. Since coming to power, Daoud had relied on Soviet support to advance his modernization program (US agencies had begun shrinking their commitment in the late 1960s), and on left-leaning supporters in the military and in parliament. Among these were a communist faction called Parcham (banner), a moderate wing of a Communist Party, The People's Democratic Party of Afghanistan, which had been founded the previous decade and quickly split into two wings. (The more radical Khalq faction generally took a harder line against Daoud's regime.) Concerned about growing Soviet influence and anxious to preserve Afghanistan's neutrality, Daoud sought to improve relations with Pakistan and Iran, both US allies.[34]

In 1978, the murder of a prominent communist leader and the ensuing protests led Daoud to attempt a decisive blow against the communists by arresting key members of both Khalq and Parcham, including Nur Mohammed Taraki, the First Secretary of the reconstituted party, and his deputy Babrak Karmal (leader of Parcham and a member of parliament). He underestimated the extent of communist support in the military, key units of which rallied in support of the arrested communists and overthrew Daoud. The Saur revolution, as its organizers called the coup, had brought an avowedly Marxist-Leninist party to power in Afghanistan.[35] From all available evidence, it seems that Moscow had not supported a takeover and was not aware of what was about to take place; Soviet leaders were unhappy with Daoud's recent realignments but had consistently urged Afghan communists to support his regime.[36]

The new communist leadership quickly turned to in-fighting, repressions against those associated with the Daoud regime (the former president and his family were assassinated the night of the revolution), and a radical program that promised to push far beyond what Daoud had tried in terms of female emancipation, land redistribution, and education. Soviet advice to take things slowly and avoid alienating the population went unheeded; by the fall, Moscow was beginning to have serious concerns about the viability of the regime. The logic of Cold War alliances dictated Soviet moves, however: once the regime professed itself to be an ideological and political ally of the USSR, the latter could hardly turn away from its junior ally. In fact, a new friendship treaty was signed in December 1978, committing both countries to cooperation in military affairs and calling for military assistance in case one of them was under attack, a clause that would be used to justify Soviet intervention a year later.

The assassination of party leader Nur Mohammed Taraki by his protégé Hafizullah Amin set off a chain of events that led to the Kremlin's decision to intervene in December 1979. Amin claimed loyalty to Moscow, but feuded with the Soviet ambassador and other advisers. There were rumors that he wanted to move closer to Washington. Finally, Soviet officials decided that he would have to be replaced by a more moderate leadership (composed of exiled Parchamis and led by Babrak Karmal) that could unite the party, reassert government control where possible, and win over the armed and unarmed opposition that was forming against its rule. Soviet special forces would take out Amin, while a larger contingent would help to man bases and protect key buildings, leaving the Afghan army free to stabilize the country. In fact, by the spring of 1980, Soviet troops were drawn into the fighting, and would take the lead in most operations almost until their withdrawal in 1988–89.

The decision to intervene and the US response need to be seen in the context of détente's collapse at the end of the 1970s. Soviet gains in the Third World throughout the 1970s had angered many politicians in the US, including President Jimmy Carter and his National Security Adviser, Zbigniew Brzezinski, who felt that Moscow was simply taking advantage of stability in Europe to make gains elsewhere. While Carter continued to work with Moscow on arms control, he also wanted to demonstrate the limits of US tolerance for Soviet Third World policies and on issues of human rights within the USSR. The result was confrontations by proxy in places like the Horn of Africa, where a war had broken out between Somalia and Ethiopia (both had been Soviet allies, but Somalia switched sides), and an increasingly tense bilateral relationship. Then, in the summer of 1979, the US Congress rejected the second Strategic Arms Limitation Treaty (SALT II), while NATO announced the placement of Pershing missiles in Germany; Soviet leaders were convinced that Washington was moving towards confrontation. Both the intervention and the response were also conditioned by Moscow and Washington's respective reading of the Iranian revolution; the former feared that, following the toppling of the pro-US Shah, Washington would look to Afghanistan as a new foothold in the region, while officials in Washington fretted that the Soviets would take advantage of US setbacks in the region and press on from Afghanistan to extend their influence into the Persian Gulf.

The intervention, interpreted in the US as only the most aggressive of Soviet moves in the Third World and one aimed particularly at an area of US weakness, destroyed whatever was left of détente. President Carter announced his administration's new policy for the region, stating that "An attempt by any outside force to gain control of the Persian Gulf region will be regarded as an assault on the vital interests of the United States of America, and such an assault will be repelled by any means necessary, including military force."[37] The US also committed to aiding the *mujahedeen*, primarily by working with the Pakistani ISI. Under President Ronald Reagan (1981–89), this aid expanded as support for the "freedom fighters" battling communism and foreign intervention became an increasingly popular cause in Congress, where the war was also seen as an opportunity to give the Soviets "their own Vietnam."

The Soviet–Afghan War and South Asia

The Soviet intervention led to yet another realignment in South Asia. The Carter administration, with its focus on human rights in international affairs, was a fervent critic of Zia, especially after the execution of Bhutto in April 1979.³⁸ Pakistan's nuclear program (begun by Bhutto to balance India's nuclear capability) was also an increasing irritant, and led the US to cut off aid. By 1979, with Pakistan's withdrawal from the Central Treaty Organization and the seizure of the US embassy in Islamabad in November 1979 by students, US–Pakistani relations, in the words of a National Security Council staff member, were "about as bad as with any country in the world, except perhaps Albania or North Korea."³⁹

The Soviet intervention in Afghanistan once again highlighted Pakistan's importance as a bulwark against Soviet expansion and salvaged the relationship with the US. Zia seems to have genuinely felt that Pakistan was in danger of Soviet aggression, especially in the early years after intervention, and this was one of the reasons why he hosted Afghan refugees and emerged as the godfather of the Afghan *jihad*. Zia thus became a hero instead of a pariah, and for most of the 1980s US politicians were more than happy to overlook his own violations of civil rights, as well as the revival of Pakistan's nuclear program.⁴⁰

Pakistani, US, and Soviet involvement in the Afghan conflict all transformed the region in ways that lasted long beyond the Cold War. The Pakistani-Indian rivalry led Pakistani officials to see Afghanistan as a sort of reserve area used to balance against the Indian threat, a notion known as "strategic depth," giving Zia another reason to support the rebels. As Ayesha Jalal and others have argued, the late 1970s saw a turn to religious alternatives in South Asia and beyond, as secular ideologies failed to bring the equality and justice they promised.⁴¹ Coordinating the resistance to communist rule and Soviet occupation allowed Pakistan to position itself as champion of the "first international Islamic brigade" (as ISI chief Hamid Gul put it), and to mobilize potential allies for its conflicts with India.⁴² The ISI set up a broad network to recruit, train, and infiltrate refugees, training some 80,000 fighters between 1982 and 1987. The whole network was funded by the United States and Saudi Arabia, with various other private and state donors, including China.⁴³ The Pakistani involvement in the Afghanistan war left the country with an enormous infrastructure of training camps and radical parties, but the fighting did not, on the whole, affect Pakistan directly. Soviet and Afghan commanders may have been frustrated by their inability to stem the flow of arms across the Afghan–Pakistani border, but they never expanded the war into that country.

The Saur revolution and the subsequent Soviet intervention also cut short a nascent Indian attempt to rebalance its foreign policy. In 1977, Indira Gandhi's Congress Party had suffered its first electoral defeat, bringing to power a new coalition government that tried to move away from Moscow, improve relations with Washington, and normalize relations with Beijing. The Soviet intervention in Afghanistan and the resumption of US military support for Pakistan forced Indian leaders to abort that re-orientation, and ultimately led India to provide tacit support for the presence of Soviet troops, balancing any criticism of the Soviet intervention with swipes at the US and Pakistan for militarizing the region and sowing chaos.⁴⁴ It was one of the few non-aligned countries to do so.⁴⁵ This policy would hold even after Indira Gandhi's assassination in 1984 and her son Rajiv's succession as Prime Minister.

Indian officials saw the Soviet presence and the Kabul regime itself as a bulwark against spreading fundamentalism and US-fueled Pakistani ambitions. And while Gandhi would also try to improve relations with Washington, very different readings of the regional situation prevented genuine rapprochements. For US policymakers, fighting the Soviets in Afghanistan superseded any other considerations on Indian policy, and it seemed strange to the Reagan administration that New Delhi would be more worried about US aid to Pakistan than about large-scale Soviet military intervention in the region.⁴⁶ Newly released documents confirm that both the Carter and Reagan administrations had nevertheless decided to basically overlook the Pakistani nuclear program, prioritizing Pakistan's role in the Afghan effort.⁴⁷

The war also changed the way that US officials thought about Soviet Central Asia. Scholars like Alexander Bennigsen had long been arguing that the USSR's Muslim population had never fully accommodated themselves to Soviet rule and could be encouraged to rise up against Moscow, but until the late 1970s no one in the US government had taken the idea seriously. But the Soviet march across the Third World, culminating in the invasion of Afghanistan in 1979, and perceived US weakness in the Middle East (where it was associated with Israel) led the Carter administration to start taking the idea more seriously by creating a Nationalities Working Group led by Paul Henze, a veteran spy and part-time scholar. The group's work, continued during the Reagan administration, led to a number of psychological and military operations targeting Soviet Central Asia, but fear that the Soviets would respond by escalating the war and doubts about the operations' effectiveness limited their scope.[48] Thousands of Central Asian soldiers, translators, and advisors served in Afghanistan throughout the war. Many returned proud of their service, believing that they had helped protect the USSR while bringing modernization to their neighbors; others were horrified by atrocities they saw committed in the name of the revolution and became critics of the Soviet system upon their return.[49] But until the Soviet Union's final days the war had very little effect on the republics of Central Asia.

Soviet officials were divided about the wisdom of intervention in 1979, and they were soon looking for a way out. Although a basic framework for disengagement was reached, with the help of UN mediation, by 1983, it was only in 1988 that Afghanistan, Pakistan, the US, and the USSR signed the Geneva Accords and the withdrawal began. Soviet leaders could countenance Afghanistan reverting to some kind of neutral status, but they feared a bloodbath after their withdrawal, chaos on their southern border, or, worse, a country that would ultimately join the western camp. Besides, Soviet leaders had to think of how a withdrawal or a defeat would look to the rest of the world, especially to Moscow's Third World allies. They fought as long as they had hope that their military could deliver a decisive blow to the *mujahedeen*, that their aid efforts would make the Kabul regime legitimate, and that the Afghan army could be trained and equipped to the point where it could stand on its own. Soviet and Afghan agents worked to bring rebel leaders over to the government side.

The reformer Mikhail Gorbachev, who came to power in 1985, made withdrawal from Afghanistan a priority. But though he called the war a "bleeding wound" publicly by 1986, he too was held back by some of the same concerns that bothered his predecessors. Every change of policy, whether military, economic, or political, had to be given a chance to work. In late 1986 Gorbachev supported another change of power in Afghanistan, pushing Babrak Karmal into retirement and promoting Mohammed Najibullah, who announced a policy of "National Reconciliation" and began positioning himself as a national, rather than as a communist leader. Meanwhile, Soviet diplomats worked furiously to get guarantees from the US and Pakistan that once Soviet troops came home outside support for the resistance would stop. But the latter would give such guarantees only if Moscow also stopped supplying the Afghan army with arms, a non-starter because the USSR would look like it was abandoning a friend.

Two things made withdrawal possible: first, a realization that the Soviet presence would never win the war for the Kabul regime, no matter how much aid was provided. Second, by 1988 there seemed to be a real opportunity to end the Cold War, and Afghanistan was one of the remaining obstacles to improving relations not just with the US, but also with China and Iran. At the Washington summit in December 1987, Soviet leaders thought they had US agreement to stop supplying weapons, something the Reagan administration then denied. But Gorbachev opted to announce a withdrawal anyway, in the hope that the US, seeing that Moscow was serious about getting out, would meet them half way. It was not to be – once it became clear that Soviet troops were coming home, there was no reason for the Reagan administration to upset the important "Afghan" lobby in Congress or pick a fight with Pakistan by cutting off aid; Soviet troops went home, but arms kept flowing from both sides, though they would gradually decrease in subsequent years as both the US and the USSR lost interest in the country. Zia, the main champion of the resistance and the only person who might have been able to push the groups into some coherent arrangement, died in a plane crash in 1988. Under Prime Minister Benazir Bhutto (daughter of Zulfikar), the ISI was given a free hand in Afghan affairs, and favored the more extreme Hizb-i Islami.[50]

The End of the Cold War

In the mid-1980s, India tried again to refashion its foreign policy, this time by improving relations with the US while maintaining its military relationship with Moscow. Both superpowers courted India. Yet, as Sergey Radchenko argues, under Rajiv Gandhi, who succeeded his mother after her assassination in 1984, India briefly "punched above its weight," but by the end of the decade its Cold War strategy was "obsolete."[51] The non-alignment New Delhi had preached (if not always practiced) lost its meaning with the end of the Cold War, while India's attempt to increase its regional power, especially vis-à-vis Pakistan and Sri Lanka, only alienated its neighbors and frustrated the superpowers.

Gorbachev developed a special relationship with Rajiv Gandhi, seeing in the young Indian Prime Minister a fellow reformer who understood what Gorbachev was trying to do domestically and internationally. Gorbachev hoped to move the Soviet–Indian relationship beyond military supplies, recognizing that the USSR had long stopped being an economic model for the Indians. In fact, Rajiv Gandhi wanted improved relations because he saw US technology as the key to India's own revitalization. The Reagan administration obliged. A 1985 "memorandum of understanding" on technical cooperation included the sale to India of a Cray XMP-24 supercomputer, a powerful machine which had no remotely close competitor on the Soviet side.[52] Although Soviet military aid to India would continue, it was no longer seen as the go-to country for economic development or the latest technology.[53]

Courted so actively by both superpowers, Rajiv Gandhi sought to expand India's regional influence. Its neighbor, Sri Lanka, descended into a civil war with its Tamil minority, many of whom looked to India, with its own Tamil state in the south-east, for support. Gandhi saw the Sri Lankans as US stooges, and found the Soviets willing to support that view. But in 1987 India went from supplying Tamil rebels with air-drops to an agreement with Sri Lanka that brought an Indian peace-keeping force to the island. It became embroiled in the civil war, effectively fighting the Tamil insurgency.[54]

If Gandhi could at least count on Soviet support for his Sri Lanka policy, on Pakistan he soon found that Soviet and Indian interests were no longer aligned. By 1987 Gorbachev was actively trying to improve relations with that country as a prelude to withdrawal from Afghanistan, and India's aggressive stand toward Pakistan was no longer welcome. Schemes to launch a joint attack on Pakistan by Afghanistan and India, muted by a few Soviet officials early in the war and now revived by Najibullah and Rajiv Gandhi, were received coldly by Moscow. By this point Gorbachev was more interested in playing peacemaker between India and Pakistan, recognizing that animosity between those two countries could only compromise his efforts to find a settlement in Afghanistan and normalize relations with the US and China.[55]

The settlement in Afghanistan never came. Soviet forces pulled out, leaving behind a shrinking pool of military advisors who helped Najibullah hold on to power. Only when the Soviet Union collapsed, and military aid dried up completely, did his regime finally fall – in

April 1992, four months after the collapse of the USSR. The US had by that point lost interest in Afghanistan, meaning that the main external player was Pakistan. Finding a lasting arrangement between the various resistance parties proved impossible, however. They soon turned their guns on each other, destroying Kabul, a city which had largely been spared the ravages of war to that point, in the process. By 1996 Pakistan was supporting a new militant group, the Taliban, composed of former anti-Soviet fighters and younger followers, many of them displaced by the war of the 1980s. In 1996 this group would take Kabul and offer refuge to one Osama bin Laden, a wealthy Saudi militant who first gained prominence fighting the Soviets, and was now trying to organize and bankroll an international battle against the United States and its allies.

Conclusion

At the dawn of the Cold War, India and Pakistan were newly independent countries seeking strategies for economic development and security that would not leave them vulnerable to a new form of imperialism. At the end, they were on their way to becoming nuclear powers, involved in global and regional alliances, and trying to pursue regional hegemony. The dreams of economic development that animated leaders in the 1950s and 1960s were now being abandoned, with India moving towards liberal market reforms. The secular visions of the countries' founders were increasingly challenged as Islamist groups gained influence in Pakistan and a nationalist party took power in India. The Cold War-era projects, whether Soviet-supported industrialization or US-supported modernization of agriculture, seemed to be forgotten. But patterns of alliances held: Russia continues to be a major arms supplier to India; the coolness that characterized Indian–Chinese relations for most of the Cold War has not abated, even as the two countries became two of the most exciting success stories of the post-Cold War decades, and India and Pakistan continue to have a troubled relationship, with periods of relative calm punctuated by war, most recently in 1998. Washington may have largely turned its back on Pakistan in the 1990s, but the 9/11 attacks and the subsequent war in Afghanistan threw the US and Pakistan into a testy and troubled alliance which neither can quit. As the US prepares to leave Afghanistan in 2014, it is clear that the Cold War casts a very long shadow indeed.

Notes

1 The author would like to thank Sergey Radchenko and Eric Pullin for their comments on earlier drafts of this chapter.
2 See, for example, Robert J. McMahon, *The Cold War on the Periphery: The United States, India, and Pakistan* (New York: Columbia University Press, 1994); H.W. Brands, *The Specter of Neutralism: The United States and the Emergence of the Third World, 1947–1960* (New York: Columbia University Press, 1989); Dennis Kux, *India and the United States: Estranged Democracies, 1941–1991* (Washington, DC: National Defense University Press, 1992); Dennis Kux, *The United States and Pakistan, 1947–2000* (Washington, DC: Woodrow Wilson Center Press, 2000).
3 Andrew J. Rotter, *Comrades at Odds: The United States and India, 1947–1964* (Ithaca, NY: Cornell University Press, 2000).
4 Nick Cullather, *The Hungry World: America's Cold War Battle against Poverty in Asia* (Cambridge, MA: Harvard University Press, 2010); Cullather, "Hunger and Containment: How India Became 'Important' in US Cold War Strategy", *India Review* 6(2) (April–June 2007): 59–90; Cullather, "Damming Afghanistan: Modernization in a Buffer State," *Journal of American History* 89(2) (2002): 512–537.

5 Sergey Radchenko, *Unwanted Visionaries: The Soviet Failure in Asia at the End of the Cold War* (New York: Oxford University Press, 2014); Vojtech Mastny, "The Soviet Union's Partnership with India," *Journal of Cold War Studies* 12(3) (Summer 2010): 50–90.
6 Mastny, "The Soviet Partnership with India," 51.
7 See Paul M. McGarr, "'India's Rasputin'?: V.K. Krishna Menon and Anglo-American Misperceptions of Indian Foreign Policymaking, 1947–1964," *Diplomacy & Statecraft* 22(2) (2011): 239–260.
8 David Engerman, "Learning from the East: Soviet Experts and India in the Era of Competitive Coexistence," *Comparative Studies in South Asia, Africa, and the Middle East* 33(2) (2013): 227–238.
9 Cullather, "Hunger and Containment," 60.
10 McMahon, *Cold War on the Periphery*, 14.
11 Cullather; "Hunger and Containment"; see also Nicole Sackley, "The Village Cold War Site: Experts, Development, and the History of Rural Reconstruction," *Journal of Global History* 6(3) (2011): 491–492.
12 Cullather, *Hungry World*, 130.
13 Odd Arne Westad, *The Global Cold War: Third World Interventions and the Making of Our Times* (Cambridge: Cambridge University Press, 2005), 299–302; Peter Tomsen, *The Wars of Afghanistan: Messianic Terrorism, Tribal Conflicts, and the Failures of Great Powers* (Washington, DC: Public Affairs, 2011).
14 Nuritdin Mukhitdinov, *Gody provedennye v Kremle* (Tashkent: Publishing House Kadyry, 1994), 312.
15 Masha Kirasirova "'Sons of Muslims' in Moscow: Soviet Central Asian Mediators to the Foreign East, 1955–1962." *Ab Imperio* 2011.4, 106–132; Artemy M. Kalinovsky, "Not Some British Colony in Africa," *Ab Imperio* 2013.2: 191–222.
16 Brands, *Specter of Neutralism*, 110–113.
17 Kux, *Estranged Democracies*, 106–115.
18 "Speech by Prime Minister Nehru before the Political Committee of the Asian–African Conference," April 24, 1955 in George McTurnan Kahin, *The Asian–African Conference* (Ithaca, NY: Cornell University Press, 1956), 64–72.
19 Brands, *Specter of Neutralism*, 110–125. On the broader significance of Bandung, see also Christopher J. Lee, "Introduction," in Christopher J. Lee, ed. *Making a World after Empire: The Bandung Moment and its Political Afterlives* (Athens, OH: Ohio University Press, 2010), 1–42; and Westad, *Global Cold War*, 97–109.
20 Brands, *Specter of Neutralism*, 116–117.
21 Kux, *Estranged Democracies*, 202. On the origins of this conflict, see Chen Jian, "The Tibetan Rebellion of 1959 and China's Changing Relations with India and the Soviet Union," *Journal of Cold War Studies* 8(3) (Summer 2006): 54–101.
22 Kux, *Estranged Democracies*, 201–208; Mastny "The Soviet Union's Partnership with India," 57–63.
23 Kux, *Estranged Democracies*, 237–239; Mastny "The Soviet Union's Partnership with India," 64.
24 Cullather, *Hungry World*, 212–213.
25 Quoted in Mastny, "The Soviet Union's Partnership with India," 69.
26 Robert J. McMahon, "Nixon, Kissinger, and the South Asia Crisis of 1971," in Fredrik Logevall and Andrew Preston, eds., *Nixon in the World: American Foreign Relations, 1969–1977* (New York: Oxford University Press, 2008), 249–268. On the US reaction, see the documents in *Foreign Relations of the United States, 1969–1976: South Asia Crisis, 1971* (Washington, DC: Department of State, U.S. Government Printing Office, 2005).
27 Jussi Hahnimaki, *The Flawed Architect: Henry Kissinger and American Foreign Policy* (Oxford: Oxford University Press, 2004), 154–184; Robert Dallek, *Nixon and Kissinger: Partners in Power* (New York: HarperCollins, 2007), 335–352.
28 Mastny, "The Soviet Union's Partnership with India," 71–73.
29 Ayesha Jalal, "An Uncertain Trajectory: Islam's Contemporary Globalization, 1971–1979," in Niall Ferguson, Charles S. Maier, Erez Manela, and Daniel R. Sargent, eds., *The Shock of the Global: The 1970s in Perspective* (Cambridge, MA: Belknap Press, 2010), 323–324.
30 Mastny, "The Soviet Union's Partnership with India," 73–74.
31 Sugata Bose and Ayesha Jalal, *Modern South Asia: History, Culture, Political Economy* (London: Routledge, 1998), 220–234.
32 Thomas Barfield, *Afghanistan: A Cultural and Political History* (Princeton, NJ: Princeton University Press, 2010), 212–213.
33 Peter Tomsen, *The Wars of Afghanistan: Messianic Terrorism, Tribal Conflicts, and the Failures of Great Powers* (Washington, DC: Public Affairs, 2011), 109–110.

34 Tomsen, *Wars of Afghanistan,* 107–108.
35 Most scholarly work on the communist period in Afghanistan and the Soviet war in Afghanistan has been carried out by scholars based in the US or UK. See, for example, the article and primary sources in Odd Arne Westad, "Concerning the Situation in A: New Evidence on the Soviet Invasion of Afghanistan," *Cold War International History Project,* Bulletin 8/9 (Winter 1996), Antonio Giutozzi, *War, Politics, and Society in Afghanistan* (London: Hurst & Co., 2000); Artemy M. Kalinovsky, *A Long Goodbye: The Soviet Withdrawal from Afghanistan* (Cambridge, MA: Harvard University Press, 2011); Rodric Braithwaite, *Afgantsy: The Russians in Afghanistan* (London: Profile Books, 2011). A number of Russian participants published memoirs, the most important of which is Alexander Liakhovsky, *Tragedia i Doblest' Afgana* [The Tragedy and Valour of Afghanistan] (Moscow: Nord, 2005). See also Vladimir Snegirev and Valerii Samunin, *Virus A: kak my zaboleli vtorzheniem v Afgnanistan* [Virus A: How We Caught the Disease of Intervening in Afghanistan] (Moscow: Rossiyskaia Gazeta, 2011), written by two veteran journalists; and V. Khristoforov *Afganistan: Praviaschaia partia i armia, 1978–1989* [Afghanistan: the ruling party and army] (Moscow: Granitsa, 2009), a study drawing on hard-to-access intelligence materials.
36 Westad, *Global Cold War,* 302.
37 State of the Union Address, 23 January 1980, online at the Carter Library http://www.presidency.ucsb.edu/ws/?pid=33079 [accessed 4 April 2014].
38 On the Carter administration and human rights, see Sarah B. Snyder's Chapter 17 in this volume. See also Samuel Moyn, *The Last Utopia: Human Rights in History* (Cambridge, MA: Belknap Press, 2010), 151–161.
39 Quoted in Dennis Kux, *The United States and Pakistan, 1947–2000: Disenchanted Allies* (Washington, DC: Woodrow Wilson Center Press, 2001), 245.
40 Kux, *The United States and Pakistan,* 245–291; Ian Talbott, *Pakistan: A Modern History* (London: Hurst & Company, 1998), 245–283.
41 Ayesha Jalal, "An Uncertain Trajectory," 319–336.
42 See Aparna Pande, *Explaining Pakistan's Foreign Policy: Escaping India* (London: Routledge, 2011), 59–87.
43 Tomsen, *Wars of Afghanistan,* 245–246; see also Zahib Shahab Ahmed, "Political Islam, the Jamaat Islami, and Pakistan's Role in the Afghan-Soviet War," in Philip E. Muehlenbeck, ed., *Religion and the Cold War: A Global Perspective* (Nashville, TN: Vanderbilt University Press, 2012c), 275–296.
44 Harish Kapur, *Foreign Policies of India's Prime Ministers* (New Delhi: Lancer, 2009), 163.
45 Peter C. Horn, *Soviet–Indian Relations: Issues and Influence* (Westport, CT: Praeger, 1982), 182.
46 Kux, *Estranged Democracies,* 384.
47 See the briefing book of declassified documents from the National Security Archive, http://www.gwu.edu/~nsarchiv/nukevault/ebb377/ [Accessed April 29, 2012].
48 Kalinovsky, *Long Goodbye,* 49–50.
49 Christian Bleuer, "Muslim Soldiers in Non-Muslim Militaries at War in Muslim Lands: The Soviet, American and Indian Experience," *Journal of Muslim Minority Affairs* 32(4) (2012): 3–5; Erica Marat, *The Military and the State in Central Asia: From Red Army to Independence* (London: Routledge, 2009).
50 See Artemy M. Kalinovsky "The Failure to Resolve the Afghan Conflict, 1989–1992," in Artemy M. Kalinovsky and Sergey Radchenko, eds., *The End of the Cold War and the Third World* (London: Routledge, 2011), 136–154.
51 Sergey Radchenko, "India and the End of the Cold War," in Artemy M. Kalinovsky and Sergey Radchenko, eds., *The End of the Cold War and the Third World* (London: Routledge, 2011), 173.
52 Radchenko, "India and the end of the Cold War," 179.
53 See Mark Kramer, "The Decline in Soviet Arms Transfers to the Third World, 1986–1991: Political, Economic, and Military Dimensions," in Artemy M. Kalinovsky and Sergey Radchenko, eds., *The End of the Cold War and the Third World* (London: Routledge, 2011), 47–100.
54 Radchenko, "India and the End of the Cold War," 181–182.
55 Radchenko, "India and the End of the Cold War," 182–186. Sergey Radchenko, *Unwanted Visionaries: The Soviet Failure in Asia at the End of the Cold War* (New York: Oxford University Press, 2014).

PART V

From Confrontation to Negotiation

14
THE ERA OF DÉTENTE

Craig Daigle

In the late 1960s, after a decade of often contentious and bitter rivalry between the two superpowers which led to a nuclear confrontation over the presence of Soviet missiles in Cuba, crises over the status of Berlin, communist control of Eastern Europe, and proxy wars in Africa, Latin America, and Indochina, the Cold War took a dramatic turn. Leaders across the globe abandoned the "heated ideological fervor" that characterized much of the early Cold War and instead pursued what one historian has called a "balance of order" in an effort to promote an era of peaceful coexistence between the major communist and capitalist powers.[1] Such a balance changed the nature of the US–Soviet relationship; it ended the longstanding political and diplomatic isolation between the People's Republic of China (PRC) and the West; and it helped produce the Helsinki Accords, which not only brought security and stability to the European continent, but also facilitated human rights activism that contributed to the end of the Cold War.

Despite the profound impact that the era of détente (1969–79) had in easing East–West tension, scholars interested in détente are only beginning to explore the full extent to which it shaped the Cold War. For decades, historians viewed détente as primarily an American-led initiative, with President Richard M. Nixon and his National Security Advisor, Henry Kissinger, as its principal architects. Many of these scholars have subscribed to the notion that détente offered an effective way to "contain" the Soviet Union without resorting to the "crisis management" system of the Kennedy–Johnson years or the ideological rigidity that defined the Eisenhower–Dulles foreign policy.[2] More recently, however, scholars have devoted increasing attention to the international dimensions of détente, acknowledging the leading role which Soviet General Secretary Leonid Brezhnev had in fostering improved relations with the United States and Western Europe, and to West German Chancellor Willy Brandt's pursuit of *Ostpolitik*.[3] Other scholars, meanwhile, have explored the limits of détente's reach, particularly in the Third World, where superpower competition persisted and where détente would ultimately meet its demise.[4]

There is no question that détente improved overall US–Soviet relations by reducing the potential for major superpower conflict in many areas of the world. But, as this chapter argues, the success of détente depended on the context. Thus, while détente found success at the global strategic level, where the United States and the Soviet Union produced the Anti-Ballistic Missile (ABM) and Strategic Arms Limitation (SALT) treaties, and in Europe where Brandt's

Ostpolitik eased longstanding differences between West Germany and Eastern Europe, at the regional level, particularly in the Third World, détente had its limits. By the end of the decade, superpower competition in Angola, the Horn of Africa, the Persian Gulf, and Afghanistan would bring an end to détente.

From Confrontation to Negotiation

"After a period of confrontation, we are entering an era of negotiation." With these words in his inaugural address on January 20, 1969, President Richard M. Nixon heralded a period of US–Soviet cooperation unmatched during the entire Cold War. After a decade of superpower crises, Nixon believed the time had come for rapprochement. To America's adversaries, he called for "peaceful competition," cooperation to "reduce the burden of arms," and "years of patient and prolonged diplomacy." He offered his "sacred commitment" to devote his office and energies to "the cause of peace" and to join with the communist world to "explore the reaches of space" and to "lift up" the poor and the hungry. "Let all nations know that during this administration our lines of communication will be open," he declared. "We seek an open world – open to ideas, open to the exchange of goods and people – a world in which no people, great or small, will live in angry isolation."[5]

Nixon's calls in his inaugural address for "peaceful negotiation" and "prolonged diplomacy" with the Soviets were somewhat surprising, coming from the man who had built his political career as a staunch anticommunist. But Nixon had largely softened his anticommunist rhetoric since his defeat to John F. Kennedy in the 1960 presidential election and his years in political exile. Traveling the world as a private citizen, and witnessing repeated crises with the Soviet Union and its allies had convinced the former vice-president that the American people were living in a "new world" – a world with new leaders, new people, and new ideas. The giants of the post-World War II era – Winston Churchill, Konrad Adenauer, Joseph Stalin, Jawaharlal Nehru, Khrushchev, and Sukarno – had all left the stage. No longer was Western Europe economically and militarily dependent on the United States, as it was for nearly a decade after the war, nor could the communist world be seen as "monolithic," given the public rift between the Soviet Union and the People's Republic of China. Most important, the United States had lost its atomic monopoly and pursued an unpopular war in Southeast Asia, causing it to lose much of its international prestige.[6]

Taking the "long view," Nixon believed that the United States needed a fundamental reappraisal of its foreign policy, particularly in moving toward more normal relations with the Soviet Union. Among the many reasons that impelled this change was the fact that by the late 1960s the Soviets had reached strategic parity in nuclear weapons with the United States. Both superpowers, therefore, needed to be able to resolve their differences through negotiations, and to avoid crises that could lead to US–Soviet conflict. Equally important, Nixon believed, was the fact that the Kremlin had vastly increased its influence around the world, while the US appeared to be losing friends. The Soviets, for example, had a major presence in the Arab states, while the United States had none, and important American allies, led by West Germany and France, increasingly sought to improve their relations with Moscow. The Soviets, moreover, still possessed considerable influence in Fidel Castro's Cuba, a constant thorn in America's side, while Eastern Europe remained largely under Soviet control.[7]

But it was Nixon's desire to extricate America from Vietnam, perhaps more than any factor, which necessitated a strategy of détente. By any objective analysis, there was simply no way to end the Vietnam War without Soviet cooperation. As late as 1968, the Soviets were providing 100 percent of the oil and 85 percent of all "sophisticated" military equipment for the North Vietnamese forces, including such modern weapons as surface-to-air missiles (SAMs), fighter airplanes and tanks. The Soviets also had several thousand technicians and "advisers" supporting the Vietnamese communists, some of them operating antiaircraft batteries and shooting down US aircraft.[8] As long as Moscow continued to supply Hanoi with these weapons, and send its forces to the region to assist North Vietnam, the Vietnam War could continue indefinitely. "It was often said that the key to a Vietnam settlement lay in Moscow and Peking rather than Hanoi," Nixon later wrote. "Without continuous and massive aid from either or both of the communist giants, the leaders of North Vietnam would not have been able to carry on the war for a few months."[9]

Although Nixon clearly had his own reasons for improving relations with Moscow, détente had its antecedents elsewhere. President Eisenhower, for example, invited Khrushchev to Camp David and his private Gettysburg farm in an effort to lessen Cold War tensions.[10] After the Cuban Missile Crisis, President Kennedy began negotiations with Moscow which led to a Nuclear Test Ban Treaty.[11] And President Johnson had called for discussions with Moscow on such issues as arms control, mutual and balanced force reductions in Germany, scientific and cultural exchanges, and the liberalization of trade and travel restrictions between East and West. He also held a major summit with Premier Kosygin at Glassboro, New Jersey to improve the prospects for a lasting peace with the Soviet Union.[12] European leaders, moreover, including France's Charles De Gaulle and Germany's Willy Brandt, had pursued rapprochement with the Eastern bloc in response to domestic pressure for change.[13] By 1968, in fact, with domestic unrest spreading globally, world leaders had a "common urge" for international stability.[14]

But, unlike these earlier efforts, which often collapsed at the first sign of disagreement, Nixon made détente a priority. He realized that when he entered office there were unique circumstances, including the militarization of the Sino-Soviet split and the Kremlin's need to expand trade with the US and the major Western powers, which allowed for improvement in US–Soviet relations that were unavailable to his predecessors. Soon after his election, he informed President Nikolai Podgorny that the American and Soviet people must work together "in a spirit of mutual respect" and "on the basis of special responsibility for the peace of the world," and had Kissinger convey to Soviet officials that under Nixon this would be "an era of negotiation not confrontation."[15]

Although many of the president's critics, especially from his own Republican Party, argued that negotiating with the Soviet Union demonstrated America's weakness, Nixon and Kissinger maintained that negotiations with the Kremlin were the most effective means of "containing" the Soviet Union. Whereas the Truman and Eisenhower administrations had treated power and diplomacy as two distinct elements in phases of policy and had often failed to negotiate from positions of strength, and the Kennedy and Johnson administrations had relied heavily on "crisis management," Nixon and Kissinger wanted to use negotiations with the communist world to lay the foundation for a "long-range" American foreign policy. They understood that the limits of the nuclear era meant that negotiations with a nuclear power could no longer wait until one side achieved the unattainable "situation of strength." As the historian John Lewis Gaddis has pointed out with regard to the Nixon–Kissinger strategy, negotiations were not in themselves a sign of weakness. "Properly managed," wrote Gaddis, "with a view to the identification of common interest as well as the frank recognition of irreconcilable antagonisms, they could become the primary means of building a stable world order, not simply a luxury to be enjoyed once stability had been achieved."[16]

Soviet Conceptions of Détente

In Moscow, Nixon's call for an "era of negotiation" was naturally received with considerable skepticism. The Politburo, in fact, unanimously believed that his "classic anticommunism" would mean "hard times" for Soviet–American relations.[17] The Soviet ambassador to the United States, Anatoly Dobrynin, also had his doubts about the new president's commitment to détente. Having served as Moscow's ambassador in Washington since 1962, Dobrynin knew that Nixon's career "was imbued with anti-Sovietism, anti-communism, and militarism, and he had skillfully used irresponsible and demagogic attacks on his political rivals and others he considered fair game to advance his position."[18] However, instead of rejecting Nixon's call for negotiations, Soviet leaders recognized the need for a thaw in superpower relations, even while questioning whether Nixon was the man they could work with to bring about such changes. To Nixon's call for an "era of negotiations," Foreign Minister Andrei Gromyko replied later in the year that "we for our part are ready."[19]

Foremost among Soviet reasons for pursuing détente with Nixon was the growing threat of China to its far east. Although China had once been an important ally to Moscow, the Sino-Soviet alliance collapsed between 1956 and 1966, due to substantive differences regarding Marxism-Leninism, disagreements over "peaceful coexistence" with the capitalist west, and competition for leadership of the socialist world.[20] In its infancy, the Sino-Soviet rivalry remained a largely ideological and political affair, but by the end of the 1960s the split turned "hot" as border clashes erupted between the armies of two communist giants along the Ussuri River.[21] By 1969, the Soviets had placed twenty-five heavily armed divisions on the border with China, far beyond the requirements for border security, suggesting to CIA analysts that Moscow might initiate "offensive operations" against North China, "should the need arise."[22] That same year, General Secretary Leonid Brezhnev condemned the Chinese as not merely "renegades" but "open enemies of the Soviet state."[23]

Facing continued tension on their border with China, the Soviets believed that hostility toward the US and the West should be muted. In part this decision stemmed from the fact that the Kremlin wanted to attract new allies in order to "contain" the Chinese.[24] But the Soviets also feared that if they failed to normalize relations with Washington, the United States would soon find ways to use the Sino-Soviet rivalry against Moscow.[25] This concern was not entirely without foundation. Following the Ussuri River incident, there were calls inside the White House for the US to recognize Albania, which supported the PRC during the Sino-Soviet split, and to promote West German contacts with Communist China as a means of making the Soviets "nervous" over a possible US–Chinese deal.[26] Recognizing that the US would exploit the situation, Gromyko circulated a telegram to Soviet embassies around the world making clear the need to avoid "pressure on the USSR from two flanks – NATO and China"; Soviet policy henceforth should "manifest restraint, moderation, and flexibility in relations with the US, [and] … refrain from complications with her which are not dictated by our important national interests."[27]

In addition to using détente to contain the Chinese threat, the Kremlin also viewed negotiations with the new president as an effective way to improve its global image following its invasion of Czechoslovakia in August 1968. In the short term, Soviet officials viewed the use of force to suppress the "Prague Spring" – the political, social, and economic reform efforts to de-Stalinize Czechoslovakia and pursue an independent course from Moscow – as a necessary move to reassert Soviet control over the Eastern bloc and to prevent "falling dominoes" in Central Europe.[28] But, in the long run, the overwhelming force and the blatant disregard for Czechoslovakia's sovereignty did more to cripple Soviet foreign policy than they did to strengthen it. Many communist countries, including China, condemned the use of troops against a socialist country, and the invasion soured the emerging US–Soviet détente. President Johnson canceled his impending visit to the Soviet Union and, according to historian Thomas Schwartz, issued a "clear warning" to Moscow to discontinue the "Brezhnev Doctrine" by taking action against either Romania or Yugoslavia, countries that had both split from the traditional orthodoxy of Moscow's foreign policy.[29]

Finally, there were a number of economic pressures pushing the Soviets in the direction of a détente with the United States. The financial burden of the nuclear arms race and the high costs of maintaining large armies in both the East and the West were no longer sustainable. Many Soviet leaders, moreover, wanted to purchase Western technology to help modernize their chemical and automobile industries, and sought to increase the rate of Western investment for future growth.[30] And there was recognition amongst the top echelons of the Politburo that the Kremlin needed to be more receptive to popular demands for material improvement, especially in the areas of food and housing.[31]

Faced with the overwhelming combination of foreign and domestic pressures to improve relations with Washington, the Kremlin undertook a major reassessment of its foreign policy objectives to better meet these challenges. On September 16, 1968 Gromyko presented the Politburo with a paper entitled "An Assessment of the State of Foreign Policy and the State of Soviet–American relations," which in effect outlined the future Soviet foreign policy doctrine. The document called for a combination of "firmness with flexibility" with the United States and for "actively using means of diplomatic maneuver." Under certain conditions, Gromyko explained to his colleagues, a "dialogue" could be initiated with the United States on a broad range of issues, preparations for which "should be conducted systematically and purposely even now."[32] The Politburo unanimously approved the paper and presaged the course of Soviet foreign policy and the scope of Soviet–American relations during the Nixon years.[33]

After hearing Nixon's call on January 20 that "our lines of communication" will be open to "all" nations,[34] the Kremlin moved aggressively to respond in kind. In early February, during a "special review" of Soviet–American relations held at a government dacha outside of Moscow, Soviet leaders drafted a message for Nixon that intended to show they "were full of goodwill and eager to move forward on a broad front." The Soviet leadership indicated their willingness to answer questions on Vietnam or "any other political problem on [your] mind,"[35] and urged the president to begin joint negotiations on the Middle East to avoid "most undesirable consequences" in the region. "We are confident that if the Soviet Union and the United States ... make full use of their possibilities and influence in order to find just and lasting settlement in the Middle East it will also greatly contribute to the general relaxation of international tensions."[36]

When Dobrynin brought the message to the White House on February 17, there could be little doubt that the president shared Moscow's desire to begin negotiations not just on the Middle East but on other areas of joint concern, including arms control, Vietnam, and a summit. According to Dobrynin, Nixon nodded his head "vigorously" to the passages in the Soviet note that "expressed our readiness to conduct a comprehensive exchange of views with him and our readiness for a joint, constructive dialogue," and he noted that it was apparent that, on the whole, Nixon liked the "balanced, constructive tone" of the Soviet statements. "Those views, he said, fully correspond to his own thoughts on the main point: the leaders of the two great powers must maintain a frank dialogue based on mutual trust and an understanding of the complex and important role that both our countries play in the modern world."[37]

It was also during that meeting that Nixon formally established a "backchannel" between the Soviet ambassador and Henry Kissinger, which would be used as the primary venue to advance détente. During their conversations, which generally took place in the Map Room of the White House, Kissinger and Dobrynin discussed topics as far ranging as arms control, Vietnam, Berlin, the Middle East, and Soviet–American trade. In part, this reflected Nixon's desire for "linkage," whereby progress on each issue, particularly issues of importance to the Soviet Union, would depend on progress on several others. Yet it also ensured, according to

Kissinger, that the "major negotiations" with the Soviet Union would be conducted from the White House, under the president's direct supervision.[38]

Despite the establishment of the backchannel and the desire of both Moscow and Washington for improved relations, Nixon also understood that détente had little chance of success if he did not also simultaneously improve relations with the People's Republic of China. Only after the Soviet leaders understood that they could not count on "permanent hostility" between Washington and Peking would they be willing to make the necessary concessions in the direction of détente. Although the president repeatedly professed in public that his policies with China were in no way "linked" to improved relations with Moscow, he skillfully exploited the fractured Sino-Soviet relationship to extract concessions from both sides. "In the conditions of the late 1960s," Kissinger later wrote, "improved Sino-American relations became the key to the Nixon Administration's Soviet strategy."[39]

Indeed, it was only after the United States and the People's Republic of China took steps toward rapprochement in late 1970 that improvements in Soviet–American relations followed. Continued disagreements on the Middle East, Cuba, and Vietnam ensured that détente remained a distant prospect during the first two years of the Nixon administration. By the spring of 1971, however, the United States and the Soviet Union took a number of steps to show that both sides were committed to improved relations. On May 20, just weeks after Mao invited the US table tennis team to Peking, the United States and the Soviet Union reached an ABM agreement that limited Washington and Moscow to one ABM site for defense of their capitals and of an intercontinental ballistic missile (ICBM) field, and helped to curb the nuclear arms race. In August, Nixon and Brezhnev, along with the British and French, signed the Quadripartite Agreement relaxing tensions over Berlin. And in October 1971, Nixon announced that he had accepted an invitation from Brezhnev to visit Moscow the following year, where the two leaders would seek a major arms control agreement.

Nixon's state visit to Moscow in May 1972 lasted eight days and turned out to be the most significant event in Soviet–American relations since the Yalta conference in the waning months of World War II. The highlight of the summit was the signing of the Strategic Arms Limitation Treaty (SALT), an interim agreement that froze the existing numbers of ICBMs already deployed or under construction. But important agreements were also reached on political, economic, strategic, and technical ties and culminated with the signing of the Basic Principles of Mutual Relations and the joint communiqué.[40] "What we have agreed upon are principles that acknowledge differences, but express a code of conduct which, if observed, can only contribute to world peace and to an international system based on mutual respect and self-restraint," Nixon said in a report to Congress after the summit. "These principles are a guide for future action" and, as the *New York Times* editorialized, an important "first step … toward a safer future for the Soviet and American peoples and for the world."[41]

The Moscow Summit was indeed a first step towards détente, but US–Soviet efforts to ease tension at the global level continued. In 1973, Nixon and Brezhnev reached further agreements on scientific and cultural exchanges, transportation, and the peaceful use of atomic energy. They also signed a treaty on the Prevention of Nuclear War, which committed the superpowers to a code of conduct that would remove the danger of nuclear war and the use of nuclear weapons and compelled officials in Washington and Moscow not to worsen relations with any country, so as to avoid a nuclear war. The following year, moreover, after Nixon resigned from office, President Gerald F. Ford continued the Nixon–Kissinger policy of détente by reaching agreements with Brezhnev at Vladivostok that set further limits on the total number of missiles equipped with multiple independently targetable reentry vehicles (MIRVs), as well as a framework to continue the SALT negotiations.

Many conservatives in Congress, such as Senator Henry "Scoop" Jackson, were critical of détente for ignoring human rights abuses behind the Iron Curtain. Others, like California Governor Ronald Reagan, were critical of détente because its policies accepted living with the communist system rather than seeking its defeat. Even critics inside the Ford administration came to see détente as sacrificing American national security interests for the sake of improved relations with Moscow. Assistant Secretary of Defense Paul Nitze, for example, wrote in a January 1976 *Foreign Affairs* article that participating in a SALT II agreement made little sense in terms of defense strategy. "Unfortunately – and to the profound regret of one who has participated both in the SALT negotiations and in a series of earlier U.S. decisions designed to stabilize the nuclear balance," wrote Nitze, "I believe that each of these conclusions is today without adequate foundation."[42] Still, for a brief period, the policies adopted by Nixon, Ford, and Brezhnev during the late 1960s and early 1970s offered an alternative to the crisis years of the 1960s and demonstrated that the potential danger of a nuclear war meant that new policies, strategies, and tactics needed to be pursued.

Ostpolitik and European Détente

Although superpower détente has generally received the most attention from scholars through the years, the era of détente was not limited to Washington and Moscow. Indeed, even before US and Soviet leaders sought improved relations at the global level, European leaders envisioned a world that saw an end to the Cold War division of Europe. France's Charles De Gaulle, for example, sought to break the Cold War order in Europe long before Nixon and Brezhnev pursued such policies. Building on his enhanced international prestige from ending the Algerian War, De Gaulle wanted a strong and independent France to act as a balancing force between the United States and the Soviet Union and he sought to establish a "real détente" between East and West. In an effort to defuse the Berlin crisis and work toward nuclear disarmament, De Gaulle invited the superpowers to Paris in May 1960 for a major summit. Khrushchev's protestation over the American U-2 reconnaissance plane caught spying over Soviet territory prevented the summit from taking place in Paris, but De Gaulle continued to press forward with trying to bridge the East–West divide. As a sign that he wanted improved relations with the East, De Gaulle established diplomatic relations with the People's Republic of China, pushed for West Germany's integration in the European Economic Community, and withdrew French participation from NATO.[43]

De Gaulle's efforts to build real détente came up short, but that did not stop other European leaders from attempting to end the Cold War division of Europe. In 1969, the new West German Chancellor, Willy Brandt, unveiled a grand design for a Western Europe living in peace with its neighbors to the East. Rejecting the long-held policies of the Adenauer era, and the Hallstein Doctrine, when the Federal Republic of Germany refused diplomatic relations with any country that recognized East Germany, Brandt instead believed that a rapprochement with the East, not isolation, was the only way to bring about a change in the East German regime. Put simply, his goal was to normalize relations with the communist countries, moving "from confrontation to cooperation," much like Nixon had proposed with the Soviets in his inaugural address. In this regard, Brandt was willing to accept the German Democratic Republic (GDR) as a separate state and to accommodate Poland on the question of the Oder–Neisse Line, which formed Poland's western frontier. He also hoped through this new policy to reduce the antagonism toward West Germany in the USSR and Eastern Europe and to make the division of Germany less severe.[44]

To understand the roots of Brandt's eastern policy – *Ostpolitik* – one need only look at the two most important events in Germany's postwar period: the suppression of the uprising in East

Berlin on June 17, 1953 and the erection of the Berlin Wall in August 1961. These events convinced Germans on both sides of the Iron Curtain that there were limits to Western power and resolve when it came to defending Berlin and West Germany. In 1953, President Dwight D. Eisenhower and Secretary of State John Foster Dulles watched on the sidelines as Soviet tanks and troops moved into East Berlin, despite pledges to "liberate" Eastern Europe and "roll back" communism.[45] Eight years later, the Kennedy administration again did nothing to challenge the Soviet and East German decision to seal the border between East and West Berlin. As Mayor of West Berlin in 1961, Brandt personally witnessed the devastation that the Wall brought to German families and understood that the Four Power commitment to a free Berlin ended at the sector border. The United States, either alone or in concert with its allies, could not bring about a solution to the German problem.[46]

Without US support, Brandt moved aggressively to find his own solution to the German problem. Along with Egon Bahr, his chief foreign policy adviser, the new German chancellor guided West Germany through four years of negotiations that led to treaties with the Soviet Union, Poland, and the GDR, and produced a Four Power Treaty on Berlin that helped to ease more than two decades of tension over the divided city. Although many of Brandt's political opponents accused him of accepting the status quo in Germany, and the permanent division of Europe, for Brandt *Ostpolitik* marked the first step in a long process toward German unification. Only by first accepting the division of Germany, and working to improve the lives of Germans in both states, could the two sides strive for unity. "In a span of a few years," the historian Jussi Hanhimaki has written, "the German question was transformed from being the focal point of East–West tension to becoming a centerpiece of détente."[47]

Many critics of *Ostpolitik* believed that by improving relations with the East, Brandt would undermine the Western alliance and bring the Federal Republic of Germany (FRG) within the Soviet sphere of influence. As for Nixon and Kissinger, in particular, they were initially reluctant to embrace Brandt's eastern policy. In a memo to Nixon on February 16, 1970, Kissinger argued that recognition of the GDR would strengthen the communist regime and could turn into a new form of "classic German nationalism." He also feared that the FRG would find itself in a "race for influence" with the GDR in the Third World, which could quickly put Bonn's policies at odds with those of its allies, for example in the Middle East. Even in Europe, particularly in Scandinavia and the United Kingdom, the FRG might find its relations "clouded" by increased GDR commercial activities. "Men like Brandt ... and Defense Minister Schmidt undoubtedly see themselves as conducting a responsible policy of reconciliation and normalization with the East and intend not to have this policy come into conflict with Germany's Western association," said Kissinger. "But their problem is to control a process which, if it results in failure could jeopardize their political lives and if it succeeds could create a momentum that may shake Germany's domestic stability and unhinge its international position."[48]

Despite early reservations from Washington about his grand design, Brandt quickly found a partner in Soviet General Secretary Brezhnev, who wanted to use *Ostpolitik* and improved relations with West Germany to reduce the potential for war between NATO and the Warsaw Pact countries, as well as to secure recognition of the post-World War II borders and to open up new markets, particularly in oil and gas.[49] In August 1970, after more than six months of negotiations, Soviet and West German leaders signed the Treaty of Moscow, which recognized existing postwar boundaries, including the Oder–Neisse Line, and brought an end to German claims on territory lost in the war. Through the treaty, moreover, Soviet and West German leaders also renounced the use of force, and any territorial claims against the other. Most important, as historian William Hitchcock has observed, the Moscow Treaty committed both

West Germany and the USSR to the "political status quo" and "marked a new era in European diplomacy."[50] Four months later, Brandt reached a similar deal with Poland. By accepting the Oder–Neisse Line as the Polish–German border and relinquishing claims to territories that had once belonged to Germany, Poland agreed to expedite the emigration of the remaining ethnic Germans living in Poland who wished to go to the FRG.

The Moscow and Warsaw treaties marked a major success of *Ostpolitik* but Brandt was not done. The following year, in what was perhaps the signature achievement of his eastern policy, the German Chancellor maneuvered the Four Powers into signing the Quadripartite Agreement on Berlin. The treaty called for the Soviets and East Germans to allow for "unimpeded" civilian traffic between West Berlin and West Germany; periodic visits by West Berliners to their families in East Berlin; and the expansion of communication and transport points from Berlin. In return, Brandt agreed to relinquish the claim that West Berlin "belongs to" and is politically part of West Germany. The treaty did nothing to push for the elimination of the Berlin Wall, nor did it carry any provisions to eliminate the shootings of individuals who tried to cross the wall. Nevertheless, the Quadripartite Agreement went a long way to easing tension between West and East Germany and improved the lives of the German people, as new possibilities were created for trade, travel, and the reconnection of family members separated by the division of Germany.

Brandt's luck would run out by 1974, as he was forced from office by a domestic scandal. Still, *Ostpolitik* opened the door for further improvements in East–West relations. With West Germany's acceptance of the Oder–Neisse Line, the Soviet Union pushed aggressively for a broader European security conference to secure formal recognition of the postwar frontiers in Central and Eastern Europe. This had been a major goal of Soviet leaders since the end of World War II, as they sought formal recognition from the West of their sphere of influence in Eastern Europe. At the Conference on Security and Cooperation in Helsinki, Finland, in the summer of 1975, delegates from thirty-five nations accepted the permanence of existing European boundaries, including adjustments made in Germany and Eastern Europe three decades earlier. The conferees pledged themselves to détente and endorsed human rights for all Europeans. In addition to reaching an agreement on the inviolability of frontiers, which was the original impetus for the Soviet desire to hold the conference, the Helsinki Final Act committed Conference on Security and Cooperation in European states to respect human rights and facilitate human contacts across East–West borders.

Right-wing critics blasted the Helsinki Final Act as putting "the American seal of approval on the Red Army's Second World War conquests,"[51] and many conservatives inside the Republican Party compelled President Ford to abandon the word "détente" during the Republican primary. In retrospect, however, it is clear that these charges were grossly misplaced. As historian Sarah B. Snyder has demonstrated, the Helsinki Accords "spurred" the development of a transnational network of politicians, dissidents, and activists that significantly contributed to the end of the Cold War. So-called Helsinki groups, from Charter 77, headed by Vaclav Havel in Czechoslovakia, and Solidarity, led by Lech Walesa in Poland, emerged in the wake of Helsinki to pressure Soviet and Eastern European leaders to adhere to the Accords, especially the provisions in Basket Three that addressed humanitarian issues.[52]

Détente and the Third World

Détente may have found success in Europe and at the global strategic level, through arms limitations agreements, *Ostpolitik*, and the Helsinki Accords, but the Soviet–American rapprochement failed to reach its full potential, due to persistent competition and the inability of either superpower to forgo its desire for predominance at the regional level, particularly in the Third World. In 1970, for example, tensions between Washington and Moscow quickly surfaced in the Caribbean, when the Soviets decided to build a nuclear submarine base at Cienfuegos, Cuba, in violation of their pledge after the 1962 missile crisis not to place offensive weapons on the island. The following year, when the civil war in Pakistan threatened Indian intervention to contain the massive flood of East Bengali refugees, the United States and the Soviet Union once again found themselves on opposing sides, backing allies for purely geopolitical purposes. Believing that "we can't allow a friend of ours and China's to get screwed in a conflict with a friend of Russia's," Nixon and Kissinger "tilted" towards Pakistan, sending weapons and a naval task force to the Bay of Bengal, while ignoring President Yahya's brutal crackdown of the Bengali refugees.[53]

But it was in the Middle East, perhaps more than any other area of the world, that the superpowers demonstrated that détente would have its limits. Despite efforts by Washington and Moscow to reach an Arab–Israeli peace agreement in 1969, Brezhnev, in February 1970, sent more than ten thousand Soviet forces to Egypt to defend its Arab ally against Israeli deep-penetration raids. The Soviet intervention in the Egyptian–Israeli war of attrition, known as Operation Kavkaz, proved to be one of the most significant military operations outside the Warsaw Pact that the Soviet Union had ever made, and weakened the prospects for a lasting détente.[54] Kissinger, in fact, described the move and the diplomacy behind it as the "first Soviet threat" to the administration, which warranted a firm reply from President Nixon.[55] Several months later, after Secretary of State William P. Rogers successfully negotiated a ceasefire agreement ending the war of attrition, the Kremlin undermined the ceasefire by colluding with the Egyptians in moving surface-to-air missiles closer to the Suez Canal, a clear violation of the "standstill" provision of the agreement.[56]

Although the superpowers reached agreements at the 1972 Moscow Summit to place their difference in the Middle East on ice and accepted the status quo in the region for the benefit of détente, US and Soviet behavior during the 1973 Arab–Israeli War saw a return to traditional Cold War politics. Both superpowers could have encouraged a quick end to the war by calling for an immediate ceasefire in the UN Security Council. Instead, both Washington and Moscow initiated massive airlifts of weapons to their respective clients, prolonging the war and exacerbating tensions in Soviet–American relations. On October 24, when the Soviets proposed sending a joint Soviet–American force to the region to end the conflict and threatened to dispatch Soviet troops unilaterally if Israel did not adhere to the United Nations Security Council's ceasefire resolution, Nixon and Kissinger chose to assume the worst in Brezhnev's motivations and placed US forces on military alert. "After all we have heard about the 'Hot Line' between the White House and the Kremlin, the trustful personal relationship between Secretary Kissinger and Ambassador Dobrynin of the Soviet Union, and the new 'partnership for peace' between the U.S. and the U.S.S.R.," James Reston wrote in the *New York Times* the day after the crisis abated, "are we to believe that the only way Mr. Nixon can send Mr. Brezhnev a message is to put American forces all over the world on alert?"[57]

Kissinger's peace efforts following the war eased Arab–Israeli tensions and put Egypt on a path towards permanent peace with Israel, but they also marked an effective end of Soviet–American cooperation in the Middle East. Instead of using the US–Soviet framework that had produced the ceasefire ending the war to conduct the postwar negotiations, Kissinger unilaterally launched his "shuttle diplomacy," ensuring that the Soviets would reap none of the benefits that came from ending the Israeli occupation. True, the December 1973 Geneva Conference, in which the Egyptians and Israelis convened for the first time since the end of the war,[58] was held under the joint auspices of the Soviet Union and the United States, but even the participants at the conference could see through Kissinger's transparent ploy to "pacify" the Soviets by letting them be part of the game without providing them with any role in the negotiations.[59] Following Geneva, Kissinger abandoned any pretext of involving the Soviets in the Middle East negotiations. By the time the secretary of state had concluded the second disengagement agreement with Egypt in 1975, he had accomplished the goal that the Nixon administration had set out from nearly day one, which sought to reduce the Soviet influence in the Middle East and to "produce a stalemate until Moscow urged compromise or until, even better, some moderate Arab regime decided that the route to progress was through Washington."[60] But at what cost?

With the Soviets facing the deterioration of their strategic position in the Arab world, all to the benefit of the United States, they had little incentive to help Washington conclude peace agreements that would bring additional Arab states further into the American sphere of influence, and they were less inclined to cooperate with future administrations on the Middle East. It should come as no surprise that in 1978 Ambassador Dobrynin, a strong advocate of US–Soviet détente, recommended that the Kremlin throw a "wrench" into the Carter administration's game plan in the Middle East by revealing the "hypocrisy" of the United States in trying to show that it was equally close to the interests of the Arabs and Israel and to "more actively use the contradiction between the American imperialistic interests in the Middle East (oil, investment in Saudi Arabia, etc.) and Israeli-Zionist interests (open territorial expansion at the Arabs' expense)."[61]

The Soviets also took aggressive steps in the mid-to-late 1970s to reclaim the strategic ground they had lost in the Middle East as a result of détente. Coinciding with its deteriorating relationship with Cairo and the expulsion of its military presence from Egypt, Moscow accelerated military aid to Aden, providing a $20 million arms deal in 1972 and doubling it the following year. Also in 1972, Moscow signed a Treaty of Friendship and Cooperation with the Ba'ath party in Iraq and assisted Baghdad with the nationalization of its oil. It later provided Iraq with enough arms to double the size of its armed forces by 1975.[62] And in 1978, the Soviets supported the coup in the People's Democratic Republic of Yemen (South Yemen) that brought to power Abd al-Fattah Ismail, first leader of the Yemeni Socialist party, which gave Moscow important air facilities in the Persian Gulf.[63]

Although the United States did agree to the Helsinki Accords in 1975, marking the high point of détente, the stabilization of the European continent allowed the superpowers to continue their competition in the Third World. Indeed the limits, and pending decline, of détente came to the forefront in 1975–76 over competition in the former Portuguese colony of Angola. Fearing that the Marxist MPLA (Popular Movement for the Liberation of Angola) would be defeated by a racist regime in Pretoria, the Kremlin joined Cuba in lending military and financial aid to the MPLA. Brezhnev insisted that in aiding Augusto Neto's MPLA forces, he had no intention of threatening détente. But, in the wake of the fall of Saigon, the Ford administration viewed Soviet involvement in Angola as a direct challenge to US credibility.

Consequently, President Ford, at the urging of Secretary of State Henry Kissinger, countered the Soviet move by authorizing in 1975 more than $30 million in covert funds to support the FNLA (National Front for the Liberation of Angola) and UNITA (National Union for the Total Liberation of Angola) forces, and drawing the United States and the Soviet Union into further competition in Africa in the waning months of his administration.[64]

The Carter administration attempted to resuscitate efforts at détente but it, too, found that competition with the Soviets in the Third World would make continuing détente a pipedream. Historian Louise Woodroofe has recently shown that in the Horn of Africa the small border war between Ethiopia and Somalia erupted into a major Cold War "hotspot." Like in Angola, after the Soviets and Cubans sent military advisors to assist their new ally in Ethiopia, the United States responded by counteracting the Soviet presence in Addis Ababa by supporting Somalia.[65]

Brezhnev professed to remain committed to détente despite continued disagreements with the United States in Africa, but his words never matched his actions. Two years after fueling a proxy war in the Horn of Africa, Soviet troops invaded Afghanistan to preserve a shaky communist government and to expand its influence in South Asia. Brezhnev in particular feared that a communist defeat at the hands of Muslim guerrillas would damage Soviet prestige worldwide and that the adjacent Muslim areas of the USSR would be destabilized.[66] For the United States, the Soviet invasion of Afghanistan was the last straw in its efforts to continue détente. Carter withdrew the SALT II treaty from the Senate, stopped high-technology sales and grain shipments to the USSR, and pulled the United States out of the summer Olympic Games scheduled for Moscow.

The resurgence of the Soviet military presence in the Middle East, combined with its activities in Afghanistan and the Horn of Africa, not only demonstrated the limits of US–Soviet cooperation but signaled the end of détente. President Jimmy Carter's warning to the Soviets in his 1980 State of the Union address that he would view any attempt by any "outside force" to gain control of the Persian Gulf region as "an assault on the vital interests of the United States of America," which would be "repelled by any means necessary, including military force," echoed the language of the Truman and Eisenhower Doctrines, extended containment to the Persian Gulf, and brought a return to traditional Cold War politics.[67]

All this is not to say that détente did not have its benefits. Certainly, détente produced the ABM and SALT treaties, helping to limit the size of US and Soviet nuclear arsenals; it brought about the Quadripartite Agreement, which removed Berlin as a frequent crisis point in the Cold War; and it led to the 1975 Conference on Security and Cooperation in Europe, which produced the Helsinki Accords. Moreover, détente improved overall US–Soviet relations by reducing the potential for major superpower conflict in many areas of the world. Nevertheless, détente was not a monolithic policy; its application and effect varied depending on the context. Nowhere was this truer than in the Third World. As American and Soviet leaders pursued détente, their policies in the Third World undermined progress towards peaceful coexistence and lasting cooperation. Clearly, competition would persist. The Cold War would continue. Détente had its limits.

Notes

1 Jeremi Suri, *Power and Protest: Global Revolution and the Rise of Détente* (Cambridge, MA: Harvard University Press, 2003), 216.
2 Raymond L. Garthoff, *Détente and Confrontation: American–Soviet Relations from Nixon to Reagan* (Washington, DC: The Brookings Institution, 1994); William P. Bundy, *A Tangled Web: The Making of Foreign Policy in the Nixon Presidency* (New York: Hill & Wang, 1998); Keith Nelson, *The Making of Détente: Soviet–American Relations in the Shadow of Vietnam* (Baltimore, MD: Johns Hopkins University Press, 1993); Jussi M. Hanhimaki, *The Rise and Fall of Détente: American Foreign Policy and the Transformation of the Cold War* (Washington, DC: Potomac Books, 2012).
3 On Brezhnev and Soviet détente, see Vladislav Zubok, *A Failed Empire: The Soviet Union in the Cold War from Stalin to Gorbachev* (Chapel Hill, NC: University of North Carolina Press, 2007); M.E. Sarotte, *Dealing with the Devil: East Germany, Détente, and Ostpolitik, 1969–1973* (Chapel Hill, NC: University of North Carolina Press, 2001); W.R. Smyser, *From Yalta to Berlin: The Cold War Struggle over Germany* (New York: St. Martin's Press, 1999), 248–255.
4 Robert J. McMahon, "The Danger of Geopolitical Fantasies: Nixon, Kissinger, and the South Asia Crisis of 1971," in Fredrik Logevall and Andrew Preston, eds., *Nixon in the World: American Foreign Relations, 1969–1977* (New York: Oxford University Press, 2008), 249–268; Tanya Harmer, *Allende's Chile and the Inter-America Cold War* (Chapel Hill, NC: University of North Carolina Press, 2011); Craig Daigle, *The Limits of Détente: The United States, the Soviet Union, and the Arab–Israeli Conflict,*

1969–1973 (New Haven, CT: Yale University Press, 2012); Piero Gleijeses, *Conflicting Missions: Havana, Washington, and Africa, 1959–1976* (Chapel Hill, NC: University of North Carolina Press, 2002); Louise P. Woodroofe, *"Buried in the Sands of the Ogaden": The United States, the Horn of Africa, and the Demise of Détente* (Kent, OH: Kent State University Press, 2013).

5 *Public Papers of the Presidents of the United States: Richard Nixon, 1969* (Washington, DC: Government Printing Office, 1970), 3–4.
6 Address by Richard M. Nixon to the Bohemian Club, July 29, 1967, *Foreign Relations of the United States* [*FRUS*], 1969–1976, vol. 1, doc. 2; Richard Nixon, *RN: The Memoirs of Richard Nixon* (New York: Grosset & Dunlap), 284–285.
7 Nixon, *Memoirs*, 344; Anatoly Dobrynin, *In Confidence: Moscow's Ambassador to America's Six Cold War Presidents* (New York: Times Books, 1995), 201.
8 Nixon, Address to the Bohemian Club, July 29, 1967; George C. Herring, *America's Longest War: The United States and Vietnam, 1950–1975*, 3rd ed. (New York: McGraw Hill, 1996), 163–164.
9 Nixon, *Memoirs*, 345.
10 William Taubman, *Khrushchev: The Man and His Era* (New York: W.W. Norton & Company, 2004), 435–439; Aleksandr Fursenko and Timothy Naftali, *Khrushchev's Cold War: The Inside Story of an American Adversary* (New York: W.W. Norton & Company, 2006), 226–232.
11 Robert Dallek, *An Unfinished Life: John F. Kennedy, 1917–1963* (Boston, MA: Little Brown, 2003), 614–620; Richard Reeves, *President Kennedy: Profile of Power* (New York: Simon & Schuster, 1993), 548–552.
12 Thomas Alan Schwartz, *Lyndon Johnson and Europe: In the Shadow of Vietnam* (Cambridge, MA: Harvard University Press, 2003), 135–136, 181–182.
13 Suri, *Power and Protest*, 44–61, 73–39, 216–226.
14 Ibid., 2.
15 Memorandum of Conversation, January 2, 1969, National Archives and Records Administration (hereafter NARA), NPMS, NSCF, box 725, Country Files, Europe, USSR, Contacts with the Soviets Prior to January 20, 1969; Memorandum of Conversation, December 18, 1968, *FRUS*, 1964–1968, vol. 14, doc. 335.
16 John Lewis Gaddis, *Strategies of Containment: A Critical Appraisal of Postwar American National Security Policy* (New York: Oxford University Press, 1982), 290; Henry Kissinger, *White House Years* (Boston: Little Brown, 1979) (hereafter cited as *WHY*), 61–62.
17 Dobrynin, *In Confidence*, 201.
18 Ibid.
19 A full text of Gromyko's July 10 speech before the Supreme Soviet is in *The Current Digest of the Soviet Press* (Columbus, OH: American Association for the Advancement of Slavic Studies), vol. 21, August 6, 1969, 6–10.
20 For more on the Sino-Soviet split, see Lorenz M. Lüthi's Chapter 6 in this volume.
21 Chen Jian, *Mao's China and the Cold War* (Chapel Hill, NC: University of North Carolina Press, 2000), 240–241.
22 See footnote 2, doc. 15, *FRUS*, 1969–1976, vol. 17; William I. Hitchcock, *The Struggle for Europe: The Turbulent History of a Divided Continent, 1945 to the Present* (New York: Doubleday, 2002), 296.
23 Kissinger to Nixon, July 23, 1969, *FRUS*, 1969–1976, vol. 12, doc. 71.
24 National Intelligence Estimate, August 12, 1969, *FRUS*, 1969–1976, vol. 12, doc. 73.
25 William Burr, "Sino-American Relations, 1969: The Sino-Soviet Border War and Steps towards Rapprochement," *Cold War History* 1:3 (2001): 73–112.
26 Kissinger to Nixon, July 26, 1969, *FRUS*, 1969–1976, vol. 12, doc. 61.
27 Helms to Rogers, July 14, 1969, ibid., doc. 66.
28 Zubok, *A Failed Empire*, 207; transcript of Leonid Brezhnev's Telephone Conversation with Alexander Dubcek, August 13, 1968, National Security Archive.
29 Schwartz, *Lyndon Johnson and Europe*, 219.
30 Zubok, *A Failed Empire*, 220.
31 National Intelligence Estimate, February 27, 1969, *FRUS*, 1969–1976, vol. 12, doc. 21.
32 Excerpts from "An Assessment of the Course of Foreign Policy and the State of Soviet–American Relations" (Approved by the Politburo), September 16, 1968, in Dobrynin, *In Confidence*, 643.
33 Dobrynin, *In Confidence*, 184.
34 *Public Papers: Nixon, 1969*, 1–4.
35 Editorial Note, *FRUS*, 1969–1976, vol. 12, doc. 12.

36 Note from the Soviet Leadership to President Nixon, undated, NARA, RG 59, Central Files, 1967–1969, POL 1 US-USSR.
37 Nixon–Dobrynin Memcon, From the Diary of Anatoly Dobrynin, February 17, 1969, *Soviet–American Relations: The Détente Years, 1969–1972*, ed. David C. Geyer and Douglas Selvage (Washington, DC: US Department of State, 2007), 14–18 (hereafter cited as *Soviet–American Relations*); Dobrynin, *In Confidence*, 203–204; *White House Years*, 143, 354; Jussi Hanhimaki, *The Flawed Architect: Henry Kissinger and American Foreign Policy* (Oxford: Oxford University Press, 2004), 38–40.
38 Henry A. Kissinger, "Foreword," in *Soviet–American Relations*, ix–xviii.
39 Henry Kissinger, *Diplomacy* (New York: Simon & Schuster, 1994), 719.
40 For details of the negotiations at the summit, see *FRUS, 1969–1976*, vol. 14; the Soviet records can be found in *Soviet–American Relations*, chap. 10. See also Dobrynin, *In Confidence*, 251–257; *White House Years*, 1202–1257; and Nixon, *Memoirs*, 609–621.
41 Richard M. Nixon, *U.S. Foreign Policy for the 1970s*, vol. 4: *Shaping a Durable Peace*, A Report to the Congress (Washington: Government Printing Office, 1973), 37; "Rules for Coexistence," *New York Times*, May 30, 1972.
42 Paul Nitze, "Assuring Strategic Stability in an Era of Détente," *Foreign Affairs* 54:2 (January, 1976): 207–232.
43 Suri, *Power and Protest*, 54.
44 Kissinger to Nixon, 16 February 1970, *FRUS, 1969–1976*, vol. XL, doc. 55.
45 For more on the events in 1953 and 1961 see Hope M. Harrison's Chapter 5 in this volume.
46 Paper Prepared in the Department of State, October 12, 1972, *FRUS, 1969–1976*, vol. XL, doc. 123.
47 Hanhimaki, *The Flawed Architect*, 86.
48 Kissinger to Nixon, February 16, 1970, *FRUS, 1969–1976*, vol. XL, doc. 55.
49 Vladislav Zubok, "The Soviet Union and Détente of the 1970s," *Cold War History* 8:4 (November 2008), 427–447.
50 Hitchcock, *The Struggle for Europe*, 297.
51 Quoted in Sarah B. Snyder, "Through the Looking Glass: The Helsinki Final Act and the 1976 Election for President," *Diplomacy and Statecraft* 21 (March 2010): 91.
52 Sarah B. Snyder, *Human Rights Activism and the End of the Cold War: A Transnational History of the Helsinki Network* (Cambridge: Cambridge University Press, 2011).
53 McMahon, "Danger of Geopolitical Fantasies." For more on the South Asia crisis of 1971, see Artemy M. Kalinovsky's Chapter 13 in this volume.
54 Isabella Ginor, "'Under the Yellow Arab Helmet Gleamed Blue Russian Eyes': Operation *Kavkaz* and the War of Attrition, 1969–70," *Cold War History* 3:1 (2002): 127–156.
55 Kissinger to Nixon, February 1, 1970, NARA, NPMS, NSCF, box 489, PTF, Dobrynin/Kissinger, 1970.
56 See Daigle, *The Limits of Détente*, chapter 4.
57 James Reston, "A Crisis a Day," *New York Times*, October 26, 1973.
58 Syria did not participate at Geneva. For more on the Geneva Conference, see Kissinger, *Years of Upheaval*, 747–798; and William B. Quandt, *Peace Process: American Diplomacy and the Arab-Israeli Conflict Since 1967* (Berkeley: University of California Press, 2005), 138–141.
59 Richard B. Parker, ed., *The October War: A Retrospective* (Gainesville, FL: University Press of Florida, 2001), 249.
60 *White House Years*, 1279.
61 Political Letter of Soviet Ambassador to the United States Anatoly Dobrynin to the USSR Ministry of Foreign Affairs, July 11, 1978, Cold War International History Project, US–Soviet Relations.
62 Galia Golan, *Soviet Policies in the Middle East: From World War II to Gorbachev* (Cambridge: Cambridge University Press, 1990), 167.
63 Ibid., 228–243.
64 Hanhimaki, *The Flawed Architect*, 413.
65 Woodroofe, *"Buried in the Sands of the Ogaden"*.
66 Odd Arne Westad, *The Global Cold War: Third World Interventions and the Making of Our Times* (Cambridge: Cambridge University Press, 2005), 316–326.
67 Terrence Smith, "Carter Warns U.S. Would Use Armed Force to Repel a Soviet Thrust at Persian Gulf," *New York Times*, January 24, 1980; Olav Njolstad, "Shifting Priorities: The Persian Gulf in U.S. Strategic Planning in the Carter Years," *Cold War History* 4:3 (2004): 21–55; William E. Odom, "The Cold War Origins of the U.S. Central Command," *Journal of Cold War Studies* 8:2 (2006): 52–82.

15
ZHOU ENLAI AND THE SINO-AMERICAN RAPPROCHEMENT, 1969–1972

Yafeng Xia

Zhou Enlai was first foreign minister (1949–58) and first premier (1949–76) of the People's Republic of China (PRC). China's paramount leader, Mao Zedong, as the chairman of the Chinese Communist Party (CCP), had sufficient power to set the foreign policy agenda and guidelines on his own. He consigned Zhou to the role of a manager overseeing day-to-day aspects of foreign affairs.[1] Zhou won both domestic and international recognition as being responsible for formulating and carrying out China's foreign policy during the Cold War. Among the PRC leaders, Zhou was known for his negotiation skills, personal patience and attention to detail. In this regard, Zhou was "indispensable" in Mao's eyes. The question of Mao's and Zhou's individual roles in the Sino-American rapprochement and their real attitudes during this period, is still a hotly debated topic. In my previous work, I have argued that "Mao was the behind-the-scenes strategist and final decision-maker."[2] Zhou was "obviously a sponsor and promoter of" China's policy of reconciliation with the United States, but "not an initiator and final decision-maker."[3] Zhou's strength lay in the execution rather than the conception of policy.

Based on currently available Chinese and U.S. primary and secondary sources,[4] this chapter examines Zhou's role as the promoter of the policy of rapprochement with the United States and as China's chief negotiator with U.S. leaders on thorny issues such as Taiwan, Indochina, and the Korean peninsula. It attempts to fill a gap in the current scholarship on the U.S.–China rapprochement and provides a new perspective to the Chinese side of the story, as seen through the prism of Zhou.[5]

Promoting the Policy of Rapprochement

By the middle of 1969, China seemed to have a more urgent need to improve its relationship with Washington in order to break its diplomatic isolation and predicament. The Chinese felt "under siege" after the Soviet Union invaded Czechoslovakia in August 1968 and declared that it had the right to intervene in any socialist country that deviated from Moscow's line. Mao interpreted this "Brezhnev Doctrine" as an attack on his own legitimacy. In 1968–69 the tension over Vietnam between China and the United States remained high. Although Richard Nixon promised during the 1968 presidential campaign to end the war in Vietnam, he escalated America's air war in the hopes of bringing Hanoi to its knees in his first year in office.[6] In June

1969, the United States restored diplomatic relations with Cambodia, a Chinese ally, which made Beijing worry.[7] Such security threats on China's southern borders were made worse by the sustained military standoff between the CCP forces and the KMT (Chinese Nationalist Party) army across the Taiwan Strait, as well as the hostile attitudes of Japan and South Korea toward the PRC. Consequently, Beijing perceived that, from Bohai Bay to the Gulf of Tonkin, all of China's coastal borders were under siege.[8] Since the Chinese–Indian border war of 1962, Beijing and New Delhi had each viewed the other as a dangerous enemy. Thus, the security situation along China's long western border with India was equally tense.

When two bloody conflicts between Chinese and Soviet border garrison forces broke out on Zhenbao Island (called Damansky Island in Russian), located in the Ussuri River, in March 1969, China's security situation dramatically worsened. Soon border conflict spread to other areas as tension increased along the entire length of the border. These incidents immediately brought China and the Soviet Union to the brink of a major military confrontation. According to Henry Kissinger, Soviet leaders even considered conducting a preemptive nuclear strike against their former Communist ally.[9] It is not surprising that Beijing's leaders felt compelled to improve their nation's security by making major changes in China's foreign and security strategy.

After the Ninth Congress of the CCP in April 1969 and the end of the radical phase of the Cultural Revolution, Mao and Zhou were again in effective control of Chinese foreign policy making and attempting to rectify some of the radical policies of the previous years. Starting in early June 1969, Chinese ambassadors, who had been recalled at the beginning of the Cultural Revolution, gradually returned to their posts.[10] Chinese diplomacy was returning to normality. The stabilization of Chinese politics was favorable to the improvement of Sino-American relations. Even before the Ninth Party Congress, Zhou had consciously selected articles regarding noticeable developments in international affairs, important commentaries and possible policy alternatives from a large quantity of information for Mao's reference. This was an oft-employed technique of Zhou's while participating in important policy-making processes, so that he could, without much notice, influence Mao's decision making.[11]

In the making of China's American policy, Mao was the key figure with the final word. Mao laid particular emphasis on philosophical issues and grand strategy, while Zhou focused on special planning details and operations. In Nixon's words, "Mao was chairman of the board ... Zhou was the chief operating officer."[12] More importantly, Zhou needed Mao's support in order to improve relations with the United States. The improvement in the Sino-U.S. relationship would also consolidate Zhou's influence and power in the domestic politics of the People's Republic.[13]

In mid-May 1969, Zhou, at Mao's behest, asked four veteran marshals – Chen Yi, Ye Jianying, Xu Xiangqian, and Nie Rongzhen – to study international affairs.[14] In their reports to Zhou and Mao, the marshals argued that in order for China to be ready for a major confrontation with the Soviet Union, "the American card" should be played. The marshals proposed that, in addition to waging "a tit-for-tat struggle against both the United States and the Soviet Union," China should use "negotiation as a means of struggle against them." Perhaps the Sino-American ambassadorial talks should be resumed "when the timing is proper."[15] The reports by the Four Marshals' Study Group provided Mao and Zhou with a strategic assessment that emphasized the benefits of improving Sino-American relations. The war scare, both strategically and psychologically, also created the necessary conditions for the CCP leadership to reconsider the PRC's long-standing policy of confrontation with the United States. The perception of an extremely grave threat from the Soviet Union to China's national security pushed Mao to decide to break through existing conceptual restrictions in order to improve relations with the United States.[16]

The Soviet Union was concerned with the U.S. stand in the Sino-Soviet confrontation. Soviet Premier Alexei Kosygin held talks with Zhou at Beijing airport on September 11. Zhou intended to utilize the occasion to provoke U.S. interest in expediting the Sino-American rapprochement process. For this purpose, Zhou tried hard to avoid "closeness" and "friendliness" with the Soviets. The subsequent Sino-Soviet border negotiation at the vice foreign ministers' level gave the Americans another impetus.[17]

The Chinese strategy seemed to work well. President Nixon was eager for the U.S. to catch up in its China policy. During the fall of 1969 and the early winter of 1970, the Nixon administration made several attempts to establish direct talks with China. The White House had been in secret contact with the Chinese through the Pakistanis and Romanians during the summer.[18] To supplement the nascent Pakistani and Romanian channels, Nixon and his assistant for National Security Affairs, Henry Kissinger, decided to reopen the long-frozen U.S.–China ambassadorial talks in Warsaw. In September 1969, they ordered Walter Stoessel, the American ambassador to Poland, to contact his Chinese counterpart for a new meeting. Stoessel acted in an unusual fashion: on December 3, he ran after Chinese diplomats after a Yugoslavian fashion show at Warsaw's Palace of Culture and was able to catch up with the Chinese interpreter, telling him that he had an important message for the Chinese embassy.[19]

Before this "encounter," China regarded Nixon's probing as only exploratory. This time Beijing's response was swift. The Chinese leaders seemed to be convinced of the seriousness of the U.S. offer. After receiving the Chinese embassy's report on the American ambassador's "unusual behavior," Zhou immediately reported to Mao that "the opportunity is coming; we now have a brick in our hands to knock at the door [of the Americans]."[20] Zhou acted at once to let the Americans know of Beijing's interest in reopening communication with Washington. As a goodwill gesture, on December 4, with Mao's approval, Zhou ordered the release of two Americans who had been held in China since mid-February 1969, when their yacht had strayed into China's territorial water off Guangdong.[21] Stoessel's "encounter" with Chinese diplomats at the Yugoslavian fashion show was a turning point in the evolution of a new relationship between the two countries. This "encounter" served as the right set of circumstances for the Chinese leaders to tell the Chinese public that "it is the Americans who need something from us, not the other way around." They would retell the story and repeat the theme time and again.[22]

But the last two sessions of the Sino-American ambassadorial talks in Warsaw in early 1970 failed to make much progress. In early May, when Nixon ordered American troops in South Vietnam to conduct a large-scale cross-border operation aimed at destroying Vietnamese Communist bases inside Cambodia, the Chinese refused to talk in Warsaw.[23] The collapse of the Warsaw talks moved the venue of communications with the Chinese to the White House, which had been in secret contact with Chinese officials through the Pakistanis since the previous summer. By late May, Nixon and Kissinger decided to covertly pursue China policy on their own. These early and indirect contacts between the Nixon White House and Beijing involved delicate exchanges on setting up an agenda for direct talks between top leaders of the two sides. In these exploratory communications, the Chinese tried to focus the anticipated talks on the withdrawal of U.S. forces from Taiwan and the establishment of U.S.–PRC diplomatic relations. The Americans attempted to define a much broader, open-ended agenda that would include discussion of global and regional security issues. Employing the Pakistani channel, the Americans and Chinese haggled over the terms for high-level meetings. Zhou stated that the sole purpose of the talks would be to discuss Taiwan, a limitation the Nixon administration could not accept.[24]

The major public breakthrough came in the spring of 1971, at an international table-tennis tournament in Japan. Zhou artfully instructed the much better Chinese players to stress "friendship first, competition second."²⁵ Evidently with Zhou's encouragement, the members of the Chinese and U.S. teams met without difficulty in a friendly atmosphere. To further prepare the Chinese people politically and psychologically for the forthcoming transformation of Sino-American relations, Mao decided to invite the American table tennis (ping-pong) team to visit China.²⁶ Zhou confided to his top aides Huang Hua and Zhang Wenjin,²⁷ after learning of Mao's approval of Beijing's invitation to the U.S. team on April 7: "This [visit] has offered a very good opportunity to open the relations between China and the United States. In our handling of this matter, we must treat it as an important event, and understand that its significance is much larger in politics than in sports."²⁸ The visit of the American Ping-Pong team to China was widely covered by the Chinese media.²⁹ The highlight of the visit was Zhou's meeting with the American and Chinese teams, together with teams from four other countries, at the Great Hall of the People on April 14. Zhou announced, "Your visit has opened a new chapter in the history of the relations between Chinese and American peoples."³⁰

In the wake of the Ping-Pong diplomacy, Beijing moved to make concrete plans for the high-level meetings with Washington that had been discussed since early 1970 through the Pakistani channel. At a meeting of the CCP Central Committee Politburo on May 26, Zhou delivered a speech in which he pointed out that the United States had been at the height of its power at the end of World War II and thus could interfere with "anything anywhere in the world" afterwards. U.S. power, however, had declined in recent years. America's intervention in Vietnam had lost the support of the American people, forcing Washington to withdraw its troops gradually from Vietnam. Under these circumstances, Zhou speculated, the American leaders had to consider whether to continue their "going-all-out" policy or to reduce America's international involvement. As a first step toward the latter choice, Washington needed to get out of Vietnam, and the Americans thus found it necessary to establish contact with China. These developments, Zhou stressed, had provided China with "an opportunity to improve Sino-American relations," which "will be beneficial to the struggle against imperialist expansion and hegemonism, beneficial to maintaining peace in Asia as well as in the world, and beneficial to maintaining our country's security and pursuing the unification of the motherland in a peaceful way."³¹

The Politburo meeting reached some consensus, which was summarized in "Politburo Report on the Sino-American Talks," drafted by Zhou after the meeting. The main points were the eight "basic principles," which became China's new guiding principles in relations with the United States.³² China set the parameters of its upcoming negotiations with the U.S.: it would not raise preconditions for opening high-level meetings. The Chinese leaders would prepare to accept partial success in the conduct of high-level talks with the United States. However, the Beijing leadership was aware of the strategic difficulties faced by Washington and saw opportunities to pressure the U.S. envoy to make concessions. The Politburo reasoned that Nixon needed a successful negotiation to support his reelection campaign. Thus, Kissinger was under great pressure to reach an agreement. After receiving the Chinese invitation, Kissinger felt relieved in particular at Zhou's acceptance of the U.S. proposal that each side should be free to raise issues of great concern. This, of course, would guarantee a discussion of global issues – such as the war in Indochina and the Soviet threat. Meanwhile, Zhou had framed the Taiwan problem in a manner most susceptible to solution: the withdrawal of U.S. forces.³³

Having established the rules at the Politburo meeting in May, the Chinese leaders now made efforts to prepare the Party and the nation for a significant change of Chinese policy toward the United States. To this end, the PRC leaders convened a series of meetings, including the CCP Central Work Conference in Beijing from June 4 to 18. Two hundred and twenty-five "leading officials" from the party, government, army and different provinces attended the meeting, where Zhou outlined "The Politburo's Report on the Sino-American Talks." He also made closing remarks on the significance of the upcoming new policy toward the United States,[34] where he stressed that it was Nixon and Kissinger who were coming to Beijing. "It is not we who need something from them, but they who need something from us," he said.[35] This tone dominated Beijing's effort to justify the Sino-American opening to the party rank and file in the years to come. The Chinese leadership, concerned about China's proper role in the world, maintained that the PRC should occupy a central position in international affairs, and not be a supplicant. On the strategic level, it would not allow any slights from the Americans.

On the tactical level, Zhou was particularly thoughtful and considerate. He would treat Kissinger and his team as state guests and accord them due respect. To achieve the desired result, Zhou demanded that the local governments should coordinate their activities with the central government and do well in their reception work. "In receiving our foreign guests," Zhou stated, "We must be courteous. Neither haughty nor humble nor chauvinistic. We should also guard against ultra-leftist tendencies and the old sycophancy."[36] China's chief policy makers had thus confirmed and provided ideological underpinnings for the new policy toward the United States.

To prepare for Kissinger's arrival, Beijing established a special task force headed by Zhou and Marshal Ye Jianying, a senior Politburo member and vice chairman of the Central Military Commission, to handle all the technical and logistical matters.[37] According to Zhang Ying, the Chinese were very meticulous. Zhang, a middle-ranking official in the Information Department of the Foreign Ministry, was assigned to read Kissinger's books and to write summaries and reports for the leaders' reference. Extensive surveys on American history, politics, society and, especially, U.S. China policy since the founding of the PRC in 1949 had been prepared. By June, all the Chinese officials who were assigned to work with the visiting Americans moved into the state guesthouse. They were warned to keep Kissinger's visit secret even from their families. Zhou discussed almost every talking-point with his senior associates and always sent the reports to Mao for his approval.[38] Zhou even squeezed the time to read Nixon's *Six Crises* and watched Nixon's favorite film, *Patton*.[39] Zhou's handwritten notes on the document "On Several Key Questions Pertinent to Sino-American Preliminary Talks," prepared by the Foreign Ministry, stating that "We will adhere to principles and make flexible adjustment if circumstances require. We will be ready for bargaining from the American side. ...,"[40] set the tone.

China's Chief Negotiator

As China's top diplomat, Zhou paid much attention to detail and "display[ed] an extraordinary personal graciousness" in dealing with the Americans even after nearly twenty-two years of hostility and confrontation. To ease any tension the Americans might have felt on the five-hour flight from Islamabad to Beijing, Zhou sent a group of four English-speaking Chinese foreign ministry officials to Pakistan to escort Kissinger and his team on their secret mission. Zhou, as China's premier, despite the difference in rank, made a point of calling on Kissinger, as National Security Advisor (equivalent to deputy Cabinet secretary, three levels down), at the state guesthouse. Kissinger remembered this as "a gesture of considerable courtesy."[41]

During Kissinger's secret visit to Beijing in July 1971, his second visit in October, and Nixon's trip to China in February 1972, the Chinese and U.S. leaders held more than twenty face-to-face talks. In accordance with Mao's instruction, Zhou served as China's chief negotiator and was present at nearly all these negotiations.[42] Although Mao set up China's grand strategy regarding negotiation with the Americans and had the final word on major policy decision,

Zhou was responsible for stipulating China's basic negotiation plan and acted as the occasion demanded during the talks. Mao also instructed that Zhou might revise the negotiation plan whenever he found it necessary during the talks.[43]

The Taiwan issue was the biggest stumbling-block in the process of U.S.–China reconciliation and high-level contacts. The fact that both the Communist government in Beijing and the Nationalist government in Taiwan held to the "one China" principle restrained U.S. options while adjusting its policy toward China. It served as a precondition for Beijing and Washington to work within this framework to achieve a breakthrough.[44]

The eight "basic principles" in the "Politburo Report on the Sino-American Talks" of May 1971 embodied three noticeable changes from China's previous position. First, while demanding that U.S. troops withdraw from Taiwan, China no longer insisted that the United States openly sever diplomatic relations with Taiwan as a precondition for exchanges between the Chinese and U.S. governments. Second, while continuing to say that liberating Taiwan was China's internal affair, China stressed only its interests in resolving the Taiwan issue through peaceful means. Third, China advanced the idea of establishing liaison offices in both capitals if the Taiwan problem would not be resolved in the immediate future.[45] These three changes reflected China's willingness to adopt a flexible and more constructive negotiating position.

During these negotiations, Zhou identified Taiwan as the most crucial issue and Vietnam as the most urgent issue, and ranked Korea the third most important issue. As a master diplomat, Zhou knew that "negotiations proceed by a combination of clear statements, hints, and suggestions."[46] Zhou was eager to get firm commitments from Kissinger and Nixon that Washington would not champion such policies as supporting "two Chinas," "one China and one Taiwan," "one China with two separate governments," "Taiwan independence" and the sovereignty over Taiwan as "an undetermined question." Zhou would employ issues such as "presidential reelection," the "Japanese expansion" to Taiwan and "the positive results of President Nixon's visit to China" as leverage in his bargaining with Kissinger and Nixon.[47] During Kissinger's second visit to Beijing, in October 1971, Zhou adroitly reminded Kissinger that Britain had decided to upgrade Sino-British relations to the ambassadorial level, recognizing "Taiwan as a province of China" and voting for the Albanian resolution.[48] Zhou attempted to force more concessions from Kissinger on the Taiwan issue and also offered new ideas for the draft communiqué. Meanwhile, Zhou was especially sensitive to the issue of Japanese expansion to Taiwan after U.S. withdrawal and continuously attempted to sound out the U.S. commitment to preventing this from happening.[49] Thus, the most important breakthrough was attained in the first meetings between Kissinger and Zhou, as each leader was trying to understand and accommodate the other's basic position.

Although Beijing had repeatedly emphasized that no other question would be discussed unless Washington made concessions on Taiwan, Zhou showed flexibility. China would not set U.S. immediate withdrawal from and severance of diplomatic relations with Taiwan as preconditions for Nixon's visit and meeting with Mao.[50] On Indochina, in his numerous talks with U.S. officials, Zhou urged the U.S. to withdraw its troops from Vietnam.[51] During these talks, on the one hand, Zhou stressed that both China and the United States should not send troops to foreign countries; on the other, he felt obliged to defend the continuous presence of Vietnamese troops in Cambodia. While Kissinger indicated that the U.S. would not ask the Chinese to suspend their aid to Vietnam, Zhou promised not to send China's combat troops to Vietnam. Zhou had to seek information from his U.S. interlocutors regarding the U.S.–North Vietnam Paris peace talks. The U.S. made concessions to the Vietnamese at the Paris peace talks partly because of Zhou's persuasion. These concessions were made between Kissinger's two visits to Beijing and Hanoi became suspicious that Beijing was trading off its interests with Washington.[52] China's relations with Vietnam deteriorated dramatically.

The two sides did not agree easily on the wording of the announcement on Nixon's trip to China during Kissinger's secret visit. Even before Kissinger's secret visit, the Chinese were anxious to receive confirmation that Nixon was in principle willing to visit China, but they also tried to show that they had responded to Nixon's request. After considerable bargaining, Zhou eventually backed away from his hard-line position that the summit should be in the context of improving Sino-U.S. relations and that the best way to accomplish the latter was through the establishment of diplomatic relations. He reluctantly acknowledged that recognition was not an "absolute" precondition for a summit, but insisted that the direction should be set by the summit.[53] Zhou showed flexibility and was considerate of the American concern. The Chinese finally presented a new draft, which Kissinger immediately found agreeable. It stated that "knowing of President Nixon's expressed desire to visit the People's Republic of China," Premier Zhou "has extended an invitation." This formulation avoided the issue of who first proposed the presidential visit.[54] The draft joint announcement bridged U.S. and Chinese objectives, yet toned down the implication that the two sides would discuss matters of international security and peace, which would gratuitously irritate the Soviets. For the convenience of the Nixon administration, the Chinese agreed that the presidential visit would be the spring of 1972.[55]

After Kissinger's secret July visit, the Chinese government began preparing the Chinese people for a public visit by Kissinger in October. An unexpected political crisis in the CCP leadership in September 1971 made Kissinger's visit easier to sell to the Party. Lin Biao, Mao's anointed successor, who had been known as Mao's "closest comrade-in-arms" and "best and most loyal student," allegedly plotted a coup to assassinate Mao. Lin, together with his wife, his son and a handful of supporters, fled from Beijing but died in a mysterious plane crash in the People's Republic of Mongolia on September 13.[56] Lin's downfall enhanced the position of Zhou in PRC politics. As the Lin Biao Incident damaged the myth of Mao's "eternal correctness," Mao now was even eager to have a major breakthrough in China's foreign relation so as to cover up the domestic political crisis and salvage his declining reputation and authority.[57]

After the Lin Biao Incident, Zhou started to change China's domestic political atmosphere. He directed a nationwide policy education, toned down anti-American propaganda and restored the names of old stores and shops. All these were permitted by Mao, as the chairman was eager to score diplomatic points. Through Ambassador Huang Zhen in Paris, Beijing notified the U.S. that the Lin Biao Incident would not change China's attitude toward the U.S., and China would proceed with the preparations for Nixon's visit. The Nixon administration was very pleased at Beijing's stance.[58]

During Kissinger's second visit to Beijing, in October 1971, the negotiations over the communiqué draft turned out to be tortuous. When Kissinger handed a draft to Zhou on October 22, the Chinese premier did not respond right away.[59] While listening to Zhou's briefing on his meetings with Kissinger, Mao told the premier, "I have said many times that all under Heaven is great chaos, so it is desirable to let each side speak out for itself." If the American side wanted to talk about "peace, security, and no pursuit of hegemony," the chairman continued, the Chinese side should emphasize "revolution, the liberation of the oppressed peoples and nations in the world, and no rights for big powers to bully and humiliate small countries." Mao acknowledged that stressing these goals was no more than "firing empty cannons," yet he stressed that "all of these points must be highlighted; and anything short of that would be improper."[60] Zhou carefully explained to Mao the Nixon administration's dilemma, but assured the chairman that he would revise the draft communiqué "in accordance with the chairman's instruction."[61] The revised communiqué reflected many of Mao's ideas on the international situation.[62] At first, Kissinger was obviously surprised to receive the Chinese draft communiqué on October 24. But after reading the document full of "empty cannons" and having time to digest it, Kissinger "began to see that the very novelty of the [Chinese] approach might resolve our perplexities."[63] He wrote that "the unorthodox format appeared to solve both sides' problem. Each could reaffirm its fundamental convictions, which would reassure domestic audiences and uneasy allies."[64] When Kissinger accepted the Chinese draft in principle and attempted to tone down the fiery nature of the Chinese rhetoric, Zhou again demonstrated flexibility, understanding and accommodation.[65]

Zhou was Nixon's primary host during the latter's historic visit in February 1972. Mao met with Nixon for only a little over an hour on the day of his arrival, lending his authoritative endorsement to the rapprochement, and then retired into the background. Zhou and Nixon participated in the vivid and dramatic drama of a U.S.–China summit after twenty-two years of hostility between the two countries. Through the television cameras, they jointly inaugurated a new chapter in U.S.–China relations. Zhou also charmed the U.S. audience through the gift to the U.S. of two giant panda bears. But during the closed-door negotiations Zhou stuck to China's established principles, arguing on the basis of reason.[66] Nixon recalled: "Zhou was tough and tenacious, but was flexible in working out our differences."[67]

Zhou's refusal to link Vietnam with Taiwan made the latter a touchy subject. The Taiwan issue needed to be addressed not just in the private talks between Nixon and Zhou, but also in the formal communiqué, which still had to be worked out between Kissinger and Vice Foreign Minister Qiao Guanhua. Nixon tried to convince Zhou that, due to domestic constraints, he could not "abandon his old friends" in Taiwan. He told Zhou there were certain forces in the U.S. who believed "that no concessions at all should be made regarding Taiwan." Nixon advanced his five principles on Taiwan on February 22, including an affirmation of a one-China policy; that the United States would not support Taiwan in any moves toward independence; that the United States would discourage any Japanese move into Taiwan; support for peaceful resolution between Beijing and Taipei; and commitment to continued normalization.[68] He also restated his intention to normalize relations with the PRC during his second term in office.

Vietnam was another tough issue. Zhou had singled out Indochina as the most "urgent" issue in Sino-American relations. During their first meeting, on February 22, Zhou tried hard to persuade Nixon to agree to a "total withdrawal" from Vietnam.[69] Zhou stated that although the question of Taiwan was very important for U.S.–China relations, China was willing to wait on Taiwan. But China had an obligation to give the Indochinese people assistance if the war continued, although this did not mean that China would intervene in their internal affairs.[70] China concentrated on the military questions, claiming that only the Indochinese people should take care of their own political problems.[71] Therefore, China would like to see Indochina removed as a distortion in U.S.–China relations and as an issue for Soviet exploitation. Nixon indicated that he agreed with Zhou and had offered to withdraw all Americans and to have a ceasefire throughout Indochina if he could get all U.S. prisoners back. He agreed that the political decision should be made by Indochinese people without outside interference. But the U.S. could not consent to remove the South Vietnamese government, as was requested by North Vietnam.[72]

The Korean issue during U.S.–China rapprochement has so far received little attention in scholarly studies. Zhou and Kissinger did discuss the Korean issue at some length in their first meeting on July 9, 1971. Zhou urged U.S. withdrawal from Korea, and Kissinger indicated that it should not be a problem.[73] Later in their conversation, when Zhou raised the issue of the entry of Japanese forces into Korea after U.S. withdrawal from the Korean peninsula,

Kissinger made it clear that the Nixon administration was opposed to "Japan's military power outside its home islands into areas for possible offensive uses." When Zhou mentioned that there was only an armistice agreement between South and North Koreas, and the North felt threatened by the presence of U.S. forces in the South, Kissinger declared U.S. opposition to military aggression by South Korea against North Korea and hoped that Beijing would use its influence with North Korea not to use force against the U.S. and South Korea. Zhou raised no objection.[74] It seems that both Washington and Beijing were interested in preserving stability in the Korean peninsula.

Selling the Policy of Rapprochement

The Sino-American reconciliation had troubling implications for China's erstwhile Communist allies outside the Soviet bloc, who had relied on China to stand up to "American imperialists." These countries included North Vietnam, North Korea and Albania. Thus, Zhou Enlai had a tough job of selling China's new policy toward Washington to its Communist allies. Soon after Kissinger left Beijing, Zhou travelled to Hanoi on July 13–14 and to Pyongyang on July 15, 1971 to explain China's new policy toward the U.S. to the Vietnamese and North Korean leaders. He failed to convince the Vietnamese, although he stated that China would never barter away principles and would continue to assist the Vietnamese in their struggle against the United States. But, in fact, China's diplomatic priority was to improve relations with the United States – to welcome Kissinger and Nixon to visit China. The North Vietnamese were so angry that they tilted more aggressively toward the Soviet Union.[75] Albania, which had vigorously supported China's policy during the Culture Revolution, felt betrayed by China's reconciliation with the United States. Enver Hoxha, the Albanian leader, wrote about it in his memoirs, stating that this development "fell like a bombshell on us Albanians, on the Vietnamese, the Koreans, not to mention the others."[76]

In his consultation with the North Korean leader, Kim Il-sung, Zhou formulated China's new strategy as forming a United Front with the American people against U.S. imperialists. It seems that Zhou was successful in convincing Kim. Kim was somewhat surprised and even shocked at first,[77] but he did not view China's improved relations with the U.S. as a betrayal. Zhou tried to persuade Kim to comprehend the prospect of the U.S.–China rapprochement and to seize the opportunity to drive the U.S. out of the Korean peninsula. He told Kim that this would match China's effort in engaging with the United States to accomplish the return of Taiwan to China. Zhou stated that China would never trade off principles and would stick to its positions. Kim soon voiced support for China's changing policy toward the United States.[78]

During Kissinger's public visit to China in October 1971, the discussion on North Korea between Zhou and Kissinger was longer than it had been in July. Zhou ranked Korea third on the agenda (immediately behind Vietnam and Taiwan in importance), giving it a higher priority than in July. He was responding to Pyongyang's request. In addition to the U.S. withdrawal from Korea, Zhou talked about letting North Korea participate in the UN debate unconditionally. It seemed that Zhou already anticipated the PRC's role at the UN – to be the champion of North Korea. Zhou stressed the importance of the UN's treating South and North Korea equally. In the end, Zhou seemed to have accepted the U.S. position that the issue of Korea would take time but that opinions could be exchanged in the interim. Zhou was more interested in the dissolution of the UN Commission for the Unification and Rehabilitation of Korea than in U.S. withdrawal. Kissinger believed that China was not particularly interested in a unified Korea.[79] During Nixon's trip to China, Zhou and Nixon briefly touched on the Korean issue – only to confirm what Zhou had previously discussed with Kissinger.[80] The

Shanghai Communiqué, which was released at the end of the presidential visit on February 27, stated that "the United States will maintain its close ties with and support for the Republic of Korea ... will support efforts of the Republic of Korea to seek a relaxation of tension and increased communication on the Korean Peninsula"; the PRC "firmly supports the eight-point program for the peaceful unification of Korea," and the stand for the abolition of the "U.N. Commission for the Unification and Rehabilitation of Korea."[81]

Zhou travelled to Pyongyang on March 7, 1972 to brief Kim Il-sung on the U.S.–China negotiations during Nixon's visit. Zhou, in particular, mentioned Nixon's tacit agreement that "the Japanese forces would not be allowed to enter [Korea in the wake of any U.S. troop withdrawal]." Although the Shanghai Communiqué stated that "neither is prepared to negotiate on behalf of any third party," Chinese officials had reminded the U.S. that "China and North Korea represent one side at the Korean Military Armistice Commission." According to the Chinese report, Kim was very pleased.[82]

Conclusion

Forty years after his secret trip to Beijing, Henry Kissinger wrote, "In some sixty years of public life, I have encountered no more compelling figure than Zhou Enlai." Kissinger was lavish in his praise, stating "Zhou's subtle and sensitive style helped overcome many pitfalls of an emerging relationship between two previously hostile major countries."[83] During the rapprochement talks, Zhou negotiated directly with Kissinger, although largely at Mao's instruction. In cultivating the new relationship, Kissinger and Nixon were both impressed by Zhou's diplomatic skills. To Kissinger, Zhou appeared "urbane, infinitely patient, extraordinarily intelligent, [and] subtle." He moved through their discussions "with an easy grace that penetrated to the essence of our new relationship as if there were no sensible alternative." Kissinger wrote that the talks between Zhou and him "were longer and deeper than with any other leader I met during my public service, except possibly Anwar Sadat." He also observed that "Chou [Zhou] never bargained to score petty points."[84] Richard Nixon was equally impressed by his interaction with Zhou during his historic China trip. He wrote: "Four things made an indelible impression on me: his stamina, his preparation, his negotiating skill, and his poise under pressure." Nixon compared Zhou with the Soviet leaders, stating that Zhou "never raised his voice, never pounded the table, never threatened to break off talks in order to force a concession."[85]

Although Zhou made every effort to keep Mao in the limelight, Western media credited China's new relations with the United States and the U.S.–China rapprochement as the achievement of "Zhou Enlai Diplomacy." It was the crowning achievement of Zhou's career and he had reached the zenith of international fame. Nonetheless, Zhou regarded himself as "Chairman Mao's good student and long trusted aid." After his triumphant China trip, Nixon said that Zhou was a great man, yet he had to "live in the shadow of" Mao, always careful to "let the limelight shine on Mao."[86] As we now know, the praise of Zhou in the Western media caused only harm to Zhou, because of Mao's jealousies. Zhou would suffer the most serious political crisis in his life at the hands of Mao in 1973.[87]

Notes

1 Yafeng Xia, "China's Elite Politics and Sino-American Rapprochement, January 1969–February 1972," *The Journal of Cold War Studies* 8:4 (Fall 2006): 4.
2 Yafeng Xia, *Negotiating with the Enemy: U.S.-China Talks during the Cold War, 1949–1972* (Bloomington, IN: Indiana University Press, 2006), 170. Portions of this chapter are adapted from this book.

3 Kuisong Yang and Yafeng Xia, "Vacillating between Revolution and Détente: Mao's Changing Psyche and Policy toward the U.S., 1969–1976," *Diplomatic History* 34:2 (April 2010): note 54 on p. 425.
4 Archival documents of American government on the U.S.–China rapprochement have been declassified since the early 2000s. But Chinese archival records on the Sino-American rapprochement talks, especially the Chinese Foreign Ministry archives for the period starting 1965, have not been declassified.
5 Important recent works on aspects of the U.S.–China rapprochement based on archival documentation include Chris Tudda, *A Cold War Turning Point: Nixon and China, 1969–1972* (Baton Rouge, LA: Louisiana State University Press, 2012); Margaret MacMillan, *Nixon and Mao: The Week that Changed the World* (New York: Random House, 2007); Xia, *Negotiating with the Enemy*; Evelyn Goh, *Constructing the U.S. Rapprochement with China, 1961–1974: From "Red Menace" to "Tacit Ally"* (New York: Cambridge University Press, 2005).
6 Robert J. McMahon and Thomas W. Zeiler, eds., *The Guide to U.S. Foreign Policy: A Diplomatic History* (New York: DWJ Books, 2012), 348–49.
7 Qiang Zhai, *China and the Vietnam Wars, 1950–1975* (Chapel Hill, NC: University of North Carolina Press, 2000), 184–85.
8 Li Ke and Hao Shengzhang, *Wenhua Dageming Zhong de Renmin Jiefangjun* [The People's Liberation Army during the Cultural Revolution] (Beijing: Zhonggong Dangshi Ziliao Chubanshe, 1989), 249–51.
9 Henry Kissinger, *The White House Years* (Boston, MA: Little, Brown & Company, 1979), 183; Henry Kissinger, *On China* (New York: The Penguin Press, 2011), 219.
10 Ma Jisen, *Waijiaobu Wenge Jishi* [The Cultural Revolution in the Foreign Ministry] (Hong Kong: Xianggang Zhongwen Daxue Chubanshe, 2003), 289.
11 Gao Wenqian, *Wannian Zhou Enlai* [Zhou Enlai's Later Years] (Hong Kong: Mirror Books, 2003), 407.
12 Richard Nixon, *Leaders* (New York: Warner Books, 1982), 238.
13 Xia, *Negotiating with the Enemy*, 144–45.
14 On February 19, 1969, Mao, through Zhou, assigned the four marshals to study international affairs. Li Ping et al. *Zhou Enlai Nianpu, 1949–1976* [Chronology of Zhou Enlai, 1949–1976, hereafter cited as ZEN] (Beijing: Zhongyang Wenxian and Renmin Chubanshe, 1997), vol. 3, 281.
15 Xiong Xianghui, *Wo de Qingbao yu Uaijiao Shengya* [My Career in Intelligence and Diplomacy] (Beijing: Zhongyang Dangxiao Chubanshe, 1999), 184–86.
16 For a discussion of the war scare in Beijing in 1969, see Yang Kuisong, "The Sino-Soviet Border Clash of 1969: From Zhenbao Island to Sino-American Rapprochement," *Cold War History* 1:1 (August 2000): 35–7; Xia, *Negotiating with the Enemy*, 138–39.
17 Gao, *Wannian Zhou Enlai*, 411–13.
18 See Steven Phillips, "Nixon's China Initiative, 1969–1972," in *Documenting Diplomacy in the 21st Century* (Washington, DC: United States Department of State, 2001), 135.
19 Xue Mouhong, chief ed. *Dangdai Zhongguo Waijiao* [Contemporary Chinese Diplomacy] (Beijing: Zhongguo Shehui Kexue Chubanshe, 1988), 219. See also "Stoessel to Secretary of State," December 3, 1969, pp. 23–28, Subject-Numeric files, 1967–1969, POL-U.S., RG 59, National Archives, College Park, Maryland (NA).
20 See Jin Chongji, et al. chief ed. *Zhou Enlai Zhuan, 1949–1976* [A Biography of Zhou Enlai, 1949–1976, hereafter cited as ZEZ] (Beijing: Zhongyang Wenxian Chubanshe, 1998), 2: 1087.
21 ZEN, 3: 336; ZEZ, 2: 1088. See also Kissinger, *White House Years*, 188.
22 Xia, *Negotiating with the Enemy*, 145.
23 Kissinger, *White House Years*, 692.
24 Xia, *Negotiating with the Enemy*, 146–52.
25 Qian Jiang, *Xiaoqiu Zhuandong Daqiu: Pingpang Waijiao Muhou* [Little Ball Moves Big Ball: Behind Ping-Pong Diplomacy] (Beijing: Dongfang Chubanshe, 1997), 267–68.
26 For details, see Xia, "China's Elite Politics," 13–17.
27 Huang Hua was then China's ambassador to Canada. Zhang Wenjin was director-general, Western European and American Department, PRC Foreign Ministry. He had been a close assistant of Zhou, dating back to the Marshall Mission in 1946.
28 Qian, *Xiaoqiu Zhuandong Daqiu*, 236; Xu Dashen, chief ed. *Zhonghua Renmin Gongheguo Shilu* [A Factual Record of the People's Republic of China] (Changchun: Jilin Renmin Chubanshe, 1994), 3: 698–99.

29 See Qian Jiang, *Pingpang Waijiao Shimo* [Ping-Pong Diplomacy: The Beginning and the End] (Beijing: Dongfang Chubanshe, 1987), 268–71.
30 Minutes, Zhou Enlai, "Conversations with the American Table Tennis Delegation," April 14, 1971, in *Zhou Enlai Waijiao Wenxuan* [Selected Diplomatic Papers of Zhou Enlai] (Beijing: Zhongyang Wenxian Chubanshe, 1990), 469–75. The Chinese media reported the meeting extensively. See, for example, *Renmin Ribao*, April 15, 1971, front page, where the quote can be found.
31 Yang Mingwei and Chen Yangyong, *Zhou Enlai Waijiao Fengyun* [Diplomatic Winds and Clouds of Zhou Enlai] (Beijing: Jiefangjun Wenyi Chubanshe, 1995), 247–48.
32 See *ZEZ*, 2: 1096; *ZEN*, 3: 458–59. Mao approved Zhou's report on May 29, 1971. See Pang Xianzhi and Jin Chongji, chief eds. *Mao Zedong Zhuan, 1949–1976* [A Biography of Mao Zedong, 1949–1976] (Beijing: Zhongyang Wenxian Chubanshe, 2003), 2: 1633.
33 Kissinger, *White House Years*, 727.
34 Tao Wenzhao, chief ed. *Zhong Mei Guanxi Shi, 1949–1972* [PRC–U.S.A. Relations, 1949–1972] (Shanghai: Shanghai Renmin Press, 1999), 536.
35 *ZEZ*, 2: 1097.
36 Tang Longbin. "A Mysterious Mission – Receiving Kissinger's Secret China Visit," in Yu Wuzhen, chief ed. *Xin Zhongguo Waijiao Fengyun* [Winds and Clouds in New China's Diplomacy] (Beijing: Shijie Zhishi Chubanshe, 1996), 4: 39.
37 Gong Li, *Kuayue Honggou: 1969–1979 nian Zhongmei Guanxi de Yanbian* [Across the Chasm: The Evolution of China–U.S. Relations, 1969–1979] (Zhengzhou: Henan Renmin Chubanshe, 1992), 108.
38 Zhang Ying, *Sui Zhang Wenjin Chushi Meiguo: Dashi Furen Jishi* [Serving in the United States with Zhang Wenjin: Account of an Ambassador's Life] (Beijing: Shijie Zhishi Chubanshe, 1996), 33–34; idem, "Random Recollection of Premier Zhou's Later Years," in Tian Zengpei and Wang Taiping, eds. *Lao Waijiaoguan Huiyi Zhou Enlai* [Senior Diplomats' Remembrance of Zhou Enlai] (Beijing: Shijie Zhishi Chubanshe, 1998), 375–76.
39 Gao, *Wannian Zhou Enlai*, 438.
40 *ZEN*, 3: 467.
41 Kissinger, *On China*, 238–39.
42 Li Danhui, "Zhou Enlai in the Sino-American Rapprochement," *Lengzhan Guojishi Yanjiu* [Cold War International History Studies] 6 (Summer 2008): 143.
43 Wei Shiyan, "Inside Stories of Kissinger's Secret Visit to China," in Pei Jianzhang chief ed., *Xin Zhongguo Waijiao Fengyun* [Winds and Clouds in New China's Diplomacy] (Beijing: Shijie Zhishi Chubanshe, 1991), vol. 2: 39–45; *ZEN*, 3: 458–59, 467–68, 489, 491, 512.
44 Li, "Zhou Enlai in the Sino-American Rapprochement," 145.
45 Gong, *Kuayue Honggou*, 104.
46 MacMillan, *Nixon and Mao*, 256–57.
47 Memorandum of Conversation, October 25, 1971, 9:50–1:40 p.m., NA, Nixon Presidential Materials Project (*NPMP*), NSCF, Box 1034; Memorandum from the President's Assistant for National Security Affairs (Kissinger) to President Nixon, November 1971, *Foreign Relations of the United States* (*FRUS*), 1969–1976, vol. 17, China, 1969–1972, 524–57; Memorandum from the President's Assistant for National Security Affairs (Kissinger) to President Nixon, February 5, 1972, *FRUS*, 1969–1976, vol. 17, 657–58.
48 For a number of years, Albania had introduced a resolution at the UN to install the PRC and expel the Government of the Republic of China in Taiwan. In 1965, for the first time the vote ended in a tie, and by 1970 it received a simple majority.
49 Memorandum of Conversation, October 21, 1971, 10:30 a.m.–1:45 p.m., *FRUS*, 1969–1976, vol. 17, 498–517. Memorandum from the President's Assistant for National Security Affairs (Kissinger) to President Nixon, November 1971.
50 Memorandum of Conversation (Kissinger and Zhou Enlai), July 10, 1971, 12:10–6:00 p.m., *FRUS*, 1969–1976, vol. 17, 411.
51 Li Danhui, "Sino-American Rapprochement and the War to Aid Vietnam and Resist America," *Dangshi Yanjiu Ziliao* [Materials on the Chinese Communist Party Studies], 11 (2002): 1–18; 12 (2002): 38–46; idem, "Vietnam and Chinese Policy Toward the United States," in William Kirby, Robert Ross and Gong Li, eds., *Normalization of U.S.-China Relations: An International History* (Cambridge, MA: Harvard University Asia Center, 2005), 175–208.
52 Wang Taiping, chief ed. *Zhonghua Renmin Gongheguo Waijiaoshi, 1970–1978* [A Diplomatic History of the People's Republic of China, 1970–1978, hereafter cited as *ZRGW70*] (Beijing: Shijie

Zhishi Chubanshe, 1999), 53; Memorandum of Conversation, July 10, 1971, 12:10–6:00 p.m., *FRUS*, 1969–1976, vol. 17, 406–407, 416–21; Memorandum of Conversation, October 21, 1971, 4:42–7:17 p.m., Box 1034; Memorandum of Conversation, February 24, 1972, 5:15–8:05 p.m., Box 87, NPMP, White House Special Files, President's Office Files.

53 Memorandum of Conversation (Kissinger and Zhou Enlai), July 9, 1971, *FRUS*, 1969–1976, vol. 17, 362, 371.
54 Memorandum of Conversation (Kissinger and Chinese officials), July 11, 1971, *FRUS*, 1969–1976, vol. 17, 437–39. Also see Wei, "Inside Stories of Kissinger's Secret Visit to China," 44–45; Kissinger, *White House Years*, 752–53. According to a Chinese account, Kissinger only added "with pleasure" to describe that "President Nixon has accepted the invitation."
55 Gao, *Wannian Zhou Enlai*, 439.
56 Wang Nianyi, *Da Dongluan de Niandai* [In the Years of Great Upheaval] (Zhengzhou: Henan Renmin Chubanshe, 1988), 415–33. For an English article, see Xia, "China's Elite Politics and Sino-American Rapprochement," 3–28.
57 Gao, *Wannian Zhou Enlai*, 427–28; Chen Jian, *Mao's China and The Cold War* (Chapel Hill, NC: University of North Carolina Press, 2001), 270.
58 Gao, *Wannian Zhou Enlai*, 442, 441.
59 POLO II – Transcript of Meeting (October 22, 1971, 4:15–8:28 p.m.), p. 40, folder 2, box 1034, NSCF.
60 Wei Shiyan, "Kissinger's Second Visit to China," in Pei Jianzhang chief ed., *Xin Zhongguo Waijiao Fengyun* [Winds and Clouds in New China's Diplomacy] (Beijing: Shijie Zhishi Chubanshe, 1994), vol. 3: 67.
61 Gao, *Wannian Zhou Enlai*, 443.
62 Wei, "Kissinger's Second Trip to China," 69.
63 Kissinger, *White House Years*, 782.
64 Kissinger, *On China*, 269.
65 Gao, *Wannian Zhou Enlai*, 444.
66 Ibid., 448.
67 Nixon, *Leaders*, 235.
68 Memorandum of Conversation, Beijing, February 22, 1972, 2:10–6 p.m., *FRUS*, 1969–1976, vol. 17, 697–99.
69 *ZRGW70*, 364.
70 Ibid. Also Memorandum of Conversation, Shanghai, February 28, 1972, 8:30–9:30 a.m., *FRUS*, 1969–1976, vol. 17, 823–24.
71 Wei, "Inside Stories of Kissinger's Secret Visit to China," 41. "The President Briefing Paper for the China Trip," Indochina–Vietnam, p. 1, folder 4, box 847, NSCF.
72 Memorandum of Conversation, Beijing, February 22, 1972, 2:10–6 p.m., *FRUS*, 1969–1976, vol. 17, 713–15.
73 Memorandum of Conversation, Beijing, July 9, 1971, 4:35–11:20 p.m., *FRUS*, 1969–1976, vol. 17, 388–91.
74 "Memorandum for Kissinger," August 6, 1971, China, HAK Memocons, box 1033, NSCF; Memorandum From the President's Assistant for National Security Affairs (Kissinger) to President Nixon," July 14, 1971, *FRUS*, 1969–1976, vol. 17, 453–55 and Document 9 in *FRUS*, 1969–1972, vol. E-13 China (online); Memorandum of Conversation: Kissinger and Chou En-lai, July 11, 1971.
75 Zhang Shuguang, *Meiguo Duihua Zhanlv yu Juece, 1949–1972* [U.S. Strategic Thinking and Policymaking toward China] (Shanghai: Shanghai Foreign Language Education Press, 2002), 158.
76 Jon Halliday ed., *The Artful Albanian: Memoirs of Enver Hoxha* (London: Chatto & Windus, 1986), 285.
77 Jong-Seŏk Lee, *Pukhan-Chungguk kwan'gye, 1945–2000* [The Sino-North Korean Relationship, 1945–2000] (Seoul: Joongshim, 2000), 252–53; Chen, *Mao's China and the Cold War*, 269; Bernd Schaefer, "Overconfidence Shattered: North Korean Unification Policy, 1971–1975," *North Korea International Documentation Project Working Paper*, no. 2 (December 2010, Washington, DC), 6.
78 *ZRGW70*, 39–40.
79 Memorandum from the President's Assistant for National Security Affairs (Kissinger) to President Nixon, November 1971, in *FRUS*, 1969–1976, vol. 17, 526.
80 Memorandum of Conversation, Beijing, February 23, 1972, *FRUS*, 1969–1976, vol. 17, 732–33.
81 Joint Statement Following Discussions with Leaders of the People's Republic of China, Shanghai, February 27, 1972, *FRUS*, 1969–1976, vol. 17, 813–14.

82 *ZRGW70*, 40–41.
83 Kissinger, *On China,* 241, 243.
84 Kissinger, *White House Years*, 745–47.
85 Nixon, *Leaders*, 234–35.
86 Ibid., 3.
87 For Zhou's political crisis after Nixon's trip to China, see Yafeng Xia, "Myth or Reality: Factional Politics, U.S.–China Relations, and Mao Zedong's Psychology in His Sunset Years, 1972–1976," *The Journal of American–East Asian Relations* 15 (Fall 2008): 107–30.

16
THE CONFERENCE ON SECURITY AND COOPERATION IN EUROPE
A Reappraisal

Angela Romano

From 22 November 1972 to 8 June 1973 the diplomatic delegations of thirty-five countries – the US, Canada, and all European states but self-excluded Albania – gathered informally in Helsinki for the Multilateral Preparatory Talks (MPT) on the Conference on Security and Cooperation in Europe (CSCE). The MPT *Final Recommendations of the Helsinki Consultations* set the rules and agenda for the negotiations and established a conference in three phases, the last of which was undefined as to date and, most importantly, the political level of the representatives.

The first phase took place in Helsinki from 3 to 7 July 1973, at ministerial level. The thirty-five foreign ministers adopted the *Final Recommendations* and set the opening date and location of the second phase. On 18 September 1973, more than six hundred delegates and experts met in Geneva for the negotiation phase of what was considered the most significant diplomatic gathering since World War II. The Geneva session was the longest non-stop non-technical negotiation of the modern era: it ended at 3:40 in the morning on 21 July 1975, after twenty-two months. As agreed in the last weeks of the negotiations, the third phase – the signing of the final document – took place in Helsinki at summit level. From 30 July to 1 August 1975 the leaders of the thirty-five countries signed the Final Act in a solemn ceremony in front of the press from all over the world.

The Helsinki Final Act was a solemn but non-legally binding agreement. It comprised three main sets of recommendations (the so-called 'baskets'): (1) Questions relating to security in Europe (ten principles guiding relations between the participating states, known as the 'Helsinki Decalogue' + Confidence Building Measures (CBMs)); (2) Co-operation in the fields of economics, of science and technology, and of the environment; (3) Co-operation in humanitarian and other fields.

Historians have for long overlooked the CSCE and its results. Considered within the wider context of the process of détente between East and West, the Helsinki Final Act was presented as a sort of seal on détente, which was indeed realized by other means, e.g. superpowers' nuclear agreements, the Federal Republic of Germany's *Neue Ostpolitik*. In the mid-1990s, a different interpretation emerged which highlighted the revolutionary charge of the Final Act. It suggested that, given the emerging role of public opinion in influencing governments and foreign policy, the document could be considered as one of the premises of the change that was about to happen in the East.[1] Indeed, movements for freedom and democracy in Eastern

Europe appealed to the moral obligations that governments had assumed by signing the Final Act, and particularly advocated full implementation of the provisions on the promotion and development of a wider circulation of ideas, information, and people, as well as of the principle of respect for peoples' right to self-determination. Several historians have focused on links between the CSCE process and these movements, and historiography now acknowledges the CSCE among the crucial factors in explaining the pace of the fall of communism in Europe.[2]

Since the early 2000s, thanks to the disclosure of sources in many national archives, the historiography on the CSCE has boomed. Virtually every aspect of the Helsinki conference and almost every participating country's policy has been analyzed and appraised. This scholarship has demonstrated that the CSCE was of major importance in most participating countries' Cold War policy. In particular, it has contributed to elucidating the different conceptions of détente and to revealing the relevant role and increasing activism of actors other than the superpowers within the European scenario.

This chapter argues that the CSCE and the Final Act, far from setting a seal on détente, constituted a step in the process of setting relations in Europe to a new pattern beyond the Cold War. This is evident in the content of the Final Act and the approach that underpins it, which is analyzed in the first part of the chapter. The innovative character of the CSCE is also the result of the proactive and, ultimately, determinant role played by the EEC member states ("the Nine"), the neutral and non-aligned countries (N+N), and independently acting Romania in shaping the content of the Final Act. Major actors' goals and actions at the CSCE are analyzed in the second part and show a striking difference between the superpowers' approach and some European countries' visions of continental relations. Indeed, the most immediate result of the CSCE, crystallized in the ensuing process, was the shift "from détente in Europe to European détente," the former being a superpower tool for stabilizing the continent, while the latter was a long-term policy aimed at overcoming the Cold War.[3]

What Kind of Détente Did the CSCE Endorse?

If détente meant the stabilization of the European situation, then there is a grain of truth in the interpretation that it had been realized by means other than the CSCE. This had been the explicit policy of the Atlantic allies, who wanted to exploit the Soviet desideratum for the conference so as to set the rhythm and priorities of détente and reach concrete solutions to fundamental European issues. In responding to the Warsaw Pact Budapest Appeal of March 1969, which called for a pan-European conference,[4] the Atlantic Council meeting in Brussels in December 1969 affirmed that the conference was a feasible option in the general East–West dialogue.[5] Before giving a green light to the opening of preparatory talks, the Atlantic allies demanded that agreements be achieved on crucial European issues, i.e. positive conclusion of the Federal Republic of Germany's *Ostpolitik* treaties with the USSR and Poland, a quadripartite agreement on Berlin, a positive development of inner-German talks, and agreement to open negotiations on mutual and balanced force reduction (MBFR).[6] This request was reiterated in the subsequent NATO communiqués and Western leaders' statements, as well as via bilateral contacts with the East. By setting these preliminary conditions, the Atlantic allies aimed to avoid the risk that the conference might end with exclusively Soviet benefits and leave the main European problems unsolved or, even worse, solved according to Moscow's wishes. Only in late May 1972, when agreements had been achieved on all four issues, did the Atlantic Alliance accept the Finnish invitation of early May 1969 to open preparatory talks for the pan-European conference.

If major European issues had already been dealt with, then the CSCE might well seem like a diplomatic parade to seal those agreements and, ultimately, the status quo in Europe. Indeed, signatory statements of the communist leaders invariably stressed the prominence of the principles on the inviolability of frontiers and territorial integrity, as well as the acknowledgement of the existing realities as a basis of mutual understanding and future cooperation.[7] Not surprisingly, most experts and commentators gave a negative appraisal of the Helsinki summit. If Raymond Aron was skeptical about the "Helsinki comedy," harsh and passionate critics of both the Final Act and détente considered the CSCE a "second Yalta," hinting at the agreement on the partition of Europe and recognition of Soviet post-World War II political and territorial acquisitions. Eugene Ionesco even considered the CSCE a re-run of the Munich Conference of 1938.[8] On the eve of US President Gerald Ford's departure for Helsinki, the *Wall Street Journal* ran a passionate headline, "Jerry, don't go!"[9] The eminent Russian dissident Aleksandr Solzhenitsyn, for whom "the countries of Western Europe will confirm the slavery of their brother countries of the East, all the while believing they are strengthening the prospects for peace," was bitter in his judgment.[10] In its major editorial on the CSCE the *Economist* stated "Mr Brezhnev has got the main thing he wanted from the security conference."[11] The most complete, disenchanted and pessimistic analysis of the Final Act came from US former diplomat and foreign policy expert George Ball, whose article was significantly headed "Capitulation at Helsinki." After mocking the US government and his allies ("*Détente* has become more an obsession than a policy"), Ball pointed out a series of Soviet gains. First, the West had solemnly recognized the inviolability of the borders set by the Red Army in its World War II advance, which were equivalent of the post-war peace treaty on Germany that the Western allies had sworn not to sign as long as Europe remained divided. Second, the Soviets, as sponsors of the conference, had gained equal status with the US in promoting détente. Third, the Helsinki "convivial summit" succeeded in achieving the first Soviet goal: the strengthening of European wishful thinking about a peace-loving Soviet Union that would eliminate the necessity for maintaining vigilance, unifying Europe and preserving a strong relationship with the US.[12]

Yet the Final Act featured recognition of the existing realities, along with a widening of the concept of détente to include the gradual liberalization of contacts between peoples and wider dissemination of information and ideas, the so-called Third Basket provisions. This had been a Western aim ever since the Atlantic Council of Brussels in December 1969;[13] once the MPT opened, the West insisted on having a specific chapter of negotiations on the subject of cooperation in the fields of culture, humanitarian measures and wider circulation of ideas and information. The emphasis on human rights and human contacts was justified in terms of a "people first" approach to détente, which also applied to proposals in the field of economic cooperation. Reversing the Soviet priorities, upon which détente related only to relations among states, Western leaders' signatory statements stressed the idea that wider and more frequent contacts among individuals were as necessary a condition to improve relations among states as were economic cooperation and military agreements.[14] However, the non-legally binding nature of the Final Act, the many nuances and compromises it endorsed and the divergent signatory statements in Helsinki all gave the impression of ambiguous and weak results. The *New York Times* caustically affirmed: "The 35-nation Conference [...] should not have happened. Never have so many struggled for so long over so little."[15] Ball, in the above-mentioned article, commented that Third Basket commitments were couched in such general terms as to produce only "minuscule holes in the Iron Curtain."[16]

Were Ball and other detractors right? Closer and more objective analysis of Final Act provisions leads to a negative answer. The kind of détente that the CSCE and the Final Act promoted was not a static preservation of the status quo. On the contrary, it was a dynamic process aimed at changing the situation in Europe, i.e. at overcoming the Cold War order. In the words of Samuel Pisar, the Final Act was "a step in the right direction."[17]

Détente as a Process to Change European Relations

Although Moscow did obtain recognition of the territorial status quo, the Final Act merely confirmed the *Ostpolitik* treaties agreements. In addition, the inviolability of frontiers was guaranteed against the threat or use of force, as Principle III spoke about "assaulting," "seizure and usurpation." Inviolability therefore did not mean immutability. More importantly, the West succeeded in introducing a specific clause on peaceful change which, after a long fight, was eventually placed in Principle I as an example of the rights inherent in sovereignty. It stated unambiguously that "frontiers can be changed, in accordance with international law, by peaceful means and by agreement." As soon as the Final Act recognized the existing borders, it created sound bases for a change and, evidently, for future reunification of Germany.

Moreover, the Soviet hold on Eastern Europe had been denied legitimization: the Decalogue amounted to a clear rejection of the Brezhnev Doctrine. In the Preamble, the signatories declared their determination to respect and apply the principles in relations with *all* other participating states, "irrespective of their political, economic or social system."[18] In defining the rights inherent in sovereignty, Principle I stated that each country has the right to define and conduct its relations with other states as it wishes, to freely choose to belong to alliances or multilateral treaties, and to freely set and develop its political, social and economic system. Principle II clearly established refraining from the threat or use of force for the purpose of inducing another participating state to renounce the full exercise of its sovereign rights, and added that no consideration might be invoked to warrant resorting to threat or use of force in contravention of this principle. This was linked to, and strengthened by, Principle IV on territorial integrity, stating that CSCE countries would refrain from military occupation or the threat of it. Principle VI was even more crystalline, as it forbade states from any intervention, direct or indirect, individual or collective, in internal or external affairs falling within the domestic jurisdiction of another state, "regardless of their mutual relations." It condemned, in all circumstances, any other act of military or political, economic or other coercion designed to subordinate to a state's own interest the exercise by another participating state of the rights inherent in its sovereignty, and thus to secure advantages of any kind.

Principle VIII vigorously affirmed peoples' right always to choose freely, when and as they wished, their internal and external political status, without external interference, and to pursue as they wished their political, economic, social and cultural development. The Soviet delegation opposed the inclusion of this principle, arguing that self-determination related to colonialism and therefore did not fit European countries. Western delegations successfully argued that the principle applied to Europe too, for peoples have *always* the right to self-determination, and might decide to change their political, economic and social system. Nobody in the West denied that 40,000 Soviet tanks deployed between the Elbe and the Urals remained a powerful means of influence upon East European countries. Nonetheless, the Final Act added an element of integrity and morality to inter-state relations, depriving the Brezhnev Doctrine of any legitimacy. Significantly, the West did not fight this battle alone. Romania and Yugoslavia, deeply concerned at the possibility that Moscow might apply the "Prague treatment" to them, had overtly pushed for the inclusion of the principle of refraining from the threat or use of force. Moreover, the attitudes and declarations of the East European countries' representatives, both at the conference and in bilateral meetings, revealed that they looked to the Helsinki provisions as a means of protecting their political independence and territorial integrity.

The Final Act adopted the Western thesis by which détente was not merely a question of good relations among states, but also had to provide concrete benefits to individuals. The participating states agreed on recognition of the universal significance of human rights and fundamental freedoms and stated that respect for such rights was "an essential factor for the peace, justice and well-being necessary to ensure the development of friendly relations and cooperation among themselves as among all states."[19] In addition, Principle VII made respect for human rights a specific subject of concrete cooperation agreements among CSCE signatories. Combined with the equal importance of all principles as stated in the Final Act, this provision was a significant innovation in international law, asserting the idea that human rights were no longer a matter of domestic jurisdiction. Even more significantly, the Final Act was conceived as an instrument for citizens too: it clearly stated the right of the individual to know and act upon his rights in the field of human rights and fundamental freedoms.[20] The Final Act thus gave both (Western) governments and (Eastern) dissidents the opportunity to legitimately claim the modification of certain communist regimes' rules and practices.

On a more concrete level, Third Basket provisions set several specific guidelines for intergovernmental cooperation and unilateral implementation on human contacts, information, culture and education. Participating states were called on to advance internal reforms or arrangements so as to comply with their international political engagements. Despite the undeniable limits and weaknesses of the Third Basket, it was markedly liberal in its contents and conception, and systematic and coherent in nature. The Third Basket widened the diplomatic tutelage of citizens to the point of concerning the latter's relations with their own government and national law. Moreover, it did not leave any room for governmental censorship. Given the intransigence of Western European countries, the Soviet request for consistency of Third Basket provisions with national laws and customs and for the definition of admissible content for informational and cultural items was rejected.

The same attempt to encourage reform in communist regimes and put the individual at the centre of détente also characterized the usually overlooked Second Basket, the potential of which was possibly even greater. "States will take measures" – a language unusually engaging for the Final Act – to improve conditions "for the expansion of contacts between" economic actors, the list of which explicitly went beyond governmental operators to include subjects of various kinds.[21] Important provisions related to economic and commercial information, the states agreeing to improve the quality, quantity and circulation of economic information and to ease related administrative procedures. These provisions applied particularly to communist countries, whose practices (though with substantial national differences) were restrictive to the point that in Romania and Czechoslovakia the diffusion of economic information constituted a violation of the laws on state secrets. Wider circulation of peoples and information also characterized the texts on scientific and technological cooperation. The Final Act recommended the exchange and circulation of books, periodicals and other scientific publications among interested organizations, institutions, enterprises, scientists and technologists, as well as exchanges and visits and other *direct contacts and communications* among scientists and technologists.[22] In this way, the CSCE affirmed the principle of individual scientific cooperation, narrowing the scope of state control on scientists, at least. This was significant, since many Soviet dissidents were scientists and academics. Ball's concept of "minor holes in the Iron Curtain" was quite short sighted; the potential of the Final Act was intended to unfold in the longer term.

Yet one may argue – and many did – that the non-legally binding nature of the Final Act weakened the opportunity for change. However, the peculiar nature of the Final Act did not diminish the engagements that states had undertaken in signing it. Jurists argue that international agreements of any kind involve the ethical and political responsibility of the signatory states, due to the fulfilment in good faith of the obligations they have assumed.[23] Moreover, non-binding agreements also have juridical relevance. Provisions either reaffirm obligations in international law or add new matters to those "of international concern," rescuing them from the untouchable domestic jurisdiction of the state. Having assumed a political engagement at the international level on a particular subject, a state could no longer appeal to the principle of non-interference in internal affairs as a means to justify its lack of compliance with the provisions it had agreed upon.[24] In fact, if the Soviets had thought that they could easily dismiss unpalatable Helsinki provisions, why did they fight for fifty-five working sessions on Principle VII? Why did they try to weaken the Third Basket as much as possible? Had they meant to elude uncomfortable provisions, they could have accepted Western requests immediately and gained a faster conclusion of the conference, which they wanted.

In conclusion, the CSCE, in its origins a Soviet design to gain recognition of the status quo in Europe, turned out to be a challenge to the European bipolar order – a challenge that the communist regimes, unlike some Western commentators and Eastern dissidents, seriously worried about. Archival evidence now reveals that intelligence and security agencies in the East fully foresaw the repercussions of the Helsinki provisions on internal stability and order.[25] This challenge, as the following paragraphs will show, was the result of an intentional, systematic, accurately prepared and firmly fought action on the part of some CSCE participating countries: the EEC Nine, the neutral and non-aligned countries (N+N) and Romania.

From Détente in Europe to European Détente

All accounts of the CSCE report that delegations teamed up in three major caucuses: NATO, Warsaw Pact and the N+N. Common positions and a more or less remarkable degree of coordination made these groups clearly identifiable. However, scrutiny of countries' goals and negotiation stance reveals a reality more complex than East/West opposition with neutrals in between. The actual CSCE dichotomy was between countries interested in stabilizing the situation in Europe and states promoting the overcoming of the bipolar order in the continent. The latter, though differing as to strategy and approach, were ultimately the true protagonists of the CSCE and makers of the Final Act.

The USSR's interest in using the CSCE to secure the status quo in Europe was evident in all its statements, proposals and stance at the negotiations. Archival sources on US–USSR diplomatic contacts also reveal that Moscow explicitly stressed the superpowers' duty to lead – i.e. control – their allies, in the name of global responsibilities.[26] The Nixon administration could not agree more. The White House had neither interest in nor enthusiasm for the CSCE, and accepted the conference because the majority of its European allies favoured it. By supporting them, the US was able to rein in West European readiness for convening the conference, and make sure that it did not engender neutralist tendencies. The White House "had no interest in a conference in 1972"; in particular, no decision on the opening of multilateral talks on the CSCE should be taken before agreements on fundamental security issues had been achieved. The priorities of Richard Nixon and National Security Adviser Henry Kissinger were never questioned: the CSCE was, first and foremost, a bargaining chip in negotiations with the Soviet Union to gain concrete solutions on Berlin, the SALT treaty, and the opening of MBFR negotiations. Once satisfaction was obtained on these issues, the CSCE was deprived of its bargaining value and became the "good carrot" for the Soviets, according to Kissinger's linkage tactics.

In 1972 the dialogue between the superpowers produced its best results, sealed during Nixon's visit to Moscow in May: the SALT treaty, economic and trade agreements, an understanding on the opening of the MBFR talks in parallel to the CSCE and a declaration on fundamental principles governing relations between the US and the USSR. In the latter, the US president had, remarkably, endorsed the concept of peaceful coexistence – a long-standing Soviet term – without even putting his own interpretation on record; neither the French–Soviet declaration nor the German *Ostpolitik* treaties had gone that far. More revealing, US statements omitted any reference to human rights issues. These attitudes were soon to apply to Washington's CSCE policy.

Nixon and Kissinger aimed at letting the Soviets have what they wanted: "a short snappy conference with little substance." Owing to the new relationship with Moscow, the White House was unwilling to introduce any contentious elements, such as the freer movement topic. In bilateral contacts Kissinger assured the Soviets that the White House did not attach importance to Third Basket provisions and would not endanger détente by playing an ideological struggle. The same concept was repeatedly and clearly conveyed to the European allies. For example, in June 1973, in a meeting with NATO permanent representatives at San Clemente, Kissinger stated that MBFR talks were much more important than the CSCE and that it was not helpful to challenge the Soviets by asking for human contact provisions or whatever else could be unacceptable to them.

Consistently, the action of the US delegation in Geneva was severely limited, especially after Kissinger became Secretary of State in September 1973. Behind the scenes, the US also pressed its allies to speed up the negotiations and conclude the CSCE at summit level, despite the fact that the Atlantic position was to agree to a top-level final phase only if the outcome was satisfactory. Kissinger told the European allies that the summit had to be accepted: "Europe cannot say no to the Soviets on this point."

Only in 1975, due to the unification of Vietnam under communist rule, did the US administration, and Kissinger himself, change stance and become more helpful to the Western cause at the CSCE. President Ford and Kissinger interpreted events in Vietnam as Soviet indirect lack of compliance to the basic code of conduct in superpower relations. Accordingly, they were no longer inclined to use the CSCE as a good carrot, all the more so in the light of Congress's change of tune (epitomized by the Jackson-Vanik amendment) and of the strains that the US attitude put on Atlantic cohesion. The CSCE changed from carrot into stick in the overall US policy towards the Soviet Union.

The EEC Nine: Overcoming the Cold War in Europe

The group that shaped most of the Final Act, and in particular promoted its vision of détente, was that of the European Economic Community (EEC) member states, i.e. the Nine.[27] Following the relaunch of the Western European integration process at The Hague summit of December 1969, the then six EEC member states had created an intergovernmental mechanism to coordinate their foreign policies – European Political Cooperation (EPC). Since its first meeting in November 1970, EPC had focused on East–West relations and, in particular, on the proposed pan-European conference. Although actively participating in NATO consultations for the CSCE, the EEC states soon developed a distinct collective approach to both the conference and East–West relations.

Two main reasons favoured this assertive attitude. First, it aimed at gaining some form of recognition of the EEC by the communist countries, whose propaganda still considered the Community a Western Cold War tool. In the new climate of détente, a pan-European conference on cooperation might well serve as a platform to change this anachronistic situation. The second reason was the meaning and substance of détente. For West European governments, détente was a means to start a gradual transformation of European relations aimed at overcoming the Cold War divide. While preserving NATO to guarantee defense, they aimed at loosening bipolar restraints and deepening the mutual interdependence between the two halves of Europe through economic and cultural exchanges, political dialogue and mutually advantageous cooperation in several fields. In the short and medium term, détente would improve the daily life of European citizens and promote wider human contacts and exchange of knowledge across the Iron Curtain. This in turn would, in the long run, engender reforms and liberalization of the communist regimes, ultimately ending the Cold War.

Recognizing that this process could only be gradual, the Nine thought it possible to engage the Soviets and their allies in a serious discussion by introducing specific proposals with reasonable argumentation and avoiding unnecessary polemics as far as possible. As clearly emerged in EPC debates, maximalist proposals would have been interpreted as an open ideological challenge, and would have then sharpened Soviet craving for security, with a consequent tightening of control over East European countries or even intervention à la Prague 1968. The apparent weakness of the Third Basket was thus the result of a conscious choice on the part of its promoters. What the Nine fought for was not an immediate change of the communist regimes, but a *locus standi* for all people in the East who were trying to promote reforms and a certain degree of liberalization of their societies.

Hence, Western European détente had in itself a dynamic and revolutionary charge that could not be compatible with the global strategy of the superpowers. The latter's bilateral dialogue engendered fears that the US might subordinate the interests of its allies to cooperative relations with Moscow, and that the Community might be "squeezed by the superpowers."[28] Kissinger's numerous statements about White House indifference to the CSCE and pointlessness of the Third Basket showed that the US government had neither endorsed nor even understood the European approach to East–West relations. Consequently, the Nine made promotion of (their) détente in Europe, notably through the CSCE, the main task of EPC. Not only did the Nine establish ad hoc mechanisms and working bodies to formulate proposals and tactics for the conference, they set procedures for close coordination within NATO, in order to safeguard their interests and promote their vision.

The most proactive and close-knit group at the CSCE, the Nine, took the leadership of the West at the CSCE negotiations. They stuck to their requests and resisted all Soviet attempts to undermine or narrow Third Basket provisions. The Nine also refused to agree to a top-level final phase until concrete results had been reached on human contacts, and even threatened not to accept the third phase altogether, had the Soviets persisted in refusing concessions. Heads of state or government also personally addressed the CSCE issues in their bilateral meetings with communist opposite numbers. As former Soviet Ambassador Yuri Kashlev later affirmed, Moscow's acceptance of the Third Basket resulted very much from the strong pressure that West European governments exerted, also at high level, on Soviet politicians.[29]

Moreover, the Nine also succeeded in gaining communist countries' de facto recognition of the EEC. EEC representatives had participated in the negotiations when Community competence so requested; moreover, Aldo Moro's signature of the Final Act, as president of the EEC Council, committed the EEC to the implementation of the Helsinki provisions in accordance with its competence and rules. This was a step forward in weakening the Soviet-driven policy of non-recognition; the acknowledgement of the EEC's existence and positive role in intra-European relations was a non-negligible change in the European scenario, as it invalidated one of the corollaries of the Cold War order in Europe.

European Security Beyond the Blocs

The CSCE and the Final Act would not have had the character and content that they did without the contribution of the neutral and non-aligned countries (N+N: Austria, Switzerland, Sweden and Finland + Yugoslavia). Although lacking an institutionalized mechanism to harmonize their different positions, and formulating joint proposals and initiatives only when their interests coincided, the N+N clearly emerged as a third group actor in the CSCE.[30]

The N+N as a group "definitely brought a new flavour to European Cold War politics."[31] By working to convene and to assure the proceeding of the CSCE, the N+N challenged the existing bloc-to-bloc dialogue and helped to establish a pan-European dialogue on continental issues.

To start with, neutral countries' concerted efforts at the MPT led to the adoption of two important procedural rules that were meant to make sure "that the CSCE would not just become another military alliance affair in the European Cold War":[32] all states would participate on the basis of sovereign and equal rights, and decisions would be taken by consensus. Both principles guaranteed to every participating state the possibility of tabling proposals and protecting its vital interests, regardless of its size, power or allies.

Secondly, the N+N succeeded in including CBMs in the CSCE agenda and Final Act. Not party to existing bloc-to-bloc negotiations on security issues, they aimed at introducing a link between the latter and the CSCE. Only there could the N+N participate on an equal basis with Cold War alliance countries to discuss European security and work for a collective system beyond the blocs.

Thirdly, the group demonstrated a remarkable – and highly appreciated – capacity for mediation between East and West when the situation was deadlocked. From the MPT definition of the agenda and the famous "baskets" to the practice of small informal working groups, the N+N's action proved particularly useful to the progress of the conference and agreement on the final document. These "administrative" tasks had high political value because they showed that actual cooperation and agreement were possible between the blocs and beyond them, in the interests of Europe as a whole.

Finally, the N+N were of paramount importance in securing at least a minimum agreement on the follow-up to the Helsinki conference, on which negotiations had long been lagging. The East, which had originally sponsored the idea, lost interest in a permanent mechanism that, due to the Third Basket, threatened to put domestic practices under scrutiny. Conversely, Western countries became gradually more inclined to envision some form of follow-up; yet they maintained a wait-and-see attitude until the content of the final document had been agreed upon. Only the N+N and Romania were firmly committed to guarantee continuity to the CSCE, since it could preserve their role in discussing many of Europe's crucial issues on an equal footing with their more powerful neighbours. The final decision was quite cautious, yet it opened up a glimmer of continuity: the participating countries would meet in Belgrade in two years' time to exchange views on Final Act implementation and discuss steps towards tighter cooperation.

Although a member of the Warsaw Pact, Romania arguably fits the group of states that pushed for a Europe beyond the blocs. Bucharest clearly aimed at gaining some guarantee of its independence, and hoped that détente would at least make it more embarrassing for the Soviet Union to put overt pressure on its allies. The Romanian government always stressed the relevance of principles that overtly denied legitimacy to the Brezhnev Doctrine, which Bucharest had never agreed to nor helped to implement. Consistently, Romania called for withdrawal of all foreign troops from the territory of European states, with evident reference to the stationing of the Red Army on Hungarian and Czechoslovak soils. Closely in line with the N+N, the Romanian government thought that security should be debated by all states, outside the blocs, and consistently supported the adoption of Confidence Building Measures. It even called for a collective system of security that might substitute for the military alliances. For the same reasons, Bucharest supported the creation of a permanent body or, at least, follow-up meetings that might guarantee continuity to the off-the-bloc dialogue on European security.

Keeping the CSCE and European Détente Alive

An appreciation of the shift towards a *genuinely European* détente would not be complete without a look at the follow-up to the Helsinki CSCE. The continuation of the Helsinki process was all but guaranteed at the time. Cold War crises in Africa and US President Jimmy Carter's vigorous stance on human rights brought a return of superpower rivalry, the consequences of which were deeply felt at the Belgrade meeting (4 October 1977 to 8 March 1978). The latter was meant to allow for an exchange of views on countries' implementation of the Final Act and on new measures to further cooperation. The communist countries, already determined to limit the review phase, due to their poor record of implementation, especially on the Third Basket and human rights, were subjected to harsh and case-by-case attacks from the US delegation. Superpower rivalry turned the atmosphere sour and impeded agreement on any of the proposals that had been tabled to advance cooperation in the three baskets. Yet the efforts of the N+N and the Nine, which attached great importance to the CSCE as an actual forum for détente and cooperation, led to a Concluding Document that, at least, recorded agreement to hold a number of meetings.[33] Besides a Scientific Forum and a Meeting of Experts on the Mediterranean, the important achievement was the convocation of the next follow-up conference, in Madrid in 1980.

The Madrid meeting (11 November 1980 to 9 September 1983) opened and proceeded in an even worse atmosphere. The Soviet invasion of Afghanistan, new US President Ronald Reagan's confrontational policy towards the Soviet Union and the Polish crisis all contrasted sharply with the nature and principles of the CSCE. The Madrid meeting became the stage for renewed Cold War tensions and suffered interruptions and a long recess. Again, the Nine and the N+N "saved" the CSCE process. "The firm and consistent commitment of the whole N+N group to the CSCE follow-up in combination with their readiness to accept the intermediary position [...] provided the conference with very important services that only this group of states could perform."[34] For their part, the Nine stood firmly committed to their collective policy of détente, distancing themselves from the US and overtly advocating the continuation of the CSCE negotiations on matters of substance.[35] Eventually, the Madrid meeting produced a substantial concluding document that not only guaranteed the next follow-up conference, but also added significantly to all Final Act baskets.[36]

The holding of follow-up meetings ultimately indicates the genuinely European nature of the CSCE, which stayed alive despite the breakdown of détente and the increased tension between the two superpowers. Despite Cold War structure and constraints, a new kind of intra-European relations "beyond the blocs" developed, laying the ground for the future of post-Cold War Europe. Not by chance, the Paris summit of November 1990 called on the CSCE to play its part in managing the historic change taking place in Europe and responding to the new challenges of the post-Cold War period. The CSCE process turned into the Organization for Security and Cooperation in Europe (OSCE).

Conclusion

The analysis of the CSCE and its results reveals that it was not a mere seal on (previously achieved) détente in Europe. The Final Act neither crystallized the status quo nor, as its most vociferous detractors at the time said, sold half of Europe's freedom in exchange for empty declarations of goodwill.

The Final Act, on the contrary, was a step in the direction of changing the status quo in Europe. Though recognizing existing frontiers, it explicitly admitted peaceful changes according to international agreements, legitimizing a future German reunification. The Final Act clearly rejected the Brezhnev Doctrine and sanctioned the rights inherent in sovereignty, irrespective of countries' belonging to a group or alliance. Finally, it endorsed the liberal concept of human rights and centrality of the individual, giving both Western governments and East European dissidents an opportunity to legitimately claim the modification of certain rules and practices of communist regimes.

The nature of the CSCE in itself constituted a step in the overcoming of the rigid Cold War bloc order in Europe. The CSCE was at one and the same time the means for and the symbol of new intra-European relations beyond the blocs. It guaranteed neutral and non-aligned countries a space to debate key European issues on an equal basis with their powerful neighbours; it made it more difficult for the USSR to force alignment on its allies; it enhanced the political role of the EEC. Indeed, the protagonists of the CSCE were the EEC Nine, the N+N, and Romania. In varying degrees, these countries were those that ultimately shaped the Final Act.

Historians now agree that détente between the US and the USSR differed from, and often conflicted with, détente between Western Europe and the communist bloc. The former aimed at stabilizing the continent and sealing the bipolar partition, whereas the latter was meant to promote a gradual overcoming of the Cold War in Europe via expanding contacts and exchanges across the Iron Curtain and deepening mutual interdependence between the two halves of the continent. The EEC Nine consistently used the CSCE to further their vision of détente and set intra-European relations to a new kind of thinking.

Also working for a Europe beyond the blocs were the N+N. Excluded from East–West dialogue on crucial European issues, they first made sure that the CSCE assured equal participation to all countries and then tried to promote the idea of a system of collective security. Although a member of the Warsaw Pact, Romania actually acted independently and fully shared the N+N's vision of intra-European relations – and security – beyond the blocs.

The CSCE and the Final Act thus signalled a shift away from détente in Europe, i.e. a superpower means to stabilize the continent, and towards a European détente, i.e. a process aimed at superseding the bipolar order in Europe. The fact that the CSCE turned into a process further highlights its genuinely European nature. Whereas the superpowers used the CSCE meetings as a battlefield of their renewed confrontational relationship, the other participants "saved" the CSCE as an actual pan-European forum for détente and cooperation, a tool for new intra-European relations appealing to both governments and citizens.

Notes

1 Ennio Di Nolfo, *Storia delle relazioni internazionali* (Roma-Bari: Laterza, 2000, 1st ed. 1994), 1210.
2 Daniel Thomas, "Human Rights Ideas, the Demise of Communism, and the End of the Cold War," *Journal of Cold War Studies* 7:2 (2005), 110–41; Adam Roberts, "An 'Incredibly Swift Transition': Reflections on the end of the Cold War," in *The Cambridge History of the Cold War*, ed. Melvin P. Leffler and Odd Arne Westad (Cambridge: Cambridge University Press, 2010), vol. III, 513–34; Rosemary Foot, "The Cold War and human rights," in *Cambridge History of the Cold War*, vol. III, 445–65; Sarah Snyder, *Human Rights Activism and the End of the Cold War: A Transnational History of the Helsinki Network* (Cambridge: Cambridge University Press, 2011).

3 With the exception of sections on the N+N, this chapter is a digest from my own book: Angela Romano, *From Détente in Europe to European Détente: How the West Shaped the Helsinki CSCE* (Brussels: Peter Lang, 2009).
4 *Warsaw Pact Communiqué*, Budapest, 17 March 1969. http://www.php.isn.ethz.ch/collections/colltopic.cfm?lng=en&id=18022&navinfo=14465.
5 *NATO Declaration on European Security*, Brussels, 5 December 1969. http://www.nato.int/cps/en/natolive/official_texts_26760.htm.
6 Ibid., para. 14.
7 Luigi V. Ferraris, *Report on a Negotiation, Helsinki–Geneva–Helsinki, 1972–1975* (Alphen aan den Rijn: Sijthoff & Noordhoff International 1979), 588–589.
8 For a review of the Western press, see P. Tigrid, *Helsinki Plus Four Months* (London: EUCORG, 1975).
9 *Wall Street Journal*, 25 July 1975.
10 Aleksandr Solzhenitsyn, "The Big Losers in World War III," in *The Atlantic Community Quarterly*, 13:3 (1975), 293–5.
11 *The Economist*, 2 August 1975.
12 Geoge W. Ball, 'Capitulation at Helsinki', in *The Atlantic Community Quarterly*, 13:3 (1975), 286–8.
13 *NATO Declaration on European Security*, par. 11.
14 Elliott to Mr Callaghan, 12 August 1975, Doc. No. 139 in *Documents on British Policy Overseas (DBPO)*, III:2, London: The Stationery Office 1997; Ferraris, *Report*, 587.
15 *New York Times*, 21 July 1975.
16 Ball, "Capitulation," 288.
17 *International Herald Tribune*, 30 July 1975.
18 *Final Act*, 1(a), para. 5. Emphasis added.
19 *Final Act*, Principle VII, para. 5.
20 Ibid., para. 6–7.
21 *Final Act*, Commercial Exchanges, Business Contacts and Facilities, para. 2.
22 *Final Act*, Science and Technology, Forms and Methods of Cooperation. Emphasis added.
23 Emmanuel Decaux, *La Conférence sur la Sécurité et la Coopération en Europe (CSCE)* (Paris: Presses Universitaires de France 1992), 56–60.
24 Luigi Condorelli, "Diritto e Non Diritto nella CSCE," in *La nuova Europa della CSCE*, ed. Giovanni Barberini and Natalino Ronzitti (Milano: Franco Angeli, 1994), 48–50.
25 See Svetlana Savranskaya and Thomas S. Blanton, "The Moscow Helsinki Group 30th Anniversary: From the Secret File," NSA EBB no. 191, http://www.gwu.edu/~nsarchiv/NSAEBB/NSAEBB191/.
26 This paragraph draws on my article: Angela Romano, "Détente, Entente or Linkage? The Helsinki CSCE in U.S.-Soviet Relations," *Diplomatic History*, 33:4 (2009), 703–22. See also Jussi Hanhimäki, "'They can write it in Swahili': Kissinger, the Soviets, and the Helsinki Accords, 1973–75," *Journal of Transatlantic Studies* 1:1 (2003), 37–58.
27 These paragraphs draw on my published articles and chapters on the EEC at the CSCE.
28 The National Archives of the UK, FCO 28/1692, A Federal Trust Report, 16 July 1972.
29 Contribution of former Soviet Ambassador Yuri Kashlev to the CIMA and CWIHP conference *The Road to Helsinki. The Early Steps of the CSCE*, Florence, 29–30 September 2003.
30 Thomas Fisher, "Getting to Know Their Limits: The N+N and the Follow-up Meeting in Belgrade 1977/78," in *From Helsinki to Belgrade. The First CSCE Follow-up Meeting and the Crisis of Détente*, ed. Vladimir Bilandzic, Dittmar Dahlmann and Milan Kosanovic (Göttingen: Vandenhoeck & Ruprecht 2012), 165. Fisher, *Neutral power in the CSCE. The N+N States and the Making of the Helsinki Accords 1975* (Baden-Baden: Nomos, 2009).
31 Fisher, "Getting to Know," 164.
32 Thomas Fisher, "Bridging the Gap between East and West," in *Perforating the Iron Curtain: European Détente, Transatlantic Relations, and the Cold War, 1965–1985*, ed. Poul Villaume and Odd Arne Westad (Copenhagen: Museum Tusculanum, 2010), 145.
33 On Belgrade see Bilandzic, Dahlmann and Kosanovic, *From Helsinki to Belgrade*.
34 Fisher, "Bridging," 168.
35 See Angela Romano, "More Cohesive, Still Divergent: Western Europe, the US and the Madrid CSCE Follow-Up Meeting," in Kiran K. Patel and Ken Weisbrode, *European Integration and the Atlantic Community in the 1980s* (Cambridge: Cambridge University Press, 2013), 39–58.
36 On Madrid see Jan Sizoo and Rudolf Jurrjens, *CSCE Decision-Making. The Madrid Experience* (The Hague: Martinus Nijhoff Publishers, 1984).

PART VI

Human Rights and Non-State Actors

17
HUMAN RIGHTS AND THE COLD WAR

Sarah B. Snyder

Scholars interested in human rights during the Cold War are increasingly producing innovative new work on the issue.[1] Unfortunately, human rights has not yet warranted serious, sustained consideration by those writing survey accounts of the Cold War. For example, John Lewis Gaddis' *The Cold War* mentions human rights in connection with only four subjects: the Jackson-Vanik Amendment, Jimmy Carter's foreign policy, the United Nations, and the Helsinki Final Act.[2] Yet, human rights mattered to international relations at far more points in the Cold War. We can think of the Cold War as bookended by two major human rights developments – agreement to the 1948 United Nations (UN) Universal Declaration of Human Rights (UDHR) and the influence of human rights and human rights advocacy on the end of the Cold War. In between, attention to human rights abuses internationally was inconsistent and often overshadowed by the perceived stakes of the Cold War in political, military, ideological, and economic terms. Existing scholarship on human rights in the Cold War has repeatedly pointed to two human rights "booms" – one in the late 1940s and one in the 1970s.[3] This chapter, however, will argue that the pattern was more undulating and that moments might be a more useful framework for understanding when human rights emerged as a priority in international relations.[4]

Human Rights during the Early Cold War

Building upon the UN Charter's affirmation of respect for human rights, the UN Human Rights Commission began drafting a document that outlined international human rights norms and protected individual freedoms in 1947.[5] Members of the Human Rights Commission considered the devastation of World War Two and former United States President Franklin D. Roosevelt's call for a postwar world dedicated to the preservation of four freedoms: freedom of speech, freedom of religion, freedom from want, and freedom from fear, to be the foundations for their undertaking. They struggled for many months, in the context of increasing East–West tension and rising conflict in other parts of the world, to formulate a declaration to which everyone would be morally bound. The Human Rights Commission initially intended to produce a declaration or bill of rights and a covenant with a means of implementation. In the end, however, it formulated only a declaration of principles with no mechanism for enforcement.

The UN General Assembly adopted and issued the UDHR on December 10, 1948, establishing an international human rights standard. The declaration includes thirty articles that enumerated specific rights. The first article declares "All human beings are born free and equal in dignity and rights." The remaining articles address three broad classes of rights: the integrity of the human being, or freedom from governmental intervention against the person; political and civil liberties; and social and economic rights. The first category includes "the right to life, liberty and security of person," and specifies the freedom from slavery, torture, arbitrary arrest or detention. The political and civil freedoms outlined include the right to own property and freedom of religion and expression. The declaration also addresses economic and social rights such as the right to employment, education, housing, medical care, and food.[6] Forty-eight countries voted in its favor and eight, including South Africa, Saudi Arabia, the Soviet Union, and its allies, abstained. No delegations opposed the declaration outright.

Consent to the declaration was an important step for the promotion of human rights internationally, but it did not guarantee that its provisions would be fulfilled consistently. Indeed, in the immediate aftermath of its 1948 adoption, the record of implementation of the UDHR was uneven as the issue of human rights became increasingly politicized.[7] In the 1950s, the attention of policymakers turned away from human rights declarations and institutions to waging the Cold War. In the United States, this was fueled by the Bricker Amendment controversy, which built upon fears that international human rights treaties could undermine the constitution.[8] Postwar recovery, the end of American atomic monopoly, the Chinese Civil War, the outbreak of war in Korea, and Third World nationalism all warranted greater attention. Nonetheless, the UDHR expressed a commitment to uphold certain principles that retained a type of "soft power" throughout the Cold War.[9]

Renewed attention to human rights internationally was heavily influenced by the establishment of Amnesty International in 1961, which directed international attention toward the plight of political prisoners and violations of human rights more broadly. Amnesty International was a participatory organization that worked to advance the cause of human rights despite the political context of the Cold War. Under Amnesty's model, fees-paying members formed groups that adopted specific prisoners of conscience; these were in turn overseen by a national section. Over the subsequent decades Amnesty International's members drew attention to the issue of political imprisonment through letter-writing campaigns to secure the release of political prisoners. Every group adopted three prisoners, one each imprisoned in the developing, communist, and Western blocs. Amnesty's one–one–one adoption model was intended to delineate human rights activism as outside the Cold War framework and to demonstrate that low-level individuals could still make a difference in an era determined by high-level power politics. Amnesty International groups were then tasked with securing their prisoners' release through individual and group activism. Most often, group members wrote letters to the officials responsible for imprisoning their adoptees, pleading for the easing of their conditions and release. Besides working for the release of political prisoners, Amnesty was also devoted to ensuring that trials were impartial and speedy and that prisoners were spared abuse and unjust treatment. As Amnesty International evolved from an initiative begun in the United Kingdom, chapters were established in Switzerland, Italy, France, and the United States, among other countries. In historian Samuel Moyn's view, Amnesty International was able to attract so many members because it offered an alternative outlet to those disappointed by the intransigence of the Cold War.[10] Amnesty International's development fitted into broader trends of growing concern about human rights, incarceration, and racial discrimination as well as the rise of a global civil society in those years.[11]

Human Rights in the 1960s

Decolonization was also a significant factor in directing increased attention to human rights. In particular, historian Brad Simpson has emphasized the extent to which anti-colonial movements saw self-determination as the "first right" that must be secured and from which other human rights would flow.[12] As decolonization expanded the number of UN member states, these newly independent countries brought with them an interest in certain human rights.[13] As an outgrowth of the increasing African membership in the United Nations, two new committees were established in the early 1960s: the Special Committee on Decolonization and the Special Committee on Apartheid. Importantly, in contrast to the Commission on Human Rights, both of these committees could listen to petitions and initiate investigations.[14]

One particularly significant moment in the wave of decolonization that focused international attention on human rights was Rhodesia's unilateral declaration of independence (UDI) from Great Britain on November 11, 1965, which was intended to prevent black majority rule. In response, the United States, Great Britain, and others put in place an embargo to pressure the white minority regime to reverse course. The UN Security Council acted as well, passing Resolution 217, which disavowed the UDI and pressed Great Britain to resolve the crisis. The following year, the Security Council implemented economic sanctions against the regime. Independent African countries were particularly active in opposing Rhodesia's racially discriminatory regime.

Cold War politics intersected with the international response to the UDI in a number of important respects.[15] First, the United States and others were attentive to black Africans' attitudes and wanted to attract newly independent states to the Western bloc. Disavowing Rhodesia's UDI and racially discriminatory policies was one measure intended to garner their support.[16] Ian Smith, the leader of the Rhodesian regime, however, sought to use the Cold War and his firm anticommunism to his advantage, suggesting that the country could be an important bulwark against the spread of communism in Southern Africa.[17] The ongoing controversy, which was not resolved until 1980, focused considerable attention on racial discriminatory regimes.

A similarly important moment was the April 21, 1967 Greek coup; the junta's human rights violations drew international attention, particularly given popular conceptions of Athens as the birthplace of democracy.[18] The United States, Amnesty International, and members of the Council of Europe each acted to express their concerns about political prisoners, island concentration camps, and the use of torture in the months that followed. As in many cases, however, revulsion at Greece's human rights abuses was balanced against Cold War and security concerns. Greece's position as a member of the North Atlantic Treaty Organization (NATO) and strategic location in the Eastern Mediterranean muffled high-level recriminations. Nonetheless, Denmark, the Netherlands, and Norway all initiated action against Greece before the European Commission on Human Rights.

Importantly for marshaling international condemnation of the Greek regime, Amnesty International documented the torture of Greek political prisoners. Reports from its December 1967 and March 1968 visits to the country identified "torture as a deliberate practice" of the Security Police and Military Police.[19] In the United States, particular concern surrounded the fate of political prisoner Andreas Papandreou, a Greek politician with longstanding ties to the American academic community. There, the U.S. Committee for Democracy in Greece developed, organized by many well-known Washington-based liberals. The nongovernmental organization (NGO) was part of a broader network of groups and individuals in Australia, Canada, Denmark, Great Britain, France, the Federal Republic of Germany, Italy, Norway, Sweden, Switzerland, and the United States, all of whom were opposed to the Greek regime.[20]

As in other instances in which concern for human rights intersected with Cold War politics, the instincts of high-level officials to ignore reports of abuses were complicated by several factors. Concerned citizens, international human rights groups, and ad hoc NGOs succeeded in keeping attention on human rights violations in Greece.[21] Furthermore, Greece's location in Europe and history meant that human rights abuses there were harder to overlook. Concerns about human rights violations in Greece persisted until the country returned to democracy in July 1974.

At the international level, the UN General Assembly's unanimous decision in 1963 to designate 1968 the International Year for Human Rights (IYHR), in honor of the twentieth anniversary of the adoption of the Universal Declaration of Human Rights, also raised the profile of human rights. The UN hoped its member states would celebrate the year with postage stamps, pamphlets on the Declaration, radio programming, and human rights prizes.[22] The year culminated with the International Conference on Human Rights, held in April 1968 in Tehran, Iran.[23] There was a degree of irony in the International Conference's location, given that the event's host, Shah Muhammad Pahlavi, did not respect civil liberties and that many of the other states represented at the conference did not have exemplary human rights records. Those attending focused primarily on economic development and national liberation rather than on individual human rights.[24] In historian Roland Burke's critical view, delegates from the Third World and even UN Secretary General U. Thant undermined the UDHR in their interventions at the Conference. In the assessment of the International Commission of Jurists, United States delegate Bruno Bitker, and others, "the conference was a failure."[25] Despite such dire assessments of the Conference, it was a moment at which international attention focused on human rights.

Human Rights in the Soviet Bloc

In Eastern Europe, the Warsaw Pact's invasion of Czechoslovakia disillusioned many about the possibilities for progress and reform under the Soviet system.[26] The invasion prompted a small group of Soviet human rights activists to protest in Moscow's Red Square. Those present were part of a movement that began in 1965 with a protest to commemorate the anniversary of the UDHR and carried forward with the establishment of the Initiative Group to Defend Human Rights in the USSR and the Moscow Human Rights Committee in subsequent years.[27] An important strand of those advocating for greater rights in the Soviet system were Jews who sought religious freedom and, barring that, the right to emigrate to Israel. Anatoly Shcharansky, one of the most prominent "refuseniks," as those denied the right to emigrate were called, described his religious awakening as coming in the wake of Israel's victory in the June 1967 war, suggesting the international connections underpinning many of these human rights developments.[28] The plight of Jewish refuseniks inspired considerable international sympathy.[29] One of the movement's most prominent supporters was Senator Henry Jackson (D-WA), who proposed legislation in 1973 to restrict Soviet–American trade, in an attempt to pressure the Soviet Union to issue more exit visas to Jews. The Jackson-Vanik Amendment, which became law despite opposition from the administration, angered Soviet leaders, who reduced rather than increased immigration. Furthermore, during these years, Soviet authorities remained effective in suppressing dissent.

A significant burst of human rights activism followed the publication of the 1975 Helsinki Final Act in Soviet newspapers.[30] The international agreement, signed in Helsinki, Finland on August 1, 1975 by Soviet General Secretary Leonid Brezhnev and thirty-four other world leaders, inspired the formation of human rights monitoring groups across the Soviet Union and

Eastern Europe. The first was the Public Group to Promote Fulfillment of the Helsinki Accords in the USSR, which was formed by eleven Soviet dissidents on May 13, 1976. Known in the West as the Moscow Helsinki Group, it monitored Soviet compliance with the Helsinki Final Act, with particular attention to the USSR's record on civil and human rights. The group's eleven founding members represented different strands of Soviet dissent, including Jews denied the right to emigrate to Israel, human rights activists, and representatives of national minorities, such as the Ukrainians. Yuri Orlov, a physicist who was barred from working in his field due to his human rights activism, became the group's leader. Other prominent members were Shcharansky, Yelena Bonner, and Ludmilla Alexeyeva.

The group was under pressure from Soviet state security even before its formation was formally announced. Thereafter, group members monitored the Soviet record; they based their reports on interviews, fact-finding missions, and other available evidence. They compiled numbered documents detailing instances of Soviet noncompliance, addressing issues as varied as national self-determination, the right to choose one's residence, emigration and the right of return, freedom of belief, the right to monitor human rights, the right to a fair trial, the rights of political prisoners, and the abuse of psychiatry.[31] In time, the group reported on the arrests of its own members.

The Moscow Helsinki Group's establishment was critical to the development of the transnational Helsinki network, which shaped East–West diplomacy in subsequent years. Groups such as the Moscow Helsinki Group dramatized the plight of dissidents and Helsinki monitors in Eastern Europe, inspiring many others to join in pressing for Helsinki implementation and, through their sacrifices, exemplifying the harsh repression of the communist regimes. Additional monitoring groups subsequently formed in Soviet republics such as Georgia, Ukraine, and Lithuania as well as beyond Soviet borders. The Charter 77 movement in Czechoslovakia was one of a number of other human rights initiatives inspired by the Moscow Helsinki Group.

Two years after the Moscow Helsinki Group's establishment, in the context of increasing international attention to Soviet and Eastern European compliance with Helsinki commitments and growing activism by non-state actors on human rights, a United States-based monitoring group made up of private citizens was formed – Helsinki Watch. Helsinki Watch supplemented the developing transnational network devoted to implementation of the Helsinki Final Act. As it later expanded its coverage to Latin America, Africa, and Asia, the organization took on a new name, Human Rights Watch, and now, with Amnesty International, is one of the two most prominent human rights organizations internationally.

Helsinki Watch was effective in focusing international attention on violations of human rights in Eastern Europe by writing comprehensive research reports that were relied upon by policy makers, journalists, and others involved in the cause. The group succeeded in reaching mainstream audiences and elite actors by issuing press releases, writing op-eds, and speaking out publicly. The organization also influenced Conference on Security and Cooperation in Europe (CSCE) diplomats by establishing an ongoing, visible presence at CSCE meetings.

Like Amnesty International, Helsinki Watch offered support to monitoring groups and individuals in Eastern Europe, which strengthened its transnational connections with human rights activists there. In addition, Helsinki Watch facilitated the formation of the International Helsinki Federation for Human Rights (IHF), an umbrella organization of Helsinki monitoring groups, in 1982. The IHF strengthened links with individuals and groups active on Helsinki implementation in Western Europe, enhancing the weight of monitoring groups' criticisms with CSCE diplomats and Eastern European political leaders. It also ensured that Helsinki activism would persist at a time of increasing repression in the Soviet bloc.

Human Rights in the Global South

Throughout much of the Cold War, there was an important distinction between the human rights violations faced by those residing in the Global North versus the Global South. Although abuses such as torture, the denial of civil and political liberties, and impingements on religious freedom affected individuals indiscriminately, those in the Global South faced far greater levels of abuses, racial discrimination, and challenges to their self-determination, due to colonialism.

General Augusto Pinochet's violent overthrow of democratically elected Chilean President Salvador Allende on September 11, 1973 and the abuses that followed shocked those concerned with human rights. Allende's death by suicide during the coup was followed by the murders of around 1,500 of his supporters in the first six weeks of the new regime. Overall, it is likely that 3,200 political opponents were killed, with tens of thousands more imprisoned, tortured, or exiled. Historian Patrick William Kelly writes, "The Pinochet junta effected a tremendous growth in a global human rights-inflected consciousness as solidarity activists concerned with rights abuses in the Americas began to latch onto the rhetoric and ideology of human rights as a means to galvanize the world against state repression."[32] The testimonies of opponents of Pinochet's regime gained an international audience and circulated widely. The rapid transmission of information drove attention to the Chilean case, and the use of evocative testimony enhanced solidarity for those suffering in Chile and elsewhere.

Although, in political scientist Kathryn Sikkink's view, the Cold War impeded or delayed efforts to press for human rights in Latin America, widespread concern at human rights violations in Chile presented a moment at which many moved beyond traditional concerns about communist infiltration in Latin America.[33] According to Sikkink, regional and international indignation was prompted both by the brutality of the coup, including bombings of the presidential palace and the public nature of the military's repression including mass imprisonment of political opponents in the national stadium, as well as by the socialist experiment abruptly cut short under Allende.[34] Attention to human rights abuses perpetrated by Pinochet's regime increased scrutiny of military dictatorships in Brazil and Uruguay.[35] In later years, the "disappeared" in Argentina and victims of paramilitary death squads in Central America would complicate traditional Cold War alliances.[36]

Beyond Southern Rhodesia, one of the most significant examples of racial discrimination was the repressive system of apartheid in South Africa. Apartheid garnered international attention and condemnation when, in June 1976, around 12,000 secondary school students from Soweto, a township in South Africa, marched to protest the requirement that they be educated in Afrikaans, which was the language of their white oppressors. The hardline police response led to widespread rioting, casualties, and property destruction. It also riveted international attention on South Africa's system of racial discrimination, apartheid. Internally, the riots signaled more militant anti-apartheid activism. Regionally, the South African response prompted isolation. Internationally, South Africa was subject to widespread condemnation, including an arms embargo imposed by the UN Security Council. Even United States Secretary of State Henry Kissinger, no strong supporter of human rights, expressed his hope that apartheid would end in the riots' aftermath.[37] The Soweto riots and the subsequent death of Steve Biko, an anti-apartheid activist, in police custody galvanized opposition to the regime.[38] External actors sought to exert pressure through reduced sports contacts, limiting economic links, introducing codes of conduct, and imposing sanctions.[39] Although the Soweto riots and the government's response marked an initial burst of international attention, unlike other human rights moments in the Cold War, they prompted prolonged and sustained anti-apartheid activism in subsequent years.

One of the most egregious violations of human rights during the Cold War was the Cambodian genocide, which was facilitated in part by the geopolitical dynamics of the late Cold War. In the aftermath of its seizure of Phnom Penh, the Cambodian capital, on April 17, 1975 the Khmer Rouge revolutionary movement declared the establishment of Democratic Kampuchea. By cutting Cambodia off from the world, the Khmer Rouge inhibited international awareness of the devastation there, and thus the years of genocide in Cambodia did not attract as much international attention as they arguably should have done.[40] In the course of a massive restructuring of Cambodian society, approximately 1.7 million Cambodians died, out of a total population of around 7 million.[41]

US officials and others found stories of atrocities in Cambodia hard to believe but also maintained that little could be done to address the crisis.[42] Kissinger and United States President Gerald Ford spoke out against the "bloodbath" and "atrocity of major proportions" taking place in Cambodia, but their pronouncements were treated with skepticism, given the administration's credibility and the earlier US record in the country.[43] Jimmy Carter's administration, which might have been expected to respond more forcefully to the genocide, prioritized normalization with China over criticizing Cambodian human rights abuses.[44] Carter did call the Khmer Rouge the "worst violator of human rights in the world today" but did not take action to match that rhetorical condemnation.[45] Self-imposed isolation made it difficult for external actors to influence the Cambodian regime. Fresh memories of the costs of intervening in Southeast Asia also limited the scope of action considered. The Khmer Rouge's killings were stopped only by a Vietnamese invasion in December 1978, which began the Third Indochina War.

The Promise of Jimmy Carter

A high point for those who hoped human rights violations would be taken more seriously at the international level was United States President Jimmy Carter's 1977 inaugural address, when he declared that the United States' commitment to human rights must be "absolute."[46] In this famous pronouncement, Carter made respect for human rights a central element in his foreign policy, asserting that during his presidency, the United States would pay greater attention to the issue in its foreign relations. He followed up his inaugural address with several high-profile actions, including corresponding with Soviet human rights activist Andrei Sakharov and admonishing Eastern European governments over their repressive activities.

Carter was motivated by a range of political and moral impulses. Faced with an eroded domestic foreign policy consensus, Carter believed that championing human rights could help him to gain political support.[47] In the wake of the war in Vietnam, American international prestige had suffered, and Carter concluded that support for human rights could change the United States' reputation. The issue could also serve as an effective rhetorical tool in the Cold War struggle with the Soviets. Finally, Carter's commitment was grounded in his religious and moral worldview.[48]

Carter sought to pressure states to improve their respect for human rights through reduced economic aid and reduced assistance from the World Bank, the International Monetary Fund, and the Inter-American Development Bank. Under previous administrations, the United States had overlooked the poor human rights records of its allies in the Philippines, South Korea, Chile, Brazil, and Argentina, to name a few. Carter's inaugural address seemed to presage a new approach to United States foreign relations, one which would no longer be captive to a Cold War framework when considering foreign governments' human rights records. Historians David F. Schmitz and Vanessa Walker argue that Carter intended to create a "post-Cold War foreign policy" with his emphasis on human rights.[49]

Despite Carter's rhetoric and several early steps to institutionalize attention to human rights in United States foreign policy, his commitment to the issue was overcome by recognition of the limits of American power, arms-control negotiations, and other Cold War priorities. His more muted approach can be identified as early as the July 1977 adoption of a Presidential Review Memorandum (PRM) that outlined a more circumscribed human rights policy than had been pursued initially, in part because the latter had complicated American relations with many governments.[50] After adoption of its human rights PRM, the Carter administration was more careful not to single out particular countries and emphasized the global nature of its focus. Nonetheless, Carter's attention to the issue captivated the American public and others, making it difficult for subsequent administrations to abandon his commitment completely.[51]

Human Rights and the End of the Cold War

The 1980s were not characterized by widespread improvements in human rights as apartheid persisted in South Africa, Poland declared martial law to repress the trade union Solidarity, and widespread extrajudicial killings marked civil wars in Central America.[52] The moment that garnered the greatest international attention, in part due to the presence of international broadcasters, was the Chinese crackdown on protesters in Tiananmen Square. Chinese students gathered in Tiananmen Square to mark the death of popular Chinese leader Hu Yaobang on April 15, 1989. The ongoing demonstration became a forum to protest for various freedoms and reforms, and the crowd swelled to as many as tens of thousands. Protests, including several hundred hunger strikes, were heightened by Mikhail Gorbachev's state visit. After his arrival on May 15, the crowd in the square may have exceeded one million.

On the night of June 3 and 4, the People's Liberation Army stormed the Square with tanks, crushing the protests with terrible human costs. It remains difficult to establish how many were killed in the crackdown. The Chinese government has asserted that injuries exceeded 3,000 and that over 200 individuals, including 36 university students, were killed that night. Western sources, however, remain skeptical of the official Chinese report and most frequently cite the toll as hundreds, and perhaps thousands killed. The crackdown was widely reported in the international press and covered to particularly dramatic effect by CNN, the Cable News Network. The image of a lone man facing a line of tanks resonated widely as an archetypal picture of the repressive nature of the Chinese government.

Although the United States was willing to quickly move beyond Tiananmen, for the sake of other aspects of Sino-American relations, other countries were more hesitant to return to normalcy in their relationship with China. Before Tiananmen, attention to human rights in China was episodic, such as in response to 1987 protests on Tibet, or focused on long-term issues such as religious freedom and the use of torture.[53] After Tiananmen, the Chinese human rights records garnered closer and more sustained attention by governments and NGOs alike.

A more positive, and even triumphal, story has been told about the significance of human rights to international relations in the other critical sphere of communist control at the time: Eastern Europe. The influence on the peaceful end of the Cold War of human rights activism and attention to human rights by high-level political actors linked the two stories more closely in the popular imagination. Efforts, in particular to improve the lives of those living in the Soviet bloc, had a long history but finally came to fruition on January 19, 1989. On that date representatives at the CSCE agreed to the Vienna Concluding Document, which included legitimate commitments to enhance religious freedom, facilitate the spread of information, and address human rights and human contacts in three subsequent conferences. The reforms implemented during the course of the meeting and its culminating agreement signaled a fundamentally new approach to East–West relations.

In the months that followed, protest movements inspired in part by Helsinki principles; reforms formulated in part to comply with Helsinki commitments; and new leaders, many of whom were active in Helsinki groups, all came to the fore. The influence of the Helsinki process was both direct and indirect. Indirectly, ideas about human rights shaped Soviet and Eastern European reform.[54] Directly, internal and external forces advocated for a new relationship between the state and society in Eastern Europe, one that respected the rights and freedoms of the people who lived behind the Iron Curtain.[55] In particular, Western leaders such as United States President Ronald Reagan, Secretary of State George Shultz, and British Prime Minister Margaret Thatcher as well as prominent foreign communists, Gorbachev's advisers, and even Soviet dissidents shaped Soviet General Secretary Mikhail Gorbachev's program of reform. In addition, Pope John Paul II's 1979 and 1983 visits to Poland, his anticommunism, and the Vatican's traditional support for religious freedom all influenced the course of reform in Eastern Europe.

One of the most important ways in which the Helsinki process enabled the revolutions in Eastern Europe was through the development of a "second society" in the Soviet Union, Hungary, Poland, Czechoslovakia, and elsewhere.[56] This "second society" was comprised of people committed to a wide range of political and social causes, including human rights activism, in which their participation uniquely prepared them to implement change and partake in post-communist governance in meaningful ways. Western states, organizations, and individuals supported these movements until Gorbachev's process of liberalization offered the opportunity for reform in Eastern Europe. Once a movement for reform began, organizations, activists, and structures already existed to replace the Communist Party.

A range of groups in Eastern Europe made up this "second society," such as the German Democratic Republic's Initiative for Peace and Human Rights. Ecoglasnost, a Bulgarian NGO, organized protests during a meeting on the environment in Sofia, in late 1989, that undermined the regime. In Czechoslovakia, Charter 77 and the Czechoslovak Helsinki Committee led protests for increased political freedom that quickly gained wider adherents. Václav Havel, a human rights activist and playwright who had risen to political prominence through his involvement with Charter 77, became a leader of these protests, and subsequently president of Czechoslovakia after the end of communism there. In Poland, Solidarity transformed into a political party and its leader, Lech Wałęsa, eventually became president of the Republic of Poland. Activism devoted to labor rights, peace, the environment, and national identity also shaped Eastern Europe as it transitioned from communist rule.

The end of the Cold War raised considerable hope among those in the human rights community that the issue would no longer be overshadowed by geostrategic concerns. Similarly, those disillusioned with or exhausted by Cold War competition anticipated a more moral approach to international relations that privileged concerns about individual human beings. A former Human Rights Watch researcher wrote, "The optimism unleashed by the end of the Cold War ushered in a period of expansion in human rights organizing."[57] In the aftermath of the Cold War, transnational advocacy networks took up new issues. One example was the campaign to ban antipersonnel land mines, which was made possible in many ways by the end of the Cold War. In addition, Amnesty International and Human Rights Watch gained greater geographic spread than ever before, significant financial resources, and considerable media attention. Yet, the end of the Cold War has not ushered in a radically different approach to human rights. Important disparities exist among non-state human rights actors in terms of access to resources, communications expertise, and influential political figures.[58] Furthermore, financial considerations and fears of international terrorism have replaced Cold War priorities as the concerns that now trump high-level attention to human rights.

Notes

1. The most important volume in this respect is Akira Iriye, Petra Goedde and William I. Hitchcock, eds. *The Human Rights Revolution: An International History* (New York: Oxford University Press, 2012), which brings together fifteen new contributions to the field.
2. John Lewis Gaddis, *The Cold War* (London: Penguin, 2007).
3. See for example, Barbara Keys, "Anti-Torture Politics: Amnesty International, the Greek Junta, and the Origins of the Human Rights 'Boom' in the United States," in Akira Iriye, Petra Goedde and William I. Hitchcock, eds. *The Human Rights Revolution: An International History* (New York: Oxford University Press, 2012), 201–21; Kenneth Cmiel, "The Emergence of Human Rights Politics in the United States," *The Journal of American History* 86:3 (December 1999): 1231–50; Mark Philip Bradley, "Approaching the Universal Declaration of Human Rights," in Iriye, Goedde and Hitchcock, eds. *The Human Rights Revolution*, 327–43; Kirsten Sellars, *The Rise and Rise of Human Rights* (London: Sutton Publishing, 2002), 113; and Samuel Moyn, *The Last Utopia: Human Rights in History* (Cambridge, MA: Harvard University Press, 2010).
4. Moyn's book has raised questions about the connections between the 1940s and 1970s "booms." I will not engage directly with his thesis but will suggest that the 1960s and early 1970s prompted more attention to human rights than has been previously recognized. Moyn, *The Last Utopia*, 3–8. Sellars also sees "moments" as a useful way to examine the influence of human rights. Sellars, *The Rise and Rise of Human Rights*, xiii.
5. The most important book on the drafting of the UDHR is Mary Ann Glendon, *A World Made New: Eleanor Roosevelt and the Universal Declaration of Human Rights* (New York: Random House, 2001).
6. Universal Declaration of Human Rights, www.un.org/Overview/rights.html (accessed April 6, 2006).
7. For further discussion of how Cold War tension increasingly overshadowed the promise of the UDHR and the UN, see Carol Anderson, *Eyes Off the Prize: The United Nations and the African American Struggle for Human Rights, 1944–1955* (Cambridge: Cambridge University Press, 2003), 5; and Glendon, *A World Made New*, 198–9.
8. For a recent take on the Bricker Amendment controversy, see Elizabeth Borgwardt, "Constitutionalizing Human Rights: The Rise and Rise of the Nuremberg Principles," Akira Iriye, Petra Goedde and William I. Hitchcock, eds. *The Human Rights Revolution: An International History* (Oxford: Oxford University Press, 2012), 73–83.
9. Roger Normand and Sarah Zaidi, *Human Rights at the UN: The Political History of Universal Justice* Bloomington, IN: Indiana University Press, 2008), 2; Joseph Nye, *Soft Power: The Means to Success in World Politics* (New York: Public Affairs, 2004); and Glendon, *A World Made New*, 236.
10. Moyn, *The Last Utopia*, 130.
11. Akira Iriye, *Global Community: The Role of International Organizations in the Making of the Contemporary World* (Berkeley, CA: University of California Press, 2002), 112–13.
12. Bradley R. Simpson, "Denying the 'First Right': The United States, Indonesia, and the Ranking of Human Rights by the Carter Administration, 1976–1980," *The International History Review* 31: 4 (December 2009): 798–826. The explicit connection between nationalist, anti-colonial movements and human rights, however, is disputed. Moyn does not see a link between decolonization and human rights, arguing that "anticolonial activists rarely invoked the phrase 'human rights' or appealed to the Universal Declaration in particular." Samuel Moyn, "Imperialism, Self-Determination, and the Rise of Human Rights," in Akira Iriye, Petra Goedde and William I. Hitchcock, eds. *The Human Rights Revolution: An International History* (New York: Oxford University Press, 2012), 160–1.
13. Roger Normand and Sarah Zaidi, *Human Rights at the UN: The Political History of Universal Justice* (Bloomington, IN: Indiana University Press, 2008), 141; and Roland Burke, *Decolonization and the Evolution of International Human Rights* (Philadelphia, PA: University of Pennsylvania Press, 2010), 1.
14. Burke, *Decolonization and the Evolution of International Human Rights*, 69.
15. For further discussion, see Sarah B. Snyder, "The Rise of Human Rights during the Johnson Years," in Francis J. Gavin and Mark Atwood Lawrence, eds. *Beyond the Cold War: Lyndon Johnson and the New Global Challenges of the 1960s* (New York: Oxford University Press, 2014); and Chapter 10 (The

United Nations), Administrative History of the Department of State: Volume I, Lyndon Baines Johnson Library, Austin, Texas.
16 Komer to Johnson, October 4, 1965, *Foreign Relations of the United States, 1964–1968: Volume XXIV* (Washington: Government Printing Office, 1999), 814.
17 Thomas J. Noer, *Cold War and Black Liberation: The United States and White Rule in Africa, 1948–1968* (Columbia, MO: University of Missouri Press, 1985), 221–2; and Thomas Borstelmann, *The Cold War and the Color Line: American Race Relations in the Global Arena* (Cambridge, MA: Harvard University Press, 2001), 198–9.
18 Barbara Keys has linked anti-junta activism and Amnesty International's initial reporting on torture as contributing to an upswing of interest internationally in human rights. Keys, "Anti-Torture Politics."
19 Amnesty International, "Situation in Greece," January 27, 1968, Trip to Greece – May 1968, Box 149G.2 (F), Donald M. Fraser Papers, Minnesota Historical Society, St. Paul, Minnesota.
20 Lyons to Colleague, n.d., Greek Committee, 1968, Box 151.H.3.3 (B), Donald M. Fraser Papers.
21 For further discussion, see Snyder, "The Rise of Human Rights during the Johnson Years."
22 UN General Assembly Resolution 2217, December 19, 1966, http://daccess-dds-ny.un.org/doc/RESOLUTION/GEN/NR0/005/20/IMG/NR000520.pdf?OpenElement (accessed July 16, 2012).
23 The conference concluded with agreement on the Proclamation of Tehran, calling for states to uphold their international commitments to respect human rights. Proclamation of Tehran, May 13, 1968, www.unhcr.ch/html/menu3/b/b_tehran.htm (accessed October 30, 2008).
24 Burke, *Decolonization and the Evolution of International Human Rights*, 100–1.
25 Ibid., 93.
26 Tony Judt, *Postwar: A History of Europe since 1945* (New York: Penguin, 2005), 567.
27 H. Gordon Skilling, *Samizdat and an Independent Society in Central and Eastern Europe* (London: Macmillan Press, 1989), 201; and Ludmilla Alexeyeva, *Soviet Dissent: Contemporary Movements for National, Religious, and Human Rights* (Middletown, CT: Wesleyan University Press, 1985), 9.
28 Natan Sharansky, *Fear No Evil* (New York: Random House, 1988), 153, 157. Anatoly Shcharansky changed his name to Natan Sharansky upon his emigration to Israel.
29 Gal Beckerman, *When They Come for Us, We'll Be Gone: The Epic Struggle to Save Soviet Jewry* (New York: Houghton Mifflin Harcourt, 2010).
30 For further discussion, see Sarah B. Snyder, *Human Rights Activism and the End of the Cold War: A Transnational History of the Helsinki Network* (New York: Cambridge University Press, 2011), 53–80 as well as Angela Romano's Chapter 16 in this volume.
31 Ludmilla Alekseeva, "O Dokumentakh Moskovskoi Khel'sinkskoi Gruppi," in Mosckovskai Khel'sinskai Gruppa – Obshchestvo "Memorial," *Dokumenty Moskovskoi Khel'sinkskoi Gruppi, 1976–1982* (Moscow: Mosckovskai Khel'sinskai Gruppa, 2006); Yuri Orlov, *Dangerous Thoughts: Memoirs of a Russian Life*, Thomas P. Whitney, trans. (New York: William Morrow & Company, 1991), 196–7; and Paul Goldberg, *The Final Act: The Dramatic, Revealing Story of the Moscow Helsinki Watch Group* (New York: Morrow, 1988), 85.
32 Patrick William Kelly, "When the People Awake: The Transnational Solidarity Movement, the Pinochet Junta, and the Human Rights Moment of the 1970s," paper presented at *A New Global Morality?: The Politics of Human Rights and Humanitarianism in the 1970s*, Freiburg Institute for Advanced Studies, Freiburg, Germany, June 2010. For further discussion, see Tanya Harmer's Chapter 10 in this volume.
33 Kathryn Sikkink, *Mixed Signals: U.S. Human Rights Policy and Latin America* (Ithaca, NY: Cornell University Press, 2004), 29.
34 Ibid., 108.
35 For further discussion of the impact on activism related to Brazil, see James N. Green, "Clerics, Exiles, and Academics: Opposition to the Brazilian Military Dictatorship in the United States, 1969–1974," *Latin American Politics and Society* 45:1 (Spring 2003): 111.
36 For further discussion, see Sikkink, *Mixed Signals*; Greg Grandin, *The Last Colonial Massacre: Latin America in the Cold War* (London: University of Chicago Press, 2004); Jason M. Colby, "'A Chasm of Values and Outlook': The Carter Administration's Human Rights Policy in Guatemala," *Peace & Change* 35:4 (October 2010): 561–93; William Michael Schmidli, "Human Rights and the Cold War: The Campaign to Halt the Argentine 'Dirty War,'" *Cold War History* 12:2 (2012): 345–65; and Jean H. Quataert, *Advocating Dignity: Human Rights Mobilizations in Global Politics* (Philadelphia, PA: University of Pennsylvania Press, 2009), 109–40.

37 James Barber and John Barratt, *South Africa's Foreign Policy: The Search for Status and Security, 1945–1988* (Cambridge: Cambridge University Press, 1990), 204, 214.
38 Barber and Barratt, *South Africa's Foreign Policy*, 211; and Aryeh Neier, *The International Human Rights Movement: A History* (Princeton, NJ: Princeton University Press, 2012), 3–4.
39 Barber and Barratt, *South Africa's Foreign Policy*, 228–9.
40 Samantha Power, *"A Problem from Hell:" America and the Age of Genocide* (New York: Harper Perennial, 2002), 90.
41 Kenton Clymer, "Jimmy Carter, Human Rights, and Cambodia," *Diplomatic History* 27:2 (April 2003): 247.
42 Power, *"A Problem from Hell"* 115, 123.
43 Ibid.,108.
44 Ibid.,127; and Clymer, "Jimmy Carter, Human Rights, and Cambodia," 255–6, 258.
45 Clymer, "Jimmy Carter, Human Rights, and Cambodia," 246.
46 Jimmy Carter, "Inaugural Address," January 20, 1977, *American Presidency Project*, http://www.presidency.ucsb.edu/ws/?pid=6575 (accessed July 16, 2012).
47 Elizabeth Drew, "A Reporter at Large: Human Rights," *The New Yorker*, July 18, 1977, 38; and David Skidmore, *Reversing Course: Carter's Foreign Policy, Domestic Politics, and the Failure of Reform* (Nashville, TN: Vanderbilt University Press, 1996), 84, 135.
48 Joshua Muravchik, *Uncertain Crusade: Jimmy Carter and the Dilemmas of Human Rights Policy* (Lanham, MD: Hamilton Press, 1986), 7; Robert A. Strong, *Working in the World: Jimmy Carter and the Making of American Foreign Policy* (Baton Rouge, LA: Louisiana State University Press, 2000), 73; and Alexander M. Haig, Jr. with Charles McCarry, *Inner Circles: How America Changed the World: A Memoir* (New York: Warner Books, 1992), 531.
49 David F. Schmitz and Vanessa Walker, "Jimmy Carter and the Foreign Policy of Human Rights: The Development of a Post-Cold War Foreign Policy," *Diplomatic History* 28 (January 2004): 113, 117.
50 Presidential Review Memorandum/NSC-28: Human Rights, July 7, 1977, Box 19, Robert J. Lipshutz Files, Jimmy Carter Library, Atlanta, Georgia; and Hauke Hartmann, "US Human Rights Policy Under Carter and Reagan, 1977–1981," *Human Rights Quarterly* 23 (2001): 410.
51 Moyn quantifies this resonance by noting that the term "human rights" was printed in the *New York Times* in 1977 five times more frequently than in any previous year. Moyn, *The Last Utopia*, 4.
52 For further discussion see Gregory F. Domber's Chapter 27 in this volume and Grandin, *The Last Colonial Massacre*.
53 Rosemary Foot, *Rights Beyond Borders: The Global Community and the Struggle over Human Rights in China* (New York: Oxford University Press, 2000), 105, 113.
54 For further discussion of the influence of dissidence on Soviet reform, see Robert Horvath, *The Legacy of Soviet Dissent: Dissidents, Democratisation and Radical Nationalism in Russia* (New York: RoutledgeCurzon, 2005), 1, 3, 237.
55 For further discussion of the influence of Helsinki activism, see Snyder, *Human Rights Activism and the End of the Cold War*.
56 Janie Leatherman, *From Cold War to Democratic Peace: Third Parties, Peaceful Change, and the OSCE* (Syracuse, NY: Syracuse University Press, 2003), 222; Sabrina P. Ramet, *Social Currents in Eastern Europe: The Sources and Consequences of the Great Transformation* (Durham, NC: Duke University Press, 1995), 317; Timothy Garton Ash, *The Magic Lantern: The Revolution of '89 Witnessed in Warsaw, Budapest, Berlin and Prague* (New York: Vintage Books, 1993), 14; J. F. Brown, *Surge to Freedom: The End of Communist Rule in Eastern Europe* (Durham: Duke University Press, 1991), 168; Grzegorz Ekiert and Jan Kubik, *Rebellious Civil Society: Popular Protest and Democratic Consolidation in Poland, 1989–1993* (Ann Arbor: The University of Michigan Press, 1999), 44; Mark R. Beissinger, "Nationalism and the Collapse of Soviet Communism," *Contemporary European History* 18:3 (2009): 331–47; and Padraic Kenney, *A Carnival of Revolution: Central Europe 1989* (Princeton, NJ: Princeton University Press, 2002).
57 Julie Mertus, "Applying the Gatekeeper Model of Human Rights Activism: The U.S.-Based Movement for LGBT Rights," in Clifford Bob, ed. *The International Struggle for New Human Rights* (Philadelphia, PA: University of Pennsylvania Press, 2009), 58.
58 Clifford Bob, "Globalization and the Social Construction of Human Rights Campaigns," in Alison Brysk, ed. *Globalization and Human Rights* (London: University of California Press, 2002), 140–1; and Daphneé Josselin and William Wallace, "Non-state actors in World Politics: the Lessons," in Daphneé Josselin and William Wallace, eds. *Non-State Actors in World Politics* (Basingstoke: Palgrave, 2001), 256.

18
U.S. SCIENTISTS AND THE COLD WAR

Paul Rubinson

The totalizing nature of the Cold War in the United States meant that all societal institutions were affected by the bipolar ideological conflict. As World War II drew to a close, U.S. culture, economy, politics, and religion all began to confront both the apparent communist menace overseas and the domestic demand for anticommunist conformity. Much like other bedrocks of the American nation at this time, science could not stand aside. As science and engineering produced the dramatic innovations of the Cold War (including lasers, computers, and nuclear missiles), leaders of the scientific community also wrestled over the direction of science and the nation.

While the technological products of science and engineering drove the arms race, many influential scientists themselves saw the Cold War as a dilemma. On the one hand, the militarization of U.S. society after World War II provided scientists with seemingly limitless research funding, while the role of the atomic bomb in ending the war gave scientists – physicists especially – an aura of heroism. Scientists accordingly played a large part in developing and defending the national security state. With Joseph Stalin leading an increasingly hostile Soviet Union, many U.S. scientists felt justified in continuing weapons work, a sentiment that helped to staff weapons laboratories throughout the Cold War.

At the same time, many scientists grew troubled by the increasing connections between science and the military. Linking science with nationalism and national security violated the internationalist ideals of science, which encouraged cooperation across national borders. The race to build an atomic bomb during World War II was meant to be an exception to the normally friendly global competition in pursuit of scientific knowledge. Many scientists, feeling empowered by growing public respect for scientific expertise, felt they could help end the Cold War and encourage peace by fusing the internationalism of science with progressive, liberal values.

Try as they might, scientific activists ultimately found it difficult to transcend the Cold War. Like any group, scientists were not a homogenous group. A powerful segment of scientists actively sought to mobilize science in the name of national security and the nuclear arms race. Not surprisingly, those scientists working to end the arms race faced a rigid Cold War consensus in the United States, whose government resisted dissent aimed against the nation's nuclear arsenal, even as presidents searched for a way out of the Cold War. Scientists proved to be a powerful, influential group, but one shaped by the Cold War despite continued attempts to transcend it.

Creating and Questioning Atomic Weapons

Gar Alperovitz and other historians have characterized the atomic bomb as the first salvo in the Cold War with the Soviet Union. Historians have challenged the notion of "atomic diplomacy" but they have not overturned the centrality of the atomic bomb in the origins of the Cold War. Credited with building the "winning weapon," scientists – mostly physicists – rose to great prominence immediately after the war. The activities of politically engaged scientists during the Cold War reflected their legacies as both creators of atomic weapons and would-be sages who held ultimate knowledge of nuclear weapons.[1]

Scientists from around the world worked to develop an atomic bomb in the United States. Refugees from the Nazi regime in Europe, including Enrico Fermi (Italy), Leo Szilard (Hungary), Edward Teller (Hungary), and Hans Bethe (Germany), relocated to the United States, where they ultimately convinced the U.S. government to undertake an atomic bomb program. The Manhattan Project eventually counted among its leaders Ernest Lawrence and J. Robert Oppenheimer, two of the leading physicists in the United States. Motivated by fear of a German atomic bomb and sharing the same eagerness to participate in the war that swept through the populace of the United States, scientists worked under military discipline to produce a massive weapon. As the bomb grew closer to completion, the military constructed a laboratory for assembling the bomb in Los Alamos, New Mexico, with Oppenheimer as director. Notably, the participants voiced hardly any dissent against developing an atomic weapon into 1945. Although some scientists questioned "the impact of the Gadget on civilization," they ultimately reconciled their concerns about building and using the bomb.[2] The lone exception, Joseph Rotblat, left Los Alamos after the German surrender rather than work on an atomic bomb for use against Japan, a nation that no one feared would develop an atomic weapon.[3] For almost all the other Manhattan Project scientists, work continued apace – speeded up, actually – in order to see that the bomb would be used in time to play a role in the war.

The seemingly inevitable construction and use of the bomb did not keep a few thoughtful scientists from pondering the future of a world in which atomic weapons existed. Particularly thoughtful was Leo Szilard, the Hungarian physicist who originally conceived of a nuclear chain reaction. From the Metallurgical Lab in Chicago, Szilard distributed a petition to his fellow scientists about the "moral responsibilities" involved in using the bomb. Szilard's petition urged President Truman to reconsider the use of the bomb against Japan without a public warning. He wrote: "a nation which sets the precedent of using these newly liberated forces of nature for purposes of destruction may have to bear the responsibility of opening the door to an era of devastation on an unimaginable scale."[4] After it garnered over one hundred signatures, the charismatic Oppenheimer quashed the petition at Los Alamos; Truman never received it. Successive attempts by scientists to shape atomic policy met with similarly uneven results.

Even as the bombs were prepped for use against Japan, the budding U.S.–Soviet rivalry heavily influenced scientists' and politicians' thinking about the atomic bomb. Meeting with Stalin at Potsdam in July 1945, Truman needed Soviet help in fighting Japan, yet feared allowing the Soviet dictator to extend his influence in East Asia. Scientists, meanwhile, including the legendary Niels Bohr, had hoped that Truman and Stalin might discuss the future of atomic weapons seriously and cautiously. But the White House quickly dismissed the internationalist ideas that scientists developed about the postwar era and atomic weapons, even though scientists had relative success in getting Secretary of War Henry Stimson to consider their proposals. After a successful test of the A-bomb at Los Alamos, Truman grew more confident that he could proceed without Stalin, simply and ominously telling the Soviet leader that the United States had acquired a significant weapon. This approach differed vastly from what many elite scientists, including Bohr, Oppenheimer, and Szilard, wanted; for the remainder of the Cold War, the bomb would become a symbol of national might, rather than an inspiration for shared global cooperation. In the following weeks, two atomic bombs were dropped on Japan, the Soviet A-bomb program sped up, and the arms race began.

As the 1940s progressed, the atomic bomb essentially mirrored the progress of the Cold War itself. As the arms race increased, the Cold War intensified. When the superpowers considered arms control, détente and reconciliation were on the horizon. In 1946 Oppenheimer expressed the desire for international control of atomic energy as a means of arms control. He influenced David Lilienthal, who, under White House orders, developed a plan for United Nations control of atomic energy based on Oppenheimer's ideas. But the newly evolving national security state was not willing to take away the military's ultimate trump card. Under the revisions of Truman's representative Bernard Baruch, the Lilienthal Plan became an attempt to strangle the Soviet atomic weapons program and make permanent the superiority of the U.S. atomic arsenal. The Soviets quickly rejected the hollow proposal, as national security trumped the impulse of scientific internationalism and cooperation.

Then, in August 1949, the Soviet Union successfully detonated an atomic bomb, demonstrating its ability to match the United States in the arms race. Adding to international tension in the months after were the revelations of atomic spies, including Klaus Fuchs, David Greenglass, and Julius Rosenberg, who had managed to infiltrate the Manhattan Project and share atomic secrets with the Soviets. In the context of the Red Scare, opposition to nuclear weapons became a suspicious cause to embrace. Amidst this turmoil, U.S. scientists and policy makers debated the next step in the arms race.

A Bigger Bomb

The size of the world's nuclear arsenals served throughout the Cold War as a barometer of international tension. In 1947 the editors of the *Bulletin of the Atomic Scientists* made this connection explicit by creating their "doomsday clock," which ticked closer to or further from apocalyptic midnight according to current geopolitical conflicts. After the Soviet development of an A-bomb, science pointed the way to the next leap in nuclear weapons development: a so-called Super bomb based on nuclear fusion, exponentially more powerful than the fission bomb. As with the atomic bomb, scientists (notably Edward Teller and Ernest Lawrence) pushed the U.S. government to pursue this thermonuclear weapon, hoping to regain the nuclear advantage over the Soviet Union. But, unlike the atomic bomb, U.S. scientists varied greatly in their support and enthusiasm for the new weapon. Concern ranged from the purely technical to the moral implications of the killing power of a Super bomb. Adding confusion to the mix was a scientific controversy over the design of the bomb itself. Ultimately the U.S. government overlooked, ignored, and in some cases punished those who questioned the wisdom of a thermonuclear weapon.

Fusing atoms together promised to release even more energy than splitting the atom through fission, and scientists had conceived of a fusion bomb even as they discussed how to build an atomic one in the mid-1940s. Pursuit of the Super was only gently pursued at Los Alamos during World War II, but as soon as that conflict ended, Teller and others argued that, rather than demobilize, Los Alamos scientists should embark on another crash program in pursuit of the Super. The Soviets, these advocates believed, would understand only the threat of force and would certainly make their own Super. In the aftermath of the Soviet A-bomb test, influential figures from the U.S. scientific and political establishments debated the Super. A surprising number of scientists lined up against it, including James B. Conant, Oppenheimer, and a majority of science advisors working for the Atomic Energy Commission (AEC). They called it "a weapon of genocide" and "necessarily an evil thing considered in any light … Its use would put the United States in a bad moral position relative to the peoples of the world."[5] Ultimately the decision was a presidential one and, for Truman, Cold War concerns prevailed. Los Alamos was ordered to pursue a crash program to develop the Super.

It is important to point out that the scientific opposition was to the Super, a specific bomb design that promised fusion bombs of theoretically unlimited explosive power. Dissent against the Super was often a matter of scale rather than of strict antinuclearism. Oppenheimer, for example, eagerly advocated a large atomic bomb build-up, arguing that the genocidal power of the Super was impractical and excessive, while trying to build the weapon would be detrimental to the nation's atomic bomb stockpile. When the Super design proved unfeasible, and was replaced with the less-powerful (but still awesome) Hydrogen bomb design, many critics, including Oppenheimer, changed their minds and supported development of the new weapon. Others relented according to circumstances: Hans Bethe joined Los Alamos to work on the bomb after the Korean War broke out, despite having previously declared the weapon "morally wrong and unwise."[6]

This subtlety and flexibility about bomb design and circumstance was lost on government officials, who in Red Scare fashion saw questions about nuclear weapons in strictly yes-or-no terms. As the Red Scare escalated, scientists with leftist pasts were criticized, and even the influential Oppenheimer suffered the humiliating removal of his security clearance for his questioning of the Super. Although Oppenheimer was far from an antinuclear advocate, his punishment served to demonstrate the penalties of questioning the commitment to ever more powerful nuclear weapons.

Nuclear Testing and the Test Ban

While the H-bomb promised to defend the United States against the Soviet threat, it also appeared to be somewhat self-defeating. Testing the device (continually necessary in order to stay ahead in the arms race) proved lethal, releasing radioactive fallout and harming those very people it was intended to protect. After H-bomb testing began in the Pacific, islanders showed signs of radioactive poisoning. When the Atomic Energy Commission moved testing to a site in Nevada, residents of nearby towns began to suffer as well. By the middle of the decade, public concern about nuclear fallout had become so great that the Democratic candidate for president in 1956, Adlai Stevenson, endorsed a ban on nuclear testing. Influential scientists supported the idea, but the scientific community remained divided over its relationship with nuclear weapons, as equally influential supporters rushed to defend and even expand testing, promising new, safe weapons that released little or no fallout.

For a number of scientists, the value of nuclear weapons did not justify the increased threat they posed to the public. As the Red Scare ended it became once again acceptable (to an extent) to question the danger of the arms race. No scientists who hoped to be taken seriously by the government argued for the complete abolition of nuclear weapons. But the influence that nuclear advocates like Edward Teller had in Congress, the Pentagon, and the AEC, convinced President Eisenhower to bring in science advisors with a different point of view. Thus he formed the President's Science Advisory Committee (PSAC), created after the Soviet launch of *Sputnik* sparked a crisis of confidence in the United States. PSAC scientists hoped to restrain the arms race by directly influencing the president. As Hans Bethe put it, "we now have a mechanism to get the ideas of scientists directly to the government."[7] Although the PSAC advised the president on a myriad of scientific and technical issues, including space exploration and federal funding of research, the committee's scientists mainly focused on developing methods of monitoring a potential nuclear test ban with the Soviet Union.

Of course, many U.S. scientists out of the limelight worked in near anonymity, neither publicly questioning nor hindering the arms race. Far from it, in fact, as a new generation of scientists and engineers, trained in the days of lavish funding for academic institutions, created rockets, missiles, and satellites. These children of Big Science accelerated the space race and the arms race, staffing Los Alamos and the second national weapons lab in Livermore, California, and working for countless military contractors. Far outnumbering the scientists mobilizing against nuclear weapons, this workforce powered the military-industrial complex and the "scientific-technological elite" that Eisenhower warned the American people about on his way out of office.[8]

Outside of government circles, individual scientists continued to crusade against nuclear weapons in an attempt to counter the militarization of U.S. science. Biologist Barry Commoner and the Committee on Public Information took an apolitical approach, demonstrating the presence of radioactivity in milk and children's teeth, building a sizable reform movement in favor of restricting testing. Other scientists, geneticist Ralph Lapp for example, made their case in the *Bulletin of the Atomic Scientists* with an array of strictly scientific arguments discussing the potential threats of nuclear fallout.

In stark contrast stood Linus Pauling, the premier chemist of his age (winner of the 1954 Nobel Prize in Chemistry), and in equal parts scientist and crusader. While not a geneticist, Pauling believed he had enough expertise as a chemist to prove that fallout from nuclear testing caused harmful genetic mutations and leukemia. Unlike other scientific critics of nuclear weapons during the 1950s and 1960s, Pauling eagerly challenged the federal government as well as those scientists whom he believed responsible for promoting nuclear weapons. His methods of protest were many: scientific articles, lawsuits, protest marches, and even a petition signed by over 11,000 scientists and delivered to the United Nations. "Each nuclear bomb test spreads an added burden of radioactive elements over every part of the world," the petition read. "Each added amount of radiation causes damage to the health of human beings all over the world and causes damage to the pool of human germ plasm such as to lead to an increase in the number of seriously defective children that will be born in future generations."[9] These actions earned Pauling an impressive following and huge public credibility. As with previous critics of nuclear weapons, Pauling drew great authority from his immense scientific reputation, and sought to link science with progressive thought and causes. Late in life he explained: "I thought that people trained to think as scientists might make valuable contributions in searching for solutions to problems in society and in shaping the human future in a positive way."[10]

Accused by his rivals (and some historians) of being loose with data, Pauling suffered because he was an outsider. Congress, fearing his potent antinuclear campaign, slandered him as a red, and the State Department restricted his travel. Pronuclear scientists like Teller challenged him publicly, and privately asked scientific organizations not to give him a platform from which to proselytize. Appealing to the American Chemical Society (which had invited Pauling to give a talk in 1963), Teller wrote, "It certainly is inappropriate to give Linus Pauling a free chance to make propaganda in the Chemical Society," and "the Chemical Society is not the right forum and I also find that Dr. Pauling has gone in his pronouncements beyond limits of really good taste."[11]

Much less public were the efforts of the Pugwash scientists, named after the Nova Scotia village where they first met in 1957. They convened after Albert Einstein and Bertrand Russell issued a manifesto urging scientists to "assemble, not as members of this or that nation, continent, or creed, but as human beings, members of the species Man, whose continued existence is in doubt."[12] Joseph Rotblat took up this charge, gathering scientists from both sides of the Iron Curtain to discuss ways to end the arms race and the Cold War. Relying on their elite status, these scientists hoped to act as catalysts to official diplomacy. One Soviet participant defiantly declared, "Diplomacy is an antiquated vehicle. Our role is to remove obstacles from the path of this antique chariot."[13] Although far less confrontational than Pauling, as they hoped to gain the ear of their governments, Pugwash scientists still embraced the internationalism of science. U.S. Pugwash relayed valuable information from their Soviet peers to the Kennedy administration during its pursuit of a test ban, while political scientist Matthew Evangelista has shown that Soviet Pugwash was able to influence policy under Khrushchev.[14]

Although Adlai Stevenson lost the 1956 election, calls for a test ban remained loud. With Pauling agitating in public, the PSAC working from within the Eisenhower administration, and Pugwash trying to work behind the scenes, a nuclear test ban gained strong political momentum. Perhaps most influential for Eisenhower were his PSAC scientists, who provided him with scientific assurances that a ban would not harm U.S. national security. On the Soviet side, official rhetoric had always been cynically antinuclear, characterizing nuclear weapons as a tool of imperialists and capitalists, while maintaining that Soviet weapons were strictly defensive. When a test ban became a legitimate possibility, therefore, the Soviets could not really object. Edging tentatively toward a test ban, each side unilaterally halted testing in 1958, a moratorium that would last until September 1961. But Cold War tensions, including the U-2 affair, ultimately thwarted Eisenhower's attempt to reach a formal agreement with Khrushchev. In addition, Teller and other pronuclear scientists promised that they could make clean weapons that would produce no fallout, a claim with just enough credibility to make Eisenhower question the need for a test ban.

Upon entering the White House, John F. Kennedy inherited Eisenhower's testing controversy, and though he angered antinuclear activists by ending the moratorium in 1961 (albeit following the Soviet lead), he ultimately pursued a test ban, particularly after the Cuban Missile Crisis of 1962. In the quest for a test ban he was influenced by Jerome Wiesner, his personal science advisor and participant in several Pugwash meetings. Wiesner convinced Kennedy of the danger of nuclear fallout and that a test ban would help protect both national security and the U.S. public – as well as U.S. nuclear superiority. In August 1963 a team of U.S. diplomats traveled to Moscow to sign the Limited Test Ban Treaty, which banned nuclear testing in the atmosphere, in space, and in the ocean; testing underground remained perfectly acceptable. About a month later the U.S. Senate ratified the treaty after an occasionally heated debate involving numerous representatives of the scientific community. Although most of the scientists who testified privately hoped the treaty would slow the nuclear arms race, the primary rationale they offered was that the treaty would not harm U.S. national security or the superiority of the U.S. nuclear arsenal.

Advocates of arms control heralded the test ban treaty, though it was far from perfect. While the restriction of tests to beneath the earth's surface all but eliminated the threat of fallout (a huge accomplishment), the measure did not lead to a dramatic decline in the arms race. In order to get the Senate's approval for the test ban, the Kennedy administration actually promised that the testing and development of nuclear weapons would continue to be a priority. In fact, testing actually increased when it moved underground. One Pugwash scientist later referred to the test ban as an "arms control disaster."[15]

Beyond Disarmament

A succession of arms control treaties followed in the years after the test ban: the Nonproliferation Treaty, the Antiballistic Missile Treaty, and the Strategic Arms Limitation Talks Treaty.

Though these measures reflected the increasingly cordial détente between the United States and Soviet Union, none of them actually eliminated nuclear weapons from the face of the earth. The rise of détente after the Cuban Missile Crisis and the Test Ban Treaty did much to quell the public's concern about the arms race and nuclear fallout. Consequently, demands for arms control stemmed more from diplomatic initiatives than grassroots protest. Scientists nevertheless remained interested in influencing the Cold War conflicts and controversies of the time. On the whole, and with notable exceptions, these efforts leaned toward the progressive, liberal side of Cold War conflicts.

For scientists who continued to be interested in ending the Cold War, the bloated nuclear arsenals of the superpowers were the most glaring problem. But mutual trust seemed to be an even bigger obstacle to achieving real disarmament. Furthermore, although détente temporarily calmed Cold War conflicts in Europe, the Third World appeared as dangerous and destabilizing as ever, as conflicts in Latin America, Africa, and particularly Southeast Asia threatened to escalate. Biophysicist Eugene Rabinowitch, the head of U.S. Pugwash, ambitiously envisioned solving all these problems by relying on the internationalist ideals of science. Specifically, Rabinowitch proposed a move toward U.S.–Soviet cooperation in massive scientific endeavors such as space exploration and assistance to developing nations. Cooperation, Rabinowitch envisioned, would help to advance science and allow the superpowers to work together; in the process, they would learn to trust each other. In this improved atmosphere, the superpowers could pursue real disarmament.

Hoping for "a change of mentality, for the replacement of obsolete attitudes,"[16] Rabinowitch organized Pugwash conferences in Ethiopia and India that explored the needs of developing nations and featured the participation of scientists from Third World nations. The Addis Ababa, Ethiopia conference concentrated on "Science in Aid of Developing Countries," with eighty-six scientists representing thirty-one countries, over half coming from Africa, Asia, and Latin America. But other scientists in Pugwash resisted Rabinowitch's shift and jealously guarded the role they played as nuclear weapons experts. As late as 1970, Rabinowitch was stating that "development of the underdeveloped countries is the key to the future of mankind."[17] But Rabinowitch ultimately grew frustrated by Pugwash's attitudes toward the development problem, blaming Soviet recalcitrance as well as Pugwash Secretary General Joseph Rotblat, who preferred to retain nuclear disarmament as Pugwash's priority. Obviously, there was no guarantee that Rabinowitch's plan would have had its intended effect, but the resistance to it shows how entrenched the scientific disarmament movement had become.

In the late 1960s, the urgency of the Vietnam War interrupted the efforts of Pugwash, as it did the rest of society. After years of serving as experts on issues related to national security and nuclear weapons, it seemed natural for influential U.S. scientists to weigh in on the Vietnam conflict. Consulted as experts by the White House, some PSAC scientists developed technology to assist U.S. military goals in Vietnam. But as the war dragged on, relations between the White House and U.S. science grew increasingly tense. Presidential science advisor Don Hornig walked a tightrope trying to keep the White House from alienating scientists over Vietnam, asking the president not to "discount the interest and influence of the scientific community ... They are among the most worried and hard to deal with in connection with Viet Nam and we continue to need their support."[18]

As the war continued, it revealed tensions within U.S. science itself. A number of scientists cut ties with the government in protest of the war, including former science advisor under Eisenhower, George Kistiakowsky, who canceled a consulting contract with the Pentagon.[19] The New Left's increasing disdain for both physical and social scientists associated with defense funding led to a loss in scientists' public authority. Mock trials punished scientists in effigy, and leftist science groups such as the Union of Concerned Scientists and Science for the People emerged to challenge not only the discipline's links to the military–industrial complex, but also its traditions of sexism and class privilege.[20] The scientific community was at odds with the public, the government, and itself; after the resignation of two science advisors, President Richard Nixon abolished the PSAC altogether.

Although extremely divisive, the Vietnam War did not dim the enthusiasm of politically active scientists in the 1970s. Much more in line with the internationalist scientific tradition was the human rights issue that reshaped the Cold War in its final years. The Helsinki Final Act of 1975 established measures to monitor the status of human rights in the Eastern bloc, and also emphasized East–West cooperation on science and technology in the internationalist tradition. But cooperation in scientific exchange programs exposed U.S. scientists to Soviet human rights abuse of their scientific peers. Upset at the deplorable treatment of prominent scientific dissidents including Andrei Sakharov, Yuri Orlov, and Anatloly Scharansky, U.S. scientists began to boycott scientific exchanges with the Soviets, issued statements of solidarity at academic conferences, and formed committees aimed at pursuing human rights action, such as the Human Rights Committee of the National Academy of Sciences (NAS). When Soviet authorities exiled Sakharov to Gorky for criticizing the invasion of Afghanistan, the NAS president declared, "These actions represent, from our perspective, an intrusion upon the human rights and scientific activities of an eminent scientist."[21] John T. Edsall, of Harvard University, echoed this new human rights mindset of scientists when he protested the imprisonment of Orlov and Scharansky: "These profoundly disturbing events seem to belong to an alien world that repels us. We are concerned with the maintenance of human rights throughout the world, and as a scientific community we are particularly concerned with the defence of the rights of our fellow scientists."[22] Defending human rights proved much less controversial than opposing nuclear weapons, scientists discovered, as numerous segments of U.S. society were eager to criticize the Soviets in the years after détente ended, including both Democrats and Republicans.

Scientific human rights activism extended beyond the Soviet Union. While boycotting scientific conferences and programs in countries with poor human rights records was common, other scientists chose to confront the perpetrators of human rights abuses directly. At the 1978 International Cancer Congress (ICC) in Buenos Aires, a few dozen scientists and doctors took the opportunity to attend Catholic mass with the families of the "disappeared," discussed their concerns with human rights activists, and even brought up the issue during a meeting with an official in the Foreign Ministry. A statement at the end of the ICC declared, "If Argentina wishes to continue its distinguished role in the world community of science … improvement [in human rights] is mandatory."[23] Like so many causes linked to the Cold War, however, scientists' human rights activism faded quickly after the end of the U.S.–Soviet conflict.

Nuclear Revival in the 1980s

The early 1980s saw a revival of the Cold War after the end of détente. With the Soviet incursion in Afghanistan, the bipolar rivalry intensified and brought an end to the superpowers' pursuit of arms control. When the United States announced plans to deploy nuclear cruise missiles in Western Europe and the Soviet Union sent SS-20 missiles to Eastern Europe, the antinuclear movement was reborn. Grassroots movements appeared in the United States on a large scale, and were dwarfed by even larger protests across Europe in the early 1980s. Interestingly, however, as grassroots sentiment against nuclear weapons rose in strength, scientists played less and less of a public role as nuclear dissenters. Scientists still spoke with authority; Carl Sagan's "nuclear winter" campaign convinced many that a nuclear war would so disrupt the global climate that even those humans far removed from a nuclear war would likely freeze or starve in the post-apocalyptic environment. But for the most part, scientists had been replaced as leading arms controllers by professional arms-control policy experts, such as Randall Forsberg, who advocated a Nuclear Freeze that would "stop the nuclear arms race quite literally, by stopping the development and production of all nuclear-weapon systems" in the United States and Soviet Union.[24] Medical professionals, including the International Physicians for the Prevention of Nuclear War, as well as Helen Caldecott and the Physicians for Social Responsibility, provided a more human perspective on the nuclear arms race, contrasting with the more technical arguments of antinuclear scientists. Amidst this outpouring of antinuclear sentiment, scientists were but one voice among many. Having for decades pushed for limited arms-control measures, antinuclear scientists suddenly appeared as moderates in the movement against nuclear weapons, as when long-time arms-control advocate Hans Bethe declared, "I don't endorse the freeze as an actual measure, but I do endorse it as an easily understood public movement."[25]

But the arms race remained central to the Cold War in the 1980s, and with the development of new, destabilizing weapons systems, scientists still served as expert critics and advocates of nuclear weapons. The Strategic Defense Initiative (SDI), envisioned as a system of satellite-based lasers capable of blasting incoming enemy missiles, sparked the most controversy. Largely conceived of and promoted by Edward Teller, the SDI served as a purely defensive measure, in the eyes of its defenders, "to replace the truly horrible idea of mutual assured destruction."[26] Critics of the SDI, however, maintained that defensive weapons could easily be turned into offensive ones. Resistance to the SDI came from the expected circles of scientists, including Sagan and Bethe, but also from newer disciplines such as computer science. The arguments leveled against the SDI focused mainly on its technical flaws, including its expense, complexity, and reliability. A system that defended against, say, 90 percent of incoming missiles – a solid success rate by many standards – meant little when a single warhead could kill millions. With Ronald Reagan squarely in favor of the SDI, scientists' objections fell largely on deaf ears, and the end of the Cold War, starting in 1989, ensured a quick decline in the public's interest in the SDI and nuclear weapons in general.

The Cold War's end dampened much scientific activism, as nuclear weapons appeared to be less of a threat with the Soviet Union dissolved. But scientists today occupy a similarly complicated place as they did during the Cold War. As public authorities, they frequently weigh in on public policy, particularly regarding environmental issues. But this expertise is often contested – intellectual brilliance and professional accomplishments are no guarantee of a sympathetic ear from the public, media, or Congress. Much of this comes from scientists' role in the debate over Cold War policy: as the global conflict redefined scientists' relation to society and its problems, it also made scientists more vulnerable to the whims, biases, and contradictions of politics.

Notes

1 Gar Alperovitz, *Atomic Diplomacy: Hiroshima and Potsdam: The Use of the Atomic Bomb and the American Confrontation with Soviet Power* (New York: Vintage, 1965); Martin Sherwin, *A World Destroyed: Hiroshima and Its Legacies*, 3rd edition (Stanford, CA: Stanford University Press, 2003); Gregg Herken, *The Winning Weapon: The Atomic Bomb in the Cold War, 1945–50* (New York: Vintage, 1982).

2 Los Alamos scientist Robert Wilson convened a meeting by this name. See Charles Thorpe, *Oppenheimer: The Tragic Intellect* (Chicago: University of Chicago Press, 2006), 154–55, and Kai Bird and Martin J. Sherwin, *American Prometheus: The Triumph and Tragedy of J. Robert Oppenheimer* (New York: Alfred A. Knopf, 2005), 287–89.

3 Joseph Rotblat, "Leaving the Bomb Project," *Bulletin of the Atomic Scientists*, Vol. 41, No. 7, August 1985, 16–19.
4 "A Petition to the President of the United States," reprinted in Cynthia Kelly, ed., *The Manhattan Project: The Birth of the Atomic Bomb in the Words of Its Creators, Eyewitnesses, and Historians* (New York: Black Dog & Leventhal, 2007), 291–93.
5 Robert C. Williams and Philip L. Cantelon, eds., *The American Atom: A Documentary History of Nuclear Policies from the Discovery of Fission to the Present, 1939–1984* (Philadelphia, PA: University of Pennsylvania Press, 1984), 126–27. The AEC's science advisors produced two recommendations: a majority that opposed the Super, and a minority that opposed the Super with the caveat that if the Soviet Union went forward with the H-bomb, the United States should follow suit.
6 Bethe to Norris Bradbury, Folder: Bethe, Hans A., Box 273: Correspondence, Personal, Edward Teller Papers, Hoover Institution, Stanford University (ET Papers).
7 Bethe to Rabinowitch, Feb. 12, 1958, Box 8, Folder 16, Eugene I. Rabinowitch Papers, Regenstein Library, University of Chicago (ER Papers).
8 "Farewell Radio and Television Address to the American People, January 17, 1961," *Public Papers of the Presidents of the United States: Dwight D. Eisenhower, 1960–61* (Washington, DC: U.S. Government Printing Office, 1961), 1035–40.
9 Pauling to Dag Hammarskjöld, Jan. 13, 1958, LP Peace 5: Nuclear Bomb Test and Proliferation Petition, 5.002: *An Appeal by Scientists to the Governments and People of the World*, 1957–58, 2.4: Correspondence: Dag Hammarskjöld, United Nations, 1957–58, Linus Pauling Papers, Special Collection Library, Oregon State University.
10 Linus Pauling, *Linus Pauling in His Own Words: Selections from his Writings, Speeches, and Interviews*, Barbara Marinacci, ed. (New York: Touchstone Press, 1995), 11.
11 Teller to Arthur Adamson, undated, Folder 1: Reading File, April–June 1963, Box 425: Chronological Correspondence, 1962–66, ET Papers.
12 Joseph Rotblat, *Pugwash – the First Ten Years: History of the Conferences of Science and World Affairs* (New York: Humanities Press, 1968), 77.
13 "Private Meeting in London to Discuss the Nuclear Test Ban Deadlock," March 16–17, 1963, part 1, 1, Box 35: Correspondence, 1961–1965, Folder: Nuclear Test Ban, HUG (FP)–94.8, George B. Kistiakowsky Papers, Harvard University Archives, Harvard University.
14 Matthew Evangelista, *Unarmed Forces: The Transnational Movement to End the Cold War* (Ithaca, NY: Cornell University Press, 1999).
15 Bernard Feld, unpublished autobiography, "VIII: Nuclear Politics in the U.S.A.," Doc. 11, March 8, 1988, Box 65: Writings, Folder unnumbered: Autobiographical, Bernard T. Feld Papers, Institute Archives, Massachusetts Institute of Technology.
16 Rabinowitch to Harrison Brown, June 10, 1964, Series IV, Addenda II, Box 6, Folder 13: General Correspondence, ER Papers.
17 Rabinowitch, "Speech for Lake Geneva Conference," 1970, Series IV, Addenda II, Box 3, Folder 10: 20th Pugwash Conference, ER Papers.
18 Hornig, Memo to the President, May 29, 1967, April–June 1967, Box 5, Chronological File, Papers of DFH, Lyndon Baines Johnson Library.
19 Evert Clark, "Top Scientist Cuts All Links To War," *New York Times*, March 1, 1968.
20 Kelly Moore, *Disrupting Science: Social Movements, American Scientists, and the Politics of the Military, 1945–1975* (Princeton, NJ: Princeton University Press, 2008).
21 UPI, "Academy Halts Soviet Exchanges," February 25, 1978, Box 58, Folder 14, National Academy of Sciences, Series I: Jeri Laber Files, Human Rights Watch Archives, Columbia University (HRWA).
22 John T. Edsall to W. A. Engelhardt, August 18, 1978, Box 63: Folder: Files of Jeri Laber: USSR: Scientists: AAAS: 1975–1979, Series I: Jeri Laber Files, HRWA.
23 Kiernan, "The International Cancer Congress," 3–5; "Statement by group of U.S. physicians attending the 12th International Cancer Congress," Oct. 11, 1978, Files of Jeri Laber: USSR: Scientists: AAAS, 1975–79, HRWA.
24 Randall Forsberg, "A Bilateral Nuclear-Weapons Freeze," *Scientific American*, November 1982, Vol. 247, No. 5, 52.
25 "The Arms Race: A Sandia Colloquium by Hans A. Bethe, July 28, 1982," 15–16, Folder 17.12: Arms Control Sandia Colloq. '82, Box 17, Hans Bethe Papers, Division of Rare and Manuscript Collections, Carl Kroch Library, Cornell University.
26 Teller to Peter Renz, July 30, 1984, Folder 3.11: Peter Renz, correspondence, Box 3, ET Papers.

19

THE CATHOLIC CHURCH AND THE COLD WAR

Piotr H. Kosicki

The Cold War was a time of fundamental transformation for the Catholic Church, as it witnessed the maturation and globalization of a Catholic modernization project whose beginnings date from the late nineteenth century. As the Cold War raged, the Catholic Church for the first time in its history officially embraced – during the Second Vatican Council of 1962–65 – freedom of conscience and dialogue with the modern world, and successive popes sought to expand the horizons of the Catholic imagination beyond Europe and the United States to the decolonizing Third World. These shifts were, at least in part, motivated by some of the same factors without which there would have been no Cold War: first, the spread of Marxist revolutionary socialism in Europe's *fin-de-siècle*, and second, the rise of Communist political parties in the wake of the Russian Revolution of 1917 and the resultant creation of the Soviet Union. The initiator of the Catholic Church's modernization, Pope Leo XIII (reigned 1878–1903), was – like Karl Marx – responding to the "social question": how to alleviate the suffering of the masses of industrial working poor flooding the European continent by the late nineteenth century as a consequence of the Industrial Revolution.

This ideological entanglement of the roots of the Catholic modernization project with revolutionary Marxism makes it understandably difficult to offer a simple, linear narrative of Catholicism's place in the Cold War. Historian Peter C. Kent may be correct to speak of Pius XII (reigned 1939–58) as having waged a "lonely Cold War,"[1] and Catholic writer George Weigel may be right to speak of the "resistance church" of John Paul II (reigned 1978–2005), but these two phrases do not even fully describe those popes, let alone Catholicism's place in the four-decade-long global confrontation between Soviet and American camps.[2] That is a story of both the theological choices and geopolitical calculations of individual popes in their capacity as leaders of the Catholic ecclesiastical hierarchy.

The traditional historiography of the Cold War has, sadly, paid scant attention to this story. Biographers of John Paul II have happily claimed since the early 1990s that he was a key – if not in fact *the* key – factor in bringing the Cold War to an end,[3] but very little systematic source-based research has appeared to confirm these contentions. Some attention has gone to correlating the origins of the Cold War with the papacy of Pius XII – in particular, Peter C. Kent's excellent monograph *The Lonely Cold War of Pope Pius XII* – but the difficulty in accessing Church archives in both the Vatican and the former Soviet bloc countries has long tied researchers' hands. Thanks to available oral history and diplomatic correspondence, the

Ostpolitik of Paul VI (reigned 1963–78) has perhaps received the most systematic attention, notably in Hansjakob Stehle's exhaustive, if now somewhat dated, *Eastern Politics of the Vatican*.[4] Happily, new research into Cold War-era grassroots and intellectual Catholic activism on both sides of the Iron Curtain has begun to fill in some of the important gaps.

This chapter makes three broad claims about the Catholic Church's role in the Cold War. First, the Catholic Church's place in the Cold War must be understood not in terms of simple "anti-Communism," but rather in terms of the Church's pre-existing competition with Marxist socialism over answers to the social question. Second, there was considerable variation in the Cold War popes' geopolitical stances, determined partly by contingent circumstances (World War II, the Cuban Missile Crisis, the Helsinki Conference of 1973–75), and partly by the Church's progressive pastoral reorientation away from Europe and the United States and towards the decolonizing Third World. Third, from Pius XII's first reluctant, then unequivocal, embrace of American democracy and the emerging American strategy of containing Communism, the Church transitioned under his successor, John XXIII (reigned 1958–63), to a more even-handed willingness to chastise both camps.

Rather than simply be party to the Cold War, John and his successors, Paul VI and John Paul II, re-centered Catholicism's international advocacy around three pillars: the dignity of the human person, nuclear disarmament, and international development. In so doing, these popes delicately balanced encouragement for reform in the Soviet bloc and support for endeavors aimed at its demise. In this final aspect, the Polish-born John Paul II's contributions – both symbolic and substantive – proved decisive, as he combined hard anti-Soviet rhetoric reminiscent of Pius XII with delicate diplomacy learned from both John XXIII and Paul VI.

The Social Question, the Bolsheviks, and Early Catholic Anti-Communism

When Leo XIII issued the Catholic Church's first official call for a modern Catholic social teaching with his 1891 encyclical *Rerum Novarum*, Marxism was but the purview of a small – albeit brilliantly organized – network of clandestine European writers and revolutionaries. Although Leo's predecessor, the controversial Pius IX (reigned 1846–78), had denounced "communism" already at mid-century, it was nationalism and liberalism that attracted the ire of the nineteenth-century popes, while Marx's "specter" of an international proletarian revolution remained but an abstraction to successive occupants of the seat of Saint Peter.

Leo XIII reoriented the Church's priorities, channeling ongoing academic debates regarding a proper Catholic response to the social question into an encyclical that deftly juggled competing aims. *Rerum Novarum* both insisted on the dignified treatment of workers by their employers and offered a definitive Catholic endorsement of the notion of private property. Although *Rerum Novarum* used the word "socialism" but once and "communism" not at all, the encyclical established a foundation for systematic Catholic thought and action in opposition to the atheistic, revolutionary demands of Marxism.[5]

With the outbreak of the Russian Revolution in 1917, however, dealing with socialist revolution became a priority for Catholicism as never before. Cardinal Achille Ratti – who would later assume the papal throne under the name Pius XI (reigned 1922–39) – as the Holy See's first nuncio to the newly re-established independent state of Poland observed at first hand in Eastern Europe the geopolitical consequences of the Bolshevik Revolution. Ratti would remember for the rest of his life the Soviet invasion of Poland in 1919 as well as the so-called "miracle" on the Vistula River, when Polish soldiers turned the Red Army back from the gates of Warsaw in August 1920. Two years later, Ratti came to the papacy fixated on the idea of containing the Bolshevik advance.[6] In this sense, then, Pope Pius XI was one of Europe's first and most determined Cold Warriors *avant la lettre*.

Drawing from the work of French Catholic philosopher Jacques Maritain, Pius XI incorporated an insistence on the dignity of every "human person" into a decade's-worth of encyclicals spanning the entire 1930s, culminating in his 1937 condemnation of Communism in *Divini Redemptoris*.[7] The implications of this encyclical were unequivocal: "Communism is intrinsically wrong, and no one who would save Christian civilization may collaborate with it in any undertaking whatsoever."[8] The document went in tandem with Pius XI's enthusiastic support for Francisco Franco in the Spanish Civil War. French Communist leader Maurice Thorez had initiated a campaign aimed at Catholic industrial workers in order both to weaken their support for the Franco war effort and to convince Catholic workers that it was not only possible but indeed natural to be at once Communist and Catholic.[9] Pius XI warned Catholics against such Communist entreaties; "without receding an inch from their subversive principles, they [Communists] invite Catholics to collaborate with them in the realm of so-called humanitarianism and charity."[10] *Divini Redemptoris* went a long way toward identifying Catholicism with anti-Communism, and both the vocabulary and the politics that it embraced launched the Catholic Church as a Cold War actor *avant la lettre*.

War and Resistance

Much has been written about the reticence of Pope Pius XII to speak out against Nazi Germany – mostly for his failure to protest the Holocaust, but also for his unwillingness to advocate for priests and lay activists rounded up, imprisoned, and killed in Poland and elsewhere.[11] Beyond the war itself, however, Pius XII's behavior toward Nazi Germany presaged the politics that he came to embody with the advent of the Cold War. One of Pius XI's closest associates and Secretary of State of the Holy See for his predecessor's last nine years as pope, Pius XII had been a key decision maker in Vatican policy already under Pius XI. *Divini Redemptoris* and the Spanish Civil War context thus hold the key to understanding not just Pius XI's anti-Communism, but that of Pius XII as well.

Pius XII's priority in World War II was to stand against the spread of Soviet Communism: hence his reticence to speak out against Nazi crimes, as well as his public equivocation regarding democracy prior to his Christmas radio message of 1944. Even in that message, however, Pius XII's goal seemed to be not condemnation of Fascism or Nazism but caution against democracy of the "masses," in other words, the Soviet "democratic" model: "the masses – as we have just defined them [i.e. 'a shapeless multitude'] – are the capital enemy of true democracy and of its ideal of liberty and equality. In a people worthy of the name, the citizen feels within him the consciousness of his personality, of his duties and rights, of his own freedom joined to respect for the freedom and dignity of others."[12] In his guarded acceptance of democracy, Pius XII thus made crystal clear the Church's stance that collectivism of any sort was undemocratic in virtue of its privation of its citizens' conscious understanding of their rights and duties as human persons. In other words, no self-styled "people's democracy" could ever be democratic, according to the Catholic Church.

During the war itself, Catholic resistance to Nazi Germany had grown more out of day-to-day experience than sheer loyalty to the Vatican. As sociologist Maryjane Osa has suggested, the fragmentation of the lines of communication across Europe during World War II reoriented Catholic activism along horizontal lines of autonomous organizational dynamics rather than top-down communication passed along from the Holy See by national bishops.[13] The wartime shift from a "feudal" Church to an "activist" Church defined the postwar Church as well.

As Christian Democratic movements in France, Italy, and West Germany transitioned out of wartime resistance into mainstream politics in 1944 and 1945, the Vatican attempted repeatedly to dictate policy to them. As historian Philippe Chenaux has demonstrated, however, Robert Schuman, Konrad Adenauer, and Alcide De Gasperi, among others, deftly traded on the perceived legitimacy granted them as Catholic politicians by Pius XII, while preventing him from turning their postwar reconstruction projects – especially European integration – into a "Vatican Europe."[14]

Meanwhile, in Poland, Czechoslovakia, and Hungary – countries both liberated and occupied by the Red Army – organized postwar Catholic political action had a very short shelf-life. Despite the popular front model of "free and unfettered elections" promised by Joseph Stalin at Yalta for Poland and the rest of the emerging Soviet bloc, by early 1947 activists operating outside the emerging Communist establishment had become targets of harassment, co-optation, and even assassination. Broken as the lines of communication had been during the war between the Holy See and Catholics in Central and Eastern Europe, the pope held even less sway among activists on the ground in the emerging Soviet bloc than in Western Europe.

Certain key bishops proved effective as opposing centers of gravity to the Communist establishment in the years 1945–48, but the tide turned against the Church in Red Army-occupied countries with Tito's defection to the Marshall Plan and the "Stalinization" of Eastern European Communism. In October 1948, the death of Polish cardinal-primate August Hlond resulted in his replacement by the young, inexperienced bishop Stefan Wyszyński, a *modus vivendi*-inclined seminary professor who bore little resemblance to the icon of Soviet bloc Catholic anti-Communism that he would become in the wake of his three-year house arrest in the mid-1950s.[15]

The key development, however, from the Holy See's standpoint came in late December 1948, with the arrest of Jozsef Mindszenty, cardinal-primate of Hungary. Imprisoned and tortured, Mindszenty confessed at a subsequent show trial to espionage for the United States, and he was sentenced on 8 February 1949 to life imprisonment. Long acquainted with Mindszenty, Pius XII followed his case closely, excommunicated everyone involved in his prosecution, and took it upon himself to publicize the case as a Communist atrocity. In the pontiff's mind, Mindszenty's arrest and conviction confirmed long-held suspicions about the detrimental effects of expanding Soviet influence. Indeed, Mindszenty's sentencing led the pope to re-evaluate the Holy See's place in the international arena, in particular, in the context of the nascent Cold War. Guarded in his embrace of the United States even in the wake of his 1944 Christmas message, Pius XII by late 1948 had wholeheartedly joined the emerging American Cold War camp.[16]

On 1 July 1949, the Holy See issued a decree threatening with excommunication anyone collaborating with Communists anywhere in the world. The decree, formulated as a series of four questions, culminated in the statement that "His Holiness Pius XII, pope by Divine Providence, in an ordinary audience accorded to the assessor of the Holy Office, approved the decision" that any Catholic "faithful professing materialist and anti-Christian doctrine as Communists and, above all, those who defend or propagate such doctrine incur, as apostates of the faith, the excommunication specially reserved to the Holy See."[17]

At first glance, the text of this decree would seem to indicate the pope's unequivocal intention to excommunicate thousands, if not tens or hundreds of thousands, of Soviet-bloc Catholics who either had chosen to embrace their new lives under Communist regimes or – in a much smaller number of cases – had actively participated in the regimes' construction. And yet the decree soon proved little more than a symbolic gesture. It was applied almost exclusively in Western Europe, and even there, some of the loudest advocates of a Catholic–Communist syncretism remained Catholics in good standing for years – a few, even as men of the cloth, like the French "red priest" Jean Boulier. A leading pro-Communist peace activist, Father Boulier wrote in 1950, "Let me do my job as a man and a priest and preach to all men the Lord's precept 'Thou shalt not kill.' Where is the Communist game in this? [...] Must you be evil because they have been good?"[18] Though defrocked in 1953, Boulier returned to the priesthood in 1963, never facing the excommunication promised by the 1949 decree.

In the Soviet bloc, meanwhile, multiple self-identifying Catholic organizations succeeded not only in maintaining a *modus vivendi* with Stalinist regimes, but indeed in profiting from their collaboration. Only in one case did the Holy See condemn such an organization, and this condemnation had nothing to do with the 1949 decree. A Polish organization started in 1945 by the ex-fascist Bolesław Piasecki succeeded in obtaining a concession to print a weekly newspaper, which Piasecki and his colleagues then grew into what behind the Iron Curtain might have passed for a commercial mini-empire: two trading companies, weekly and daily newspapers, a private high school, a private bus line, and the only publishing house in Poland with permission to print the Bible in large quantities.

The movement, known from 1952 as "PAX," coaxed Primate Wyszyński into signing a *modus vivendi* agreement with the Polish government in 1950, only to switch course in 1953. Following its public condemnation of Kielce bishop Czesław Kaczmarek, convicted in a show trial of espionage for the United States, PAX praised the Communist establishment for stripping Primate Wyszyński of his functions when the primate declined to condemn Kaczmarek. At the same time, PAX continued to advertise itself as a "social-Catholic" organization. PAX faced condemnation for none of this, incurring censure only when denounced to the Holy See in 1955 with copious documentation of PAX leader Piasecki's theologically suspect writings put together by an erstwhile family friend. In the end, PAX agreed to withdraw the heretical texts and shutter its weekly journal, and none of its members incurred any judgment of excommunication.[19]

Given Pius XII's reputation as the ultimate Catholic Cold Warrior, it is difficult to understand such cases. Catholic writers at the time argued that canon law prohibited the Holy See from coming down too harshly on subjects of Communist regimes for simply living according to the principle of rendering unto Caesar that which is Caesar's.[20] Yet, given PAX's use of its role as a prominent arbiter of Polish Catholic opinion to denounce its own episcopal leadership, this argument seems intensely problematic.

The best explanation seems to be that Pius XII followed the geopolitics of his predecessor. Although he was quick to condemn repressions against high officers of the ecclesiastical hierarchy behind the Iron Curtain – not just Mindszenty, but also Alojzije Cardinal Stepinac in Yugoslavia and Archbishop Josef Beran in Czechoslovakia – Pius XII very quickly assimilated the American Cold War containment strategy. The immediate priority was thus not to win back the Soviet bloc, but to prevent any other territory from being lost to the Soviet camp. Pius XII's first test in this respect came with the Italian parliamentary elections of April 1948, for which he turned Italy's Catholic Action into a field organization for Christian Democratic politicians and asked priests to underscore to the faithful that their political choice was to proceed "with Christ or with Lenin." In the end, the pontiff could claim success in staving off a Communist parliamentary victory.[21]

Won over to American democracy from Franco's paradigm of order through dictatorship by the understanding that the former alone could contain the spread of Soviet Communism, Pius XII openly applauded the Marshall Plan, the creation of NATO, the Schuman Plan, and the American Cold War strategy. In effect, the anti-Communism that he inherited from Pius XI, combined with his inability to prevent the loss of Eastern Europe, led him to commit fully to a two-track strategy of supporting the American camp geopolitically and rebuilding Catholic activist networks everywhere outside the containment zone of Communism. In view of these priorities, the "Catholic Communism" of Boulier and PAX seems less germane, in the first case because the "red priest" ultimately submitted to defrocking, and in the latter because PAX became a danger to Pius XII's containment policy only when its leader attempted to promote his Catholic-Communist writings outside the zone of containment.

Peace on Earth

Pius XII, who died in 1958, played a smaller and smaller role in the Holy See's decision making as his health began to fail in the second half of the 1950s. The events of 1956 in the Soviet bloc – Khrushchev's Secret Speech in February, the Poznań Bread Riots in Poland in June, the rehabilitation and return to power of once-disgraced national Communist Władysław Gomułka in Poland in October, and the bloody Soviet suppression of the Hungarian Revolution of October–November – fell precisely within this period.

As a result, national Church leaders and lay activists in the Soviet bloc were heard much more loudly than the Holy See itself. Jozsef Cardinal Mindszenty, released from prison on 30 October 1956, praised the ongoing – socialist, but anti-Soviet – uprising in Budapest, only five days later to have to seek asylum in the American embassy, where he would remain for fifteen years, unaided by two successive popes. Poland's Gomułka released Stefan Cardinal Wyszyński from house arrest on 26 October 1956, at which point a new movement ("Znak" – Sign) of Catholic writers and activists came into public life to serve as intermediaries between the bishops and the Party. Both the episcopate and the laity carved out a substantial space for their own public activism in Communist Poland after 1956.[22] Meanwhile, in Hungary and Czechoslovakia, the events of 1956 led to a progressively deeper co-optation of the bishops, such that by 1960 the regime, not the Vatican, had the decisive say in episcopal appointments.[23]

On a global scale, however, the transition from Pius XII to his successor, John XXIII, marked a watershed in Catholicism's place in the Cold War. Illusory as the "thaw" heralded by Nikita Khrushchev's rise to power in the Soviet Union proved to be – instead yielding both the Berlin Crisis and the Cuban Missile Crisis – John XXIII made a concerted effort both to shift the Catholic Church toward a more neutral stance in the global Cold War and to move Catholicism's center of gravity away from Europe and the United States and toward the decolonizing Third World. These geopolitical shifts came in tandem with the most significant event in modern Catholic history: the calling of the Second Vatican Council. In 1959, announcing an *aggiornamento* – literally, an "updating" – of the Church's place in the modern world, the new pope called for an ecumenical council. Optimistic as John XXIII was, he could not have anticipated the revolutionary effect that the council would have, not only on Catholicism itself, but on relations among organized religious faiths across the world.[24]

John XXIII inherited from Pius XII a strong, close relationship with the United States. Three years into his pontificate, he found himself in the unique position of dealing with the first Catholic ever elected U.S. president, John F. Kennedy. However, it was Kennedy who, alongside the thaw-promising Soviet leader Khrushchev, drove John XXIII to pursue his own foray into geopolitics, seeking concessions from Soviet and American camps alike. The encyclical originally intended to define his papacy, *Mater et Magistra*, issued in 1961 on the seventieth anniversary of *Rerum Novarum*, reiterated the continued centrality of the social question to Catholicism. In April 1963, however, John took a drastic step in a different direction, toward substantive political advocacy. *Pacem in Terris*, his response to the Cuban Missile Crisis, argued explicitly and tersely for both the United States and the Soviet Union to stop stockpiling nuclear weapons: "justice, right reason, and the recognition of man's dignity cry out insistently for a cessation to the arms race. The stock-piles of armaments which have been built up in various countries must be reduced all around and simultaneously by the parties concerned. Nuclear weapons must be banned. A general agreement must be reached on a suitable disarmament program, with an effective system of mutual control."[25]

For more than a decade, the arms race had been the elephant in the room in Vatican dealings with the United States. The most prominent Catholics to agitate for peace had been radicals like the "red priest" Jean Boulier, aligning themselves with the Communist-sponsored peace movement. Boulier himself had been one of the principal international exponents of the Stockholm Appeal of 1950, written by Ilya Ehrenburg to call for "the absolute prohibition of the atomic weapon."[26] The Stockholm Appeal had, however, itself been a creation of the Soviet propaganda machine. In contrast, in 1963, it was the head of the Roman Catholic Church who called for the prohibition of nuclear weapons.

This shift, however, was in the making even before *Pacem in Terris*, and it did not go unnoticed by Soviet bloc leaders, especially since John XXIII had received Khrushchev's daughter and son-in-law for a private audience at the Vatican. Jerzy Zawieyski, a prominent Catholic author and representative on the Polish State Council, was granted a personal audience with John XXIII in November 1962. Prior to his departure from Warsaw, he met with Polish Communist party leader Władysław Gomułka, who declared with respect to John XXIII: "The pope is a great statesman because he understands the conflicts of our world, and he understands, in particular, what nuclear war might mean. [...] The pope represents a Church of peace and wisdom, a Church of love, as you all call it. The pope extends his hand to everyone, which is why he has won the hearts of everyone, including those outside the Church."[27] Indeed, Gomułka even went so far as to give Zawieyski the following message to transmit to the pope during his audience: "May the Lord God grant him health!"[28]

The Polish Communist leader's warmth toward John XXIII suggests also the ire that this pontiff faced at the hands of the numerous cardinals remaining from the papacy of Pius XII. Although John XXIII died within two months of issuing *Pacem in Terris*, his successor, Paul VI, inherited his predecessor's ecumenical council, his geopolitics, and the ire of Vatican conservatives. Advised among others by American priest John Courtney Murray, the Second Vatican Council accepted *Dignitatis Humanae*, a declaration centering on the "dignity of the human person" who "has a right to religious freedom."[29] Intended to promote freedom of conscience above all in the Soviet camp, *Dignitatis Humanae*, along with the council's other closing documents, simultaneously fell prey to criticism that it was soft on Communism, even affording a loophole for Communists to feel legitimated in their political choices by freedom of conscience. Likewise, *Gaudium et Spes*, the council's key document on "the Church in the modern world," stipulates that only through "sincere and prudent dialogue" between believers and unbelievers could everyone "work for the rightful betterment of this world in which all alike live."[30]

These documents signaled a renewed interest by the Holy See in the life of Catholics behind the Iron Curtain. Polish bishop Karol Wojtyła, the future John Paul II, played a role in preparing both texts. Paul VI was the first pope to send official representatives behind the Iron Curtain, relying on the diplomatic skill of future cardinal Agostino Casaroli, whose so-called *Ostpolitik* included negotiating Vatican recognition of Polish sovereignty over the so-called Western lands of Silesia and Pomerania, which had been transferred from Germany to Poland by Allied agreement at the Potsdam Conference in 1945. (Prior to 1972, Polish archbishops on this territory were accredited by the Holy See only as administrators of ostensibly German diocesees.)[31]

Although the Second Vatican Council was not principally concerned with the Cold War, the project of bringing Catholicism "up to date" for the "modern world" necessarily impacted the Church's priorities, and thereby also its position within the Cold War. This was the first ecumenical council to have brought to Europe bishops from all over the world: from Accra, Santiago, and Manila, among many other places. Reacting to this unprecedented global participation in the reinvention of Catholicism, Paul VI made good on his predecessor's declared priority of making the social question no longer just about class in Europe, but about the "progressive development of peoples" and the "hungry nations of the world."[32]

His signature 1967 encyclical *Populorum Progressio* suggested that the pope had had enough of Soviet–American conflict, with extensive collateral damage in proxy wars in Vietnam or various de-colonizing African states. Instead, Paul VI argued, "it is largely your task to see to it that senseless arms races and dangerous power plays give way to mutual collaboration between nations, a collaboration that is friendly, peace-oriented." Between *Populorum Progressio*, which made the argument to both Cold War camps of their responsibility vis-à-vis the rest of the world, and the infamous 1968 encyclical *Humanae Vitae* – in which Paul VI made explicit the Church's prohibition of all artificial means of birth control, thereby provoking an uproar among American and Western European Catholics – Paul VI lit a new path for the Church. Not only was he shifting the horizons of Catholicism, but he was indeed moving its center of gravity in a manner that made the concerns of the United States and the Soviet Union alike seem less central.

At the same time, particularly during the Helsinki Conference of 1973–75, the Catholic phrase "dignity of the human person" that had featured so prominently in the documents of the Second Vatican Council became a key operative phrase of agreements signed by statesmen of both the Soviet and American camps as they committed themselves to protecting human rights. It would be Karol Wojtyła, a close ally of Paul VI, who, on his election to the papacy following the one-month reign of John Paul I, would redefine Catholicism's role in the global promotion of human rights.

The Pope from Behind the Iron Curtain

Much has been written about the contribution of Pope John Paul II to the end of the Cold War. Together with Ronald Reagan, Margaret Thatcher, and Mikhail Gorbachev, this pope is often lauded as one of the "great leaders" responsible for bringing down the Iron Curtain.[33] Undoubtedly, from the moment of his election on 16 October 1978, John Paul II transformed the collective imagination of Catholics and non-Catholics alike behind the Iron Curtain. In addition to directly influencing events in the People's Republic of Poland, he also developed a close partnership with the American administration of President Ronald Reagan, and he made the struggle against the Soviet Union a top priority of his papacy.

That said, to think of John Paul II's papacy as the quintessential resistance church, or simply a continuation or even intensification of Pius XII's Cold War papacy, is to miss part of its essence. The historian Agostino Giovagnoli is correct to underscore that John Paul II's papacy was very much marked by his experience as a Catholic living in Poland first during the Nazi occupation and then under the Soviet-installed Communist regime.[34] Wojtyła, however, was no eternal anti-Communist. He completed a Ph.D. thesis in Rome in 1948, having spent substantial time in France, Belgium, and the Netherlands learning the ways of the worker-priest movement, a short-lived initiative devoted to ministry among industrial workers that required its participants to have a keen understanding of Marxism.

As a young priest and professor in Stalinist Poland, Wojtyła was no rabble-rouser or guerrilla fighter. Indeed, it was not until his elevation to archbishop of Kraków that Wojtyła first began to come into conflict with the regime. Intense involvement in the debates of the Second Vatican Council helped him to develop both a sense of responsibility for the overall direction of Catholicism and a personal affinity and loyalty to Paul VI. Wojtyła was an ardent advocate of Paul VI's *Ostpolitik*, of his recentering of Catholicism on the Third World, of his prohibition of artificial birth control, and of the emphasis on human rights promoted during the Helsinki Conference.[35]

It is perhaps the great paradox of John Paul II's papacy that he is remembered principally as a Cold Warrior when his two priorities were, first, to promote human rights in the Soviet bloc and, second, to promote justice and the development of the Third World. Unlike Pius XII, he sought not to contain the Soviet Union, but rather to promote human rights in all of the countries behind the Iron Curtain. He made an unprecedented first papal pilgrimage to Poland in June 1979, speaking from a platform on Warsaw's Victory Square to thronging crowds, reminding Poles of their death tolls in battles over centuries in the pursuit of their "rights of man, indelibly inscribed in the inviolable rights of people."[36] As George Weigel has put it, "Thirteen million Poles heard John Paul speak the hitherto unspeakable during nine stunning days in June 1979. Neither they, nor the system which falsely claimed to govern in their name, would be the same again."[37] John Paul II created an entire symbolic canon upon which, fourteen months later, the founders of the Solidarity trade union movement would draw in their protests and negotiations with the Polish regime.[38]

Under the Polish pope, the Vatican also became a haven for interfaith dialogue. The Second Vatican Council had pioneered systematic Catholic–Protestant and Catholic–Orthodox dialogue, and it also produced the declaration *Nostra Ætate*, which reversed centuries of Christian anti-Jewish and anti-Muslim teachings with the proclamation that "[t]he Church reproves, as foreign to the mind of Christ, any discrimination against men or harassment of them because of their race, color, condition of life, or religion."[39] That said, it would take more than a decade for the spirit of *Nostra Ætate* to take root in papal practice. When Paul VI had journeyed to Israel in January 1964 – the first-ever papal pilgrimage to the Holy Land – he had neither visited Yad Vashem nor used the word "Israel" in any of his sermons or public statements.

John Paul II, on the other hand, made Catholic–Jewish dialogue a cornerstone of both his theology and his geopolitics. In his June 1979 pilgrimage to Poland, he visited Auschwitz and honored its Holocaust victims, invoking "the nation whose sons and daughters were destined for total extermination."[40] In 1986, he became the first modern pope to enter a synagogue. Although it was not until after the Cold War's end that John Paul II established diplomatic relations between the Vatican and Israel, personally traveled to Israel, and issued the document "We Remember: A Reflection on the Shoah," from the beginning of his papacy it was clear that the Catholic Church would no longer accept the geopolitical instrumentalization of religion.

The Polish pope's gift for public speaking and public relations turned him overnight into the global spokesman for human rights in the Soviet bloc, and he used this role to advance his priorities. In his September 1981 encyclical *Laborem Exercens* – handed down three months before the 13 December imposition of martial law in Poland, i.e. while the Solidarity trade union network could still function freely – John Paul II drew on the experience of the Solidarity protests to call global attention to "the dignity and rights of those who work."[41] For the ninetieth anniversary of *Rerum Novarum*, then, John Paul II gave new meaning to the social question by pointing to the Solidarity movement as an incarnation of Catholic social teaching, while at the same time underscoring a fundamental shift in the place of the social question in the late twentieth century from "the 'class' question" to "the 'world' question," thereby decrying the "world sphere of inequality and injustice." In this respect, then, John Paul II continued a shift initiated by John XXIII and Paul VI.

It is in the context of this shift that John Paul II faced perhaps his greatest doctrinal challenge: liberation theology. Often misunderstood and misrepresented, the confrontation between the Holy See and the vanguard of Latin American social theology at the turn of the 1970s and 1980s was the culmination of a long-standing conflict within the Latin American bishops' conference (CELAM) that predated the Second Vatican Council. John XXIII and Paul VI had strongly advocated a "continental" solution for Latin America to the problem of a widening rich–poor gap and a fragmented Church hierarchy, part of which openly aligned with dictators and *juntas*. Nonetheless, both popes were unwilling to distinguish the permissible from the impermissible amidst a new flood of theological propositions coming from Latin America suggesting that Catholic social teaching's "preferential option for the poor" should serve as the point of departure for a new, radical theology targeting only the Third World poor at the expense of the rest of the world. John Paul II, on the other hand, in the first year of his papacy, declared when opening the 1979 CELAM conference in Puebla, Mexico, that the revolutionary rhetoric of certain liberation theologies and the potential for their co-optation by Third World Marxist revolutionaries was unacceptable. The pope insisted, "this idea of Christ as a political figure, a revolutionary, as the subversive man from Nazareth, does not tally with the Church's catechesis."[42]

On behalf of the new pope, the Congregation for the Doctrine of the Faith, headed by Joseph Cardinal Ratzinger (later to become Benedict XVI), went on the offensive, undertaking extensive reviews of the most recent writings of Latin America's most famous Jesuit and Franciscan liberation theologians. Some, like the Dominican Gustavo Gutiérrez, escaped outright condemnation, while the Franciscan Leonardo Boff – now a layman – did not. In the end, the Congregation of the Doctrine of the Faith in its two published "instructions" on liberation theology – from 1984 and 1986 respectively – absorbed, as theologian Peter Hebblethwaite has argued, much of the social justice-centered vocabulary and agenda of liberation theology while censuring many of its original exponents.[43] The Congregation's 1984 instruction, for example, speaks of "deviations, and risks of deviations, damaging to the faith and to Christian living, that are brought about by certain forms of Liberation Theology which use, in an insufficiently critical manner, concepts borrowed from various currents of Marxist thought."[44] The struggle to define the contours of an orthodox liberation theology thus shored up global perceptions of John Paul II as both a warrior against Marxism and an engaged statesman with a clear vision of the type of Third World development that he was willing to countenance.

In some sense, then, John Paul II juggled a new sort of Cold War participation with his advocacy of international development in the Third World. The example of Latin American liberation theology underscores the widespread perception that he and U.S. president Ronald Reagan, his contemporary, agreed more than they differed in both ideological and geopolitical terms. Indeed, Reagan's presidency coincided with the birth of a vibrant American Catholic neo-conservative milieu that attempted to link Reagan and the pope inextricably in the minds of their American audiences. Richard John Neuhaus and other Catholic authors connected, beginning in 1981, to the Institute on Religion and Democracy combined anti-Communism, ecumenical dialogue, and social conservatism. Theirs were clarion voices of the American Culture Wars of the 1980s, combining a domestic political agenda centered on a refusal to accept the 1973 U.S. Supreme Court *Roe v. Wade* decision legalizing abortion with a geopolitical agenda directed against the Soviet Union.[45] It was in large part through the pens of Neuhaus and his younger colleague George Weigel that John Paul II's American presence transcended Catholic milieux, with the Polish pontiff becoming a household name across the American spectra of political and religious affiliation.

Despite his prominence in the symbolic canon of American public life, it would be erroneous to suggest that the coordination of Cold War policy with the Reagan administration took precedence for John Paul II. True, the pontiff and the president maintained open channels of communication, and the Vatican took advantage of those channels, in particular during the years of martial law in Poland. Nonetheless, as historian Marie Gayte has underscored, John Paul II pressed the Reagan administration hard on the matter of Third World armed interventions and aid. Even though the Vatican did not speak out against Reagan's Strategic Defense Initiative, there is evidence of substantial negotiation between John Paul II and Reagan's advisors on the matter.[46] Indeed, when he felt that he had no choice, the pontiff did not hesitate to criticize the United States, as he did in his 1987 encyclical *Sollicitudo Rei Socialis*, when he wrote, "each of the two blocs harbors in its own way a tendency toward imperialism, as it is usually called, or towards forms of new colonialism: an easy temptation to which they frequently succumb."[47]

In the end, John Paul II long outlasted the Iron Curtain. In December 1989, he had the opportunity to establish a direct dialogue with Mikhail Gorbachev, to speak about ecumenical dialogue between Catholics and Orthodox Christians, and to discuss internal reforms within the Soviet Union. The pope's following comment to Gorbachev makes clear that he thought about the Cold War not in terms of conflict or competition but precisely in terms of rights and development:

> I would like to speak about the elements related to the word "perestroika," which has deeply touched all aspects of life for the Soviet people, and not only them. This process allows us together to look for a way to enter a new dimension of people's common existence, which would reflect to a greater degree the requirements of the human spirit, of different nations, of the rights of individuals and nations. The efforts you are making are not only of a great interest to us. We share them.[48]

Conclusion

The Roman Catholic Church had been anti-Communist since long before the Cold War began, and even before Communist parties as such came into existence. Yet anti-Communism alone cannot explain the meandering path of the Church's engagement in the Cold War. The evolution of the social question, the geopolitical extension of Marxism with the Red Army's advance across Europe in 1944–45, the increasingly realistic prospect of nuclear annihilation, the project of updating the Church for the modern world – all of these factors shaped the Vatican's stance toward Soviet and American camps alike. Whereas Pope Pius XII inherited his predecessor's visceral desire to contain Communism at all costs within its existing boundaries, his successors offered an extended hand across the Iron Curtain, all the while opening the horizons of the Catholic Church to a modern world defined by the need for nuclear disarmament, international development, and the safeguarding of human rights.

John Paul II incorporated all of these elements into his papacy. Falsely seen by some as a blindly anti-Communist warrior, this pontiff learned sufficiently from Marxism in his youth to strike a balance between pursuing dialogue on behalf of human rights and drawing lines in the sand to crack down on Latin American liberation theology. A staunch ally of Ronald Reagan, John Paul II was nonetheless willing to criticize American geopolitical expansionism. Without a doubt, John Paul II as Roman Catholic pontiff played a central role in the Cold War's end, yet his role lay not so much in the conduct of the Cold War itself, but rather in his status as a source of inspiration and symbolic capital. Having helped to guide Poles toward the Solidarity trade union movement, having initiated serious interfaith dialogue, John Paul II drew firm lines within the Catholic world, piercing the veil of neutrality pursued by his immediate predecessors and maintaining ideological discipline. Whether or not his stance ultimately served the causes of *aggiornamento*, international development, and social justice beyond 1991 remains an open question, but, as of the collapse of the Soviet Union, Rome played a far more nuanced and complex role in the restructuring of the international system than many understood at the time – or have come to understand since.

Notes

1. P.C. Kent, *The Lonely Cold War of Pope Pius XII: The Roman Catholic Church and the Division of Europe, 1943–1950* (Montréal: McGill-Queen's University Press, 2002).
2. G. Weigel, *The Final Revolution: The Resistance Church and the Collapse of Communism* (New York: Oxford University Press, 1992).
3. For example, G. Weigel, *Witness to Hope: The Biography of Pope John Paul II* (New York: Cliff Street Books, 1999).
4. H. Stehle, *Eastern Politics of the Vatican, 1917–1979*, trans. Sandra Smith (Athens, OH: Ohio University Press, 1981). On Vatican *Ostpolitik* toward East Germany, see R. Cerny-Werner, *Vatikanische Ostpolitik und die DDR* (Göttingen: V & R Unipress, 2011).
5. Leo XIII, *Rerum Novarum* (15 May 1891), Online at http://www.vatican.va/holy_father/leo_xiii/encyclicals/documents/hf_l-xiii_enc_15051891_rerum-novarum_en.html.
6. N. Pease, "Il Papa Polacco: The Making of Pius XI, 1918–1922," in *Rome's Most Faithful Daughter: The Catholic Church and Independent Poland, 1914–1939* (Athens, OH: Ohio University Press, 2009, pp. 30–53).
7. S. Moyn, "Personalism, Community, and the Origins of Human Rights," in S.-L. Hoffmann (ed.), *Human Rights in the Twentieth Century* (New York: Cambridge University Press, 2011, pp. 85–106).
8. Pius XI, *Divini Redemptoris* (19 March 1937), Online at http://www.vatican.va/holy_father/pius_xi/encyclicals/documents/hf_p-xi_enc_19031937_divini-redemptoris_en.html.
9. M. Thorez, *Communistes et catholiques. La main tendue...* (Paris: Éditions du comité populaire de propagande, 1937).
10. Pius XI, *Divini Redemptoris*.
11. For example, C. Rittner and J.K. Roth (eds.), *Pope Pius XII and the Holocaust* (New York: Continuum, 2002).
12. Pius XII, "Democracy and a Lasting Peace: 1944 Christmas Message of His Holiness Pope Pius XII," Online at http://www.papalencyclicals.net/Pius12/P12XMAS.HTM.
13. M. Osa, "Resistance, Persistence, and Change: The Transformation of the Catholic Church in Poland," *East European Politics and Societies*, 1989, vol. 3 no. 2, 268–299, at 296.
14. P. Chenaux, *Une Europe Vaticane? Entre le Plan Marshall et les Traités de Rome* (Bruxelles: Éditions Ciaco, 1990).
15. For example, P.H. Kosicki, "Between Catechism and Revolution: Poland, France, and the Story of Catholicism and Socialism in Europe, 1878–1958," Ph.D. Dissertation, Princeton University, 2011, pp. 256–266.
16. Kent, *The Lonely Cold War of Pope Pius XII*, pp. 217–236.
17. Decree of the Holy Office of the Roman Catholic Church, 1 July 1949, in Y. Tranvouez, *Catholiques et communistes: la crise du progressisme chrétien, 1950–1955* (Paris: Cerf, 2000), p. 42. Author's translation.
18. J. Boulier, *Why I Signed the Stockholm Appeal to Ban the Atom Bomb* (Sydney: New South Wales Peace Council, 1950), pp. 8–9, 10–11.
19. Kosicki, "Between Catechism and Revolution," pp. 357–409.
20. For example, O. Laffoucrière, "L'Église de Pologne entre Rome et l'État. I: Un accord de raison," *Le Monde*, 1–2 November 1953.
21. R.A. Ventresca, *From Fascism to Democracy: Culture and Politics in the Italian Election of 1948* (Toronto: University of Toronto Press, 2004).
22. A. Michnik, *The Church and the Left*, trans. and ed. David Ost (Chicago: University of Chicago Press, 1993).
23. N. Bauquet, "Une Église d'agents? L'Église catholique hongroise face à l'héritage du kadarisme," *La Nouvelle Alternative*, 68, Autumn 2006.

24 J.W. O'Malley, *What Happened at Vatican II* (Cambridge, MA: Belknap Press of Harvard University Press, 2010).
25 John XXIII, *Pacem in Terris* (11 April 1963), Online at http://www.vatican.va/holy_father/john_xxiii/encyclicals/documents/hf_j-xxiii_enc_11041963_pacem_en.html.
26 Reprinted in F. Joliot-Curie, "A Proposal toward the Elimination of the Atomic Danger," *Bulletin of the Atomic Scientists*, 1950, 6, 166–167, at 166.
27 J. Zawieyski, Diary (2 November 1962), in *Dzienniki*, Vol. 2: *Wybór z lat 1960–1969* (Warszawa: Ośrodek KARTA/Dom Spotkań z Historią, 2011), pp. 191–195, at p. 193. Author's translation.
28 Zawieyski, Diary, p. 194. Author's translation.
29 *Dignitatis Humanae* (7 December 1965), Online at http://www.vatican.va/archive/hist_councils/ii_vatican_council/documents/vat-ii_decl_19651207_dignitatis-humanae_en.html.
30 *Gaudium et Spes* (7 December 1965), Online at http://www.vatican.va/archive/hist_councils/ii_vatican_council/documents/vat-ii_const_19651207_gaudium-et-spes_en.html.
31 J. Luxmoore and J. Babiuch, *The Vatican and the Red Flag: The Struggle for the Soul of Eastern Europe* (New York: Continuum, 1999), pp. 165–166.
32 Paul VI, *Populorum Progressio* (26 March 1967), Online at http://www.vatican.va/holy_father/paul_vi/encyclicals/documents/hf_p-vi_enc_26031967_populorum_en.html.
33 J. O'Sullivan, *The President, the Pope, and the Prime Minister: Three Who Changed the World* (Washington: Regnery, 2006).
34 A. Giovagnoli, "Karol Wojtyla and the End of the Cold War," in Silvio Pons and Federico Romero (eds.), *Reinterpreting the End of the Cold War: Issues, Interpretations, Periodizations* (London: Frank Cass, 2005), pp. 82–90.
35 J. Moskwa, *Droga Karola Wojtyły*, Vol. 1: *Na tron Apostołów, 1920–1978* (Warszawa: Świat Książki, 2010).
36 John Paul II, "Apostolic Journey to Poland, Holy Mass: Victory Square, Warsaw, 2 June 1979," Online at http://www.vatican.va/holy_father/john_paul_ii/homilies/1979/documents/hf_jp-ii_hom_19790602_polonia-varsavia_en.html.
37 Weigel, *The Final Revolution*, p. 133.
38 J. Kubik, "John Paul II's First Visit to Poland as an Example of the Ceremonial Transformation of Society," in *The Power of Symbols against the Symbols of Power: The Rise of Solidarity and the Fall of State Socialism in Poland* (University Park, PA: Pennsylvania State University Press, 1994), 129–152.
39 *Nostra Ætate* (28 October 1965), Online at http://www.vatican.va/archive/hist_councils/ii_vatican_council/documents/vat-ii_decl_19651028_nostra-aetate_en.html.
40 John Paul II, Sermon at Auschwitz-Birkenau (7 June 1979), Online at http://mateusz.pl/jp99/pp/1979/pp19790607c.htm. Author's translation.
41 John Paul II, *Laborem Exercens* (14 September 1981), Online at http://www.vatican.va/holy_father/john_paul_ii/encyclicals/documents/hf_jp-ii_enc_14091981_laborem-exercens_en.html.
42 John Paul II, Address to the Third General Conference of the Latin American Episcopate (28 January 1979), Online at http://www.fjp2.com/pl/jan-pawel-ii/podroze-apostolskie/59-apostolic-journey-to-the-dominican-republic-mexico/16023-to-the-3rd-general-conference-of-the-latin-american-episcopate-puebla---republic-of-mexico-january-28-1979.
43 P. Hebblethwaite, "Liberation Theology and the Roman Catholic Church," in Christopher Rowland (ed.), *The Cambridge Companion to Liberation Theology*, 2nd ed. (Cambridge: Cambridge University Press, 2007), pp. 209–228.
44 Congregation for the Doctrine of the Faith, *Instruction on Certain Aspects of the "Theology of Liberation"* (6 August 1984), Online at http://www.vatican.va/roman_curia/congregations/cfaith/documents/rc_con_cfaith_doc_19840806_theology-liberation_en.html.
45 For example, R.J. Neuhaus, *The Naked Public Square: Religion and Democracy in America* (Grand Rapids, MI: W.B. Eerdmans Publishing Co., 1984). For background, see J.D. Hunter, *Culture Wars: The Struggle to Define America* (New York: Basic Books, 1991).
46 M. Gayte, "The Vatican and the Reagan Administration: A Cold War Alliance?" *Catholic Historical Review*, 2011, vol. 97 no. 4, 713–736.
47 John Paul II, *Sollicitudo Rei Socialis* (30 December 1987), Online at http://www.vatican.va/holy_father/john_paul_ii/encyclicals/documents/hf_jp-ii_enc_30121987_sollicitudo-rei-socialis_en.html.
48 Record of Conversation of M.S. Gorbachev and John Paul II, 1 December 1989, trans. Anna Melyakova, On File at National Security Archive, http://www.gwu.edu/~nsarchiv/NSAEBB/NSAEBB298/Document%208.pdf.

PART VII

Nuclear Weapons, Technology, and Intelligence

20
NUCLEAR WEAPONS AND THE COLD WAR

Ruud van Dijk[1]

Even without the nuclear revolution there would, in all likelihood, still have developed a cold war. It would probably still also have been *the* Cold War: an escalating, ideology-driven rivalry between a United States-led West and the Soviet Union and its allies over the shape of the post-World War II world, and influence in it, that dominated international affairs until one side decided to yield to the other. However, it would not have been the Cold War as we have come to know it, characterized by the widespread fear of nuclear annihilation but also the absence of a new great-power war. The post-World War II world was shaped in profound ways by the development of nuclear weapons and the subsequent nuclear arms race, but these remained, in some cases only just, secondary to politics and ideology.

Nuclear weapons made the Cold War at once more dangerous and less likely to lead to a new world war. The development of the hydrogen bomb by both sides in the 1950s, the mass deployment of these warheads on intercontinental missiles the decade after, and the development, for example, of so-called "launch on warning" war-fighting systems threatened the extinction of most life on earth in case of an all-out war. However, as thermonuclear weapons became part of arsenals and planners drew up scenarios plotting the course of a great-power war involving nuclear weapons, successive American and Soviet leaders eventually all came to the conclusion that the military use of nuclear weapons could, in the end, serve no meaningful political purpose. Ultimately all came to share the conviction of the American strategist Bernard Brodie, who wrote in 1946: "[t]hus far the chief purpose of our military establishment has been to win wars. From now on its chief purpose must be to avert them. It can have almost no other useful purpose."[2]

This "nuclear learning" did not mean that political decisions could not, or did not, create situations where an accidental escalation leading to a major nuclear exchange could not have taken place. The Cuban Missile Crisis of October 1962 demonstrates that Cold War politics in the nuclear age remained the work of human beings, and that individual actors are capable of taking irresponsible risks (while fortuitously also being able to choose the opposite course of action at key moments).[3]

This crisis was a turning point because in its wake leaders in Washington and Moscow came to see the containment of the nuclear danger as a shared interest. The nuclear arms race continued, in part because it gradually created its own logic and momentum that proved hard for policy makers to control.[4] Still, for the remainder of the Cold War, the two sides together sought ways to avoid an accidental nuclear exchange; agreed upon limits on the testing of nuclear devices; worked to prevent the proliferation of nuclear weapons; and eventually also took joint steps toward nuclear arms reduction. Arms reduction helped make the end of the Cold War possible, but it was not the main cause.[5]

The Nuclear Arms Race Begins: 1945–52

The first use of the atom bomb played a part in the emergence of the Cold War, but not a central one. America's nuclear incineration of the Japanese cities of Hiroshima and Nagasaki in August 1945 primarily sought to bring about a rapid end to World War II – not to launch a new conflict against the Soviet Union.[6] The Truman administration did, however, have some general expectations that this new display of power would make the Soviet regime more willing to discuss postwar problems on American terms. The opposite happened, because in response to reports of the devastation in Japan, Stalin ordered an all-out attempt to develop a Soviet bomb, thus launching in earnest the nuclear arms race that was to characterize the Cold War until the end. In East–West diplomacy the Soviet leader became even more determined not to show weakness toward the United States and instead increasingly defined the relationship with Washington as a "war of nerves."[7]

Already during the years of the United States atomic monopoly, 1945–49, questions about their military effectiveness, but also ethical considerations, made the actual use of nuclear weapons unlikely. In the wake of Hiroshima and Nagasaki, President Harry S. Truman refused to contemplate more bombings, and later that fall questioned whether nuclear weapons could "ever be used" again.[8] In 1948, during the Berlin blockade, the president refused to give custody to the military of any atomic bombs, but by sending several B-29 bombers to Great Britain his administration did signal to Moscow the potential risks of further escalation. (Some B-29s were capable of carrying atomic bombs, though the planes sent to Britain were not.) After Communist China's intervention in the Korean War in late 1950, with the U.S. atomic monopoly still virtually intact, there was increasing talk of a possible use of nuclear weapons, and Truman added to the chorus during a poorly handled press conference. In early 1951 he did give the military custody of several atomic bombs, but his administration did not seriously contemplate their use because the military pay-off seemed highly questionable.

The determination of political leaders such as Truman to keep civilian control of nuclear weapons – itself an increasingly controversial issue – does not mean that nuclear arms control in the early Cold War was possible. On the contrary, international control of atomic energy was an illusion, in part because in the United States there was little political support for it. News of Soviet espionage within America's wartime Manhattan Project, breaking in early 1946, made sure of this. Washington did put forward a proposal for arms control, the 1946 Baruch Plan, but it could hardly be taken as a serious offer, and the Soviet Union quickly rejected it. The Atomic Energy Act that created the Atomic Energy Commission, passed by Congress the same year, explicitly banned the sharing of nuclear technology with other nations (including Great Britain, America's partner in the wartime Manhattan Project to develop a nuclear weapon). Given his fundamental mistrust of the capitalist world, and his determination to obtain his own nuclear capability, it is extremely unlikely that Stalin would have accepted any plan that limited his own options.[9]

The successful Soviet nuclear test on August 29, 1949 ended the U.S. monopoly and, together with the Communist victory in the Chinese civil war, led to an intensification and militarization of the Cold War. (The Cold War also turned hot in Korea in 1950, but Stalin's permission to North Korea's leader Kim Il Sung for an attack on the South had more to do with general strategic considerations than his acquisition of the atom bomb.) Already before the outbreak of war in Korea, political upheaval – internationally and in the United States – made a new phase in the nuclear arms race almost a foregone conclusion. Only a few of Truman's advisers (though not the least) argued against the development of a thermonuclear weapon, the "Super." In the Soviet Union, there was not even a discussion.[10]

Nuclear Bluff, Fear, and the Years of Maximum Danger: 1952–63

A series of Soviet and American tests between 1952 and 1955 launched a second nuclear weapons revolution with the introduction of thermonuclear weapons, hundreds, even thousands of times more powerful than the bombs dropped on Hiroshima and Nagasaki.[11] The frightening force of these new weapons convinced most statesmen, nuclear scientists, strategists, and military leaders (not to mention anti-nuclear activists) of the need to prevent them from ever being fired in anger. Ideas on how to achieve this differed widely. While the military use of nuclear weapons was increasingly called into question, the thinking about their political, diplomatic, or psychological uses, however, entered its heyday, along with, not surprisingly, so-called "nuclear fear" among the general population, especially in the United States.[12]

From the mid-1950s to the mid-1960s speculation about the possibility of nuclear war was at an all-time high, also because the period saw the acceleration of a third dimension of the nuclear arms race, in the area of missile technology. The lack of reliable tools with which to verify the capabilities of the adversary added to the uncertainty. An even greater destabilizing factor was the imbalance between the arsenals of the two principal nuclear powers to the advantage of a United States apparently willing to press its advantage, and Soviet leader Nikita Khrushchev's counterproductive efforts to make up for this and other Soviet weaknesses by way of bluff and intimidation. A final destabilizing factor in this period was projects that both superpowers initiated to share nuclear weapons technology with allies. Apparent U.S. willingness to find a way for the Federal Republic of Germany (FRG) to gain access to nuclear weapons caused great political turmoil, especially in Moscow. The nuclear arms race was an important driver of East–West confrontation at the height of the Cold War, but so were competition in the Third World, the struggle over Germany and Europe, and, most fundamentally, ideology. Eventually, containment of the nuclear danger would also become a way through which East and West sought to stabilize their rivalry (like the eventual mutual recognition of the European status quo, but unlike relations with the Third World or, except at the very end of the Cold War, ideology), but the opening decade of the thermonuclear age was not the time for this.

In both Washington and Moscow after 1952, new leaders developed new ideas on the role of nuclear weapons in the East–West conflict. President Dwight D. Eisenhower initially argued that nuclear weapons were no different from other means of war. Concerned also about the fiscal consequences of the vast conventional re-armament begun under his predecessor, Eisenhower gave nuclear weapons, and their potential military use, a prominent place in his national security strategy, the "New Look." (Washington expected regional allies around the world to shoulder much of the burden of conventional options.) At the same time, in December 1953, the president put forward ideas for international cooperation on nuclear energy matters in his "Atoms for Peace" proposal. Although this initiative led to the founding of the International Atomic Energy Agency, dedicated to monitoring nuclear proliferation and peaceful uses of atomic energy, Eisenhower's emphasis was on the integration of nuclear weapons in America's war-fighting arsenal and on the further development of U.S. thermonuclear capabilities. On March 1, 1954, the U.S. tested an unprecedented fifteen megaton thermonuclear device (Castle Bravo) in the Pacific, casting doubt on the sincerity of the earlier "Atoms for Peace" initiative. In several international crises in the 1950s, particularly in Asia, the Eisenhower administration indeed signaled that, if necessary, the United States would not hesitate to use atomic bombs to protect its interests or those of its allies.

This may have been a serious threat during much of Eisenhower's first term, but after 1955 the president's insistence on a (thermo)nuclear option in a military crisis became a way to impress upon both friend and foe the catastrophic consequences of a nuclear exchange. Such a war – or any war between the United States and the Soviet Union, for that matter – he argued, could not possibly be contained. Instead, it would escalate to a major war in which all had everything to lose. By giving the United States no other realistic military option except the thermonuclear one, Eisenhower sought to focus everyone's attention on this reality, thereby creating – in his own eyes, though not those of all of his subordinates – the best possible deterrent to an actual nuclear war.[13]

In its "peace offensive" following Stalin's death in March 1953, the new, collective Soviet leadership moved away from the old tyrant's dictum that a great-power war was inevitable. The following year, probably in response to scientists' reports on the destructive power of thermonuclear weapons, the chairman of the Council of Ministers and apparent head of the leadership group, Georgy Malenkov, even stated publicly that continued conflict between the United States and the Soviet Union could lead to "the end of world civilization."[14] However, the balance of power between East and West was too much in favor of the latter, and the internal leadership struggle in Moscow too much in flux, for a détente to have a real chance. Khrushchev, Malenkov's main rival in the leadership, soon used the pronouncement to weaken Malenkov's influence. It was Khrushchev who, in July 1955, was the de facto leader of the Soviet delegation at the first great-power summit since 1945, the Geneva heads-of-government meeting between France, Great Britain, the Soviet Union, and the United States. In spite of a certain stabilization of the East–West rivalry, the time for a genuine détente that included arms control had not yet arrived. Khrushchev reportedly considered calling Eisenhower's bluff when the president put forward his "Open Skies" proposal for observation flights over each other's military installations, but in the end the summit meeting yielded nothing substantial.[15]

Like Eisenhower (and Malenkov), Khrushchev also believed that in the thermonuclear age general war between the Soviet Union and the United States was unthinkable. But just like the president, Khrushchev understood – indeed, eagerly embraced – that nuclear weapons had to play a part in policy. Like Stalin, Khrushchev thought it was all a matter of strong nerves. The new Soviet leader consciously and aggressively used nuclear bluff to compensate for Soviet strategic and military weakness vis-à-vis the United States. Eisenhower may have concluded that his veiled nuclear threats had paid political dividends in the cases of Korea (1953) and the Chinese off-shore islands of Quemoy and Matsu (1954–55), but the president primarily used his nuclear bluff as a deterrent, that is, as a way to keep an adversary from doing certain things. Khrushchev, on the other hand, believed he could use nuclear bluff proactively to compel the resolution of international questions on Soviet terms, a much more dangerous approach, as events were to demonstrate. With few internal challenges to his handling of foreign affairs after 1956, Khrushchev was able to put a major imprint on international developments between 1958 and 1963. In part, his actions were driven by domestic and international challenges – for example the emerging rift with China's Mao Ze Dong – but mostly, he acted by choice. His case is the best example of how, in the nuclear age, individual leaders, especially those who manage to evade accountability to their constituents, can have an enormous influence on matters of war and peace – for better or for worse.[16]

At Geneva, Khrushchev had noticed that the West was equally afraid of war, and this bolstered his self-confidence. Furthermore, he appears to have concluded from the Suez crisis (1956), when he threatened France and Britain with nuclear missile strikes, that a strategy of nuclear intimidation could take him far. When, the following October, the Soviet Union became the first nation to launch a satellite into orbit (*Sputnik*), seemingly getting ahead of the United States in the race to develop intercontinental missiles, Khrushchev's confidence in the feasibility of his strategy only grew. *Sputnik* was a psychological blow to the United States. Many felt themselves vulnerable to surprise nuclear attack. Democrats, including the party's nominee in the 1960 presidential election, John F. Kennedy, charged that under the Republicans a "missile gap" in Moscow's favor had emerged. Knowing from CIA overflights of Soviet territory that a Soviet lead was fiction, Eisenhower remained calm, but at the same time his administration intensified missile development and increased science and technology spending across the board. Civil defense initiatives proliferated during the late 1950s and early 1960s, as did the production of nuclear-themed science-fiction films, literature, and cartoons. Public protests against the nuclear arms race, particularly the effects of atmospheric testing, also became a common feature of public life.[17]

By the early 1960s, both Soviet and American leaders believed they needed to bring the arms race under control. Over the previous decade the Cold War had escalated and intensified, and it had continued to spread through the Third World. Moreover, the arms race seemed to be taking on a semi-autonomous momentum, driven by ever greater technological progress in nuclear weapons development (smaller devices with higher yields) and means of delivery (aircraft, submarines, missiles, guidance systems). Various constituencies on both sides – the military, politicians, science, business – not only developed a stake in further development of nuclear weapons capabilities but also began to drive research and development, even war planning, semi-independently from the political leadership.[18] In his Farewell Address in early 1961, Eisenhower warned against the influence of this, as he labeled it, "military-industrial complex." Many, including a growing number of nuclear scientists on both sides, feared that nuclear war, inadvertent or not, could be the result in a crisis-prone international system where political and military leaders were having an ever harder time keeping a grip on the development of new weapons systems and the way governments planned for their use. In 1958, both the United States and the Soviet Union voluntarily decided to stop atmospheric nuclear testing, a practice deeply resented around the world due to the potentially lethal effects of nuclear fall-out. Both sides also began talks about a test ban treaty, but these quickly became bogged down in disagreements over verification rules. The search for arms control, therefore, became an important aspect of the 1958–63 period, but it would take the bankruptcy of the policy of nuclear bluff, and Khrushchev's reckless approach in particular, for progress to become feasible.[19]

Nuclear bluff for Khrushchev was a tool to achieve political ends and to improve a weak Soviet position quickly. In spite of his bluster, he was well aware of his country's economic backwardness compared to the West, and of the fact that the purported Soviet lead in missile technology was imaginary. He knew the Soviet nuclear arsenal was no match for that of the United States. The Soviet system, Khrushchev knew, could not afford the arms race if it was to realize greater prosperity for Soviet citizens and, ultimately, superiority over the West – both things he fervently believed were possible. Khrushchev needed détente, but believed he could not reveal weakness in its pursuit. Equally pressing, developments in Central Europe, especially Germany, threatened to undermine Soviet influence in the area most vital for Soviet national security. Located in the center of Soviet-dominated East Germany (the German Democratic Republic, GDR), the open city of Berlin, one half of it occupied by Britain, France, and the

United States, served as an escape route for tens of thousands of well-educated East Germans seeking a better life in the West. In order to ensure the stability and long-term viability of the GDR, Khrushchev, pushed by GDR leader Walter Ulbricht, wanted the Western powers out of Berlin, and through repeated ultimatums between 1958 and 1962 he seemed willing to go to the brink of a major confrontation to get his way.[20]

Another important reason for Khrushchev's Berlin ultimatums was the apparent willingness of the United States to give its German ally access to nuclear weapons. Controversial also in the Western alliance, this issue had entered onto the agenda as Britain and France began to pursue their own nuclear weapons capability in the mid-1950s – the former in close cooperation with the U.S., the latter less so. The Eisenhower administration had long believed that eventually the European allies should be able to defend themselves without reliance on U.S. forces. Through "nuclear sharing" Washington hoped to achieve this goal. Nuclear weapons, both strategic and tactical, had been important in the North Atlantic Treaty Organization's (NATO) strategy since 1954, also because the West European countries seemed unable to raise sufficiently large conventional armies. However, as the U.S. lead over the Soviet Union gradually diminished, the credibility of the U.S. nuclear guarantee would also weaken. As Soviet capacities to strike U.S. territory grew, would Washington really risk the survival of Chicago in order to save Munich? For a credible deterrent against Soviet aggression in Europe, the West Europeans needed their own access to nuclear weapons, Eisenhower believed. It was unhealthy for the United States to have all the power and all the responsibility in the alliance; the West Europeans should have some influence over military matters affecting their own survival, and they needed to take more responsibility for their own defense. West German chancellor Konrad Adenauer, obsessed with equal treatment for his country, wanted his country to be included in any sharing of nuclear weapons technology, in spite of a formal renouncement of aspirations to atomic weapons at the time of the FRG's entry into NATO in 1954–55. Washington did not feel it could deny the chancellor, who was increasingly suspicious of America's commitment to German unification (a more and more remote prospect), but whose allegiance to the Western alliance was essential to NATO's viability and the fragile European status quo. Of course, giving the FRG access to nuclear weapons was just as likely to upset this status quo, but by 1958 NATO seemed well on its way to doing just that.[21]

The problem of a possible West German nuclear role bedeviled East–West as well as West–West relations well into the 1960s, and it added significantly to international tensions between 1958 and 1963. For the Soviet Union, a nuclear-armed West Germany still seeking unification with the GDR on its own terms, a "revanchist" Germany in Soviet parlance, represented a major threat. In any case, through its willingness to consider a West German nuclear role, the West had made the 1945 Potsdam agreement, the basis of its presence in Berlin, meaningless, Moscow argued. Through his Berlin ultimatums Khrushchev, therefore, sought to stabilize the GDR, incorporate all of Berlin within the communist state, and achieve Western recognition of a permanently divided Germany curtailed militarily by the World War II victors. Khrushchev's ultimatums failed to move the West (in August 1961 Moscow and its German ally built the Berlin Wall to save the GDR) but they did raise the overall temperature of the Cold War. The Wall notwithstanding, Khrushchev stuck to the objectives that were behind his Berlin ultimatums until the end of 1962, and he kept searching for a way to corner the Americans (who, he argued, would not risk a nuclear war) and force them to do business on Soviet terms.[22]

Khrushchev also felt pressure from the People's Republic of China (PRC). The PRC and the Soviet Union had collaborated closely since 1950, also on nuclear weapon development. However, Mao was growing increasingly critical of the Soviet leader's policies, especially

Khrushchev's search for a détente with the United States. Mao also began to challenge Khrushchev for pre-eminence in the anti-capitalist camp, particularly in relations with newly independent countries and liberation movements in the Third World. In 1959, Moscow stopped helping China to develop a nuclear weapon, but by then China's program was far enough along to enable the country to complete its first nuclear device independently (successfully tested in 1964). The Sino-Soviet Split contributed to Khrushchev's militancy in his search for an agreement with the United States, and nuclear bluster remained an important tool.

Thus, it was a confident but also impatient Khrushchev who met with Eisenhower's successor, John F. Kennedy, in Vienna in early June 1961. Two months earlier, the new U.S. president had been humiliated in a failed, CIA-sponsored invasion of Cuba at the Bay of Pigs. Through the use of Cuban exiles, the Americans had attempted to reverse Fidel Castro's 1959 revolution on the island. The operation definitively gained the Soviet Union a new ally in the Western hemisphere, as Castro now eagerly welcomed Soviet military and economic support. That same month, the Soviet Union celebrated yet another first in the space race with the manned space flight by cosmonaut Yuri Gagarin. At their Vienna meeting, the two leaders talked at cross-purposes, the Soviet leader failing to get any U.S. concessions on the Berlin–Germany issue, the American seeing his pleas for serious discussions on a nuclear test ban go unanswered. Khrushchev believed he had had the upper hand, and even more than in 1955 came away from the summit with increased self-confidence. It was, however, a grim kind of determination, as once again the Soviet leader had failed to make any headway on Berlin. Time was not on his side, also because his domestic policies had not lived up to expectations. In subsequent months, both sides took measures that further raised the stakes, but it was Khrushchev who acted most aggressively.[23]

Reassured by new satellite imagery confirming a vast United States lead in the intercontinental missile race, and seeking a greater array of military options under the new strategy of "flexible response," Kennedy announced an increase in conventional forces in July, some destined for Europe. He warned that the West would fight to maintain its position in Berlin; and he talked to the American people of ways to prepare themselves for war. When the Wall went up three weeks later, however, the U.S. response was restrained. The same month, Moscow announced it would end the self-imposed moratorium on atmospheric nuclear testing. In October, the Soviets detonated a fifty-megaton thermonuclear weapon (Tsar Bomba), the largest nuclear device ever, over Novaya Zemlya. Kennedy responded by authorizing the resumption of underground testing in the U.S. That fall also saw a tense stand-off between American and Soviet tanks at a checkpoint in Berlin. With the stakes in the Third World also being raised by both sides, it appeared the Cold War could lead to real war after all.

Continued U.S. pressure on Cuba and Khrushchev's commitment to his Latin American ally, Moscow's inferior strategic position vis-à-vis the United States and U.S. superiority in all areas of the nuclear arms race, growing skepticism among Soviet elites about Khrushchev's leadership, and his frustration at the lack of progress toward an East–West agreement on Germany and Berlin – all these problems made Khrushchev decide in May of 1962 to address them through one bold stroke. As part of a massive military build-up on the island of Cuba, the Soviet Union would, he announced to his colleagues, station nuclear missiles there, just like the United States recently had placed nuclear missiles near Soviet territory, in Italy and Turkey. It would be done in secret, and after the U.S. mid-term elections in November the missiles would be revealed – then Washington would have to leave Castro alone and would have no choice but to negotiate on Soviet terms.[24]

When, in mid-October, the United States discovered the Soviet missile sites on Cuba, nuclear weapons quickly became a driver of politics and diplomacy rather than the tool Khrushchev intended them to be. The Kennedy administration demanded a withdrawal of the missiles, imposed a naval blockade (a "quarantine") around Cuba, and began preparations for an invasion.

A high-stakes stand-off in the nuclear missile age, both sides quickly discovered, leaves political leaders very little time for communication or deliberation. At the same time, such a confrontation creates mini-crisis upon mini-crisis where small incidents can escalate quickly without political leaders having much, if any, control. Through a series of such high-pressure mini-crises – around the U.S. blockade, connected with U.S. overflights of Cuba, because of continued U.S. missile testing during the crisis – both Khrushchev and Kennedy discovered to their great dismay that they were losing control of the situation. A nuclear war might develop even though nobody wanted one. Aware of this danger, Khrushchev reversed the orders of the Soviet commander in Cuba, who had been authorized to use the tactical nuclear weapons at his disposal in the event of a U.S. attack (in Washington at the time, and long after, nobody knew that this type of nuclear missile was also present in Cuba). Khrushchev, however, had no control over the decisions taken by officials on nuclear-armed Soviet submarines when they came under pressure from U.S. ships.[25] For his part, Kennedy felt growing pressure from his military to authorize an invasion of Cuba – a move, he feared, that might well provoke Soviet retaliation in Berlin, to which the West would then have to respond. The president did not believe he could resist this pressure indefinitely, or even for very long.[26]

The fear that they were quickly losing control of developments was the primary reason why both men, through intermediaries, worked out an agreement by the end of the second week of the stand-off. In a definitive defeat for Khrushchev's nuclear-bluff policies, the Soviet missiles would be withdrawn in return for Kennedy's pledge not to attack Cuba. Secretly, Kennedy also promised to withdraw the U.S. missiles from Turkey.[27] U.S. strategic superiority (throughout the confrontation and for about a year afterwards the United States maintained the ability to knock out most if not all of the Soviet Union's nuclear weapon capabilities in a first, preemptive strike) was an important aspect of the crisis, and a contributing factor to its anti-climactic outcome. However, given the strong objections, moral and practical, to the use of nuclear weapons that existed throughout the U.S. political and military leadership, U.S. strategic superiority was of only secondary importance in the resolution of the crisis. Most important was that both leaders became convinced that events were spinning out of control and nuclear war might ensue.

Taming the Nuclear Danger: 1963–79

The Cuban Missile Crisis was a major turning point in the history of the Cold War because it brought home to leaders in Moscow and Washington the realization that in their nuclear rivalry their countries had created a situation where nuclear war could erupt unintentionally and that together they were increasing the nuclear danger to a point where it could overwhelm everything. Khrushchev, Kennedy, and their successors started working together in earnest to establish some measure of arms control. At the same time, the outcome of the crisis gave a new impetus to the nuclear arms race. As Soviet Deputy Foreign Minister Vasily Kuznetsov told his American counterpart, John D. McCloy, in the negotiations on the implementation of the missile withdrawal deal: "We will honor this agreement. But never will we be caught like this again."[28] Thus, both sides working together began to build a global arms control regime, while the Soviet Union, for the remainder of the decade, dedicated itself to achieving strategic nuclear parity with the United States.

During the 1970s, the years of "détente," both sides together pursued arms control agreements, without, however, abandoning the arms race. Due to the firm hold of the "military-industrial complex" on policy making in each camp, the intensification of East–West competition in the Third World rather than its abatement, and, as always, the persistence of ideologically based rivalry and mistrust, arms control increasingly came under siege by the end of the decade while the nuclear arms race intensified and accelerated.[29]

Fittingly, in the wake of their confrontation over Cuba, Kennedy and Khrushchev together took the first steps to implement the lessons learned. Although the two leaders were not to meet in person for a second time, their governments soon took steps to improve lines of communication, most famously through the establishment of a direct telex (later telephone) "hotline" between the Kremlin and the White House, so as to limit the chances of nuclear war breaking out unintentionally due to technical or human error. The year 1963 also saw a breakthrough in the long-languishing discussions over a nuclear test ban. In August, the two countries, joined by Great Britain, signed a treaty banning nuclear tests in the atmosphere, in outer space, and under water: the Partial Test Ban Treaty (PTBT).

A third consequence of the Cuban Missile Crisis was that the United States and the Soviet Union began to see the non-proliferation of nuclear weapons as a shared interest. China was one concern, especially early on. Its deepening and increasingly public conflict with the Chinese probably contributed to Moscow's agreement to the PTBT. China's nuclear program was certainly a concern in Washington. The Americans believed that the nuclear danger was bound to be increased by unpredictable, revisionist regimes such as Mao's getting control of nuclear weapons. Subsequent developments showed these fears to be overdrawn, but in 1963 the Kennedy administration indicated to Moscow that it might be willing to act jointly to stop China from developing a nuclear bomb. Moscow, however, did not respond. In spite of his own fears of the consequences of a nuclear China, collaboration with the capitalist opponent against another communist regime was a bridge too far for Khrushchev.[30]

Another source of concern was the FRG, or rather, ongoing discussions within NATO over a possible nuclear role for the country. From the time it came into office, the Kennedy administration had been much less interested in nuclear sharing with the European allies than its predecessor had been. However, it was faced with the same problem: if – as was practically a given after the first French nuclear test in February 1960 – Britain and France were going to have access to nuclear weapons, probably their own; and if, as seemed essential to the future of NATO, the West Germans ought to be treated equally, how could Bonn be denied a nuclear role? A possible solution had become the so-called Multilateral Force (MLF): in order to enhance the credibility of the U.S. nuclear umbrella for Western Europe, the European allies were to get joint control over several strategic nuclear weapons.

The MLF became a major stumbling block in U.S.–Soviet negotiations over a non-proliferation treaty (NPT). Khrushchev appeared willing to accept the MLF, and thus a West German nuclear role, if that would lead to an NPT. With an NPT he hoped to put pressure on China to abandon its nuclear ambitions. His Warsaw Pact allies, particularly Poland and the GDR, objected vehemently, and Khrushchev, his power diminished, could not impose his will on them. Only in the wake of Khrushchev's fall in October 1964 (also the time of China's first nuclear test) did there develop a clear Soviet position against nuclear sharing with smaller allies (i.e. the FRG) under an NPT. The United States – led after November 1963 by Kennedy's successor, Lyndon B. Johnson – needed even more time to sort out its official position on non-proliferation, the consequences for the NATO alliance in general, and the future of the MLF in particular. Negotiations over an NPT, conducted by representatives of eighteen governments, took until 1968 to bear fruit. A second reason for the slow progress was the U.S. escalation of the war in Vietnam, where North Vietnam, Moscow's ally, bore the brunt of the American onslaught.[31]

By 1965 it was clear that the MLF lacked the unified European support it needed. France and Britain preferred, indeed for reasons of national pride insisted on, their own nuclear forces. It also became clear that for West Germany interest in a nuclear role was much less about being an actual nuclear power than about being able to count on U.S. protection, and about having a meaningful role in NATO's decision making on nuclear weapons. While NATO in 1966 formalized its Nuclear Planning Group (NPG) to ensure the latter, the Johnson administration worked hard to assure Bonn of the former. The NPT played a role here too, as a broad international commitment to non-proliferation singled out the FRG less. Important also was the FRG's own changing sense of the connection between nuclear issues, on the one hand, and the goal of German unification, on the other. As Bonn, under a new coalition government from late 1966, moved to a new policy toward Eastern Europe and the Soviet Union, seeking areas of common interest became more important than the principled hard line of the early Adenauer years. Aspirations to control over nuclear hardware ran counter to this changing Eastern policy.[32]

France's withdrawal in 1966 from NATO's military structures eventually aided in this process toward an East–West détente in which nuclear arms control would gain a central place. NATO managed to turn this crisis into an opportunity by formulating a new dual strategy of deterrence and détente in its 1967 Harmel Report. It found a willing partner in Moscow – now simultaneously less insecure, thanks to the build-up of its strategic nuclear forces, more able to act, due to the ascendancy of Leonid Brezhnev, and deeply concerned about an increasingly unpredictable and hostile China. In 1967 Mao's state had successfully tested its first thermonuclear device, just one year after the Great Leader had plunged his country into the infamous Cultural Revolution.[33]

By 1968 East and West had established sufficient common ground for the NPT to be finalized and signed. The year before, the countries of Latin America had pronounced their region to be the world's first nuclear weapons-free zone under the Treaty of Tlatelolco. Also in 1967, the Outer Space Treaty, banning the militarization of outer space, went into force. But although Moscow and Washington also began preliminary discussions on arms control, including missile defense systems (Anti Ballistic Missile systems, ABM), it was too early for a genuine détente. The Warsaw Pact suppression of the reformist Prague Spring in August 1968 was a set-back, and, following it, the U.S. presidential election ensured that a new administration would need some time to develop its own Cold War strategy. Finally, on the Soviet side the powerful military-industrial sector remained strongly opposed to any limits on weapons development or the idea of sharing sensitive national security information with the West in the context of what in 1969 nonetheless would become formal negotiations over a Strategic Arms Limitation Treaty (SALT). Told that the head of the Soviet delegation knew nothing about armaments, even Brezhnev is reported to have said: "All the better; then at least no secrets will be betrayed."[34]

In the post-Cuban Missile Crisis era the superpowers refrained from using nuclear bluff or brinkmanship in dealing with each other. Instead, both sides had come to appreciate the apparent stability provided by a nuclear balance of terror under which each side had sufficient second-strike capability to make a pre-emptive first strike a suicidal proposition: Mutually Assured Destruction (MAD). The new U.S. president, Richard M. Nixon, however, deliberately sought to intimidate opponents through what he himself called a "madman" strategy. The communists should think that the president might do anything to have his way. Genuinely interested in détente for a variety of reasons, Nixon also hoped to extricate the United States from an unwinnable war in Vietnam quickly and "with honor." Especially in 1969, he employed "madman" tactics – a partial, worldwide nuclear alert – to force the North

Vietnamese enemy, perhaps pressured by their Soviet ally, to make peace on U.S. terms. Neither Hanoi nor Moscow was much impressed, however, and Nixon, never intending to follow through with nuclear weapons anyway, had to accept defeat.[35] A potentially more dangerous situation developed the same year between the Soviet Union and China. Military clashes between these two nuclear-weapons states led to a virtual war scare in Peking, where Mao's regime worried about a Soviet nuclear strike.[36] And in August a Soviet official in Washington did ask an American colleague about the U.S. position on a possible Soviet strike on Chinese nuclear facilities. The Nixon administration, already looking for a way to exploit the Sino-Soviet Split and normalize U.S. relations with Peking, did not want to see China "smashed."[37] Soviet posturing was most likely for diplomatic purposes, and both Moscow and Beijing together managed to defuse the crisis soon afterwards.

U.S.–Chinese normalization got underway gradually after 1969, which was one reason why U.S.–Soviet détente also began to take shape. Negotiations over the SALT and ABM were at the center, and they led to treaties that Nixon and Brezhnev were able to sign at their summit in Moscow in May 1972. SALT I, in spite of its indisputable significance as the first major arms control agreement between the superpowers, stipulated only how and to what extent the strategic arsenals of both sides could grow. The treaty took account of the development of multiple independently targetable reentry vehicles (MIRV), or the ability to place multiple nuclear warheads in one and the same missile, but because it failed to contain their numbers, SALT I did not stop, let alone reverse the arms race. The ABM treaty, on the other hand, did stop a looming competition in missile defense systems. Furthermore, because these were not developed beyond the two sites permitted to each side under the treaty, the U.S. and the Soviet Union did not get a new incentive to build more offensive systems (to ensure that, in spite of AMB systems, enough missiles could still reach their targets).

Enough other forces continued to push the nuclear arms race onward and upward, however, primarily because détente did not permanently stabilize, let alone end, the Cold War. While Soviet leaders, especially Brezhnev, appreciated the apparent stability that détente brought to East–West relations, they primarily viewed their newly acquired influence and prestige as evidence of a global communist ascendancy that was both ongoing and inevitable. Washington, meanwhile, never ceased to see the relationship as fundamentally adversarial and, temporarily weakened because of Vietnam, mostly viewed détente as a way to contain a further increase of Soviet power and influence.[38]

Competition in the Third World continued during the 1970s, and intensified after 1974, contributing to growing doubts, especially in the United States, about the sustainability, even desirability, of the search for common ground. Domestic critics in the United States questioned the wisdom and morality of doing business with the Soviet regime, emphasizing the flaws in SALT I and U.S.–Soviet follow-up negotiations over a second treaty. Strong pressures for further weapons development and deployment continued to emanate from the military-industrial complexes on both sides. On the Soviet side the military operated virtually autonomously from a weakening, compliant political leadership. In the United States, opponents of SALT became more organized and influential as the decade wore on and East–West disagreements replaced the optimism of a few years before. The opponents of détente charged that the Soviet Union had never stopped striving for strategic superiority over the West, and that by clinging to a naively benign vision of the adversary the United States and its allies were putting themselves in great danger. The critics were right and wrong at the same time, for while Soviet missile development and deployment maintained its steady pace during the 1970s and early 1980s, and the number of Soviet warheads came to exceed that on the American side, the U.S. technological lead was never threatened, and neither was MAD.[39]

Modernization of Soviet intermediate-range missiles, U.S.–Soviet agreements on strategic weapons, and Warsaw Pact conventional superiority did cause old West-European concerns about the credibility of the U.S. nuclear umbrella to manifest themselves again in the mid-1970s. SALT did not address so-called "grey area" weapons, between the strategic and battlefield levels (since 1973, the latter had been covered in the Mutually Balanced Force Reduction talks – MBFR). While Washington believed its NATO allies to be sufficiently provided for, the Europeans themselves, pointing to the deployment of new Soviet SS-20 missiles and Warsaw Pact tank superiority, disagreed. Led by West German chancellor Helmut Schmidt, they requested that the issue be addressed – in the context of SALT, but also by maintaining a complete spectrum of (nuclear) military options for the European theater. The effort to address the problem through the introduction of the anti-tank neutron bomb into NATO's arsenal failed in 1977–78, due to a combination of popular resistance and political indecisiveness.[40] Covert Soviet and East German support for anti-nuclear movements in Western Europe played a part, also to elevate the stakes when NATO attempted to address the problem a second time, through its "Dual Track" decision of December 1979. This plan, consisting of the deployment of 572 Pershing II and cruise missiles in Western Europe and an offer to Moscow for negotiations, definitively launched the "Euromissile crisis" of the late 1970s and early 1980s.[41]

The Euromissile crisis was political, as much as it dealt with military-strategic questions. Once NATO had announced its decision, member states saw it as crucial for the future of the alliance to see things through. A failure to deploy if negotiations with Moscow failed would be a major victory for the Soviets (who throughout the stand-off kept adding to the number of SS-20s). But staying the course placed significant strain on West European societies, where resistance to what many saw as a new stage in the nuclear arms race was widespread (supporters preferred to call it a modernization) and in some cases caused governments to postpone participation in the deployment scheme.[42] Eventually, all participating NATO members accepted the missiles, although complete deployment was pre-empted by the 1987 Intermediate Nuclear Forces (INF) Treaty, under which all SS-20, cruise, and Pershing missiles were withdrawn and dismantled.

The Primacy of Politics: 1980–89

The 1980s began as a new era of confrontation, crisis, and danger, but at the end of the decade the Cold War was over, and the nuclear arms race had been put in reverse. Organized popular resistance against the nuclear arms race played a bigger part than in the earlier crisis years, but it took a gradual meeting of the unusual minds of new leaders in the United States and the Soviet Union for this to happen. Ronald Reagan and Mikhail Gorbachev broke with their predecessors in their rejection of the inevitability of the nuclear weapons stand-off. Reagan's and Gorbachev's challenge to the Cold War conventional wisdom on nuclear arms was closely entwined with their rejection of the alleged inevitability of the Cold War itself. After 1984, in a near-symmetrical reversal of the emergence and escalation of the Cold War forty years earlier, shifting ideological and political calculations interacted to reduce mistrust and danger to such an extent that nuclear arms *reduction* became possible and the conflict itself could come to a peaceful conclusion in 1989.

The battle over the Euromissiles paralleled the collapse of détente and the onset of a new chill in East–West relations, but it was not the only or even the main cause. In 1979 Brezhnev and U.S. president Jimmy Carter managed to sign the SALT II treaty, but in hindsight it was détente's last gasp. The Soviet invasion of Afghanistan, two weeks after NATO's Dual Track decision, completed the demise. The United States and Soviet governments gradually ceased most meaningful diplomatic contact. In the Kremlin, an aging and seriously ill Brezhnev was incapable of effective leadership or policy coordination, and his geriatric colleagues in the Politburo were not much help; in the United States, the 1980 elections brought Republican Ronald Reagan to power. Reagan had rejected détente virtually since it began and now pledged to rebuild U.S. strength before committing to new negotiations. In response to Cold War setbacks and an ongoing expansion of the Soviet nuclear arsenal, the United States had begun its new build-up already during Carter's last two years in office. However, especially between 1981 and 1985, many in East and West believed themselves to be living in a new era of acute nuclear danger.

Neither side ever considered using nuclear weapons in these years. Nuclear brinkmanship was not on anyone's agenda either. However, the combination of an accelerated nuclear arms race, hostile rhetoric on both sides, a series of small crises, and, most significantly, an almost total lack of meaningful U.S.–Soviet diplomatic contacts made the early 1980s, and especially the year 1983, one of the most dangerous of the entire Cold War era. In November of that year a war-scare erupted in Moscow in response to NATO's Able Archer exercises. Since 1981 the Soviet leadership had been gathering and analyzing intelligence on the premise that the Reagan administration could launch a surprise attack, and by 1983 this premise had become a self-fulfilling prophecy.[43]

Reagan, personally deeply skeptical about the nuclear balance of terror, had nevertheless facilitated this kind of thinking. Not only did he label the Soviet Union as an "evil empire" destined for the ash-heap of history, in March of 1983 he also put forward the Strategic Defense Initiative (SDI). In Reagan's own mind, this revival of (space-based) missile defense was a precondition for the reduction and eventual abolition of nuclear weapons; for the Soviets it signified a new phase in the arms race and a reaching for first-strike capability. The Reagan administration's double-zero proposal for the INF negotiations (begun in 1981) appeared disingenuous against this background. There were plenty of critics of Reagan's policies in the United States also, and in late 1983 Reagan himself was shaken after viewing the apocalyptic made-for-TV movie *The Day After*, depicting a nuclear attack on eastern Kansas. The president was also shocked to hear of the Kremlin's response to Able Archer. Also in November 1983, the West German and Italian parliaments voted to start deployment of NATO's intermediate nuclear missiles as envisioned by the Dual Track decision. In response, Soviet negotiators walked out of the INF talks.[44]

It was as if all lessons learned in the 1958–63 crisis period had been forgotten. There was no showdown as in 1962, no nuclear blackmail by either side, but in the fall of 1983 both the Kremlin and the White House, like Khrushchev and Kennedy, worried nonetheless that their confrontation might spin out of control, even though nobody wanted it to. Public opinion in the West was equally anxious, as witness numerous mass-demonstrations in Western countries at this time. Nuclear weapons were not primarily responsible. Responsible was the fact that, in spite of all the so-called nuclear learning and the unceasing diplomatic efforts after 1953 to create a *modus vivendi*, the Cold War remained a fundamentally unstable rivalry. The crisis of 1979–85 was different in many ways from that of 1958–63, and less dangerous, but the two had in common that political leaders – mostly through acts of commission in the earlier crisis, primarily through acts of omission in the latter – allowed the rivalry to drift. With giant nuclear-armed militaries on both sides nervously working on worst-case scenarios, the stakes, the potential price for such failure of political leadership, were very high. In this sense, nuclear weapons made an enormous difference.

The year 1984 brought a different tone in Washington, and 1985 brought the first Soviet leader in some years capable of acting. When Mikhail Gorbachev took charge, the Soviet

Union had many more international obligations than it could afford, and the economy was in a crisis. The need to pare down internationally in order to reform at home was therefore an important reason why Gorbachev pursued arms control. But just as important was his rejection of the logic of MAD. To the surprise of many, he found a partner in Reagan. SDI would complicate their discussions for several years, but in the course of their first two summit meetings the two leaders nonetheless came to trust and respect each other. Most significantly, they discovered a joint desire to reverse the nuclear arms race. Both countries turned out to have leaders who were terrified of nuclear weapons.

Meeting at Reykjavik in October 1986, Reagan and Gorbachev came close to agreeing to a phased abolition of intercontinental nuclear missiles. Gorbachev's demand for, and Reagan's rejection of, major limits on SDI research kept a deal out of reach, but the meeting still made both leaders realize that they could do business, albeit on a less ambitious scale. In this, the two leaders were well ahead of most of their advisers, and after Reykjavik progress toward arms reduction came to rest as much on the ability of each to overcome resistance in his own ranks as on negotiators' ability to work out specifics.[45]

Gorbachev faced the biggest hurdles, but he also had the biggest incentive to move forward. Thus, in the wake of Reykjavik he decided no longer to make a deal on INF conditional on U.S. concessions on SDI, and he made the Soviet military fall into line. Where Brezhnev had left the initiative to the Soviet Union's military-industrial sector, Gorbachev restored the balance. In the U.S., many mistrusted Gorbachev's motives, but it was difficult to fault the double-zero outcome of the INF negotiations, although some tried. Progress on a strategic arms reduction treaty (START) was slower, but by the spring of 1988 enough had changed for Reagan, during his visit to Moscow, to confirm in public that talk of the Soviet Union as an "evil empire" belonged to a different era.[46]

The Cold War indeed was in the process of dissolving, although in spring 1988 most still believed they were witnessing a new era of détente. To bring about the end of the Cold War, it would take the more fundamental choice by Gorbachev essentially to withdraw from the East–West rivalry by abandoning the anti-Western ideology that had driven Soviet policy since 1917. Nuclear arms control helped in creating an international climate conducive to these revolutionary steps. But the real cause of the end of the Cold War, and the reason why the nuclear arms race was brought under control and put in reverse, were choices by leaders, first and foremost Gorbachev, to reject the logic of the inevitability of a Cold War.[47]

Notes

1 The author thanks Maarten Brands, Patrick J. Garrity, Ronald Havenaar, Timothy McDonnell, and the two editors of this volume for many helpful comments. All imperfections remain the sole responsibility of the author!
2 Bernard Brodie, ed., *The Absolute Weapon: Atomic Power and World Order*, quoted in Gregg Herken, *Counsels of War*, Expanded Edition (New York: Oxford University Press, 1987), xii, 9–10.
3 John Lewis Gaddis, Philip H. Gordon, and Ernest R. May, eds., *Nuclear Statesmen Confront the Bomb: Nuclear Diplomacy since 1945* (New York: Oxford University Press, 1999).
4 A path-breaking study, from the U.S. perspective, on what could be called nuclear risk management and its limits is Scott D. Sagan, *The Limits of Safety: Organizations, Accidents and Nuclear Weapons* (Princeton, NJ: Princeton University Press, 1993). See also, Francis J. Gavin, "Politics, History, and the Ivory Tower-Policy Gap in the Nuclear Proliferation Debate," *Journal of Strategic Studies* 35:4 (2012), 573–600.
5 For general background on the role of nuclear weapons during the Cold War, see: McGeorge Bundy, *Danger and Survival: Choices About the Bomb in the First Fifty Years* (New York: Random House, 1988); Francis J. Gavin, *Nuclear Statecraft: History and Strategy in America's Atomic Age* (Cornell, NY: Cornell

University Press, 2012); Steven J. Zaloga, *The Kremlin's Nuclear Sword: The Rise and Fall of Russia's Strategic Nuclear Forces, 1945–2000* (Washington, DC: Smithsonian Institution Press, 2002). From the *Cambridge History of the Cold War*, Melvyn P. Leffler and Odd Arne Westad, eds. (Cambridge: Cambridge University Press, 2010), Vol. 1: David Holloway, "Nuclear Weapons and the Escalation of the Cold War, 1945–1962", 376–397; Vol. 2: William Burr and David Alan Rosenberg, "Nuclear Competition in an Era of Stalemate, 1963–1975," 88–111; Francis J. Gavin, "Nuclear Proliferation and Non-proliferation during the Cold War," 395–416. Also, the National Security Archive's Nuclear Vault: http://www.gwu.edu/~nsarchiv/nukevault/.

6 Historians have long argued over the motives behind the use of the bomb, and research continues to broaden our knowledge from the perspective of the United States, the Soviet Union, and Japan. Many experts, however, would agree that ending the war was foremost on U.S. officials' minds. A good overview of the debate is J. Samuel Walker, "Recent Literature on Truman's Atomic Bomb Decision: A Search for Middle Ground," *Diplomatic History* 29:2 (2005), 311–334.

7 David Holloway, *Stalin and the Bomb: The Soviet Union and Atomic Energy, 1939–1956* (New Haven, CT and London: Yale University Press, 1994), 127–133; chapter 8.

8 Alonzo Hamby, *Man of the People: A Life of Harry S. Truman* (New York: Oxford University Press, 1995), 336–339; Robert H. Ferrell, *Harry S. Truman: A Life* (Columbia, MO: University of Missouri Press, 1994), 343–344.

9 Campell Craig and Sergey Radchenko, *The Atomic Bomb and the Origins of the Cold War* (New Haven, CT: Yale University Press, 2008).

10 Herbert F. York, *The Advisors: Oppenheimer, Teller, and the Superbomb*, Expanded Edition (Stanford, CA: Stanford University Press, 1989, first edition 1976). Holloway, *Stalin and the Bomb* chapters 13 and 14. Kai Bird and Martin J. Sherwin, *American Prometheus: The Triumph and Tragedy of J. Robert Oppenheimer* (New York: Alfred A. Knopf, 2005), chapter 30.

11 Richard Rhodes, *Dark Sun: The Making of the Hydrogen Bomb* (New York: Simon & Schuster, 1995).

12 Stephen R. Weart, *Nuclear Fear: A History of Images* (Cambridge, MA: Harvard University Press, 1988).

13 Campbell Craig, *Destroying the Village: Eisenhower and Thermonuclear War* (New York: Columbia University Press, 1998).

14 Vladislav Zubok, *A Failed Empire: The Soviet Union in the Cold War from Stalin to Gorbachev* (Chapel Hill, NC: University of North Carolina Press, 2007), 125–126.

15 Anatoly Dobrynin, *In Confidence: Moscow's Ambassador to America's Six Cold War Presidents, 1962–1986* (New York: Times Books, 1995), 37–38.

16 William Taubman, *Khrushchev: The Man and His Era* (New York: W. W. Norton & Company, 2003), chapter 14.

17 Lawrence S. Wittner, *The Struggle against the Bomb*, 3 vols (Stanford, CA: Stanford University Press, 1993–2003).

18 Stuart W. Leslie, *The Cold War and American Science: The Military-Industrial-Academic Complex at MIT and Stanford* (New York: Columbia University Press, 1993). Sharon Ghamari-Tabrizi, *The Worlds of Herman Kahn: The Intuitive Science of Thermonuclear War* (Cambridge, MA: Harvard University Press, 2005).

19 Zubok, *A Failed Empire*, chapter 5.

20 Hope Harrison, *Driving the Soviets up the Wall: Soviet–East German Relations, 1953–1961* (Princeton, NJ: Princeton University Press, 2003), chapters 3 and 4. James G. Richter, *Khrushchev's Double Bind: International Pressures and Domestic Coalition Politics* (Baltimore, MD: Johns Hopkins University Press, 1994).

21 Marc Trachtenberg, *A Constructed Peace: The Making of the European Settlement, 1945–1963* (Princeton, NJ: Princeton University Press, 1999), part II.

22 Gerhard Wettig, *Chruschtschows Berlin-Krise 1958 bis 1963: Drohpolitik und Mauerbau* (Munich: Oldenbourg, 2006).

23 Alexsandr Fursenko and Timothy Naftali, *"One Hell of a Gamble": Khrushchev, Castro, and Kennedy, 1958–1964: The Secret History of the Cuban Missile Crisis* (New York: W.W. Norton & Company, 1997).

24 Zubok, *A Failed Empire*, 143–149.

25 Svetlana V. Savranskaya, "New Sources on the Role of Soviet Submarines in the Cuban Missile Crisis," *The Journal of Strategic Studies* 28:2 (2005), 233–259.

26 Ernest R. May and Philip D. Zelikow, eds., *The Kennedy Tapes: Inside the White House during the Cuban Missile Crisis* (Cambridge, MA: Harvard University Press, 1997).

27 On the story of the Jupiter missiles since 1957 see Philip Nash, *The Other Missiles of October: Eisenhower, Kennedy, and the Jupiters, 1957–1963* (Chapel Hill, NC: University of North Carolina Press, 1997).
28 Walter Isaacson and Evan Thomas, *The Wise Men: Six Friends and the World They Made, Acheson, Bohlen, Harriman, Kennan, Lovett, McCloy* (New York: Simon & Schuster, 1986), 630.
29 It is possible, though controversial, to see the Soviet build-up of the 1970s as going "beyond parity." See Zaloga, *The Kremlin's Nuclear Sword*, chapter 5.
30 William Burr and Jeffrey T. Richelson, "'Whether to Strangle the Baby in the Cradle': The United States and the Chinese Nuclear Program, 1960–64," *International Security* 25:3 (2000/2001), 54–99. Zubok, *A Failed Empire*, 152.
31 Douglas Selvage, "The Warsaw Pact and Nuclear Nonproliferation, 1963–1965," *Cold War International History Project Working Paper No. 32* (Washington, DC: Woodrow Wilson International Center for Scholars, April 2001); Vojtech Mastny, "The 1963 Nuclear Test Ban Treaty: A Missed Opportunity for Détente?" *Journal of Cold War Studies* 10:1 (2008), 3–25.
32 Thomas Alan Schwartz, *Lyndon Johnson and Europe: In the Shadow of Vietnam* (Cambridge, MA: Harvard University Press, 2003). See also Hal Brands, "Alliances and Armaments: Non-Proliferation and the Dynamics of the Middle Cold War: The Superpowers, the MLF, and the NPT," *Cold War History* 7:3 (2007), 389–423.
33 Frédéric Bozo, "Détente versus Alliance: France, the United States and the Politics of the Harmel Report (1964–1968)," *Contemporary European History* 7:3 (1998), 343–360. Andreas Wenger, Crisis and Opportunity: NATO and the Multilateralization of Détente, 1966–1968," *Journal of Cold War Studies* 6:1 (2004), 22–74.
34 Quoted in Jonathan Haslam, *Russia's Cold War: From the October Revolution to the Fall of the Wall* (New Haven, CT: Yale University Press, 2011), 261.
35 Scott Douglas Sagan and Jeremi Suri, "The Madman Nuclear Alert: Secrecy, Signaling, and Safety in October 1969," *International Security* 27:4 (2003), 150–183; William Burr and Jeffrey Kimball, "Nixon's Nuclear Alert: Vietnam War Diplomacy and the Joint Chiefs of Staff Readiness Test, October 1969," *Cold War History* 3:2 (2003), 113–156.
36 Yang Kuisong, "The Sino-Soviet Border Clash of 1969: From Zhenbao Island to Sino-American Rapprochement," *Cold War History* 1:1 (2001), 21–52.
37 Henry Kissinger, *White House Years* (Boston: Little, Brown, 1979), 183.
38 Raymond L. Garthoff, *Détente and Confrontation: American-Soviet Relations from Nixon to Reagan* (Washington, DC: Brookings Institution, 1985).
39 For an account emphasizing the willingness of political leaders on both sides to salvage great-power détente, Melvyn P. Leffler, *For the Soul of Mankind: The United States, the Soviet Union, and the Cold War* (New York: Hill & Wang, 2007), chapter 4. For an account emphasizing the Soviet Union's disregard for restraint, see Haslam, *Russia's Cold War*, chapter 10. Both authors acknowledge the growing influence of anti-détente forces in the United States.
40 Kristina Spohr Readman, "Germany and the Politics of the Neutron Bomb, 1975–1979," *Diplomacy and Statecraft* 21:2 (2010), 259–285.
41 Kristina Spohr Readman, "Conflict and Cooperation in Intra-Alliance Nuclear Politics: Western Europe, the United States, and the Genesis of NATO's Dual-Track Decision, 1977–1979," *Journal of Cold War Studies* 13:2 (2011), 39–89. The influence of Soviet-bloc manipulation in the West European anti-nuclear movement of the late 1970s and early 1980s is controversial. See for example Gerhard Wettig, "The Last Soviet Offensive in the Cold War: Emergence and Development of the Campaign against NATO Euromissiles, 1979–1983," *Cold War History* 9:1 (2009), 79–110; Holger Nehring and Benjamin Ziemann, "Do All Paths Lead to Moscow? The NATO Dual-Track Decision and the Peace Movement – a Critique," *Cold War History* 12:1 (2012), 1–24; Gerhard Wettig, "Der Kreml und die Friedensbewegung Anfang der achtziger Jahren," *Vierteljahrshefte für Zeitgeschichte* 60:1 (2012), 143–149.
42 For the Dutch case, see Ruud van Dijk, "'A Mass Psychosis': The Netherlands and NATO's Dual-Track Decision, 1978–1979," *Cold War History* 12:3 (2012), 381–405.
43 Assessments of the real danger in late 1983 differ. See Vojtech Mastny, "How Able was 'Able Archer'?: Nuclear Trigger and Intelligence in Perspective," *Journal of Cold War Studies* 11:1 (2009), 108–123; Arnav Manchanda, "When Truth Is Stranger than Fiction: the *Able Archer* Incident," *Cold War History* 9:11 (2009), 111–133.
44 Frances FitzGerald, *Way Out There in the Blue: Reagan, Star Wars, and the End of the Cold War* (New York: Simon & Schuster, 2000). John Lewis Gaddis, *Strategies of Containment: A Critical Appraisal of*

American National Security Policy during the Cold War, revised and expanded edition (New York: Oxford University Press, 2005), chapter 11.
45 Peter J. Westwick, "'Space-Strike Weapons' and the Soviet Response to SDI," *Diplomatic History* 32:5 (2008), 955–979.
46 The so-called "Reagan victory school" notwithstanding, there is an emerging consensus among specialists that President Reagan and General Secretary Gorbachev together, in collaboration, made the end of the Cold War possible, although most would argue that Gorbachev's policies had the bigger impact. The effect of Reagan's anti-Soviet rhetoric and U.S. programs such as SDI may, on balance, have been more to strengthen Soviet hard-liners than to compel concessions. Celeste A. Wallander, "Western Policy and the Demise of the Soviet Union," *Journal of Cold War Studies* 5:4 (2003), 137–177; Archie Brown, *The Rise and Fall of Communism* (New York: HarperCollins, 2009), chapters 23–25; Jack F. Matlock Jr., *Reagan and Gorbachev: How the Cold War Ended* (New York: Random House, 2004). Also, Beth A. Fischer, *The Reagan Reversal: Foreign Policy and the End of the Cold War* (Columbia, MO: University of Missouri Press, 2000). For a debate between Brown and one of his critics: Archie Brown, "Perestroika and the End of the Cold War," *Cold War History* 7:1 (2007), 1–17; Andrew Patman, "Some Reflections on Archie Brown and the End of the Cold War," *Cold War History* 7:3 (2007), 439–445.
47 James Graham Wilson, "Bolts from the Blue: The United States, the Soviet Union, and the End of the Cold War," PhD Dissertation, University of Virginia, 2011.

21

TECHNOLOGY AND THE COLD WAR

Elidor Mëhilli

Rockets, reactors, missiles, submarines, fighter jets: For decades, the Cold War conjured images of an imminent military confrontation and the terrifying prospect of nuclear weapons deployment. The arms race between the United States and the Soviet Union was intense, its impact profound. With the introduction of high-tech nuclear weapons, vast military industries developed in both countries. The result could have been mass destruction on an unprecedented scale. Much attention has been paid to this aspect of the Cold War conflict – and rightly so. But the intense focus on military topics and high-level political actors in Moscow and Washington often overlooked other kinds of technologies and exchange processes. In addition to struggles over fighter-bombers and warheads, in fact, the technological competition between East and West also extended to consumer desires and living standards. Reviewing a number of more recent contributions on this subject, this chapter looks at the connections between Cold War politics, technological innovation, and material demands. This, too, was a complicated affair involving state bureaucrats and communist parties, information agencies and espionage, ambitious planners, engineers, designers, advertisers, itinerant experts dispensing advice, and propagandists of all colors. At its most conspicuous, this was a race between capitalism and socialism over consumption: everyday conveniences like televisions, washing machines, and modern kitchens. But underlying this race in mundane consumer artifacts were aspirations for a better life, shared by millions across the world, and the pursuit of international prestige and modernization.

Studying scientific and technological developments and exchanges during the Cold War presented numerous challenges, including high levels of secrecy, unreliable data, and limited sources. Still, the work of scholars like Zhores Medvedev, Kendall Bailes, Alexander Vucinich, and Loren Graham proved illuminating.[1] More was written about the physical and natural sciences rather than technology, and specifically on the question of what was "Soviet" about Soviet science. As telling examples, scholarship focused on the assault against genetic research in the Soviet Union, launched under Stalin, and the momentous transformations within the Soviet Academy of Sciences.[2] But the literature on Soviet science and technology developed largely in isolation from the major debates among historians and sociologists in the West. The "constructivists" of the 1970s and 1980s, for example, who sharply emphasized the social, economic, and political factors shaping scientific and technological knowledge, did not engage with comparisons across socio-political systems.[3] In more recent years, another generation of historians of science and technology has revisited the complex relationship between scientists and the state, officials and designers, planners and engineers. Based on declassified Soviet archival sources, these works include studies by Asif Siddiqi, Ethan Pollock, and authors inspired by Thomas Hughes' influential analysis of large-scale technological systems.[4] Not confined to Big Science, authors have turned to transnational interactions among experts and the rise of new fields like computing.[5] Nevertheless, works that cross the Iron Curtain, or that adopt a transnational angle within the communist world, like Paul Josephson's highly evocative studies of technologies under authoritarian rule, remain the exception.[6] Finally, only recently have Cold War historians seriously engaged with the connections between technology, economic planning, and consumption.

As some of the best new works illustrate, designing and deploying technologies, industrial blueprints, and consumer goods became crucial to how ordinary inhabitants across the East–West divide perceived Cold War relations. In large part, this was because the superpowers used technology as a measure of their political supremacy and economic success. In the communist world, party leaders promised that modern technology would enable them to create the basis for a new, non-capitalist version of society. In the United States, government agencies deployed technological inventions to convince the rest of the world of the power of free markets and liberal democracy. Fueled by political interests, ideology, and envy, this competition showed that socialist and capitalist states were in constant interaction. How this competition played out, in the end, had as much to do with Western postwar achievements as with the internal constraints of state-run socialist economies and the unexpected outcomes of technological circulation.

Rockets and Kitchens

On 24 July 1959, eager throngs of Soviet residents spent hours waiting in line to get a glimpse of life under capitalism. At the American National Exhibition in Moscow's Sokol'niki Park, they were particularly drawn to the *Splitnik*, a spacious prefabricated suburban house specially designed to woo the Soviets. Inside that ranch-style house, Vice President Richard M. Nixon and Soviet Premier Nikita S. Khrushchev took a tour of a fully equipped yellow General Electric kitchen and argued over the relative merits of their political systems. Pointing to female housewife impersonators operating modern ovens, Nixon hailed the wonders of American capitalism. The Soviets were ahead in space exploration, he admitted, but the Americans had "miracle kitchens" and color television. "Would it not be better," Nixon asked, "to compete in the relative merits of washing machines than in the strength of rockets?"[7] Khrushchev came across as unimpressed. Nobody in the Soviet Union would be interested in what American capitalist companies had to offer, he insisted. Soviet inhabitants enjoyed housing, health care, social security, and free education. In the US, the Soviet premier pointed out, people with no money could not afford such kitchens anyway.

Snapshots of the two leaders arguing over a washing machine quickly made the news across the world. The images told a simple but poignant story: parallel to the intense race in developing nuclear technology, the two superpowers were also engaged in "psychological warfare," played out in the realm of industrial technology, consumption, and domestic material culture. Already in 1951, in a satirical essay titled "The Nylon War," the American sociologist David Riesman had provided a glimpse of this peculiar war fought with "soft weapons" like household appliances and supermarket products. Composed as a fictitious war report, Riesman's essay described a military campaign against the Soviet Union during which US planes dropped tons of consumer goods instead of bombs. If the Soviets were given the opportunity "to sample the riches of America," the tongue-in-cheek report concluded, "the Russian people would not long tolerate masters who gave them tanks and spies instead of vacuum cleaners and beauty parlors." Riesman's "Operation Abundance" envisioned US military aircraft bombing the Soviets into submission with copious amounts of "nylon hose," cigarettes, radios, yo-yos, and wristwatches.[8] Tellingly, some readers seem to have believed that Riesman's report was genuine, a fact that baffled the author, who had merely wanted to take issue with what he deemed narrow-minded US foreign policy debates in the late 1940s. Within a few years, US officials would become fully involved in psychological warfare to demonstrate the superiority of American life.[9]

A new battleground between capitalism and socialism emerged by the late 1950s: the modern home. Soviet and US leaders disagreed on virtually every aspect of economic policies, but they "found common diplomatic ground in the idea that science and technology were the true yardsticks of society's progress."[10] At the same time, the Soviets were acutely aware of the economic strides made in the US and Western Europe. By the middle of the 1950s, the US was purchasing three-quarters of all domestic appliances produced in the world (and, in turn, produced a sizeable share of those goods and services).[11] The average personal income of American families and single individuals doubled between 1936 and 1960.[12] By the early 1960s, West Germans had become "affluent Europeans with high rates of expenditure on kitchens, automobiles, and holidays."[13] This was the advent of mass consumption, and though it did not develop uniformly everywhere, it presented Soviet and Eastern bloc leaders with a troubling new reality. On both sides of Germany, this emerging competition in "soft weapons" involved information agencies, cultural and economic institutions, engineers, inventors, entrepreneurs, spies, and millions of users (consumers). Though clearly not terrifying like the threat of nuclear confrontation underlying the Cold War, it nevertheless proved corrosive to communist regimes that had proclaimed that they would successfully compete with – and overcome – the capitalist West.[14]

This drive to engineer an alternative form of modern life was deeply rooted in the Soviet experiment, but Khrushchev's rise was momentous for a number of reasons. At the Twentieth Congress of the Communist Party of the Soviet Union (CPSU) in February 1956, he astonished delegates by criticizing Stalin and cataloguing his crimes and political errors. He championed the idea of peaceful coexistence with the West, thus clearing the way for borrowing Western technical advances and setting in motion reformist urges across the Eastern bloc. Against the financial excesses of Stalinism, made visible in the gigantic ornate skyscrapers dotting Moscow, Khrushchev proposed rational industrial methods and building much-needed apartment blocks quickly out of reinforced concrete. Indeed, for tens of millions of ordinary Soviet residents, the 1950s and 1960s were the years when they moved from collective housing to single-family apartments. Khrushchev advocated forcefully for advanced technology as the vehicle for Soviet economic success. Mechanization became the mantra in agriculture; the hydroelectric power plants and massive canals of the early Five Year Plans would later be supplanted by massive systems of railroads, dams, and vastly ambitious projects to divert the flow of Siberian rivers. Finally, for some elites in the cultural sphere, the period referred to as "the Thaw" also brought closer contacts with their Western counterparts.

Crucially, in 1957, the Soviets launched the world's first intercontinental ballistic missile and the world's first artificial satellite, *Sputnik-1*. At the 1958 World Fair (EXPO) in Brussels, Soviet designers proudly displayed replicas of the *Sputnik*, which attracted millions of visitors.[15] In contrast, the US pavilion failed to generate the same level of enthusiasm.[16] Moscow appeared confident and eager to impress the world, which helps explain why the Soviets permitted Washington to bring American kitchens to Sokol'niki Park in 1959 in the first place. The decision to allow the American exhibition, in other words, was informed both by the desire to open the country to Western technological innovations and by the underlying belief that the Soviet Union had the moral prerequisites and determination to outdo the capitalists. Two years later, the Soviets sent Yuri Gagarin into space. It was in this context that "catching up and overtaking" the West became a dominant mantra. And why many observers, both inside and outside of the Soviet Union, found Khrushchev's rallying cry plausible.

Sputnik shook the confidence of Americans in their absolute technological supremacy. In its aftermath, US officials pumped funding into aeronautics research and electronics. Federal organizations like the National Science Foundation also channeled increasing amounts of money into defense programs, whereas private organizations like the Ford Foundation were galvanized in the effort to mount a "cultural Cold War" in Europe.[17] In devising their propaganda effort, however, US officials shifted from military hardware to everyday technologies, consumer goods, and the modern conveniences made possible by industrial innovations under capitalism. Employing special advertising consultants and engineers, they designed and shipped generously appointed prefabricated homes to the Soviet Union as examples of the "American Way of Life." They also brought Soviet delegations to the US to "convert" them to the conveniences of American suburban homes. These carefully designed campaigns, as one author has put it, "encouraged the Soviet bloc to measure its progress through direct comparisons with Western per-capita private consumption, the Achilles heel of economies based on state-owned heavy industries."[18] But World Fair pavilions, technology shows, and industrial propaganda would not have been as effective if socialist leaders themselves had not intentionally submitted to the competition with Western capitalism in terms of innovation and consumption. Nuclear arms and space exploration had already placed science and technology at the center of the Cold War. By entering the single-family home, however, the competition in "conventional" science and technology (rockets and missiles) gained another important dimension: the challenges of satisfying individual desires and the unpredictable consequences of envy.

Superiority and Envy

The United States and the Soviet Union offered two different models of development in the postwar period: On the one hand, there was the market economy on view at Sokol'niki Park, heavily reliant on private enterprises, competition, global capitalist trade, and vigorously targeting the desires and behavior of consumers. The other model was illustrated by the economy of the Soviet Union and replicated in the early 1950s across the Eastern bloc. It was marked by state-led growth, mass mobilization of the labor force, and a predominant focus on heavy industry. The American model, the historian Odd Arne Westad has observed, "was tainted by the association of US capitalism with the capitalism of the colonial oppressors." But the Soviet model also suffered from a plethora of problems, including "the image of the Soviet Union as the 'secondary' superpower and from what was often seen as second-rate Soviet products and technology. Both, however, offered a road to high modernity through education, science, and technological progress."[19]

This belief in scientific knowledge and technological innovations as a means for attaining progress was widespread and enduring. Under both capitalism and socialism, it was largely the state that enabled research and innovation and created institutions to educate and train new professional elites. Large-scale technologies, moreover, were not limited to party-states and centralized economies. From metallurgical factories to massive railway systems and hydropower plants, technocrats both East and West, when given resources and power, often opted for utopian projects with radical social, economic, and environmental outcomes.

Yet there were important differences in how capitalist and socialist states dealt with science and technology. Soviet party authorities operated on the basis of an egalitarian ideology and they saw science and technology as a vehicle for radically restructuring society. "Closely connected to this ideological proclivity to embrace modern technology," one author has observed, "was the practical necessity of employing high technology in order to attain one of the major goals of state socialism: detailed, precise, and timely planning of economic and social development."[20] Extensive engineering programs were established across the Soviet republics and ambitious youths were enrolled in polytechnic institutes. As a result, there emerged a Soviet scientific–technical elite, constituting a large military-industrial complex. Under the socialist system of the division of labor, the technical professions – especially engineering – proved crucial in ensuring upward social mobility for eager youths.[21] In return for political loyalty, this new class of engineers and other highly skilled technical personnel enjoyed social status and received a range of material perquisites denied to others. Material privileges were crucial in a society of chronic shortages, but it is also true that members of this expanding Soviet technical elite were profoundly committed to the Soviet project of creating an alternative society to the capitalist one. In the context of a large-scale social engineering program, their technocratic orientation could be advantageous.

As powerful as the centrally planned economy could be in marshalling and redistributing resources, it had a hard time encouraging innovation. Restricting professional associations outside of the state was necessary for political reasons but it also negatively impacted science and technology. The Soviet regime, writes David Holloway, "supported science, but also destroyed scientific disciplines."[22] The absence of property rights and limited patent protections facilitated copying and sharing inventions but also stifled any sense of competition between innovators and industrial agents. Technological improvements were governed by the need to satisfy socialist planning targets. Having suppressed consumption, the state's planning favored large-scale projects: nuclear reactors, hydroelectric power plants, and aeronautics. Virtually everything was supposed to be governed by the plan, including the allocation of cadres to enterprises and factories, students to university faculties, materials, goods, and the labor force. "It became impossible to conceive of a solution to personnel problems involving anything other than more or better planning," one author has observed in reference to the Soviet Union. "Planning had to be more specific, based on better data, or conducted according to new formulas. It was unthinkable to question the idea of planning itself."[23]

Unlike in the US, the civil and military industrial sectors in the Soviet Union remained firmly distinct from one another. Scientists and engineers were deemed crucial to the socialist modernization project, but they also aroused intense suspicion, especially under Stalin. This was particularly the case with physicists and engineers, but communist authorities (Khrushchev first and foremost) also meddled into the affairs of agriculture experts, urban planners, architects, and industrial designers. State controls on scientists and technical disciplines also isolated them from universities and academies. In communist Albania, where the Soviet socio-economic model was vigorously embraced and diligently copied, the engineering profession similarly held the promise of social status, but also the major risk of being labeled a wrecker or accused of imitating the West – even decades after such policies were relaxed elsewhere in the Eastern bloc. A rift developed between the widely shared desire to provide a modern alternative to Western capitalism and the internal constraints of the centralized economy, the politics of censorship, and the constant preoccupation with enemies (both real and imagined). Across the communist world, centrally planned economies mobilized millions of individuals, built vast systems of cities and massive factories, invested in education and created science academies. But they also struggled when it came to infusing technical innovations into light industries, and they were notoriously bad in enacting workplace safety provisions. Impressive as they seemed, state-sponsored large-scale big technologies – dams, reactors, massive metallurgical factories – also had a deleterious impact on the environment that is still visible today across Eurasia.

Underlying the socialist policy of "catching up and overtaking" the West, then, was a persistent paradox: the Soviet establishment deemed its mission of creating a new type of society as being morally superior to social policies under capitalism. It viewed technology, as Paul Josephson observes, "as value-neutral, independent of the system in which it was created."[24] This meant that the Soviets could borrow freely from the latest inventions of capitalist scientists and engineers insofar as these borrowings would further their goal of creating an alternative advanced society. At the same time, by the late 1950s, Soviet leaders had become acutely aware of their inferior economic performance, outmoded technology, and inability to develop a viable socialist alternative to the consumer society being celebrated in the United States. One author has described this contradictory situation as superiority mixed with inferiority, a combination that deeply affected "the mentality of the communist elite and their seemingly capricious oscillations between the extremes of offensive or defensive, integrationist or isolationist policies."[25] To put it another way, Soviet government planners both extensively borrowed from the West, as we shall see, and endlessly sought to reinvent their own socio-economic system on the basis of an ideological alternative to capitalism, the deployment of large-scale technologies, and continued mass mobilization.

A similar contradictory outlook could be found in the Eastern bloc. Just as the Soviets were trying to make sense of American consumer culture, East German party elites faced the immediate challenge of another postwar economic success story: West Germany. The building of the Berlin Wall drastically reduced the number of scientists fleeing the German Democratic Republic (GDR), but news of West German technological innovations and consumer successes had a way of trickling in through the airwaves. As East German leader Walter Ulbricht explained in 1963, "even after the closing of state borders, the high living standard [in West Germany] strongly affects the population of the GDR and its political attitudes."[26] Determined to outdo the capitalists, Eastern-bloc states borrowed technologies from abroad and rebranded them as "socialist." They also increasingly circulated technologies, blueprints, and industrial practices among themselves, creating a parallel system of exchange spanning almost all of Eastern Europe (the so-called Second World). In this sense, the 1959 Nixon–Khrushchev kitchen debate signaled not only the advent of a new consumer-related dimension to Cold War competition, but also the simple fact that, for all the military barriers and enforced censorship, the two sides of the Iron Curtain were in constant communication, both formal and informal, direct and indirect. In this particular postwar moment, marked by "multidirectional exchanges of products, people, cultural values, and gender regimes," socialist states institutionalized a kind of technological envy of the West.[27]

Copying and Circulating

Technological innovations cross over from country to country through a number of channels. Official ones include trade agreements between governments, license purchases, and the exchange of delegations of experts. These are relatively easy to trace in documents or official publications. Informal channels of exchange, however, though crucial, are far more difficult to identify. During the Cold War, these included illegal copying, industrial espionage, and reverse engineering, which involves working back from a finished product to obtain a primary design that can be reproduced. In the early stages of the Cold War, US officials grew alarmed that Western technologies could fall into Soviet hands. As deterrence, Washington pushed for a strategic embargo against the Soviet Union and the Eastern bloc. The result was the Coordinating Committee for Multilateral Export Controls (CoCom), established in 1949 and entrusted with the task of controlling the transmission of sensitive technology from NATO countries to the Eastern bloc. In addition to weapons, lists of embargoed items also included a range of industrial blueprints and raw materials that US officials thought might serve the Soviet military (so-called dual-use items). The more intense struggles to control Western technology, as a result, often occurred in Cold War "border-zones" like Austria and Finland.

As much as they tried, US officials could not control all technical transfers. Reverse engineering allowed Soviet specialists to obtain valuable technical information, as did, to varying degrees, circulating Western professional journals and displays at trade fairs. Both superpowers relied on military and industrial espionage, as did the East Germans.[28] American, British, and West German intelligence operatives, in fact, actively sought information on Soviet innovations and weapons, and they also encouraged the defection of high-skilled East German specialists and scientists to West Germany in the 1950s.[29] Through a combination of formal and informal mechanisms, the Soviets adopted Western technology, especially in the chemical and motor industries, while limiting purchases to Western equipment and machines.[30] As trade in manufactured goods with West European countries increased under Khrushchev, Soviet officials also created new institutions to attract imported technology in areas like transportation and energy. But it was one thing to borrow or import machines and technology from Western Europe. It was quite another to effectively absorb them. On that front, as one economic historian has concluded, "the Soviet economic system impeded not only domestic innovation but also the assimilation of imported technology."[31]

Elsewhere in the Eastern bloc, Western technology became increasingly appealing in the 1960s and 1970s. Western licenses, for example, allowed the Hungarians to improve their Ikarus bus line. The country was one of the world's major producers and exporters of large-size buses, which it traded for Soviet oil.[32] By the 1970s, Western companies like the Finnish Nokia and the West German Siemens had developed direct ties to the Soviet Union through technical transfer agreements.[33] In the people's democracies, certain high-skilled specialists were permitted to attend international meetings and scholarly conferences, where they connected with their Western counterparts. Architects and urban planners from the Eastern bloc interacted with their Western colleagues during the meetings of the Union Internationale des Architectes (International Union of Architects, UIA), which held congresses in Moscow (1958), Havana (1963), Prague (1967), and Varna, Bulgaria (1968). Still, as important as these international contacts were, they did not necessarily transcend Cold War ideological barriers. East German architects attending the Moscow UIA Congress in 1958, for example, took the Soviets to task for being too uncritical of Western architects.[34] Many of the technical elite types in the Eastern bloc were intensely drawn to Western innovations, which they sought to emulate, but they also took issue with capitalism and the logic of free markets. Under socialism, in any case, opportunities for international exposure had to be negotiated with suspicious superiors, government bureaucrats, and, frequently, narrow-minded party apparatchiks.

Parallel to this contentious East–West exchange, the Soviets developed a system of technical transfer and reorganization within the communist world. The immediate pattern for these interactions, as the historian Austin Jersild has observed, largely grew out of Soviet policies and encounters in Europe and Asia in the immediate aftermath of the Second World War. Soviet operatives and managers "scavenged" war-torn Eastern Europe to appropriate German factories and enterprises, and also native industrial components, blueprints, and technical knowledge. They shipped entire factories from China to the Soviet Union and eagerly took ownership of Japanese military equipment. Over the years, they also kept an eye on East European laboratories, factories, and enterprises for inventions or innovations they could similarly adopt. This became particularly important in the context of the US-led strategic embargo and it involved a lot of calculations about where Soviet economic and industrial interests would be best served. "The Soviets looked to Prague for automobile and tractor production," writes Jersild, "as well as film production and candy making, to Budapest for electronic computing devices, to Dresden for material-testing equipment, and to Warsaw for factories, technology, and workers in the coke and coal industry."[35] Deeming China technically inferior, Soviet managerial elites looked instead towards the Eastern bloc, which could serve both as a direct supplier of components and as an avenue for "smuggling" Western technology.

Yet it is also true that socialist countries became increasingly involved in technical exchange among themselves. This type of exchange involved a variety of actors at the national and transnational levels. The most obvious was the Council for Mutual Economic Aid (Comecon, or CMEA), established in 1949, whose official task was to foster closer economic relations among the people's democracies. It was originally composed of Bulgaria, Czechoslovakia, Hungary, Poland, Romania, and the Soviet Union (Albania joined later that year; East Germany in 1950). In the 1960s, Mongolia, Vietnam, and Cuba also joined. The organization had an executive committee, a secretariat, and special commissions covering a range of economic issues from trade in raw materials to transfers of machinery and industrial equipment. During its early existence, however, the Comecon merely served to reinforce Moscow's economic orientations for the Eastern bloc. Each country devised its own plan for "technical-scientific cooperation" and reached bilateral agreements on a host of prearranged "themes" (like metallurgy, fuel, mass-produced housing, prefabrication, transportation, or telecommunications). Typically, this was done by a special sector within branch ministries or the government, tasked with overseeing relations with other socialist countries. Increasingly, a host of other actors, including scientific academies, cultural unions, and special commissions, also became involved in technical exchange. Through regular meetings of bilateral technical delegations and Comecon-based commissions, socialist countries arranged for the transfer of engineers, blueprints, documentation, formulas, patents, and industrial products.

Under Khrushchev, there was a greater push for socialist economic integration and a division of labor. The Soviet leader boldly envisioned a kind of socialist world system without markets and private property. "International distribution networks would supply standardized and unified production lines from Berlin to Shanghai," one scholar has described it, "research and training would be shared between socialist countries, as would innovations in technology, defense, and planning, and ideological questions would be decided at international congresses."[36] The adoption of a Comecon Charter in 1959, however, did little to change the nature of the organization and Khrushchev's ambitious ideas faced resistance from member states like Romania. Tension persisted between bilateral technical agreements (which were, on the whole, more efficient) and the drive for multi-lateral exchange in the framework of Comecon. Over the years the organization grew more bureaucratic and complex, spanning permanent commissions and working groups, coordinating centers, research institutes, international organizations, cross-country scientific teams, and experimental laboratories. But branch ministries within the individual member states continued to engage directly with their counterparts abroad to trade personnel, trainees, and postgraduate students.

Increased exchange among socialist countries also highlighted technological differences within the Eastern bloc. Take, for example, the Czechoslovaks and their achievements in design and the construction industry. Prague's pavilion for the Brussels World Fair in 1958, featuring modern examples of industrial design and ceramics, won numerous accolades from visitors and critics alike. In industrialized housing construction, the country was far ahead from the rest of the Eastern bloc. Czechoslovak architects developed standard building types for single-family apartment blocks in the 1940s and they also pioneered the prefabricated panel technology that became so ubiquitous across the communist world over the following four decades.[37] In large part, Czechoslovak architects and planners were served by the significant prewar experience with industrial building technologies. This was also the case with East Germans and Hungarian planners and civil engineers, who also developed a number of advanced systems of panel prefabrication in the 1960s and 1970s.

To be sure, prefabrication was not a socialist invention. Indeed, the Soviets had long been fascinated with American industrial innovations, especially Fordism and Frederick Winslow Taylor's ideas about "scientific management." In the interwar period, a number of prominent European architects (Walter Gropius, Marcel Lods, Hans Scharoun) flirted with the idea of concrete slabs and factory-made houses. Crucially, the Second World War served as a major catalyst for extending military methods and materials into the civilian construction industry, whether in postwar France or in the Eastern bloc. Socialist planners quickly adopted European prefabrication models like the Danish Larsen-Nielsen system or systems developed by the French engineer Raymond Camus. When coupled with the immense housing shortages across the Eastern bloc and the Soviet Union, as well as Khrushchev's calls for more rational construction methods in the mid-1950s, it is easy to see why socialist states found this particular technology so appealing. Once imported into the Eastern bloc, such technological systems could be circulated, reinvented, and adopted in a variety of contexts. Like the Hungarians and the East Germans, the Soviets were constantly on the lookout for novelties in West European prefabrication technology, though, owing to the logic of central planning, innovations were often delayed or deferred in the interest of reducing costs. Within a matter of years, socialist states were measuring technological success by the thousands of concrete apartment blocks they could quickly build each year. Up until the collapse of communism, tens of millions of prefabricated apartment blocks sprung up, from the Adriatic shores to the farthest reaches of Siberia in the most unprecedented industrial construction campaign in the world.

While extensively borrowing from Western Europe and the Eastern bloc, the Soviets also deployed a considerable amount of technical aid abroad. Apart from fully equipped textile mills, factories, and tractors shipped to Albania in the 1950s, this technical aid extended to North Korea, Egypt, Indonesia, and a number of other countries. In the 1950s, thousands of Soviet and East European advisers and specialists were sent to China and trade between Beijing and other communist countries grew significantly. The Chinese received industrial equipment for the energy sector and the defense and shipbuilding industries. Factories often came fully equipped with machines made in the Soviet Union or the Eastern bloc, assembly teams, and groups of engineers who were supposed to train the local workforce.[38] Soviet scientific and technology transfer to China between 1955 and 1958 was a significant factor in Beijing's development of nuclear infrastructure (though both sides denied it). All of this exchange was no mean fit. It involved a myriad of logistical challenges, from the enormous hurdles involved in shipping entire plants and massive machinery halfway across Eurasia to the more basic – but equally crucial – challenges of translating technical literature from the Russian language, negotiating financial terms, and dealing with servicing and repairs.

Soviet and Eastern-bloc achievements in science, technology, and prefabrication also attracted leaders in the developing world. The Soviets became involved with the metallurgical industry in India, while the Czechoslovaks furnished the Institute for Metal Working Machinery in Bangalore, and the Poles assisted with the shipbuilding industry. The fate of these projects varied from country to country. "The experience of such countries as Algeria, Syria, Ethiopia, and others," one official Soviet publication observed, "shows that the socialist orientation of their development greatly facilitates and accelerates the use of scientific and technological knowledge."[39] According to official sources, in 1978 some 41,000 students from over 100 developing countries were enrolled in universities located in various Comecon member states.[40] Comecon assistance, similarly, was used to establish technological institutes in Afghanistan, Ethiopia, and Burma. Finally, there were a number of technical inventions transferred from the Eastern bloc to the West. Two examples include the BD 200 open-end spinning machine and the soft (hydrogel) contact lens – both Czechoslovak inventions purchased and eventually distributed in the United States and elsewhere.[41] But these were rare examples. As György Péteri has concluded, "Out of fifty major technological advances that were made during the post-war era and still shape our lives today, only three appeared first in a socialist country."[42]

Tracing these exchanges of technological systems, it becomes clear that they were shaped both by the specific interests of the agents involved and by the institutional links created by socialist states. Soviet bureaucrats were fond of insisting that technical cooperation among socialist countries was fundamentally different from similar practices in the capitalist world. They argued that socialist states engaged in "relations of a new type," based not on exploitation and greed but on proletarian solidarity and friendship. It turned out, needless to say, that techno-scientific exchange was as much driven by national interests and economic calculations as by Cold War security concerns and ideological considerations. In the context of Cold War geopolitics, this kind of exchange could take unexpected turns. In Asia, for example, Soviet provisions of technical assistance contributed to a growing rivalry with the Chinese, who sought to reorient themselves in the region.[43] (After Mao Zedong's death in 1976, Deng Xiaoping would enthusiastically seek advanced US technology, including weapons technology, and Washington happily cooperated with Beijing in the interest of countering the Soviets.) Just as it could facilitate the self-induced Soviet competition with American-style capitalism, then, the acquired sphere of influence in Eastern Europe and Asia could also produce unexpected challenges.

Competition and Control

Heavy industry and big technological projects propelled the Soviet Union and Eastern-bloc countries on a far-reaching recovery program from relative "backwardness" in the postwar period. Nuclear weapons and military technologies brought international prestige, and they also shaped the conflict between the superpowers and their allies. But parallel to this military competition there was also a race over standards of living, the mass provision of consumer goods, and the achievement of small-scale technological innovations. In this sense, "politically neutral" objects like General Electric washing machines on display in Sokol'niki Park or slabs of prefabricated concrete became, like nuclear reactors, infused with a specific kind of politics.[44] The competition between capitalism and socialism, which Soviet leaders forcefully embraced, encouraged borrowing and circulation. Political, economic, and institutional mechanisms peculiar to centrally planned economies, in turn, shaped the manner in which borrowed technologies were deployed. Yet, the intentions of political leaders, ambitious planners, and state-funded engineers did not guarantee any particular outcomes. Soviet and Eastern-bloc governments could imitate, borrow, and they could seek further technical integration between the socialist states. But they had no control over US and West European innovations or the future implications of exchanged technologies.

Economic discrepancies between the communist world and Western Europe only became more pronounced over the years. To keep up in providing the consumer goods that inhabitants had been led to expect, a number of Eastern-bloc regimes increasingly borrowed money from Western Europe. But no matter how hard they tried, socialist states found it challenging to assimilate foreign technological innovations and still furnish housing, clothing, consumer goods, or even basic staples. This was also true for the Soviet Union, but Eastern-bloc states directly faced "a capitalist world – in many cases right across the border – that had undergone its greatest-ever consumer boom in the 1950s and 1960s."[45] The East Germans, for example, though more advanced than other socialist countries in a number of industries, struggled to remain competitive. They enacted economic reforms in the 1960s, only to abandon them one decade later. Some elements of market research were introduced and various offices and planning agencies flirted with elements of Western-style consumerism. Nevertheless, Eastern-bloc ideologues recognized that these mechanisms were fundamentally alien to socialism.[46] At the time, the East German model of "technocratic modernization" seemed plausible to some Western observers, who vastly exaggerated, as the political scientist Jeffrey Kopstein has put it, the power of a so-called German technocratic culture over Leninist structures.[47] Fantasies of rescuing socialism by deploying high-tech technologies and electronics, similarly, ultimately amounted to little.[48] In comparison to East Germany, some countries (like Albania) were significantly more insulated, which allowed native communist regimes to keep a strong grip on power and coerce residents into tightening their belts. In any case, all socialist states had to grapple with Western technical and consumer advances at one point or another. And they had to do this in increasingly unfavorable conditions: while centrally planned economies were left out of major global capital flows, innovations in communications made socialist state-enforced controls over information immensely difficult.

Notes

1. Zhores Medvedev, *Soviet Science* (New York: Norton, 1978); Kendall E. Bailes, *Technology and Society under Lenin and Stalin: Origins of the Soviet Technical Intelligentsia, 1917–1941* (Princeton, NJ: Princeton University Press, 1978); Alexander Vucinich, *Empire of Knowledge: The Academy of Sciences of the USSR (1917–1970)* (Berkeley, CA: University of California Press, 1984); Loren R. Graham, *Science in Russia and the Soviet Union: A Short History* (Cambridge: Cambridge University Press, 1993).
2. For a useful overview, see Michael Gordin, "Was There Ever a 'Stalinist Science'?" *Kritika: Explorations in Russian and Eurasian History* 9:3 (Summer 2008): 625–639.
3. Loren R. Graham, *What Have We Learned about Science and Technology from the Russian Experience?* (Stanford, CA: Stanford University Press, 1998), 2–3.
4. Asif A. Siddiqi, *Sputnik and the Soviet Space Challenge* (Gainesville, FL: University Press of Florida, 2003); Ethan Pollock, *Stalin and the Soviet Science Wars* (Princeton, NJ: Princeton University Press, 2006); Gabrielle Hecht (ed.), *Entangled Geographies: Empire and Technopolitics in the Global Cold War* (Cambridge, MA: MIT Press, 2011).
5. One example is Atsushi Akera's *Calculating a Natural World: Scientists, Engineers, and Computers during the Rise of U.S. Cold War Research* (Cambridge, MA: MIT Press, 2007).
6. Paul R. Josephson, *Totalitarian Science and Technology* (Atlantic Heights, NJ: Humanities Press, 1996); *Industrialized Nature: Brute Force Technology and the Transformation of the Natural World* (Washington, DC: Island Press, 2002); *Would Trotsky Wear a Bluetooth? Technological Utopianism Under Socialism 1917–1989* (Baltimore, MD: Johns Hopkins University Press, 2010).
7. Victoria de Grazia, *Irresistible Empire: America's Advance Through Twentieth-Century Europe* (Cambridge, MA: Harvard University Press, 2005), 456.
8. David Riesman, *Abundance for What? And Other Essays* (Garden City, NY: Doubleday, 1964), 65–77.
9. Walter L. Hixson, *Parting the Curtain: Propaganda, Culture, and the Cold War, 1945–1961* (Basingstoke: Macmillan, 1997).
10. Ruth Oldenziel and Karin Zachmann, "Kitchens as Technology and Politics," in Oldenziel and Zachmann (eds.), *Cold War Kitchen: Americanization, Technology, and European Users* (Cambridge, MA: MIT Press, 2009), 3.

11 Mary Nolan, "Consuming America, Producing Gender," in Laurence R. Moore and Maurizio Vaudagna (eds.), *The American Century in Europe* (Ithaca, NY: Cornell University Press, 2003), 248.
12 James T. Patterson, *America's Struggle against Poverty in the Twentieth Century, 1900–1985* (New York: Basic Books, 1986), 42.
13 De Grazia, *Irresistible Empire*, 359.
14 For this extended argument, see Stephen Kotkin, with a contribution by Jan T. Gross, *Uncivil Society: 1989 and the Implosion of the Communist Establishment* (New York: Modern Library, 2009).
15 Lewis Siegelbaum, "Sputnik Goes to Brussels: The Exhibition of a Soviet Technological Wonder," *Journal of Contemporary History* 47:1 (January 2012): 120–136.
16 Susan E. Reid, "Who Will Beat Whom? Soviet Popular Reception of the American National Exhibition in Moscow, 1959," *Kritika: Explorations in Russian and Eurasian History* 9:4 (Fall 2008): 855–904.
17 Volker R. Berghahn, *America and the Intellectual Cold Wars in Europe* (Princeton, NJ: Princeton University Press, 2001).
18 Greg Castillo, *Cold War on the Home Front: The Soft Power of Midcentury Design* (Minneapolis, MN: University of Minnesota Press, 2010), xi.
19 Odd Arne Westad, *The Global Cold War: Third World Interventions and the Making of Our Times* (Cambridge: Cambridge University Press, 2007), 92.
20 Raymond Stokes, *Constructing Socialism: Technology and Change in East Germany, 1945–1990* (Baltimore, MD: Johns Hopkins University Press, 2000), 195.
21 Harley Balzer, "Engineers: The Rise and Decline of a Social Myth," in Loren Graham (ed.), *Science and the Soviet Social Order* (Cambridge, MA: Harvard University Press, 1990), 141–167.
22 David Holloway, *Stalin and the Bomb: The Soviet Union and Atomic Energy, 1939–1956* (New Haven, CT and London: Yale University Press, 1994), 4.
23 Balzer, "Engineers," 160–161.
24 Josephson, *Would Trotsky Wear a Bluetooth?*, 4.
25 György Péteri, "Nylon Curtain – Transnational and Transsystemic Tendencies in the Cultural Life of State-Socialist Russia and East-Central Europe," *Slavonica* 10:2 (November 2004): 113–123.
26 Quoted in Mark Landsman, *Dictatorship and Demand: The Politics of Consumerism in East Germany* (Cambridge, MA: Harvard University Press, 2005), 211.
27 Nolan, "Consuming America," 245.
28 Kristie Macrakis, *Seduced by Secrets: Inside the Stasi's Spy-Tech World* (Cambridge: Cambridge University Press, 2008).
29 Paul Maddrell, *Spying on Science: Western Intelligence in Divided Germany, 1945–1961* (Oxford and New York: Oxford University Press, 2006).
30 Philip Hanson, *Trade and Technology in Soviet-Western Relations* (New York: Columbia University Press, 1981).
31 Philip Hanson, "The Soviet Union's Acquisition of Western Technology after Stalin: Some Thoughts on People and Connections," in Sari Autio-Sarasmo and Katalin Miklóssy (eds.), *Reassessing Cold War Europe* (London and New York: Routledge, 2011), 16–32.
32 S.R. Mikulinski and R. Richta (eds.), *Socialism and Science* (Prague: Academia, 1983), p. 336; Paul Marer, *East–West Technology Transfer: Study of Hungary 1968–1984* (Paris: Organization for Economic Cooperation and Development, 1986).
33 Sari Autio-Sarasmo, "Knowledge through the Iron Curtain: Soviet Scientific-Technical Cooperation with Finland and West Germany," in Sari Autio-Sarasmo and Katalin Miklóssy (eds.), *Reassessing Cold War Europe* (Abingdon and New York: Routledge, 2011), 66–82.
34 Elidor Mëhilli, "The Socialist Design: Urban Dilemmas in Postwar Europe and the Soviet Union," *Kritika: Explorations in Russian and Eurasian History* 13:3 (Summer 2012): 635–665.
35 Austin Jersild, "The Soviet State as Imperial Scavenger: 'Catch Up and Surpass' in the Transnational Socialist Bloc, 1950–1960," *American Historical Review* 116:1 (February 2011), 127.
36 Westad, *The Global Cold War*, 69.
37 Kimberly E. Zarecor, *Manufacturing a Socialist Modernity: Housing in Czechoslovakia, 1945–1960* (Pittsburgh, PA: University of Pittsburgh Press, 2011).
38 Shu Guang Zhang, *Economic Cold War: America's Embargo against China and the Sino-Soviet Alliance, 1949–1963* (Washington, DC: Woodrow Wilson Center Press; Stanford, CA: Stanford University Press, 2001), 163.
39 Mikulinski and Richta (eds.), *Socialism and Science*, 343.

40 A. Semenov, "Stabil'nyi faktor vsestoronnego progressa (K itogam XXXIII sessii SEV)," *Mirovaia ekonomika i mezhdunarodnye otnosheniia* 9 (September 1979): 12–13.
41 Karen Johnson Freeze, "Innovation and Technology Transfer during the Cold War: The Case of the Open-End Spinning Machine from Communist Czechoslovakia," *Technology and Culture* 48:2 (April 2007): 249–85; Riika Nisonen-Trnka, "Soft Contacts through the Iron Curtain," in Sari Autio-Sarasmo and Katalin Miklóssy (eds.), *Reassessing Cold War Europe* (Abingdon and New York: Routledge, 2011), 100–118.
42 Péteri, "Nylon Curtain," 118.
43 Stephen Kotkin and Charles Armstrong, "A Socialist Regional Order in Northeast Asia After World War II," in Kotkin and Armstrong (eds.), *Korea at the Center: Dynamics of Regionalism in Northeast Asia* (New York: M.E. Sharpe, 2006), 110–25.
44 Gabrielle Hecht, "Introduction," in Hecht (ed.), *Entangled Geographies*, 3.
45 Kotkin, with Gross, *Uncivil Society*, 27.
46 Landsman, *Dictatorship and Demand*.
47 Jeffrey Kopstein, *The Politics of Economic Collapse in East Germany, 1945–1989* (Chapel Hill, NC: University of North Carolina Press, 1997).
48 Dolores Augustine, *Red Prometheus: Engineering and Dictatorship in East Germany, 1945–1990* (Cambridge, MA: MIT Press, 2007).

22

INTELLIGENCE AND THE COLD WAR

Ben de Jong[1]

During the Cold War substantial financial and human resources were spent on intelligence by both sides of the Iron Curtain. Intelligence and security services in the East and West fought their own war, largely hidden from public view and mostly not in a very gentlemanly way. This chapter will discuss the ebb and flow of this "intelligence war" in general terms and in particular with respect to intelligence from human sources (Humint), signals intelligence (Sigint) and covert action, called "active measures" by the KGB.[2] The main protagonists in this war were the KGB and the CIA. Both services were assisted at crucial junctures by allied services of member states of the Warsaw Pact and NATO, and by services from other parts of the world. The cooperation between US intelligence and security services and British services, which dated from the Second World War, was particularly close and far reaching.

At the beginning of the Cold War the main Western powers, the United States and Great Britain, found themselves in the intelligence field at a clear disadvantage vis-à-vis the Soviet Union. Both countries had spent their financial and human resources in previous years primarily on fighting the Axis Powers and had not made a serious effort of spying on the Soviet Union, their main ally in the war against Nazi Germany after June 1941. Indeed, the British had suspended intelligence operations against the Soviet target for the duration of the war, even though the leadership of the NKVD, the main intelligence and security service of the USSR in 1934–46, could hardly believe this when it was told so by one of its most valuable British agents during the war.[3] As far as the United States was concerned, it did not have a foreign intelligence service worth mentioning at the beginning of the Second World War. The Office of Strategic Services (OSS), the forerunner of the CIA, was established only in June 1942, and abolished by President Truman immediately after the war. The British had much more experience in the field of intelligence and security than the Americans. Both the British Security Service, also known as MI5, and the Secret Intelligence Service (SIS, also known as MI6), were founded in 1909.[4]

Immediately after the October Revolution of 1917, Soviet leaders had established a security apparatus to which, in 1920, a foreign intelligence component had been added. In the 1920s, Soviet intelligence had penetrated anti-communist Russian exile organizations abroad and, in a very sophisticated operation, lured some of their leading figures back to the USSR, where they had been dealt with.[5] Soviet intelligence also managed from the 1930s onwards to lay the foundation of many successful Humint operations in the West.

Humint

At the end of the 1940s and in the early 1950s, US and British authorities discovered that Soviet intelligence had been running several hundred agents in their countries, dating from before the Second World War. Of these agents, dozens were in vital positions in government departments and ministries. To give but two examples: Alger Hiss, a high official at the US State Department and a member of the American delegation at the Yalta conference in 1945, had been an agent of the GRU, Soviet military intelligence, since the mid-1930s. Harry Dexter White, who became Assistant Secretary of the Treasury in 1945 and the first American director of the International Monetary Fund in 1946, had originally also been a GRU agent, but was later handled by the NKVD. Julius Rosenberg, later executed, along with his wife Ethel, on account of espionage for the Soviet Union, was recruited by the NKVD at the end of 1941. He did not occupy a position within the US government, but ran a network of agents that engaged in industrial and technological espionage on a large scale. Soviet agents, two from Rosenberg's group among them, had also penetrated the Manhattan Project, America's top-secret program that produced the first atomic bomb, as well as the British atomic project codenamed Tube Alloys.[6] The information that Soviet intelligence acquired from the Manhattan Project played an important part in the development of the first Soviet atomic bomb in the 1940s, and the acquisition of Western, in particular American, military technology had a high priority for the KGB and the military intelligence service GRU throughout the Cold War period.

The best-known Soviet penetration of the British establishment is the case of the Cambridge Five, freshly graduated students from Cambridge who were recruited by the NKVD in the mid-1930s and managed to get various government positions that gave them access to many secrets for Soviet intelligence. Kim Philby, probably the most productive agent of the five, became SIS liaison with US services in Washington in 1949, which meant that he was in a position to betray not just British intelligence secrets, but many American ones as well.[7] In the first ten or fifteen years of the Cold War, American and British security managed to uncover many of these Soviet agents, though arguably not all of them. The first break came with several important defections to the West of Soviet intelligence officers or agents who brought with them documents and other information on intelligence operations and agents. But it was the Venona project that undoubtedly made the biggest contribution to the unmasking of many important agents in the US and Great Britain in the early phase of the Cold War.

The Venona project – the name is a code name without particular meaning – was originally an American code-breaking, or Sigint, program which began in 1943 and continued to operate until 1980. Venona decrypted encoded messages exchanged between *rezidenturas* (i.e. stations) of the NKVD and GRU in the United States and Moscow headquarters or vice versa, through a very slow and difficult process. Most of the messages were sent in 1942–45; only a tiny portion were decrypted, and in many cases only partly.[8] Almost all big cases involving Soviet espionage in the United States or Great Britain in the beginning of the Cold War were discovered by information from Venona. This applies to the network of the Rosenbergs, to other important cases of atomic espionage in Great Britain and the United States in the beginning of the 1950s, and to the Cambridge Five. The fact that in the end only a tiny part of the Venona traffic could be decrypted had a serious drawback, however. This relatively small amount of information still resulted in about 350 code names of Americans who had been in contact with the NKVD or GRU in the 1940s, out of which more than half could not be identified properly. These discoveries led to a general fear, within the American and British services, particularly during the 1960s, that they still had Soviet agents within their ranks. This fear can partly be attributed to the fact that the tiny portion of decrypted Venona messages already contained references to many Soviet agents. The part that was not decrypted therefore probably contained references to many more that would never be discovered. Also, at the end of the 1950s and in the 1960s, American and British services did not have the kind of agents-in-place in the KGB that could give leads to KGB penetrations of the West in the way that they had come out of Venona. This fear of Soviet penetration led to a series of "misdirected molehunts," inside the CIA and MI5 in particular, with often disastrous results for the careers of officers who were wrongly suspected or against whom suspicions could at the very least not be confirmed.[9]

An important characteristic of most Soviet agents in the West in the 1930s and 1940s was that they were "ideological agents" who worked for Soviet intelligence out of communist sympathies or convictions. They were usually highly motivated, barely needed recruiting for that reason and were generally not interested in receiving a financial reward from their Soviet masters. Indeed, had they been offered payment for their services they would probably have been offended. The ideological Soviet agent was mostly a phenomenon of the beginning period of the Cold War. From roughly the 1960s onwards, as the political attraction of Soviet communism gradually waned, the motivation of agents was more likely to be financial. Frustrations of some kind about the employer or the workplace would also often play a role in many individual cases. During the whole Cold War period, the KGB and GRU would also make use of Western Communist parties or their individual members for their intelligence operations,[10] even though they went about this in a circumspect way after Western security services had discovered at the end of the 1940s the important role that dedicated communists had played in spying for the Soviet Union.

A typical example of agents and their motivations in the later period of the Cold War was the Walker spy ring, which operated for the KGB between 1968 and 1985 and had US Navy Chief Warrant Officer and communications specialist John Walker at its center. Walker and his three associates were spying primarily for financial gain. They succeeded in handing over so much information about US Navy codes, and other technical information, to the Soviets that they probably changed the military balance considerably, to the detriment of the United States, at least for the period in which they were active as agents.[11]

American and British governments suffered from a serious lack of information on the USSR in the 1940s and 1950s, especially as far as the intentions of the Soviet leadership were concerned. Even the state of Soviet military readiness was largely a mystery to Western intelligence services. A telling example is the explosion of the first Soviet atomic bomb in 1949, of which the Americans became unexpectedly aware that it had taken place when the US government detected radioactive material resulting from the test in the atmosphere. One of the main concerns on the Western side during the Cold War, especially during its early phase when intelligence was scarce, had to do with the possibility of a surprise attack by the Soviets. Indeed, the first question posed to a defector from the communist East in the early days was if he knew of any signs of an impending war.[12] The serious lack of intelligence on the Soviet Union and its allies was made worse by the presence of "fabrication factories" in the early Cold War period: political exiles from the East and all kinds of shady characters in need of cash who provided "intelligence" on demand to Western services in dire need of it.[13]

The little real information in the field of Humint came from defectors from the KGB and other Soviet organizations who decided to stay in the West when they were on a mission abroad. Due to the very strict security environment inside the USSR (the KGB ran very successful counterintelligence and surveillance departments), it was almost impossible for a service like the CIA to run an agent in Moscow. Maintaining vital communication with an agent, often causing headaches in the best of circumstances, is an almost insurmountable obstacle in a non-democratic state with a ruthless and ubiquitous security apparatus. The CIA managed to place its first operational officers at the US Embassy in Moscow only at the beginning of the 1960s, but even then it was very difficult for them to escape the attention of the KGB when moving about the Soviet capital.

It is telling that the most important human source in the Soviet Union for both the SIS and the CIA in the beginning of the 1960s, GRU colonel Oleg Penkovsky, was a British-American agent for only a year and a half. Luckily for the CIA and SIS, his handlers could arrange meetings with him in hotels in London, Leeds and Paris when he was in the West as a member of a Soviet delegation. In Moscow, dead-drops or brush-passes were the only possibility to exchange information with Penkovsky. The CIA and SIS were not able to run him in Moscow for very long and, like most Western agents in the Soviet Union, he paid for his spying with his life. The stationing abroad of a Soviet citizen for a long period as a diplomat or KGB officer offered practically the only way for the CIA to approach him and run him as an agent. What often was missing, however, was intelligence on the mindset and intentions of the Soviet leadership. Sources in the Kremlin or very close to it, closer still than Penkovsky had been, would have been necessary to achieve this, but they never materialized.

It was American technological prowess that filled some important gaps in Western knowledge about the Soviet Union from the end of the 1950s. Important information was acquired by the US U-2, by far the most famous photo and electronic reconnaissance plane of the Cold War, which made altogether twenty-four overflights of Soviet territory in 1956–60. The downing of a U-2 above Soviet territory on 1 May 1960, however, led not only to a major international crisis but to the end of U-2 overflights of Soviet territory.[14] Fortunately for the West, U-2 overflights were soon to be followed by another important development which took off in the early 1960s: putting into orbit satellites that generated more and more intelligence on the Soviet Union from signals (Sigint) and images (Imint). The US was always far ahead of the Soviet Union in this technology, and, just like the overflights of the U-2, it gave Washington and London vital information about the Soviet order of battle, i.e. the number of tanks, missiles and other weapon systems, that could not have been acquired by Humint.[15]

In the later stages of the Cold War, roughly from the end of the 1970s, American technology again made an important contribution to a safe way of running agents on Soviet territory by rapid advances in communications technology. The CIA developed a short-range agent communication device (SRAC), for instance, which could be used by agents to send text messages to receivers placed on several locations in Moscow.[16] The CIA also developed sophisticated operational methods to avoid the usually heavy KGB surveillance in Moscow and thus to maintain contact with valuable agents. That virtually all CIA and FBI agents in the Soviet Union and at the Soviet Embassy in Washington DC were arrested by the KGB in the mid-1980s, about a dozen of whom were subsequently executed, was not the result of thorough KGB surveillance in Moscow but of betrayal on a grand scale from the American side by Aldrich Ames of the CIA and Robert Hanssen of the FBI.

Sigint

Sigint (signals intelligence) refers to the interception and analysis of "foreign communications and non-communications radio-electronic transmissions."[17] As far as intercepting radio communications is concerned, every Sigint organization tries to read another state's messages, even if it is a close ally diplomatically, the US and the UK being a possible exception in this regard. To give but one example: by the end of the Second World War the United States had not only broken the codes of the three Axis Powers, but it was also reading the encrypted diplomatic and military traffic of more than forty other countries, among them allies and neutral states.[18]

The role of Sigint during the Cold War tends to be underestimated by historians, which is partly due to the fact that daring exploits by human agents fire the imagination much more than the tedious work of installing antennae, breaking codes and reading other people's messages in nondescript government buildings. The main factor, however, for the lack of information on Sigint during the Cold War until fairly recently has to do with the fact that governments in both East and West, though more so in the former, for obvious reasons tended to keep their Sigint capabilities as secret as possible.

The importance of Sigint can be seen from the number of reports based on intercepts sent to other government agencies and officials by the National Security Agency (NSA), the US Sigint organization. In 1964, for instance, the NSA distributed 150,000 intelligence reports among its customers in Washington – more than 400 a day. This figure had more than doubled just a few years later, at the end of the decade. The KGB, on the other hand, decrypted 188,400 diplomatic messages sent by seventy-two countries in 1967 alone, a rate of 516 decryptions a day.[19] A particular problem that applies to Sigint is what is called by some authors the "wheat versus chaff problem": the amount of material coming in is often so huge that it is not possible to process and evaluate it in a timely fashion and thereby to separate the valuable items from background noise. The outbreak of the October 1973 Arab–Israeli War, which caught the Nixon administration by complete surprise, is a case in point. One of the reasons for the Arabs' surprise lay in the fact that "NSA intercepts of Syrian and Egyptian war preparations in the period preceding the attack were so voluminous – an average of hundreds of reports each week – that few analysts had time to digest more than a small portion of them. Even fewer analysts were qualified by technical training to read raw NSA traffic."[20]

As was often the case with intelligence generally during the Cold War, Sigint successes for one side in the struggle could easily be followed by dismal failures; such was the ebb and flow of the intelligence war between East and West. The so-called Black Friday episode, which occurred in 1948, offers a prime example. In cooperation with the British, the Army Security Agency (ASA), a forerunner of the NSA, had succeeded in breaking several low-grade ciphers of the Soviet army, navy and air force, which resulted in important information on the order of battle. Very suddenly, on Friday, 29 October, called Black Friday in the history of the NSA, the Soviet government started a massive change of practically all its main cipher systems, which went on for several months after that date. Newer and more sophisticated cipher machines were also introduced by the Soviets, all of which resulted in the Americans and British not being able to break Soviet ciphers for almost thirty years. Eventually, it became clear that the Soviets had carried out this massive change as a consequence of information obtained by them from a human source inside the ASA.[21]

The disaster of Black Friday forced the Americans and British to look for other ways to eavesdrop on Soviet communications. Tapping into Soviet landlines would have the additional advantage that such communications would not be encrypted, since they would be considered inaccessible and therefore secure by the KGB. This is exactly what the British and Americans did, often with great success. In late 1948 in Vienna, the SIS managed to dig a tunnel in the British sector to a Soviet underground cable, and a further two tunnels would follow later. In February 1954 in Berlin, in a joint operation with the CIA codenamed Gold, the SIS started work on a tunnel from the American sector to a Soviet underground cable not far away in the Eastern sector. This listening post operated for only little over a year, until April 1956, when it was discovered by the KGB. The SIS officer and KGB agent George Blake had betrayed the

Berlin tunnel operation when it was still in the planning phase. American and British intelligence services considered the material from the tunnel operation as a good source of early warning in case of a Soviet attack.[22]

On many occasions during the Cold War the United States displayed a very high level of technological inventiveness, such as it had done in the case of the high-altitude U-2 reconnaissance plane during the 1950s. Highly advanced American technology also played an important part in an operation code-named Ivy Bells, carried out jointly by the NSA and the US Navy, which involved eavesdropping on a Soviet underwater communications cable in the Sea of Okhotsk in the Soviet Far East. This operation, revealed in 1980 by a KGB agent in the US, resulted in vast amounts of intelligence on the Soviet Pacific Fleet, including early warning of a possible Soviet military attack.[23]

Intelligence cooperation between the US and Great Britain during the Cold War was generally very close. Services of the two countries sometimes cooperated in the field of Humint, as in the case of the GRU colonel Penkovsky, but especially with respect to Sigint. The Sigint alliance between the United States and Great Britain, also known as "UKUSA," is a stable and long-lasting intelligence liaison which dates from the Second World War, when the two Western allies worked closely together in breaking German and Japanese codes. UKUSA consists of a series of sometimes overlapping agreements, the first concluded in 1943 and 1946, to which other agreements were added over the years and which also came to include Canada, Australia and New Zealand.[24]

The Sigint effort of the Soviet Union was more fragmented than the one of the US, since it involved participation from both the KGB and GRU. Judging from available evidence, it seems that Soviet Sigint successes during the Cold War resulted largely from installing bugs (hidden microphones) in Western embassies and other establishments and from operations with agents, rather than from cryptanalysis pure and simple.[25] It is well known that Western embassies in Moscow, the American and British ones in particular, were a constant target for the KGB, and its efforts in this regard were often successful. From roughly the 1970s onwards, the KGB also installed specialized listening posts in Soviet embassies and other establishments abroad with which it could eavesdrop on local communications. By 1970 the KGB residency in Washington could listen in on the communications of a host of US government agencies, including the White House, the FBI, the State and Defense Departments and the local police.[26] Humint operations, i.e. agents, were used frequently by the KGB to acquire Sigint from the West. A good example of this was the Walker spy ring, already mentioned. Geoffrey Prime, who in the 1970s and the beginning of the 1980s worked at the Government Communications Headquarters (GCHQ), the main British Sigint establishment, was also a very valuable KGB agent.[27]

Covert Action

The American term "covert action" is formally defined as an "activity or activities of the United States Government to influence political, economic or military conditions abroad, where it is intended that the role of the United States Government will not be apparent or acknowledged publicly."[28] The scope of covert action is very broad. It can take different forms, from common propaganda and political activities such as giving financial support to political parties, to organizing a coup and different kinds of paramilitary action. The KGB used the term "active measures" during the Cold War to refer to roughly the same as "covert action."[29]

Both the CIA and the KGB practiced covert action, though arguably the CIA did this in a way which was the most haphazard and inconsistent of the two. The collection and analysis of information were and are ongoing activities of the CIA. Covert action, if carried out properly at least, needs to be based on accurate information, i.e. intelligence, but its goal, of course, goes further than that. In the American system, covert action during the Cold War was very much a tool of presidential politics and, depending on the spirit of the times and the preferences of the president and his advisers, it could be practiced somewhat reluctantly or with great fervor, the latter being especially the case in roughly the first decade of the CIA's existence. At least until the mid-1970s legal arrangements hardly played a role in CIA covert action and congressional oversight did not exist.

The 1950s became the "golden era" of CIA covert action, in which almost everything seemed legitimate that served the greater purpose of countering and undermining the threat from the Soviet Union and its allies. The extent to which the idea of such a threat had taken hold of leading circles in the US government becomes clear from the content of a document drafted by a team of high officials from the State Department and the Department of Defense in 1950, which became known as NSC 68 (National Security Council Paper 68). In the document, the Cold War between the West and the Soviet Union was seen in terms of a struggle between forces of Good and Evil and it called for the "intensification of ... operations by covert means in the field of economic warfare and political and psychological warfare."[30] The so-called Doolittle Report, written at the request of President Eisenhower in September 1954, saw the struggle in equally apocalyptic terms:

> It is now clear that we are facing an implacable enemy whose avowed objective is world domination by whatever means and at whatever cost. There are no rules in such a game. Hitherto acceptable norms of human conduct do not apply. If the United States is to survive, long-standing American concepts of "fair play" must be reconsidered. We must develop effective espionage and counterespionage services and must learn to subvert, sabotage and destroy our enemies by more clever, more sophisticated and more effective methods than those used against us. It may become necessary that the American people be made acquainted with, understand and support this fundamentally repugnant philosophy.[31]

This thinking was the ideological basis for the ample use of covert action by the CIA during the Cold War, especially in the 1950s and 1960s.

In the late 1940s and well into the 1950s, Europe was the primary focus of CIA covert action, the funding of the Christian Democrats against the Communists at the elections in Italy in 1948 being a good example. Apparently, money was spent by the CIA on Italian political parties during election time well into the 1970s.[32] In the same way, the CIA also routinely meddled in elections in Chile in the 1960s and the beginning of the 1970s. The agency was apparently not directly involved in the coup against President Salvador Allende in September 1973, but at the behest of the White House it had done its best to destabilize his government in the preceding years.[33] Supporting friendly, i.e. anti-communist or at the very least non-communist political parties and other organizations all over the globe was to be one of the CIA's main activities during the Cold War. In the first years after the end of the Second World War the CIA, together with the British SIS, also actively supported resistance movements against the establishment of communist rule in the Eastern periphery of the Soviet empire in such regions as the Baltic states, Poland, Western Ukraine and Albania. These movements were spectacularly unsuccessful, since most of them had been penetrated by the KGB or its East European counterparts from the outset. British and American support for them therefore came to nothing.

During the 1950s, after the Iron Curtain had been firmly established in Europe, the focus of the CIA shifted increasingly to the Third World. Coups were organized in Iran in 1953 and Guatemala in 1954, for instance, against regimes that were perceived to be friendly towards the Soviet Union or simply not friendly enough towards the United States. The ignominious failure of the Bay of Pigs invasion in 1961 by Cuban anti-Castro exiles trained and financed by the CIA was a very public event and came as a shock to many. It was openly trumpeted by Fidel Castro and led to the resignation of Director of Central Intelligence Allen Dulles.[34] In the 1960s the CIA continued on its by now well-trodden path of intervention in the Third World by supporting Joseph Mobutu in taking power in the Congo in 1965, after having looked the other way, at the very least, when the first elected Congolese leader after independence, Patrice Lumumba, was murdered in 1961.[35]

Front organizations were used widely by both sides throughout the Cold War. On the surface, such organizations were not connected to the CIA or the KGB, but behind the scenes the ties could be very strong indeed. The CIA, especially, set up many front organizations during the Cold War, so-called proprietaries, to carry out tasks connected with its many covert actions, such as arms deliveries and air transport in general. Several air corporations were established during the wars in Indochina in the 1960s and 1970s, the best-known of which was Air America. Both the CIA and the KGB made wide use of radio and television stations, print journals, other media and individual journalists for propaganda purposes, in most cases, of course, without proper attribution. The best-known use by the CIA of radio as a propaganda tool concerned Radio Free Europe (RFE) and Radio Liberty (RL), founded in 1949 and 1951 respectively. RFE broadcast to communist Eastern Europe and RL to the Soviet Union. Both stations were subject to almost constant jamming by the communist authorities. They were funded and run by the CIA until the early 1970s, and thereafter by the US Congress. In many cases, the CIA also set up radio stations within the wider context of the coups and paramilitary actions it carried out.[36]

A series of congressional investigations in the mid-1970s led to revelations about the CIA's involvement with repressive regimes in the Third World, tarnishing its relationship with the US Congress and its image in the eyes of US public opinion. These investigations started in the wake of the Watergate affair, and led to severe criticism of the CIA because of its involvement in several surveillance operations against US citizens which were expressly prohibited by law. Several CIA plots to assassinate foreign leaders, some of them quite exotic, also became publicly known as a result of these investigations, most notoriously those directed against Cuban leader Fidel Castro. As a result of these revelations, President Ford issued an Executive Order in 1976 prohibiting political assassinations. Further, from the mid-1970s onwards the activities of the CIA came under a measure of congressional oversight. It is important to keep in mind, however, that whenever the CIA breached the law or displayed other activities deemed undesirable, the agency had never acted as a "rogue elephant," as some critics later called it, but on the President's instructions.[37]

With hindsight, one of the striking aspects of covert actions in the American political context is the extent to which they created periodic problems for the CIA when they became public. The congressional oversight instituted after the scandals of the mid-1970s did not prevent the agency from supporting the Contras in Nicaragua and mining the country's harbors in the first half of the 1980s, in contravention of resolutions by the US Congress, after which another scandal ensued.[38] As a consequence of all this, periods of feverish CIA activity were often followed by others in which the agency and the US president it served seemed to engage in covert action only reluctantly and with some trepidation. The CIA ended the Cold War against the Soviet Union, again, with a period of great activity in Afghanistan, where it successfully financed and armed, together with Pakistan and Saudi Arabia, the Mujahedeen resistance against the Soviet invasion. This, of course, would all come back to haunt the CIA and the US in September 2001.

From Stalin's time the KGB had a tradition of assassinating or abducting enemies of the Soviet state abroad, mostly anti-communist exiles and defectors. Several leading opponents of the Soviet regime were murdered in the 1950s, mainly in West Germany, and often with poison in a very sophisticated manner. From the beginning of the 1960s onwards the number of KGB assassinations abroad abated considerably, probably due to bad publicity from earlier failed attempts, even though the KGB is said to have given essential technical assistance to Bulgarian state security in connection with the murder of the Bulgarian exile Georgi Markov in London in 1978. The operation was carried out with a rare poison, ricin, inserted into the victim's body with the use of an umbrella converted into a silent gun.[39]

As far as setting up proprietaries was concerned, the KGB seems to have practiced this art to a much lesser extent than the CIA, although it had a long tradition of using firms as a cover for intelligence operations, especially in countries where no Soviet embassies existed. It also routinely used Soviet press agencies and other Soviet organizations to provide cover positions for its intelligence officers abroad. During the Cold War the KGB was also very keen on using media outlets and agents to disseminate reports that reflected positively on the USSR or served Soviet interests in other ways. Furthermore, within the KGB there existed a strong tradition of distributing disinformation, mostly a mixture of facts and rumors or outright lies, which was used to discredit the West, in particular the United States. In the 1960s and 1970s, for instance, the KGB used its many contacts in the world of journalism to promote the conspiracy theory that President John F. Kennedy had been assassinated on the orders of US right-wing circles or by the CIA.[40] Another example of KGB disinformation was the campaign carried out in 1983–88 by the KGB and other Eastern-bloc communist services, in particular the East German Hauptverwaltung Aufklärung (Main Reconnaissance Administration, HVA), in which reports were circulated, especially through media outlets in the Third World, that the virus which caused AIDS was developed in biological warfare laboratories of the Pentagon, after which it was used to deliberately target gay communities and other minority groups.[41]

During the Cold War, the KGB also offered ample support in the form of arms deliveries and training to many communist groups and liberation movements in the Third World. In Central America in the 1970s, for instance, the KGB trained several of the Sandinista guerrillas who were to seize power in Nicaragua in 1979. After the Sandinista takeover it was primarily the KGB which stayed close to the new revolutionary government and not the Soviet Ministry of Foreign Affairs. In the Middle East in the 1970s, one of the leading figures of the Popular Front for the Liberation of Palestine (PFLP), according to Andrew and Mitrokhin, was a KGB agent. The KGB was involved in arms deliveries to the PFLP and also cooperated closely with it in several terrorist operations. The KGB also established contact with other Palestinian terrorist groups. Around 1980, both the KGB and East German state security had extensive contacts with the PLO and the KGB provided military training to some of its guerrillas. Moscow always had doubts, however, about closely cooperating with the PLO and its leader Yasser Arafat.[42] With all these operations, the KGB acted under orders and with the consent of the top leadership of the Communist Party of the Soviet Union (CPSU) in Moscow, just as the CIA carried out its covert actions at the behest of the president of the United States.

Historiography

Especially during the first three decades of the Cold War, writings on intelligence were very few in number and often of questionable quality. In an article originally written in 1955, the founder of CIA intelligence analysis, Sherman Kent, noted the fact that intelligence as a discipline lacked a body of literature. In his words, "you are unlikely to have a robust and growing discipline without one [i.e. a body of literature]."[43] It was to remain this way for quite some time. Two British scholars edited a volume published in 1984 in which intelligence was aptly referred to as "the missing dimension" in the history of international relations.[44]

In the Soviet Union the workings of the "organs of state security" were naturally shrouded in a cloak of secrecy, which made research into this topic for Western scholars extremely difficult. Indeed, it can be said that the first scholarly work discussing the many different aspects of KGB activities inside and outside of the USSR, including its place in the Soviet political system and not just its intelligence operations, was published in the West only in 1988.[45] Even in a relatively open political system such as the United States, the operations of the CIA in the 1950s and 1960s were barely spoken about publicly. The situation in other Western countries in that period was not much different and change came slowly. In the beginning of the 1970s the secret of "Ultra," the breaking of German codes during the Second World War, was revealed, which deeply changed historians' understanding of the period and stimulated an interest in intelligence generally. The scandals involving the CIA in the mid-1970s meant that from that moment the interest of the public and of historians in the doings of this organization was guaranteed. Indeed, in combination with the release of records from CIA archives that took place over the two decades since the end of the Cold War, it can be said that there is no intelligence or security service in the world about which so many books and articles have been written as the CIA. The declassification of US intelligence records was strongly influenced by the end of the Cold War: since the mid-1990s millions of documents of the CIA and other US intelligence agencies have been made available by the US government. Since 1995, the National Security Agency in the US also has released over 3,000 Venona messages into the public domain, containing important information on Soviet intelligence operations in the US in the 1930s and 1940s.[46] Regular releases of material from the archives of MI5 and MI6 now also take place in the United Kingdom and much of this material naturally finds its way into the works of intelligence historians in both the US and the UK.

Due to the nature of the Soviet state and the Russian state that followed it, the availability of material from KGB archives would always be problematic, even in the best of circumstances. By the end of the 1980s, however, when the Soviet "organs of state security" had come under a lot of criticism from the liberal media in the USSR, even the KGB leadership, under its then chairman, Vladimir Kryuchkov, realized that there was some use in cultivating a positive public image of the organization by releasing records selectively.[47] These records mostly had to do with past Soviet intelligence successes in the West, such as the Cambridge Five, of which the outlines in most cases were already known.[48] Significantly, they did not deal with, for instance, the KGB suppression of the dissident movement in the USSR since the 1960s. Under the auspices of the Russian intelligence service SVR, a six-volume series covering the whole Soviet period and more, *Essays on the History of Russian Foreign Intelligence*, was also officially published in Moscow in 1999–2006.[49] Even more important, however, was the uncensored material from the KGB archives that was smuggled to the West by the KGB defector Vasili Mitrokhin at the beginning of the 1990s. This resulted in two volumes that offer the most complete overview of KGB intelligence operations in the West and the Third World that has been published so far.[50] In the mid-1990s, the former KGB officer Alexander Vassiliev managed to bring to the West, unbeknownst to the Russian authorities, a fair amount of information from the KGB archives on Soviet intelligence operations in the US in the 1930s and 1940s. Vassiliev's material partly confirmed earlier information from Venona and resulted in two important publications.[51]

In sum, the number of serious publications on intelligence, especially relating to the Cold War period, is much larger nowadays than could even have been imagined little over two decades ago, and it is still growing.

Did Intelligence Matter?

Arguably the most important function of intelligence during the Cold War, at least for the West, was that of early warning of an enemy attack and, related to this, the acquisition of intelligence about the other side's order of battle. Initially, the West was in a weak position in this respect, having as its opponent a Soviet system that practiced extreme secrecy with respect to the most mundane matters. Largely thanks to new American technology such as the U-2 and satellites, from the late 1950s the West managed to receive enough imagery and other information about Soviet weaponry and its disposition to make an unexpected attack unlikely. There always remained ample room, however, for exaggerated estimates and worst-case analysis, as is exemplified by the "missile gap" of the end of the 1950s, when there was high uncertainty in the US intelligence community about Soviet capability in the field of intercontinental ballistic missiles (ICBMs). The number of ICBMs was hugely overestimated, at least in some parts of the US government. The Democrat presidential candidate John F. Kennedy aptly made use of the non-existent missile gap during the 1960 campaign by making a Republican administration responsible for it. Khrushchev himself was at least partly to blame for the US misperception, since in his efforts to intimidate the West he had grossly exaggerated Soviet capabilities to deliver nuclear weapons.[52] Even though gaps remained in Western knowledge of Soviet military power, in the 1970s and 1980s there was, generally speaking, good intelligence, largely thanks to American technology operating from a distance, on the Soviet military dispositions and the specifications of Soviet missiles, for instance. Estimating military effectiveness, however, remained difficult and information on the intentions of Soviet leaders was also mostly lacking.[53]

The KGB had an aggressive intelligence program targeted at the West right from the beginning of the Cold War, especially in the field of Humint. From what has become known about these operations one can conclude that the results were often spectacular. About the acquisition of Western military secrets by the Soviet Union it has been said that "it is clear that every military secret of any significance was betrayed."[54] It is generally assumed that the Soviet Union had no great difficulty in using the Western technology it acquired for its own needs. The question is, however, if it also managed to do this with the huge amounts of political intelligence received from the West. The Soviet worldview, which was the worldview of the KGB as well, was highly conspiratorial and ideologically extremely one-sided. It accepted only information which was slanted towards this worldview and which confirmed the idea of the West and its intelligence services as constantly plotting and scheming for the downfall of the Soviet Union as their ultimate objective.[55]

Extreme Soviet suspicion towards the West, the US in particular, manifested itself on several occasions during the Cold War. When relations between the US and the Soviet Union reached a new low during President Reagan's first term in office at the beginning of the 1980s, the old guard in the Kremlin took the possibility of a surprise nuclear attack by the West, a first strike, very seriously and ordered its intelligence services, in particular the First Chief Directorate of the KGB and the GRU, to look out for preparations for such a first strike.[56] According to Andrew and Gordievsky, Soviet fears of a nuclear first strike by the West reached their climax in November 1983, during a NATO military exercise codenamed Able Archer which had to do with nuclear release procedures.[57] It has been said that KGB experts on the US and other intelligence officers regarded this fear with considerable skepticism, but the chief of the First Chief Directorate, Vladimir Kryuchkov, took it very seriously.[58] On another occasion about two decades earlier, in June 1960, the KGB in Moscow had received a document apparently sent by a NATO liaison officer at the CIA to his own government. It said that the US military leadership in the Pentagon was hoping to launch a preventive war against the Soviet Union before the military balance between East and West, especially in the field of nuclear missiles, would change in favor of the USSR. Apparently KGB chairman Alexander Shelepin took this information very seriously and sent a report on it to the party leadership, including First Secretary Nikita Khrushchev. Measures were taken to get its contents confirmed from other sources.[59] Almost two years later, it was the turn of the military intelligence service GRU to raise the alarm about the danger of an American nuclear first strike. According to two GRU intelligence reports received in March 1962, based on a source within the US national security establishment that was usually considered reliable, the United States had decided in June 1961 to launch a nuclear surprise attack on the USSR a couple of months later, in September of that year. It was only the huge Soviet nuclear tests in the fall of 1961 which had deterred the US government from proceeding with plans to launch such an attack.[60]

In spite of such misunderstandings with potentially disastrous consequences, it is possible to argue that intelligence about the order of battle and military preparedness of the other side tended to take away to a large extent the danger of surprise from the military confrontation which the Cold War partly also was. This seems to have held true for Western governments generally, but probably not to the same extent for the Soviet leadership, judging by the episodes just mentioned. Intelligence also played an important role in the verification of the arms control treaties of the 1970s, mainly SALT I and SALT II, especially by "national technical means," i.e. satellites and the like. In this sense intelligence could be said to have played a stabilizing role during the Cold War.

Remarkably, inside the KGB there was scant attention paid to intelligence analysis. Traditionally, Soviet leaders were presented mostly with "raw" intelligence on which they did the analysis themselves. Both Stalin and Khrushchev largely were their own intelligence analysts. According to two authors on KGB foreign intelligence reporting at the time of the Cuban Missile Crisis, it was seriously hampered by having to conform to prevailing Party orthodoxy, as expressed in the views of members of the CPSU Politbureau. The reports of the First Chief Directorate were characterized as "largely compilations of information collected on a topic," which lacked "any overarching argument."[61] They were, in other words, not intelligence estimates in the proper sense of the term. The new KGB chairman after the failed coup of August 1991, Vadim Bakatin, when discussing the reporting by the KGB to the leadership of the country, complained in his memoirs about the "Practically undigested pieces of information that came together on the desk of the KGB Chairman, who chose from them as he saw fit for the state leadership."[62] This process, of course, further tended to confirm the leadership's existing worldview. In the United States and Great Britain the situation was different, since there was a system of all-source intelligence in place during the Cold War in which, ideally, intelligence from a variety of sources, Humint, Sigint or open sources, among others, was combined into reports for policy makers.

It has always been notoriously difficult to analyze the concrete input of intelligence into the decision-making process of governments at the highest levels. Policy makers tend to take decisions for a combination of reasons, often of a domestic nature or for other reasons not related to available intelligence. Sometimes, but not always, intelligence plays a role. At the time of the Cuban Missile Crisis in October 1962, for example, intelligence handed over by the British-American agent Oleg Penkovsky played a role in the decision-making process on the US side. One could argue that intelligence occasionally tended to reinforce the hostility between the two camps during the Cold War because of the role it played in particular incidents or crises. If an important part of the struggle between East and West was between competing ideologies, then incidents related to intelligence such as the downing of the American U-2 plane over Soviet airspace in 1960 could be said to have reinforced this mutual hostility.[63]

The same could be said about several politically and emotionally charged individual spy cases, such as the one against the Rosenbergs in the beginning of the 1950s in the United States, in which the two main defendants in the end died on the electric chair. Similarly, the British and American covert actions in the opening phase of the Cold War, in which armed resistance fighters were infiltrated into the Soviet Union and some satellite states, clearly must have fed the omnipresent suspicions on the part of the KGB and the Soviet leadership against the West and its intelligence services. In some ways, Soviet suspicions of the West, though often grossly exaggerated, were not entirely without foundation. Neither were those of the West against the Soviet Union, for that matter.

Notes

1 The author is grateful to W.P.J. Keller M.A. in Overijse, Belgium, and Dan Mulvenna in Leesburg, VA, USA, for their comments on an earlier draft of this chapter.
2 Terminology differs considerably between countries and even between intelligence and security services of one country, but Humint's human sources are in most cases called "agents." As to covert action, some authors do not see it as a part of "intelligence," because its primary focus is not on the collection of secret information, but on influencing the political situation in a country or other target in a variety of ways. Covert action was such an important part of the activities of intelligence services during the Cold War, however, of the CIA and the KGB in particular, that it will be discussed here.
3 Christopher Andrew and Vasili Mitrokhin, *The Mitrokhin Archive: The KGB in Europe and the West* (London: Allen Lane, 1999), 157–158. This valuable agent was Kim Philby, among others. The Russian acronym NKVD stood for "People's Commissariat of Internal Affairs," of which state security (including the intelligence service) was an important component.
4 Gordon Corera, *The Art of Betrayal: Life and Death in the British Secret Service* (London: Weidenfeld & Nicolson, 2011), 28.
5 Andrew and Mitrokhin, *The Mitrokhin Archive*, 43–46.
6 The case of Alger Hiss has long been extremely controversial in the United States, but there can now be no doubt that he was a GRU agent. See, for instance, John Earl Haynes, Harvey Klehr and Alexander Vassiliev, *Spies: The Rise and Fall of the KGB in America* (New Haven, CT and London: Yale University Press, 2009), ch. 1. On Harry Dexter White, see ibid., pp. 258–262. For the case of the Rosenbergs and the Soviet penetration of the American and British atomic projects see ibid., ch. 2 and passim. The case of the Rosenbergs was equally controversial during the Cold War and many historians and others rejected the US government version, insisting the couple were innocent. Apart from all the other evidence, including Venona (see below), their innocence can no longer be maintained, however, since one of Julius Rosenberg's NKVD controllers, Alexander Feklisov, wrote his memoirs in which he detailed his contacts with this highly productive Soviet agent. See Alexander Feklisov and Sergei Kostin, *The Man Behind the Rosenbergs* (New York: Enigma Books, 2001).
7 On Philby see Genrikh Borovik, *The Philby Files: The Secret Life of the Master Spy – The KGB Archives Revealed* (London: Little, Brown & Company, 1994); Andrew and Mitrokhin, *The Mitrokhin Archive*, passim.
8 John Earl Haynes and Harvey Klehr, *Venona: Decoding Soviet Espionage in America* (New Haven, CT and London: Yale University Press, 1999); Nigel West, *Venona: The Greatest Secret of the Cold War* (London: Harper Collins, 2000).
9 David Wise, *Molehunt: How the Search for a Phantom Traitor Shattered the CIA* (New York: Avon Books, 1994), on the molehunts inside the CIA. Christopher Andrew, *The Defence of the Realm: The Authorized History of MI5* (London: Allen Lane, 2009), 503–521 on MI5.
10 Andrew and Mitrokhin, *The Mitrokhin Archive*, 360–382.

11 Andrew and Mitrokhin, *The Mitrokhin Archive*, 268–269; Pete Earley, *Family of Spies: Inside the John Walker Spy Ring* (Toronto: Bantam Books, 1988).
12 Corera, *The Art of Betrayal*, 164–65, 215.
13 Former Director of Central Intelligence Richard Helms has a whole chapter on these fabrication factories in his memoirs. Richard Helms with William Hood, *A Look over My Shoulder: A Life in the Central Intelligence Agency* (New York: Random House, 2003), chapter 9.
14 Michael R. Beschloss, *Mayday: Eisenhower, Khrushchev and the U-2 Affair* (New York: Harper & Row, 1986).
15 Matthew M. Aid, *The Secret Sentry: The Untold History of the National Security Agency* (New York: Bloomsbury Press, 2009), 129, 155, 183 and passim.
16 Robert Wallace and H. Keith Melton, with Henry R. Schlesinger, *Spycraft: The Secret History of the CIA's Spytechs from Communism to Al-Qaeda* (New York: Dutton, 2008), 110–158 and passim.
17 Matthew M. Aid and Cees Wiebes, "Introduction: The Importance of Signals Intelligence in the Cold War," *Intelligence and National Security, Special Issue on Secret of Signals Intelligence during the Cold War and Beyond*, Matthew M. Aid and Cees Wiebes (eds.), 16 (2001), 1–4. The terminology used by different authors can be confusing and is not always consistent. Mark M. Lowenthal, *Intelligence: From Secrets to Policy*, 4th ed. (Washington DC: CQ Press, 2009), 91.
18 Aid, *The Secret Sentry*, 3.
19 Aid and Wiebes, "Introduction: The Importance of Signals Intelligence in the Cold War," 9.
20 As quoted from a House Select Committee on Intelligence report in Christopher Andrew, *For the President's Eyes Only: Secret Intelligence and the American Presidency from Washington to Bush* (London: Harper Collins, 1996), 391. Especially in the internet era, the problem of wheat versus chaff certainly applies to Open Source Intelligence (OSINT) as well, i.e. intelligence acquired from regular media and other outlets.
21 Aid, *The Secret Sentry*, 11–19. Black Friday was in fact not just one day but covered a longer period of several months.
22 Richard J. Aldrich, *GCHQ: The Uncensored Story of Britian's Most Secret Intelligence Agency* (London: HarperPress, 2010), 169–173.
23 Aid, *The Secret Sentry*, 184.
24 Aldrich, *GCHQ*, ch. 5, esp. 89–90.
25 See Andrew and Mitrokhin, *The Mitrokhin Archive*, 439–461 for Soviet Sigint during the Cold War.
26 Oleg Kalugin, with Fen Montaigne, *The First Directorate: My 32 Years in Intelligence and Espionage Against the West* (New York: St. Martin's Press, 1994), 92.
27 Aldrich, *GCHQ*, 367–386.
28 As quoted in Lowenthal, *Intelligence: From Secrets to Policy*, 4th ed., 165.
29 See Abram N. Shulsky and Gary J. Schmitt, *Silent Warfare: Understanding the World of Intelligence*, Third Edition (Washington, DC: Potomac Books, 2002), 76–77 for the difference between the two.
30 Andrew, *For the President's Eyes Only*, 181–183.
31 As quoted in John Ranelagh, *The Agency: The Rise and Decline of the CIA* (New York: Simon & Schuster, 1986), 277.
32 Kevin A. O'Brien, "Interfering with Civil Society: CIA and KGB Covert Political Action during the Cold War," in Loch K. Johnson and James J. Wirtz, eds., *Strategic Intelligence: Windows into a Secret World. An Anthology* (Los Angeles, CA: Roxbury Publishing Company, 2004), 262–263.
33 Andrew, *For the President's Eyes Only*, 370–374, 390.
34 On the coups in Iran and Guatemala, and on the Bay of Pigs see Andrew, *For the President's Eyes Only*, 202–206, 206–211, 262–267.
35 Corera, *The Art of Betrayal*, 127–130; Andrew, *For the President's Eyes Only*, 253, 406.
36 O'Brien, "Interfering with Civil Society," 264–267.
37 Andrew, *For the President's Eyes Only*, 275–276; Ranelagh, *The Agency*, 338–345, 383–390 and passim. On President Ford's Executive Order see ibid., 627. Similar Executive Orders were issued by Presidents Jimmy Carter and Ronald Reagan in 1978 and 1982, respectively.
38 Andrew, *For the President's Eyes Only*, 466–467, 478–479.
39 Andrew and Mitrokhin, *The Mitrokhin Archive*, 507–508.
40 Andrew and Mitrokhin, *The Mitrokhin Archive*, 293–297.
41 Thomas Boghardt, "Operation Infektion: Soviet Bloc Intelligence and its AIDS Disinformation Campaign," *Studies in Intelligence*, 33, 4 (December 2009), 1–19.
42 Christopher Andrew and Vasili Mitrokhin, *The Mitrokhin Archive II: The KGB and the World* (London: Allen Lane, 2005), 117–122, 246–250, 252–253, 255, 145.

43 Sherman Kent, "The Need for an Intelligence Literature," in Donald P. Steury (ed.), *Sherman Kent and the Board of National Estimates: Collected Essays* (History Staff, Center for the Study of Intelligence, Central Intelligence Agency, Washington D.C., 1994), 14.
44 Christopher Andrew and David Dilks (eds.), *The Missing Dimension: Governments and Intelligence Communities in the Twentieth Century* (Basingstoke: Palgrave Macmillan, 1984).
45 Amy W. Knight, *The KGB: Police and Politics in the Soviet Union* (Boston, MA: Unwin Hyman, 1988).
46 See http://www.nsa.gov/public_info/declass/venona/index.shtml, accessed on 15 July 2012.
47 Andrew and Mitrokhin, *The Mitrokhin Archive*, 26–29.
48 Examples of publications based on such records are John Costello and Oleg Tsarev, *Deadly Illusions* (London: Century, 1993); Nigel West and Oleg Tsarev, *The Crown Jewels: The British Secrets at the Heart of the KGB Archives* (London: HarperCollins, 1998). Both volumes contain important new information on the Cambridge Five and other Soviet intelligence operations.
49 *Ocherki Istorii Rossiyskoy Vneshney Razvedki tom 1–6* (Moscow: Mezhdunarodnye Otnosheniya, 1999–2006).
50 Andrew and Mitrokhin, *The Mitrokhin Archive*; Andrew and Mitrokhin, *The Mitrokhin Archive II*. The US editions of these two volumes are entitled *The Sword and the Shield* and *The World Was Going Our Way*, respectively.
51 Allen Weinstein and Alexander Vassiliev, *The Haunted Wood: Soviet Espionage in America – the Stalin Era* (New York: Random House, 1999); Haynes, Klehr and Vassiliev, *Spies*.
52 John Lewis Gaddis, *The Cold War: A New History* (New York: The Penguin Press, 2005), 69–74.
53 Michael Herman, "What Difference Did It Make?" *Intelligence and National Security* 26, 6 (2011), 886–901.
54 Gordon S. Barrass, *The Great Cold War: A Journey through the Hall of Mirrors* (Stanford, CA: Stanford University Press, 2009), 393, as quoted in Herman, "What Difference Did It Make?" 895.
55 Andrew and Mitrokhin, *The Mitrokhin Archive*, 720–725. For the conspiratorial worldview prevalent within the KGB see Julie Fedor, "Chekists Look Back on the Cold War: The Polemical Literature," *Intelligence and National Security* 26, 6 (2011), 842–863.
56 Christopher Andrew and Oleg Gordievsky, *KGB. The Inside Story of its Foreign Operations from Lenin to Gorbachev* (London: Hodder & Stoughton, 1990), 488–507; *Instructions from the Centre. Top secret files on KGB foreign operations 1975–1985*, edited by Christopher Andrew and Oleg Gordievsky, (London: Hodder & Stoughton, 1991), 67–90; Benjamin B. Fischer, *A Cold War Conundrum: The 1983 Soviet War Scare*, https://www.cia.gov/library/center-for-the-study-of-intelligence/csi-publications/books-and-monographs/a-cold-war-conundrum/source.htm. Accessed on 11 May 2012.
57 Andrew and Gordievsky, *KGB*, 502. Cold War scholar Mark Kramer, speaking at the conference "Need to Know: Intelligence and Politics: Western and Eastern Perspectives" in Brussels on 8–9 November 2012, did not believe that in fall 1983 there was a real fear of a nuclear surprise attack by the West among the Soviet political and military leadership.
58 Andrew and Gordievsky, *KGB*, 488; *Instructions from the Centre*, 69.
59 Aleksandr Fursenko and Timothy Naftali, *"One Hell of a Gamble": Khrushchev, Castro and Kennedy, 1958–1964: The Secret History of the Cuban Missile Crisis* (New York: W.W. Norton & Company, 1997), 51–52.
60 Fursenko and Naftali, *"One Hell of a Gamble,"* 155. According to the authors, it is not clear to whom, within the Soviet political establishment, these reports went.
61 Aleksandr Fursenko and Timothy Naftali, "Soviet Intelligence and the Cuban Missile Crisis," in *Intelligence and National Security, Special Issue on Intelligence and the Cuban Missile Crisis*, edited by James G. Blight and David A. Welch, 13(3) (1998): 66. On Stalin and Khrushchev doing their own intelligence analysis, see also Andrew and Mitrokhin, *The Mitrokhin Archive*, 240, 720.
62 Wadim Bakatin, *Im Innern des KGB* (Frankfurt am Main: S. Fischer, 1993), 59. In this quotation Bakatin is not referring to reports from the First Chief Directorate, but from the KGB leadership as a whole. There existed, to be sure, within the First Chief Directorate a Directorate of Information and Analysis, which prepared reports for the party leadership. Nikolai Leonov, chief of this directorate in 1973–1983, is somewhat skeptical in his memoirs about the amount of attention the leadership paid to them. According to Leonov, Soviet leader Gorbachev often did not respond at all to reports. Nikolai Leonov, *Likholetye* [Stormy Years] (Moscow: Mezhdunarodnye Otnosheniya, 1994), 112–113, 288, 317, 321.
63 Herman, "What Difference Did It Make?" 899–900.

PART VIII

Psychological Warfare, Propaganda, and Cold War Culture

23
PROPAGANDA AND THE COLD WAR

Nicholas J. Cull and B. Theo Mazumdar

Propaganda – broadly defined here as mass political persuasion – deserves a place of prominence in the field of Cold War studies. Much of the world experienced the conflict in the realm of communication and culture rather than that of physical combat. At the height of the Cold War the contending powers sought to use ideas and persuasion to rally, sustain and extend their respective blocs and bombarded one another's home populations with messages to elicit political advantage. The bloated capitalist plutocrat of Soviet propaganda matched the dull, doctrinaire Red Fascist of American stereotype. But propaganda was not just a symptom of the conflict. The propaganda deployed by East and West had a profound impact on the course of the Cold War: it surged in the early years; it flourished in the Third World during the middle years of the conflict; it reshaped during the period of détente and arguably played a key role in the ending of the Cold War. No less significantly, propaganda played a role in the outbreak of the conflict and it is with that story that this chapter must begin.

Propaganda and the Origins of the Cold War

William Shakespeare had King Henry IV counsel his son Prince Hal: 'Be it thy course to busy giddy minds with foreign quarrels; that action hence borne out may waste the memory of the former days.'[1] Whatever their genuine political differences, both the US, Britain and their allies and the post-revolutionary Soviet Union shared King Henry's understanding of the value of a foreign threat to rally domestic opinion. The Soviet Union generated a stream of anti-Western propaganda throughout the 1920s and 1930s, stereotyping Western governments as creatures of big business manipulation in newspaper cartoons, in publications like the satirical journal *Krokodil* [Crocodile] (1922–91), in official speeches and in the wider cultural output of the country.[2] Conversely, anti-communism was a cornerstone of Western politics in the interwar period, encouraged by sectors as diverse as the political right, big business, the church and non-communist left, sometimes out of proportion to the real scale of the revolutionary threat; in Western speeches, sermons and motion pictures the Soviets were the unschooled, unsmiling Ivan with a penchant for swift executions, bent on upturning the social order.[3] Both sides repressed such rhetoric during the period of alliance against Hitler, but these strategies returned in earnest at the war's end. The best-known case is Stalin's so-called 'election speech', broadcast on 9 February 1946, in which he spoke of war with the West as inevitable. Winston Churchill answered on 5 March 1946 in his famous speech characterizing the border between the Soviet-dominated eastern portion of Europe and the rest of the continent as an 'Iron Curtain'. It represented a further escalation in the war of words. President Truman's announcement of the Truman Doctrine, in which he committed the United States to the 'containment' of 'foreign subversion', which meant military aid to the anti-communist governments of Greece and Turkey, filled the need, as Senator Arthur H. Vandenberg put it, to 'scare the hell out the American people' and moved the Cold War decisively to the forefront of American political life.[4]

A surge of mutual demonization followed – the film industries of Moscow and Hollywood alike traded the Nazi villains of wartime for monstrous renderings of one another. But this was more than a return to business as usual. Part of the problem sprang from the wartime attempt to promote the alliance between East and West. The wartime propaganda bureaucracies of the West oversold their new ally to their home populations, creating images of heroic and friendly Russian allies, portrayed in propaganda films by leading men of the era such as Lawrence Olivier and Gregory Peck.[5] The scale of this pro-Soviet sentiment in US wartime culture provoked an anti-communist backlash against the perceived infiltration of left-wingers into the propaganda bureaucracy and entertainment industry. The issue was perfect for conservative Republicans eager to roll back Democratic Party power after more than a decade of the New Deal. This anti-communist rhetoric found a ready audience in part because the rosy wartime portrait of the Soviet Union set up the American public for a fall when Stalin failed to behave as an avuncular, reformed and tolerant ally in the war's aftermath. The parallel overselling of Chiang Kai-shek and the Republic of China as an ally resulted in similar confusion in the US when that government fell in the late 1940s. It was easier to look for an enemy within who had 'lost China' than to grasp that, despite war-era propaganda, China had never been America's to lose in the first place.

Over-reactions to unforeseen events and the consequences of old ideological baggage alone do not explain the onset of Cold War. Psychological pressures pushed the blocs towards polarization: Senator William Fulbright once compared the situation to two dogs who find themselves clawing at one bone.[6] It was only to be expected that the two largest powers of any age would view each other with suspicion and begin defining themselves in opposition to each other, but in this case the differences were genuine and the reasons for mutual suspicion were considerable. Both sides adhered to mutually incompatible ideologies. Both sides had explicit ideological agendas and each created a bureaucratic apparatus to promote those agendas. Moreover, an awareness of one another's ideological projects became a further motor of escalation. It is to those projects and the respective bureaucracies that we must now turn.

The Eastern Bloc's Propaganda Machine

Propaganda was not an optional extra to the Soviet state – some sort of auxiliary function added on a whim – it was part of the DNA of the Bolshevik regime, and an essential element in the revolution and its consolidation of power. During the years of struggle against the tsar, Bolshevik theorists had developed a sophisticated sense of political communication. The revolutionary thinker Georgi Plekhanov famously drew a distinction between 'propaganda' as a complex political education and the mere stirring-up of feelings in the masses (termed 'agitation'). His dictum ran: 'A propagandist gives many ideas to one or a few people while an agitator gives only one or only a few ideas but to masses of people.'[7] It was only to be expected that as the state looked to its international relationships its leaders would seek to deploy the same methods. They began with grand gestures like Foreign Minister Leon Trotsky's opening of the secret diplomatic archives of the tsar but soon brought forth full-scale institutions such as the International Book Company (known by its Russian abbreviation as *Mezhkniga*) in 1923 to publish books about communism overseas and the All-Union Association for Cultural Relations with Foreign Countries (*Vsesoiuznoe obshchestvo kulturnykh sviazei s zagranitsei*, known by the acronym VOKS), created in 1925 to build links with sympathetic foreign intellectuals, to manage international visits and promote the exchange of publications.[8] VOKS created local partner organizations like the American Society for Cultural Relations with Russia, founded in the USA in 1927.[9] Aiming for more of a mass market, Radio Moscow addressed people around Europe, and working-class audiences around the world (where their censors permitted it) viewed films by Sergei Eisenstein and others which valorized the events of the revolution and made the visions of Socialist ideology palpable on the screen.[10] The Communist International of 1919 (COMINTERN, also known as the Third International) established a mechanism to export the revolution, while operators like the German communist publisher Willi Münzenberg became adept at setting up front organizations to spread the Party line across Europe, the United States and beyond.[11] The Soviet revolutionary ideals of the 1920s generally withered in the 1930s. Stalin eviscerated the leadership of the Third International with purges and his alliance with Hitler in 1939 disillusioned all but its most doctrinaire adherents, at least in the West. In 1943 Stalin suspended the COMINTERN to reassure his capitalist allies, but in September 1947, as the wartime grand alliance dissolved into suspicion, Moscow launched a new incarnation: the Communist Information Bureau, COMINFORM. COMINFORM purported to be non-hierarchical and hence was housed at arm's length from the Kremlin, first in Belgrade, Yugoslavia and then, after the split with the Tito regime, in Bucharest, Romania. COMINFORM published a stream of propaganda in support of the global communist project. Its true nature as a device of Soviet power was soon apparent.[12]

The Cold War brought new initiatives from both old and new Soviet propaganda agencies. A host of front organizations reached out for world opinion in the name of youth and peace. The initiative used Pablo Picasso's famous cartoon drawing of a dove as its logo. The Soviet state threw itself into sporting diplomacy, competing in the Olympic Games for the first time in 1952 and turning it and subsequent Olympics into showcases for the vitality of the socialist system. In 1954 the internal security service of the USSR was reorganized into the Komitet gosudarstvennoy bezopasnosti (Committee for State Security), known by the dreaded initials KGB. The KGB played its own role in the propaganda war by recruiting agents of influence, subsidizing sympathetic newspapers and planting disinformation: invented stories carefully crafted to undermine the reputation of its enemies.[13] Favourite themes in KGB disinformation included the existence of elaborate conspiracies within Western societies. The assassination of President Kennedy in 1963 would be grist to its mill.

Soviet outreach hit its zenith under the leadership of Stalin's charismatic successor, Nikita Khrushchev. He understood that the key battleground of the Cold War would be one of culture and political imagination and moved the apparatus of communication out from under the authority of the foreign ministry.[14] He also brought the USSR into the United Nations' cultural forum, UNESCO, and began a program of cultural outreach. Folk-dancing troupes and the Bolshoi ballet toured the world; invitations to study in the Soviet Union abounded and the state began exporting prestige motion pictures which reflected a willingness to flirt with artistic freedom.[15] Khrushchev's confidence in the power of the Soviet image was such that he also sought out a series of bilateral cultural agreements with Western countries, which allowed Western access to Soviet audiences in exchange for his access to publics in the US, UK, France and elsewhere, beginning with a treaty with the US in 1958. The USSR prepared exhibitions for display in the West, created magazines like *Soviet Weekly* to impress Western audiences with the achievements of the state, marshalled students and scientists for exchanges, and waited for the images of Soviet industrial achievement, bountiful grain harvests and prowess in outer space to work their magic. The space story was especially effective and convinced many around the world of the vitality and technical superiority of the Soviet system.[16]

The golden age of Soviet outreach did not last. The fall of Khrushchev in 1964 brought institutional retrenchment. Leonid Brezhnev brought international propaganda back under the control of the foreign ministry.[17] By 1970, even with the US still bogged down in Vietnam, the Soviet Union began losing ground. The Soviet intervention in Czechoslovakia in 1968 showed the brutal side of the regime's approach and the United States belatedly trumped its prowess in space by landing on the moon in 1969. Increasingly, Moscow looked to the covert techniques of the KGB to carry the burden of its propaganda war.

The satellite states of the Soviet bloc boosted Moscow's propaganda drive. In the early years there was a synergy with the propaganda of Mao's China. Perhaps the most damaging allegation spread by Soviet media originated with the Chinese: the claim that the United States had launched bacteriological warfare attacks against North Korea and North East China. Pictures of empty leaflet canisters were claimed to depict the delivery devices for the pathogens and prisoners confessed complicity. Despite the best efforts of historians, the story continues to surface six decades on from its launch.[18] By the end of the 1950s the Chinese had become a rival for the attention of the non-aligned world.

East Germany had a substantial propaganda operation aimed at subverting West Germany, directed by a former journalist and Politburo member, Albert Norden. West Germany reported that some 10 million leaflets found their way into the country in the first quarter of 1960 alone. Fake documents created in East Berlin also circulated, including a set of Pentagon documents responding to the excessive drinking, mental illness and 'sex perversion' in the US air force, designed to undermine allied confidence in the Straegic Air Command.[19]

Moscow's radio propaganda campaign was helped by the existence within the Warsaw Pact of pre-communist radio stations, including Radio Prague (Czecholovakia) and Radio Polonia (Poland) broadcasting in multiple languages (both were founded in 1936 in response to the pre-war threat of Germany). Hungary launched Radio Budapest in 1950 and East Germany provided Radio Berlin International from 1959, which played a key role in encouraging liberation movements in the developing world. Strong film exports from Poland and Hungary supplemented the USSR's film propaganda output and the Olympic prowess of East Germany, Romania and other states joined that of the Soviet Union in international sports. Soviet allies also took part in high-profile projects in the Third World, the most notable being the propaganda and aid work of Cuba in Latin America and West Africa. Universities across the Eastern bloc hosted scholars from developing countries. While the contributing powers doubtless saw these efforts as projecting their own cultural distinctiveness and nuanced ways of life, the West saw a communist world in lock-step marching forward, and responded in kind.

The Western Propaganda Machine

It is ironic, given America's domination of international popular culture, that the US government initially lagged behind the Soviet in its international outreach. It is no less ironic that once the American effort was underway there were a surprising number of parallels between the approaches of the systems that were officially diametrically opposed. The foundations for the Western campaign were laid in Europe, where America's allies had long since established quasi non-governmental organizations to promote foreign policy goals by facilitating the export of culture. Key institutions included the Alliance Française (founded 1883), Italian Cultural Institute (founded

1926), British Council (founded 1934) and West German cultural operations, which were re-launched in 1951 as the Goethe Institute. The same nations also had international broadcasting capacity: important players included Radio Netherlands (founded 1927), Radio Vaticana (founded 1931), the external services of the BBC (founded 1932) and German international broadcasting (re-launched as Deutsche Welle in 1953).

While these national institutes of culture were competing as much with each other as with the shadow of global communism, the Western broadcasters were certainly mindful of the Soviet threat and slipped readily into a Cold War posture at the conclusion of the Second World War. Fascist Spain added an unfortunate dimension to the radio war by beginning to jam Soviet broadcasts. Moscow responded by jamming a wide range of broadcasts from across the West.[20]

British rearmament for the Cold War predated that of the United States in part because Britain was more suspicious and because the British political system was more conducive to new initiatives. The leaders of Britain's post-war Labour government had no illusions as to the benevolence of communists. The BBC launched a Russian Service as early as 1946 and in 1948 the Foreign Office initiated a secret counter-propaganda department called the Information Research Department (IRD). IRD developed a range of research materials, journals and briefs to promote Britain's perspective on the Cold War which were discreetly made available to policy makers and journalists in the UK and around the world. Its first publication, in 1948, was a short briefing paper entitled *The Real Conditions in Soviet Russia*, which put the lie to Kremlin claims of freedom and prosperity. The IRD operation was extensive and showed enough results to survive into the late 1970s. The IRD's materials aimed directly at the USSR included a major role in the British magazine for Soviet consumption under the exchange agreement, *Anglia*. The unit also commissioned and promoted translations of such valuable anti-Soviet texts as George Orwell's novel *Animal Farm*.[21]

Britain also had the British Council for its cultural work and a British Information Service for overt publicity attached to its diplomatic posts. The Foreign Office also recognized the value of the country's global news agency, Reuters, which provided much of the raw news for the world's newspapers with a British slant. The Foreign Office surreptitiously subsidized Reuters by contracting for news to be supplied to all UK diplomatic posts at a level quite beyond their true needs.[22] Other European governments jumped into anti-communist propaganda as part of their effort to retain control of their colonial possessions. In the case of Italy, where the Communist Party was a major force in domestic politics, anti-communist propaganda was part of the struggle to retain control of the government at home.

For the United States, anti-communism was a corollary of the American political system and there was no shortage of precedent for American opposition to revolutionary regimes around the world, but the United States was reluctant to deploy state-funded media overseas; while other nations advanced rapidly in the interwar years, American propaganda moved in baby steps. The Department of State set up a Cultural Department only in 1938, and then with a focus solely on Latin America. The Second World War saw the creation of Voice of America (VOA) radio and a network of US Information Service posts as part of the Office of War Information. Key American embassies acquired cultural attachés, but as the war ended Congress seemed initially unwilling to continue to fund any such work.[23] In the end, the scale of Soviet propaganda around the world scared America into action. During the course of 1947 multiple groups of American legislators visited Europe. They reported back to hearings on Capitol Hill that the continent was teetering on the brink of communism. Deeply concerned, in early 1948 Congress finally passed the Smith-Mundt Act, thereby providing a proper budget to continue international information and exchange work.

The later 1940s saw a host of new communication initiatives, both overt and covert. In 1947 VOA launched its Russian Service and the Central Intelligence Agency (CIA) began work with authority to conduct covert propaganda activities. In 1948 the first Fulbright exchange scholars set sail (for Burma). The United States injected vast sums of money and other aid into the Italian election to head off a communist victory and launched its most dramatic example of propaganda by deed: the Marshall Plan to aid European recovery. The Marshall Plan included a lively communication component to promote knowledge of America's generosity and spread associated ideas of modernization and regional cooperation. Its propaganda techniques included posters, films and even, in the south of Italy, puppet shows to explain its principles to illiterate people. The emphasis was on the need for cooperation and integration within Europe. Later the output took on a more ideological anti-Soviet bent.

In 1949 the CIA began a new initiative – a propaganda radio network staffed by refugees from the Eastern bloc, known as Radio Free Europe (RFE). Unlike VOA it had no pretence at journalistic objectivity and pulled no punches in its criticism of the communist system. Its output included the broadcasting of a 'Black Book': claims of outrages perpetrated by particular local communist officials which refugees had made known in the West. RFE's parent Committee for a Free Europe floated printed propaganda into the Eastern bloc by balloon. In 1950 President Truman himself launched a 'Campaign of Truth' to contest Soviet claims to international virtue and the policy document known as NSC 68 codified the Cold War in terms of a zero-sum clash of image and ideology in which a defeat anywhere was a defeat everywhere.

America's propaganda apparatus grew in an uncoordinated fashion and suffered from the same turf battles that plagued the Soviet equivalent. Its inefficiency and even the loyalty of those involved became a major political issue, exploited by the political opportunist of the era: Senator Joseph McCarthy. In 1953 the incoming president, Dwight D. Eisenhower, rationalized America's international information apparatus by grouping most of its overt elements within a single United States Information Agency (USIA), which set its face to engage the peoples it described as the 'uncommitted, the wavering, the confused, the apathetic, or the doubtful within the free world' and did what it could to reach into the communist bloc.[24] Eisenhower invested in cultural outreach and he authorized a wide range of 'people-to-people' exchanges. He invested in the US presence at exhibitions and World's Fairs, which showcased America's industrial output and design and he sent jazz musicians and shows like *Porgy and Bess* on international tours. This use of musical diplomacy was especially effective. By selecting works which showcased African American talent – often in partnership with white performers – it conveyed an image of the United States as open to and respectful of its black citizens and thereby helped to counter the accounts of American racism emphasized in the Kremlin's portrait of the United States. While the musical diplomacy could take the edge off such criticism, Eisenhower also knew that only real change in the racial situation could undercut Moscow's claims. As historians like Mary Dudziak have shown, the president's desire to deny propaganda to the Russians propelled his firm response to white resistance to desegregation. Thus, Cold War propaganda helped to propel domestic reform within the USA.[25]

Besides the overt activity, Eisenhower also authorized an expanded covert propaganda campaign. The brain behind Eisenhower's effort was a magazine executive named C.D. Jackson, who served as the president's special assistant for psychological warfare. Jackson was a veteran of the wartime propaganda effort and a leading light in support of RFE. He was prepared to emulate his enemy's propaganda methods. With Jackson's encouragement, the CIA began its own campaign of setting up propaganda front organizations, some of which were not aware of their real funder's identity. Student, labour and intellectual groups like the

Congress for Cultural Freedom flourished under their patronage in what became known as the cultural Cold War.[26] Memorable documents distributed as part of the cultural Cold War included translations of a book originally created in Britain in 1950 called *The Got that Failed*, which was a set of autobiographical essays written by respected former-communist intellectuals of the period, including Arthur Koestler, in which they explained why they had quit the Party. The element of personal testimony gave an edge to its message and the book proved an effective tool.[27]

The durability of the Eastern regimes caught the Eisenhower administration by surprise, and following the repression of the Hungarian uprising in 1956 the US moved away from a policy of encouraging the 'roll back' of Soviet power in Europe and towards a game of proxy war in the developing world. When Khrushchev opened the door to exchanges, the US responded by circulating an illustrated magazine about life in the country, called *Amerika*, and creating a string of exhibitions, beginning with the American National Exhibition in Moscow in 1958. Traveling exhibits followed, featuring US technical accomplishment in fields such as medicine, plastics and graphic design. USIA found that one secret of success at exhibitions was the employment of lively young Americans with appropriate language skills as guides to engage audiences.[28]

Back in the US, USIA and VOA backed away from propaganda, and a new approach emerged which emphasized objectivity. In 1960 VOA acquired a charter embedding an obligation of balance in presenting the news. In 1961 Kennedy's new director of USIA, Edward R. Murrow, said in his confirmation hearing that credibility required honesty, and that meant discussing America's faults. Much programming about the Civil Rights struggle followed. By 1965 the determination to devise a democratic approach to international information created a new vocabulary with the term 'public diplomacy' at its heart. It remained to be seen whether the benign term would be filled with benign meaning, or revert to a mere euphemism for propaganda. The place where the difference would have to be demonstrated was the key battleground of the middle years of the Cold War: the developing world.

The Battle in the Developing World

By the end of the 1950s the developing world, with its newly independent nations and spreading calls for reform, became the most hotly contested battleground of the Cold War. Both superpowers recognized at an early stage the importance of propaganda to achieving their strategic goals in Asia, Africa, the Middle East and Latin America. The story of the evolution of USIA is the story of a shift of resources from an East–West and North Atlantic emphasis to a North–South focus; hence, by 1960, of USIA's roughly 200 posts around the world 84 were in the Middle East and Asia, 40 were in Latin America and 34 were in Africa.[29] Soviet leaders were no less concerned with winning hearts and minds in the so-called Third World. In 1947 Andrei Zhdanov, organizer of COMINFORM, had established the Soviet doctrine that there were only two clearly defined camps in the world: communist and capitalist-imperialist.[30] But in the early 1950s the Soviet Union publicly identified itself with the nationalist aspirations of colonial and newly decolonized peoples. Soviet universities began recruiting students from the developing world, Soviet propaganda channels carried messages from nationalist leaders and nationalist fighters carried Soviet-made or Soviet-designed weapons. The efficient design of the AK-47 assault rifle became as effective an ambassador for the system of the East as the smooth running of the Mercedes-Benz S-class was for the system of the West.

As USIA's own polling regularly demonstrated, the US initially won fewer friends than the USSR in the global South. The reasons for this were manifold, and while the Americans tended to point simply to Soviet budgets and success with *Sputnik*, there were deeper-seated factors at work. Above all, throughout the 1950s and 1960s two related strategic failures undermined American work. First and perhaps most damaging, was the failure of the Americans to take Third World nationalism seriously. Successive administrations did not understand that the newly empowered citizens of the developing countries, with their recent memory of the shackles of the old European colonial powers, tended to fear imperialism far more than they feared communism.[31] The United States, with its segregation and history of racism, had little credibility as a champion of the non-white world. For this reason, as already noted, the need for positive Cold War propaganda became a major driver of Federal support for Civil Rights reform, and USIA worked hard to publicize the achievements of the Civil Rights movement (albeit with a frame that tended to make the Federal government rather than leaders like Martin Luther King, Jr. the heroes). Significant examples of this include a USIA documentary film chronicling the March on Washington of August 1963 called *The March*. Civil Rights elements were also prominently woven into the USIA's memorialization of President Kennedy. The approach helped a little but was countered by the wave of racial riots, polarization and the assassination of King in the later 1960s.[32]

Besides the ongoing race problem, American leaders consistently underestimated many Third World actors' commitment to reform, their cultural resiliency and, in some cases, their resolve to remain unaligned. In the crucial early years of the 1950s US officials clung to an oversimplified binary worldview, expecting an inevitable and swift alignment of the developing world with either the Soviet Union or the United States. This misperception was part of the logic underpinning America's disastrous involvement in the war in Vietnam.

By the 1960s the leadership in the United States understood that the country would be judged by its deeds in the developing world. Practical gambits included the Kennedy administration's creation of the Peace Corps, which deployed young American volunteers in developing countries to variously build clinics, run schools and teach modern agricultural techniques. The Vietnam War was also an attempt at propaganda by deed, intended to prove the vitality of the American system in the field against a communist insurgency. The US selected the Vietnam situation from a number of crises in the early 1960s as one with particular potential for exploitation as a symbol. Saigon had excellent communication with the outside world and anything the US did would be seen. The intervention itself included a wide range of propaganda activity, including leaflet appeals for the enemy to defect, intense media support for the client government of South Vietnam and efforts to 'spin' the war for the world's media. The media campaign around Vietnam would call forth the largest budgets for propaganda of the entire period. But the communication could not counter ill-conceived strategy. Military setbacks drew ever deeper US military commitment in the name of protecting America's credibility. The intervention had disastrous results in the region and, thanks to division, it wrought havoc within the United States also. It was a propaganda gift to America's detractors and became a staple of Eastern-bloc outreach to audiences in the developing world. They circulated pictures of dead civilians, burned villages and other atrocities of the conflict. With such appalling images in play it helped that there were other images and accounts of democratic life circulating besides the American one. During the mid-1960s Britain's BBC stepped up its broadcasting to the developing world and rebranded its operation as the World Service.

The Soviet Union, by contrast, had an immediate strategic advantage in its approach to the developing world. It was the enemy of the old colonial powers and had no history comparable to either European imperialism or American racism. Its struggles to manage its ethnic diversity were conducted away from the world's gaze, though the ubiquity of the theme of happy minority groups in Soviet cultural propaganda now looks like an attempt to paper over the inter-communal cracks. While the Soviet Union initially shared the rigid binary outlook of the Americans, Soviet officials pivoted to a flexible worldview more quickly than did their Western counterparts. After Stalin's death in 1953 the Soviets both famously declared their support for national wars of liberation and publicly abandoned their opposition to non-alignment.[33] However, Soviet propaganda still pushed a modified version of the binary Cold War; the Soviets may have ostensibly embraced Third World non-alignment, but they actively sought to manipulate it.[34] Soviet propaganda cited non-alignment as supportive of the Soviets' vision of the world political economy: a developing nation's independent political policies denied that nation's addition to the American side, while independent, non-capitalist economic policies could be trumpeted as a kind of endorsement of Soviet socialism. No matter how they chose to view a developing nation's non-alignment, the Soviets placed their own global interests ahead of the local concerns of the developing nations.[35]

Of the Asian countries, India became a particularly important battleground for Cold War propaganda. By 1950 American leaders feared not only that the ideological loss of India would be a symbolic victory for the Soviets, but also that such a development might serve as a powerful example to other nations in the manner of Mao's China.[36] American administrations from Eisenhower on directed significant resources to India in an effort to promote America's image. But beyond the control of the Americans, Jawaharlal Nehru, India's first prime minister, viewed independence as fundamentally equated with nonalignment. Nehru resented the American 'advertisement approach'[37] to propaganda and viewed it as a threat to India's foreign policy and sovereignty.[38] Indian government officials proved a considerable impediment to American aims, closing propaganda offices, directing local police to harass and investigate American information officers and limiting the types of messages that US officials could disseminate.[39] US officials adjusted their messaging after the 1955 meeting of postcolonial African and Asian nations at the Bandung Conference; US propaganda ceased trying to pull India into the West and moved to convince Indians that US behaviour was superior to that of the Soviets. Still, Indian officials and non-state actors like journalists and cultural leaders resisted propaganda efforts and tended to collaborate only when their interests were served. The Soviets also made early concerted attempts to persuade India into their camp, including propaganda to foment revolution within the country. Their stridency in India and elsewhere, however, soon gave way to conciliatory initiatives like Khrushchev's 1955 'People's Diplomacy'.[40] Although few Indians abandoned non-alignment, the Soviet Union enjoyed a good image and Indian journalists tended to favour information from Soviet sources over US campaigns. Nevertheless, the bottom line was that in India – and elsewhere in South and East Asia – the Cold War agenda simply did not fit the concerns of governments or people: decolonization, nationalism and other local processes such as women's liberation, regional relations and local inter-ethnic politics. Propaganda created in the framework of Cold War bipolarity often missed the mark.[41]

The superpowers also waged a fierce competition for influence in Latin America. Interventions there, especially in the three decades after Castro's triumphant revolution, were characterized by military and covert intervention as much as by propaganda. But the Soviets and Americans still launched aggressive information campaigns. The US had propaganda outlets in Latin America dating back to the 1930s and needed merely to re-orientate against the new enemy. The Soviets used the familiar pattern of press and Party work and added cultural outreach into the mix. The US won friends by teaching English, and in Chile the Soviets responded by mounting their own English-language classes to beat the Americans at their own game. American innovations in the 1960s included a successful anti-communist *telenovela* for the region called *Nuesta Barrio* which told the story of a neighbourhood in which a good doctor battled against an evil communist boss.[42] Nevertheless, the general pattern of underestimating the agency of the Third World's actors held true: Latin America went its own way.[43] In the 1960s and 1970s major changes to the region came from hard power interventions and clientism – as with US sponsorship of Pinochet in Chile or Soviet in-roads in Central America – rather than from the soft power of persuasion.

Africa was also aggressively contested by East and West. Concerns like Egyptian Islamism, Pan-Africanism, tribal rivalry and sectionalism occupied the agendas of Africans, but as in the cases of South and East Asia, local issues tended to be ignored.[44] Instead, the superpowers sought out client states and worked to sell their respective systems. The surge of Chinese propaganda work in Africa in both the 1960s and 1970s rallied both Moscow and Washington to still greater efforts on the continent. The East's sponsorship of the colonial liberation movements which came to power in the late 1950s and 1960s helped its credibility. By the same token, the readiness of the United States and Western Europe to do business with the last and worst colonial regimes on the continent – those of the white minorities in South Africa and Rhodesia, and of Portugal in Angola and Mozambique – hurt their credibility. Behind the scenes the US and Britain used public diplomacy to promote reform but their efforts seemed paltry compared to the material support for radical change flowing from the Eastern bloc. The South African Communist Party contributed much to the organization and operation of the African National Congress (ANC). South Africa exploited the connection between the communist bloc and the ANC to undermine the ANC at home and abroad. The apartheid state defended its existence as a necessity of the Cold War, peaking in the early 1970s with some of the most outrageous propaganda gambits of the period, including an attempt to covertly acquire control of the *Washington Star* newspaper. Settlement in South Africa could be reached only as Cold War propaganda dropped out of the international equation in the late 1980s.[45]

In Cold War propaganda to the Middle East the Soviet Union made play on its openness to nationalism, while US propaganda sought to reverse anti-American public opinion and to channel 'the revolutionary and nationalistic pressures throughout the area into orderly channels not antagonistic to the West'.[46] The US again neglected local agendas, and messages of American wealth and success displaced engagement on political and economic reform. As the US came to be identified with the repressive status quo, US propaganda outlets became regular targets of local anger.[47] No local issue was more neglected than the plight of the Palestinians and US support for Israel. Despite later US rhetoric attempting a more neutral posture in the Israel–Palestine dispute, the effects of the Palestine situation on public opinion in the Arab world were nothing short of 'overwhelming'.[48] US Cold War outreach in the Middle East became a tragedy of sorts. The only way that America could communicate effectively in the region was to create a professional cadre of Arabic-speaking information specialists who would address the region on its own terms. But the Middle East's sanctions against the United States, imposed in the wake of the disastrous Arab–Israeli war of 1967, so reduced the number of American information posts in the Arab world that they not only rendered the region a dead end for anyone seeking a career at USIA, but also hobbled the US approach to that part of the world for a decade.[49] In one important respect both Moscow and Washington missed the mark. Washington backed away from its early attempts to identify the West with religious faith – which in the Middle East meant compatibility with Islam – and allowed its confrontation with the Soviet Union to become a clash of two materialisms. This opened the door for a different kind of non-aligned politics: the religious fundamentalism of radical Islam which defied both East and West. Both Washington and Moscow would be bloodied by this unintended consequence of their propaganda duel – in Iran and Afghanistan respectively – but the challenge was fated to endure into the post-Cold War era.[50]

Détente

Although at the time the Cold War world seemed utterly polarized, in hindsight it is possible to track important undercurrents towards a mutual quest for understanding and conflict resolution. These undercurrents were periodically manifest in events like the Khrushchev–Eisenhower rapprochement in the late 1950s, the Johnson–Kosygin Glassboro Summit of 1967 and the Strategic Arms Limitation Talks (SALT) process which began under Nixon. The leaders concerned understood the international public relations value of being associated with compromise – 'Blessed are the peacemakers' – and absolute value of lowered risk, greater stability and smaller military budgets. The détente of the 1970s had its own layer of propaganda attached, as participants vied for position and alternately spun the behaviour of the other to cement their own standing.

Détente did not preclude continued manoeuvring for ideological position between East and West. International organizations became a key theatre for this. Soviet sponsorship of Third World nationalism gave the Soviet Union an edge in many quarters, especially the United Nations Educational Scientific and Cultural Organization (UNESCO), where a new director general, Amadou-Mahtar M'Bow of Senegal, played directly into Soviet hands by launching a campaign for what was termed a New World International Communication Order (NWICO). NWICO purported to promote an antidote to the domination of Western news channels, but, by guaranteeing the rights of nations to police their own media environment, could also be read as a ploy to establish a right to censorship, which would hinder the spread of democratic media practices. The battle around NWICO laid the foundation for the departure of the United States and Britain from UNESCO in the 1980s.[51]

The economic challenges of the 1970s led to smaller budgets for external propaganda in the West. There was also a reassessment of purposes. Of America's allies, the UK's British Council moved into new territory, financing much of its operation through paid services such as English-language teaching. The organization also moved beyond a crude model of simply exporting British values and culture, introducing a strand of mutuality into its operations by facilitating the entry of foreign arts and culture into the UK.[52] Similar notions arose in the United States. During the Carter administration the entire structure of US public diplomacy underwent a major revision and re-branding under the name of United States International Communication Agency (USICA), which brought with it a new or 'second' mandate to inform Americans about the rest of the world. Unlike the British efforts in the same field, the American version lacked any budget to mount anything more than a couple of token projects.[53] The Soviet Union continued to seek influence through cultural and educational work, but as some portions of the globe seemed to cool in their admiration for the USSR, Moscow came to rely on cruder methods. The KGB simply hired crowds to demonstrate in support of the nation when Soviet leaders toured the world, and faked evidence of continued global admiration for the Soviet way of life. In this way the manipulation of international opinion became a subset of Soviet domestic propaganda, and a part of the Kremlin's claim to legitimacy before its own people. It was an addictive brew and it sometimes seemed that the Brezhnev regime had lost touch with reality and become a dupe of its own propaganda.[54]

Détente spawned its own eccentric attempts at the co-creation of propaganda. There was the joint US–Soviet space link-up in 1975 and a co-produced lackluster children's fantasy film called *The Blue Bird* which brought together the stars of the Bolshoi Ballet with American performers such as Elizabeth Taylor and Jane Fonda.[55] The real impact of détente was felt elsewhere. The Soviets traded the appearance of success at the negotiating table for increased vulnerability to dissident criticism when they signed up to universal principles of human rights in the Helsinki Accords in 1975. The Accords also opened new channels of East–West trade, cooperation and exchange and started the Soviet bloc on a path to change. In the wake of Helsinki, Western ideas flowed more freely into Eastern Europe. Mutual media coverage became easier, just in time for the Western press to have a front-row seat for the stagnation of the Soviet economy.[56] The news of increased dissident activity and economic crisis became grist to the mill of Western international broadcasters like RFE, VOA or the BBC World Service, or the official information apparatus of the USIA/USICA. Carter-era work was dominated by the theme of human rights, despite the irony of his government's cosy relationship with the Shah of Iran.

The Second Cold War

As the Soviet economy became bogged down in the 1970s Brezhnev and his successors manoeuvered to shore up their position in the wider world. Propaganda gave way once again to military intervention. Soviet adventurism in Southern and Eastern Africa, Central America and – most especially – Afghanistan pushed the East–West relationship beyond its breaking point and mutual hostility returned. The formal propaganda bureaucracies of the rivals recommenced sniping at one another in earnest. Soviet gambits sank to the level of covert attacks on Western broadcasters, most famously the BBC Bulgarian Service broadcaster Georgi Markov, who was shot in the leg with a poisoned pellet fired from an umbrella while crossing London's Waterloo Bridge in 1978. The West expanded its operations, adding to the mix new technologies such as the American government's satellite news feed WORLDNET, which was launched in 1983. Some of the oldest methods remained the most effective. The KGB stepped up its use of rumours, gaining considerable mileage from promoting the idea that a new disease known as HIV/AIDS had begun as an American bio-weapon, while the USIA (which had regained its old title soon after the election of Ronald Reagan) promoted awareness of the economic difficulty within the Soviet world by circulating the jokes which Russians themselves told to make light of their privations.[57]

The market-driven US film industry and official Soviet film industry both plunged back into shameless stereotyping.[58] But the Cold War propagandists were not the only forces vying for international opinion. Non-state actors challenged the Cold War's logic and methods. In Europe the Campaign for Nuclear Disarmament challenged the deployment of new kinds of weapon and artists created anti-nuclear materials. One of the most affecting post-nuclear war pieces was a comic book drawn by British children's author Raymond Briggs, *When the Wind Blows* (1982), which told the story of a nuclear attack through the eyes of an elderly couple who obediently followed all the civil defence instructions issued by the government of Margaret Thatcher. Comment from the world of popular music included '*99 Luftballons*' (released in an English version as '99 Red Balloons') by the German singer Nina (1983), in which a balloon accidentally triggers nuclear war; Sting's 1985 song 'Russians', which suggested that 'Russians love their children too', and 'Two Tribes' by Frankie Goes to Hollywood (1984), whose video featured doubles of Reagan and Soviet premier Chernyenko grappling in a wrestling ring and the lyric: 'When two tribes go to war, one is all that you can score.'

The strength of anti-nuclear feeling posed a severe political problem for the US delegation to NATO as it sought to balance the Soviet deployment of SS20 missiles with its own Pershing II cruise missiles. The campaign which they launched, feeding arguments to local news outlets, was as skilled a piece of advocacy work as any in the Cold War era and, while not wiping out anti-nuclear sentiment, moved feeling enough to permit deployment of the missiles on European soil.

Much East–West exchange suffered as a result of the renewed conflict. Sporting exchange was a prominent casualty. The US organized a clumsy boycott of the Moscow Olympics of 1980 and the Soviet Union stayed away from the Los Angeles games of 1984. But other exchanges survived the renewal of tension, perhaps because the East gambled on learning technical skills that could revive economic growth. The trend towards a greater knowledge of the Western way of life continued. The pressure for reform brought forth a new kind of politician in the East, typified by Mikhail Gorbachev. Media savvy and open to negotiation, Gorbachev understood the value of communication and image as well as any Western executive. He branded his political project *Perestroika* (restructuring) and *Glasnost* (openness) and impressed opinion in the West. Both sides used a full range of news-management techniques to present the spectacle of negotiation and compromise to their respective audiences. Negotiations included attention to the realm of propaganda, including what amounted to disarmament talks and agreements to tone down such behaviours as mutual vilification and rumour mongering.[59]

Western broadcasting flourished and VOA, the BBC, RFE and Radio Liberty (which had been re-born in a post-CIA incarnation with a strong news culture) became part of the everyday life of many people in the Eastern bloc. The KGB and RFE/Radio Liberty analysts both estimated listenership in the vicinity of 10 percent a week.[60] Music remained popular content and DJs like the veteran jazz man Willis Connover of VOA or the more youthful rock disk jockey Seva Novgorodsev on the BBC Russian service were stars in the Eastern world. RIAS TV, established by the United States in West Berlin, had an immense impact in East Germany, bringing a glimpse of the MTV culture to the land of the Stasi. East Germans living near Dresden were prevented by their surrounding topography from receiving signals from the West and were disparaged as being from 'the valley of the people who know nothing'. Ironically, it may have been a final example of the negative form of broadcast propaganda – censorship – which sealed the decline of Soviet power in the East. In April 1986 the nuclear power plant at Chernobyl near Kiev went into a catastrophic meltdown. The Soviet government said nothing of the incident for many days, while the Western broadcasters and the internal grapevine carried the truth of the disaster to the region, destroying the credibility of the Kremlin as they did so.[61]

The final phase of Cold War propaganda came in 1989, as pressure for reform expressed in songs, banners and speeches from the street – encouraged by exchanges with and news from the West – finally brought change to the Eastern bloc. Western broadcasters, some of whom had begun the Cold War with crude slogans, contributed to its end with honest news coverage of the march of reform, encouraging one movement with news of developments in its neighbour. A spectacular chain reaction followed, and by the end of 1989 Gorbachev and the new US president, George H.W. Bush, spoke of the Cold War as history. It was fitting that the Cold War, which had always rendered ordinary people impotent spectators, ended with the people acting decisively and governments, both East and West, watching from the sidelines.

Conclusion

While the mutual vitriol which characterized the early years of the first and second Cold Wars suggests that the Cold War was a static ideological slugging match in which contending blocs simply bombarded one another with messages, the reality was one of surprising ebb and flow, and nuance. It is remarkable how successful Soviet propaganda was for much of the period, if only because the early Soviet grab for the nationalist high ground in the imagination of the developing world left the West wallowing at the bottom of the slope with whichever local status quo power would accept its sponsorship. In the West, Cold War propaganda became a learning process as the practitioners (if not the policymakers) learned the limited value of unbridled rhetoric and the importance of such things as listening to their audience, basing their approach on truth, and aiming for dialogue and mutual learning. The new approach in the US became identified with a new term – public diplomacy – which would be widely used internationally in the years following the Cold War, in recognition both of its role in the Cold War's end-game and of the expanded scope for international communication provided by the end of bipolar international politics.

One irony of the post-Cold War period has been that the analysis of the Cold War has become a site of propaganda in its own right. In Scandinavia much ink has been spilled over the positions taken by various journalists towards the Soviet Union or the US camp. In the former Soviet Union the conclusion of the Cold War was constructed as a result of internal economic problems rather than the prowess of an adversary. In the United States, the end of the Cold War sparked a victory culture in which the political right wing emphasized lessons of self-assertion and strength at the expense of negotiation and exchange. No branch of government suffered more in post-Cold War America than the organs of public diplomacy and in 1999, after a decade of underfunding and neglect, USIA ceased to exist and its functions and remaining personnel were transferred into the State Department. At the same time a new enemy – the Al Qaida network – made extensive use of a victory narrative of its own, arguing that the role of Islamic militants in driving the Soviet Union from Afghanistan was instrumental in the collapse of the whole regime and that its philosophy was the true victor in the Cold War and the wave of the future. Thus – as with the Cold War itself – the distortion of one conflict became an overture for the next.

Despite the emergence in the twenty-first century of multiple challenges, from terrorism to the climate, and the rise of China as a major player on the world stage, the Cold War division between Washington and its allies and Moscow is still periodically evident, like ominous rumblings along a geological fault-line. Barbs of mutual criticism still fly and public diplomacy can still find itself on the front line. The rhetoric of Russian President Vladimir Putin and US presidential candidate Mitt Romney in 2012 indicated that the 'Henry IV' approach to domestic politics was still alive and well. It remains to be seen whether such rumblings are aftershocks of yesterday's conflict or a foretaste of hostility to come. People of goodwill on both sides need to remember the lessons of the propagandized past, work to build real understanding across the international divide and resist the glib resort to stereotype and mutual demonization which fuelled both sides of the Cold War.

Notes

1 *Henry IV* pt. II, Act 4, scene 5.
2 Examples include such feature films as *Potomok Chingiskhana* [The Heir to Genghis Khan, released in the West as *Storm Over Asia*] (Vsevolod Pudovkin dir., 1928).
3 Commercially generated examples of anti-Soviet propaganda still available today include the Greta Garbo comedy *Ninotchka* (Ernst Lubitsch, dir. 1939) or the first outing in a Belgian newspaper for the character Tintin: *Les Adventures de Tintin ... au Pays des Soviets* [The Adventures of Tintin ... in the land of the Soviets] (1929–30).
4 Quoted in Eric F. Goldman, *The Crucial Decade and After: America, 1945–1960* (New York: Vintage Books, 1961), p. 59.
5 Famous feature film examples include the Lawrence Olivier film *Demi-Paradise* (Anthony Asquith dir., 1943) in the UK or Warner Brothers' wildly pro-Stalin *Mission to Moscow* (Michael Curtiz dir., 1943) in the US, and documentary examples include the *Battle for Russia* episode of *Why We Fight* in the US or an even more enthusiastic profile of Russia put out in the *Canada Carries On* series. On the

distortions of US propaganda in the Second World War see M. Todd Bennett, *One World, Big Screen: Hollywood, the Allies and World War II* (Chapel Hill, NC: University of North Carolina Press, 2012).
6 R.W. Apple Jr., 'J. William Fulbright, Senate Giant, Is Dead at 89', *New York Times*, 10 February 1995.
7 Georgi Plekhanov, 'The Tasks of the Social-Democrats in the Famine' (1892), quoted in Jonathan Frankel (tr./ed.) *Vladimir Akimov on the Dilemmas of Russian Marxism: 1895–1903* (Cambridge: Cambridge University Press, 1969), p. 17.
8 For a survey of the Soviet propaganda structure see Frederick C. Barghoorn, *The Soviet Cultural Offensive* (Princeton, NJ: Princeton University Press, 1960) and *Soviet Foreign Propaganda* (Princeton, NJ: Princeton University Press, 1964).
9 See *The Soviet Union: Facts, Descriptions, Statistics* (New York: Soviet Information Bureau, 1929). The US affiliate organization had a distinguished board including the anthropologist Franz Boas, with Shakespearian scholar William Allan Neilson as its president.
10 Ludmila Stern, 'The All-Union Society for Cultural Relations with Foreign Countries and French Intellectuals, 1925–29', *Australian Journal of Politics and History* 45 (1999), 99–109; Anthony Swift 'The Soviet World of Tomorrow at the New York World's Fair of 1939', *Russian Review* 57, (1998), 364–379.
11 For a biography see Sean McMeekin, *The Red Millionaire: A Political Biography of Willi Münzenberg, Moscow's Secret Propaganda Tsar in the West* (New Haven, CT: Yale University Press, 2003).
12 For a British report on the formation of COMINFORM see the National Archives, Kew (hereafter TNA) FO 975/88 'Some facts about the COMINFORM', IRD report B.257, September 1955. This report notes that by 1955, of the forty or so delegates to the first three COMINFORM meetings, ten had been purged or executed.
13 Barghoorn, *Soviet Foreign Propaganda*, p. 238.
14 Khrushchev replaced the old apparatus with a free-standing Union of Soviet Societies of Friendship and Cultural Relations with Foreign Countries (SSOD) and State Committee for Cultural Ties (GKKS). In the later Khrushchev years the regime also set up a new press agency, NOVOSTI, to feed its version of global events to the world, and a new international propaganda station called Radio Peace and Progress.
15 Barghoorn, *Soviet Foreign Propaganda*, p. 241. Examples of films of the era include *Letyat zhuravli* [The Cranes are Flying] (Mikhail Kalatozov dir., 1957) or *Ballada o soldate* [Ballad of a Soldier] (Grigori Chukrai dir., 1959).
16 Barghoorn, *The Soviet Cultural Offensive*, p. 336.
17 Nigel Gould-Davies, 'The Logic of Soviet Cultural Diplomacy', *Diplomatic History* 27 (2003), 193–214, esp. 203, 205–6.
18 For a British report on the story see TNA FO 975/62 'The Communist Germ Warfare Campaign', IRD, June 1952.
19 TNA FO 295/975 'East Berlin Lie Factory', IRD, FB (G) revised May 1960.
20 The story of Western Cold War broadcasting is well told in Michael Nelson, *War of the Black Heavens: The Battles of Western Broadcasting in the Cold War* (London: Brassey's, 2003). On the origins of jamming see ibid., p. 21.
21 For a history of the IRD see Andrew Defty, *Britain, America and Anti-Communist Propaganda 1945–53: The Information Research Department* (London: Routledge, 2004). The first report can be found in TNA FO 975/1 'The Real Conditions in Soviet Russia', IRD, 1948.
22 John Jenks, *British Propaganda and News Media in the Cold War* (Manchester: University of Manchester Press, 2006).
23 The best source on US cultural diplomacy is Richard T. Arndt, *The First Resort of Kings: American Cultural Diplomacy in the Twentieth Century* (Washington, DC: Potomac Books, 2005).
24 For a complete history of USIA see Nicholas J. Cull, *The Cold War and the United States Information Agency: American Propaganda and Public Diplomacy, 1945–1989* (Cambridge: Cambridge University Press, 2008). The quote is from Kenneth Osgood, 'Words and Deeds: Race, Colonialism, and Eisenhower's Propaganda War in the Third World', in K.C. Statler and A.L. Johns (eds.), *The Eisenhower Administration, the Third World, and the Globalization of the Cold War* (Lanham, MD: Rowman & Littlefield, 2006), pp. 3–26, at p. 7).
25 On the race issue see Mary Dudziak, *Cold War Civil Rights: Race and the Image of American Democracy* (Princeton, NJ: Princeton University Press, 2000). On the Cold War use of jazz see Penny Von Eschen, *Satchmo Blows Up the World: Jazz Ambassadors Play the Cold War* (Cambridge, MA: Harvard

University Press, 2004) and Lisa E. Davenport, *Jazz Diplomacy: Promoting America in the Cold War Era* (Jackson, MS: University of Mississippi Press, 2009).

26 Accounts of the covert propaganda war include Scott Lucas, *Freedom's War: The American Crusade Against the Soviet Union* (New York: New York University Press, 1999) and Gregory Mitrovich, *Undermining the Kremlin: America's Strategy to Subvert the Soviet Bloc, 1947–1956* (Ithaca, NY: Cornell University Press, 1999).
27 Athur Koestler et al., *The God that Failed* (London: Hamilton, 1950).
28 On US exhibitions see Conway Lloyd Morgan and Jack Masey, *Cold War Confrontation: US exhibitions and Their Role in the Cultural Cold War, 1950–1980* (Zürich: Lars Müller Publishers, 2008).
29 USIA Strategic Principles, n.d. [March 1954], OCB Central files, box 20, OCB 040 USIA (1), EL., cited in Osgood, 'Words and Deeds', p. 7.
30 Pullin, 'Noise and Flutter', p. 65.
31 Osgood, 'Words and Deeds'.
32 On *The March* see Nicholas J. Cull, 'Auteurs of Ideology: USIA Documentary Film Propaganda in the Kennedy Era as seen in Bruce Herschensohn's *The Five Cities of June* (1963) and James Blue's *The March* (1964)', *Film History* 10(3) (1998), 295–310.
33 Osgood, 'Words and Deeds', p. 10; Pullin, 'Noise and Flutter', p. 317.
34 Pullin, 'Noise and Flutter'.
35 Pullin, 'Noise and Flutter', p. 317.
36 Pullin, 'Noise and Flutter'.
37 Jawaharlal Nehru, 15 March 1948, *Constituent Assembly on India Debates, Official Report*, Volume III, 1948, 2190–2191, cited in Pullin, 'Noise and Flutter', p. 90.
38 Pullin, 'Noise and Flutter'.
39 Pullin, 'Noise and Flutter', p. 10.
40 Pullin, 'Noise and Flutter'.
41 Michael Szonyi and Hong Liu, 'New Approaches to the Study of the Cold War', in Zheng Yangwen, Hong Liu and Michael Szonyi (eds.), *The Cold War in Asia: The Battle for Hearts and Minds* (Boston, MA: Brill, 2010), 7.
42 Cull, *The Cold War and the United States Information Agency*, p. 240.
43 Chester J. Pach Jr., 'Thinking Globally and Acting Locally', in Kathryn C. Statler and Andrew L. Johns (eds.), *The Eisenhower Administration, the Third World, and the Globalization of the Cold War* (Lanham, MD: Rowman & Littlefield, 2006), pp. xi–xxii, at p. xvi.
44 Osgood, 'Words and Deeds'.
45 On South Africa's propaganda policies see James Sanders, *South Africa and the International Media 1972–1979*, (London: Routledge, 1999).
46 NSC 5428, United States Objectives and Policies with Respect to the Near East, 23 July 1954, cited in Joyce Battle (ed.), *U.S. Propaganda in the Middle East – The Early Cold War Version*, National Security Archive Electronic Briefing Book No. 78. (December 13, 2002). See http://www.gwu.edu/~nsarchiv/NSAEBB/NSAEBB78/essay.htm#7.
47 Battle, *U.S. Propaganda in the Middle East*.
48 Battle, *U.S. Propaganda in the Middle East*.
49 William A. Rugh, *American Encounters with Arabs: The 'Soft Power' of U.S. Public Diplomacy in the Middle East* (Westport, CT: Praeger, 2006), p. 65.
50 This point is made in the conclusion to Nicholas J. Cull, *The Decline and Fall of the United States Information Agency: American Public Diplomacy, 1989–2001* (New York: Palgrave, 2012), p. 188.
51 On UNESCO see William Preston, Jr., Edward S. Herman and Herbert I. Schiller, *Hope and Folly: The United States and UNESCO 1945–1985* (Minneapolis, MN: University of Minnesota Press, 1989).
52 Ali Fisher, *A story of engagement: the British Council 1934–2009* (London: Counterpoint/British Council, London, 2009), pp. 45–46.
53 On Carter-era public diplomacy see Cull, *The Cold War and the United States Information Agency*, p. 360–98; on token projects see p. 384.
54 Details of disinformation work and the self-deception point are dealt with at length in Christopher Andrew and Vasili Mitrokhin, *The World Was Going Our Way: The KGB and the Battle for the Third World* (New York: Basic Books, 2005). See also Nicholas J. Cull, 'Karen Hughes and the Brezhnev Syndrome: The Trial of Public Diplomacy as Domestic Performance', in Ali Fisher and Scott Lucas (eds.), *Trials of Engagement: The Future of US Public Diplomacy* (Leiden: Brill, 2010).

55 For a case study of *The Blue Bird* see Tony Shaw, 'Nightmare on Nevsky Prospekt: *The Blue Bird* as a Curious Instance of U.S.–Soviet Film Collaboration during the Cold War', *Journal of Cold War Studies* 14:1 (Winter 2012): 3–33.
56 Yale Richmond, *U.S. Soviet Cultural Exchanges, 1958–1986: Who Wins?* (Boulder, CO: Westview, 1987), p. 100; Yale Richmond, *Cultural Exchange and the Cold War: Raising the Iron Curtain* (University Park, PA: Pennsylvania State University Press, 2003), p. 209.
57 Cull, *The Cold War and the United States Information Agency*, p. 424.
58 Tony Shaw and Denise Youngblood, *Cinematic Cold War: The American and Soviet Struggle for Hearts and Minds* (Lawrence, KS: University of Kansas Press), esp. pp. 189–213. American films like *Red Dawn* were matched with a crop of Russian spy thrillers like *Gruz bez markirovki* [Unmarked Load] (Vladimir Popkov, dir., 1984) *Kankan v angliyskom parke* [Can-Can in English Park] (Valeri Pidpaly, dir., 1984), or the TV series *TASS upolnomochen zayavit* ... [TASS is Authorized to Announce] (Vladimir Folkin, dir., 1984).
59 Cull, *The Cold War and the United States Information Agency*, pp. 466–68.
60 For a full treatment of audience data see R. Eugene Parta, *Discovering the Hidden Listener: An Empirical Assessment of Radio Liberty and Western Broadcasting to the USSR during the Cold War* (Palo Alto, CA: Hoover Institution, 2007).
61 Nelson, *War of the Black Heavens*, pp. 167–168; Cull, *The Cold War and the United States Information Agency*, pp. 457–9.

24
THE COLD WAR AND FILM

Andrei Kozovoi

The interconnection between the Cold War and cinema is a relatively new topic of research, even if it has been studied at least since Nora Sayre's *Films of the Cold War* (1982). Walter J. Hixson's *Parting the Curtain* (1997), engaging with the cultural dimension of the Cold War, certainly had a huge influence in this field, famously stating that the Cold War's outcome "could only be decided on cultural ground."[1] That said, historiography in its current state still has many shortcomings, which leads us to start by stressing "the Five Commandments" which should be considered by any Cold War cinema historian.

First, he or she shall remember that the Cold War did not end in the 1950s (or in 1962, after the Cuban Missile Crisis), since to this day Hollywood and the "anti-Red" films of the 1940s and 1950s still receive overwhelming attention from scholars. Similarly, Russian/Soviet historiography has almost exclusively focused on the Stalin years and its images of "the enemy." Second, current research has a natural tendency toward a self-centered view of things, often forgetting the merits of comparative history. Hence, when tackling this area of the cultural Cold War, one should not favor the United States, nor forget that the fate of the "blacklisted" in the U.S. pales in comparison with the fate of cinematographers in the Soviet Union. Third, the motivational factors: why use the Cold War enemy in a script? One should remember that the demonization of the Soviet enemy – either explicit, as in *Invasion U.S.A.* (1952), or implicit, as in *Invasion of the Body Snatchers* (1956) – was not always the main goal of American film producers. The same goes for the demonization of the American fiend in Soviet cinema: Soviet film directors were not particularly anti-American, but in order to work, one had to make concessions to the Communist Party, and follow an ideological line. Fourth, one should focus not only on feature films, but also on television productions, which contained numerous Cold War references. Last, but certainly not least, one should carefully study the historical background against which these films were made – internal (social interactions) and external (international relations) – as the study of films in a vacuum is a sterile exercise.

Situated at the crossroads of various academic disciplines and cultural genres, the study of the cinematic Cold War relies on a number of key principles. First, the Cold War must be understood as a *system of interactions*, both belligerent and cooperative, between the different "blocs" or "camps." Second, despite their various definitions and manifestations, "propaganda," "psychological warfare" and "cultural diplomacy" are still legitimate concepts, and hereafter they will mean more or less the same thing. They encompass numerous practices dealing with information production and communication common to both the Soviet Union and the "free world." This being said, the historian must remember that both sides, communist and capitalist, used propaganda techniques and were influenced by stereotypes which long preceded the Cold War per se. Third, standing at the core of filmmaking, the process of "representation" presupposes a conscious act of creation and tends to favor particular forms of reception. The effect of propaganda on popular perceptions, however, was often subliminal and the message, as well as the image, was not always obvious. Hence it would be more appropriate to use the notion of "presences," which not only transcends the notion of genre but acknowledges the existence of a specific image on screen, thus introducing a vast array of previously ignored movies.[2] For instance, Glenn Miller's famous tune "In the Mood," included in both the opening and closing scenes of the Soviet musical *The Hat* (1981), on the ups and downs of a trumpeter gone "commercial," bore the weight of the Cold War. Conversely, the absence of the Other where *it should have been* also manifests an important characteristic of the celluloid Cold War. One of the most striking Soviet examples is the biopic *Aleksandr Popov* (1949), on the Russian radio inventor: the film mentioned the Italian pioneer Marconi but remained conspicuously silent about the American scientist Nikola Tesla, who had paved the way for Popov.

As a conflict of ideologies and social models, the cinematic Cold War involved a global (i.e. interacting) network of filmmaking. For both the U.S. government and Hollywood, economic imperatives overlapped with political and ideological ones: the stakes involved were as much about revenues as about projecting one's identity and model and winning over the audience, both domestic and foreign. On the other side of the barricade, the Soviet film industry, directed by the Party, was also striving to compete for its place on the global arena with the same objectives in mind, although with a lot less money and glamor. Ever since the 1930s, Stalin had played the role of a producer, imposing his will upon the industry and the spectator; after his death, things tended to loosen up, with frequent debates and even conflicts between Party watchdogs of the Central Committee, "realist" thinkers within the government (the Ministry of Cinematography in its various incarnations) and "artistic workers" (Union of Cinematographers) on the nature of cinema – entertainment or art, industry or ideology.

The cinematic Cold War was a confrontation that engulfed all continents, involving mass media and communication as well as millions of spectators around the globe. It was a battle between images, social and political models, but also individuals, groups and cultures, which eventually ended with the demise of the Communist cinematic model. The limited scope of our discussion in this chapter does not allow us to look beyond the cinematic rivalry between the U.S. and the Soviet Union, as well as beyond feature films and films made for television, excluding for example documentary cinema – particularly developed in the USSR when it came to politics.

Presences

Negative stereotypes apparent in "topical films" of the Cold War period were not new. From the end of the eighteenth century, Americans grew increasingly wary of Russia as they observed the rise of conservative and anti-Semitic sentiments under Tsar Alexander III. The geopolitical rivalry in the Far East, culminating in the Russo-Japanese War of 1904–5, reinforced these negative perceptions.[3] America's support of the Japanese and the resultant anti-American travelogues such as Gorky's *City of the Yellow Devil* (1906) in turn aroused suspicion in Russia, although Russians' attitudes towards the U.S. were far more ambivalent, exhibiting a mixture of negative and positive stereotypes. For example, Americans were perceived as a nation particularly prone to efficient business, but also a nation without a "real culture."[4]

The Bolshevik ascent to power ignited a new wave of anti-Russian sentiment in the U.S., with the first feature, *Darkest Russia*, coming out as early as 1917. It was followed by other productions reflecting both the domestic and international situation, such as the American "first Red Scare" and the Russian Civil War, but also the importance of the Russian emigration to Hollywood.[5] *Ninochka* (1939), with its Bolshevik protagonist eventually converted to the capitalist cause (played by Greta Garbo, known for her depictions of Anna Karenina) became the epitome of American hostility towards the Soviet regime: it pictured a totalitarian system bent on absolute control, brainwashing and depriving its subjects of the most basic goods.[6] To some historians, it became a model to which all Soviet Cold War films would be compared.[7] In the Soviet Union, there was a similar cinematic obsession with everything American during the interwar period, growing increasingly anti-American over the years. In *The Circus* (1936), an American actress came to Soviet Russia to rescue her black child from a racist milieu. Such unsympathetic representations were deemed inappropriate during the years of the Grand Alliance (1941–45), when the American idealization of Soviet Russia went as far as to justify the infamous Moscow Trials, exemplified in *Mission to Moscow* (1943), based on the memoirs of the ambassador Joseph Davies.

Mission to Moscow is a perfect example of motion pictures playing the role of a "barometer of East-West relations," even more so than books.[8] In the U.S., after the launch of spy scandals in 1946, and after the proclamation of the Truman Doctrine in 1947, the time was ripe for a new surge of anti-Soviet features. Contrary to the first Red Scare, the emphasis was no longer on the enemy's race, ethnicity or nationality, but on ideology.[9] Between 1948 and 1953, Hollywood produced over seventy feature films – with twenty-two movies dealing with Russians and/or Communism released in 1952, during the height of the Korean War. But contrary to common knowledge, during the 1950s, Hollywood did not depict Russians only as caricatures. The year 1952, for example, saw the release of *My Son John*, a depressing tale of Communist infiltration, but also *Walk East on Beacon*, a realist depiction of Soviet espionage and the ambiguous western *High Noon*, famously characterized by John Wayne as "the most un-American thing I've seen in my whole life."[10] That being said, critics of McCarthyism[11] had to wait until 1956 for *Storm Center*, the first feature tackling the controversial subject of anti-Communist censorship in libraries.

During the same period, the Soviet Union released less than twenty feature films with explicit anti-American presences (images and/or discourses). Considering the weak industry output in the Soviet Union at the time (*malokartinie*), it was nevertheless an important figure. One of the more (in)famous titles, *The Meeting on the Elbe* (1949), rejected blunt anti-Americanism and divided American society along class lines, represented by the "good America" (simple workers, "progressive" individuals, ethnic minorities and ordinary soldiers) and the "bad America" (Wall Street fat cats, Pentagon hawks and CIA/FBI agents) – a common feature in all anti-American films in the USSR. To these one should add numerous anti-American scenarios which were never produced either because of their crudeness or because of their reliance on a volatile international context. Such was the fate of Alexander Dovzhenko's *Goodbye, America* (1951) based on the real-life story of a former American embassy employee, Annabelle Bucard, it was put "on the shelf" after she defected back to America. Topicality, thus, was a crucial factor for Soviet propaganda and the presence of the Other on screen directly depended on it.[12]

After March 1953, the presence of the screen "Other" became less obvious and menacing, especially in the West. The year 1956 saw the re-introduction of the notion of "peaceful coexistence." Cold War films adapted – as with the replacement of the Red Army counter-intelligence agency (SMERSH) by an imaginary supranational organization, "SPECTRE" –

in the adaptation of the James Bond novels. The context was sometimes transferred onto the screen: the first James Bond installment, *Dr. No* (1962), "acquired a sudden topicality" when the film was projected in England, in the fall of 1962, after the Cuban Missile Crisis: the villain's island was compared to Cuba.[13] Here and there, American films were reminding spectators of the evil side of the Soviet regime, for example in *Nicholas and Alexandra* (1971), depicting the murder of the last Russian tsar. But globally, despite the indirect confrontation in Southeast Asia, "fear of the evil Russian" was more or less outdated: anti-Russian stereotypes were ridiculed in the comedy *The Russians Are Coming, the Russians Are Coming* (1966) and Americans and Soviets played together against danger coming from space in *Meteor* (1979). On the Soviet side, cinema had to remain vigilant even if, more often than not, the United States was replaced by the anonymous NATO or West Germany. *The Resident's Mistake* (1968) told the story of a foreign spy of Russian aristocratic descent (Mikhail Tul'ev, played by Georgi Zhzhenov, himself a former prisoner in a Stalin labor camp), sent by the Germans and captured by the KGB, to become a double agent. Contrary to the U.S., in the USSR during the détente years, the danger coming from the West was sustained, even if not as forcefully as before: *50 on 50* (1972) cemented the image of Anglo-American collusion in espionage against the Soviet camp; the popular television mini-series *Seventeen Moments of Spring* (1973) brought the myth of the "Nazi-American war pact" to a new generation of viewers; *Heavy Water* (1979) told the story of an atomic submarine protecting Soviet waters against *provocateurs* from the West.

This imperfect "cinematic truce" lasted until the beginning of the 1980s. The mistreatment of dissidents in the USSR (Solzhenitsyn was expelled in 1974 and Sakharov arrested in 1980), the invasion of Afghanistan in 1979, the American boycott of the Olympic Games in Moscow in 1980, the Euromissiles crisis and the downing of a Korean civilian airliner by the Soviets in 1983, the Soviets' refusal to participate in the Los Angeles Summer Olympics of 1984 – all this heralded another cycle of mutual obsession and, more often than not, thrashing. In the period of 1984–86, the American film industry produced and released over thirty pictures with a strong Russian presence, mostly negative. Revived fears of an invasion were reflected in *Red Dawn* (1984), a film depicting the Soviet invasion of the United States from a "small middle-west city point of view," while *Rocky IV* (1985), with its depiction of the Soviet boxer's (Ivan Drago, played by Dolph Lundgren) sheer athleticism, dwelled on imaginary Soviet technological and physical superiority. The Soviets followed suit with their own depiction of foreign interventionists, as in *Coordinates of Death* (1985), which condemned the American war in Vietnam.

Explicit presences were only one part of the story, though, and filmmakers often employed other means to convey the belligerent atmosphere. The key Cold War geographic locations in Europe, such as the divided cities of Berlin and Vienna (until 1955), and in Southeast Asia, specifically Korea and Vietnam, served as the backdrop of numerous movie scripts, eventually leading to new subgenres in Western cinematography. In one such film, Vienna itself became one of the protagonists (*The Third Man*, 1949). Emotions, most prominently fear, were an important feature of contemporary celluloid art as well. In the 1950s, Hollywood filmmakers, following government-funded programs for Civil Defence training, exploited fears of a nuclear holocaust using various genres, among others science-fiction allegories (*The Day the Earth Stood Still*, 1951).[14] While those pictures ended well for the free world, pessimistic depictions of nuclear war became common on screen after the Cuban Missile Crisis (*Fail-Safe*, 1964). Fear of the Soviets provoking a nuclear strike in Europe lingered until the 1980s, not only in the U.S., but also among British filmmakers (*The Fourth Protocol*, 1987). Further east, a more amiable relationship with the Soviet Union ensured that French cinematographers were not as concerned about nuclear war in Europe as were their British colleagues, although the international context did find its way into a feature with a gloomy tone – *Spy, Stand Up* (1982), a film along dozens of the same type in which Western and Soviet secret services were put on the same level, the prototype being *The Spy Who Came in from the Cold* (1965).

Examples given above showed that both sides favored the spy film, which dwelled on the risk of foreign terrorism. However, whereas Western heroes did not limit themselves to certain geographic areas and traversed the world, either in a romanticised fashion, like in the James Bond franchise, or in the fairly mundane manner of the Harry Palmer trilogy (especially *The Ipcress File*, 1965), the Soviet spy film accentuated the hallowed nature of state borders, representing Soviet territory as perpetually in danger from foreign agents trying to corrupt Soviet people or to stage terrorist attacks (*Marked Atom*, 1972). With the spy film genre as well as other genres, the representation of foreign countries on the Soviet screen was as delicate (filmmakers had to be "realist" without appearing too admiring of the opulent West) as it was popular – cinema fulfilling here its first function as a "window to the world." Forbidden to travel abroad freely, Soviet viewers praised comedies depicting "cruises movies" with a Cold War aftertaste: in one of the most famous comedies, *The Diamond Arm* (1968), one tourist was asked whether he drank Coca-Cola, a question many Soviet citizens certainly wanted to ask, but rarely dared to, in public at least. The Second World War was another common feature of cinematic warfare. Both American and Soviet filmmakers often alluded to the Grand Alliance as a necessary but shameful affair. Soviet cinema closely followed the official American and British "historiophoty," to quote a term coined by historian Hayden White, i.e. the representation of history in visual images and filmic discourse.[15] But where American war cinema was silent on the crucial role of the Soviet ally, Soviet films insisted whenever they could on the "treacherousness" of the Americans, slowing the opening of the Second Front, dealing with the Nazis in order to prevent the Red Army from occupying Germany (*Secret Mission*, 1950).

Interactions

The political context is insufficient to understand the reasons behind the variations of Cold War representations on screen, and one must consider not only the interactions between the fictional world of cinema and the real world of politics, but also commercial and ideological factors.

It is commonly accepted that in Hollywood producers generally had the last word, and only a few famous and financially successful directors could have it their way, such as Cecil B. DeMille, creator of the "Cold War epic" genre.[16] However, even during the years of the "Hays code" (1934–68), an internal motion picture censorship system, Hollywood players were never *forced* to follow a particular standard of representation; there were *incentives* to do so, which is a different matter. On the the other hand, the cinematic version of "socialist realism," implemented in the USSR by the Party cinema organ, could hardly be circumvented. Soviet studios had "thematic plans" to fulfill (films on the Revolution, on the Great Patriotic War …), Party resolutions to implement and an enormous censorship machine to please, which made sure that directors did not overstep the line. If, in the West, the FBI and the Pentagon often interfered with the movie business, there was always a way to do a film without their help,[17] whereas "friendly advice" from the KGB or Soviet military could not be challenged. Ideological constraints explain, for example, why, during most of the Soviet period, the horror genre, so successfully employed by Western cinema, was considered decadent and "post-apocalyptic" features à la Mad Max were unthinkable. Until 1987 the doctrine of Mutually Assured

Destruction (MAD) was not part of Soviet operational thinking; nuclear war was considered a "strong possibility"[18] and propaganda aimed to instil confidence in the invincibility of the Soviet army. This explains a dearth of films depicting a nuclear strike as a disaster for humanity (*The Silence of Dr. Evans*, 1973). It was not before 1986 that the Soviets produced their "answer" to the post-apocalyptic *The Day After* (1983): *Letters of a Dead Man*. (Those features, while relatively successful, did not match the success of the American TV film, which is said to have had an impact even on Ronald Reagan.)

It should be stressed that the Soviet Communist regime, while preaching peace, actually *needed* the Cold War to assert its legitimacy. A certain amount of tension was a "structural necessity," since the Western enemy could be blamed for the lackluster state of the economy and the deprivations endured by the Soviet population. This is why there was always room for a capitalist conspiracy, even during (late) détente, as in *The Right of the First Signature* (1978), where a young Soviet representative dealt with American businessmen – good and bad. Outside of the détente years, at times of heated confrontation, the Soviet Communist Party responded to perceived "Western psychological warfare" by launching concerted anti-American campaigns in the media. There were at least two such campaigns, characterized by a high production output of Cold War films, in 1948–53 and in 1982–86. Interestingly enough, the first Cold War film that was released was Soviet: *The Russian Question* (8 March 1948); its counterpart, *The Iron Curtain*, had its premiere on 12 May of the same year.

When creating those films, American cinematographers and scriptwriters drew their inspiration from various sources. Personal or ideological connections to Russia and/or Communism certainly played a part. As many others, Ernst Lubitsch, the director of *Ninochka*, who had Russian roots and was fond of Russian people and traditions, came back from his honeymoon in Moscow a disillusioned man in 1936.[19] John Wayne's patriotic bravado found expression in *Big Jim McLain* (1952), a tale of a Communist infiltration in Hawaii, just as John Milius's anti-communist feelings influenced his *Red Dawn* (1984). The film's violence shocked its viewers, including the Soviets who had a chance to see it.[20] This, of course, does not mean that films presenting Communist ideas in a favourable light were not made in the U.S., even when the political context was unfavorable. The invasion of Afghanistan and the election of Ronald Reagan made *Reds* (1981), the biopic of the "first American communist" and the only American to be buried in the Kremlin, John Reed, even more "daring." Loaded with big stars (Warren Beatty, Diane Keaton and Jack Nicholson), it was nominated for nine Academy awards and won three, but was a disappointment at the box-office. *Reds*' very existence was a testimony to the freedom of speech in America, in contrast to the tightened censorhip in the Soviet Union during the same period.

Personal factors played a certain role in Soviet Russia too. Many cinematographers, such as Anatoli Bobrovski, Venyamin Dorman and Mikhail Tumanishvili, who specialized in action, adventure or espionage films, were not so much interested in the demonization of the Other than in the exploration of a given genre. At the same time, Soviet cinematography had its own John Waynes, the most famous of them Tatyana Lioznova. A former prisoner of war, she became a film director and the creator of the cult TV series *17 Moments of Spring* (1973), but also of the lesser known *On the Islands of Grenada* (1980), the first and perhaps only anti-American film to include a scene with an American president (seen from the back). But even in this production, an ambivalent vision of the West – dangerous and opulent – prevailed: a scene depicted a "typical American kitchen" with a full refrigerator – something that the Soviet people could only dream of in 1980.[21]

Another important aspect to consider here is cinematic diplomacy. Ever since the 1920s, State Department and film industry representatives considered American film export as the greatest factor in the "Americanisation of the world," seen as the globalization of culture.[22] The logic of the Cold War only reinforced this thinking, as cinema became an instrument in the ideological struggle for audiences' hearts and minds. During the Eisenhower presidency, "psychological warfare" shaped not only diplomatic, economic and military policies, but also cultural exchanges,[23] including film. In the end, the goals of Hollywood and those of the American government converged. As European markets opened up to the American film industry, the latter, in order to thrive (in fact to survive), had to export movies that projected "democracy's spiritual as well as material values."[24] The "Americanization" of the European market had financial incentives behind it as well; Britain became a particularly attractive destination for filmmakers in the 1950s and 1960s, owing to low production costs. Producers benefited from the Film Production Fund (known as the Eady Levy), which allowed additional revenue from ticket sales on profitable features. This explains why the James Bond franchise was financed with American money but involved British working teams.[25]

The Soviet Union also tried to compete with American cinema for a long time, even on American soil, using the help of Artkino, a distribution firm created originally by dedicated fans of Soviet films.[26] After Stalin's quasi-autarky years of cinematic contact, the 1950s witnessed an opening of the Soviet cinema industry to the West; even if French filmmakers were active in creating opportunities for collaboration right after Stalin's death, the true revolution came after the signature of the Lacy–Zarubin agreement on cultural exchanges of January 27, 1958. Films, technology and filmmakers began to flow between East and West on an unprecedented scale. Soveksportfilm, the organization in charge of promoting and exporting Russian films abroad, did its best to make Soviet productions visible at various international film festivals around the globe, particularly in the Third World. Cinema and television were playing a crucial part in the project of a "socialist cultural model" which emerged in the 1930s, but had to "prove itself both sovereign and superior" on a global arena after the war.[27] The Soviet golden age of export lasted a decade – from the end of the 1950s to the end of the 1960s, during the so-called "thaw," from *The Cranes Are Flying* (Palme d'Or at the Cannes Film festival in 1958), to *War and Peace*, which won an Academy Award in 1969 (it was originally intended as a reply to the American–Italian version of 1956). This was also the period when Goskino, the Soviet Ministry of Cinema, acquired a taste for money under the leadership of Alexei Romanov and, particularly, his successor, Filipp Ermash, two cunning apparatchiks with a "producer's mind."[28] Disregarding the bitter criticisms of several hardliners, the two men secured a quiet agreement from the Party to allow certain directors with "dissident" inclinations, such as Andrei Tarkovsky, who was very successful abroad, to serve as diplomats of Soviet cinema culture, as well as to opt for co-productions as a convenient financing opportunity.

This "golden age" did not last long. There was a great deal of improvisation and amateurism in Soviet commercial policy: when Sergei Solovyov's TV feature *The Postmaster* (1972) was whisked away by its West German co-producer to the Venice festival, where the film won the Golden Lion Award, the Party quickly took the credit, proudly calling the award a victory for Soviet cinematography.[29] Globally, Soveksportfilm lacked efficiency in its dealings, as it was "half owned by the KGB, one third by Vneshtorg [and only] the rest by Goskino,"[30] and hence ridden with institutional conflicts and contradictions over its real objectives. Also, tensions in the international arena often impacted Soviet efforts: in 1981, Solovyov and Tarkovsky, seen as "the last hope" by Ermash, were refused American visas to attend the Los Angeles Film Festival. In a mirror-like accusation often reserved by Soveksportfilm for American films, the State Department condemned Tarkovsky's *Mirror* (1975) and Solovyov's *The Savior* (1980) as "militaristic."[31] Partnerships for co-produced features were often commercial failures, as with the American–Soviet film *The Blue Bird*

(1976), a good symbol of the failure of détente.³² Eventually, Hollywood took over – not only in numbers, but also in hearts and minds.

Impacts

In order to study Cold War cinema, one needs also to focus on its social repercussions. The most publicized and controversial episode in this history took place in Hollywood in the 1940s. Long before Joseph McCarthy became a household name, "whistle blowers" across the country had warned against the threat that Communist infiltration posed for national security and for democracy. Public pressure led to the creation in 1938 of the House Committee on Un-American Activities (HUAC). Ten years later, HUAC launched its investigation of Communist activities in Hollywood, seen as a fifth column. Among those who testified as a "friendly witness" was the Russian-born writer and philosopher Ayn Rand. Unlike some of her colleagues who visited and supported the Soviet Union before the Second World War, Rand had intended to unmask the realities of the Bolshevik regime, although she was questioned only on one movie, *Song of Russia* (1944), an American propaganda feature made by the conservative Louis B. Mayer of Metro Goldwyn Mayer, starring the conservative Robert Taylor but written predominantly by members of the U.S. Communist Party. Many of the witnesses were "unfriendly" and their options were limited to three: "naming names", i.e. giving the names of Communists they knew in the industry; to invoke the First Amendment (guarantee of free speech and association) and to risk being sentenced for contempt by Congress; to invoke the Fifth Amendment (privilege against self-incrimination) and lose their job and be blacklisted.³³ The successful playwright and screenwriter Lilian Hellman, a "Rand *doppelgänger* on the Red side," nominated for her screenplay for *The North Star* in 1944, chose the latter. The "Hollywood Ten," a group of Communist members, chose the second option and went to jail. Among them, only the director Edward Dmytryk fully repudiated his Communist past.³⁴

The controversy of HUAC's often conflictual hearings still lingers, even after the revelations made by the FBI and the Russian archives on the realities of the Communist infiltration in Hollywood. Ironically, it was the French Communist Party that first used the word "redlisted" (i.e. blacklisted) in 1945, when its "Committee for the Liberation of the French Cinema" suspended dozens of artists for their supposedly collaborationist attitudes during the Nazi occupation.³⁵ And while the Hollywood Ten and other Communist sympathizers continued working as ghost writers or, in the worst case, left the United States (the case of Charlie Chaplin is well studied³⁶), in the Soviet Union, the "rootless cosmopolites" accused of "adulating the West" were much more numerous and their fate was far more dramatic. After 1946, the Soviet cinema was "purged" of hundreds of "politically suspect" employees, who were often "blacklisted" for many years to come, unable to leave the country. In February 1947, famous actress Zoya Fedorova was sentenced to twenty-five years in a hard labor camp in a fabricated case of espionage. In February 1949, director Leonid Trauberg, who stressed the importance of Western influence on Soviet cinema during his cinema courses, was accused of being a "rootless cosmopolitan" and became an outcast in his own country until the thaw.³⁷ Stalin's death in 1953 brought some respite in the purging of filmmakers, although blacklisting practices, less violent, continued until 1986, when the Fifth Congress of Cinematographers officially adopted democratization and glasnost.

Yet another impact of the cinematic Cold War was Americanization and hybridization. Hollywood had exerted a profound influence on Soviet filmmakers from the early days of Bolshevik rule – much more than the other way round. At least until the mid-1930s, Soviet screens were largely dominated by Western productions, while new Soviet films were practically invisible.[38] Russian audiences' admiration of American films gave rise to the term *amerikanshchina*, coined by the famous director and film theorist Lev Kuleshov.[39] One of Eisenstein's most able pupils, Grigori Aleksandrov, closely studied American musicals during the 1930s and used them in his own films.[40]

Despite attacks on "the cult of the West" during the Stalin years, the economic imperatives of the post-war reconstruction forced the Party to release the so-called "trophy films." Acquired by the Red Army on its march across Germany, these American, Italian, Austrian and German films of various genres were often renamed to make them sound more "progressive." For instance, *The Roaring Twenties* (1939) came out under the evocative title *The Fate of a Soldier in the US*.[41] After the ending of the "trophy films" policy, Goskino and Soveksportfilm continued to import foreign motion pictures, increasing their number to attract larger audiences and counteract the impending crisis in the Soviet cinema industry. Among all foreign productions, *The Magnificent Seven* (1960) enjoyed the greatest acclaim. It not only became the all-time favorite among Soviet audiences, but also greatly influenced Soviet filmmakers who began producing the so-called "Easterns," action taking place in the USSR (*The Elusive Avengers*, 1966) and even "Red Westerns," which deconstructed the "Wild West" myth, such as *The Man from the Boulevard of Capuchines* (1987). Likewise, television productions relied heavily on the adaptation of American "progressive" literature (*Rich Man, Poor Man*, based on Irwin Shaw's novel, 1983), in fact reflecting the spectators' tastes more than the ideologues'.[42] Commercially speaking, foreign films – American, Italian, French, but also Mexican[43] – were always among the hits at the Soviet box office, contrasting with the poor results of the Soviet films abroad. Even the striking popularity of Indian cinema[44] was largely due to its role as a "substitute" for American features: *Disco Dancer* (1982), which was released in 1984, attracted 60.9 million viewers; it was more of a rehash of *Saturday Night Fever* (1977), a film that millions of Russians could only fantasize about after reading their favorite cinema journal, *Sovetski ekran* (*The Soviet Screen*), an institution in itself.

Conclusion

The study of the cinematic Cold War appears complex. As ideological supports, films were thermometers of the Cold War, measuring the degree of tension between the states. As art objects, they epitomized one society's collective psyche, fears and expectations, fantasies and nightmares: films were products of an era, but they influenced the way people thought, especially when it came to stereotypes. As products of massive industries, films were Cold War weapons in themselves, reflecting one model's achievements or weaknesses. The cinematic battle was certainly as important as the military confrontation. It had international and domestic repercussions that cannot be overestimated. Domestically, the cinematic Cold War could induce a real trauma, shaking democracies and reinforcing the climate of fear among societies. But, as with the Cold War itself, the cinematic Cold War was not all about confrontation: it was also about money and cultural transfers, human, technological and financial exchanges – which certainly helped to "part the Iron Curtain."[45]

Today, the cinematic Cold War remains a fascinating field for research. The role of Western, particularly American, films in the final demise of the Communist system is yet to be assessed. After all, from the beginning of the Cold War, Soviet viewers were aware that American cinema was a perfect cultural weapon – and it was considered such by Motion Picture Association of America directors, from Hays to Valenti.[46] Another area of research deals with contemporary Russian cinema as a result of globalization developed during the Cold War. Last, one obvious field of investigation is concerned with the memory of the Cold War in contemporary cinema. Presences of the Cold War in recent film are numerous, particularly in the U.S. after 9/11. What makes their study particularly appealing is the capacity Cold War history has to reflect present-day anxieties: the story of the FBI agent-turned-Soviet spy Robert Hanssen in *Breach* (2007) can illustrate fears of Islamist subversion in post-9/11 America; the Cuban missile crisis in *X-Men: First Class* (2011) echoes fears of nuclear war in the context of the Iranian re-armament program. And so, the history of the Cold War continues to be written on the screen.

Notes

1 Walter L. Hixson, *Parting the Curtain: Propaganda, Culture and the Cold War, 1945–1961* (New York: Palgrave Macmillan), 1997, 233.
2 Andrei Kozovoi, *Par-delà le Mur. La culture de Guerre froide soviétique entre deux détentes.* [*Beyond the Wall. The Soviet Cold War culture between two détentes.*] Paris: Complexe, 2009, 31.
3 Norman E. Saul, *Concord and Conflict: The United States and Russia, 1867–1914* (Lawrence, KS: University Press of Kansas, 1996), 589.
4 Kozovoi, *Par-delà le Mur*, 39–42.
5 Tony Shaw and Denise J. Youngblood, *Cinematic Cold War: The American and Soviet Struggle for Hearts and Minds* (Lawrence, KS: University Press of Kansas, 2010), 17; Harlow Robinson, *Russians in Hollywood, Hollywood's Russians: Biography of an Image.* (Lebanon, NH: Northeastern University Press, 2007).
6 Tony Shaw, *Hollywood's Cold War* (Edinburgh: Edinburgh University Press), 2007, 11.
7 Shaw and Youngblood, *Cinematic Cold War*, 21, 41.
8 Jonathan Petley, quoted in James Chapman, *Licence to Thrill: A Cultural History of the James Bond Films*, new revised edition (London and New York: I.B. Tauris), 2007, 206.
9 Jennifer Frost, *Hedda Hopper's Hollywood: Celebrity Gossip and American Conservatism* (New York and London: New York University Press), 2011, 108.
10 Shaw, *Hollywood's Cold War*, 144.
11 McCarthyism is a term to be used with extreme care, for Senator Joseph McCarthy had nothing to do with the Hollywood investigations. The same goes for "zhdanovshchina," as Andrei Zhdanov (Stalin's ideologue-in-chief) was not the inspirer of the climate of post-war cultural terror, only the executioner of Stalin's design.
12 Andrei Kozovoi, "'This Film Is Harmful.' Resizing America for the Soviet Screen," in Sari Autio-Sarasmo and Brendan Humphreys, eds., *Winter Kept Us Warm: Cold War Interactions Reconsidered* (Helsinki: Aleksanteri Cold War series, 1/2010), 140–141.
13 Chapman, *Licence to Thrill*, 70–71.
14 Melvin E. Matthews, *Duck and Cover: Civil Defense Images in Film and Television from the Cold War to 9/11* (Jefferson, NC: MacFarland, 2011), 34.
15 Hayden White, "Historiography and Historiophoty," *American Historical Review*, 93:5, December 1988, 1193–1199.
16 Alan Nadel, "God's Law and the Wide Screen: *The Ten Commandments* as Cold War 'Epic'." *PMLA* 108:3, 1993, 415–430.
17 John Sbardellati, *J. Edgar Hoover Goes to the Movies: The FBI and the Origins of the Hollywood Cold War* (Ithaca, NY and London: Cornell University Press, 2012); David L. Robb, *Operation Hollywood: How the Pentagon Shapes and Censors the Movies* (New York: Prometheus Books, 2004).
18 David M. Glanz, *The Military Strategy of the Soviet Union: A History* (London: Frank Cass, 1992 and 2004), 203.
19 Harlow Robinson, *Russians in Hollywood*, 104–105.
20 Kozovoi, "'This Film Is Harmful'," 140–141.
21 Kozovoi, *Par-delà le Mur*, 94, 109
22 Melvyn Stokes and Richard Maltby, eds., *Hollywood Abroad. Audiences and Cultural Exchange* (London: BFI Publishing, 2004), 1.
23 Kenneth Osgood, *Total Cold War: Eisenhower's Secret Propaganda Battle at Home and Abroad* (Lawrence, KS: University Press of Kansas, 2006, 364.

24 Shaw, *Hollywood's Cold War*, 105.
25 Chapman, *Licence to Thrill*, 39–40.
26 James H. Krukones, "Peacefully Coexisting on a Wide Screen: Kinopanorama vs. Cinerama, 1952–1966." *Studies in Russian and Soviet Cinema* 4:3, 2010, 283–306.
27 Kristin Roth-Ey, *Moscow Prime Time: How the Soviet Union Built the Media Empire that Lost the Cultural Cold War* (Ithaca, NY: Cornell University Press, 2011), 4–5.
28 Sergei Solovyov, *Nichego chto ia kuru? Zapiski konformista. Kniga vtoraya*. Saint-Petersburg: Amfora/Seans, 2008, 56.
29 Sergei Solovyov, *To da së ... Zapiski konformista. Kniga pervaya*. Saint-Petersburg: Amfora/Seans, 2008, 297–299.
30 Solovyov, *Nichego chto ia kuru?* 105.
31 Solovyov *To da së ...*, 246–247.
32 Tony Shaw, "Nightmare on Nevsky Prospect. The Blue Bird and the Curious Episode of Soviet–American Film Collaboration during the Cold War." *Journal of Cold War Studies* 14:1, 2012, 3–33.
33 Victor S. Navasky, *Naming Names* (New York: Hill & Wang, 2003 (original edition 1980)), x.
34 Robert Mayhew, *Ayn Rand and Song of Russia: Communism and Anti-Communism in 1940s Hollywood* (Lanham, MD: The Scarecrow Press, 2005), ix, xii, 103.
35 Jean-Paul Török, *Pour en finir avec le MacCarthysme. Lumières sur la Liste Noire à Hollywood* [*To end with MacCarthyism. Lights on the Black List in Hollywood*] (Paris: L'Harmattan, 2000), 17.
36 Sbardellati, *J. Edgar Hoover Goes to the Movies*.
37 A.S. Deryabin, ed., *Letopis' rossiiskogo kino, 1946–1965* (Moscow: Kanon-Plus, 2010), 111–113, 128–129.
38 Jamie Miller, *Soviet Cinema: Politics and Persuasion under Stalin* (London and New York: I.B. Tauris, 2010), 25–26.
39 Shaw and Youngblood, *Cinematic Cold War*, 37.
40 Sergei Kapterev, "Illusionary Spoils. Soviet Attitudes toward American Cinema during the Early Cold War." *Kritika* 10:4, 2009, 779–807, p. 789.
41 A.S. Deryabin, ed., *Letopis' rossiiskogo kino, 1946–1965*. Moscow: Kanon-Plus, 2010, 74–75.
42 Andrei Kozovoi, "Les États-Unis réinventés sur les écrans soviétiques, 1975–1985." [The United States reinvented on Soviet screens, 1975–1985.] *Communisme* 90, 2007, 119–139.
43 The most popular film of all time in the Soviet Union is the Mexican melodrama with a gypsy theme, *Yesenia* (1971), released in 1975 to 91 million viewers. Roth-Ey, *Moscow Prime Time*, 43–44.
44 Sudha Rajagopalan, *Leave Disco Dancer Alone: Indian Cinema and Soviet Movie-going after Stalin* (New Delhi: Yoda Press, 2008).
45 Hixson, *Parting the Curtain*.
46 For Jack Valenti, see his memoir, *This Time, This Place: My Life in War, the White House, and Hollywood* (New York: Harmony Books, 2007).

25
SOVIET STUDIES AND CULTURAL CONSUMPTION

Sergei I. Zhuk

During the Cold War, especially before the 1980s, Soviet society was presented as a one-dimensional, monolithic and predictable entity on both sides of ideological divide – in the Soviet studies in the West and in histories of the USSR/Communist Party in the Soviet Union as well. Despite the prevailing different theoretical models of interpretation – a totalitarian/modernization model in the West and orthodox Marxism-Leninism in the USSR – Soviet studies in both capitalist West and socialist East explained the major developments in a similar way, emphasizing mostly political, economic and ideological moments in a never-changing stability of the Soviet civilization. During the 1970s and the 1980s, the sudden rise of the "revisionist" school in Western historiography, especially with the publication of the brilliant studies by Sheila Fitzpatrick, Stephen Cohen, Leopold Haimson and other Western scholars, revealed new data from the Soviet/Russian archives and introduced the fresh ideas and theories of a new social and new cultural history. A new generation of Western scholars, including Richard Stites, Vera Dunham, Laura Engelstein, Sheila Fitzpatrick, Jeffrey Brooks and Denise Youngblood replaced the traditional, one-dimensional interpretation of Soviet society with one that took into account the wealth and variety of different cultural practices which these scholars had "discovered" in the everyday life of Soviet people. This has changed the development of Soviet studies, and eventually contributed to the tremendous popularity of cultural studies among both Western and post-Soviet historians.[1]

The rise of the Western "revisionist" school coincided with and was stimulated by the events of *perestroika* and the resulting collapse of the Soviet Union in 1991. During this period new archival collections were opened in the Soviet Union and post-Soviet states. Many former Soviet scholars could travel abroad and use funding and resources (both financial and theoretical) from Western research centers. A unique scholarly dialogue and collaboration between Western and former Soviet scholars was established during this time. Many talented Soviet intellectuals with different professional backgrounds, such as Serhii Plokhy (trained as a historian of early modern Ukraine), Yuri Slezkine (an expert in the Portuguese language), Irina Paperno (trained as an expert in Russian literature and associated with the Tartu school), Dmitry Shlapentokh (a historian of France and Russia), Aleksei Yurchak (a radio engineer and producer of famous Leningrad rock bands), Andrei Znamenskii (a historian of American Indians), Vladislav Zubok (trained as an expert in US politics) and myself (a historian of colonial British America), left their post-Soviet countries and joined Western academia, and now teach Soviet/Russian/

Ukrainian studies in American universities. All this experience has contributed to expansion and change in the field of Soviet studies, which has now become a real international phenomenon.[2] This has particularly affected studies of Soviet society during the Cold War. The most interesting and innovative of these international Soviet studies are devoted to the history of cultural consumption, media and the Soviet youth.

Cultural Consumption

During the 1980s and 1990s various British studies of cultural consumption and identity became influential in shaping international Soviet studies. According to one of the pioneers of cultural studies, John Storey, "it is important to include cultural consumption in a discussion of identities because human identities are formed out of people's everyday actions and interaction in different forms of consumption."[3] New cultural studies concentrate on the effects of globalization, the consumption of Western cultural products such as pop music and films on local identities on the margins of the Western world and in non-Western countries.[4] Cultural products from the West became an important factor in the formation of local identity, especially during the Cold War. As sociologists of music have noted, "in appropriating forms of popular music, individuals are simultaneously constructing ways of being in the context of their local everyday environments."[5] The consumption of foreign cultural products was (and still is) a process of selective borrowing and appropriation, translation and incorporation into the indigenous cultural context.[6] These ideas influenced the new school of Russian/Soviet cultural studies, whose representatives such as Hilary Pilkington and Catriona Kelly began to study the effects of globalization, cultural consumption and local youth cultures in Soviet and post-Soviet Russia.[7] The most important idea for Soviet cultural studies was the role of the local cultural context in which the consumption of foreign cultural products is "embedded" and took very different forms from their original meaning. Another concept which derived from cultural studies was the idea of "cultural fixation." According to sociologist Thomas Cushman, the limited sources of foreign cultural practices always produce "an intense idealization" of the early available forms of such practices in societies with strong ideological control and limitations. In the closed Soviet society during the Cold War, literature, music and film of "an important, but limited range," Cushman explained, "was seized upon early on and became the central objects" upon which subsequent cultural practice was based.[8] Western cultural products became a point of cultural fixation for Soviet youth, who exaggerated the cultural significance of these products.

In the early 1990s, Richard Stites was the first historian to write a complete, and still the most popular, history of popular culture and entertainment in Russia/the Soviet Union since 1900. He covered the major media of popular culture and various cultural forms, including music, film, television, variety shows and popular literature. He had already included a description of various forms of cultural practices, known later as "cultural consumption," in his pioneering efforts to analyze the popular culture and everyday life of Soviet society during the Cold War.[9] Then a former Soviet émigré from Leningrad, Svetlana Boym, tried to present her own impressionistic vision of cultural consumption in her Soviet home-town before the collapse of communism.[10] Missing from all these pioneering efforts was a general theoretical framework for the cultural history of Soviet society during the Cold War. But by the end of the 1990s, the rise of cultural studies in Great Britain and cultural anthropology in the United States contributed to the creation of a theoretical foundation for new Soviet cultural studies.

The first serious attempt to analyze cultural consumption in Soviet society during the Cold War after Stalin was a study by another émigré from Leningrad, anthropologist Alexei Yurchak, who tried to explore the ideological aspects of everyday life, theories and practices of late socialism, and discursive practices and identity formation in post-Stalin Soviet society. Yurchak investigated "internal shifts that were emerging within the Soviet system during late socialism at the level of discourse, ideology, and knowledge but that became apparent for what they were only much later, when the system collapsed."[11] According to Yurchak, after Khrushchev's de-Stalinization, communist ideology in Soviet society underwent a so-called "performative shift," when Stalin's authoritative discourse lost its importance and became mere ritual for many Soviet people, who had tried to exist *vnye* – outside – this communist ideological discourse since the 1950s. Yurchak primarily used material from his home-town, Leningrad, to show how different forms of cultural production and consumption of late socialism, especially rock music and Western fashion influenced Soviet youth, including Komsomol activists and officials. According to Yurchak, "rock-n-roll culture" became a part of "nonofficial discourses and practices in late socialism." In contrast to authors such as Thomas Cushman, who insisted on the countercultural character of rock music in the Soviet Union, Yurchak argued that non-official practices (such as listening to and playing rock-n-roll) "involved not so much countering, resisting, or opposing state power as simply *avoiding* it and carving out symbolically meaningful spaces and identities away from it. This avoidance included passive conformity to state power, pretense of supporting it, obliviousness to its ideological messages, and simultaneous involvement in completely incongruent practices and meanings behind its back."[12]

In fact, the entire theoretical framework of Yurchak's study was directly influenced by French thinkers like Michel Foucault and Michel de Certeau. According to Certeau, in modern European society, "the imposed knowledge and symbolisms become objects manipulated by practitioners who have not produced them." In de Certeau's interpretation, such practitioners usually subverted practices, and representations that were imposed on them from within – not by rejecting them or transforming them (though that occurred as well), but in many different ways. Practitioners of knowledge production "metaphorized the dominant order: they made it function in another register. They remained other within the system which they assimilated and which assimilated them externally. They diverted it without leaving it."[13] These ideas, combined with Mikhail Bakhtin's concept of "authoritative discourse," became the foundation of Yurchak's theoretical framework.[14]

The Imaginary West and the Soviet Post-War Generation

As Alexei Yurchak argued, the obsession with Western cultural products became the most important feature of cultural consumption in the closed socialist society of the post-Stalin era during the Cold War. He focused especially on the cultural and discursive phenomenon known among social scientists as the "imaginary West."[15] According to Yurchak, the imaginary West is "a local cultural construct and imaginary that was based on the forms of knowledge and aesthetics associated with the 'West,' but does not necessarily refer to any 'real' West, and that also contributed to 'deterritorializing' the world of everyday socialism from within."[16] Yurchak rejects a confrontational/countercultural character of the imaginary West in Soviet cultural consumption. He offers a consensual/conformist interpretation of this metaphor. Using the ideas of the Russian cultural critic Tatyana Cherednichenko, Yurchak tries to show how western music (as a part of the imaginary West) contributed to "the production of a whole generational identity" for the last Soviet generation.[17]

At the same time, he ignores the problems of regional, national and religious identities which were shaped by the consumption of Western cultural products in various parts of the Soviet Union. Yurchak discarded connections between Soviet dissidents and the idea of the

West, which was very important for the practice of political dissent in the USSR. Yurchak's interpretation exaggerates the role of discursive practices. In his interpretation, the visual elements, especially Western film, lost their role of influencing both ideological discourse and local identity of the Soviet consumers.[18] Therefore, Yurchak interprets Soviet society during late socialism as a society void of any serious social problems or conflicts. Prevalent problems of this period, like the involvement of Soviet officials in black market activities, Russification, the street gang culture, popular religiosity, nationalism and anti-Semitism are ignored in Yurchak's study. Yurchak also underestimated the importance of the KGB and police interference in the cultural consumption of late socialism, which especially affected the provincial cities, where the majority of the Soviet youth lived.[19]

Yurchak's ideas influenced new studies about post-war Soviet history, especially the history of Soviet youth. One of the best books about Soviet post-war youth, called *Stalin's Last Generation*, demonstrated an obvious following of Yurchak's ideas and approaches. But in contrast to Yurchak, its author, Juliane Fürst, not only used material from the Soviet capital cities, like Leningrad and Moscow, but introduced archival documents from various Russian and Ukrainian regional archives and created a lively picture of cultural consumption among Soviet young people during the late 1940s and early 1950s. She greatly enriched the historiographical terrain of late Stalinism, based on the classic studies of Soviet/Russian historian Elena Zubkova, and added new concepts of Western cultural studies, including Yurchak's ideas. Again in contrast to Yurchak, Fürst convincingly demonstrated that the roots of the liberalization and mass Westernization of post-war Soviet society should be located in late Stalinism, rather than in Khrushchev's Thaw.[20] Trying to avoid an excessive conceptualization of Yurchak the anthropologist, the historian Vladislav Zubok wrote an excellent study of post-war Soviet intellectuals, whom he called "Zhivago's Children," in reference to the eponymous hero of Boris Pasternak's novel. Again, in contrast to Yurchak, Zubok showed how important was the legacy of World War II for Soviet intelligentsia.[21] An overwhelming majority of recent studies, including research by Zubok, Fürst, Stephen V. Bittner, Stephen Lovell, Benjamin Tromly and Gleb Tsipursky, has emphasized the role of the post-war period, rejected the simplistic portrayal of the Khrushchev era as a revolutionary predecessor of *perestroika*, and offered a more nuanced portrayal of late socialism than the "speech act" analysis presented by Yurchak.[22]

The Cold War and the Brezhnev Era

Leonid Brezhnev replaced Khrushchev as the General Secretary of the Central Committee of the Communist Party of the Soviet Union (CPSU) in October 1964. His rule (1964–82) began a new chapter in "socialist consumption" in the Soviet Union.[23] All Soviet leaders, beginning with Lenin and Stalin, understood that communist society needed to prove its superiority over capitalism. However, before Brezhnev, no one had publicly announced and included the idea of "socialist consumption" in the official social policy of the Communist Party and Soviet state. Brezhnev pointed out that the production of consumer goods had to be the main goal of the entire socialist economy. In contrast, both Stalin and Khrushchev had emphasized investment in heavy industry as the priority for both the Soviet state and people. During the 24th CPSU Congress in March–April 1971, Brezhnev changed the emphasis in the directives of the USSR's Ninth Five-Year Plan. Instead of making heavy industry a top priority, the Soviet leadership turned their attention to goods for mass consumption. Brezhnev introduced "Soviet consumerism" into the official Soviet discourse as a legitimate precondition of what communist ideologists had called "developed socialism" since 1967. The Soviet leadership planned to increase investment in the agricultural, food and textile industries to satisfy the growing demands of Soviet consumers during "the developed socialism," which was, according to Brezhnev's new theory, the "last stage before the final phase of communist social and economic formation." In February 1976, during the 25th CPSU Congress, Soviet leaders were still prioritizing growth in the consumer sector.[24] In reality, the official emphasis on providing socialist consumers with necessary goods worked poorly, and a black market with a system of personal favors known as *blat* compensated for a lack of products and services.[25]

During the 1960s and 1970s, Soviet ideologists paid more attention to the organization of leisure time and cultural consumption among the Soviet population. Soviet consumers had to be provided not only with consumer goods, but also with new services and new, healthy goals for consumption. According to the ideological requirements of developed socialism, socialist consumption differed from "the capitalist consumerism" and excluded notions of individual profitability and accumulation of wealth. Soviet ideologists tried to combine traditional Stalinist goals of "rational consumption" and the "rational use of leisure" with the new requirements of the "developed socialism" theory.[26] As Hilary Pilkington argues, this theory "attempted to show the difference between cultural relations in socialist and capitalist versions of modernity. Whilst in both societies emphasis was placed on high standards of living and development of consumer industries, Soviet society, it was claimed, was characterized by rational consumption and not cheap consumerism."[27]

In spite of the fact that Western Sovietologists have published extensively about Soviet politics, economy, society and culture during the Cold War, the Brezhnev era is still mostly ignored by historians. The current historiography includes Svetlana Boym's and Nina Tumarkin's general surveys of "mythologies" of everyday life in Soviet Russia from Lenin to Gorbachev, where "the Brezhnev period" is mentioned as a period of "stagnation and reaction."[28] Frederick Starr, Timothy Ryback and Richard Stites also wrote chapters on the "era of stagnation" in their historical analyses of entertainment and music in Russia and Eastern Europe.[29] Some scholars such as Ellen Propper Mickiewicz, Anne White, Dmitry and Vladimir Shlapentokh, and Denise J. Youngblood devoted a few chapters in their books to problems of film consumption during the Brezhnev era.[30] Historians of book consumption analyzed paradoxes of "the reading revolution" in the post-Stalin era.[31] After the collapse of the Soviet Union, more scholars devoted their studies to "the national question in the USSR" during late socialism.[32] A few historians, especially Anne Gorsuch and Andrei Kozovoi, have explored the problems of tourism in the Brezhnev era.[33] Many Western scholars noted Soviet intellectuals' fascination and idealization of the imaginary West, especially during late socialism.[34] However, the overwhelming majority of social historians have ignored the history of the Brezhnev era, preferring to study the "Stalinist terror" or "Khrushchev thaw," rather than the supposedly boring "period of stagnation."

The scholarly neglect of this period is indicative of a stereotypical view of Brezhnev's rule as an unimportant time for Soviet history.[35] British scholars, such as Edwin Bacon, have recently noted that one of the primary reasons why the Brezhnev era attracted so little "posthumous" analysis was because of "the reforming discourse of the political project known as perestroika and overseen by the last Soviet leader Mikhail Gorbachev," which declared the Brezhnev years to be "an era of stagnation." Unfortunately, this discourse became the "overwhelmingly dominant conceptualization of the almost two decades during which Brezhnev oversaw the Soviet state." They considered this to be an inaccurate approach because Brezhnev "brought an unprecedented stability to the Soviet system, oversaw a continuing rise in living standards for his people, consolidated the USSR's position as a global superpower, and played a part in the prevention of the global nuclear conflict which many observers considered likely during those years. He stands as the most popular leader of the USSR/Russia in the twentieth century."[36]

Only recently have a few scholars made the first attempts to explore in depth the social and cultural history of everyday life in the Brezhnev era. Weaving together diaries, interviews, oral histories and KGB and Party archival documents, my study provided a vivid account of how Soviet cultural repression and unrest during the Brezhnev period laid the groundwork for a resurgent Ukrainian nationalism in the 1980s. The book explored the connections between cultural consumption, ideology and identity formation in one industrial city, Dniepropetrovsk, which the KGB closed to visits by foreigners in 1959 because it became the location for one of the biggest missile factories in the Soviet Union. Given its closed, sheltered existence, Dniepropetrovsk became a unique Soviet social and cultural laboratory in which various patterns of late socialism collided with the new, Western cultural influences. Using archival documents, periodicals, personal diaries and interviews as historical sources, the book focuses on how different moments of cultural consumption (reading books, listening and dancing to music, watching movies) among the youth of the Soviet "closed city" contributed to various forms of cultural identification which eventually became elements of post-Soviet regional identity.[37]

In another recent path-breaking study about consumption during the Brezhnev era, Natalya Chernyshova demonstrates how urban Soviet consumers became more technologically savvy and responsive to new developments; how they became more selective and autonomous in their decision making, choosing not only the level of sophistication of their machines but also their brands, just as one would expect a Western consumer to do. She also uses the example of household gadgets to demonstrate the rise of late Soviet consumerism. Ultimately, her study demonstrates how, despite the ideological peculiarities of Soviet economic policies and the generally closed nature of Soviet society, late Soviet consumer culture developed in ways that had many parallels with Western consumer societies, raising interesting questions about the nature of consumerism as a global or local phenomenon.[38]

Unfortunately, an overwhelming majority of the recent studies about post-Stalin socialism in the Soviet Union are still based on material from two Westernized "open" capital cities of the USSR (Moscow and Leningrad), which were exposed to direct Western influences through foreign tourists and journalists.[39] As a result, the history of cultural consumption, media and youth in "closed" Soviet provincial cities and villages is missing from the analysis. It is difficult to generalize about the social and cultural history of the Soviet Union when the focus is only on Moscow and Leningrad.[40] Only recently, new research by Kate Brown about the closed cities, an oral history of Saratov by Donald Raleigh, Christopher Ward's social history of the Baikal–Amur railroad project, Karl D. Qualls' analysis of urban culture in Sevastopol, Paul Stronski's book about Tashkent and the brilliant study of Soviet L'viv by William Risch have started to shift away from the traditional emphasis of Western historians on Moscow and Leningrad.[41] To some extent all of these authors tried to cover a history of cultural practices, involvement of the local population in cultural consumption and the role of media.

Media and Cultural Politics of Détente

A comprehensive analysis of Soviet media after Stalin, especially in the Brezhnev era, was offered by a representative of the new young generation of Western scholars, who had already been influenced by post-Soviet cultural studies. Kristin Roth-Ey wrote her fascinating book about the most popular forms of media in the Soviet Union – movies, radio and television. Although many good studies had already been written in both Russian and English about each of these media, Roth-Ey's book is an interesting research experiment, offering a story of all of them together, concentrating mainly on two decades, the 1950s and 1960s (although some of her information partly covers the beginning of the 1970s). Rejecting traditional approaches to the history of Soviet culture that are prevalent in Western historiography, her book looks beyond "the fabled intelligentsia gatherings around the kitchen table to consider cultural terrains of a different type: bureaucracies, technologies, social networks, and everyday life practices."[42] The major theme of the entire book is the increasing bureaucratization and regulation of all of Soviet visual culture, especially films and television, from the post-Stalinist 1950s to the Brezhnev era.

Roth-Ey's major goal is to show how the Soviet Union became a media empire after Stalin. The USSR was fundamentally a "propaganda state": culture in the Soviet context was always in the business of educating, training, motivating, and mobilizing Soviet citizens to build communism. Various media had to be tools in this process, whose major goal was to elevate everyone and fight against "cheap" mass culture, associated with the capitalist West; and the consumption of socialist art was supposed to further this goal of the moral education and political mobilization of the population of the USSR *en masse*.

Roth-Ey notes that the most important contradiction in the Soviet film industry as an ideological category "was its definition of success and its relationship to markets." Soviet cinema identified itself as anti-commercial art, but also as drawing huge audiences and generating revenues for the state. Thus, success in the Soviet film industry "was framed in ways that encouraged people across the spectrum to blur the lines between art and commerce, self-expression and self-interest, and public service and budgetary windfall." In the USSR during the mid-1960s gross movie ticket sales were roughly 1 billion rubles annually, of which the state was said to have collected 440 million in "pure profit."[43]

Eventually, the notion of commercial success in the Soviet film industry led to its internationalization and the purchase of more foreign movies, which brought more profits to this industry. For every ruble in its budget, Soviet officials estimated income from foreign film purchases at five rubles; in the case of commercial Western films, it could reach 250 rubles. The Soviet Ministry of Culture began to purchase large numbers of films from abroad: 63 in 1955, 113 in 1958, with plans for over 150 in 1960. According to Roth-Ey's calculations, based mainly on material of Valery Golovskoy and Sudha Rajagopalan, in the period 1954 to 1991 the USSR imported 206 films from India, 41 from the USA and 38 from France. In 1960 each film from the capitalist world drew an average audience of more than 500,000 in Moscow, while Soviet productions averaged 357,000 and socialist-bloc pictures 133,000.[44]

According to my own research on Soviet film consumption during the Brezhnev era, in 1973 alone, the main Soviet authority for the acquisition and distribution of foreign films, Soveksportfilm, bought more than 150 feature films from seventy countries. During the period of détente, this number grew. More Western films reached Soviet moviegoers by the end of the 1970s than in the previous decade. During the entire Brezhnev era the few Western movies which were released in the Soviet Union played a more significant role in the "Westernization" of Soviet youth than did Western popular music or books. In 1966 almost 60 percent of all movies shown in Ukrainian cities were of foreign origin, 50 percent of them being films from the "capitalist" West. Ten years later, in 1975, almost 90 percent of the films were foreign movies, and almost 80 percent were Western ones. In 1981 more than 95 percent of all movies were of foreign origin, and 90 percent came from Western capitalist countries. More than 90 percent of all Western films came from Western Europe, and fewer than 10 percent from the USA. According to the personal diaries of Ukrainian middle school students, during a normal school week in the 1970s they would each watch two or three movies per week. During the school breaks they watched six to seven films per week, and 90 percent of all these films were from Western European countries.⁴⁵

Both radio and television followed the same trajectory which the Soviet film industry had taken after Stalin. Both failed to offer elevated forms of socialist culture and became, instead, the major media for mass entertainment. Roth-Ey shows how Soviet radio failed in an ideological and cultural contest with Western radio as early as the 1950s and the 1960s. Paradoxically, new technologies (the replacement of wired with wireless radio) and consumer demand for more efficient home-based wireless radio sets exposed Soviet radio audiences to Western radio broadcasting by introducing them to new models for media which were more attractive and more modern than the traditional Soviet ones. In the 1950s, the shift from wired to wireless radio had far-reaching implications: for one thing, it meant that what had been a predominantly collective and public activity was now moving into the realm of private experience and was thus far less simple to quantify, monitor and control – "indeed, it was beginning to look less and less like a traditional Soviet phenomenon altogether," and secondly "was the fact that a large number of these sets could receive shortwave broadcasts, including foreign ones."⁴⁶ Soviet jamming of foreign radio did not help; it jammed even Soviet home broadcasting, so periodically the Soviets removed jamming. But it was too late: more than a half of all residents in Soviet urban centers in 1968 listened to foreign radio on a regular basis using their Soviet wireless radio sets. Soviet radio tried to adjust to the new requirements of ideological confrontation by adopting some Western forms of broadcasting. Soviet radio administration introduced the new elements in its foreign radio service. In 1964, using Western forms of radio broadcasting, Soviet radio introduced a new radio station, Maiak (Beacon), with a round-the-clock five-minute news and twenty-five minute entertainment show. Using Russian memoir literature, Roth-Ey describes in detail the efforts of Soviet radio engineers to organize the new Soviet radio stations, like Maiak, with "a second-rate imitation of foreign broadcasting."

Unfortunately, in her description of the new Soviet radio station, Roth-Ey completely ignores a fascinating and well-known story of radio journalist Viktor Tatarskii, who came to Maiak in 1967 and created the most popular music radio shows in the history of Soviet broadcasting, which influenced the tastes and cultural preferences of millions of Soviet radio listeners. In 1967 he founded a music show called *Vstrechi s pesnei* (Meetings with a Song), which popularized Soviet popular (*estrada*) song. From 1968 to 1975, the Moscow radio station Maiak broadcast a special music show by Tatarskii and the journalist Grigorii Libergal with the title *Zapishite na vashi magnitofony* (Please Make Your Own Tape Recording). Sometimes Tatarskii managed to broadcast his show for one hour each Sunday. Usually, he had only twenty-five minutes for his show. Tatarskii included the latest Western music hits along with his professional commentary. The radio station's administration tried to control him and stop him from playing "loud music." Several times Maiak closed his show. After 1976, Tatarskii moved to other Moscow stations and devoted his new shows to jazz music and Soviet *estrada*. Together with the central radio station Yunost (the Youth), Viktor Tatarskii and other young radio journalists, such as Ekaterina Tarkhanova, Vladimir Pozner and Igor Fesunenko, organized two new radio shows: *Na vsekh shirotakh* (On All Latitudes) and *Muzykal'nyi globus* (Musical Globe). These shows covered various categories of modern popular music, including jazz and rock and roll, and they became the major source of information about Western pop music for millions of Soviet rock music fans.⁴⁷

The most interesting part of Roth-Ey's book is her chapters about Soviet television. Using mainly the memoirs of a Russian author, Fedor Razzakov, as her source, she shows the pioneering efforts of Soviet engineers to organize television broadcasting during the 1950s, when the USSR ranked fourth in the world in the national total number of television sets, after the USA, Canada and Great Britain. By 1970 television reached 70 percent of the Soviet population, with 35 million television sets; by 1985 it reached 93 percent, with 90 million sets. Television sets became the most popular object of Soviet consumption. For Soviet ideologists, television became a symbol of modernity. They presented television as "fundamental to a modern lifestyle and as a symbol of Soviet science's power to deliver that lifestyle and draw together people from across the USSR."[48]

The first stage in the development of Soviet television was live transmission, with many experiments introduced by local enthusiasts of the new medium. Roth-Ey describes the new live TV shows such as *Goluboi ogoniok* (Little Blue Flame), *Kinopanorama* and *Klub veselykh nakhodchivykh* (KVN – Club of the Merry and Quick-Witted), which became the most original and popular shows on Soviet television during the 1960s and 1970s. But at the same time, Roth-Ey notes an increasing centralization and Russification of television broadcasting, which led to a replacement of the original live shows with pre-recorded broadcasts by 1970.[49]

Soviet television professionals saw all culture as a mechanism for moral education and political mobilization; Soviet television viewers "were understood to be culture's patients rather than its patrons." But Soviet television viewers ignored the ideological messages and the shows about elevated cultural events such as opera or ballet. They became the passive consumers of TV entertainment, watching feature films on television more often than any other form of programming. As a result, the most popular Soviet television show through the entire 1970s was the Soviet TV mini-series, like *Seventeen Moments of Spring* about the adventures of Stirlitz (Viacheslav Tikhonov), a Soviet agent posing as a Nazi officer in Hitlerite Germany in the spring of 1945, during the final months of World War II.[50] In her book, Roth-Ey ignored another group of popular TV mini-series – television movies from socialist countries. They included tremendously popular movies from Poland, such as a film about a Polish intelligence officer during World War II, *Stavka bol'she chem zhizn'* (A Stake is More than Life), and also the TV film series for children such as a Polish film about the adventures of a Polish tank crew during WWII, *Chetyre tankista i sobaka*, and a Hungarian historical adventure film, *Captain Tenkesh*. Despite some mistakes and misinterpretations in her portrayal of Soviet television, overall, Roth-Ey is correct to present Soviet television in the 1970s as "a domestic empire in two senses: an all-Union broadcasting empire ruled from Moscow and an every-day empire based in tens of millions of homes."[51] In post-Soviet Russia, television is still the major medium for millions of Russian consumers of visual culture; it is more popular than comics, radio and the movie-theater, which has become very expensive for the ordinary Russian citizen.

Recent Western studies are an important contribution to the growing literature about the role of visual media in the cultural consumption of contemporary Russian history. Although recent studies implicitly present also a history of the Westernization of Russian visual culture, showing "the influence of the West on Soviet-Russian culture" and in "the place of mass-media culture, leisure, and pleasure" in modern Russian life, they miss a crucial moment in this Westernization – the détente of the 1970s, especially the period from 1972 to 1979. The majority of recent studies miss and ignore the role of détente in the Westernization of Soviet media. During this period, the Soviet administration bought official licenses to manufacture popular music records from the West, the first comic books from the West were reprinted in the USSR and officially licensed Western movies were shown. Soviet television broadcast the concerts of Western popular musicians and Western rock music was incorporated into official Soviet television shows, such as *International Panorama* and *Vesiolye rebiata* (Funny Guys). During détente, Soviet ideologists officially sanctioned and controlled the organization of disco clubs with Western dance music all over the Soviet Union.[52]

For Soviet rock music consumers during the Cold War, the first and most popular source of rock and roll was not foreign radio stations such as the Voice of America or the BBC (especially Seva Novgorodtsev shows). Most developed their first taste of, and enthusiasm for, new music on the dance floor in their schools and offices or at private parties, when they had their first exposure to the new rhythms and melodies. Through their friends in school they began to listen seriously to rock music recordings. They began creating their own audiotapes, which they then exchanged with their friends. Some of them went to the black market, while others went to the city music studios to ask about new tape recordings. For many rock music consumers who wanted to avoid the black market, the state label Melodia (Melody) became another, albeit incomplete and belated, source of music information by 1975. This state-owned recording company responded to the growing demands among young music consumers. The first attempt to satisfy their demands was a release of two songs (three years after their original release in England!) – "Girl" by the Beatles and "(I Can't Get No) Satisfaction" by the Rolling Stones – in a Soviet compilation of popular music in 1967–68. But Melodia did not reveal the true names of the famous rock bands. It put only the words: "English people's (*narodnaia*) song: vocal and instrumental ensemble (England)."[53] From 1971 to 1975, without any official permission from the Western record companies, Melodia released six small musical records (*minions*) with the most popular Beatles hits. The Soviet recording company also released at least two *minions* with songs by the Rolling Stones, "As Tears Go By," "Paint It Black," "Ruby Tuesday" and some others. The Moscow rock band *Vesiolye rebiata* covered the Beatles songs "Ob-La-Di, Ob-La-Da" in English and "Drive My Car" in Russian and released their own *minion* on Melodia. In 1975 a new compilation, "Vocal Instrumental Ensembles from England," featured the Beatles song "Birthday," from the White Album of 1968.[54] From 1974 to 1984, Melodia released two *minion*-compilations with John Lennon's songs from the "Imagine" album, and two *minions* with a few songs from the albums "Ram" and "Band on the Run" by Paul McCartney and Wings.[55] By 1976, in many cases without revealing the names of the performers or songwriters, Melodia's compilations included music by the Animals, Bob Dylan, Simon and Garfunkel, Elton John, Creedence Clearwater Revival, the Bee Gees, Deep Purple, Slade, Sweet and T. Rex. Released without any official permission from the Western music record companies, all of these Melodia recordings became the first available source of music for the youngest Soviet rock music fans, mainly middle and high school students, who had just begun their search for information about their favorite music.

As a reaction to the rising interest in jazz and rock music, the USSR Radio Committee created a special music journal to promote new forms of arts and music – *Krugozor* (Wide vision). Melodia was involved in the release of this journal, which included small musical records with popular songs by foreign musicians and sometimes even rock music from Europe and the USA. The Soviet recording company provided the journal with the necessary music information. Other journals, such as *Club and Amateur Art Activities*, followed the example of *Krugozor* and released small records of popular Western musicians in special "music appendices."[56] By 1968 popular youth magazines like *Rovesnik* (Person of the Same Age), *Smena* (Successors) and *Yunost'* (Youth) began publishing material about Western rock music. Many Soviet rock and roll fans turned to these publications for more information about their favorite musicians.[57] According to contemporaries and library statistics, the most popular publication among Soviet consumers of popular music was the Soviet youth journal *Rovesnik*, which was established in 1962 by the All Union Komsomol to cover the major issues of international youth culture and politics.

During détente this periodical published information mainly (almost 80 percent of its material) on Western popular culture (especially rock and disco music). Contemporaries noted that during the 1970s young enthusiasts of rock music would sign the list of readers to get a fresh issue of this popular magazine in the public library's reading room. Some librarians complained that young zealots of rock music would vandalize the issues of this magazine by cutting out the pages with the sheet music and lyrics of their favorite songs, which were published by *Rovesnik*. It happened for the first time in the spring of 1968, when *Rovesnik* reprinted the Animals' song "House of the Rising Sun" as "The old American folk song."[58] In its December 1968 issue, *Rovesnik* reprinted the Beatles song "A Hard Day's Night." During the January school break of 1969, young beat music enthusiasts in the reading rooms of Soviet public libraries cut out the pages of the magazine with the sheet music and lyrics of this song.[59] The same thing happened in 1969 and 1970, when *Rovesnik* reprinted the sheet music and lyrics (sometimes in Russian) of hits such as "Lady Madonna," "Yesterday," "Girl," and "Back in the USSR," and John Lennon's "Give Peace A Chance."[60] Some of these issues of *Rovesnik* just disappeared from the libraries; they were stolen by Beatles fans. Even the central Lenin Library of the Soviet Union in Moscow suffered from the numerous Beatles fans who cut out the pictures of their idols from the issues of *Rovesnik* in the 1970s.[61]

As a result of détente, in 1976, Melodia signed its first official contract with the Dutch recording company OLD ARK to facilitate the release of the album of the Dutch rock band Teach-In.[62] It was the first original Western music record that Melodia had released with an official license. After this, many Western music records reached Soviet consumers through official channels. These records represented different styles of Western music – from Billie Holliday's "Greatest Hits in Jazz" to the ex-Beatles John Lennon's "Imagine" and Paul McCartney and the Wings' rock album "Band on the Run." The latter album appeared on the Melodia label in 1977, four years after its original release in England.[63] Popular journals such as *Krugozor* and *Klub i khudozhestvennaia samodeiatel'nost* released various compilations of Western music on the flex discs which were included as the music appendices to these journals.[64] In general, Melodia was too slow and inefficient to satisfy the growing demand of Soviet cultural consumption in the 1970s and 1980s. In contrast to the slow reaction of the official recording company, the Soviet black market provided young consumers with all the fashionable Western music products without any delay.

The beginning of détente in US–Soviet relations and the relaxation of international tensions also resulted in some changes in youth cultural consumption.[65] Young Western pop music enthusiasts could not only listen to Soviet music records with popular Western music hits, but could also watch their music idols on Soviet television. The Central Soviet TV station always prepared a special music variety show which was shown on New Year's eve. During the late 1960s and early 1970s, this show usually included a long concert with famous Soviet and foreign musicians and actors who were predominantly from socialist countries. This show was called *Novogodnii Ogoniok*. Various Soviet celebrities, politicians, journalists, artists, musicians and singers were invited to *Ogoniok* as guests. Some sat at tables with wine, champagne and snacks, while others played music, danced or sang. Classical music, traditional folk and Soviet popular songs dominated the show. Sometimes popular singers from socialist countries, such as Karel Gott from Czechoslovakia, or even Dean Reed from the US, appeared as guests of the *Ogoniok* TV show. Millions of Soviet fans of Western pop music were pleasantly surprised when, after a traditional, long and boring *Novogodnii Ogoniok* show in the early morning of January 1, 1975, the Central Soviet TV station broadcast an unusually long concert of Western pop music stars. These stars included the most popular names played in Soviet discotheques, such as ABBA, Boney M, Dowley Family, Donny Osmond, Silver Convention, Joe Dassen, Amanda Lear, Smokey and Baccarat. After 1975, Soviet TV aired similar shows at least once a year, usually very late at night. From January 11, 1977, Soviet TV organized a special show called "Melodies and Rhythms of Foreign Estrada," which included the most popular stars of Western rock and disco music. Until *perestroika*, "Melodies and Rhythms" was the only television show which gave a unique opportunity to millions of Soviet fans to see their idols on the Soviet television screen at least once a year. During the 1970s, Soviet television also organized the broadcasting of variety shows, which included covers of the most popular Western hits in Russian by various Soviet vocal and instrumental ensembles. The "TV Benefit Performances" of famous Soviet film stars such as Larisa Golubkina (1975) and Liudmila Gurchenko (1978) and Evgenii Ginzburg's show "Magic Lantern" (1976) offered very good covers of songs from the British rock opera *Jesus Christ Superstar*, and also from the Beatles and Paul McCartney's albums, by various Soviet rock bands (VIA) such as Vesiolye rebiata from Moscow and Poiushchie gitary from Leningrad.[66]

Cultural consumption and various forms of media, especially television, became the most influential moments of everyday life in the Soviet Union during the Cold War. The Soviet traditions of this cultural consumption, visual media and patterns of Westernization still play an important role in post-Soviet states, such as Russia and the Ukraine. Recent books are a serious reminder to post-Soviet experts of how important media, especially television, and cultural consumption are for our understanding of present-day post-Soviet society and culture. Recent research on cultural consumption in the USSR during the Cold War highlights the complete failure of Soviet ideologists to protect Soviet society from "ideological pollution" in the Cold War confrontation between the "capitalist West" and the socialist ideological system. At the same time, it shows how the tastes and activities of the new "Westernized" culture created new values and demands for cultural consumption that gradually transformed and replaced traditional Soviet values and communist ideological practices.

Notes

1 For revisionism in American Soviet studies see David C. Engerman, *Know Your Enemy: The Rise and Fall of America's Soviet Experts* (New York: Oxford University Press, 2009), 9, 286, 294, 305–308. For the new popularity of cultural studies and mutual influences between Western and former Soviet scholars see Laura Engelstein, "Culture, Culture Everywhere: Interpretations of Modern Russia, across the 1991 Divide," *Kritika*, 2(2) (Spring 2001): 363–393. Soviet historians were also influenced by such a charismatic medievalist as Aron Gurevich, who popularized the ideas of the French *Annales* among the Soviet reading audience. See Roger D. Markwick, "Cultural History under Khrushchev and Brezhnev: From Social Psychology to *Mentalités*," *The Russian Review*, 65 (April 2006): 283–301. See also Catriona Kelly, Hilary Pilkington, David Shepherd and Vadim Volkov, "Introduction: Why Cultural Studies," in *Russian Cultural Studies: An Introduction*, edited by Catriona Kelly and David Shepherd (New York: Oxford University Press, 1998), 1–17.
2 See Engelstein, "Culture, Culture Everywhere," 389ff.
3 John Storey, *Cultural Consumption and Everyday Life* (London: Arnold, 1998), 135, 136. As Madan Sarup observes, "Our identities are in part a result of what we consume. Or to put it another way, what we consume and how we consume it says a great deal about who we are, who we want to be, and how others see us. Cultural consumption is perhaps one of the most significant ways we perform our sense of self. This does not mean that we are what we consume, that our cultural consumption practices determine our social being; but it does mean that what we consume provides us with a script with which we can stage and perform in a variety of ways the drama of who we are." Madan Sarup, *Identity, Culture and the Post Modern World* (Edinburgh: Edinburgh University Press, 1996), 105, 125. According to British scholars, "human self is envisaged as neither the product of an external symbolic system, nor as a fixed entity which the individual can immediately and directly grasp; rather the self is a symbolic project that the individual actively constructs out of the symbolic materials which are available to him or her, materials which the individual weaves into a coherent account of who he or she is, a narrative of self-identity." See John B. Thompson, *The Media and Modernity: A Social Theory of the Media* (Stanford, CA: Stanford University Press, 1995), 207, 210; Storey, *Cultural Consumption*

and Everyday Life, 135, 136, 147. Simon Frith emphasized that consumption of books, music and film "constructs human sense of identity through the direct experiences it offers of the body, time and sociability, experiences which enable people to place themselves in imaginative cultural narratives." See Frith, "Music and Identity," in *Questions of Cultural Identity*, edited by S. Hall and P. du Gay (London: Sage, 1996), 122, 124. As John B. Thompson noted, "these are narratives which people will change over time as they draw on new symbolic materials, encounter new experiences and gradually redefine their identity in the course of a life trajectory." See his *The Media and Modernity*, 210.

4 On globalization and the consumption of Western popular music in Eastern Europe, Asia, Latin America and Africa see Peter Manuel, *Popular Music of the Non-Western World: An Introductory Survey* (New York: Oxford University Press, 1988); *Music at the Margins: Popular Music and Global Cultural Diversity*, edited by Deanna Campbell Robinson et al. (London: Sage Publications, 1991); Nabeel Zuberi, *Sounds English: Transnational Popular Music* (Urbana, IL: University of Illinois Press, 2001); *Global Pop, Local Language*, edited by Harris M. Berger and Michael Thomas Carroll (Jackson, MS: University Press of Mississippi, 2003); Mel van Elteren, *Imagining America: Dutch Youth and Its Sense of Place* (Tilburg: Tilburg University Press, 1994). See also for the connection of cultural consumption to ideology during the Cold War, Uta G. Poiger, *Jazz, Rock, and Rebels: Cold War Politics and American Culture in a Divided Germany* (Berkeley, CA: University of California Press, 2000). Compare with Mark Fenemore, *Sex, Thugs and Rock 'n' Roll: Teenage Rebels in Cold-War East Germany* (New York: Berghahn Books, 2007).

5 Andy Bennett, *Popular Music and Youth Culture: Music, Identity and Place* (New York: St. Martin's Press, 2000), 198.

6 The consumption of foreign goods and services "is always embedded in local circumstances." See van Elteren, *Imagining America*, 4, 18.

7 See especially Hilary Pilkington, "'The Future is Ours': Youth Culture in Russia, 1953 to the Present," in *Russian Cultural Studies: An Introduction*, edited by Catriona Kelly and David Shepherd (New York: Oxford University Press, 1998), 368–385.

8 Thomas Cushman, *Notes from Underground: Rock Music Counterculture in Russia* (New York: State University of New York Press, 1995), 43.

9 Richard Stites, *Russian Popular Culture: Entertainment and Society since 1900* (New York: Cambridge University Press, 1992), 98–203.

10 Svetlana Boym, *Common Places: Mythologies of Everyday Life in Russia* (Cambridge, MA: Harvard University Press, 1994).

11 Alexei Yurchak, *Everything Was Forever, Until It Was No More: The Last Soviet Generation* (Princeton, NJ: Princeton University Press, 2005), 32.

12 Ibid., 36–76. This thesis had already been criticized and analyzed by Sheila Fitzpatrick in *London Review of Books*, 28(10) (May 25, 2006): 18–20, and by Kevin Platt and Benjamin Nathans in *Novoe literaturnoe obozrenie*, 101(2010): 167–184 (in Russian), and in Kevin Platt and Benjamin Nathans, "Socialist in Form, Inderreminate in Content: The Ins and Outs of Late Soviet Culture," *Ab Imperio*, 2, (2011): 301–323 (in English).

13 Michel de Certeau, *The Practice of Everyday Life*, translated by Steven Rendall (Berkeley, CA: University of California Press, 1989 [1st printing 1984]), 31.

14 As he explained, "for Bakhtin, authoritative discourse coheres around a strict external idea or dogma ... and occupies a particular position within the discursive regime of a period," while "all other types of discourse are organized around it." Yurchak *Everything Was Forever*, 14. See especially an American edition of Bakhtin's work with insightful comments in Mikhail Bakhtin, *The Dialogical Imagination: Four Essays by Mikhail Bakhtin*, edited by Michael Holquist (Austin, TX: University of Texas Press, 1994), 342–343. Compare with Slava Gerovitch, *From Newspeak to Cyberspeak: A History of Soviet Cybernetics* (Cambridge, MA: MIT Press, 2004); Stephen Lovell, *The Russian Reading Revolution: Print Culture in the Soviet and Post-Soviet Eras* (New York: St. Martin's Press, 2000); Juliane Fürst, *Stalin's Last Generation: Soviet Post-War Youth and the Emergence of Mature Socialism* (New York: Oxford University Press, 2010).

15 See how various scholars used this metaphor before Yurchak: Gordon K. Lewis, *The Growth of the Modern West Indies* (New York: Monthly Review Press, 1968), 57ff.; Robert D. English, *Russia and the Idea of the West: Gorbachev, Intellectuals and the End of the Cold War* (New York: Columbia University Press, 2000), 22.

16 Alexei Yurchak, *Everything Was Forever*, 34–35, 161–162.

17 See in Tatyana Cherednichenko, *Tipologiia sovetskoi massovoi kul'tury. Mezhdu Brezhnevym i Pugachevoi* (Moscow: RIK Kul'tura, 1994).
18 Most of Yurchak's material and interviews are from the Leningrad area. Moreover, a majority of his material and information came from the educated elite of this city, the loyal representatives of the Soviet middle and upper classes, and conformist Soviet intellectuals from Leningrad. He entirely ignores working-class youth, the major consumers of heavy metal and adventure films in Soviet society. Another problem with Yurchak's study is his uncritical attitude to interviews. Many of Yurchak's interviewees tended to idealize or exaggerate their "idealist socialist experience" without any conflicts in contrast to the bandit capitalism of the Yeltsin era. In many cases, using his "speech acts" approaches, Yurchak took his interviewees' information at face value, uncritically, without checking archival sources. For his methods see Yurchak, *Everything Was Forever*, 29–33.
19 Even the list of forbidden rock bands, which Yurchak published in his book, came from the Ukrainian provincial town of Nikolaev. With only a few exceptions, all Yurchak's information derived from his home-town, Leningrad/St. Petersburg. See Yurchak, *Everything Was Forever*, 214–215.
20 Fürst, *Stalin's Last Generation*, 25, 100, 103, 297, 301, 362. Compare with Elena Zubkova, *Russia after the War: Hopes, Illusions, and Disappointments, 1945–1957*, translated and edited by Hugh Ragdale (Armonk, New York: M.E. Sharpe, 1998).
21 Vladislav Zubok, *Zhivago's Children: The Last Russian Intelligentsia* (Cambridge, MA: The Belknap Press of Harvard University Press, 2009). This project originated from another excellent study of the Cold War, Vladislav M. Zubok, *A Failed Empire: The Soviet Union in the Cold War from Stalin to Gorbachev* (Chapel Hill, NC: University of North Carolina Press, 2007).
22 Zubok, *Zhivago's Children*, Fürst, *Stalin's Last Generation*; Stephen V. Bittner, *The Many Lives of Khrushchev's Thaw: Experience and Memory in Moscow's Arbat* (Ithaca, NY: Cornell University Press, 2008); Stephen Lovell, *Shadow of War: Russia and the USSR, 1941 to the Present* (Oxford: Wiley-Blackwell, 2010); Benjamin Tromly, "An Unlikely National Revival: Soviet Higher Learning and the Ukrainian 'Sixtiers,' 1953–65," *The Russian Review*, 68 (October 2009): 607–622; Gleb Tsipursky, "'As a Citizen, I Cannot Ignore These Facts': Whistleblowing in the Khrushchev Era," *Jahrbücher für Geschichte Osteuropas*, 58(1) (March 2010): 52–69; idem, "Citizenship, Deviance, and Identity: Soviet Youth Newspapers as Agents of Social Control in the Thaw-Era Leisure Campaign," *Cahiers du monde russe* 49(4) (October–December 2008): 629–49. Comapre with Sergei I. Zhuk, "Inventing America on the Borders of Socialist Imagination: Movies and Music from the USA and the Origins of American Studies in the USSR," *REGION: Regional Studies of Russia, Eastern Europe, and Central Asia*, 2(2) (2013): 249–288.
23 See the first scholarly biography of Brezhnev, published as a book in a Russian (formerly Soviet) series "Life of the Remarkable People": Leonid Mlechin, *Brezhnev* (Moscow: Molodaia gvardia, 2008). In the 1930s during the Stalinist regime, the Communist Party and Soviet leadership always had to think of material consumption under socialism as a measure of their achievements in the historical struggle of a socialist system against a capitalist one. For "Soviet consumption" under Stalin see: Elena Osokina, *Za fasadom "stalinskogo izobilia". Raspredelenie i rynok v snabzhenii naseleniia v gody industrializatsii, 1927–1941* (Moscow, 1998); Catriona Kelly and Vadim Volkov, "Directed Desires. 'Kulturnost' and Consumption," in *Constructing Russian Culture in the Age of Revolution: 1881–1940*, edited by C. Kelly and D. Shepherd. (New York: Oxford University Press, 1998); Natalia Lebina, *Povsednevnaia zhizn' sovestskogo goroda. Normy i anomalii. 1920/1930 gody* (St. Petersburg: Neva/Letnii, 1999); Sheila Fitzpatrick, *Everyday Stalinism: Ordinary Life in Extraordinary Times: Soviet Russia in the 1930s* (New York: Oxford University Press, 1999); Jukka Gronow, *Caviar with Champagne: Common Luxury and the Ideals of the Good Life in Stalin's Russia* (Oxford: Berg, 2003), esp. pp. 69–86. For tourism and consumption during late Stalinism see: Anne E. Gorsuch, "'There's No Place Like Home': Soviet Tourism in Late Socialism," *Slavic Review*, 62(4) (Winter 2003): 760–785. On "Stalinist culture as a particular Soviet incarnation of modern mass culture" see also David L. Hoffmann, *Stalinist Values: The Cultural Norms of Soviet Modernity, 1917–1941* (Ithaca, NY: Cornell University Press, 2003), 10; on mass consumption under Stalin, ibid., 118–145.
24 Leonid I. Brezhnev, *Report to the 24th Congress of the CPSU 1971* (Moscow: Progress, 1971), 12–53; ibid., *Report to the 25th Congress of the CPSU 1976* (Moscow: Progress, 1976), 99; Leonid I. Brezhnev, *Leninskim kursom* (Moscow: Politizdat, 1972), Vol. 3, 24, 124, 235.
25 For a pioneering English-language study of this system see: Alena V. Ledeneva, *Russia's Economy of Favours: Blat, Networking and Informal Exchange* (New York: Cambridge University Press, 1998).

26 In the new interpretation of Soviet consumerism, the Stalinist "noble objectives of education and cultural growth of Soviet citizens" still dominated the ideological discourse of the Brezhnev era. See Gorsuch, "'There's No Place Like Home'," 781, and Kelly and Volkov, "Directed Desires," 293.
27 Pilkington, "The Future is Ours," 373.
28 See Mlechin, *Brezhnev*; Boym, *Common Places*; Nina Tumarkin, *The Living and the Dead: The Rise and Fall of the Cult of World War II in Russia* (New York: Basic Books, 1994); idem, *Lenin Lives!: The Lenin Cult in Soviet Russia* (Cambridge, MA: Harvard University Press, 1997).
29 The best studies about popular music consumption in the Soviet Union explore mainly "indigenous" popular music production by the famous Soviet and post-Soviet bands in the major capital cities. See S. Frederick Starr, *Red and Hot: The Fate of Jazz in the Soviet Union 1917–1980* (New York: Limelight Editions, 1985), especially his chapter "The Rock Inundation, 1968–1980," 289–315; Artemy Troitsky, *Back in the USSR: The True Story of Rock in Russia* (London: Omnibus Press, 1987); Timothy W. Ryback, *Rock Around the Bloc: A History of Rock Music in Eastern Europe and the Soviet Union* (New York: Oxford University Press, 1991), 50–65, 102–114, 149–166, 211–222; Stites, *Russian Popular Culture*, especially his chapter "The Brezhnev Culture Wars 1964–1984," 148–177; *Rocking the State: Rock Music and Politics in Eastern Europe and Russia*, edited by Sabrina Petra Ramet (Boulder, CO: Westview Press, 1994). See also studies based on Moscow and Leningrad sources: Cushman, *Notes from Underground*; Yngvar Bordewich Steinholt, *Rock in the Reservation: Songs from the Leningrad Rock Club, 1981–86* (New York and Bergen: Mass Media Music Scholars' Press, 2004); Michael Urban with Andrei Evdokimov, *Russia Gets the Blues: Music, Culture, and Community in Unsettled Times* (Ithaca, NY: Cornell University Press, 2004); Polly McMichael, "'After All, You're a Rock and Roll Star (At Least, That's What They Say)': *Roksi* and the Creation of the Soviet Rock Musician," *The Slavonic and East European Review*, 83(4) (2005): 664–684, and Alexei Yurchak, *Everything Was Forever*. See also: Eric Shiraev and Vladislav Zubok, *Anti-Americanism in Russia: From Stalin to Putin* (New York: Palgrave, 2000), 19–21, and Yale Richmond, *Cultural Exchange and the Cold War: Raising the Iron Curtain* (University Park, PA: Pennsylvania State University Press, 2003), 11–13, 205–209. See also a collection of essays about Soviet youth: *Soviet Youth Culture*, edited by Jim Riordan (Bloomington, IN: Indiana University Press, 1989), and a study of youth entertainment in the Soviet Palaces of Culture: Anne White, *De-Stalinization and the House of Culture: Declining State Control over Leisure in the USSR, Poland and Hungary, 1953–89* (London: Routledge, 1990). Compare with David MacFadyen, *Red Stars: Personality and the Soviet Popular Song, 1955–1991* (Montreal: McGill-Queen's University Press, 2001).
30 Ellen Propper Mickiewicz, *Media and the Russian Public* (New York: Praeger Publishers, 1981); White, *De-Stalinization and the House of Culture*; Dmitry Shlapentokh and Vladimir Shlapentokh, *Soviet Cinematography 1918–1991: Ideological Conflict and Social Reality* (New York: Aldine de Gruyter, 1993); Denise J. Youngblood, *Russian War Films: On the Cinema Front, 1914–2005* (Lawrence, KS: University of Kansas Press, 2007); Tony Shaw and Denise Youngblood, *Cinematic Cold War: The American and Soviet Struggle for Hearts and Minds* (Lawrence, KS: University Press of Kansas, 2010). On the cultural consumption of Indian films by Soviet movie goers after Stalin see Sudha Rajagopalan, "Emblematic of the Thaw: Hindi Films in Soviet Cinemas," *South Asian Popular Culture*, 4(2) (October 2006): 83–100; and her book, *Indian Films in Soviet Cinemas: The Culture of Movie-going after Stalin* (Bloomington, IN: Indiana University Press, 2009).
31 See especially Lovell, *The Russian Reading Revolution*.
32 Ben Fowkes, "The National Question in the Soviet Union under Leonid Brezhnev: Policy and Response," in *Brezhnev Reconsidered*, edited by Edwin Bacon and Mark Sandle (New York: Palgrave Macmillan, 2002), 68–89; Gerhard Simon, *Nationalism and Policy toward the Nationalities in the Soviet Union: From Totalitarian Dictatorship to Post-Stalinist Society*, translated by Karen Forster and Oswald Forster (Boulder, CO: Westview Press, 1991); Yitzhak M. Brudny, *Reinventing Russia: Russian Nationalism and the Soviet State, 1953–1991* (Cambridge, MA: Harvard University Press, 1998).
33 G.P. Dolzhenko, *Istoria turizma v dorevoliutsionnoi Rossii i SSSR* (Rostov: Izd-vo Rostovskogo universiteta, 1988), 150. See also Denis J.B. Shaw, "The Soviet Union," in *Tourism and Economic Development in Eastern Europe and the Soviet Union*, edited by Derek R. Hall. (London: Belhaven Press, 1999), 137–140. For tourism and Soviet trade unions see Blair Ruble, *Soviet Trade Unions: Their Development in the 1970s* (Cambridge: Cambridge University Press, 1981). See also chapters in the collection about tourism in socialist countries, especially Karl D. Qualls, "'Where Each Stone Is History': Travel Guides in Sevastopol after World War II," *Turizm: The Russian and East European Tourist under Capitalism and Socialism*, edited by Anne S. Gorsuch and Diane P. Koenker (Ithaca, NY:

Cornell University Press, 2006), 163–185, and Christian Noack, "Coping with the Tourist: Planned and 'Wild' Mass Tourism on the Soviet Black Sea Coast," in ibid., 281–304. See Anne Gorsuch, *All This Is Your World: Soviet Tourism at Home and Abroad after Stalin* (New York: Oxford University Press, 2011) and various publications of Andrei Kozovoi in French and English, especially his, "Eye to Eye with the 'Main Enemy': Soviet Youth Travel to the United States," *Ab Imperio*, 2 (2011): 221–236.

34 See especially Maurice Friedberg, *A Decade of Euphoria: Western Literature in Post-Stalin Russia, 1954–64* (Bloomington, IN: Indiana University Press, 1977); idem, *Russian Culture in the 1980s* (Washington, DC: Georgetown University, Center for Strategic and International Studies, 1985); Ellen Mickiewicz, *Split Signals: Television and Politics in the Soviet Union* (New York: Oxford University Press, 1988), 32–34; Vladimir Shlapentokh, *Public and Private Life of the Soviet People: Changing Values in Post-Stalin Russia* (New York: Oxford University Press, 1989), 139–152; idem, *Soviet Intellectuals and Political Power: The Post-Stalin Era* (Princeton, NJ: Princeton University Press, 1990), 120–121, 123–125, 150, 225–226; English, *Russia and the Idea of the West*.

35 For a good summary of the post-Soviet sociological studies in Russia devoted to problems of "Homo Soveticus" in historical anthropology during late socialism see L.D. Gudkov, "Pererozhdeniia 'Sovetskogo cheloveka' (Ob odnom issledovatel'skom proekte Levada-Tsentra)," *Odissei: Chelovek v istorii. 2007: Istoria kak igra metaphor* (Moscow: Nauka, 2007), 398–436.

36 Bacon and Sandle (eds.) *Brezhnev Reconsidered*, 1, 4, 19.

37 Sergei I. Zhuk, *Rock and Roll in the Rocket City: The West, Identity, and Ideology in Soviet Dniepropetrovsk, 1960–1985* (Baltimore, MD: Johns Hopkins University Press; Washington, DC: Woodrow Wilson Center Press, 2010).

38 See Natalya Chernyshova, "Consuming Technology in a Closed Society: Household Appliances in Soviet Urban Homes of the Brezhnev Era," *Ab Imperio*, 2 (2011): 188–219, and her recent book, *Soviet Consumer Culture in the Brezhnev Era* (London and New York: Routledge, 2013).

39 See Boym, *Common Places*, and Hilary Pilkington, *Russia's Youth and Its Culture: A Nation's Constructors and Constructed* (London: Routledge, 1994). Sociology of rock music consumption in Leningrad is covered in Cushman, *Notes from Underground* and Yurchak, *Everything Was Forever*.

40 See recent post-Soviet studies that added two provincial Russian towns such as Samara and Ulianovsk to a traditional focus on Moscow: Hilary Pilkington, Elena Omel'chenko et al., *Looking West? Cultural Globalization and Russian Youth Cultures* (University Park, PA: Pennsylvania State University Press, 2002), and Elena Omel'chenko, *Molodiozh: Otkrytyi vopros* (Ulianovsk: Simbirskaia kniga, 2004).

41 See a detailed analysis of the recent literature about the Soviet "closed" cities in Sergei Zhuk, "Closing and Opening Soviet Society (Introduction to the Forum *Closed City, Closed Economy, Closed Society: The Utopian Normalization of Autarky*)," *Ab Imperio*, 2 (2011): 123–158. See especially Kate Brown, "The Closed Nuclear City and Big Brother: Made in America," *Ab Imperio*, 2 (2011): 159–187, and her recent book, *Plutopia: Nuclear Families, Atomic Cities, and the Great Soviet and American Plutonium Disasters* (New York: Oxford University Press, 2013). Compare with Ekaterina Emeliantseva, "The Privilege of Seclusion: Consumption Strategies in the Closed City of Severodvinsk," *Ab Imperio*, 2 (2011): 238–258. See also *Russia's Sputnik Generation: Soviet Baby Boomers Talk about Their Lives*, translated and edited by Donald J. Raleigh (Bloomington, IN: Indiana University Press, 2006), and Donald J. Raleigh, *Soviet Baby Boomers: An Oral History of Russia's Cold War Generation* (New York: Oxford University Press, 2012); Christopher J. Ward, *Brezhnev's Folly: The Building of BAM and Late Soviet Socialism* (Pittsburgh, PA: University of Pittsburgh Press, 2009); Karl D. Qualls, *From Ruins to Reconstruction: Urban Identity in Soviet Sevastopol after World War II* (Ithaca, NY: Cornell University Press, 2009); Paul Stronski, *Tashkent: Forging A Soviet City, 1930–1966* (Pittsburgh, PA: University of Pittsburgh Press, 2010); William Jay Risch, *The Ukrainian West: Culture and the Fate of Empire in Soviet Lviv* (Cambridge, MA: Harvard University Press, 2011).

42 Kristin Roth-Ey, *Moscow Prime Time: How the Soviet Union Built the Media Empire That Lost the Cultural Cold War* (Ithaca, NY: Cornell University Press, 2011), 12. Compare with the first history of Russian comic books in José Alaniz, *Komiks: Comic Art in Russia*. (Jackson, MS: University Press of Mississippi, 2010). See also recent research on the history of Soviet television in: Christine E. Evans, "A 'Panorama of Time': the Chronotopics of *Programma Vremia*," *Ab Imperio*, 2 (2010); idem, "*Song of the Year* and Soviet Culture in the 1970s," *Kritika*, 12(3) (Summer 2011).

43 Roth-Ey, *Moscow Prime Time*, 27. Compare with the old literature on Soviet cinema in Mickiewicz, *Media and the Russian Public*, 73–88. For film consumption in the USSR see also Anna Lawton, *Kinoglasnost: Soviet cinema in our time* (New York: Cambridge University Press, 1992), 7–51; George Faraday, *Revolt of the Filmmakers: The Struggle for Artistic Autonomy and the Fall of the Soviet Film Industry*

(University Park, PA: Pennsylvania State University Press, 2000), 87–109; Youngblood, *Russian War Films*. For Soviet film audiences during the Khrushchev era see Josephine Woll, *Real Images: Soviet Cinema and the Thaw* (London: I.B. Tauris, 2000). On the popularity of Indian films among Soviet movie goers see Rajagopalan, *Indian Films*.

44 Roth-Ey, *Moscow Prime Time*, 36.
45 Zhuk, *Rock and Roll in the Rocket City*, 125, 126, 166. See also my essays: Sergei I. Zhuk, "Richard Stites, the Soviet West, Media, and the Soviet Americanists," in *Cultural Cabaret: Russian and American Essays for Richard Stites*, edited by David Goldfrank and Pavel Lyssakov (Washington, DC: New Academia Publishing, 2012), 159–177; idem, "The 'Closed' Soviet Society and the West: Consumption of the Western Cultural Products, Youth and Identity in Soviet Ukraine during the 1970s," in *The Crisis of Socialist Modernity: The Soviet Union and Yugoslavia in the 1970s*, edited by Marie-Janine Calic, Sabine Dabringhaus, Dietmar Neutatz and Julia Obertreis (Göttingen: Vandenhoeck & Ruprecht, 2011), 87–117.
46 Roth-Ey, *Moscow Prime Time*, 138.
47 See Zhuk, *Rock and Roll in the Rocket City*, 90, 97, 246 (in my book, his first name is printed incorrectly as Aleksandr). See also information in Western media about his show: *Billboard*, February 19, 1972, and an internet interview with him: "Viktor Tatarskii: 'Vstreche s pesnei' reitingi ne nuzhny," http://www.radioportal.ru/5005/viktor-tatarskii.
48 Roth-Ey, *Moscow Prime Time*, 210, 212.
49 Ibid., 212.
50 Ibid., 224.
51 Ibid., 281.
52 See chapter 12 of my book: Zhuk, *Rock and Roll in the Rocket City*, 215–238.
53 See memoirs of Andrei Makarevich, a representative of the Soviet generation of "the Beatles men" and a leader of the Soviet rock band "Time Machine" from Moscow: Andrei Makarevich, *"Sam ovtsa": Avtobiograficheskaia proza* (Moscow: Zakharov, 2002), 53–54; see also A. Bagirov, *"Bitlz" – liubov' moia* (Minsk: "Parus", 1993), 3, 157.
54 The Soviet Beatles' songs compilations included "Can't Buy Me Love," "I Should Have Known Better" (from the album "A Hard Day's Night"), "With A Little Help From My Friends," "When I'm Sixty Four," "Lovely Rita" (from the album "Sgt. Pepper's Lonely Hearts Club Band"); "Eleanor Rigby," "Penny Lane," "Lady Madonna"; "Come Together," "Something," "Maxwell's Silver Hammer," "Here Comes the Sun," "Octopus Garden," "Because" (from the album "Abbey Road") and "Let It Be," "I, Me, Mine," "Across the Universe" (from the album "Let It Be"). For some reason the last three tracks from "Abbey Road" ("Golden Slumbers," "Carry That Weight" and "The End") were released as one track on one of these *minions* under the title "Beatles Potpourri." For a complete list of the Melodia discs with Beatles recordings see Bagirov, *"Bitlz" – liubov' moia*, 157–58. Bagirov mistakenly wrote that VIA Blue Guitars (instead of Happy Guys) was the first Soviet rock band which covered a song "Ob-La-Di, Ob-La-Da." See Bagirov, *"Bitlz" – liubov' moia*, 82.
55 Eventually Melodia agreed to buy a license for a release of "Imagine" and "Band on the Run" in the Soviet Union in the mid-1970s. Bagirov, *"Bitlz" – liubov' moia*, 160–162.
56 For *Krugozor* see: Alexei Kozlov, *Dzhaz, rok i mednye truby* (Moscow: EKSMO, 2005), 187–88. For an example a special appendix with a good article about a British band, Jethro Tull, and a *minion* with this band's music see: A. Troitskii, "Folk-Rock," *Klub i khudozhestvennaia samodeiatel'nost'*, 18 (1978). See also *Krugozor*, 4 (1974), "The Luck of the Irish" and "New York City" by John Lennon; *Krugozor*, 12 (1974) with songs "My Sweet Lord," "Awaiting On You All" and "Bangla Desh" by George Harrison; and Krugozor, 3 (1981) with "(Just Like) Starting Over" and "Dear Yoko" by Lennon. More compilations were released on flex discs of *Klub i khudozhestvennaia samodeiatel'nost'*. See McCartney's songs "Man, Who Was Lonely" and "Give Ireland Back to the Irish" in *Klub i khudozhestvennaia samodeiatel'nost'*, 10 (1972), "You Gave me the Answer" and "Mrs. Vanderbilt" in ibid., 12 (1976), "With a Little Luck" and "Mull of Kintyre" in ibid., 10 (1978), "Ebony and Ivory" and "Tug of War" in ibid., 8 (1984). See also the Beatles songs in ibid., 13 (1980), and Lennon's songs "Working Class Hero" and "Isolation" in ibid., 13 (1981).
57 For the role of *Rovesnik*, a magazine which was most influential for Soviet rock music fans, see chapter 13 of my book.
58 *Rovesnik*, 4 (April 1968): 25.
59 *Rovesnik*, 12 (December 1968): 25.

60 *Rovesnik*, 7 (July 1969): 25; ibid., 2 (February 1970): 24; ibid., 3 (March 1970): 25; see sheet music and lyric in Russian of "Back in the USSR" in *Rovesnik*, 8 (August 1970): 24. The English lyric of "Give Peace a Chance" was shortened in reprint to remove "the awkward words" for the Soviet reader such as "masturbation." See *Rovesnik*, 11 (November 1970): 25.
61 In July of 2007 this author discovered that the pictures of the Beatles had been cut out of issues of the youth magazine in the Russian (Lenin) State Library in Moscow. See *Rovesnik*, 7 (1973): 21 and 10 (1973): 21–22 in the library's collection.
62 The band Teach In became popular among Melodia administrators because it won the Eurovision contest in 1975. Officially, a Teach-In record was released under license from CNR b. v. Grammofoonplaten Maatschappij (Leiden, the Netherlands). The Melodia record's number was GOST 5289-73 (C60-07403), and its price was 1.90 rubles.
63 Bagirov, *"Bitlz" – liubov' moia*, 160–162.
64 They were songs by the major stars of Western rock music, from Elton John and Pink Floyd to Jethro Tull. For these journals see Ryback, *Rock Around the Bloc*, 161. *Krugozor* was very popular among Ukrainian consumers. In 1981 the local periodical devoted a long essay to this musical magazine, which started publication in 1963 with 100,000 copies and reached its height of popularity in 1980 with a circulation of 500,000 (including a popular journal for children *Kolobok*). See S. Avdeenko, "Zvuchashchie gorizonty "Krugozora"," *Dnepr vechernii*, January 5, 1981, p. 4.
65 For détente from the American point of view see: Walter LaFeber, *America, Russia, and the Cold War, 1945–2006* (New York: McGraw-Hill, 2007), esp. 282–298.
66 See Zhuk, *Rock and Roll in the Rocket City*, 239, 240.

PART IX

The End of the Cold War

26
EXPLANATIONS FOR THE END OF THE COLD WAR

Artemy M. Kalinovsky and Craig Daigle

Few topics of Cold War history have provoked as much scholarly debate as its beginning and its end. In one camp are those who insist on the primacy of the US role in ending the conflict, and especially the vision of Ronald Reagan.[1] For these scholars, it was the combination of Reagan's vision of a world without nuclear weapons, his toughness in relations with Moscow, and his ability to articulate the superiority of the American way of life that helped to demonstrate the bankruptcy of the Soviet model. Nonsense, say others – the Cold War ended not because of anything Reagan did, but because of Soviet leader Mikhail Gorbachev's determination to reform the Soviet Union and, in so doing, end the Cold War competition with the United States.[2] International Relations theorists have been vocal as well, arguing that explanations for the end of the Cold War need to be found in structural causes – namely, Soviet economic problems and the large debts of East European states.[3] Others have justly argued that any account of the Cold War's end needs to pay equal, if not greater, attention to what took place in Europe and the actions of elites there.[4] And as the chapters that follow demonstrate, one must also take into account the role of transnational institutions and movements like Solidarity in Poland and of paradigms like neoliberalism, in order to understand the end of the Cold War.

One of the reasons that these debates have such resonance is because, like the debates about the Cold War's origins, debates about its end have had and continue to have serious implications for contemporary politics. Debates about the Cold War's origins in the 1960s and 1970s were inevitably tied to the critiques and justifications of US Cold War policies, particularly American involvement in the Vietnam War. Debates about how it ended are linked to questions about America's place in the world, its proper relations with its allies, and even which vision of America, precisely, triumphed over communism – the New Deal vision that promised state intervention to promote equality, or the more individualistic version espoused by Ronald Reagan. Those who believe, for example, that Reagan's toughness played a key role in ending the Cold War have used their reading of history to justify a more interventionist role for the US in the post-Cold War world. Differing interpretations of the end of the Cold War, and the terms on which it was negotiated, continue to have an impact on Russia's relations with the United States and in Europe, including with former Soviet republics and East European satellites.

This chapter does not make an intervention in the debate so much as sum up its development. It reviews what we know about the Cold War's end by looking at it from the perspectives of the United States, the Soviet Union, and Eastern Europe, as well as that of the Third World and transnational forces. Following historian Melvyn P. Leffler, we take structures and ideologies as contexts in which the end of the Cold War took place, but nevertheless place emphasis on the role of individual leaders within that context.[5]

How the Cold War Ended

Leffler has argued that four factors that created the context for the onset of Cold War in its first decade had changed so significantly by the end of the 1980s that an end to confrontation was finally possible. The first was the threat perception of the two superpowers after the destruction of Germany and Japan; the second was the debate about political economies that grew out of the experience of the Great Depression and the mobilization for the war; the third was decolonization and the "perceptions of threat and opportunity" that it engendered for the superpowers; and the fourth was atomic weapons. By the 1980s, competition in the Third World had become largely de-ideologized; that is, Marixst-Leninism had little appeal; the European states had settled into prosperous social democracy, and there was a growing realization, promoted in part by anti-nuclear campaigners, that the vast nuclear arsenals of both superpowers made the use of nuclear weapons unlikely. Both Reagan and Gorbachev would move most enthusiastically to nuclear reduction, steps that would in turn build greater trust.[6]

Over the four decades of the Cold War, both US and Soviet leaders had sought ways to end or at least defuse the conflict. In 1953, soon after Stalin's death, Lavrentii Beria, Stalin's chief of the secret police and one of several contenders for power, made an attempt to offer the Western powers a deal on Germany (it was soon used to build a case against him).[7] Later in the decade, Nikita Khrushchev tried to lessen hostility between the two superpowers by promoting "peaceful co-existence," but his own temper, problems with political opponents at home, and the pull of revolutions abroad led to some of the most tense moments of the Cold War, including the showdown over Berlin in 1958 and the Cuban Missile Crisis in 1962. But these same crisis moments also encouraged Khrushchev's successors after 1964 to seek, with some success, a broader détente with the United States.[8]

What is now often forgotten is that for at least some observers at the time, détente seemed to herald not just a temporary phase but the end of the Cold War. The arms control agreements signed between the United States and the Soviet Union in May 1972, the Agreement on the Prevention of Nuclear War in 1973, the Vladivostok Accords in 1974, and the Helsinki Final Act of 1975 all demonstrated that a new era had emerged where both sides were prepared to accept the Cold War division of Europe. But competition in the Third World, which climaxed with the Soviet invasion of Afghanistan in 1979, helped to bring that period to a close. The early 1980s were thus seen by some as the "Second Cold War," and in fact the rhetoric of the Reagan administration and the government of British Prime Minister Margaret Thatcher, the domestic propaganda on both sides, and the breakdown in arms control negotiations amounted to the greatest period of superpower confrontation the world had seen since the early 1960s.[9] This phase reached a head in the fall of 1983, when Soviet military pilots shot down a Korean Air Lines passenger plane that had inadvertently strayed over Russian air space, killing all 269 people aboard, including 61 Americans, and NATO went forward with a military exercise called Able Archer, which was briefly misinterpreted by the Soviets as preparation for a nuclear strike.

The two autumn crises of 1983 in turn set the stage for a reassessment in US and Soviet foreign policy, which are discussed in more detail below. Reagan had been looking for a Soviet leader with whom he could engage, but was frustrated that one after another Soviet leader died soon after taking office – first Yuri Andropov, a former KGB chairman who, despite his security background, seemed to have reformist inclinations, then Konstantin Chernenko, a grey and sickly figure who died after just nine months in office. In March 1985 he got Mikhail Gorbachev, at 55 a relatively young, energetic politician who seemed equally excited to engage with his counterpart.

Thus began the series of famous summit meetings – at Geneva (1985), Rejkavik (1986), Washington (1987), and Moscow (1988) – that in many ways set the stage for the end of the Cold War. The first two dealt primarily with nuclear weapons, but the latter expanded to include other issues such as the war in Afghanistan and other Third World hotspots, human rights, and trade. The first two summits were not promising. Gorbachev left Geneva feeling he was talking to a man who was a prisoner of the military-industrial complex, had little intellectual capacity, and was a "political dinosaur." Reagan liked Gorbachev more, but was not prepared to make concessions.[10] The following year, the Rejkavik summit collapsed because Reagan refused to give up testing of his beloved Strategic Defense Initiative (SDI), a space-based missile defense system which critics had derisively called "Star Wars." In retrospect, however, these summits laid the groundwork for the relationship that later developed between these leaders.

New thinking and New Personalities

Writing history from the point of view of great men or women has largely gone out of fashion. Yet, in the debates on the end of the Cold War it is impossible to ignore the imprint of Reagan and Gorbachev. Too myopic a focus on their personalities and personal roles can obscure larger trends, structural forces, and a constellation of actors, leading to a kind of hero-worship and hagiography. A review of their evolution as leaders and actions in power, if placed in their intellectual, political, and cultural context, can help us develop an appreciation for how they interpreted the structural conditions they inherited, and how they responded.

Realist scholars have argued that Gorbachev's domestic and foreign policy reforms were determined by the USSR's economic failures up to that point. Soviet growth had slowed down in the 1970s, a weakness papered over by high oil prices throughout the decade. When oil prices dropped in the early 1980s, Moscow was left without a key source of hard-currency earnings and was compelled to confront its problems head on. For the first time since Khrushchev's attempt to shrink the Soviet military, Moscow confronted the huge imbalance in its distribution of resources towards the military-industrial complex. Yet, whatever the weaknesses of the Soviet economy (and it had suffered a downturn when oil prices dropped in the early 1980s), the reality is that it was not in crisis, and therefore reform was ultimately a choice, not a necessity.[11] Similarly, the decisions that led to the end of the Cold War – the engagement with the United States, the withdrawal from Afghanistan, the non-interventions in Eastern Europe – were conditioned by the choices Gorbachev faced, but not forced by them. Rather, the generational change brought with it the rise of new ideas and a new approach to problems, one that became known as "New Political Thinking."

The roots of new thinking go back to the Khruschev era and the political and intellectual thaw that began with Khruschev's Secret Speech in 1956. Khruschev's denunciation of Stalinism ushered in an era of relative intellectual freedom and debate that had not existed in the Soviet Union since the 1920s. New directions were taken in history and the social sciences, where many of the assumptions of the Stalinist period were challenged or pushed aside.[12]

Gorbachev did not belong to this group of young intellectuals, but the age did not entirely pass him by. Gorbachev had attended Moscow State University from 1950 to 1955, at a time when Stalin was still revered as the leader from the Great Patriotic War. Still, he made some important friendships with future reformers, including a leader of the "Prague Spring" movement, Zdenek Mlynar.[13] After his move to Moscow in 1978, which took place with the support of then KGB chairman Yuri Andropov, he became acquainted with some of the reform-minded intellectuals working in the Central Committee and the institutes, including Georgi Arbatov and Anatoly Chernayev. Gorbachev's interests quickly evolved beyond the agricultural sphere, his official domain, to larger questions of domestic and foreign policy.[14] Acting on Andropov's instructions he also commissioned some 110 papers from the reformers on various domestic and foreign policy issues. As he put it in 1989, these conversations and papers "formed the basis of the decisions of the April [1985] plenum and the first steps thereafter."[15] Once Gorbachev was in power, he promoted these advisers, who were given stronger platforms to present their ideas for reforming Soviet domestic and foreign policy.

Gorbachev's views on domestic and foreign policies evolved year by year as he grew frustrated with his early reforms and foreign policy initiatives. Though he had made withdrawing from Afghanistan a priority, in 1987 Soviet forces were still fighting there and it appeared that there was no quick end to the war in sight. His attempts to bring the US into an agreement that would give the Soviet client a chance to survive had been unfruitful. Other issues were stalled as well. That summer Gorbachev told one of his assistants that he was prepared to go "far, very far" in pursuing reforms. That year became a turning point for his approach to domestic and foreign policy. He was coming to see Soviet–US relations as stalled because of a lack of trust, and recognized that the Soviet failure to get out of Afghanistan was one of the key obstacles.

Gorbachev's adoption of reformist ideas made it possible for him to present to the Politburo a memo critical of Soviet policy in Eastern Europe in 1986. Gorbachev argued that the USSR should tolerate a greater diversity of socialist approaches and focus on "ideational-political influence" rather than issuing directives to their allies.[16] With the help of "new thinkers" and the reform-minded military men he had promoted, Gorbachev also took unprecedented steps in redefining the Soviet position on the arms race and the United States. In January 1986 he called for the abolition of nuclear weapons by the year 2000, a call that was soon echoed by one of his key allies in the military, Marshal Sergey Akhromeev, Chief of the General Staff. The notion of "two camps," capitalist and socialist, was replaced by interdependency. "Reality is such that we cannot do anything without them, nor they without us," Gorbachev told the Politburo that year. "We live on one planet. And we cannot preserve peace without America."[17]

The most controversial aspects of Gorbachev's foreign policy, from a Russian perspective, need to be understood in these terms. Gorbachev's vision of a Europe no longer divided by military blocks (the "common European home") is perhaps the best example of this. Although the idea had been muted by Brezhnev in the détente years, with Gorbachev it became, in the words of historian Marie-Pierre Rey, "a Utopian proposal for a new diplomatic and societal order within the whole European continent."[18] Gorbachev used the metaphor of a four-floor house, the first being collective security and disarmament, the second peaceful resolution of conflicts, the third economic integration, and the fourth a European cultural community, built upon respect for the Helsinki principles. This was not just propaganda; Gorbachev's advisers and foreign policy institutions were geared to work towards this goal. Though it achieved few actual diplomatic gains, it was nevertheless indicative of Gorbachev's thinking by this point, and it also helped to change the way European leaders, especially French President François Mitterand, thought about the USSR.[19]

Gorbachev's policies cannot be understood without an appreciation of the extent to which he was a true believer in a reformed communism. In Gorbachev's mind there may have been problems in the USSR, but the dream of communism was redeemable. His message to East European communists that they were on their own should be understood in that vein; he encouraged them to reform because he believed that they could still create socialist systems that would have broad social acceptance.

Gorbachev's beliefs also made it possible for him to go along with what was arguably one of the most controversial of his foreign policy decisions – agreeing to the unification of Germany. Following the opening of the Berlin Wall and the collapse of the Social Democratic Party in East Germany the momentum moved very quickly towards unification. For the West German Chancellor, Helmut Kohl, then struggling in the polls, unification provided a huge political opportunity and he exploited it to the fullest. Skeptical voices within Germany were drowned out; so were the doubts of the English and French, who had participated in Germany's dismemberment at the end of World War II and were worried about the weight a reunified Germany might throw about in a post-Cold War Europe.[20]

It was particularly risky for Gorbachev. The USSR's role in Germany was too closely tied up with the costly victory in the Great Patriotic War, in which many of his advisers, as well as his political enemies, had taken part. But Gorbachev's whole approach by this point was predicated on the belief that the Cold War had ended; if earlier he had proposed a return to the four-power arrangement of the immediate post-World War II years, by early 1990 he had switched to what Mary Louise Sarotte calls a "*heroic model* of multinationalism," which included the utopian version of the Common European Home.[21] Of course, his ultimate agreement (which went against public opinion within the USSR and the views of many of his advisers) to German unification within NATO was also made easier by the financial aid promised by Chancellor Kohl. But there is no doubt that Gorbachev's acceptance of such an arrangement would have been impossible without a broad change in his thinking on how the world and Europe was to look, and a firm commitment to get beyond the Cold War.[22]

Morning in America

By the late 1970s in the United States, the post-war consensus on domestic policy was coming apart. "Stagflation," oil shocks, rising urban crime, and budgetary crises in cities like New York all contributed to the erosion of faith in the New Deal and Great Society programs and the fracturing of the political coalitions that had made them possible. The humiliation in Vietnam, the Soviet march across the Third World in the 1970s, and growing attention to human rights issues all helped to undermine the central premises of détente as articulated under presidents Richard Nixon and Gerald Ford.[23] This was the context for the foreign policy of Jimmy Carter and the more fundamental transformation of domestic and Cold War politics undertaken by Ronald Reagan that would help to bring an end to the Cold War.

Although Reagan entered the White House in January 1981 with no foreign policy experience, he possessed firmly held convictions that contributed to the demise of the communist system and the collapse of the Soviet Union. Reagan was imbued with an unshakable optimism in the superiority of the American system, and firmly believed that the United States possessed a "missionary impulse." In Reagan's view, the United States remained the "shining city on a hill" that Puritan leader John Winthrop had articulated in 1630, and its promise, its peoples, and its ideals were boundless. Speaking at a commencement address at Williams Woods College in June 1952, Reagan declared that in his own mind he had always thought of America as "a place in the divine scheme of things that was set aside as a promised land … Any person with the courage, with the desire to tear up their roots, to strive for freedom, to attempt to dare to live in a strange and foreign place, to travel halfway across the world was welcome here."[24]

This steadfast faith in the superiority of American ways, and the belief in American exceptionalism, led Reagan to reject the détente policies of his Republican predecessors, since they accepted living with the communist system rather than seeking its defeat. Challenging Ford for the Republican nomination in 1976, Reagan criticized the Nixon–Ford policies as an abandonment of American national interests. He (mistakenly) opposed Ford's endorsement of the Helsinki Final Act for putting the American "seal of approval on the Red Army's Second World War conquests" and questioned Ford and Secretary of State Henry Kissinger for negotiating with communist countries. Reagan vowed to change the Soviet–American relationship if he were elected: "There is little doubt in my mind that the Soviet Union will not stop taking advantage of détente until it sees that the American people have elected a new President and appointed a new Secretary of State."[25]

Although Reagan fell just short of receiving the Republican nomination in 1976, his critique of détente resonated with conservatives, many of whom believed the United States had sacrificed its defense for better relations with Moscow, and Reagan took advantage of his growing popularity from the campaign to articulate a new vision of foreign policy that conservatives could support. Following his defeat to Ford, Reagan used nationally syndicated radio commentary, speeches, and daily commentaries to articulate a vision of foreign policy that aimed to reassert America's preeminence in the world. He entered the White House, therefore, not as an "intellectual lightweight" who acted more on instinct than on "patient reasoning,"[26] as many historians and political analysts originally concluded, but as someone who had a clear vision to reshape Soviet–American relations and bring the Cold War to an end.[27]

As part of this new strategy, Reagan embarked on a massive military build-up meant to intimidate Moscow. In the President's view, the Soviets were far too weak economically to compete in an expanded arms race and would be compelled to the bargaining table instead. "Defense is not a budget item," he told the Pentagon. "Spend what you need." Between 1980 and 1985, the number of dollars devoted each year to defense spending more than doubled, from $143.9 billion to $294.7 billion.[28] The navy added nearly fifty combat ships to its fleet, while the army purchased thousands of new Abrams tanks and Bradley fighting vehicles and introduced the Apache helicopter.[29] The Reagan administration also launched a host of new weapons systems, including the B-1 bomber; the MX missile; the Trident Submarine; the neutron bomb; the F-14 fighter jet; the Stealth bomber; and mobile midgetman missile programs. In addition, Reagan pursued new research projects that sought to take advantage of recent developments in particle beam technology, such as high-energy lasers and space weapons.[30]

As part of the administration's military build-up, moreover, Reagan also expanded the US military presence in the Middle East and Persian Gulf. Before the 1980s, as historian Olav Njølstad has argued, the United States remained unprepared to conduct a major military operation in the broader Middle East. The inability to respond to the Soviet invasion of Afghanistan and the failed Desert One Operation – the attempted rescue of the US hostages in Iran – highlighted the fact that American forces, equipment, and command-and-control structure were inadequate for dealing with the conditions of the Persian Gulf and underlined the need to strengthen the US military presence in the area. Continuing the efforts that began during the Carter administration,[31] Reagan, on January 1, 1983, established the United States Central Command, increased the US base presence in the Persian Gulf, strengthened US ties to Saudi Arabia, and continued Operation Bright Start, a joint US–Egyptian military exercise.[32] The new command structure helped to contain the expansion of Soviet power in the Middle East and would later prove decisive in the US-led effort in 1991 to remove Iraq from Kuwait during the Persian Gulf War.

Although the defense build-up ran up huge federal deficits, Reagan justified these costly programs by arguing that the United States must negotiate with the Kremlin from a position of strength. In a major address to the British Parliament, the President argued that "our military strength is a prerequisite to peace" and he wanted to use the "vast resources at our command" to "leave Marxism-Leninism on the ash-heap of history."[33] Much of the reason why Reagan detested the SALT agreements that personified the détente era was because they accepted limits on what the United States could do with its vast defense arsenal and accepted parity with the Soviet Union. What Reagan wanted instead was to demonstrate to the Soviets that there were no limits on American capabilities, especially when it came to defense matters.[34]

Beyond placing pressure on the Soviets through increased defense spending, Reagan also embarked on a campaign to support anti-communist "freedom fighters" around the world seeking to overthrow Soviet-supported governments. Much like the "roll back" strategy during the Eisenhower administration, which sought to actively push back the influence of the Soviet Union in Eastern Europe, Reagan aimed to reverse Soviet encroachment, particularly in the Third World. This strategy, later dubbed the "Reagan Doctrine" by conservative columnist Charles Krauthammer,[35] found its most prominent articulation in the 1983 National Security Decision Directive (NSDD) 75. Making it clear that US policy towards the Kremlin would consist of "external resistance" to Soviet imperialism, NSDD 75 made it official US policy "to support effectively those Third World states that are willing to resist Soviet pressure or oppose Soviet initiatives hostile to the United States, or are special targets of Soviet policy." To carry this out, Reagan supported increased "security assistance" and "foreign military sales," as well as readiness to use US military forces where necessary "to protect vital interests and support endangered Allies and friends."[36]

The application of the Reagan Doctrine extended to almost every part of the globe. In Southwest Africa, the United States covertly sent millions of dollars to Jonas Savimbi, the leader of anti-Marxist UNITA rebels, who continued to resist Soviet and Cuban influence in Angola. The economic aid may not have been decisive in bringing about a political settlement to end the long civil war in Angola, but it did help to produce a military stalemate, which compelled the withdrawal of outside powers.[37] Reagan also used covert assistance to support the mujahedeen in Afghanistan. Between 1981 and 1988, the US funneled more than $600 million dollars of economic and military aid to the Afghan resistance, including Stinger missiles, which were effectively used against Soviet helicopter gunships.[38]

In keeping with this doctrine, moreover, the Reagan administration aggressively supported the Contras to overthrow the Sandinista government in Nicaragua. Beginning in 1981, the President authorized $20 million in covert funds to support the Contras, and later imposed an economic embargo and blocked loans to Nicaragua from the World Bank.[39] Nicaragua became such an obsession for hardliners in the Reagan administration that the White House actively sought ways to circumvent congressional restrictions on economic and military support to the Contras, including illegally selling arms to Iran at inflated prices and siphoning off the profits to fund the contra war.[40] Critics of Reagan's aggressive support of freedom fighters around the world argued that the President would lead the US into another Vietnam, but Reagan would not back down. "We must not break faith with those who are risking their lives ... on every continent ... to defy Soviet aggression and secure rights which have been ours from birth," he declared in his 1985 State of the Union Address. "Support for freedom fighters is self-defense."[41]

Despite his aggressive military build-up and his support for freedom fighters around the world to resist communism, Reagan's confident militarism did not extend to nuclear weapons. He possessed a deep abhorrence of nuclear weapons and the doctrine of Mutual Assured Destruction (MAD), unmatched by any US president during the Cold War. As early as 1976, he warned of the "horrible missiles of destruction that can, in a matter of minutes ... destroy virtually the civilized world we live in".[42] Three years later, during a tour of North American

Aerospace Defense Command headquarters at Cheyenne Mountain, Colorado, Reagan was shocked to learn that the United States possessed no capabilities to prevent a nuclear attack. Relying on MAD, therefore, left the President with what he considered two untenable alternatives: either do nothing and watch the destruction of a major US city; or retaliate by launching a nuclear war. "Both those alternatives are wrong," Reagan told his advisers. "There has to be a third alternative."[43]

The "third alternative" that Reagan pursued was the Strategic Defense Initiative (SDI). First proposed to Reagan in the fall of 1982 by the controversial physicist and father of the hydrogen bomb, Edward Teller, SDI was intended to defend the United States from a Soviet nuclear attack by developing a space-based missile defense program that would intercept incoming intercontinental ballistic missiles at various phases of their flight. As historian Frances Fitzgerald has shown, SDI depended on the costly development of a laser and particle beam shield that could be deployed above the atmosphere. This seemed impossible to achieve in the 1980s, but Reagan presented SDI to the American people as a barrier that had to be overcome to help bring the Cold War to an end. If successful, the system would render nuclear weapons obsolete.[44] "Wouldn't it be better to save lives than to avenge them?" Reagan asked in his 1983 address to the nation in which he proposed the SDI. "Are we not capable of demonstrating our peaceful intentions by applying all our abilities and our ingenuity to achieving a truly lasting stability? I think we are. Indeed, we must."[45]

Although SDI remained far from achievable during the 1980s, Reagan's commitment to SDI never wavered and he used his desire to move forward with the new system as leverage with the Soviets to make deep concessions when it came to reducing the size of their nuclear arsenals. This was evident at the 1986 summit meeting at Reykjavik, Iceland, where the Soviet leader insisted on restricting SDI to laboratory research. Reagan reacted, as special assistant Jack F. Matlock Jr. wrote later, "as if he had been asked to toss his favorite child into an erupting volcano" and walked out of the meeting.[46] The Reykjavik summit quickly collapsed over the two leaders' disagreement on the future of SDI, but the summit laid the groundwork for the Intermediate-Range Nuclear Forces (INF) Treaty the following year and for future US–Soviet cooperation.

Reagan's aggressive pursuit of SDI, in addition to the defense build-up and the Reagan Doctrine, opened the door for his successor, George H.W. Bush, to help bring an end to the Cold War within two years of taking office. Initially, Bush and some of his more hawkish foreign policy advisers were reluctant to place the faith in Gorbachev that Reagan had done and to allow Gorbachev to use his global popularity to continue seeking the initiative. Along with his national security adviser, Brent Scowcroft, Bush feared that because of the improved relations between Moscow and Washington that had occurred during the Reagan administration, Gorbachev would seek the removal of US troops from Europe, which could lead to a fracturing of the NATO alliance.[47] But Bush soon came under intense pressure from East European leaders, who were facing dramatic changes in their countries, to reach out to Gorbachev in an effort to allow for the changes to continue in the East. "I realized that to put off a meeting with Gorbachev was becoming dangerous," Bush later wrote in his memoirs. "Too much was happening in the East – I had seen it myself – and if the superpowers did not begin to manage events[!], those very events could destabilize Eastern Europe and Soviet-American relations."[48]

When Bush and Gorbachev met at Malta in December 1989, just weeks after the fall of the Berlin Wall, they declared an end to the Cold War and the Soviet–American rivalry that had characterized the post-World War II era. Gorbachev made it clear that he would cease considering the US an enemy, while Bush offered support for *perestroika* and other reforms taking place within the communist bloc. The building of the personal relationship at Malta was extremely important for the next two years, especially as Bush worked toward German unification – a move that Gorbachev and British Prime Minister Margaret Thatcher strongly opposed. Yet, even with their opposition, Bush pressed ahead for a unified Germany so long as it would be a member in NATO. Less than a year after the fall of the Berlin Wall, US and German officials produced the Two Plus Four Agreement, which finally brought an end to conflict that emerged in post-war Germany. Gorbachev not only accepted the unification of Germany, at Bush's urging, but also agreed to its participation in NATO. "For me, the Cold War ended when the Soviets accepted a united Germany in NATO," said Scowcroft. Gorbachev agreed: "The transformation of NATO is apparent … A great step towards casting off the fetters of the past has been taken."[49]

The Transnational Movement to End the Cold War

Against the backdrop of European revolutions, Soviet economic and military policies, and the oversized personalities of Reagan, Bush, and Gorbachev, the role that transnational organizations and non-state actors played in contributing to the Cold War's end appears relatively minor. Still, over the past decade historians and political scientists have given increasing attention to the importance that these "citizen-activists" and their transnational networks had in altering the rigid attitude of policy makers on both sides of the Iron Curtain, especially when it came to issues such as human rights, nuclear weapons, Soviet Jewry, and the environment.[50]

Indeed, long before Gorbachev withdrew Soviet forces from Eastern Europe and Ronald Reagan called for liberty and freedom behind the Iron Curtain, a "transnational network" of human rights activists were aggressively pushing Soviet and East European leaders to modify their behavior when it came to human rights. Taking advantage of the provisions of the 1975 Helsinki Accords, which called for greater respect for human rights and the free movement of people and information,[51] a loose network of Western politicians, Soviet dissidents, journalists, and organizations such as Helsinki Watch, the International Helsinki Federation, Charter 77, and the Commission on Security and Cooperation in Europe, catalogued repeated violations of the Helsinki Final Act and used the follow-up meetings in Belgrade (1977), Madrid (1980–83), and Vienna (1986–89) as a mechanism to pressure Eastern states to live up to their commitments in the Accords.[52]

Inside the Soviet Union, the plight of Soviet Jews became a central issue for human rights activists and dissidents. For nearly three decades *refuseniks* – Soviet Jews who were denied permission to emigrate – combined with the increasing numbers of politicized American Jews who pressured their own government on their behalf, compelled Soviet and American leaders to pay greater attention to the plight of these Jews. American politicians initially responded to the pressure with the passage of the Jackson-Vanik amendment to the 1974 Trade Act, making trade with the United States dependent on how many Jews, among others, would be allowed to emigrate.[53] These activists continued to pressure successive US administrations to keep the pressure on the Soviet Union when it came to Soviet Jewry. During his meeting with Gorbachev at Reykjavik, for example, Reagan presented the Soviet leader with a list of 1,200 Soviet Jews who sought to emigrate, and the following year, in Washington, he gave Gorbachev another list of Soviet dissidents and members of separated families who wanted to rejoin their relatives in the United States.[54]

Although Gorbachev at first showed little interest in human rights issues and was reluctant to make concessions when it came to the issue of Soviet Jewry, he quickly understood that for *perestroika* to succeed, the Soviet government would have to modify its behavior on human rights. In the late 1980s, Gorbachev pledged to make human rights a regular and legitimate part of any bilateral US–Soviet dialogue; he freed leading Soviet dissidents, including Yuri Orlov, Andrei Sakharov, and Elena Bonner; and he opened the gates to Soviet Jewish emigration and allowed the freedom of religious practice for the first time in Soviet history. This was far short of where the Soviets needed to go. Still, it offered major improvements from the Kremlin and demonstrated a new commitment to human rights that had been missing throughout Soviet history.

In this regard, historian Sarah B. Snyder has argued, the ending of the Cold War can be seen as early as January 1989, when the communist leaders attending the Conference on Security and Cooperation in Europe Review Meeting in Vienna eased restrictions on emigration, freed political prisoners, and accepted the concluding document containing provisions supporting religious freedom and the protection of civil liberties. Most fundamental, during the meeting Soviet foreign minister Eduard Shevardnadze declared that Moscow attached "paramount significance" to the Helsinki Final Act's human rights provisions and he proposed an international human rights conference to take place in Moscow.[55] "Such changes," Snyder claims, "signaled a dramatically different approach to East–West relations as well as between state and society in Eastern Europe, which suggested the Cold War had ended or that, at least, its framework had been meaningfully altered."[56]

Many historians may see January 1989 as too early a date for the ending of the Cold War, as it discounts the impact of the European revolutions later that year, as well as the other factors discussed in this chapter, but Snyder is certainly correct in that the Cold War framework had in large part been altered by transnational forces. Indeed, beyond human rights activism, transnational activists worked to reduce the threat of nuclear war and to alter the public discourse on nuclear deterrence which had been the foundation of Soviet and American defense policy throughout the Cold War. Leading the charge in this anti-nuclear movement were prominent scientists and physicians in the Pugwash Movement (Conference on Science and World Affairs), Physicians for Social Responsibility, and the International Physicians for the Prevention of Nuclear War.[57] These scientists and doctors challenged policy makers and government officials on both sides of the Iron Curtain not only to reduce the potential of a nuclear war but to show that nuclear weapons were fundamentally unusable. Astronomer Carl Sagan argued forcefully that the phenomenon of a "nuclear winter" – the prospect that the use of nuclear weapons would ignite fires and block out the sun, leading to dramatic climatic changes – as well as the radioactive fallout and concerns about the health consequences of nuclear testing and of nuclear war itself were just several of the reasons why nuclear weapons could never be used.[58]

The rise of the nuclear freeze campaign in the early 1980s, moreover, was an outgrowth of the public outrage when it came to the superpower reliance on nuclear weapons. Thousands of "freeze chapters" sprang up across the country demanding the resumption of arms control negotiations that had ended with the Soviet invasion of Afghanistan, or the adoption of unilateral disarmament. The movement's scale was apparent on June 12, 1982, when more than 750,000 people gathered in New York City's Central Park to protest the escalating arms race and the continued reliance on Jimmy Carter's Presidential Directive 59 (PD-59), which sought to give US Presidents more flexibility when it came to planning and executing a nuclear war.[59] Marches were also held in Western Europe to protest the Pershing II and NATO cruise missile deployments, as well as Tridents to be purchased by Great Britain. By the end of 1982, the United Nations had passed by overwhelming margins two resolutions calling on the superpowers to halt the testing, production, and deployment of all nuclear weapons, a major victory for the anti-nuclear movement.[60]

Combined with the effort of the scientific community to show the harmful effects of nuclear weapons and testing, the transnational activists in the freeze movement were particularly influential in shaping Soviet foreign policy, especially on matters of nuclear testing, antiballistic missile defense, and the reduction of conventional forces. According to the political scientist Matthew Evangelista, transnational organizations took advantage of Gorbachev's "new thinking" by presenting to him and the reformers in his government scientific evidence of the dangers of nuclear weapons. Following the Chernobyl disaster in 1986, when an explosion and fire at a nuclear power plant in the Ukraine released large amounts of radioactive particles into the atmosphere and killed thirty people as a result of radioactive poisoning, Gorbachev became more receptive to the anti-nuclear movement and especially to scientists' calls to extend the Soviet moratorium on nuclear testing. At a 1987 summit in Washington, Gorbachev agreed to sign the INF Treaty, the first pact to reduce US and Soviet arsenals, and accepted a joint verification experiment at each other's test sites. US and Soviet scientists and technicians were present at both experiments, demonstrating the influence of these "unarmed forces."[61]

Europe and the End of the Cold War

In addition to the growing importance of transnational forces on the end of the Cold War, the role of European states has been the subject of a number of studies – primarily European ones.[62] The seeming unwillingness of US academics to take the European role into account was one factor that led Michael Cox to wonder about a new "transatlantic split" emerging, this time over Cold War historiography.[63] As Cox points out, key European initiatives from the 1970s and 1980s helped to define the end of the Cold War: the inter-European détente, which developed contacts between states within the bloc and provided loans to Hungary and Poland that left those countries deeply indebted by the late 1980s. Though these developments did not bring on the end of the Cold War, they did shape it, because they conditioned the behavior of East European elites and limited Moscow's options.[64]

Nor were European leaders and diplomats passive observers of the events of 1987–91. The role of UK Prime Minister Margaret Thatcher in helping to convince Ronald Reagan of Gorbachev's real interest in reform is relatively well known. Frederic Bozo has explored the role of French President François Mitterrand. Bozo argues that, despite holding very different political views from Reagan, the socialist Mitterrand not only established a good working relationship with the US president but even shared some of his views regarding the necessity of being "tough" with the Soviets after the collapse of détente. This led him to support the installation of the so-called "Euromissiles," an issue that had divided Europe in the 1980s. "If we hold good on the missiles," Mitterrand had confided to the British Prime Minister Margaret Thatcher in October 1983, "we will be in a position to lend a hand to the Soviets."[65] But Mitterrand also thought Reagan went too far in trying to broaden the conflict with the USSR and pushed back against US plans to wage "economic Cold War." Once the missiles were installed, he pushed Reagan to resume détente. How much influence Mitterrand had, if any, is difficult to determine, but Reagan seems to have taken note of Mitterrand's opinions. By 1986, Bozo says, Mitterrand was playing "honest broker" between Washington and Moscow, and Mitterrand may have also played a role in convincing the George H.W. Bush administration to re-engage after the latter's "pause" with Gorbachev in 1989.[66]

As Cox and others have pointed out, the figure of German Chancellor Helmut Kohl looms large in the events of 1989 and 1990. Kohl was crucial in moving the two German states to unification, allaying the concerns of the French, British, and Americans, mobilizing German public opinion, and sweetening the deal for Gorbachev with economic aid. Cox is fully justified in saying that "in the road to 1989 and after, European nations staked out a position that if never quite fully independent of the US, represented more than a mere prop."[67]

The end of the Cold War also accelerated European integration. France and Germany had been the locomotives of European integration in the post-war period, but the prospect of German unification caused unease in Paris and other European capitals – would a newly reunited Germany once again dominate its neighbors? Kohl sought to assuage these fears by emphasizing Germany's commitment to European integration.[68] The independence movements in the Baltic states and the commitment of East European leaders after 1989 to secure their escape from Moscow's orbit led to further integration through economic aid, democracy promotion, security ties, and ultimately membership in NATO and the European Union.

The Cold War, it has been pointed out, began with the confrontation over Eastern Europe and ended when Soviet influence in Eastern Europe collapsed. By 1989, a reformist leadership had come to power in Hungary, while Poland had its own working-class movement, Solidarnost, and intelligentsia that had been contesting communist rule for the better part of the decade. Over the previous decades, these countries had accumulated debts to Western countries. They borrowed ostensibly to fund the modernization of their economies, but in fact to prop up the living standards of their workers and limit discontent. By the mid 1980s the weight of the debt and failure to keep pace with changes in Moscow were discrediting the old guard. A reformist faction gained power first in Hungary, paving the way to democratic elections, while round-table talks between the Party and opposition leaders in Poland achieved the same. In East Germany, Erich Honecker, denying that there was any unrest in the country or that democratization was necessary, tried to hold on to power, but was finally pushed out of the leadership in October. His successors also accepted free elections, which in turn led to German unification. Domestic social movements, dissident leadership, and internal Communist Party splits had a somewhat different effect on the outcome in each of these cases.[69] In all of them, however, Gorbachev's encouragement of the reformers and firmness in rejecting intervention as a policy option played an important role.[70]

The End of the Cold War and the Third World

If the end of the Cold War in Europe could be marked with summits, elections, and declarations, no similar endpoint is visible for the parts of the world where the Cold War was bloodiest. Regional conflicts were second only to nuclear weapons on the agendas of diplomats, statesmen, and even non-state actors. Inevitably, however, the end of the Cold War confrontation was felt throughout the world, although in a variety of ways.

Several of the chapters in this volume have addressed modernization and development in post-colonial states as Cold War practices, reflecting the growth of scholarship. But the paradigms of economic aid and development had begun shifting in the late 1960s. Faith in large industrialization, irrigation, and infrastructure projects, and state-led development in general had begun to ebb, especially after the economic shocks of the 1970s. China's "defection" to the market in the early 1980s was a shock to leaders who had held on to planning as a key to development.[71] The US abandoned the liberal model of economic aid and began encouraging recipient countries to accept a more limited goal for the state and to focus instead on creating the conditions necessary to attract Foreign Direct Investment – what became known as the "Washington consensus". The fact that the Soviet Union seemed largely unwilling or unable to intervene in the Latin American debt crisis of the 1980s encouraged the US to pursue this new agenda more actively.[72]

At the same time, the USSR's relationship with these countries was changing as well. Faith in the Soviet economic model was in decline, but so was interest in Soviet technology, as the USSR was seen as falling behind the US. This was most evident in the case of the Soviet relationship with India, but applied elsewhere as well. The result was that by the 1980s Moscow was less a model for Third World states and more of an arms dealer. Between 1980 and 1986, 32 percent of tanks and combat helicopters produced in the USSR were destined for the Third World, as were 39 percent of fighter airplanes. Some 70 percent of these deliveries were paid for with hard currency, much needed after the prices of oil, gas, and other commodities that the USSR used to earn dollars plummeted in the early 1980s.[73] Many of these arms were used by states to suppress internal dissent, or to fight insurgencies against US- and/or Chinese-backed challengers, as was the case in Afghanistan, Angola, Ethiopia, to name a few.

Thus, if the ideological Cold War seemed to be dying out even before Reagan and Gorbachev started finding a common language, the military one was in full swing. The Afghanistan conflict, before it was over, would take some one million lives; half a million would die as a result of the war in Angola. Would it not make sense for the US and Soviet Union to cooperate? Up until 1988, Gorbachev's policies towards the Third World (with the exception of Afghanistan) did not change much. As late as March 1987, he continued to tell the foreign ministers of socialist countries that the commitment to the Third World must be maintained: "If we lose Mozambique, if we lose in Ethiopia, Angola, then we will lose Africa ... We cannot afford to lose."[74] But from 1988, "new thinking" began to apply increasingly to Third World problems. Gorbachev tried to engage the US to help untangle the mess in Afghanistan, Angola, the Persian Gulf, and even Latin America, but the end of superpower confrontation had uneven effects. US–Soviet cooperation was arguably most successful in the case of Angola, where pressure on their respective allies and persistent diplomacy led to the New York Accords ending foreign intervention and providing for power sharing in August 1988 (although the conflict flared up again in the late 1990s).

It has also been argued that the end of the Cold War helped to speed the end of apartheid, as it separated the African National Congress from global communism, making it more palatable, and destroying any reason for the US to tolerate the apartheid regime.[75] Elsewhere, however, the end of the Cold War did not bring a peace dividend. In Afghanistan, the US and the USSR never did find a way to cooperate, killing any chance for a settlement after the Soviet withdrawal in 1989. In Somalia, the US-allied but still nominally socialist regime of Siad Barre collapsed, paving the way for the collapse of the state and twenty years of civil war.

What had clearly changed was that the Soviet Union was no longer going to play the same kind of balancing role that it had in previous decades. Nowhere was this more evident than in the Persian Gulf crisis of 1990–91. When Iraq, seeking a way out of its debts from the war with Iran, invaded Kuwait in August 1990 and refused to pull back, the US began assembling a coalition to push Iraqi forces out. Iraq had long been a Soviet ally, but while Moscow tried to play mediator, it ultimately acquiesced to Washington's military operation. Saddam Hussein's Soviet-equipped forces were easily defeated, and US President George H.W. Bush spoke confidently of a "new world order."[76]

A New History of the Cold War's End

The various explanations offered for the end of the Cold War have enriched our understanding of it. The time has come, it seems, to write a comprehensive history of its end. For all their merits, many of the new accounts that stress the role of the transnational actors, or regional powers, seem to favor their area of research as the key piece of the puzzle a bit too heavily. This is a necessary corrective to the early accounts that focused primarily on Reagan and Gorbachev (and often just on Reagan), but it still leaves us unsatisfied. Individually, neither the human rights movement, nor the anti-nuclear movements, nor any other movement focusing on a (relatively) narrow set of issues could have forced the superpowers and their allies to declare their confrontation finished. To put it another way, having expanded the definition of the Cold War and its histories as substantially as we have, we need a suitable explanation of its end.

What might a comprehensive history of the end of the Cold War look like? First, it would account for the way in which all the major actors (not just the leaders, but their bureaucracies, militaries, and other institutions) responded to the challenges posed by the various changes located in the late 1970s, and how their changing perceptions influenced their behavior in the 1980s. Second, it would link this analysis to the emerging literature on transnational networks. This would require some old-fashioned political and diplomatic history, drawing on archival sources, diaries, and oral history to trace the impact of these networks and their discourses. Third, just as scholars have pushed their analysis of the start of the Cold War to the inter-war period and even earlier, we would need to broaden our periodization of its end from a focus on the late 1980s. This broader periodization is necessary not just to integrate the new histories of transnational networks and ideas, but also to take account of where the Cold War may have ended long before anyone was ready to declare it so. The most obvious case, perhaps, is that of the competition in economic development, where the game was effectively over by the late 1970s, even if the military relationships and superpower interventions lasted through the 1980s.

Some years ago, one of us interviewed the former Soviet intelligence chief Leonid Shebarshin. He began the interview by remarking, with a coy smile, that the Cold War "was a conflict that had never begun and never ended." It is not clear how serious Shebarshin was about this insight, but in one sense he was right. The deliberately pro-Western and pro-American foreign policy of the early 1990s had evaporated with disagreements over the war in Yugoslavia, the NATO operations in Kosovo, and later the US-led invasion of Iraq. NATO's inclusion of former Warsaw Pact members and, ultimately, former Soviet republics also led to tensions. By the 2000s, journalists were publishing books about a "new Cold War." All of these developments, ultimately, are linked to differing interpretations of the Cold War, what it was, and how it ended.

Notes

1 Francis FitzGerald, *Way Out There in the Blue: Reagan, Star Wars and the End of the Cold War* (New York: Simon & Schuster, 2001); Paul Kengor, *The Crusader: Ronald Reagan and the Fall of Communism* (New York: Harper, 2006); Peter Schweizer, *Reagan's War: The Epic Struggle of His Forty Year Struggle and Final Triumph Over Communism* (New York: Doubleday, 2002); John Lewis Gaddis, *Strategies of Containment: A Critical Appraisal of American National Security Policy during the Cold War*, revised and expanded edition (New York: Oxford University Press, 2005), 342–379.
2 For example, Archie Brown, "Perestroika and the End of the Cold War," *Cold War History*, Vol. 7, No. 1, (February 2007): 1–17, and Melvyn P. Leffler, *For the Soul of Mankind: The United States, the Soviet Union, and the Cold War* (New York: Hill & Wang, 2007).
3 Stephen G. Brooks and William C. Wohlforth, "Economic Constraints and the Turn towards Superpower Cooperation in the 1980s," in Olav Njølstad, *The Last Decade of the Cold War: From Conflict Escalation to Conflict Resolution* (London: Frank Cass, 2004), 69–98; See also, Brooks and Wohlforth, "Clarifying the End of Cold War Debate," *Cold War History*, Vol. 7, No. 3 (August 2007): 447–454.
4 Michael Cox, "Another Transatlantic Split? American and European Narratives and the End of the Cold War," *Cold War History*, Vol. 7, No. 1 (February 2007): 121–146.
5 Melvyn P. Leffler, "The Beginning and the End: Time, Context and the Cold War," in Olav Njølstad, *The Last Decade of the Cold War: From Conflict Escalation to Conflict Resolution* (London: Frank Cass, 2004), 23–49.
6 Ibid.
7 Leffler, *For the Soul of Mankind*, 114–122.

8 For more on early efforts at détente, see Craig Daigle's Chapter 14 in this volume.
9 See Fred Halliday, *The Making of the Second Cold War* (London: Verso, 1986).
10 James Graham Wilson, "Bolts from the Blue: The United States, the Soviet Union, and the End of the Cold War" (PhD dissertation, University of Virginia, 2011), 168–172.
11 See Stephen F. Cohen, "Was the Soviet System Reformable?," *Slavic Review*, Vol. 63, No. 3 (Autumn, 2004), pp. 459–488 and responses in the same issue.
12 Robert D. English, *Russia and the Idea of the West: Gorbachev, Intellectuals and the End of the Cold War* (New York: Columbia University Press, 2000), 49–80.
13 Brown, *The Gorbachev Factor*, 29.
14 English, *Russia and the Idea of the West*, 183; Anatoly Chernayev, *Shest' let s Gorbachevym* (Moscow: Progress, 1993), 9.
15 Sarah Mendelson, *Changing Course: Ideas, Politics, and the Soviet Withdrawal from Afghanistan* (Princeton, NJ: Princeton University Press, 1998), 82. Gorbachev made this comment to a group of scholars in January 1989. See *Pravda*, January 7, 1989.
16 Archie Brown, "Perestroika and the End of the Cold War," *Cold War History*, Vol. 7, No. 1 (February 2007): 3.
17 Wilson, "Bolts from the Blue," 173–174.
18 Marie-Pierre Rey, "'Europe Is Our Common Home': A Study of Gorbachev's Diplomatic Concept," *Cold War History*, Vol. 4, No. 2 (January 2004): 41.
19 Rey, "Europe is Our Common Home," 53–54.
20 See Jacque Lévesque, "Qualms about Kohl's rush to German Unification," in Frédéric Bozo et al., eds., *Europe and the End of the Cold War: A Reappraisal* (London: Routledge, 2008), 95–106.
21 Mary Elise Sarotte, *1989: The Struggle to Create Post-Cold War Europe* (Princeton, NJ: Princeton University Press, 2009), 7–8.
22 See Svetlana Savranskaya, "In the Name of Europe: Soviet Withdrawal from Eastern Europe," in Frédéric Bozo et al., eds., *Europe and the End of the Cold War*, 36–48. On the negotiations, see Sarotte, *1989*, 150–194.
23 Sean Wilentz, *The Age of Reagan: A History* (New York: HarperCollins, 2008).
24 Quoted in Paul Kengor, *God and Ronald Reagan* (New York: HarperCollins, 2004), 94–96.
25 Quoted in Sarah B. Snyder, "Through the Looking Glass: The Helsinki Final Act and the 1976 Election for President," *Diplomacy and Statecraft*, Vol. 21 (March 2010): 87–106.
26 Thomas G. Paterson, et al., *American Foreign Relations: A History, Vol. 2: Since 1895* (Boston, MA: Wadsworth, 2009).
27 Gaddis, *Strategies of Containment*, 342–379.
28 Paterson, et al., *American Foreign Relations: A History*, Vol. 2, 426.
29 James Kitfield, *Prodigal Soldiers: How the Generation of Officers Born of Vietnam Revolutionized the American Style of War* (New York: Simon & Schuster, 1995).
30 Wilson, "Bolts from the Blue"; Leffler, *For the Soul of Mankind*, 346.
31 Presidential Directive/NSC 63, "Persian Gulf Security Framework," January 15, 1981, Jimmy Carter Presidential Library, Presidential Directives.
32 William E. Odom, "The Cold War Origins of the US Central Command," *Journal of Cold War Studies*, Vol. 8, No. 2 (Spring 2006): 52–82; Olav Njølstad, "Shifting Priorities: The Persian Gulf in US Strategic Planning in the Carter Years," *Cold War History*, Vol. 4, No. 3 (April 2004): 21–55.
33 Address to Members of the British Parliament, June 8, 1982, *Public Papers: Reagan, 1982*.
34 Gaddis, *Strategies of Containment*, 352.
35 *Time*, April 1, 1985.
36 NSDD 75, "US Relations with the USSR," January 17, 1983, Ronald Reagan Presidential Library and Museum, National Security Decision Directives, 1981–1989.
37 Lou Cannon, *President Reagan: The Role of a Lifetime* (New York: Simon & Schuster, 1991), 321.
38 Alan J. Kuperman, "The Stinger Missiles and U.S. Intervention in Afghanistan," *Political Science Quarterly*, Vol. 114, No. 2 (1999), 245.
39 George Herring, *From Colony to Superpower: American Foreign Relations since 1776* (New York: Oxford University Press, 2011), 889.
40 Lawrence E. Walsh, *Firewall: The Iran–Contra Conspiracy and Cover-Up* (New York: W.W. Norton, 1997).
41 Address Before a Joint Session of the Congress on the State of the Union, February 6, 1985, *Public Papers of the President: Reagan, 1985*.

42 Quoted in Gaddis, *Strategies of Containment*, 357.
43 Cannon, *President Reagan*, 275–276.
44 FitzGerald, *Way Out There in the Blue*.
45 "Address to the Nation on Defense and National Security," March 23, 1983, *Public Papers of the President: Reagan, 1983*.
46 Lou Cannon, "Actor, Governor, President, Icon," *Washington Post*, June 6, 2004.
47 George Bush and Brent Scowcroft, *A World Transformed* (New York: Alfred A. Knopf, 1998), 40–43, 71–178. For more on the Bush administration's early views of Gorbachev, see Thomas Blanton, "U.S. Policy and the Revolutions of 1989," in Svetlana Savranskaya, Thomas Blanton and Vladislav Zubok, eds., *"Masterpieces of History": The Peaceful End of the Cold War in Europe, 1989* (Budapest: Central European University Press, 2010).
48 Bush and Scowcroft, *A World Transformed*, 130.
49 Leffler, *For the Soul of Mankind*, 441–448. For more on German unification, see Hope M. Harrison's Chapter 5 in this volume.
50 Matthew Evangelista, "Transnational Organizations and the Cold War," in Melvyn P. Leffler and Odd Arne Westad, eds., *The Cambridge History of the Cold War, Vol. 3: Endings* (Cambridge: Cambridge University Press, 2010), 400–421.
51 For more on the Helsinki Accords, see Angela Romano's and Sarah B. Snyder's Chapters 16 and 17 (respectively) in this volume.
52 Sarah B. Snyder, *Human Rights Activism and the End of the Cold War: A Transnational History of the Helsinki Network* (Cambridge: Cambridge University Press, 2011), 110.
53 Gal Beckerman, *When They Come for Us, We'll be Gone: The Epic Struggle to Save Soviet Jewry* (Boston: Houghton Mifflin Harcourt, 2010), 497.
54 Cannon, *President Reagan*, 703–704.
55 Beckerman, *When They Come for Us, We'll be Gone*, 497.
56 Snyder, *Human Rights Activism and the End of the Cold War*.
57 For more on the US scientists and the Pugwash Movement, see Paul Rubinson's Chapter 18 in this volume.
58 Carl Sagan, "Nuclear War and Climatic Catastrophe: Some Policy Implications," *Foreign Affairs*, Vol. 62 (Winter 1983–84): 258–292.
59 William Burr, ed. "Jimmy Carter's Controversial Nuclear Targeting Directive PD-59 Declassified," National Security Archive; Michael Getler, "Carter Directive Modifies Strategy for a Nuclear War," *Washington Post*, August 6, 1980.
60 Bernard D. Nossiter, "UN Assembly Asks a Nuclear Freeze," *New York Times*, December 14, 1982.
61 Matthew Evangelista, *Unarmed Forces: The Transnational Movement to End the Cold War* (Ithaca, NY: Cornell University Press, 1999).
62 Bozo et al., eds, *Europe and the End of the Cold War*.
63 Michael Cox, "Another Transatlantic Split?"
64 Cox, "Another Transatlantic Split?" 135–136.
65 Bozo, "'Winners' and 'Losers': France, the United States, and the End of the Cold War," *Diplomatic History*, Vol. 33, No. 5 (November 2009), 934.
66 Bozo, "'Winners' and 'Losers'", 936.
67 Cox, "Another Transatlantic Split?" 136–137.
68 See Frederick Bozo, "France, German Unification, and European Integration" and Helga Haftendorn, "German Unification and European Integration Are but Two Sides of one Coin," in Frédéric Bozo et al., *Europe and the End of the Cold War: A Reappraisal*.
69 See Geir Lundestad, "The European Role at the Beginning and Particularly the End of the Cold War" in Njolstad, *The Last Decade of the Cold War; 60–79*.
70 See Svetlana Savranskaya, "In the name of Europe: Soviet withdrawal from Eastern Europe," in Frédéric Bozo et al., eds., *Europe and the End of the Cold War: A Reappraisal* (Abingdon: Routledge, 2008), 36–48.
71 Odd Arne Westad, "Epilogue: The Cold War and the Third World," in Robert J. McMahon, ed., *The Cold War in the Third World* (Oxford: Oxford University Press, 2013), 215–216.
72 See Duccio Basosi, "The 'Missing Cold War': Reflections on the Latin American Debt Crisis, 1979–1989," in Artemy Kalinovsky and Sergey Radchenko eds., *The End of the Cold War and the Third World* (London: Routledge, 2011), 208–228.

73 Mark Kramer, "The Decline in Soviet Arms Transfers to the Third World, 1986–1991," in Kalinovsky and Radchenko, eds., *The End of the Cold War and the Third World*, 56–57.
74 Quoted in Svetlana Savranskaya, "Gorbachev and the Third World," in Kalinovsky and Radchenko, eds., *The End of the Cold War and the Third World*, 29–30.
75 Chris Saunders, "The Ending of the Cold War and Southern Africa," in Kalinovsky and Radchenko, eds., *The End of the Cold War and the Third World*, 264–276.
76 "Address Before a Joint Session of the Congress on the Persian Gulf Crisis and the Federal Budget Deficit" http://bushlibrary.tamu.edu/research/public_papers.php?id=2217&year=1990&month=9 [Accessed January 23, 2013].

27

HUMANITARIAN AID, SOFT POWER, AND THE END OF THE COLD WAR IN POLAND

Gregory F. Domber

Since the late 1990s, literature on the role of non-governmental organizations in East–West interactions has provided complex pictures of how the West influenced the revolutionary movements that transformed the Soviet Union and Eastern Europe at the end of the Cold War. Robert English has explored the transnational flow of ideas from West to East that shaped Soviet General Secretary Mikhail Gorbachev and his advisors' worldviews, to lay the foundation for Soviet "New Thinking" – the revolutionary doctrine that paved the way for *perestroika*, *glastnost*, and a new strategic doctrine that allowed greater independence for East European Communists.[1] Matthew Evangelista's work has shed light on how transnational activists and nongovernmental organizations (NGOs) impacted Soviet thinking on nuclear and conventional war, ultimately shaping Soviet decisions to disarm unilaterally as well as through negotiations with the United States.[2] Most recently, Sarah B. Snyder has illustrated how a transnational network of NGOs and activists, inspired by the Helsinki Final Act, successfully persuaded the Soviet Union to embrace human rights norms, ending an essential point of competition and confrontation between the superpowers.[3] Each of these books tells a story, not of one superpower triumphing over another, but of the nuanced ways that independent organizations influenced the dynamics between East and West, shaping the United States relationship with the Communist world over the long term.

Including NGOs in the discussion of Poland's revolutionary moment in 1989 – when Poles formed their first non-Communist government since World War II – provides a similarly useful angle to view the complexities and nuances of American influence. U.S. policy toward Warsaw for the final decade of the Cold War took shape at the conclusion of the "Polish Crisis" – a roughly eighteen-month period of time which began with the creation of the Independent Self-Governing Trade Union "Solidarity" (Solidarność) in August 1980 and ended with military rule in December 1981. In the wake of the Polish United Workers' Party's (*Polska Zjednoczona Partia Robotnicza* or PZPR) decision to declare martial law and jail Solidarność activists, the Reagan administration pursued a two-track policy: on the one hand, declaring political and economic sanctions against the government until it returned to the *status quo ante*; and, on the other, implementing a program to politically and monetarily support the Solidarność movement.[4] Complementing Washington policies, NGOs provided the needed humanitarian aid, coordinated with the Polish Catholic Church. These humanitarian groups served as an important counterweight to sanctions, significantly enhancing American soft power. While there were numerous long-term sources of American soft power, humanitarian aid sent during the 1980s enhanced the United States' "attractive force," thereby solidifying the United States' bargaining position against the Polish government, improving the effectiveness of American sanctions, and shaping East–West interactions at the end of the Cold War.

The "Polish Crisis" began with a series of strikes along the Baltic coast that led to the signing of the Gdańsk Agreements in August 1980, which, most importantly, allowed for the creation of an independent trade union. Solidarność quickly became a national organization and spent the next eighteen months pushing the PZPR to live up to the agreements made in Gdańsk: to register the union, improve working conditions, and provide mechanisms for greater worker input into economic decisions. Solidarność's primary means to pressure the PZPR was to call for national strikes and work stoppages. While these efforts produced some political success, they slowed an already weak economy to a crawl. According to PZPR documents, national production income dropped 6.0 percent in 1980 and 12.1 percent in 1981, investment dropped 12.3 percent in 1980 and 22.7 percent in 1981, and industrial production remained flat in 1980 and dropped 15.6 percent in 1981.[5] These economic troubles, in turn, led to significant shortages of consumer goods and eventually rationing for foodstuffs, sugar, and meat.

Adding to the disarray, Poland was also ensconced in a wider battle between the superpowers. Recognizing that an independent trade union clearly upended the PZPR's ideological *raison d'etre*, both Moscow and Washington kept a close eye. The United States utilized economic incentives to promote continued political liberalization, while the Soviet Union consistently pressed the PZPR to retake control.[6] Talk of a Prague Spring-style Soviet invasion quickly emerged on both sides, with full-scale invasion scares occurring in December 1980 and March 1981. The Soviets never made a final decision to intervene militarily, but did successfully coerce the head of the PZPR, General Wojciech Jaruzelski, to declare martial law.[7] In response, President Reagan announced a series of economic and political sanctions that would be lifted only if the PZPR ended martial law, released all political prisoners, and sought political accommodation with Solidarność. The Soviets and Warsaw Pact member states rewarded martial law with increased economic packages, but it was not enough to counteract the break with the West. Poland's economy collapsed further.

In the shadows of this superpower confrontation, NGOs worked to ensure that the political crisis did not turn into a humanitarian one. In March 1981, in an effort to ease suffering in his native country, Pope John Paul II called on Catholics around the world to send aid. The PZPR responded to the initiative by opening the way for Western charitable groups to operate independently of PZPR intrusion to distribute assistance by promising "to deliver such gifts from overseas benefactors intended for the specific agencies." In the United States, the Polish American Congress Charitable Foundation (PACCF), the charitable wing of the national organizational and lobbying group for Polish-American fraternal organizations, opened a drive called a "Tribute to Poland," raising funds for food, medicine, and sanitary supplies.[8] CARE, Catholic Relief Services (CRS), and Project HOPE (Health Opportunities for People Everywhere, a group specializing in medical aid and equipment) also all heeded the Pope's request.

CRS initiated a particularly large aid program. In May 1981 Reverend Terrance J. Mulkerin, CRS's coordinator for disaster and relief services, traveled to Poland, and by the summer CRS was "finalizing an agreement with the U.S. Department of Agriculture to purchase dairy products – milk, cheese, butter – at favorable prices for shipment to Poland."[9] A month later, Father Mulkerin had finished the outline of a "Family Feeding Program" to distribute just under $15 million in USAID (US Agency for International Development) wheat-flour, rice, and vegetable oil. The aid sailed to Gdańsk on vessels paid for by the Catholic Church and the Polish government. From there it was handed over to the Charitable Commission of the Polish

Episcopate (*Komisja Charytatywna Episkopatu Polski* or KCEP), which sent the food to each of Poland's twenty-seven Catholic dioceses, where it was distributed at the parish level by local priests, free from government interference over who should receive support.[10] In a nearly homogenous Catholic society, where parish priests either saw everyone at mass or at least knew everyone in their community, this dispersal program provided complete coverage. By December 10, 1981, CRS had "responded to urgent requests initiated by the Polish-American community and the Church in Poland by shipping 16,921,128 lbs. of food valued at a total of $10,181,512.89."[11]

During the first eleven months of 1981, the Reagan White House oversaw a separate policy to provide significant amounts of government-to-government aid to reward the PZPR for political liberalization and to keep the country from collapsing economically. This aid policy (inherited from the Carter administration) was calibrated to sustain Solidarność. As Secretary of State Alexander Haig advised, the United States could strengthen the Solidarność movement's negotiating position with the PZPR by averting the possibility of further economic declines precipitating a crisis that "could demoralize and discredit the democratic forces and lead to the re-imposition of an inflexible Soviet-style Communist dictatorship."[12] Even as late as December 1981 the CIA supported the idea of providing long-term agricultural aid to the PZPR, because U.S. national security was "well served by gambling $740 million (or other sums) in credits in the hope that it will allow the Polish experiment to continue and in the knowledge that the experiment's very survival will contribute to the long-term unraveling of the Soviet position in Eastern Europe."[13]

On December 12, 1981, all of the political calculations explicit in government-to-government aid changed drastically when Jaruzelski declared martial law. One of the White House's earliest moves as part of the sanctions regime was to rescind $740 million in aid (approved just days earlier), which included suspending shipment of $100 million in emergency agricultural aid for the poultry industry. This was not a trivial issue. Chicken was an important source of protein in a country where most ham was sold for export.[14] The U.S. also cut off all rights to fishing in American waters and the possibility of future credits through the Ex-Im Bank and the Credit Commodity Corporation, blocking funding necessary for purchasing food and consumer goods in the United States. Within a few months, Poland's most-favored-nation trading status was also rescinded.

To make matters worse, the winter weather of 1981–82 turned harsh. Voluntary organizations, however, responded decisively to Poland's humanitarian needs. By mid-January 1982, CRS and CARE had raised $3.7 million in cash and $1.5 million in private donations. CARE planned to send dairy products valued at $29 million in 1982. In January 1982, CRS shipped about one million pounds of food and clothing every two weeks. CRS also purchased tires, batteries, and spare parts to service the trucks that delivered materials to KCEP distribution centers.[15] Smaller organizations like the protestant Church World Services and Lutheran World Relief, shipped blankets, quilts, clothing, and hygienic items like water purification tablets and soap.[16] As the *Christian Science Monitor* reported: "[Humanitarian aid officials] agree that as Poland's difficulties have increased, so has the generosity of contributors."[17]

Despite the decision to suspend government-to-government support, Reagan adamantly believed that the U.S. government needed to keep Poland from descending into a humanitarian crisis.[18] He consistently stated that sanctions were meant to punish the PZPR, not the Polish people. But just how the U.S. government would walk this fine line was unclear. Competing interests in Reagan's policy became evident early: at the same time $100 million in emergency agricultural aid was suspended, $30 million in Food for Peace aid already earmarked for CRS and CARE continued to flow.[19] Moreover, a final decision about continuing humanitarian shipments became embroiled in concerns about extracting political concessions from the PZPR.[20]

During this transition period, CRS worked to increase its U.S. government-supported programs while simultaneously distributing private aid. In January CRS sent a proposal to the State Department with requests for $3.5 million in food, diapers and formula for children, and spare parts and fertilizer for farmers,[21] but when Father Mulkerin attended a meeting of an interagency Task Force on Poland in March, he left the meeting with "very negative vibes ... Unless high level intervention is forthcoming the final answer will be negative."[22] Nonetheless, Mulkerin and others forged ahead, successfully dispersing huge amounts of privately funded aid in the first quarter of 1982: 4,277,000 butter packages, 1,134,000 cheese packages, 1,383,750 dried milk cartons, 754,000 wheat-flour rations, 1,152,300 rice rations, and 1,648,500 vegetable oil rations. Unfortunately, this was still not enough: KCEP asked that CRS increase programs for infants, providing hard-to-find items like diapers, cotton shirts, diaper covers, layettes, bottles, and nipples.[23]

By the end of May, the White House had finally reached a conclusion on how to proceed. According to a draft report, an interagency group decided to provide increased aid, but for political, not humanitarian reasons. People were not starving, nor were they on the brink of starvation: "Despite the gloomy economic situation and outlook ... Poland's situation is not so poor that it would meet the normal criteria for granting of [Title II Food for Peace] aid." But, as the report argued, humanitarian aid offered certain political advantages: "Our assistance is widely visible in Poland, undermining regime propaganda and providing material evidence of Western support for Solidarity and the Church. Our continued assistance would help refute European criticism of sanctions and the view that Poland is a screen for a U.S. policy of confrontation with the Soviets. Our assistance also undermines Soviet propaganda portraying themselves as the only true friends of Polish workers."[24]

These political arguments found support within the White House. The president authorized $60 million in humanitarian aid, targeted toward needy children, the elderly, and handicapped people. Of this, $23.7 million was marked to be spent for the remainder of fiscal year (FY) 1982 and $37.5 million in the first quarter of FY 1983.[25] CRS and CARE would receive enough Title II assistance to maintain their programs' current levels through the end of December 1982 "with the understanding that the program[s] ... would be continued through the balance of FY 1983 at a total not to exceed $40.0 million." The president also approved $5 million for Project HOPE.[26]

Six months after the declaration of martial law, non-governmental organizations were utilizing U.S. government funds to alleviate humanitarian needs. The final program was not as large as the $740 million aid package that had been agreed to before martial law, but neither had Poland been completely cut off. Meat, protein, and luxury goods remained scarce, but with Western support the country had enough vegetables and grain to feed its people. American governmental aid combined with private donations and other Western European support eased hardship, but the picture remained bleak. As Mulkerin reported at the end of summer 1982:

> The [grain] harvest was not so good in 1982 as it was in 1981 ... The sugar beet crop, which is a cash crop, and the potato crop, which provides a staple food, were not so good this year as they were last year. There is some distress slaughtering of animals taking place because of the lack of feed grains. The broiler [chicken] industry, with its 200,000 tons of chicken, no longer exists. Food prices have doubled and, in some instances, tripled since February. The target groups we serve continued to be in need. The food supply situation has deteriorated.[27]

The White House was walking the tightrope, balancing punishing the Polish government against supporting its people. While the Reagan administration made no attempt to flood the country with new aid to fulfill all needs, Washington ensured that the public was not in danger of starving. Funding was appropriated because both the American public and the administration felt strongly that the Polish people should not be abandoned. The United States rewarded Poland for its steps toward greater pluralism before the introduction of martial law; now was no time to revoke that commitment to the Polish people. However, as declassified documents show, humanitarian aid was approved for primarily political reasons, not humanitarian ones.

Significant amounts of American humanitarian aid continued to flow from 1982 through 1985, with Congress adding to the effort. Charitable aid in the form of frozen turkey, rice, oil, milk, cheese, flour, and used clothing formed the brunt of American aid, with CRS running the largest program. In 1982 and 1983, CRS oversaw nearly weekly shipments.[28] According to Polish government records, between 1981 and 1985 CRS was responsible for sending 266 thousand tons of aid through KCEP, worth $188 million.[29] PACCF sent additional humanitarian support: 701 tons in 1982, 1,384 tons in 1983, 706 tons in 1984, and 842 tons in 1985.[30] CARE and Project HOPE also continued their work, with CARE providing 120 thousand tons of aid worth $60 million and Project HOPE sending 1 thousand tons of medical equipment worth $23 million.[31] Between 1981 and 1985, total American humanitarian aid sent through NGOs totaled 402 thousand tons worth $362 million.[32]

After 1985, humanitarian needs subsided. Even according to opposition figures, by 1984 the consumption of bread, vegetables and vegetable products, fish, and eggs had returned to 1980 levels, although meat consumption remained at 83 percent.[33] In addition, the thriving black market supplemented the domestic market with much-needed consumer goods. Despite government-mandated price increases, real wages increased roughly 2 percent per year from 1983 to 1986. Over the same period of time the country's net material product per capita increased about 4 percent per year.[34] In macroeconomic terms, Poland's economy began to rebuild and rebound in 1983, and had returned to pre-1980 levels by 1987.[35]

These improvements, however, meant that Poland's humanitarian needs had only decreased, not disappeared. NGO programs continued, but at much lower levels. In 1986, the KCEP distributed 19,775 tons of humanitarian aid, compared to 180,000 tons in 1982.[36] By 1986 the focus of humanitarian assistance also changed from fulfilling basic food needs to prioritizing medical shipments and clothing. For example, in FY 1986, 73 percent of aid from PACCF was medical supplies and 19 percent was clothing and shoes.[37]

Political normalization also progressed slowly from December 1981 to December 1986. Martial law was temporarily lifted in December 1982 and then fully suspended in summer 1983, although the PZPR maintained a number of broad powers through legal changes. Pope John Paul II, a strong supporter of Solidarność, made a pilgrimage in 1983. Lech Wałęsa, Solidarność's chairman, was released from jail in November 1982, followed by a number of partial amnesties for political prisoners in 1983 and 1984.[38] Over these same years, Solidarność rebuilt itself as an underground political and social movement, maintaining its ability to call for strikes and protests.[39] Under pressure from the United States and Western Europe, in September 1986 the PZPR declared a complete political amnesty, releasing all Solidarność activists for the first time.[40] In this new atmosphere, Solidarność inaugurated a public leadership body to complement its underground structures, an essential step toward the Round Table negotiations of 1989.[41]

Between 1981 and 1986, American aid successfully ameliorated humanitarian needs in Poland. While life remained difficult for average Poles because of the problems associated with a shortage economy, Poland never descended into a full-fledged humanitarian crisis. Poles had to live without much meat and with very limited access to consumer goods, but at no point did the country plunge into starvation. Malnutrition remained a concern, but foreign aid forestalled any precipitous increase in hunger. However, as the Reagan administration decision in June 1982 to support humanitarian aid efforts made clear, the purposes of American aid were never purely humanitarian; they were primarily political. But, how effective was humanitarian aid in promoting American political goals?

In terms of internal trends, American humanitarian aid had a number of positive effects. First, while political relations between the opposition and the PZPR were tense and occasionally led to marches, localized riots, and strikes, tensions between the government and the people never flared into nationwide violence. The political pot continued to simmer but never boiled over, which could have provoked a civil war or an intervention by Soviet troops. By precluding conditions that could have led to widespread violence, American humanitarian aid decreased tensions so that political changes could develop incrementally through reform, negotiation, and elections rather than outright revolution. Certainly other endogenous factors – mediation by the Catholic Church; legacies of violence from revolts in 1956, 1970, and 1976; and the opposition's militant commitment to non-violence – influenced domestic patterns of change; but, it is logical to argue that humanitarian aid amplified the domestic tendencies for controlled change, supporting non-violent reform and (ultimately) political transformation.

Second, by funneling aid through KCEP, American NGOs buttressed the Catholic Church's independence, simultaneously undercutting the PZPR's legitimacy. When Poles needed help they turned to representatives of the church, not the government. The KCEP's humanitarian programs showed that the church remained strong in the face of increasing governmental power and that they had common Poles' best interests in mind. The Catholic Church had served as a defender of the Polish nation since the nineteenth century, when the country had been partitioned between the Russian, Autro-Hungarian, and Prussian empires, so the importance of cooperation with American NGOs should not be overemphasized. However, by sending aid through channels independent of the PZPR, American NGOs accentuated existing trends. In an authoritarian, one-party state the church's independence inherently undermined the government's claim to legitimacy.[42] The PZPR's inability to provide basic foods and consumer goods also highlighted the Party's own incompetence.

Finally, humanitarian assistance maintained the United States' positive image. By the end of 1986, a growing body of anecdotal evidence was surfacing to show that work by American humanitarian groups had not gone unnoticed. Church officials who worked with the Americans began publicly voicing their thanks. In September 1985, Cardinal Jozef Glemp (the highest Catholic official in Poland) visited CRS's offices to offer his "warmest thanks for the work done for the benefit of [his] countrymen." In June 1986 the head of the KCEP, Bishop Czesław Domin, presented CRS with a Medal of Gratitude, and described "prayers and masses offered to God for the donors." He also wrote of his "high esteem and prayerful gratitude" for all the work CRS had done with its "great material importance but also enormous spiritual value."[43] Similarly, the Bishop of Kraków wrote to the PACCF, "We thank you! Your kindness and generosity move us deeply, because we are aware that ultimately all men have their own problems, and despite this the people of the United States willingly hurry to send help where that help is needed."[44] Father Bronisław Dąbrowski from the Primate's Charitable-Social Committee wrote, "We thank you from the bottom of our hearts. ... We are truly moved by such effective remembrance of our wards. Your help has not only a material significance for us, but also a spiritual [*moralny*] one. It is proof of the solidarity of people of good will that are always eager to provide help for those who are in need."[45] Even a simple shipment of used clothes was meaningful. As a priest noted:

We liked the clothes very much. At present they are fashionable in our country. Both young people and the old were very pleased. And those rather fat were satisfied. Clothes are very expensive and all these people can't afford to buy them. Pensions and salaries are very low. Four brides were dressed in these white Californian dresses. They were all very happy! We pray for God's bless[ing] for all of you and may the Good Lord keep you all in his loving care at work and in your life.[46]

Evidence of the effects of NGO work also came directly from aid recipients, not just the clergy who oversaw its distribution. Moreover, these gifts took on a symbolic as well as practical meaning. Like the church leaders, individuals wrote about the gifts' spiritual (*moralny* or *duchowo*) importance. Writers frequently referred to a sense of no longer being alone in their struggle. As one explained: "I thank you very, very much for this – not only for the contents in your good things, but above all for the awareness that somewhere far away someone thinks about us and wants to help us."[47] As a former political prisoner put it, "Whoever remembers us [reminds us] that we are not alone, gives us strength and stimulates us in our future work."[48] Or as another recipient wrote, "The best part for me is that shortly after finishing my thirteen-month stay [in prison], I discover here an unfamiliar person from the other end of the earth, and what's more he impartially gives me articles in short supply in our country ... Even the smallest impulse of support for the desires and ideas for which I lost my freedom reminded me of the correctness of what I do and fills me with hope for the future."[49] American aid was reminding Poles that they were not alone and they had not been forgotten.

More generally, these thank you notes represent the sincere closeness Poles felt with Americans. In their letters, Poles included stories about their families and their children. They included pictures as well, often of notable events like christenings. They sent Christmas cards with warm words and "heartfelt" [*serdeczny*] thanks. Many notes also included their own symbolic gesture: *opłatek*. These wafers are traditionally shared at Christmas Eve dinner, with each guest breaking off a piece before offering good wishes for the coming year. While the cards, pictures, and wafers were not grand deeds, they are important indicators of the emotional response American aid evoked. The messages of thanks, stories of family events, pictures, and wafers were all gestures Poles would traditionally share with close friends and family. In these cases, however, there were no preexisting connections between donors and recipients. The two sides did not know each other, nor did they necessarily know the individuals involved, only the groups that organized the packages. Responding to strangers with stories, pictures, and acts generally reserved for friends and family members illustrates just how close Poles felt to the nameless Americans who sent help. American charity created intimate connections. As a young seminarian from Lublin explained, humanitarian aid was a "unifier of people in distant lands."[50]

More importantly, this sense of good will existed despite years of PZPR propaganda to demonize the United States. Jaruzelski consistently spoke out against the Reagan administration and American economic sanctions, particularly in the first eighteen months after the declaration of martial law. He attacked Washington as the "main inspirer of anti-Polish actions," and derided Reagan for being "blinded by an anti-Polish obsession."[51] As one member of the Polish opposition in exile explained, "Official propaganda in Poland has begun to exploit the fact of the existence of [American] sanctions by flaunting them as the major cause for a successive increase in the price of food and other basic goods."[52] Throughout the first half of the 1980s, Jaruzelski vehemently attacked the Reagan administration and blamed Poland's deep economic problems on American economic sanctions.

The Polish people remained unconvinced. Whether it was bags of rice, gallons of cooking oil, blocks of surplus yellow American cheese, or sacks of flour sent in cargo ships and distributed by local priests, or tubes of toothpaste, cans of coffee, candy, a new dress, and soap sent directly by American NGOs, the message received by the Polish people was the same: you are not alone, you are not forgotten, you are not suffering unnoticed. In turn these gifts provided moral support and instilled hope that circumstances would improve. While Jaruzelski looked to find a scapegoat for Poland's problems to relieve pressure on his own government, American aid served as evidence that sanctions and U.S. policies were not intended to hurt the Polish people.

In the big picture, the PZPR's inability to place blame for its economic problems on the U.S. or the West had consequences. Although the PZPR tolerated Solidarność after the full amnesty in 1986, initially the opposition and the government did not hold any substantive talks on reform. It was only after a series of strikes in April and then in August 1988 – prompted by government price increases and dissatisfaction with the PZPR's new economic reforms – that Jaruzelski pushed to actually sit down with Solidarność. These early secretive talks led directly to the opening of the Round Table talks in February 1989, where representatives from the opposition and the PZPR agreed to share power and to hold semi-free elections in June 1989. After sweeping these elections, Solidarność successfully navigated shifting political alliances caused by the break-up of the Communist coalition and gained a mandate to form its own government.[53] By undermining PZPR attempts to blame the country's economic woes on the United States, NGO-led humanitarian programs insured that Poles' dissatisfaction with their own government remained high, high enough to force the PZPR to pursue a negotiated settlement with the opposition in 1989.

As Joseph Nye has observed, "When the Berlin Wall finally went down in 1989, it collapsed under the assault of hammers and bulldozers, not an artillery barrage," meaning that hard power was conspicuously absent from the scenes that symbolized the end of Communist power in Eastern Europe. For Nye, the obvious place to look for Western influence, therefore, is soft power, the "attractive force" emitted by the United States.[54] In Poland, the United States' positive public image and its notable soft power were apparent throughout the 1980s. For example, when Vice President George H.W. Bush visited Poland in September 1987, hundreds of Poles greeted him wherever he went. In the most emotionally charged moment of the visit Bush appeared with Wałęsa on a balcony of Stanisław Kostka church, where the two had just laid a wreath on the grave of Solidarność hero Father Jerzy Popiełuszko. When Bush gave a short speech and waved his hands in the Solidarność "V," thousands of Polish citizens responded by chanting, "Long live Bush! Long Live Reagan!"[55]

The sources of this soft power are of course complex. A significant part of the Polish diaspora lives in the United States and the two countries have a long shared history: Poles were some of the first artisans at the Jamestown colony, and Tadeusz Kosciuszko and Kazimierz Pulaski fought with American troops in the Revolution War. In 1926, Varsovians named a traffic circle after President Woodrow Wilson for his support of Polish statehood at the Versailles Conference. The United States ran an extensive scholarly exchange program from 1956 through the 1970s, exposing Polish academics and students to American culture and ideas.[56] And, certainly, Poles have enjoyed American pop culture: iconic images of Gary Cooper in *High Noon* featured prominently in campaign posters from 1989. An annual summer Jazz Jamboree has run continuously in Warsaw since 1958, growing from a few nights in a Warsaw club to numerous performances in the Congress Hall of the Palace of Culture and Science (where the PZPR would meet for Party Congresses).[57] American humanitarian aid in the first half of the 1980s should be included in any list of the sources of American soft power.

Importantly, American humanitarian aid would not have functioned as it did without NGOs. NGO networks provided the distribution support and political cover to allow aid to continue to flow and gave the Reagan administration an important tool to fine-tune its policies. When it suspended $100 million in emergency agricultural aid in December 1981, the Reagan administration was using humanitarian aid as a hard-power tool like many of its predecessors: Lyndon Johnson used Food for Peace aid to promote American-style agricultural reforms in both South Vietnam and India, and the Carter administration linked Food for Peace aid to human rights conditions.[58] By mid-1982, the Reagan White House understood that this traditional exercise of hard power was not enough. Cutting off humanitarian aid threatened to turn the United States into the "bad guy," a possible scapegoat for Jaruzelski to blame for economic problems. Humanitarian aid sent through NGOs provided an avenue to prove to the Polish people that economic sanctions were focused on those in power, not the common worker or farmer who had supported Solidarność. Each time a sack of rice with an American flag printed on it, a box of surplus cheese, or a tube of toothpaste arrived from across the Atlantic it maintained and strengthened the positive image of the United States.

America's surplus of soft power is all the more striking because the usual conduits for it were blocked in the wake of the declaration of martial law. As part of its sanctions regime the Reagan administration suspended cultural programs, cancelled academic meetings and exchanges, and ended American participation in trade shows. The PZPR responded in kind, further hindering American soft power by increasing the jamming of Radio Free Europe broadcasts, expelling journalists, blockading the American library at the U.S. embassy, and greatly restricting American diplomats' interactions with the Polish public. Humanitarian aid was one of the few ways Poland could come in contact with anything American.

In this way, NGOs acted as a kind of bridge between hard and soft power.[59] Private organizations enabled the Reagan administration to pursue a dual policy of punishing the PZPR while supporting common Poles. Government-to-government aid was not politically palatable after Jaruzelski declared martial law. Private humanitarian groups provided an alternative mechanism to exercise what was traditionally used as one of many hard-power tools. From 1981–86, aid filtered through Polish society and reemerged on the other side in the form of increased soft power. American NGOs offered the path and mechanism for a traditionally hard-power policy to become an asset for promoting American soft power.

Overall, the Polish example shows that U.S. policy did have meaningful effects on the revolutions of 1989, although rarely in direct or obvious ways. Washington's ability to act in Eastern Europe was much more limited than triumphalist accounts would have readers believe.[60] In Budapest, Prague, Berlin, Warsaw, and Bucharest revolts against Communist rule were driven by local conditions and local players.[61] American influence was also certainly weaker than dynamics within the Soviet bloc and leadership provided by Mikhail Gorbachev.[62] The Polish case shows that the United States was not a proximate cause of the anti-Communist revolution. In fact, a close analysis of short-term American policy in 1989 suggests that the U.S. attempted to limit the revolutionary process in Eastern Europe by promoting stability over ringing in systemic change.[63] Nevertheless, over the longer term Washington did influence the indigenous revolutionary forces. American soft power, enhanced by American humanitarian policies, provided one of a few mechanisms for influencing developments in Eastern Europe, pulling the citizens of Eastern Europe toward the West when they rejected the Communist policies of the past. The United States did not cause the end of the Cold War in Eastern Europe, but it did shape the outcome at the margins.

Notes

1. Robert D. English, *Russia and the Idea of the West: Gorbachev, Intellectuals and the End of the Cold War* (New York: Columbia University Press, 2000).
2. Matthew Evangelista, *Unarmed Forces: The Transnational Movement to End the Cold War* (Ithaca, NY: Cornell University Press, 1999).
3. Sarah B. Snyder, *Human Rights Activism and the End of the Cold War: A Transnational History of the Helsinki Network* (New York: Cambridge University Press, 2011). In the Polish case, recent analyses have been buttressed by the work of the Institute of National Remembrance, which has published numerous document collections from the Solidarność period. As a single example, see: *Solidarność, Zachód i Węże: Służba Bezpieczenstwa wobec emigracyjnych struktur Solidarności 1981–1989* (Warsaw: IPN, 2011).
4. For a complete discussion of American policy toward Poland during the Reagan and Bush administrations, see Gregory F. Domber, *Empowering Revolution: America, Poland, and the End of the Cold War* (Chapel Hill, NC: University of North Carolina Press, 2014).
5. Informacja o skutkach gospodarczych wywołanych restrykcjami wprowadzonymi przez państwo zachodnie przeciwko Polsce, June 9, 1983, Archive of Modern Records, Warsaw (hereafter AAN), KC PZPR, V/203, 13.
6. For the best scholarship on the Polish Crisis and its international context, see: Mark Kramer, *Soviet Deliberations during the Polish Crisis, 1980–1981*, Working Paper No. 1, Cold War International History Project, 1999; Vojtech Mastny, *The Soviet Non-Invasion of Poland in 1980/1981 and the End of the Cold War*, Working Paper No. 23, Cold War International History Project, 1998; Matthew J. Ouimet, *The Rise and Fall of the Brezhnev Doctrine in Soviet Foreign Policy* (Chapel Hill, NC: University of North Carolina Press, 2001); Andrzej Paczkowski and Andrzej Werblan, *"On the Decision to Introduce Martial Law in Poland in 1981": Two Historians Report to the Commission on Constitutional Oversight of the Sejm of the Republic of Poland*, Working Paper No. 21, Cold War International History Project, 1997; Douglas MacEachin, *U.S. Intelligence and the Confrontation in Poland, 1980–1981* (University Park, PA: Pennsylvania State University Press, 2002); and Andrzej Paczkowski and Malcolm Byrne, eds., *From Solidarity to Martial Law: The Polish Crisis of 1980–1981. A Documentary History* (Budapest: Central European University Press, 2006).
7. For scholarship on the possibility of Soviet intervention, see the sources listed in note 6, as well as: Mark Kramer, "The Anoshkin Notebook on the Polish Crisis, December 1981," *Cold War International History Project Bulletin* no. 11 (Winter 1998): 17–31; Wilfried Loth, "Moscow, Prague, and Warsaw: Overcoming the Brezhnev Doctrine," *Cold War History* 1, no. 2 (January 2001): 103–118; and *Wejdą nie Wejdą: Polska 1980–1982: Konferencie w Jachrance* (London: ANEKS, 1999).
8. Letter from PAC President Aloysius Mazewski to Members of the Board, July 31, 1981, Catholic Relief Services Archive (hereafter CRS), EURMENA XVII-C, Box 4, Poland Correspondence 1970–1986, 1981 Poland Food Aid.
9. Letter from Edwin Broderick to Most Reverend Albert Abramowicz, August 21, 1981, CRS, EURMENA XVII-C, Box 4, Poland Correspondence 1970–1986, "1981 Poland Food Aid."
10. Memorandum, "Poland Operational Plan Coverage Outline," October 16, 1981, CRS, EURMENA, XVII-C, Box 4, Poland Correspondence 1970–1986, "1981 Poland Gen." For information on KCEP, see Gabriela Kreihs, *Dobro Ukryte w Archiwach* (Cieszyn, Poland: Cieszyńska Drukarnia Wydawnicza, 2004). Food aid from AID generally came from resources provided as part of the Food for Peace program. Food for Peace (or Title II of Public Law 480) allowed the U.S. government to provide food aid to be distributed by private voluntary organizations when humanitarian need existed. For a full explanation of the program's roots, see Kristin Ahlberg, *Transplanting the Great Society: Lyndon Johnson and Food for Peace* (Columbia, MO: University of Missouri Press, 2008), 11–41.
11. Letter from CRS Director of Operations Jean J. Chenard to Russel Stover Candy Company, December 10, 1981, CRS, EURMENA, XVII-C, Box 4, Poland Correspondence 1970–1986, "1981 Poland Gen."
12. "Memorandum from Alexander Haig to President Reagan, 'U.S. Assistance Program to Poland,' December 1, 1981," in Paczkowski and Byrne, *From Solidarity to Martial Law*, 409–411.
13. Memorandum from Robert M. Gates to the Director of Central Intelligence, "Assistance to Poland: Tuesday's NSC Meeting," December 4, 1981, National Security Archive (hereafter NSA), Soviet Flashpoints Originals, Box 1. This sentiment was reiterated by the CIA in a Memorandum, "Poland," December 10, 1981, NSA, Soviet Flashpoints Originals, Box 1.

14 For Jaruzelski's response to the news, see: "Protocol No. 19 of PUWP CC Politburo Meeting, December 13, 1981," in Paczkowski and Byrne *From Solidarity to Martial Law*, 461–472; quoted at 470.
15 Letter from Robert Charlebois to Janet Turner, January 5, 1982, CRS, EURMENA Program Correspondence Box 11, 1982 Poland: PL-IE-002 Spare parts for Trucks: Tires and Accumulators.
16 For a laundry list of assistance sent to Poland in January 1982, see "Emergency in Poland Operations Report #2, January 14, 1982," CRS, EURMENA, Program Correspondence Box 11, 1982 Poland: Agreement/Operational Plan and Relate (Bi-Lingual).
17 Rushworth Kidder, "US Helping Hand Extends to Poles," *Christian Science Monitor*, December 31, 1981, 14.
18 Alexander Haig, *Caveat* (New York: Macmillan Publishing Company, 1984), 250.
19 See, Memo from Father Mulkerin to File, December 15, 1981, CRS, EURMENA XVII-C, Box 4, Poland Correspondence 1970–1986, 1981 Poland Gen.
20 Jaruzelski requested $100 million in feed grain aid to be administered by CARE, but this option was rejected because the U.S. made the aid contingent upon the Poles releasing political prisoners and lifting martial law. The PZPR refused. See: Memorandum for William Clark, "General Jaruzelski's Request for Humanitarian Assistance (Feed Grain for Poultry)," January 16, 1982, NSA, Soviet Flashpoints, Box 27, January 1982; Notatka, January 20, 1982, Polish Ministry of Foreign Affairs Archive (hereafter MSZ), 30/85, W-3, Dep III (1982), AP 39-4-82; and Briefing Memorandum from H. Allen Holmes to the Deputy Secretary, "Your Meeting with Mr. Philip Johnston, Executive Director of Care, February 26, 10:00 a.m.," February 26, 1982, NSA, Soviet Flashpoints, Box 27, February 13–29.
21 See proposal in CRS, EURMENA, Program Correspondence Box 11, Poland 1981–1983.
22 Memo from Bishop Broderick to Anthony Foddai, "Poland," March 24, 1982, CRS, EURMENA, XVII-C, Box 4, Poland Correspondence 1970–1986, 1981 Poland Gen.
23 "Overview of the CRS Program in Poland," undated, CRS, EURMENA, Program Correspondence, Box 11, Poland 1981–1983.
24 See Confidential Memorandum, "Draft Decision Memo on Options for Humanitarian Assistance to Poland," May 12, 1982, NSA, Soviet Flashpoints, Box 27, April–June 1982.
25 *Wall Street Journal*, May 28, 1982.
26 Letter from W. Antoinette Ford to Bishop John Broderick, June 28, 1982, CRS, EURMENA, Program Correspondence, Box 11, 1982 Poland: Agreement/Operational Plan & Relate (Bi-Lingual).
27 Report to File, "Overview of the CRS Program in Poland," undated, CRS, EURMENA, Program Correspondence, Box 11, Poland 1981–1983.
28 Report, "Shipments to Poland as of May 5, 1983," May 5, 1983, CRS, EURMENA, Program Correspondence Box 11, "1983 Poland: Shipping Reports."
29 W nawiązaniu do ustaleń telefonicznych z Tow. V-dyrektorem Pawliszewskim podajemy informację nt. dostaw humanitarnych z USA w latach 1981–85, October 24, 1985, MSZ, 2/89, W-8, Dep III (1985), AP 39-2-85.
30 Kreihs, *Dobro Ukryte*, 69.
31 See note 29.
32 Ibid. According to Polish government documents, KCEP distributed over 530 thousand tons of aid from 1981 to 1985, so the CRS contribution amounted to about half of the final distributed amount. Adding in PACCF, CARE, and Project HOPE amounts would mean that over 70 percent of the humanitarian aid distributed by KCEP came from the United States. Other aid came primarily from Western Europe, particularly West Germany.
33 *Polska 5 lat po Sierpniu* (London: Aneks, 1986), 186.
34 World Economy Research Institute, *Poland International Economic Report 1990/91* (Warsaw: Warsaw School of Economics, 1991), 199, 205.
35 For statistics, see Global Financial Data's Poland Real Per Capita GDP in 2004 Zlotych (available at https://www.globalfinancialdata.com/).
36 Informacja o Zagranicznych Dostawach Humanitarnych w Latach 1982 – I Kwartał 1987, July 31, 1987, MSZ, 35/90, W-6, Dep III (1987), AP 39-4-87.
37 PACCF Relief for Poland Report, November 1, 1985 to June 30, 1986, June 27, 1986, and PACCF Relief for Poland, July 1 to October 31, 1986, November 21, 1986, both in Polish American Congress Washington, D.C. Archives (hereafter PAC), Books 9, "PACCF Registration as a Private Voluntary Organization with AID."

38 The best single-volume English-language analysis of Poland's internal transformation remains Andrzej Paczkowski, *The Spring Will Be Ours: Poland and the Poles from Occupation to Freedom* (University Park, PA: Pennsylvania State University Press, 2003).
39 For broad studies of the underground opposition, see: Andrzej Friszke, ed. *Solidarność Podziemna 1981–1989* (Warsaw: Instytut Studiów Politycznych PAN, 2006) and Maciej Łopiński, Marcin Moskit, and Maruisz Wilk, *Konspira: Solidarity Underground* (Berkeley, CA: University of California Press, 1990).
40 See chapter 4 of my *Empowering Revolution*, and Gregory Domber, "Rumblings in Eastern Europe: Western Pressure on Poland's Moves toward Democratic Transformation," in Frédéric Bozo, Marie-Pierre Rey, N. Piers Ludlow, and Leopoldo Nuti, eds., *Europe and the End of the Cold War* (Abingdon: Routledge, 2008).
41 Andrzej Paczkowski, "From Amnesty to Amnesty: the Authorities and the Opposition in Poland, 1976–1986," paper presented at the conference, "From Helsinki to Gorbachev, 1975–1985: the Globalization of the Bipolar Confrontation," Artimino, Italy, April 27–29, 2006.
42 For an overview of church–state relations see, Antoni Dudek and Ryszard Gryz, *Komuniści I Kościół w Polsce (1945–1989)* (Kraków: Wydawnictwo ZNAK, 2003).
43 Speech by Bishop Czesław Domin in New York, June 27, 1986, CRS, EURMENA, XVII-C, Box 4, Poland Correspondence 1970–1986, "Charity Commission of the Polish Episcopate '86."
44 Excerpts from thank you letters received, attached to PACCF Relief for Poland Report, November 1, 1985 to June 30, 1986 in PAC, Books 9, "PACCF Registration as a Private Voluntary Organization with AID."
45 Excerpts from thank you letters received, attached to Relief for Poland Report, November 1, 1986 to May 31, 1987, June 12, 1987, PAC, Books 9, "PACCF Registration as a Private Voluntary Organization with AID."
46 Thank you letter from Father Edward Dajczak, June 9, 1986, CRS, EURMENA XVII-C, Box 114, General Correspondence 1987–1995, "Poland: General Correspondence 1985–1986." The original is in English.
47 Unsigned thank you letter from Warsaw, September 26, 1986, Hoover Institution Archives (hereafter Hoover), Assistance Committee for the Democratic Opposition in Poland, Box 3. The Assistance Committee for the Democratic Opposition in Poland was a small, presumably grass-roots organization that sent care packages with hard-to-get items (coffee, toothpaste, cooking oil, etc.) to recently released prisoners and their families
48 Thank you letter from Marek Łukarz, September 3, 1986, Hoover, Assistance Committee for the Democratic Opposition in Poland, Box 3.
49 Thank you letter from Bogdan Guść, October 11, 1986, Hoover, Assistance Committee for the Democratic Opposition in Poland, Box 3.
50 Thank you letter from Polish Seminarian, September 24, 1987, CRS, EURMENA XVII-C, Box 114, General Correspondence 1987–1995, "Poland: General Correspondence 1985–1986." Numerous cards with opłatki can be found in Hoover, Assistance Committee for the Democratic Opposition in Poland, Box 3.
51 John Kifner, "Poland's Leader, in Bitter Speech, Threatens to Restrict ties to U.S.," *New York Times*, December 4, 1982, A7. Jaruzelski's focus on the United States as the cause of Poland's problem was repeated in private in a speech he gave to the Political Coordinating Commission of the Warsaw Pact on January 4, 1983. See "Przemówienie Przewodniczącego delegacji polskiej na posiedzeniu Doradczego Komitetu Politycznego Układu Warszawskiego I Sekretarza KC PZPR, prezesa Rady Ministrów, gen. armii Wojciecha Jaruzelskiego, wygłoszone w Pradze, 4 stycznia 1983 r," AAN, KC PZPR, V/189, 8–17.
52 Telex Message from Jerzy Milewski to Lane Kirkland, December 6, 1983, AFL-CIO Unprocessed Records (hereafter AFL-CIO), Lane Kirkland Presidential Files, inactive records, "Wałęsa on Sanctions."
53 On the dynamics of change in 1986–1989, see Paczkowski, *The Spring Will be Ours*, as well as: Padraic Kenney, *A Carnival of Revolution: Central Europe 1989* (Princeton, NJ: Princeton University Press, 2002), Marjorie Castle, *Triggering Communism's Collapse: Perceptions and Power in Poland's Transition*, Harvard Cold War Studies Book Series, vol. 3 (Boulder, CO: Rowman & Littlefield, 2003); and David Ost, *The Politics of Anti-Politics: Opposition and Reform in Poland since 1968* (Philadelphia, PA: Temple University Press, 1990). For Polish-language surveys, see: Antoni Dudek, *Reglamentowana rewolucja: Rozkład dyktatury komunistycznej w Polsce 1988–1990* (Kraków: Arcana Historii, 2004);

Andrzej Garlicki, *Karuzela* (Warsaw: Czytelnik, 2003); and Jan Skórzyński, *Rewolucja Okrągłego Stołu* (Kraków: Wydawnictwo Znak, 2009).

54 Quote from Joseph Nye, Jr., "Public Diplomacy and Soft Power," *Annals of the American Academy of Political and Social Science* 616 (March 2008): 98. For a full exploration of his ideas on soft power, see Nye, *Soft Power: The Means to Success in World Politics* (New York: Public Affairs, 2004).

55 David Hoffman, "Chanting Polish Crowds Provide Bush with Footage for '88 Campaign," *Washington Post*, October 4, 1987.

56 On the role of cultural exchanges, see: Yale Richmond, *Cultural Exchange and the Cold War: Raising the Iron Curtain* (College Park, PA: Pennsylvania State University Press, 2003).

57 On jazz as a conduit of American influence, see Penny M. von Eschen, *Satchmo Blows up the World: Jazz Ambassadors Play the Cold War* (Cambridge, MA: Harvard University Press, 2004); and Lisa Davenport, *Jazz Diplomacy: Promoting America in the Cold War Era* (Jackson, MS: University of Mississippi Press, 2009).

58 Alhberg, *Transplanting the Great Society*, chapters 4 and 6.

59 On the role of NGOs in international relations see Akira Iriye's *Global Community: The Role of International Organizations in the Making of the Contemporary World* (Berkeley, CA: University of California Press, 2002).

60 "Triumphalist" accounts of the end of the Cold War – scholarship that emphasizes American agency in beating the Soviet Union to conclude the Cold War – often highlight the Reagan administration's policy toward Poland as an offshoot of the Reagan Doctrine to support freedom fighters and as part of his overall goal to undermine Soviet and Communist power around the world. The most forthright scholar of this triumphalist view is Peter Schweizer. See his books, *Reagan's War: The Epic Story of his Forty Year Struggle and Final Triumph over Communism* (New York: Doubleday, 2002) and *Victory: The Reagan Administration's Secret Strategy that Hastened the Collapse of the Soviet Union* (New York: Atlantic Monthly Press, 1994). This strain of scholarship has also been championed by public historians. In his best-selling book, *The Cold War: A New History* (New York: Penguin, 2005), John Lewis Gaddis argues that "promoting democracy became the most visible way that the Americans and their West European allies could differentiate themselves" from their Communist opponents, and was therefore a central and effective part of policy that led to the Cold War ending with the United States emerging as the only remaining superpower (p. 225). One need only look at the laudatory coverage (both in America and abroad) of Ronald Reagan following his death in 2004, to get a sense of how pervasive this view has become. As an example, the cover of the international edition of the *Economist* featured a picture of Reagan with the simple title, "Ronald Reagan: The Man Who Beat Communism" (*Economist*, June 10, 2004).

61 See: Timothy Garton Ash, *The Magic Lantern: the Revolution of '89 Witnessed in Warsaw, Budapest, Berlin, and Prague* (New York: Vintage Books, 1993); Stephen Kotkin and Jan Gross, *Uncivil Society: 1989 and the Implosion of the Communist Establishment* (New York: Modern Library, 2009); Stephen Meyer, *The Year That Changed the World: The Untold Story behind the Fall of the Berlin Wall* (New York: Scribner, 2009); and Constantine Pleshakov, *There Is No Freedom without Bread! 1989 and the Civil War That Brought Down Communism* (New York: Farrar, Strauss & Giroux, 2009).

62 On Gorbachev's role in the end of the Cold War, see: Jacques Levesque, *The Enigma of 1989: The USSR and the Liberation of Eastern Europe* (Berkeley, CA: University of California Press, 1997); Victor Sebestyen, *Revolution 1989: The Fall of the Soviet Empire* (New York: Pantheon, 2009); Vladislav Zubok, "Gorbachev and the End of the Cold War: Different Perspectives on the Historical Personality," in William Wohlforth, ed., *Cold War Endgame: Oral History, Analysis, Debates* (University Park, PA: Pennsylvania State University Press, 2003), 207–241.

63 Gregory Domber, "Skepticism and Stability: Reevaluating U.S. Policy toward Poland's Democratic Transformation in 1989," *Journal of Cold War Studies* 13, no. 3 (Summer 2011): 52–82.

28
NEOLIBERALISM, CONSUMERISM AND THE END OF THE COLD WAR

David Priestland

As the Berlin Wall fell, the American academic Francis Fukuyama declared that state socialism had collapsed because it was on the wrong side of History in two respects: its rejection of liberal democracy had failed to grant the mass of people the 'dignity' they demanded; and its hostility to the market had prevented it from providing decent living standards for populations that had been living under it.[1] And while Fukuyama's thesis on the inevitable victory of liberal capitalism has come under a great deal of criticism, his analysis of the reasons for communism's failure has become commonplace – and especially its economic side. Some scholars may want to stress the importance of the American military build-up in the 1980s to the defeat of state socialism, and others emphasize political issues, such as loss of faith in the ideology on the part of elites, or popular hostility to communist high-handedness and corruption.[2] But it is probably more common in the popular historical literature to see state socialism's fatal flaw as economic, rather than military or political, and to assume that the struggle between capitalism and communism was a simple one between the 'market' and the 'plan', which communism was inevitably going to lose. As the historian Martin Malia put it, the history of the USSR in essence consisted of the implementation of 'Marx's fantasy of socialism as noncapitalism'; this could be achieved only through Leninist totalitarianism and Stalinist terror, and the foundations of this 'impossible utopia' were so fragile it was bound to collapse, thus forcing Moscow to concede defeat in the Cold War.[3]

Clearly, economic weaknesses played a major role in the end of the communist system and of the Cold War: communist states were unable to provide their citizens with the consumer goods their capitalist rivals could offer, and from the later 1960s it was clear to many of the world's elites – both communist and non-communist – that the state socialist economic model was not competing effectively with its capitalist rivals. However, as this chapter will argue, the notion that the Cold War between East and West was the story of a long battle between a non-market 'utopia' and a 'natural' market, which the market inevitably won, is an oversimplified one. Firstly, the nature of the 'capitalism' which challenged the state socialist model changed drastically over time as did the interests of the main capitalist power, the United States; secondly, the attitudes of communist regimes to the market, consumerism and market mechanisms were much more varied than the conventional story suggests; and thirdly, economics was not all-powerful in determining the course of the Cold War, and other issues – such as attitudes to militarism and democracy – were also crucial, especially in ending the conflict.

We therefore need to see the ideological struggle between state socialist and capitalist economic models in the broader context of changes in the world economy and attitudes towards it in the course of the twentieth century. Both 'plan' and 'market' responded to economic and ideological environments, and to their rivals, and changes in those environments were hugely important for the viability of each system. Thus the collapse of the laissez-faire, finance-dominated capitalist system after the 1929 Wall Street crash not only contributed to the development of the communist 'command economy' under Stalin, but also propelled the capitalist world towards a more statist 'Social Democratic' model, especially after World War II. And at the same time, following Stalin's death, state socialist economies became less oriented towards war, more consumerist and less hostile to the market. Between the 1930s and the 1970s, therefore, the competing capitalist and state socialist systems became more similar economically (though not politically).[4] It was only from the 1970s, with the crisis of statist models and economic thinking throughout the world, and the revival of a finance-dominated, more laissez-faire international economy that the systems diverged again, and state socialist economies came under increasing economic and ideological pressure. Even so, the extent of the victory of free markets and the political-economic philosophy that justified them – neoliberalism – was not the result of an inevitable triumph of the 'market' over the 'plan'. It was the consequence of a conjunctural crisis, driven by a mixture of social, economic and ideological change and reinforced by American Cold War strategy. Both the USSR and China sought to introduce a statist 'third way' between planning and markets, and China had much greater success than the USSR, ensuring the survival of a version of communist politics, though at the cost of major retreats from communist economics.

The Early Cold War Confrontation: Militarism versus Consumerism

It would be wrong to deny the centrality of the debate over markets and planning to the Cold War ideological conflict. The version of Marxism promoted by Lenin, the Bolsheviks and their successors saw the ultimate society of the future, 'communism', as one free of markets and all market mechanisms: people would work for the love of it, and receive goods, produced in abundance, according to their needs.

However, Marxist-Leninists were not implacably opposed to markets in all circumstances. Following Marx, they argued that before 'communist' society could emerge, humanity would have to go through two prior stages: a 'capitalist' one, where markets survived; and a 'socialist' one, where production was determined and organized by state planners rather than the market, but where people were still incentivized using market mechanisms: the harder they worked, the more they earned.[5] Implicit within this model was an element of consumerism, for the state realized that to make the extra money seem worth earning, it had to stimulate the production of, and desire for, consumer goods.

Marxist-Leninists, therefore, could justify various types of relationship between state and market, depending on which stage of history they judged society to have reached. In practice, combinations of three different models were available to communist rulers: the first founded on quasi-military mobilization, the second based on top-down technocratic planning, and the third an explicitly 'market socialist' one, in which the state controlled the main industrial sectors of the economy, and the market operated in some areas of retail and consumer industry.

Throughout most of the 1920s, when the world economy was operating according to relatively laissez-faire principles, the Soviet Union, a poor, fundamentally agrarian country, pursued a policy of market socialism and integration into the global market. However, the weakness of that system for commodity producers like the USSR at the end of the 1920s, and its collapse after the Wall Street crash of 1929, contributed to the conviction among Soviet leaders that the capitalist economy had to be abandoned completely.[6] The Stalinist system was largely founded on a mixture of mobilization and technocratic planning, with markets confined to the margins.

The regime did rely on elements of consumerism: even in the USSR of the mid-1930s, Stakhanovite 'hero-workers' were both mobilized in a quasi-military way and incentivized with gramophones and bicycles, while a burgeoning educated 'middle class' was encouraged to aspire to a life-style of 'comfort' – pianos, pink lampshades and Hollywood-style comedy musicals.[7] Stalinist communists always presented rises in living standards as the ultimate goal of the regime, and after the end of World War II Stalin hoped to demobilize the economy, explaining in February 1946 that now the war was over 'special attention will be devoted to the expansion of the production of consumers' goods, to raising the standard of living of the working people'.[8]

However, even at his most relaxed, Stalin was never an advocate of consumerism, in the sense of an economy largely directed towards the production of consumer goods, in which consumer desire was encouraged by mass advertising, citizens competed for these goods, and social status was largely judged by one's consumption. And with the start of the Cold War, as the focus changed to remilitarization, it is no surprise that promises of improved living standards were abandoned from 1947 to 1948.[9] Stalin was convinced that this militarized model of technocratic planning and mobilization, not that of consumerism and market incentives, was the only way to win the new war. As he told his loyal lieutenant Andrei Zhdanov in 1947: 'There is only one thing which these gentlemen who long for the "Western way of life" cannot explain: why we beat Hitler.'[10]

The result was a political and economic system that was particularly skewed against the interests of industrial workers and peasants; paradoxically, given Soviet regimes' claims to be 'Dictatorships of the Proletariat'. Wage differentials between white- and blue-collar workers may have been much smaller than those in the West, but post-war Stalinist socialism, purged of a populism that had survived into the 1930s, was politically very hierarchical. While it massively expanded educational opportunities for the educated, gave them high status and granted power to managers in factories and officials in offices, the peasantry suffered from collectivization and pro-urban policies, while the working class bore the burden of harsh discipline, high production targets and squeezed consumption.[11] It is no surprise that it was the working class that became the most rebellious group when the system entered a period of crisis after Stalin's death in 1953 – especially in occupied Eastern Europe.

The Challenge of 'Social Democratic' Consumerism

Therefore the 'Soviet model' that confronted the West at the beginning of the Cold War was a highly militarized and hierarchical version of state socialism. And partly in response, Western Europe developed a new model, very different from the laissez-faire capitalism that had failed so spectacularly in the inter-war period – what might be called a 'Social Democratic' (or, for a slightly more conservative version, 'Christian Democratic') consumerism. Given the dominance of these versions of 'communism' and 'capitalism', it is not surprising that the Soviet bloc was on the defensive in the battle of economic ideas in Europe in the immediate post-war years.

The production and consumption of consumer goods has played an important role in many economies in history, but most historians agree that it was only in the pre-World War I United States that a truly 'consumerist' economy and society emerged. Previous societies were divided between the mass of people who had subsistence living standards and the small elite who consumed luxury products. However, the United States saw for the first time a new economic model which allowed the mass of the population to become consumers.[12] Production lines on the model of Henry Ford's automobile plant achieved the economies of scale that allowed employers both to make high profits and to pay workers enough to buy the products they made. Professional advertising and attractive shops then helped to create the desire for consumer goods, and after World War I consumer credit helped the averagely paid to buy washing machines, cars and houses.

Consumerism was therefore closely associated with the United States, especially after World War I, when American branded goods, together with advertising and Hollywood films, arrived in Europe in profusion for the first time. However, the American mass production/consumerist economic model was not exported as a whole: European consumption remained highly segmented, and general living standards remained low. Wartime debt, the laissez-faire economic framework, the gold standard fixed currency system and overly short-termist international capital markets all precluded the necessary resources needed for investment and expansion of consumption.

Banks did allow high levels of consumption in the United States, but the result was debt, share speculation and the collapse of the economy in 1929, triggering a worldwide depression. The result was a gradual reassessment of the role of the state in capitalism. As the increasingly influential economist John Maynard Keynes argued, consumerist economies could only grow in a stable way if governments helped ordinary people to consume, by stimulating economic activity, creating jobs and establishing welfare systems. This would avoid excessive reliance on private banks, and debt.[13]

These ideas lay behind Franklin D. Roosevelt's New Deal in the 1930s – effectively a centre-left, 'Social Democratic' programme – and it was an even more statist and welfarist version of this model which the United States promoted in Western Europe after World War II. The threat of communist electoral victories empowered New Dealers in Washington, who could successfully argue that state intervention in free markets was vital in order to avoid social conflict. And, with Marshall Aid, US government help was given to Western Europe on the understanding that states became involved in its investment, and that welfare systems were established.[14] Most importantly, all this was underpinned by a new international trading and monetary system established at Bretton Woods in 1944, by which governments, led by that of the United States, cooperated to curb the power of an international finance that was seen as volatile and unreliable. Free trade was balanced by capital controls, managed currencies and institutions like the International Monetary Fund (IMF) and the World Bank which could rescue countries in distress.[15] Governments were no longer reliant on international investors, who could punish them for potentially inflationary policies such as spending money on welfare and developing their economies.

Post-war Europeans, both social democrats and the more influential conservative Christian Democrats, welcomed this project. After the disastrous social conflicts of the inter-war era, elites and middle classes were much more willing to accept the American notion that economic policy should be directed towards 'a decent standard of living' for the whole population. As Victoria de Grazia has argued in her seminal work, *Irresistible Empire: America's Advance Through Twentieth Century Europe*, there were differences between the European vision, which emphasized a concept of 'social citizenship', with standard of living as a matter of right for citizens, guaranteed by the state; and an American 'sovereign consumer' model, which stressed the free play of the market, especially dominant as American politics turned to the right after the war.[16]

State spending on war helped the mass-production, high-consumption model to revive in the United States after the Depression, though it was rather longer before it took hold in

Western Europe. This was because rebuilding production had to come before consumption, and Marshall Aid was founded on a 'politics of productivity', which required wage restraint and austerity in the early years; it was also based on organized labour accepting the Fordist 'contract' – the end of union and craft autonomy, and managerial and production-line discipline in return for higher wages.

In the early years of the Cold War, the Marshall Aiders therefore had to put a great deal of effort into propagandizing this new, mass-consumerist economic model, especially at a time when the socialist world was posting high growth rates. In Japan and those parts of Germany and Austria occupied by the United States the propaganda was particularly direct, sometimes operating through newspapers financed by the United States government; Reinhold Wagnleitner has described this process of cultural imperialism as 'coca-colonization'.[17]

From the early 1950s, as trade recovered, economies grew, more was spent on welfare and ordinary West Europeans very gradually benefited from higher living standards, perceived differences between the American and Soviet models became sharper. However, there was still a great deal of admiration for the Soviet model in Western Europe, which preserved a high culture of opera, ballet and literature, while it also seemed to be achieving major feats of reconstruction. When French workers were asked by pollsters to rank countries according to their standards of living, a quarter saw the USSR as the best place, with a slightly larger proportion as the worst; of those on the left, half thought that American workers had the best life-styles, while half preferred the Soviet model because workers were granted more respect and were working for the collective good rather than for their employers.[18]

The Eisenhower administration became particularly concerned about the appeal of the Soviet message, and poured much greater resources into promoting the benefits of American consumerism.[19] The Americans were particularly worried about the positive effect of Soviet propaganda at trade fairs, and they staged a number of exhibitions. Particularly popular were model houses and kitchens, full of consumer appliances and price tags showing how many days it took American workers to pay for them.[20] From 1956, the central message of these exhibitions was the claim that the United States had achieved a democratic 'People's Capitalism', in which everybody was equal as a consumer, destroying the old social snobberies and hierarchies. Exhibits would be entitled 'CLASS LINES BEGIN TO DISAPPEAR' and 'ALMOST EVERYBODY BECOMES A CAPITALIST'.[21]

It was therefore hoped that material comfort would overcome not only the siren calls of communism, but also the appeal of cultural egalitarianism.[22] And there is a great deal of evidence that in the course of the 1950s and 1960s it did precisely that. Stephen Gundle, in his book *Between Hollywood and Moscow*, argues that the Italian Communist Party, the largest and most successful in Western Europe, found the challenge of consumer culture extremely difficult to counter.[23] Its leadership was committed to bringing high culture to the masses and was highly critical of consumer culture, but found itself on the defensive as its main opponents, the right-wing Christian Democrats, embraced it. And although it remained the largest and most successful communist party in Western Europe, its stance on culture weakened it among an increasingly consumerist Italian public.

Indeed, it seems that consumerist culture, in combination with state economic intervention, did reduce previously sharp social conflicts – much as it had in the United States of the 1920s. As the French intellectual Raymond Aron famously argued in 1957, 'The affluent society banks the fires of indignation'.[24] In part this was because material comfort reconciled workers to the status quo: they were happier to accept discipline in the workplace in exchange for the promise of higher living standards. But it was also because consumerism challenged old status hierarchies and played a role in integrating society, as it had in the United States of the 1920s. It was easier for workers to aspire to become 'middle class' through wealth and consumption than it was to become culturally 'bourgeois'. Critics of American-inspired 'materialism', from left and right, could therefore appear snobbish and elitist.

The Rise of 'Consumer Socialism'

By the mid-1950s, the challenge of consumerism was affecting the Eastern bloc as well, and, led by the Soviet leadership, communist regimes found themselves making significant alterations to the Stalinist model. The communist turn to higher levels of consumption was the result of a number of internal factors, and not only the Western 'demonstration effect'. As has been seen, higher living standards were always a goal of the communist regimes, and even before Stalin's death the new generation of Soviet leaders had concluded that this militarized system, reliant on increasingly ineffective top-down controls, was undesirable and unsustainable.[25] All of the three major leadership contenders – Lavrenty Beria, Georgii Malenkov and Nikita Khrushchev – were convinced by 1953 that socialist regimes had to increase living standards in the bloc, especially for workers and peasants, and the first two accepted that this involved less emphasis on the military and the heavy industries associated with it.[26]

The rebellions sparked by Stalin's death in 1953 and by the official denunciation of Stalin's use of terror in 1956 merely confirmed the need for change. Protest was not entirely caused by economic discontent; nationalist resentments at Soviet imperialism (especially in Poland and Hungary), and anger at the rigid political hierarchies of the communist states were crucial reasons for discontent. But the late Stalinist economic model, relying on extracting maximum production from workers while keeping consumption to a minimum, combined with the weak legitimacy of these regimes, inevitably brought crisis – especially in the northern and western part of the region, which had enjoyed higher living standards before the war, which had lower growth after it and where there was the greatest awareness of living standards in Western Europe, most notably in East Germany.[27]

The response of Khrushchev and the post-Stalin Soviet-bloc leadership was to improve living standards, and particularly those of the working class. Blue-collar wages rose throughout the Soviet bloc – in the USSR, for instance, the differential between an engineer and a worker fell from 2.15 in 1940 to 1.11 in 1984. Soviet-bloc leaderships also sought to improve the consumer economy for everybody, partly in order to compete with the West. This was especially the case in the German Democratic Republic (GDR), where Party leader Walter Ulbricht declared 'we simply cannot choose against whom we would like to compete. We are simply forced to square off against West Germany.'[28] However, Soviet-bloc leaders were determined that consumerism should be controlled and not 'fall prey to capitalist decadence and commodity fetishism'.[29]

Over the next two decades, consumerism and markets became an increasingly important part of people's lives, as some regimes relaxed restrictions on private business activity, though to varying degrees.[30] Market socialism was at its most powerful in Yugoslavia outside the Soviet bloc, and in Hungary within it: by the end of the 1960s, a substantial proportion of Hungarian workers were taking second jobs in the private sector to earn money for ever more plentiful consumer goods.[31] In Albania, by contrast, the old, Stalinist economic order largely remained.

So how far did this new model of consumer socialism go in stabilizing the system? There is a case for arguing that it had a great deal of success in shoring up regimes that had initially suffered from a major legitimacy deficit, and in meeting the challenge of Social Democratic consumerism. Indeed, East European regimes were moving closer to the Social Democratic model, in social and economic respects, if not in political ones. Overall living standards were lower than those in the West, but wages became very equal, basic goods were kept cheap and consumer goods gradually became more plentiful.[32]

The system at least defused opposition, even if it did not satisfy populations as much as social democracy satisfied its Western counterparts. The dissident playwright Václav Havel was convinced that the majority of Czechoslovaks had been bought off by consumer goods, and he and his fellows felt very isolated.[33] And, in some respects, he seems to have been right. Opinion surveys from Hungary in the 1980s show that while majorities wanted more political liberties and more market reforms, they had egalitarian attitudes to welfare and the economy and did not want a capitalist system, which they regarded as less just in its willingness to accept higher levels of poverty; opinion surveys among Soviet émigrés show a similar set of attitudes.[34]

Also, while consumerism undermined the collectivism that socialist regimes hoped to encourage this was not necessarily incompatible with the survival of, or even support for, socialism. As Alexei Yurchak has shown in his study of the 'last Soviet generation' in the USSR, love of the Beatles and Western heavy metal was as strong amongst idealistic communist youth members as it was among the much smaller number of dissidents.[35]

On the other hand, the acceptance of consumerism could be seen to have corroded socialist regimes. A major reason was that they were now competing on the same ground as their capitalist neighbours and, in that competition, they were bound to fail. Economic plans that targeted quantity rather than quality were bound to be less effective in responding to the demands of consumers than was the market, which is driven by consumer preferences. The result was that consumer goods were less attractive and well made than were their Western equivalents. Also, the continuing political influence of heavy industry and the military, combined with the absence of important market mechanisms (such as a market-based price system and bankruptcy) to ensure capital was used efficiently, led to a chronic lack of investment in consumer industries. The result was black markets and queues: in 1989, East Germans were still waiting for cars they had ordered in 1976.[36] These failures inevitably entrenched the association of desirable consumer goods, and the associated culture of Romanticism and self-expression, with the West, particularly among young people who admired rock music and youth fashion. They also undermined the prestige of socialist states among the population. As an 'Institute of Market Research' established by the GDR Communist Party reported, the 'gap between supply and demand' of modern well-made furniture deepened resentment towards and criticism of the state.[37]

The new power of consumerism upset the legitimacy of socialist states in other ways too. It fuelled a more individualistic culture of self-expression, as it had in the West: opinion surveys in Poland showed that the principle of self-sacrifice for the collective became less important for ordinary people between 1966 and 1977 (though that of equality became more so).[38] Also, in contrast to capitalist societies, where inequalities are often seen as the consequence of a 'natural' market, distribution was a highly politicized issue, and competition over consumer goods in short supply only drew attention to allocations that many believed were unjust. In many states, officials used their power to secure privileged access to goods, inevitably undermining the prestige of the regime among ordinary citizens. Poland was a particularly egregious example of this. But other groups were also seen as benefiting from unearned privileges – the increasing numbers of semi-legal black-marketeers, and those with access to hard currency (such as those GDR citizens with relatives in the West). The educated also resented workers who benefited from egalitarian wage policies and sometimes had better access to consumer goods through their workplaces.

The convergence of 'Social Democratic' consumerism and economic egalitarianism therefore both strengthened and undermined state socialist systems, but the balance sheet was probably more negative when it came to the younger and more educated. Most, of course, were not politically active and were deterred from speaking out by threats of repression. However, as in the West, many educated members of the generations that grew up after the war were more individualistic and hostile to state paternalism than their parents. But this 'sixties' generation was much more influential in some areas than in others – most notably in the former Austro-Hungarian areas of Eastern and Central Europe.[39] It was these people who created what Padraic Kenney has called the 'carnivalesque' culture of 1989.[40] And while the small group who actually drove political change in the late 1980s – the communist reformers around Mikhail Gorbachev – were more impressed by the success of Western social democracy and consumerism, as will be shown, their Romantic politics, both Marxist and, increasingly, liberal, gave them a very un-Social Democratic radical, even revolutionary, hostility to technocratic authority.

The Struggle over Development

If in the global 'North' – East and West – both laissez-faire capitalism and state socialism adapted to each other and to the environment and converged on a Social Democratic consumerism, in the global 'South' the confrontation between the two systems was much sharper because scepticism of the market was greater. In these largely agrarian societies, many of them shaking off the bonds of European empire, inter-war laissez-faire was perceived not only as a failure but as a tool of empire. Businessmen were often seen by nationalists as a 'comprador' elite that had collaborated with the imperial power and had little interest in developing the country as a whole. Nationalists were even more negative towards foreign and multinational companies; they were convinced that collective effort and states were much more able than 'chaotic' and 'selfish' markets to achieve the huge tasks of development their countries required.

Compounding this was the failure of the dominant United States to moderate the market as effectively in the South as it did in the North by incorporating these countries fully into the Bretton Woods system. The United States did throw its weight behind statist development programmes, usually to help Cold War allies like South Korea.[41] But there was no general Marshall Aid-style program for the Third World, nor, despite Keynes's appeals, was there any attempt to deal with the problem of low commodity prices which had plagued the developing world between the wars. After a brief period of high commodity prices after World War II, prices for most goods (except for oil) drifted downwards from the 1950s as technology improved production. The advantages of involvement in international trade were therefore not decisive.

In this environment, the Soviet Union had a considerable advantage over the United States in the war of ideas. As Odd Arne Westad has argued in *The Global Cold War*, the Cold War in the developing world was as much an ideological struggle between rival visions of development as a military confrontation, and the Soviet model seemed to have more relevance than did its American rival: Stalin had industrialized his country, dragged it out of agrarian backwardness and secured its independence from imperialist rivals.[42] Soviet advocacy of land redistribution also seemed to meet demands for social justice. The United States did seek to provide an attractive alternative developmental model – that of 'modernization' – which promoted a 'middle-class revolution', as Kennedy's adviser Arthur Schlesinger put it.[43] However, given the low esteem in which trader and business classes were held, the negative terms of trade for commodity producers and the increasing association between Washington's 'modernization' projects and its efforts to support authoritarian Cold War allies (most notoriously in South Vietnam) understandably discredited American strategies among many nationalists.[44]

High tariffs, nationalization and import-substituting industrialization became much more fashionable and most of the first generation of nationalist, post-colonial rulers adopted some form of socialism. But, as hopes of rapid development were disappointed, a more orthodox Marxism-Leninism became more fashionable among Third World nationalists from the late 1960s. In the course of the 1970s several Soviet-backed Marxist-Leninist regimes, such as Ethiopia and Mozambique, embarked on full-scale Soviet-style campaigns of industrialization.[45]

Yet, even many non-Marxist-Leninist regimes – from India to Mexico, and Syria to South Korea, pursued strategies of national development in which the state played a major role. And this made sense during the Bretton Woods era: international finance was weak, there was little international capital available for investment and at the same time there were few external constraints on states pursuing economic policies that were not oriented towards the market.

Soviet-style command systems suffered from particular problems of over-centralization, which was difficult for the new state apparatuses to manage. But these post-war statist economies, both capitalist and command, had similar flaws. The absence of competition allowed the new industries to become inefficient and dependent on subsidies, and the heavy involvement of the state ensured that political priorities often trumped economic ones. It was where these state capitalisms were subject to international competition, as in the 'Asian tiger' exporting economies of East Asia, that they were most successful. It is therefore no surprise that by the 1970s, many from both left and right were criticizing this model and the old nationalist forces who had established it – whether the Institutional Revolutionary Party in Mexico, or the Congress Party in India.[46]

The Rise of Neoliberalism and Global Finance

By the late 1960s, weaknesses in state socialist systems in the communist world, state capitalist systems in the developing world and Social Democratic systems in the West were becoming evident, and they all had their critics on the left and the right. But that did not make their demise inevitable. Rather, it was changes in the international environment, and the response of political and intellectual elites to those changes, which brought about the rise of their great rival – global finance – and the free-market ideology which justified its pre-eminence – neoliberalism.

Central to those changes were the increasing difficulties that the United States had in meeting the challenge of communism and nationalism in the global South in the 1960s, and the resulting demise of the Bretton Woods system in 1971. In Vietnam, Washington found itself having to finance an expensive war at a time when its economy was losing competitiveness to its allies, especially Germany and Japan. It therefore unilaterally devalued the dollar, and in doing so destroyed the currency system that had underpinned governmental power over the international economy.[47]

The result was a decade of economic turmoil. The devaluation of the dollar caused worldwide inflation – reinforced by the oil price hikes of 1973 and 1979 – and this exacerbated the conflicts between workers and employers brought by full employment and 1960s radicalism. Increasing inflation led workers to demand higher wages to compensate, while capitalists refused to invest as profitability fell.[48] And all this was happening at a time of fundamental technological transition, when old, heavy industries were suffering from overcapacity and the future lay in new, high-tech industries. Western governments tried to keep the welfarist, high-employment, Social Democratic order going with regular Keynesian infusions of state spending, but this just intensified inflation and, with it, industrial conflict. Countries with high degrees of social solidarity, such as West Germany and Sweden, were able to survive the storm and maintain high levels of state involvement in the economy. But where tensions were greater — and especially in the United States — economic crisis fuelled a powerful pro-market backlash.[49] The free-market ideas of the 1920s, promoted by 'neoliberal' economists like Milton Friedman, were back in fashion and it became increasingly fashionable to demand fundamental reductions in state spending and trade union power as the only way to defeat inflation and create economic stability.[50]

The end of the Bretton Woods era also permitted the eclipse of government control in the international arena, and the beneficiaries were the international banks which had been disgraced in the 1930s. This process had begun in the late 1950s as the United States and Britain informally relaxed controls on capital movements, but the 1970s saw a significant increase in the international banks' power, further encouraged by the United States.[51] Flush with recycled oil wealth, they now had cash to lend, which benefited poorer, developing countries, who could tap a source of capital other than the US-controlled IMF or World Bank. But this was a Faustian pact, for the money had to be paid back and it was often not being borrowed for revenue-generating purposes. In the 1970s, communist states, especially in oil-poor Eastern Europe, borrowed heavily from Western banks, in part to fund consumer socialism, in part to invest in heavy industries whose profitability was declining at a time when markets for their products were saturated; import-substituting industrializers did the same.

The 1970s, then, saw a conflict between the old, state-dominated order — both domestically and internationally — and international and domestic financial interests, a conflict which the latter were increasingly winning. But the decisive moment came in October 1979, when Paul Volcker, the free-market liberal head of the American central bank, the Federal Reserve, decided to hike interest rates to very high levels to attract international capital back to the crisis-ridden dollar and to restore business profits. This was the beginning of a fundamental change in American strategy. American governments began to depend on borrowing from international capital markets and pursued economic policies such as a strong currency and low inflation, which benefited them, often at domestic industry's expense. Reagan's 'second Cold War' military build-up was effectively financed by Japanese loans, and for the next three decades American defence and consumption would rely on international borrowing, initially from Japan and later from China.

Volcker's alliance with the international financial markets not only helped the American military, but also dealt a severe blow to its enemies. As capital flowed into the high interest-rate United States, it fled the indebted parts of the communist and Third Worlds, causing major economic crises. A $46.8 billion outflow from the rich G-7 countries became a $347.4 billion inflow.[52] Most East European countries had to impose severe austerity at home, breaking socialist consumerist promises of higher living standards. Romania defaulted on its debt in 1981 and banned the use of refrigerators and vacuum cleaners to save energy. The crisis brought political collapse in Poland as government limits on the distribution of meat brought strikes and the rise of the Solidarity movement, which threatened to topple the regime in 1980–81. And this crisis in Eastern Europe put huge pressure on the oil-producing USSR, which by the mid-1980s was no longer in a position to bail out its satellites, now that oil prices had fallen from their 1970s highs.

Volcker's high interest-rate policies and the ensuing debt crises empowered international finance, with its preference for low state spending and market reforms, and this was reinforced by the IMF and World Bank, which abandoned their old Keynesianism for the free-market so-called 'Washington Consensus'. Loans for debtor nations were tied to radical market reforms and forced many communist and left-leaning nationalist regimes to abandon their old statist policies, from Latin America to communist Mozambique, which accepted IMF prescriptions in exchange for loans in 1987. Though there was one region where neoliberalism had less purchase – in East Asia, where statist capitalist economies, like Japan's and those of the 'Asian tigers', were more resilient and consensual.

These new conditions accelerated the transformation of economic thinking throughout much of the world. Development economists and governments were already becoming sceptical about the efficacy of large-scale, state-led industrialization projects.[53] State management of the economy – whether Keynesian efforts to maintain high demand or statist efforts to direct production, were in crisis and neoliberal ideas seemed to offer a viable alternative. And at the same time, there were neoliberal intellectual elites waiting in the wings in many countries (in the case of Latin America, often trained in the United States) who were eager to displace what they saw as a failed older generation.[54]

Consumerism, Neoliberalism and the End of the Cold War

The rise of neoliberalism may have made the world a less comfortable place for long-established communist regimes, like China's and the USSR's, but it had less impact on the thinking of communists in the early–mid 1980s.[55] More influential among communist elites was the appeal of mixed state–market economies – whether 'Social Democratic' or capitalist developmental in nature.

In China, the post-Mao leadership sought an alternative to the strongly anti-market mobilizational economy of the Cultural Revolution era by emulating the statist developmentalism of its 'Asian tiger' neighbours. Deng Xiaoping inaugurated a gradual, state-led transition to the market, insisting that the state should retain a role in the industrial 'commanding heights' of the economy. It was only in the 1990s that marketization was accelerated. However, even though China resisted neoliberalism at home, it benefited from global neoliberalism and the investment and trade that it promoted. Between 1972 and 1990, American investment in China rose from nothing to $2 billion, while in the same period US–China trade rose nearly twenty times, from $100 million to $20 billion.[56] And from 1983, the United States ran a trade deficit with China – one that became increasingly substantial.[57] Washington's desire to divide the communist world and outflank the USSR gave it a strong interest in tolerating the imbalance. Meanwhile, China's increasing dependence on foreign trade gave it ever stronger incentives not to rejoin the Cold War against the United States.

Soviet elites also sought to establish a mixed economy, though they looked west, emulating their West European Social Democratic neighbours, not east and south, as China did. Yet, Gorbachev and his group were not straightforward social democrats: central to their worldview was a Romantic Marxism which, paradoxically, allowed them to forge a temporary alliance with neoliberal currents against communist technocrats. And we need to understand this complex relationship between social democracy, communist statism, Romantic Marxism and neoliberalism – in addition, of course, to the political tactics pursued by Gorbachev and his opponents – if we are to explain the end of the Cold War and the collapse of the command economy.

One of the main reasons for the end of the Cold War was the Gorbachev group's determination that it should end. In part, economics and consumerist pressure drove that conviction: the East European debt crisis and the rapid fall in the oil price after 1985 made it clear to the leadership that less had to be spent on the military if the system was to compete with the West on consumption and living standards. But, arguably, more important was the hostility to Stalinist militarism, rooted in the Romantic Marxism so popular among the educated of Gorbachev's 'sixties' (*shestidesiatnik*) generation.

Gorbachev's Romantic Marxism was also a central element in his (distinctly uninformed) economic thinking. Early in his General Secretaryship, he was convinced that the main problem with the Soviet economy lay in the absence of proper labour incentives, and a significant part of the solution consisted in strengthening 'moral' incentives – that is, improving people's commitment to their work by encouraging more democratic participation. As he put it, the 'human factor' in the economy needed to be activated, and one of the main obstacles was 'bureaucratic styles of leadership' by officials, which suppressed these popular energies. These ideas were made more concrete in the 1987 Law on the State Enterprise, which introduced the election of enterprise directors.

However, none of these reforms dealt with the root of the Soviet economy's difficulties: the almost complete dominance of planners and plan targets, and the extreme marginalization of market mechanisms. Gorbachev, like much of the leadership, accepted that market reforms were essential if consumers were to be satisfied and the economy was to become more efficient in its use of resources. Yet the problem was how to make the transition from a system in which plan targets ruled to one in which markets and prices regulated the economy, in a way that, firstly, did not destroy a whole swathe of industry that would be unprofitable in free market conditions, and secondly, preserved the living standards of a population that was accustomed to a great deal of economic security. One group surrounding Nikolai Ryzhkov, a former planning official, advocated a Chinese-style solution – a gradual transition to markets, under the auspices of a powerful state which retained control of (and subsidized) much of industry and involved staged price rises to bring them to market levels.[58] Another group – the radical economists – were strongly anti-communist, were increasingly aware of and enthusiastic about neoliberal Western economics, and had considerable support from Western commentators. Determined that the communist state should be destroyed, and strongly opposed to any transitional measures that might justify the continuation of its power, they found in neoliberalism an ideology that reinforced their conviction that the state was unnecessary and gave them a new status as part of a global community of economists. The market, they argued, had to be introduced rapidly, through a form of 'shock therapy'; any 'third way' between state and market would only allow communists to thwart any market reform.[59]

Gorbachev was never a neoliberal, and as he learnt more about other countries as leader, he increasingly became attracted to the Social Democratic model of welfare, regulated markets and consumerism.[60] However, his Romantic Marxism and 'sixties' values gave him a very un-Social Democratic sympathy with the neoliberals' dislike of technocrats and state bureaucracies – a hostility that became greater as he sought to blame officials for the failures of his economic policies. There was also a more cynical reason for his alignment with neoliberal economists. Ryzhkov and the gradualists were calling for state-managed price rises as a way of making prices effective economic signals – crucial to a market economy – without too much social disruption. But Gorbachev, sensitive to the unpopularity of any price increases, repeatedly delayed them and used the neoliberals' opposition to state-managed, gradual reforms as cover.[61]

Gorbachev therefore refused to decide between the gradualists and the radicals; and at the end of 1989 he even appointed the radicals' leader, Nikolai Petrakov ('a kind of Russian Milton Friedman', according to one American specialist[62]), as a personal adviser while Ryzhkov, as Prime Minister, was formulating his economic reform plan.[63] Gorbachev also delayed the price reforms that would bring in serious market discipline, while simultaneously undermining the state structures that had traditionally imposed order on the economy – for instance, devolving power from the planners to enterprise managers, as demanded by the radical economists.[64] The result was the complete collapse of discipline in the economy, resulting in food shortages, high inflation and the 'stealing of the state' by managers, officials and 'entrepreneurs', as Steve Solnick has put it.[65]

However, Gorbachev refused to accept that there were structural reasons for the failure of his policies; rather, he blamed it on 'conservative bureaucrats' in the Communist Party and his solution was to put pressure on them by subjecting all Party bosses to popular elections. It was no surprise that the vast majority did badly, given the increasing economic disruption, together with the critique of abuses and past communist violence under Gorbachev's pursuit of 'openness' (*glasnost*). Having undermined power structures in the economic sphere, he did the same in the political sphere, and the result was ultimately the collapse of the Soviet state in 1991.

Conclusion

The Cold War, then, was not a simple conflict between the plan and markets, which markets won because they were more efficient and responsive to consumers, as the Fukuyaman story goes. To appreciate the real role of this struggle between economic systems during the Cold War, we need to understand both the changing economic environment, on the one hand, and the often unpredictable ways in which political leaderships and populations responded to it, on the other.

The economic environment was clearly of enormous importance. From an economic perspective, communism can be seen as a system that had much in common with Keynesian systems in the developed world and statist economic systems in the global 'South'. Like them, it emerged in response to the crises of the 1930s and World War II. And when that system in turn crumbled in the 1970s and a version of the free-market systems of the pre-World War I era and the 1920s became dominant internationally, it collapsed, along with many of its socialist and Social Democratic rivals.

However, the story is more complicated than one of a simple collapse in the face of inexorable economic change. For in many ways it was the appeal of Western social democracy to Gorbachev that propelled the collapse of communism. And European social democracy was, in itself, partly a response to the perceived successes of communists after World War II.

Some economic systems are undoubtedly more sustainable than others, in that they are more able to produce wealth; but they emerge and survive as a consequence of a whole range of other forces, including intellectual fashions, perceptions of the past and leaders' decisions. State socialism and consumerist capitalism were no exception.

Notes

1 Francis Fukuyama, *The End of History and the Last Man* (London: Penguin, 1992).
2 For a debate between those who stress the American build-up and those who emphasize internal political change, see Robert Patman, 'Some Reflections on Archie Brown and the End of the Cold War', *Cold War History* 7 (3), August 2007, 439–445.
3 Martin Malia, *The Soviet Tragedy: A History of Socialism in Russia* (New York: Free Press, 1990), 503.
4 Though this is not to argue for some form of political 'convergence', as some did in the 1970s and 1980s.
5 For an accessible account of Marxist-Leninist attitudes to the market, see Mark Sandle, *A Short History of Soviet Socialism* (London: UCL Press, 1999).
6 For the influence of global economic change on Stalin's 'Great Break' of 1928–31, see Oscar Sanchez-Sibony, 'Red Globalization: The Political Economy of Soviet Foreign Relations in the 1950s and 1960s' (PhD Dissertation, University of Chicago, 2009), ch. 1.
7 On Stalinist consumerism, see Vera Dunham, *In Stalin's Time. Middle-Class Values in Soviet Fiction* (Cambridge: Cambridge University Press, 1976); J. Grunow, *Caviar with Champagne. Common Luxury and the Ideals of the Good Life in Stalin's Russia* (Oxford: Berg, 2003).
8 J. Stalin, 'Speech at a Meeting of the Stalin Electoral District, February 9, 1946', in *J. Stalin. Speeches Delivered at Meetings of Voters of the Stalin Electoral District* (Moscow: Foreign Languages Publishing House, 1950), 40–41.
9 Mark Pittaway, *Eastern Europe, 1939–2000* (London: Arnold, 2004), ch. 2.

10 Quoted in Erik Van Ree, 'Heroes and Merchants. Stalin's Understanding of National Character', *Kritika: Explorations in Russian and Eurasian History* 8 (2007), 58–59.
11 For the relative power of white and blue collar in these systems, see David Priestland, *The Red Flag: Communism and the Making of the Modern World* (London: Penguin Press, 2010), ch. 7.
12 See Gary Cross, *An All-Consuming Century: Why Commercialism Won in Modern America* (New York: Columbia University Press, 2000).
13 For the influence of Keynes, see Peter Hall (ed.), *The Political Power of Economic Ideas: Keynesianism across Nations* (Oxford: Oxford University Press, 1989).
14 Michael Hogan, *The Marshall Plan: America, Britain and the Reconstruction of Western Europe* (Cambridge: Cambridge University press, 1987).
15 For this regime, see Jeffry A. Frieden, *Global Capitalism: Its Fall and Rise in the Twentieth Century* (New York: W.W. Norton, 2006), ch. 12.
16 Victoria de Grazia, *Irresistible Empire: America's Advance through Twentieth-Century Europe* (Cambridge, MA: Harvard University Press, 2005), 342–343.
17 Reinhold Wagnleitner, *Coca-Colonization and the Cold War: The Cultural Mission of the United States in Austria after the Second World War*, translated by Diana T. Wolf (Chapel Hill, NC: University of North Carolina Press, 1994), 75–76.
18 De Grazia, *Irresistible Empire*, 354–355.
19 Kenneth Osgood, *Total Cold War: Eisenhower's Secret Propaganda Battle at Home and Abroad* (Lawrence, KS: University of Kansas Press, 2006).
20 Greg Castillo, 'The American "Fat Kitchen" in Europe: Postwar Domestic Modernity and Marshall Plan Strategies of Enchantment', in Ruth Oldenziel and Karin Zachmann (eds), *Cold War Kitchen: Americanization, Technology and European Users* (Cambridge, MA: MIT Press, 2009), 33–58
21 Walter L. Hixson, *Parting the Curtain. Propaganda, Culture and the Cold War* (New York: St. Martin's Griffin, 1998), 138–139.
22 De Grazia, *Irresistible Empire*, 354–355.
23 Stephen Gundle, *Between Hollywood and Moscow. The Italian Communists and the Challenge of Mass Culture, 1943–1991* (Durham, NC: Duke University Press, 2000).
24 Raymond Aron, *The Opium of the Intellectuals*, cited in Victoria de Grazia, *Irresistible Empire*, p. 373.
25 Yoram Gorlizki and Oleg Khlevniuk, *Cold Peace: Stalin and the Soviet Ruling Circle* (Oxford: Oxford University Press, 2004).
26 For these conflicts, see Philip Roeder, *Red Sunset: The Failure of Soviet Politics* (Princeton, NJ: Princeton University Press, 1993).
27 Paulina Bren and Mary Neuberger, *Communism Unwrapped: Consumption in Cold War Eastern Europe* (Oxford: Oxford University Press, 2012), 10.
28 J. Kopstein, *The Politics of Economic Decline in East Germany, 1945–1989* (Chapel Hill, NC: University of North Carolina Press, 1997), 41.
29 Cited in P. Betts, *Within Walls: Private Life in the German Democratic Republic* (Oxford: Oxford University Press, 2010), 134. See also Bren and Neuberger, *Communism Unwrapped*, 9.
30 See David Crowley, 'Warsaw's Shops, Stalinism and the Thaw', in Susan Reid and David Crowley (eds), *Style and Socialism: Modernity and Material Culture in Post-War Eastern Europe* (Oxford: Berg, 2009), pp. 25–47.
31 Pittaway, *Eastern Europe*, 73.
32 For an account of this era, see Priestland, *The Red Flag*, 430–450.
33 Václav Havel, *The Power of the Powerless* (London: Faber & Faber, 1987), 37–40.
34 R. Tokes, *Murmur and Whispers: Public Opinion and Legitimacy Crisis in Hungary, 1972–1989* (Pittsburgh, PA: Center for Russian and East European Studies, University of Pittsburgh, 1997), 37–39; D. Bahry, 'Society Transformed? Rethinking the Social Roots of Perestroika', *Slavic Review* 52 (1993), 516–517.
35 See, for instance, Alexei Yurchak, *Everything Was For Ever, Until It Was No More* (Princeton, NJ: Princeton University Press, 2006), 234.
36 J. Zatlin, 'The Vehicle of Desire: The Trabant, the Wartburg, and the End of the GDR', *German History* 15, 3 (1997), 358.
37 Betts, *Within Walls*, 135.
38 D. Mason, *Public Opinion and Political Change in Poland* (Cambridge: Cambridge University Press, 1985), p. 63.
39 For 'sixties' style revolutions in these regions, see Padraig Kenney, *Carnival of Revolution: Central Europe 1989* (Princeton, NJ: Princeton University Press, 2002).

40 Kenney, *Carnival of Revolution*.
41 See especially D. Ekbladh, *The Great American Mission: Modernization and the Construction of an American World Order* (Princeton, NJ: Princeton University Press, 2010).
42 Odd Arne Westad, *The Global Cold War: Third World Interventions and the Making of Our Times* (Cambridge: Cambridge University Press, 2005), chs 1–2.
43 Quoted in Westad, *The Global Cold War*, 35. For American modernization ideologies and strategies, see N. Gilman, *Mandarins of the Future: Modernization Theory in Cold War America* (Baltimore, MD: Johns Hopkins University Press, 2003); Ekbladh, *The Great American Mission*; Nicholas Cullather, *The Hungry World: America's Cold War Battle against Poverty in Asia* (Cambridge, MA: Harvard University Press, 2010); Michael E. Latham, *The Right Kind of Revolution. Modernization, Development, and U.S. Foreign Policy from the Cold War to the Present* (Ithaca, NY: Cornell University Press, 2011).
44 Ekbladh, *The Great American Mission*, ch. 6.
45 C. Clapham, *Change and Continuity in Revolutionary Ethiopia* (Cambridge: Cambridge University Press, 1988); M.A. Pitcher, *Transforming Mozambique: The Politics of Privatization, 1975–2000* (New York: Cambridge University Press, 2002).
46 For criticisms among Mexican economists, see Sarah Babb, *Managing Mexico: Economists from Nationalism to Neoliberalism* (Princeton: Princeton University Press, 2001), ch. 5.
47 For an accessible account, see Frieden, *Global Capitalism*, ch. 15.
48 See A. Glyn, *Capitalism Unleashed. Finance, Globalization and Welfare* (Oxford: Oxford University Press, 2006), 13–15; B. Eichengreen, *The European Economy since 1945: Coordinated Capitalism and Beyond* (Princeton, NJ: Princeton University Press, 2007), 220.
49 See Eichengreen, *The European Economy since 1945*, 222, 242; Monica Prasad, *The Politics of Free Markets: The Rise of Neoliberal Economic Policies in Britain, France, Germany and the United States* (Chicago, IL: Chicago University Press, 2006).
50 On the origins of neoliberal ideas, see Philip Mirowski and Dieter Plehwe (eds), *The Road from Mount Pelerin: The Making of Neoliberal Thought* (Cambridge, MA: Harvard University Press, 2009). For the role of neoliberal ideas in the changes of the 1970s and 1980s, see Mark Blyth, *Great Transformations: Economic Ideas and Institutional Change in the Twentieth Century* (Cambridge: Cambridge University Press, 2002).
51 For the role of the United States, see L. Panitch and S. Gindin, *The Making of Global Capitalism: The Political Economy of the American Empire* (London: Verso, 2012), chs 6–7.
52 Giovanni Arrighi, 'The World Economy and the Cold War, 1970–1990', in Melvyn P. Leffler and Odd Arne Westad (eds), *The Cambridge History of the Cold War*, vol. 3 (Cambridge: Cambridge University Press, 2010), 16, 22.
53 For this intellectual crisis, see Gilman, *Mandarins of the Future*, ch. 7.
54 For this process in Latin America, see Yves Dezalay and Bryant Garth, *The Internationalization of Palace Wars: Lawyers, Economists, and the Contest to Transform Latin American States* (Chicago, IL: University of Chicago press, 2002), part 3.
55 Though there was some Western influence on non-official thinking in Eastern Europe. See Paul Aligica and Anthony Evans, *The Neoliberal Revolution in Eastern Europe: Economic Ideas and the Transition from Communism* (Cheltenham: Edward Elgar, 2009), ch. 2.
56 See H. Harding, *A Fragile Relationship: The United States and China since 1972* (Washington, DC: The Brookings Institution, 1992), 8–9.
57 Dong Wang, 'China's Trade Relations with the United States in Perspective', *Journal of Current Chinese Affairs* 3 (2010), 179.
58 J. Hough, *Democratization and Revolution in the USSR, 1985–1991* (Washington, DC: The Brookings Institution, 1997), ch. 4
59 For the 'radical economists', see Hough, *Democratization*, 118–22; P. Reddaway and D. Glinski, *The Tragedy of Russia's Reforms. Market Bolshevism against Democracy* (Washington, DC: United States Institute of Peace Press, 2001), 236–41.
60 Archie Brown, 'Did Gorbachev as General Secretary Become a Social Democrat?', *Europe–Asia Studies*, 65 (2013), 198–220.
61 Hough, *Democratization*, 132.
62 *New York Times*, March 25, 1990.
63 Hough, *Democratization*, 352–353.
64 Hough, *Democratization*, 121.
65 S. Solnick, *Stealing the State: Control and Collapse in Soviet Institutions* (Cambridge, MA: Harvard University Press, 1998).

BIBLIOGRAPHY

Adas, Michael. *Dominance by Design: Technological Imperatives and America's Civilizing Mission* (Cambridge, MA: Harvard University Press, 2006).

Allison, Graham and Zelikow, Philip. *Essence of Decision: Explaining the Cuban Missile Crisis, 2nd Edition* (New York: Longman, 1999).

Alperovitz, Gar. *Atomic Diplomacy: Hiroshima and Potsdam: The Use of the Atomic Bomb and the American Confrontation with Soviet Power* (New York: Vintage Books, 1965).

Anderson, Carol. *Eyes Off the Prize: The United Nations and the African American Struggle for Human Rights 1944–1955* (Cambridge: Cambridge University Press, 2003).

Andrew, Christopher. *The Defence of the Realm: The Authorized History of MI5* (London: Allen Lane, 2009).

Andrew, Christopher and Mitrokhin, Vasili. *The Mitrokhin Archive: The KGB in Europe and the West* (London: Allen Lane, 1999).

Arndt, Richard T. *The First Resort of Kings: American Cultural Diplomacy in the Twentieth Century* (Washington, DC: Potomac Books, 2005).

Ashton, Nigel John. *Eisenhower, Macmillan and the Problem of Nasser: Anglo-American Relations and Arab Nationalism, 1955–59* (Basingstoke and New York: Palgrave Macmillan, 1996).

Autio-Sarasmo, Sari and Miklóssy, Katalin, eds. *Reassessing Cold War Europe* (Abingdon and New York: Routledge, 2011).

Barfield, Thomas. *Afghanistan: A Cultural and Political History* (Princeton, NJ: Princeton University Press, 2010).

Barnett, Michael. *Empire of Humanity: A History of Humanitarianism* (Ithaca, NY: Cornell University Press, 2011).

Barrass, Gordon S. *The Great Cold War: A Journey through the Hall of Mirrors* (Stanford, CA: Stanford University Press, 2009).

Beinin, Joel and Lockman, Zachary. *Workers on the Nile: Nationalism, Communism, Islam, and the Egyptian Working Class, 1882–1954* (Princeton, NJ: Princeton University Press, 1987).

Belmonte, Laura A. *Selling the American Way: U.S. Propaganda and the Cold War* (Philadelphia, PA: University of Pennsylvania Press, 2010).

Bird, Kai and Sherwin, Martin J. *American Prometheus: The Triumph and Tragedy of J. Robert Oppenheimer* (New York: Alfred A. Knopf, 2005).

Borgwardt, Elizabeth. *A New Deal for the World: America's Vision for Human Rights* (Cambridge, MA: Harvard University Press, 2005).

Borstelmann, Thomas. *The Cold War and the Color Line: American Race Relations in the Global Arena* (Cambridge, MA: Harvard University Press, 2001).

Borstelmann, Thomas. *The 1970s: A New Global History from Civil Rights to Economic Inequality* (Princeton, NJ: Princeton University Press, 2012).

Bozo, Frédéric, Rey, Marie-Pierre, Ludlow, N. Piers and Nuti, Lopoldo, eds. *Europe and the End of the Cold War: A Reappraisal* (London: Routledge, 2008).

Bradley, Mark Philip. *Imagining Vietnam and America: The Making of Postcolonial Vietnam, 1919–1950* (Chapel Hill, NC: University of North Carolina Press, 2000).
Braithwaite, Rodric. *Afgantsy: The Russians in Afghanistan* (London: Profile Books, 2011).
Brands, H.W. *The Specter of Neutralism: The United States and the Emergence of the Third World, 1947–1960* (New York: Columbia University Press, 1989).
Brands, Hal. *Latin America's Cold War* (Cambridge, MA: Harvard University Press, 2010).
Brazinsky, Gregg. *Nation Building in South Korea: Koreans, Americans, and the Making of a Democracy* (Chapel Hill, NC: University of North Carolina Press, 2007).
Brown, Archie. *The Gorbachev Factor* (Oxford: Oxford University Press, 1996).
Brown, Archie. *Seven Years that Changed the World: Perestroika in Perspective* (New York: Oxford University Press, 2007).
Brown, Archie. *The Rise and Fall of Communism* (New York: HarperCollins, 2009).
Brown, Kate. *Plutopia: Nuclear Families, Atomic Cities, and the Great Soviet and American Plutonium Disasters* (New York: Oxford University Press, 2013).
Bundy, William P. *A Tangled Web: The Making of Foreign Policy in the Nixon Presidency* (New York: Hill & Wang, 1998).
Burke, Roland. *Decolonization and the Evolution of International Human Rights* (Philadelphia, PA: University of Pennsylvania Press, 2010).
Byrne, Jeffrey James. *Mecca of Revolution: Algeria, Decolonization, and the Global Third World Project* (Oxford: Oxford University Press, 2014).
Castillo, Greg. *Cold War on the Home Front: The Soft Power of Midcentury Design* (Minneapolis, MN: University of Minnesota Press, 2010).
Chamberlin, Paul Thomas. *The Global Offensive: The United States, the Palestine Liberation Organization, and the Making of the Post-Cold War Order* (New York: Oxford University Press, 2012).
Chapman, James. *Licence to Thrill. A Cultural History of the James Bond Films*, new revised edition (London and New York: I.B. Tauris, 2007).
Chapman, Jessica M. *The Mirage of Nation Building: Diem, the U.S., and the Struggle for Power in Southern Vietnam* (Ithaca, NY: Cornell University Press, 2013).
Citino, Nathan J. *From Arab Nationalism to OPEC: Eisenhower, King Sa'ud, and the Making of U.S.-Saudi Relations* (Bloomington, IN: Indiana University Press, 2nd edition 2010).
Connelly, Matthew. *A Diplomatic Revolution: Algeria's Fight for Independence and the Origins of the Post-Cold War Era* (New York: Oxford University Press, 2003).
Cooper, Frederick, and Stoler, Ann. *Tensions of Empire: Colonial Cultures in a Bourgeois World* (Berkeley, CA: The University of California Press, 1997).
Costigliola, Frank. *Roosevelt's Lost Alliances* (Princeton, NJ: Princeton University Press, 2012).
Coyne, Michael. *Hollywood Goes to Washington: American Politics on Screen* (London: Reaktion Books, 2008).
Craig, Campbell. *Destroying the Village: Eisenhower and Thermonuclear War* (New York: Columbia University Press, 1998).
Craig, Campell, and Radchenko, Sergey. *The Atomic Bomb and the Origins of the Cold War* (New Haven, CT: Yale University Press, 2008).
Cull, Nicholas J. *The Cold War and the United States Information Agency: American Propaganda and Public Diplomacy, 1945–1989* (Cambridge: Cambridge University Press, 2008).
Cullather, Nick. *The Hungry World: America's Cold War Battle against Poverty in Asia* (Cambridge, MA: Harvard University Press, 2010).
Daigle, Craig. *The Limits of Détente: The United States, the Soviet Union and the Arab-Israeli Conflict, 1969–1973* (New Haven, CT: Yale University Press, 2012).
Dallek, Robert. *Nixon and Kissinger: Partners in Power* (New York: HarperCollins, 2007).
Davenport, Lisa E. *Jazz Diplomacy: Promoting America in the Cold War Era* (Jackson, MS: University of Mississippi Press, 2009).
de Grazia, Victoria. *Irresistible Empire: America's Advance Through Twentieth-Century Europe* (Cambridge, MA: Harvard University Press, 2005).
Deighton, Anne. *Britain and the First Cold War* (London: Palgrave Macmillan, 1990).
Del Pero, Mario. *The Eccentric Realist: Henry Kissinger and the Shaping of American Foreign Policy* (Ithaca, NY: Cornell University Press, 2010).
Deryabin, A. S., ed. *Letopis' rossiiskogo kino, 1930–1945* (Moscow: Materik, 2007).
Deryabin, A. S., ed. *Letopis' rossiiskogo kino, 1946–1965* (Moscow: Kanon-Plus, 2010).

Domber, Gregory F. *Empowering Revolution: America, Poland, and the End of the Cold War* (Chapel Hill, NC: University of North Carolina Press, 2014).
Dudziak, Mary. *Cold War Civil Rights: Race and the Image of American Democracy* (Princeton, NJ: Princeton University Press, 2000).
Eisenberg, Carolyn. *Drawing the Line: The American Decision to Divide Germany, 1944–1949* (Cambridge: Cambridge University Press, 1996).
Ekbladh, David. *The Great American Mission: Modernization and the Construction of an American World Order* (Princeton, NJ: Princeton University Press, 2010).
Ellwood, David. *The Shock of America: Europe and the Challenge of the Century* (Oxford: Oxford University Press, 2012).
Engerman, David C. *Know Your Enemy: The Rise and Fall of America's Soviet Experts* (New York: Oxford University Press, 2009).
Engerman, David, Gilman, Nils, Haefele, Mark H., and Latham, Michael E., eds. *Staging Growth: Modernization, Development, and the Global Cold War* (Amherst, MA: University of Massachusetts Press, 2003).
English, Robert D. *Russia and the Idea of the West: Gorbachev, Intellectuals and the End of the Cold War* (New York: Columbia University Press, 2000).
Escobar, Arturo. *Encountering Development: The Making and Unmaking of the Third World* (Princeton, NJ: Princeton University Press, 1995).
Evangelista, Matthew. *Unarmed Forces: The Transnational Movement to End the Cold War* (Ithaca, NY: Cornell University Press, 1999).
Falk, Andrew J. *Upstaging the Cold War. American Dissent and Cultural Diplomacy, 1940–1960* (Amherst and Boston, MA: University of Massachusetts Press, 2010).
Fenemore, Mark. *Sex, Thugs and Rock 'n' Roll: Teenage Rebels in Cold-War East Germany* (New York: Berghahn Books, 2007).
Fischer, Beth A. *The Reagan Reversal: Foreign Policy and the End of the Cold War* (Columbia, MO: University of Missouri Press, 2000).
FitzGerald, Frances. *Way Out There in the Blue: Reagan, Star Wars, and the End of the Cold War* (New York: Simon & Schuster, 2001).
Frieden, Jeffry A. *Global Capitalism: Its Fall and Rise in the Twentieth Century* (New York: W.W. Norton, 2006).
Frost, Jennifer. *Hedda Hopper's Hollywood. Celebrity Gossip and American Conservatism* (New York and London: New York University Press, 2011).
Fursenko, Aleksandr and Naftali, Timothy. *"One Hell of a Gamble": Khrushchev, Castro, and Kennedy, 1958–1964: The Secret History of the Cuban Missile Crisis* (New York: W.W. Norton & Company, 1998).
Fursenko, Aleksandr and Naftali, Timothy. *Khrushchev's Cold War: The Inside Story of an American Adversary* (New York: W.W. Norton & Company, 2006).
Gaddis, John Lewis. *We Now Know: Re-Thinking Cold War History* (Oxford: Oxford University Press, 1997).
Gaddis, John Lewis. *Strategies of Containment: A Critical Appraisal of American National Security Policy during the Cold War*, revised and expanded edition (New York: Oxford University Press, 2005).
Gaddis, John Lewis. *George Kennan: An American Life* (New York: Penguin, 2011).
Gaiduk, Ilya V. *Confronting Vietnam: Soviet Policy Toward the Indochina Conflict, 1954–1963* (Stanford, CA: Stanford University Press, 2003).
Gardner, Lloyd C. *Architects of Illusion: Men and Ideas in American Foreign Policy* (Chicago, IL: Quadrangle Books, 1970).
Garthoff, Raymond L. *Détente and Confrontation: American-Soviet Relations from Nixon to Reagan* (Washington, DC: The Brookings Institution, 1994).
Gati, Charles. *Failed Illusions: Moscow, Washington, Budapest, and the 1956 Hungarian Revolt* (Stanford, CA: Stanford University Press, 2006).
Gavin, Francis J. *Nuclear Statecraft: History and Strategy in America's Atomic Age* (Cornell, NY: Cornell University Press, 2012).
Gilman, Nils. *Mandarins of the Future: Modernization Theory in Cold War America* (Baltimore, MD: Johns Hopkins University Press, 2004).
Giutozzi, Antonio. *War, Politics, and Society in Afghanistan* (London: Hurst & Co., 2000).
Glanz, David M. *The Military Strategy of the Soviet Union. A History* (London: Frank Cass, 2004 (reprint of 1992 edition)).
Gleijeses, Piero. *Shattered Hope: The Guatemalan Revolution and the United States, 1944–1954* (Princeton, NJ: Princeton University Press, 1995).

Gleijeses, Piero. *Conflicting Missions: Havana, Washington, and Africa, 1959–1976* (Chapel Hill, NC: University of North Carolina Press, 2002).

Gleijeses, Piero. *Visions of Freedom: Havana, Washington, Pretoria, and the Struggle for Southern Africa, 1976–1991* (Chapel Hill, NC: University of North Carolina Press, 2013).

Goh, Evylyn. *Constructing the U.S. Rapprochement with China, 1961–1974: From "Red Menace" to "Tacit Ally"* (New York: Cambridge University Press, 2005).

Golan, Galia. *Soviet Policies in the Middle East: From World War II to Gorbachev* (Cambridge: Cambridge University Press, 1990).

Gorlizki, Yoram, and Khlevniuk, Oleg. *Cold Peace: Stalin and the Soviet Ruling Circle* (Oxford: Oxford University Press, 2004).

Gorsuch, Anne. *All This Is Your World: Soviet Tourism at Home and Abroad after Stalin* (New York: Oxford University Press, 2011).

Gough, Roger. *A Good Comrade. János Kádár. Communism and Hungary* (London: I.B. Tauris, 2006).

Grandin, Greg. *Empire's Workshop: Latin America, the United States, and the Rise of the New Imperialism* (New York: Metropolitan Books, 2006).

Gray, William Glenn. *Germany's Cold War: The Global Campaign to Isolate East Germany, 1949–1969* (Chapel Hill, NC: University of North Carolina Press, 2003).

Hahnimaki, Jussi M. *The Flawed Architect: Henry Kissinger and American Foreign Policy* (Oxford: Oxford University Press, 2004).

Hanhimaki, Jussi M. *The Rise and Fall of Détente: American Foreign Policy and the Transformation of the Cold War* (Washington, DC: Potomac Books, 2012).

Harmer, Tanya. *Allende's Chile and the Inter-American Cold War* (Chapel Hill, NC: University of North Carolina Press, 2011).

Harrison, Hope M. *Driving the Soviets up the Wall: Soviet–East German Relations, 1953–1961* (Princeton, NJ: Princeton University Press, 2003).

Hartman, Andrew. *Education and the Cold War: The Battle for the American School* (New York and London: Palgrave Macmillan, 2008).

Hasegawa, Tsuyoshi. *Racing the Enemy: Stalin, Truman, and the Surrender of Japan* (Cambridge, MA: Harvard University Press, 2005).

Haslam, Jonathan. *Russia's Cold War: From the October Revolution to the Fall of the Wall* (New Haven, CT: Yale University Press, 2011).

Haynes, John Earl, Klehr, Harvey, and Vassiliev, Alexander. *Spies: The Rise and Fall of the KGB in America* (New Haven, CT and London: Yale University Press, 2009).

Hershberg, James G. *Marigold: The Lost Chance for Peace in Vietnam* (Palo Alto, CA: Stanford University Press, 2012).

Hess, Gary R. *Vietnam: Explaining America's Lost War* (Malden, MA: Blackwell Publishing, 2009).

Hixson, Walter L. *Parting the Curtain: Propaganda, Culture, and the Cold War, 1945–1961* (New York: Palgrave Macmillan, 1997).

Hogan, Michael J. *The Marshall Plan. America, Britain and the Reconstruction of Western Europe* (Cambridge: Cambridge University Press, 1987).

Hogan, Michael J. *A Cross of Iron: Harry S. Truman and the Origins of the National Security State, 1945–1954* (Cambridge: Cambridge University Press, 1998).

Holloway, David. *Stalin and the Bomb: The Soviet Union and Atomic Energy, 1939–1956* (New Haven, CT and London: Yale University Press, 1994).

Hopf, Ted. *Reconstructing the Cold War: The Early Years, 1945–1958* (New York: Oxford University Press, 2012).

Iriye, Akira. *Global Community: The Role of International Organizations in the Making of the Contemporary World* (Berkeley, CA: University of California Press, 2002).

Iriye, Akira, Goedde, Petra and Hitchcock, William I., eds. *The Human Rights Revolution: An International History* (New York: Oxford University Press, 2012).

Irwin, Ryan M. *Gordian Knot: Apartheid and the Unmaking of the Liberal World Order* (Oxford: Oxford University Press, 2012).

Jian, Chen. *China's Road to the Korean War* (New York: Columbia University Press, 1999).

Jian, Chen. *Mao's China and the Cold War* (Chapel Hill, NC: University of North Carolina Press, 2001).

Judt, Tony. *Postwar: A History of Europe since 1945* (New York: Penguin, 2005).

Kaiser, David. *American Tragedy: Kennedy, Johnson, and the Origins of the Vietnam War* (Cambridge, MA: The Belknap Press of Harvard University Press, 2000).

Kalb, Madelaine. *The Congo Cables: The Cold War in Africa from Eisenhower to Kennedy* (New York: Macmillan, 1982).

Kalinovsky, Artemy M. *A Long Goodbye: The Soviet Withdrawal from Afghanistan* (Cambridge, MA: Harvard University Press, 2011).

Kalinovsky, Artemy M. and Radchenko, Sergey, eds. *The End of the Cold War and the Third World: New Perspectives on Regional Conflict* (London: Routledge, 2011).

Kempe, Frederick. *Berlin 1961: Kennedy, Khrushchev and the Most Dangerous Place on Earth* (New York: Putnam, 2011).

Kent, P.C. *The Lonely Cold War of Pope Pius XII: The Roman Catholic Church and the Division of Europe, 1943–1950* (Montréal: McGill-Queen's University Press, 2002).

Khalidi, Rashid. *Sowing Crisis* (Boston, MA: Beacon Press, 2010).

Kotkin, Stephen. *Magnetic Mountain: Stalinism as Civilization* (Berkeley, CA: The University of California Press, 1995).

Kotkin, Stephen, with a contribution by Jan T. Gross. *Uncivil Society: 1989 and the Implosion of the Communist Establishment* (New York: Modern Library, 2009).

Kozovoi, Andrei. *Par-delà le Mur: La culture de Guerre froide soviétique entre deux détentes* [*Beyond the Wall: The Soviet Cold War Culture between Two Détentes*] (Paris: Complexe, 2009).

Kux, Dennis. *India and the United States: Estranged Democracies, 1941–1991* (Washington, DC: National Defense University Press, 1992).

Kux, Dennis. *The United States and Pakistan, 1947–2000: Disenchanted Allies* (Washington, DC: Woodrow Wilson Center Press, 2001).

Kuzmarov, Jeremy. *Modernizing Repression: Police Training and Nation-Building in the American Century* (Amherst, MA: University of Massachusetts Press, 2012).

Kwon, Heonik. *The Other Cold War* (New York, Columbia University Press, 2010).

Kyle, Keith. *Suez* (London: I.B. Taurus, 2003).

Laron, Guy. *Origins of the Suez Crisis: Postwar Development Diplomacy and the Struggle over Third World Industrialization, 1945–1956* (Baltimore, MD: Johns Hopkins University Press, 2013).

Latham, Michael E. *Modernization as Ideology: American Social Science and "Nation Building" in the Kennedy Era* (Chapel Hill, NC: University of North Carolina Press, 2000).

Latham, Michael E. *The Right Kind of Revolution: Modernization, Development, and U.S. Foreign Policy from the Cold War to the Present* (Ithaca, NY: Cornell University Press, 2011).

Lawrence, Mark Atwood. *Assuming the Burden: Europe and the American Commitment to War in Vietnam* (Berkeley, CA: The University of California Press, 2005).

Lawrence, Mark Atwood and Logevall, Fredrik, eds. *The First Vietnam War: Colonial Conflict and Cold War Crisis* (Cambridge, MA: Harvard University Press, 2007).

Lee, Christopher J., ed. *Making a World after Empire: The Bandung Moment and its Political Afterlives* (Athens, OH: Ohio University Press, 2010).

Leffler, Melvin P. *A Preponderance of Power: National Security, the Truman Administration and the Cold War* (Stanford, CA: Stanford University Press, 1992).

Leffler, Melvin P. *For the Soul of Mankind: The United States, the Soviet Union and the Cold War* (New York: Hill & Wang, 2007).

Leslie, Stuart W. *The Cold War and American Science: The Military-Industrial-Academic Complex at MIT and Stanford* (New York: Columbia University Press, 1993).

Levesque, Jacques. *The Enigma of 1989: The USSR and the Liberation of Eastern Europe* (Berkeley, CA: University of California Press, 1997).

Little, Douglas. *American Orientalism: The United States and the Middle East since 1945* (Chapel Hill, NC: University of North Carolina Press, 2002).

Logevall, Fredrik. *Choosing War: The Lost Chance for Peace and the Escalation of War in Vietnam* (Berkeley, CA: The University of California Press, 1999).

Logevall, Fredrik. *Embers of War: The Fall of an Empire and the Making of America's Vietnam* (New York: Random House, 2012).

Logevall, Fredrik and Preston, Andrew, eds. *Nixon in the World: American Foreign Relations, 1969–1977* (New York: Oxford University Press, 2008).

Louis, William Roger. *Suez 1956* (New York: Oxford University Press, 1989).

Lucas, Scott. *Freedom's War: The American Crusade Against the Soviet Union* (New York: New York University Press, 1999).

Lüthi, Lorenz M. *The Sino-Soviet Split: Cold War in the Communist World* (Princeton, NJ: Princeton University Press, 2008).
McAlister, Melani. *Epic Encounters: Culture, Media, and U.S. Interests in the Middle East since 1945* (Berkeley, CA: University of California Press, 2001).
MacFarquhar, Roderick. *The Origins of the Cultural Revolution*, vol. 2 (New York: Columbia University Press, 1983).
Machcewicz, Pawel. *Rebellious Satellite: Poland 1956* (Palo Alto, CA: Stanford University Press, 2009).
McMahon, Robert J. *The Cold War on the Periphery: The United States, India, and Pakistan* (New York: Columbia University Press, 1994).
McMahon, Robert J., ed. *The Cold War in the Third World* (Oxford: Oxford University Press, 2013).
McNeill, J.R. *Something New Under the Sun: an Environmental History of the Twentieth Century World* (New York: Norton, 2000).
McVety, Amanda Kay. *Enlightened Aid: U.S. Development as Foreign Policy in Ethiopia* (New York: Oxford University Press, 2012).
Manela, Erez. *The Wilsonian Moment: Self-Determination and the International Origins of Anticolonial Nationalism* (New York: Oxford University Press, 2009).
Mastny, Vojtech. *The Cold War and Soviet Insecurity: The Stalin Years* (New York: Oxford University Press, 1996).
Matlock, Jack F. *Reagan and Gorbachev: How the Cold War Ended* (New York: Random House, 2004).
Matthews, Melvin E. *Duck and Cover. Civil Defense Images in Film and Television from the Cold War to 9/11* (Jefferson, NC: MacFarland, 2011).
Mayhew, Robert. *Ayn Rand and Song of Russia. Communism and Anti-Communism in 1940s Hollywood.* Lanham, MD: Scarecrow Press, 2005).
Mazov, Sergey. *A Distant Front in the Cold War: The USSR in West Africa and the Congo, 1956–1964* (Stanford, CA: Stanford University Press, 2010).
Mazower, Mark. *No Enchanted Palace: The End of Empire and the Ideological Origins of the United Nations* (Princeton, NJ: Princeton University Press, 2009).
Milward, Alan. *The Reconstruction of Western Europe* (London: Methuen, 1984).
Mirowski, Philip and Plehwe, Dieter, eds. *The Road from Mount Pelerin: The Making of Neoliberal Thought* (Cambridge, MA: Harvard University Press, 2009).
Mitchell, Timothy. *Rule of Experts: Egypt, Techno-Politics, Modernity* (Berkeley, CA: University of California Press, 2002).
Moyn, Samuel. *The Last Utopia: Human Rights in History* (Cambridge, MA: Belknap Press, reprint edition, 2012).
Muehlenbeck, Philip E. *Betting on the Africans: John F. Kennedy's Courting of African Nationalist Leaders* (New York: Oxford University Press, 2012a).
Muehlenbeck, Philip E., ed. *Race, Ethnicity and the Cold War* (Nashville, TN: Vanderbilt University Press, 2012b).
Muehlenbeck, Philip E. *Religion and the Cold War: A Global Perspective* (Nashville, TN: Vanderbilt University Press, 2012c).
Naimark, Norman. *The Russians in Germany: A History of the Soviet Zone of Occupation, 1945–1949* (Cambridge, MA: Belnap Press of Harvard University Press, 1997).
Namikas, Lise. *Battleground Africa: Cold War in the Congo, 1960–1965* (Stanford, CA: Stanford University Press, 2013).
Navasky, Victor S. *Naming Names* (New York: Hill & Wang, 2003 (first published 1980)).
Nelson, Keith. *The Making of Détente: Soviet–American Relations in the Shadow of Vietnam* (Baltimore, MD: Johns Hopkins University Press, 1993).
Nelson, Michael. *War of the Black Heavens: The Battles of Western Broadcasting in the Cold War* (London: Brassey's, 2003).
Ngyuen, Lien-Hang T. *Hanoi's War: An International History of the War for Peace in Vietnam* (Chapel Hill, NC: University of North Carolina Press, 2012).
Njølstad, Olav. *The Last Decade of the Cold War: From Conflict Escalation to Conflict Resolution* (London: Frank Cass, 2004).
Oren, Michael. *Six Days of War* (New York: Oxford University Press, 2002).
Osgood, Kenneth. *Total Cold War: Eisenhower's Secret Propaganda Battle at Home and Abroad* (Lawrence, KS: University Press of Kansas, 2006).

Ouimet, Matthew J. *The Rise and Fall of the Brezhnev Doctrine in Soviet Foreign Policy* (Chapel Hill, NC: University of North Carolina Press, 2001).

Paczkowski, Andrzej, and Byrne, Malcolm, eds. *From Solidarity to Martial Law: The Polish Crisis of 1980–1981. A Documentary History* (Budapest: Central European University Press, 2006).

Patel, K. and Weisbrode, K. *Europe and America in the 1980s: Old Barriers, New Openings* (Cambridge: Cambridge University Press 2013).

Poiger, Uta G. *Jazz, Rock, and Rebels: Cold War Politics and American Culture in a Divided Germany* (Berkeley, CA: University of California Press, 2000).

Prados, John. *Vietnam: The History of an Unwinnable War, 1945–1975* (Lawrence, KS: the University Press of Kansas, 2009).

Prazmowska, Anita J., *Civil War in Poland: 1943–1948* (London: Palgrave Macmillan, 2004).

Preston, Andrew. *Sword of the Spirit, Shield of Faith* (New York: Alfred A. Knopf, 2012).

Priestland, David. *The Red Flag: Communism and the Making of the Modern World* (London: Penguin Press, 2010).

Quétel, Claude, ed. *Dictionnaire de la Guerre froide* (Paris: Larousse, 2008).

Rabe, Stephen G. *The Killing Zone: The United States Wages Cold War in Latin America* (New York: Oxford University Press, 2012).

Radchenko, Sergey. *Two Suns in the Heavens* (Stanford, CA: Stanford University Press, 2008).

Radchenko, Sergey. *Unwanted Visionaries: The Soviet Failure in Asia at the End of the Cold War* (New York: Oxford University Press, 2014).

Radosh, Ronald and Radosh, Allis. *Red Star over Hollywood: The Film Colony's Long Romance with the Left* (San Francisco, CA: Encounter Books, 2005).

Rainer, János M. *Imre Nagy: a biography* (London: I.B. Tauris, 2009).

Rajagopalan, Sudha. *Leave Disco Dancer alone: Indian Cinema and Soviet Movie-Going after Stalin* (New Delhi: Yoda Press, 2008).

Ro'i, Yaacov et al., eds. *The Soviet Union and the June 1967 Six Day War* (Palo Alto, CA: Stanford University Press, 2008).

Robb, David L. *Operation Hollywood: How the Pentagon Shapes and Censors the Movies* (New York: Prometheus Books, 2004).

Roberts, Geoffrey. *Stalin's Wars: From World War to Cold War, 1939–1953* (New Haven, CT: Yale University Press, 2008).

Robinson, Harlow. *Russians in Hollywood, Hollywood's Russians: Biography of an Image* (Lebanon, NH: Northeastern University Press, 2007).

Romano, Angela. *From Détente in Europe to European Détente: How the West Shaped the Helsinki CSCE* (Brussels: Peter Lang, 2009).

Romero, Federico. *Storia della Guerra Fredda: L'ultimo conflitto per l'Europa* [History of the Cold War: The Last Conflict Over Europe] (Torino: Einaudi, 2009).

Roth-Ey, Kristin. *Moscow Prime Time. How the Soviet Union Built the Media Empire That Lost the Cultural Cold War* (Ithaca, NY: Cornell University Press, 2011).

Rotter, Andrew J. *Comrades at Odds: The United States and India, 1947–1964* (Ithaca, NY: Cornell University Press, 2000).

Sarotte, Mary Elise. *Dealing with the Devil: East Germany, Détente, and Ostpolitik, 1969–1973* (Chapel Hill, NC: University of North Carolina Press, 2001).

Sarotte, Mary Elise. *1989: The Struggle to Create Post-Cold War Europe* (Princeton, NJ: Princeton University Press, 2009).

Saul, Norman E. *Concord and Conflict. The United States and Russia, 1867–1914* (Lawrence, KS: University Press of Kansas, 1996).

Sayre, Nora. *Running Time. Films of the Cold War* (New York: Doubleday, 1982).

Sbardellati, John. *J. Edgar Hoover Goes to the Movies: The FBI and the Origins of the Hollywood Cold War* (Ithaca, NY: Cornell University Press, 2012).

Schwartz, Richard A. *Cold War Culture: Media and the Arts, 1945–1990* (New York: Facts on File, 1998).

Schwartz, Thomas Alan. *Lyndon Johnson and Europe: In the Shadow of Vietnam* (Cambridge, MA: Harvard University Press, 2003).

Scott, James C. *Seeing Like a State: How Certain Schemes to Improve the Human Condition Have Failed* (New Haven, CT: Yale University Press, 1998).

Segrave, Kerry. *American Films Abroad. Hollywood's Domination of the World Movie Screens from the 1890s to the Present* (Jefferson, NC: MacFarland, 1997).

Bibliography

Shaw, Tony. *British Cinema and the Cold War. The State, Propaganda and Consensus* (London: I. B. Tauris, 2006).

Shaw, Tony. *Hollywood's Cold War* (Edinburgh: Edinburgh University Press, 2007).

Shaw, Tony and Youngblood, Denise J. *Cinematic Cold War: The American and Soviet Struggle for Hearts and Minds* (Lawrence, KS: University Press of Kansas, 2010).

Sherwin, Martin. *A World Destroyed: Hiroshima and Its Legacies,* 3rd edition (Stanford, CA: Stanford University Press, 2003).

Siddiqi, Asif A. *Sputnik and the Soviet Space Challenge* (Gainesville, FL: University Press of Florida, 2003).

Snyder, Sarah B. *Human Rights Activism and the End of the Cold War: A Transnational History of the Helsinki Network* (New York: Cambridge University Press, 2011).

Sorel, Eliot and Padoan, Pier Carlo, eds. *The Marshall Plan: Lessons Learned for the 21st Century* (Paris: OECD Publishing, 2008).

Staples, Amy L.S. *The Birth of Development: How the World Bank, Food and Agriculture Organization, and World Health Organization Changed the World, 1945–1965* (Kent, OH: Kent State University Press, 2006).

Statler, Kathryn C. *Replacing France: The Origins of American Intervention in Vietnam* (Lexington, KY: University Press of Kentucky, 2007).

Statler, K.C. and Johns, A.L., eds. *The Eisenhower Administration, the Third World, and the Globalization of the Cold War* (Lanham, MD: Rowman & Littlefield, 2006).

Stokes, Melvyn and Maltby, Richard, eds. *Hollywood Abroad: Audiences and Cultural Exchange* (London: BFI publishing, 2004).

Strada, Michael and Troper, Harold. *Friend or Foe? Russians in American Film and Foreign Policy, 1933–1991* (Lanham, MD: Scarecrow Press, 1997).

Strong, Robert A. *Working in the World: Jimmy Carter and the Making of American Foreign Policy* (Baton Rouge, LA: Louisiana State University Press, 2000).

Suri, Jeremi. *Power and Protest: Global Revolution and the Rise of Détente* (Cambridge, MA: Harvard University Press, 2003).

Tareke, Gebru. *The Ethiopian Revolution: War in the Horn of Africa* (New Haven, CT: Yale University Press, 2009).

Taubman, William. *Khrushchev: The Man and His Era* (New York: W.W. Norton & Company, 2004).

Taylor, Frederick. *The Berlin Wall: A World Divided, 1961–1989* (New York: Harper Collins, 2006).

Thomas, Daniel C. *The Helsinki Effect: International Norms, Human Rights, and the Demise of Communism* (Princeton, NJ: Princeton University Press, 2001).

Tomsen, Peter. *The Wars of Afghanistan: Messianic Terrorism, Tribal Conflicts, and the Failures of Great Powers* (Washington, DC: Public Affairs, 2011).

Török, Jean-Paul. *Pour en finir avec le Maccarthysme. Lumières sur la Liste Noire à Hollywood.* [*To End with MacCarthyism. Lights on the Black List in Hollywood*] (Paris: L'Harmattan, 2000).

Trachtenberg, Marc. *A Constructed Peace: The Making of the European Settlement, 1945–1963* (Princeton, NJ: Princeton University Press, 1999).

Tudda, Chris. *The Truth is Our Weapon: The Rhetorical Diplomacy of Dwight D. Eisenhower and John Foster Dulles* (Baton Rouge, LA: Louisiana State University Press, 2006).

Tudda, Chris. *A Cold War Turning Point: Nixon and China, 1969–1972* (Baton Rouge, LA: Louisiana State University Press, 2012).

Von Eschen, Penny. *Satchmo Blows Up the World: Jazz Ambassadors Play the Cold War* (Cambridge, MA: Harvard University Press, 2004).

Westad, Odd Arne. *Brothers in Arms: The Rise and Fall of the Sino-Soviet Alliance 1945–1963* (Washington, D.C.: Woodrow Wilson Center, 1998).

Westad, Odd Arne, *The Global Cold War: Third World Interventions and the Making of Our Times* (New York: Cambridge University Press, 2007).

Westad, Odd Arne. *Restless Empire: China and the World since 1750* (New York: Basic Books, 2012).

Westad, Odd Arne and Judge, Sophie Quinn, eds. *The Third Indochina War: Conflict between China, Vietnam, and Cambodia, 1972–1979* (New York: Routledge, 2006).

Wilentz, Sean. *The Age of Reagan: A History* (New York: HarperCollins, 2008).

Williams, William Appleman. *The Tragedy of American Diplomacy* (New York: World Publishing Company, 1959).

Wilson, James Graham. *The Triumph of Improvisation: Gorbachev's Adaptability, Reagan's Engagement, and the End of the Cold War* (Ithaca, NY: Cornell University Press, 2014).

Wittner, Lawrence S. *The Struggle against the Bomb,* 3 vols (Stanford, CA: Stanford University Press, 1993–2003).

Bibliography

Woodroofe, Louise P. *Buried in the Sands of the Ogaden: The United States, the Horn of Africa, and the Demise of Détente* (Kent, OH: Kent State University Press, 2013).

Xia, Yafeng. *Negotiating with the Enemy: U.S.–China Talks during the Cold War, 1949–1972* (Bloomington, IN: Indiana University Press, 2006).

Yaqub, Salim. *Containing Arab Nationalism: The Eisenhower Doctrine and the Middle East* (Chapel Hill, NC: University of North Carolina Press, 2004).

Young, Marilyn B. *The Vietnam Wars, 1945–1990* (New York: Harper Collins, 1991).

Zaloga, Steven J. *The Kremlin's Nuclear Sword: The Rise and Fall of Russia's Strategic Nuclear Forces, 1945–2000* (Washington, DC: Smithsonian Institution Press, 2002).

Zhai, Qiang. *China and the Vietnam Wars, 1950–1975* (Chapel Hill, NC: University of North Carolina Press, 2000).

Zhuk, Sergei I. *Rock and Roll in the Rocket City: The West, Identity, and Ideology in Soviet Dniepropetrovsk, 1960–1985* (Baltimore, MD: Johns Hopkins University Press, and Washington, DC: Woodrow Wilson Center Press, 2010).

Zhishua, Shen. *Mao, Stalin, and the Korean War: Trilateral Communist Relations in the 1950s* (London: Routledge, 2013).

Zhushia, Shen and Li, Danui. *After Leaning to One Side: China and its Allies in the Cold War* (Stanford, CA: Stanford University Press, 2011).

Zubok, Vladislav M. *A Failed Empire: The Soviet Union in the Cold War from Stalin to Gorbachev* (Chapel Hill, NC: University of North Carolina Press, 2007).

Zubok, Vladislav M. and Constantine Pleshakov. *Inside the Kremlin's Cold War: From Stalin to Khrushchev* (Cambridge, MA: Harvard University Press, 1996).

INDEX

Acheson, Dean 8, 20
Aden 205
Adenauer, Konrad 56–7, 57–8, 63, 67, 69, 262
Afghanistan 176, 178, 334; American aid 180; American policy 185; American troops in 189; casualties 383; CIA operations 312; destabilization 184–5; the Geneva Accords 187; National Reconciliation 187; and Pakistan 184; the Saur revolution 184, 186; Soviet aid 180; Soviet invasion of 67–8, 84, 114, 178, 185–8, 206, 372; Soviet policy 184–5; Soviet withdrawal 187–8, 188–9, 374; the Taliban 189
Africa 149–60; American aid 159; American interventions 156, 158–9; American policy 152, 154, 155, 158; American support for 155; the Congo Crisis 153; Cuban interventions 156, 157; and détente 205–6; development of Cold War in 149–51; economic collapse 158–9; end of the Cold War in 158–60; European domination 150; GNP 159; labor movements 150; propaganda battle 332; proxy wars 149, 151–5, 155–8, 159–60; radical anticolonialism 151–2; revolutionary movements 153–5; Soviet interventions 155–8, 205–6; Soviet policy 152–3; Soviet support for 155; spread of Communism's influence 149–50, 150–1; Wafd (delegation) movement 151
African National Congress' (ANC) 151, 154, 332, 383
Afro-Asian Movement 80, 82–3, 83
Akhromeev, Sergey 374
Al Qaida 336
Albania 79, 296, 300, 302, 406
Aleksandr Popov (film) 341
Algeria 82, 122, 126, 151, 152, 154, 159
Algerian Front de Libération Nationale 122, 152, 154

Allende, Salvadore 311
Alperovitz, Gar 250
American liberalism 120–1
American Relief Administration (ARA) 22
American Society for Cultural Relations with Russia 325
Americanization 10, 347–8, 405
Amnesty International 238, 239, 241
Anderson, Carol 26
Andrew, Christopher and Mitrokhin, Vasili 313
Andropov, Yuri 373, 374
Anglo-American alliance 18
Angola xvii, 115, 149, 154, 156, 160, 196, 205, 332, 377, 383
Angolan Civil War xviii, 149, 154–5, 156, 205, 383
Annan, Kofi 33
Anti-Ballistic Missile (ABM) Treaty 195, 254, 285
ANZUS pact 37
apartheid 242, 244
Arab Nationalism 167–8
Arab–Israeli peace process 171–2, 204
Arab–Israeli wars 37, 165–6, 169–71, 176, 183, 204, 309, 332
Arafat, Yasser 313
Arbenz, Jacobo 135, 140
Arendt, Hannah 25
Argentina 138, 139
arms control 40, 40–1, 200, 254, 254–5, 257, 276, 282–4, 372, 374
arms race. *see* nuclear weapons
Aron, Raymond 4, 225
assassinations 312, 313
Association of Southeast Asian Nations (ASEAN) 38–9
Atlantic Charter, the 18–9, 95
Atlantic Council 224
atomic diplomacy 250

Index

Atomic Energy Commission (AEC) 252
Attlee, Clement 23
Australia, ANZUS pact 37
Austria 405
authoritative discourse 353
Aydin, Cemil 92
Azikiwe, Nnamdi 150

Bacon, Edwin 355
Baghdad Pact, the 166–7, 181
Bahr, Egon 67, 202
Bailes, Kendall 292
Bakatin, Vadim 316
Bakhtin, Mikhail 353
Balfour Declaration 165
Bandung Conference, 1955 27, 37, 81, 97, 180, 181, 181–2, 331
Bangladesh 81, 183
Barre, Muhammad Siad 156
Baruch, Bernard 251
Basic Principles of Mutual Relations 200
Basic Treaty 67
Bay of Pigs 135, 281, 312
BBC 327, 330, 334, 335, 359
Begin, Menachem 172
Belgian Congo 152, 153
Bennigsen, Alexander 187
Berger, Mark T. 122, 124
Berlin 59; division of 61; East German migration to 63–4; Four Power Treaty 203
Berlin Blockade, the 10–1, 34–5, 61, 276
Berlin Crisis, 1958-61 56–7, 61–6, 195, 201–2, 264, 279–80, 280, 372; the Berlin Wall 65–6; border closed 63–4; Checkpoint Charlie Crisis 66; lessons from 66; stalemate 64–5; Vienna summit 64. *see also* Brandt, Willy.
Berlin Wall 11, 202; Checkpoint Charlie Crisis 66; construction 65–6; fall of 56, 68, 375, 378–9, 395
Berman, Jakub 47
Betancourt, Rómulo 141
Bethe, Hans 250, 252, 257
Bethell, Leslie 134
Bevin, Ernest 11
Big Jim McLain (film) 345
Biggs, David 126
Biko, Steve 242
bin Laden, Osama 189
Bitker, Bruno 240
black markets 407
blame xvii
Bohlen, Charles 35
Bohr, Niels 250–1
Bolivia 138
Bond, James 343, 344
Borgwardt, Elizabeth 18
Boulier, Jean 263, 264, 265

Boym, Svetlana 352, 355
Bozo, Frederic 381
Brands, Hal 135
Brandt, Willy 66, 66–7, 69, 70, 195, 197, 201–3
Brazil 138, 139, 142, 242
Brazinsky, Gregg 126
Bretton Woods agreement 20–1, 404, 408; end of 409–10
Brezhnev, Leonid 80, 84, 156, 171, 185, 195, 198, 200, 202, 204, 205, 206, 285, 286–7, 326, 334, 354–6
Brezhnev Doctrine 198–9, 209, 226, 231, 233
Bricker Amendment 238
Briggs, Raymond, *When the Wind Blows* 334
British Council, the 327, 333
British Information Service 327
Brodie, Bernard 275
Brooks, Jeffrey 351
Brown, Kate 356
Bruce, David 64
Brussels, Treaty of 11–2
Brzezinski, Zbigniew 155
Bulgaria, and the Sino-Soviet rift 79
Bull, Hedley 40
Bunche, Ralph 100
Burke, Roland 240
Bush, George H. W. 68, 335, 378–9, 381, 395
Byrne, Jeffrey James 126

Caamaño, Francisco 142
Calles, Plutarco Elías 138
Cambodia 84, 113, 210
Cambodian genocide 243
Camp David Peace accords 172
Campaign for Nuclear Disarmament 334
Carter, Jimmy 84, 155, 158, 172, 173, 175, 185, 185–6, 187, 205, 205–6, 232, 243, 243–4, 286–7, 333, 375, 396
Castro, Fidel xviii, 39, 140–1, 143, 281, 312
Catholic Church 259–69, 393; activist shift 261; American influence 264, 268–9; anti-Communism 260, 260–1, 262, 268, 269–70; and the Cuban Missile Crisis 264–5; excommunication decree 262–3; interfaith dialogue 267; John Paul II's papacy 259, 260, 266–9, 269–70; John XXIII's papacy 264–5; and liberation theology 268; modernization 259, 260, 266; and nuclear weapons 265; *Ostpolitik* 260, 265, 267; Paul VI's papacy 265–6; Pius XII's papacy 261–4, 269; *Populorum Progressio* 266; role of 259, 260, 270; Second Vatican Council 259, 264, 266, 267, 268; Soviet bloc 262–3; Soviet Bloc organizations 263; and World War II 261–2
Catholic Communism 263, 264
Catholic Relief Services (CRS) 23, 389–90, 390–1, 392

Index

Central America 143
Central Treaty Organization (CENTO) 37, 181
Certeau, Michel de 353
Chaplin, Charlie 347
Charter 77 203, 241, 245, 379
Chavez, Hugo 143
Chen Jian 97
Chenaux, Philippe 262
Cherednichenko, Tatyana 353–4
Chernenko, Konstantin 373
Chernobyl disaster 381
Chernyshova, Natalya 356
Chile 133, 138, 140–1, 141, 242, 332
China, People's Republic of: African policy 154, 156; alliance with Soviet Union 77; American investment in 411; Cultural Revolution 38, 76, 78, 113, 411; development model 118; establishment of 12–3; foreign policy 78, 209, 210; foundation of 97; Four Marshals' Study Group 210; Great Leap Forward 38, 75–6, 79, 81; and human rights 244; Kissinger's secret visit 213–6; Korean policy 216–7, 217–8; and the Korean War 35; the Lin Biao Incident 215; Nixon visits 84, 214, 216, 217–8, 218; and the nonaligned movement (NAM) 37; nuclear weapons 82, 280–1, 283, 284; and Pakistan 182–3; and Poland 51, 54; propaganda 326; Sino-American rapprochement 74, 81, 84, 183, 200, 209–18, 285; Sino-Indian friendship 182; Soviet support for 77; stabilization of politics 210; support for North Korea 38; Taiwan policy 214, 216; technological development 299; technological transfers 300; Third World policy 81–3; Third World propaganda 332; Tiananmen Square protests 244; trade policy 83; UN Security Council membership 95; and the Vietnam War 76, 108, 112, 113; Warsaw talks 211. *see also* Sino-Soviet rift
Christian Democratic movements 262
Churchill, Winston 18–9, 46, 95, 324
CIA: covert action 305, 310–2; front organizations 312; historiography 313–4; Humint 308; Poland policy 390; propaganda 328, 329; technological developments 308
cinema. *see* film and the film industry
cinematic diplomacy 346
Circus, The (film) 342
Civil Rights Movement 26, 101, 150, 329, 330
Cleveland, Harlan 100
coca-colonization 405
Cohen, G. Daniel 30n63
Cohen, Stephen F. 351
Cold War studies xviii–xix
collective security 19, 33
colonialism 91–2, 99; and decolonization 126; legacies 178

Combined Food Board 22
Comecon 299, 301
Cominform 9, 47
Comintern 133, 138–9, 151, 325
Commission on Security and Cooperation in Europe 379
Common Market, the 36
Commoner, Barry 253
communism: as monolith 13; in Soviet satellite states 45–54
Communist Information Bureau 325
Conference on Questions of Economic Development, Cairo, 1962 118, 127
Conference on Security and Cooperation in Europe 203, 206, 223–33; caucuses 228; Concluding Document 232; Confidence Building Measures 231–2; continuation of process 232; delegations 223; and détente 224–9; EEC and 229–30; and the fall of communism 224; Final Act 223, 224, 225, 226–8, 230, 231, 232, 233, 240–1, 256; Helsinki Accords 203, 205, 206, 334, 379; and human rights 240–1, 244–5; Madrid meeting 232; Multilateral Preparatory Talks (MPT) 223; neutral and non-aligned countries 231–2; Principle I 226; Principle II 226; Principle III 226; Principle VII 227, 228; Principle VIII 226; Second Basket provisions 227; Third Basket provisions 225, 227, 229, 230, 231; Vienna Concluding Document 244–5
confrontation, move from collaboration to 6–9
Congo 155
Congo Crisis, the 153
Congregation of the Doctrine of the Faith 268
Congress for Cultural Freedom 329
Congress on the Mutual Security Program 27
Connelly, Matthew 122, 123, 154
consumer desires 292; competition 293–5, 301–2; propaganda 295
consumer socialism 406–8
consumerism 401; American model 404–6; and the end of the Cold War 411–3; social democratic 403–4; Soviet model 406–8
consumption 292, 294, 404–6, 406–8. *see also* cultural consumption
containment 34, 165, 206
Contras, the 312, 377
Cooper, Frederick 96
Cooperative for American Remittances to Europe (CARE) 23
Coordinates of Death (film) 343
Coordinating Committee for Multilateral Export Controls (CoCom) 298
Côte d'Ivoire 159
Council for Mutual Economic Aid (Comecon) 299, 301
Council for Mutual Economic Assistance 27

Council of Europe 35
Cox, Michael 381
Cranes Are Flying, The (film) 346
Cuba 134, 139, 196–7; African interventions 156, 157; Cienfuegos crisis 204; survival 143–4
Cuban Missile Crisis xviii, 39, 40, 66, 133, 195, 197, 254, 264, 264–5, 275–6, 281–2, 316, 372
Cuban Revolution 140–2, 331
Cullather, Nick 22, 100, 122–3, 126, 179–80
cultural Cold War 295
cultural consumption 352–6; Brezhnev era 354–6; and détente 359–60; film and the film industry 357–8; ideological pollution 360; music 352, 353, 359–62; mythologies of everyday life 355; radio 358–9; television 357–8; youth cultures 352, 354; Yurchak's study 352–3, 353–4
cultural diplomacy 163
cultural egalitarianism 405
cultural essentialism 123–5, 127
cultural imperialism 405
cultural studies 352
Cushman, Thomas 352, 353
Czechoslovakia 167, 245; American food aid 24; Catholic Church and 262, 264; consumer socialism 407; coup, 1948 10; invasion of 67, 84, 240, 326; Prague Spring 54, 198; technological development 299–300

Daoud, Mohammed 184–5
Darkest Russia (film) 342
de Gaulle, Charles 63, 66, 83, 152, 197, 201
debt crisis 382, 410
Declaration of a New Asian African Strategic Partnership, 2005 37
decolonization xvii, 37, 82, 91–103, 127, 152–3; America and 91, 94–7, 100–1, 107–8; and capacity building 100–1; and development 118; and human rights 239; impact of 101–3; and imperialism 91–4; and international interdependence 94–8; and Mao Zedong 97; nation-state formation 98–101; and pan-Africanism 99–100; and self-determination 95, 97; self-determination debate 93; and United Nations membership 95–7, 98–9, 100–1
defectors 307–8
DeMille, Cecil B. 344
Democratic People's Republic of Korea 13–4, 38, 216–7, 217–8
Democratic Republic of Vietnam (DRV) 80, 217
Deng Xiaoping 74, 84
dependency theory 101
de-Stalinization 49–50, 53, 75, 353
détente xviii, 102, 155, 195–206; collapse of 185; and CSCE 224–9; and cultural consumption 359–60; European 201–3, 228–9, 230, 232, 233; and the German question 202; impact 195–6; limits 205–6; and the Middle East 204–5; Moscow Summit 201, 204; and nuclear weapons 255; origins 196–7; and propaganda 333–4; Reagan's critique 375–6; Soviet conceptions of 197–201; and the Third World 203–6
developed socialism theory 355
development and development aid 26–7, 118–27; America and 120–2, 122–3, 126, 408–9; American aid 119, 119–20; American model 118, 120; and American racism 124–5; and anti-colonialism 126; communist models 118; cultural essentialism 123–5, 127; and decolonization 118; funding 123; global analysis 125–7; as a global discourse 121–2; global turn toward 118–9; modernization discourse 127; national 122–3; Nile valley 125–6; objectives 123; rapid 118; regional analysis 125–6; Soviet aid 119, 408–9; superpower competition 119; transnational 122–3; underdevelopment problem 119; universalism 123–5, 127
Diamond Arm, The (film) 344
Diem, Ngo Dinh 106, 108–10
Dien Bien Phu, Battle of 108
Disarmament Committee 40
Dniepropetrovsk 356
Dobrynin, Anatoly 198, 199, 205
Dominican Republic 141
domino theory 64, 109, 198
Doolittle Report 311
Dr No (film) 343
Dubois, W.E.B. 92, 97, 150
Dudziak, Mary 328
Dulles, Allen 312
Dulles, John Foster 51, 181, 202
Dumbarton Oaks conference 19–20
Dunham, Vera 351

economic collapse, Third World 158–9
economic discrepancies 301–2
economic interdependence 4–5
economic management 17
economic security 34
Eden, Anthony 19
Edsall, John 256
Egypt 82–3, 98, 150, 151–2; Arab–Israeli war, 1967 169; Aswan High Dam 126, 152, 167; Camp David Peace accords 172; development policy 127; Nile valley development 125–6; revolution 166–7; war of attrition 204; Yom Kippur War 170–1. *see also* Nasser, Gamal Abdel; Sadat, Anwer
Ehrenburg, Ilya 265
Einstein, Albert 253
Eisenhower, Dwight D. 54, 60–1, 61, 63, 64, 98, 109, 111, 153, 166, 167, 168, 197, 202, 253, 277, 279, 328–9, 405
Eisenhower Doctrine 167–8

Ekbladh, David 120
El Salvador 139, 143
Élysée Friendship Treaty 66
Empire 91–2
end of the Cold War debate 371, 371–84; and American defense build-up 376–7; America's role 375–9, 396; dating 380; development 372–84; Europe's role 381–2; events 372–3; Gorbachev's reforms 373–5; new history 383–4; nuclear freeze campaign 380–1; Third World role 382–3; transnational movements role 379–81
Engelstein, Laura 351
Engerman, David C. 119, 123, 179
Eritrea 149
Escobar, Arturo 121
Ethiopia 149, 157, 205–6
Euromissile crisis 286, 381
Europe: American food aid 23–4; division of 35; end of the Cold War in 381–2; post-war reconstruction 9–12
European Coal and Steel Community 36
European Community (EC) 36
European Convention on Human Rights 25, 30n63, 35
European Court of Human Rights 35
European Defense Community 36
European Economic Community 229–30
European Political Cooperation (EPC) 229, 230
European Security and Defense Policy 36
Evangelista, Matthew 381, 388

Famine Emergency Committee 23
Fanon, Franz 97
fear, freedom from 17, 18–21
Federal Republic of Germany (FRG): Basic Treaty 67; East German migration to 61–2, 63–4; Economic Miracle 59, 297; end of occupation 58; establishment of 11, 52; and the fall of the GDR 69; foundation of 57–8; GDR policy 66–7; joins NATO 36, 58; and the Korean War 57–8; nuclear role 280, 283, 284; nuclear weapons deployed 61, 62; *Ostpolitik* 66–7, 201–3; relations with GDR, 1980s 68; Soviet Treaty of Non-Aggression 67. *see also* Adenauer, Konrad; Bahr, Egon; Brandt, Willy; Hallstein Doctrine
Ferguson, James 121
Fermi, Enrico 250
Ferris, Jose 126
film and the film industry 334, 340–9; Americanization 347–8; cinematic diplomacy 346; cinematic truce 342–3; demonization of America 340; demonization of Soviet Union 340; hybridization 347–8; ideological constraint 344–5; impacts 347–8, 348; interactions 340–1, 344–7; locations 343; negative stereotypes 341–2; and nuclear war 343–4; presences 341, 341–4; propaganda 341; psychological warfare 345, 346; representation 341; Soviet consumption 357–8; Soviet golden age 346–7; Soviet historiography 340; spy films 344; trophy films 348
First Indochina War 106–8
Fish, Hamilton 24
Fitzgerald, Frances 378
Fitzpatrick, Sheila 351
Food and Agriculture Organization (FAO) 22–3, 27, 33
Ford, Gerald R. 156, 205, 225, 229, 243, 312, 375, 376
Ford Foundation 295
Fordism 300
Forsberg, Randall 257
Foucault, Michel 353
Four Power Treaty 202, 203
France: decolonization 95, 96; détente 201; Fall of 46; First Indochina War 106–8; intervention in Lebanon 174–5; nuclear weapons 40, 280, 283, 284; and the Sino-Soviet rift 83; withdrawal from NATO 284. *see also* de Gaulle, Charles
free trade 404
freedom: essential 17; from fear 17, 18–21; from want 17, 21–5
free-market ideology 409–11
Frei, Eduardo 141
Fukuyama, Francis 401, 413
Fulbright, William 324

Gaddis, John Lewis 237
Gandhi, Indira 183, 186
Gandhi, Rajiv 188
Gasperi, Alcide De 262
Gayte, Marie 269
Gendzier, Irene 124
General Agreement on Tariffs and Trade (GATT) 33
German Democratic Republic (GDR) 279–80; Construction of Socialism program 59; economic discrepancies 302; economic weaknesses 407; end of the Cold War in 382; envy 297; establishment of 11; fall of 68–9, 69; foundation of 57, 58; FRG policy 66–7; Initiative for Peace and Human Rights 245; joins Warsaw Pact 60; living standards 406; migration to West 61–2, 63–4; militarization of border 59, 61–2; propaganda machine 326; recognition 202; relations with FRG, 1980s 68; Republikflucht 63–4; Soviet support for 60, 65; technocratic modernization model 302; uprising, 1953 59–60, 201–2
German question 52, 202
Germany 405; American policy 6; background 56–7; division of 6, 11, 35, 52, 56; end of the Cold War role 381–2; interests 56–7; occupation

of 6, 58; Occupation Statute 58; peace treaty 57, 58, 62; position 56; role of 56–70; and the Sino-Soviet rift 79; Soviet policy 5–6, 6; Stalin proposes neutrality 58–9; strategic situation 60–1; unification 57, 58, 62, 68–9, 70, 375, 379, 382. *see also* Berlin; Federal Republic of Germany (FRG); German Democratic Republic (GDR)
Ghana 101, 152, 155, 159
Giap, Vo Nguyen 107
Gilman, Nils 120
glasnost 68, 388, 413
Gleijeses, Piero 156
Glendon, Mary Ann 25
global economic system 20–1
global finance, rise of 409–11
globalism 4–5
globalization 40, 91, 93, 96, 349
Golovskoy, Valery 357
Goodbye, America (film) 342
Gorbachev, Mikhail 68, 69, 70, 74; background 373–4; beliefs 375, 411–2; Bush meetings 378–9; economic thinking 411–2; human rights policy 379–80; and India 188; John Paul II and 269; nuclear policy 286–8, 374, 381; propaganda 335; reforms 143, 245, 371, 373–5, 388, 408, 411–3; Rejkavik summit 378; Romantic Marxism 411–2; Sino-Soviet relations 84; and the Soviet–Afghan War 187; takes office 373; Third World policy 383; withdrawal from Afghanistan 374
Gorsuch, Anne 355
Goswami, Manu 99
Gowing, Margaret 39
Graham, Loren 292
Grandin, Greg 135
Grazia, Victoria de 404
Great Britain: decolonization 95, 96, 98–9; film and the film industry 344; and the foundation of NATO 11–2; Government Communications Headquarters (GCHQ) 310; imperial preference 20; Information Research Department (IRD) 327; intelligence 305, 307–8, 308–10; Middle East policy 164–6; nuclear weapons 39, 276, 280, 283, 284; post-war situation 3–4, 8; propaganda machine 327; Sigint 308–10; Soviet agents in 306–7; Third World propaganda 330. *see also* Bevin, Ernest; Churchill, Winston; Thatcher, Margaret
Greece 8–9, 12, 36, 123, 165, 239–40
Gromyko, Andrei 198, 199
Guatemala 133, 140, 143, 312
Guevara, Ernesto 'Che' 140, 141
Gulf of Tonkin incident 111
Guinea 152
Gumede, Josiah (J.T.) 151
Gundle, Stephen 405

Hadj, Messali 151
Hague summit 229
Haig, Alexander 390
Haimson, Leopold 351
Hallstein Doctrine of nonrecognition 67
Hanhimaki, Jussi 202
Harrison, Hope M. xviii
Hasegawa, Tsuyoshi 13
Hat, The (film) 341
Havel, Vaclav 203, 245, 407
Hellman, Lilian 347
Helsinki Accords. *see* Conference on Security and Cooperation in Europe
Helsinki Group 241
Helsinki groups 203
Helsinki Watch. *see* transnational groups
High Noon (film) 342
Hiroshima 276
Hitchcock, William 202–3
HIV/AIDS 334
Hixson, Walter J. 340
Ho, Chi Minh 97, 105, 106, 107, 150
Hobson, John 91
Holloway, David 296
Hollywood 341, 342, 344, 347–8
Honecker, Erich 68, 69, 382
Hoover, Herbert 22, 23–4
Hornig, Don 255–6
Hot Springs conference, 1843 21–2
housing shortages 300
Hoxha, Enver 79
Huang, Hua 212
Hughes, Thomas 293
Hull, Cordell 19
human rights 18–9, 19, 25–6, 158, 227, 232, 237–46; in the 1960s 239–40; and aid 243; America and 238, 243, 243–4; and Amnesty International 238; Cambodian genocide 243; China and 244; CSCE and 240–1; and decolonization 239; and the end of the Cold War 244–6; end of the Cold War role 379–80; in the global South 242–3; Greek violations, 1960s 239–40; International Year for Human Rights (IYHR) 240; in Latin America 242; monitoring groups 241; scientific community activism 256; Soviet Bloc 240–1, 244–5; Universal Declaration of Human Rights adoption 237–8; Vienna Concluding Document 244–5
Human Rights Watch 241, 245
humanitarian aid 388–96; impacts 393–6
humanitarianism 23–4
Hungary: Catholic Church and 262, 264; consumer socialism 407; de-Stalinization 75; end of the Cold War in 382; market socialism 406; and the Sino-Soviet rift 79; technological exchanges 298; uprising, 1956 36, 45, 51–3, 264, 329

hunger 22
Hussein, Saddam 173–4, 175, 383

ideological pollution 360
imaginary West, the 353–4
imperial preference 20
imperialism 91–2, 96, 99
imperial-revolutionary paradigm 7
India 95, 178, 189; American policy 179, 188; decolonization 96, 99; development 119; neutralism 181, 182; and the nonaligned movement (NAM) 37; nuclear weapons 40, 184; propaganda battle 331; regional influence 188; relations with Soviet Union 183; Sino-Indian friendship 182; and Sino-Soviet rift 80–1; Soviet policy 179; and the Soviet–Afghan War 186; State of Emergency 183; strategic importance 179; technological transfers 300; wars with Pakistan 37, 81, 182. *see also* Gandhi, Indira; Nehru, Jawarlahal
Indian–Pakistani wars 37, 81, 182
Indonesia 38
industrial espionage 297–8
industrialization 94
intelligence 305–17; analysis 316–7; Black Friday episode 309; cooperation 310; counterintelligence and surveillance 307; covert action 305, 310–3; defectors 307–8; front organizations 312; historiography 313–4; Humint 305, 306–8, 315; ideological agents 307; industrial espionage 297–8; Sigint 305, 308–10; significance 315–7; technological developments 308, 310, 315; the Venona project 306–7, 314; the Walker spy ring 307; World War II 305
Inter-American Development Bank 243
Intermediate Nuclear Forces (INF) Treaty 286, 378
International Atomic Energy Agency (IAEA) 39, 40, 277
International Bank for Reconstruction and Development 21
international bill of rights 20
International Helsinki Federation for Human Rights (IHF) 241
international interdependence 91, 94–8
international law 33
International Monetary Fund (IMF) 21, 33, 159, 243, 404, 410
international order, restoration of 4–5
International Refugee Organization 23
international relations, post-war reform 20
International Year for Human Rights (IYHR) 240
internationalism: core beliefs 17; early Cold War 17–28; freedom from fear 17, 18–21; freedom from want 17, 21–5; limitations 25–8
Invasion of the Body Snatchers (film) 340

Invasion U.S.A. (film) 340
Iran 7, 166, 176, 311
Iran Crisis 164
Iranian Revolution 173–4, 185
Iran-Iraq War 174
Iraq 166, 168, 173–4, 175, 205, 383
Iron Curtain, The (film) 345
Islamism 127
Israel: Arab–Israeli peace process 171–2; Arab–Israeli wars 37, 165–6, 169–71, 183, 204, 309, 332; Camp David Peace accords 172; foundation of 165–6; intervention in Lebanon 174–5; war of attrition 204; Yom Kippur War 170–1. *see also* Begin, Menachem; Meir, Golda
Italy 23–4, 311

Jackson, Henry 240
Jacobs, Matthew F. 124
Jacobs, Seth 125
Jalal, Ayesha 186
Japan 40, 83, 93, 405
Jaruzelski, Wojciech 389, 390, 394, 396
Jersild, Austin 298–9
John Paul II, Pope 259, 260, 265, 266–9, 269–70, 390
John XXIII, Pope 260, 264–5
Johnson, Lyndon B. 106, 111, 111–2, 159, 197, 198, 396
Joint Four-Nation Declaration, 1943 19
Jordan 168, 170
Joseph, Gilbert M. 135, 138, 141
Josephson, Paul 293, 297
Judt, Tony 3, 23, 24

Kádár, János 52
Kashlev, Yuri 230
Kazakhstan 180
Kazennov, A. 63
Kelly, Catriona 352
Kelly, Patrick 242
Kennan, George F. 7, 34, 39, 136, 165
Kennedy, John F. 197, 202; African policy 152; Alliance for Progress xviii; arms control 283; assassination 313; assassinations 325; and the Berlin Crisis 63, 64, 66; and the Berlin Wall 65; Catholicism 264; Cuban missile crisis 281–2; and development 119, 120; and the NAM 182; nuclear policy 254, 315; propaganda 329; and the Vietnam War 110, 111
Kent, Peter C. 259
Kent, Sherman 313–4
Kenya 159
Keynes, John Maynard 21, 404, 408
KGB: assassinations 313; counterintelligence and surveillance 307; covert action 305, 310, 313; front organizations 312; historiography 314; Humint 306–7, 315; intelligence analysis 316;

Middle East involvement 313; propaganda role 325, 333; Sigint 309, 310
Khmer Rouge 243
Khrushchev, Nikita 45, 48, 51–2, 69, 98, 197, 277, 293; African policy 152–3; arms control 283; and the Berlin Crisis 62–3, 63–4, 64–5, 66; Cuban missile crisis 281; development aid 119; economic model 406; Middle East policy 167; and the NAM 182; nuclear bluff policy 278–80; People's Diplomacy 331; propaganda machine 325–6; Secret Speech 49, 75, 79, 264, 294, 373; and the Sino-Soviet rift 74, 75–6, 78, 80, 280–1; South and Central Asia policy 179, 180; and the Vietnam War 108
Kim Il-sung 217–8, 276–7
King and I, The (musical) 125
Kissinger, Henry A. 67, 102, 113, 156, 171–2, 183, 195, 196, 197, 199, 202, 204–5, 210, 211, 212, 213–6, 216–7, 217–8, 218, 228–9, 230, 242, 243
Kistiakowsky, George 255
Klein, Christina 125
Klubock, Thomas 138
Kohl, Helmut 68, 375, 381
Kopstein, Jeffrey 302
Korean War xviii, 13, 35, 37, 38, 40, 57–8, 80, 97, 98, 108, 276, 276–7
Kosygin, Aleksei 80, 197, 211
Kotkin, Stephen 94
Kozovoi, Andrei 355
Kramer, Paul 95
Krauthammer, Charles 377
Kryuchkov, Vladimir 314, 315
Kuleshov, Lev 348
Kuzmarov, Jeremy 120
Kuznetsov, Vasily 282
Kwan, Heonik 124, 125, 127

LaFeber, Walter 121
Lapp, Ralph 253
Latham, Michael E. 120, 121
Latin America xviii, 33–5, 34, 133–44, 144; American interventions 133, 135, 139–40, 142, 143, 144; American policy 139–40; anti-communism 138, 144; arrival of Marxist thought in 137–8; casualties 135; Central America 143; chronology 137–42; counter-revolutions 141–3; debt crisis 382; defining characteristics of Cold War in 135–6; democratization 134; dictatorships 142–3; human rights in 242; ideological divides 136; impact of the Cuban Revolution on 140–2; international context 139; international relations 144; intra-regional and transnational history 144; liberation theology 268; links to the Soviet Union 133; models of transformative nationalism 141; National Security Doctrine 142; New Cold War Historians and 136; nuclear-free zone 40, 284; propaganda battle 331–2; proxy wars 135; Regional Civil War 136; revolutions 135; sources 134; Soviet interventions 143; and World War II 139
Lawrence, Ernest 251
League Against Imperialism 94, 151
League of Nations 19, 22, 92–4, 121, 150
Lebanon 168, 172, 174–5, 176
Leffler, Melvyn P. 8, 372–84
Leguía, Augusto B. 138
Lenin, Vladimir 93–4, 97, 99, 102, 149
Leo XIII, Pope 259, 260
Lewis, John 197
liberation theology 268
Libya 159
Lightner, Allan 66
Lilienthal, David 251
Lilienthal Plan, the 251
Limited Test Ban Treaty, 1963 40, 254
Lin Biao Incident 215
Lioznova, Tatyana 345
Liss, Sheldon 137
living standards 292, 293–5, 295, 401, 403, 404, 404–5, 405, 406, 406–7
Logevall, Fredrik 111–2
long peace, the 14
Lugard, Frederick 93
Lumumba, Patrice 152, 153
Lundestad, Geir 10

McCarthy, Joseph 328, 347
McCloy, John D. 282
Macmillan, Harold 62–3, 98–9
Mahoney, Michael 126
Malaysia 38
Malenkov, Georgy 278
Malia, Martin 401
Mandela, Nelson 18
Manela, Erez 122
Manhattan Project 250–1, 276, 306
Mansfield, Mike 125
Mao, Zedong 12, 38, 97, 150; and decolonization 97; and Sino-American rapprochement 209, 210, 211, 212, 215–6, 218; and the Sino-Soviet rift 74, 75–6, 77, 78; Third World policy 81–2; and the Vietnam War 108, 112, 113
Marcuse, Herbert 101
Mariam, Mengistu Haile 157
Mariátegui, José Carlos 138
market: American model 404–6; rise of global finance 409–11; Soviet model 401–2, 402–3, 405, 406–8; Soviet reforms 411–3
market socialism 406
Markov, Georgi 313, 334
Marshall, George C. 9, 24
Marshall Plan, the 9–10, 24, 34, 263, 328, 404, 405
Mazower, Mark 25

Measures for the Economic Development of Under-Developed Countries (ECOSOC) 27, 118–9
Medvedev, Zhores 292
Meeting on the Elbe, The (film) 342
Meir, Golda 172
Mexican Revolution, the 137
Mexico 138, 139
Mickiewicz, Ellen Propper 355
Middle East 163–76; American policy 163, 164–6, 168, 171–2, 176, 204–5, 376; American relations with 163; Arab–Israeli wars 37, 165–6, 169–71, 176, 183, 204; the Baghdad Pact 166–7; Cold War legacies 176; containment strategy 165; cultural diplomacy 163; and détente 204–5; development of Cold War in 164–6; Egyptian revolution 166–7; end of the Cold War in 175; instability 163; the Iran Crisis 164; Iranian Revolution 173–4; KGB involvement 313; Lebanese Civil War 172, 174–5; Nasser era 167–8; peace process 171–2, 204; propaganda battle 332–3; Saudi influence 172; scholarship 163; Soviet involvement 163, 164, 167, 168, 169, 170; Soviet policy 176, 205; strategic importance 163, 176; and World War II 164
militarization 33–5
Mindszenty, Jozsef 262, 264
Mission to Moscow (film) 342
Mitchell, Timothy 125–6
Mitrokhin, Vasili 314
Mitterand, François 381
Mlynar, Zdenek 374
modernity 91, 119
modernization theory 124
Molotov, Vyacheslav 19
Monnet, Jean 36, 96
Monroe Doctrine 33, 94, 144
Morgenthau, Henry 20–1
Moro, Aldo 230
Moscow Summit (1972) 200, 204
Moscow Treaty 202–3
Moyn, Samuel 21, 25
Mozambique 126, 158
Mulkerin, Terrance J. 390–1, 391
Multilateral Force (MLF) 283–4
multipolarity 102
Munich Olympics Massacre, 1972 170
Münzenberg, Willi 325
Murrow, Edward R. 329
music 352, 353, 359–62, 407
Muslim Brotherhood 127
mutual and balanced force reduction (MBFR) 224
My Son John (film) 342

Nagasaki 276
Nagy, Imre 52, 53
Namibia 158

Nasser, Gamal Abdel 82–3, 98, 118, 119, 127, 151–2, 166–7, 167–8, 169, 170
National Association for the Advancement of Colored People (NAACP) 26
National Security Doctrine, Latin America 142
national state building 122–3
nationhood, and race 94
nation-state, the 91, 98–101, 102–3
Nehru, Jawarlahal 80–1, 96, 97, 99, 119, 123, 151, 179, 181, 181–2, 331
neocolonialism 101
neo-liberalism 127, 158, 401–13; and the end of the Cold War 411–3; rise of 402–11; rise of global finance 409–11
Neuhaus, Richard John 268
neutralism 181–2
New Cold War Historians 136
New International Economic Order 101–3, 159
New World International Communication Order (NWICO) 333
New Zealand, ANZUS pact 37
Nguyen, Lien-Hang T. 126
Nicaragua 133, 138, 143, 312, 313, 377
Nicholas and Alexandra (film) 343
Niebuhr, Reinhold 35
Nigeria 150, 159
99 Luftballons 334
Ninochka (film) 342
Nitze, Paul 201
Nixon, Richard M. 67, 84, 102, 106, 113–4, 171, 171–2, 183, 204, 256, 293, 375; China visit 84, 214, 216, 217–8, 218; and CSCE 228–9; détente policy 195, 196–7, 199–200, 202; inaugural address 196; Middle East policy 204; Moscow visit 200; nuclear bluff policy 284–5; Sino-American rapprochement 200, 211, 285; Soviet view of 197–8; Warsaw talks 211
Njølstad, Olav 376
Nkrumah, Kwame 99, 101, 119, 151
Nokia 298
Non-Aligned Movement (NAM) 37–9, 82, 99–100, 181–2
nongovernmental organizations (NGOs), end of the Cold War role 388–96
Nonproliferation Treaty (NPT), 1968 40–1, 254, 283–4
Norden, Albert 326
North Atlantic Treaty 11–2
North Atlantic Treaty Organisation (NATO) 26, 35–6, 185, 379; and CSCE 229–30; foundation of 11–2, 34–5; France withdraws 284; FRG joins 58; Nuclear Planning Group (NPG) 284; nuclear strategy 280, 283–4; West Germany joins 36
North Korea. *see* Democratic People's Republic of Korea

Index

North Vietnam. *see* Democratic Republic of Vietnam (DRV)
Novikov, Nikolai 7–8
nuclear disarmament 40, 255
nuclear energy 39
nuclear learning 275
Nuclear Test Ban Treaty, 1962 78–9, 82, 83
nuclear weapons 275–88, 334–5; American bluff policy 284–5; arms control 276, 282–4, 285–6, 286–8; arms race 275, 276–7, 277, 279, 292, 374; and Catholic Church 265; China 82, 280–1, 283, 284; deployed in FRG 61, 62; deployment 275; and détente 255; development 249–54, 275, 276–7, 277; financial burden 199; France 280, 283, 284; freeze campaign 380–1; Great Britain 276, 280, 283, 284; impact of 275; India 184; intelligence 306; Mutually Balanced Force Reduction talks – MBFR 286; NATO strategy 280, 283–4; opposition to 250, 252, 253–4, 265, 334; proliferation 39–41, 184, 277, 280, 283, 285; Pugwash scientists and 253–4, 255; Reagan policy 377–8; scientific community justification of 249; second Cold War deployment 68; Soviet 39, 199, 251, 276–7, 281; Soviet bluff policy 278–80; strategy 40; test ban 254, 279; testing 252, 253, 277–8, 281; threat of 78; US nuclear monopoly ended 12, 251, 276–7
nuclear winter 256–7
Nye, Joseph 395

Ochab, Edward 50
oil 164, 373, 410; OPEC embargo, 1973 159, 171
One World 91, 94–8, 100
OPEC, oil embargo, 1973 159, 171
Oppenheimer, J. Robert 250–1, 252
Organization of African Unity (OAU) 154
Organization for Economic Cooperation and Development 34
Organization for Security and Cooperation in Europe (OSCE) 232
Organization of American States (OAS) 34, 139
Orientalism 123–4, 127
Orlov, Yuri 241
Orr, Sir John Boyd 22
Orwell, George 136; *Animal Farm* 327
Osa, Maryjane 261
Ostpolitik 66–7, 69, 195, 201–3, 224, 229, 260, 265, 267
Oxfam 23

Padmore, Goerge 151
Pakistan 166, 178, 180, 181, 188, 189, 204; and Afghanistan 184, 189; America and 183, 185–6; and China 182–3; nuclear weapons 40, 186; and Sino-Soviet rift 81; and the Soviet-Afghan War 186; wars with India 37, 81, 182; Zia coup 183–4

Palestine, British Mandate 165–6; *Intifada* 175
Palestine Liberation Organization (PLO) 169–70, 172, 174, 175
Palmer, Harry 344
pan-Africanism 91, 99–100, 150
pan-Arabism 167–8
pan-Asianism 91, 92, 100
pan-Islamism 92
Panchsheel Treaty, 1954 37, 97
Paris Agreements, 1954 58
Parsons, Talcott 123
Partial Test Ban Treaty (PTBT) 283
Paul VI, Pope 260, 265–6, 267
Pauling, Linus 253
PAX 263, 264
peaceful coexistence, principle of 54
peacekeeping 33
Penkovsky, Oleg 308, 310, 316
perestroika 68, 388
Perón, Juan Domingo 139
Persian Gulf War (1991) 175, 383
Peru 138
Petrakov, Nikolai 412
Philby, Kim 306
Pierre-Rey, Marie 374
Pilkington, Hilary 352, 355
Ping-Pong diplomacy 211–2
Pinochet, Augusto 242, 332
Pisar, Samuel 225
Pius XI, Pope 260–1
Pius XII, Pope 259, 260, 261–4, 269
Plekhanov, Gregori 324
Pleshakov, Constantine 7
Podgorny, Nikolai 197
Poland 244, 245, 410; American policy 388–96; Bush visits 395; Catholic Church and 262, 264, 265, 266–7, 269; Catholic Church organizations 263; and China 54; communism in 45, 45–6, 46, 47–51, 52–3, 53–4; consumer socialism 407; de-Stalinization 49–50, 53, 75; diaspora 395; economic collapse 389; economic development model 48–9; economic recovery 392; end of the Cold War in 382; foreign policy 54; humanitarian aid 388–96; Hungarian Revolution and 52; John Paul II visits 267; martial law declared 389, 390; Polish Communist Party 46; Polish United Workers' Party (PZPR) 46, 388, 389, 390, 392, 393, 395, 396; political normalization 392; Pope John Paul II visits 245; post-war borders 46; Poznañ riots 54; Poznañ strike, 1956 50; purge, 1951-53 47–8; rehabilitation 53–4; relations with the Soviet Union 48, 51, 52–3, 53–4; relations with the Western democracies 54; revolutionary moment 388; Round Table talks, 1989 395; and the Sino-Soviet rift 79; Solidarity movement in 388–96; Soviet

434

military assistance 54; strikes 389, 395; and the Warsaw Pact 54
Polish American Congress Charitable Foundation (PACCF) 389
Polish United Workers' Party (PZPR) 46, 388, 389, 390, 392, 393, 395, 396
political Islam, rise of 172, 173–4, 175
Pollock, Ethan 293
popular culture 352
Popular Front strategy 139
poverty 121
Poznañ riots 54
Poznañ strike, 1956 50
Prague Spring 54, 198
Project HOPE 391, 392
propaganda 323–36; American 323, 324; China 326; co-creation 333–4; cultural institutes 327; definition 323; and détente 333–4; in the developing world 329–33; film industry 334, 341; and the origins of the Cold War 323–4; radio 326, 327, 328, 334, 335; second Cold War 334–5; Soviet 323, 323–4; Soviet machine 324–6; Soviet outreach 325–6; and sport 325; technological developments 295; Vietnam War 330; wartime 323–4; Western machine 326–9
proxy wars xviii, 135, 149, 151–5, 155–8, 159–60, 185, 195, 266
psychological warfare 293–5, 328–9, 345, 346
Public Group to Promote Fulfillment of the Helsinki Accords 241
Pugwash Movement 253–4, 255, 380
Putin, Vkadimir 336

Quadripartite Agreement, 1971 67

Rabin, Yitzhak 175
Rabinowitch, Eugene 255
race, and nationhood 94
racism 26, 91, 328, 330
Radchenko, Sergey 188
radio broadcasting 326, 327, 328, 334, 335, 358
Radio Free Europe (RFE) 50, 312, 328, 334, 335, 396
Radio Liberty (RL) 312
Radio Moscow 325
Rajagopalan, Sudha 357
Rákosi, Mátyás 52
Rand, Ayn 347
rational consumption 355
Ratzinger, Joseph 268
Reagan, Ronald 68, 158, 159, 175, 185, 186, 188, 201, 245, 266, 268–9, 286, 371, 372–3, 379; background 375–6; end of the Cold War role 375–8, 381; nuclear policy 286–7; Poland policy 390, 391–2, 393, 396
Reagan Doctrine 376–7
Recabarren, Luis 137

Red Dawn (film) 343
Reds (film) 345
refuseniks 240
regionalization 33–5
Rejkavik summit 373, 378
religion 17
religious freedom 245
Republic of Korea 126, 216–7
Republic of Vietnam 108–11
Resident's Mistake, The (film) 343
Reston, James 204
Reuters 327
revisionists xvii
Rhodesia, unilateral declaration of independence 239
Riesman, David 293–4
Right of the First Signature, The (film) 345
Rist, Gilbert 121, 127
Roberto, Holden 154
rock-n-roll culture 353
Rocky IV (film) 343
Rodney, Walter 101
rogue states 40
Rokossovky, Konstantin 51
Romania 226; and CSCE 231–2; debt crisis 410; and the Sino-Soviet rift 79–80
Romantic Marxism 411–2
Romney, Mitt 336
Roosevelt, Franklin D. 17, 18, 21, 33, 46, 107, 404
Rostow, Walter W. 120
Rotblat, Joseph 250–1, 253–4, 255
Roth-Ey, Kristin 356–9
Roxborough, Ian 134
Rusk, Dean 112
Russell, Bertrand 253
Russian Question, The (film) 345
Russian Revolution 137
Russians Are Coming, the Russians Are Coming, The (film) 343
Rustow, Dankwart A. 123
Ryback, Timothy 355
Ryzhkov, Nikolai 411–2

Sadat, Anwar 170–1, 172
Sagan, Carl 256–7, 257, 380
Said, Edward 123–4
Sakharov, Andrei 243
Sandino, Augusto César 138
Sarotte, Mary Louise 375
Saudi Arabia 172
Sayre, Nora 340
Sayward, Amy L. 21
Schabowski, Günter 68
Schlesinger, Arthur 408
Schmidt, Helmut 68, 286
Schmitt, Carl 94, 97
Schmitz, David 243

Schuman, Robert 262
Schuman Plan 36, 263
Schwartz, Thomas Alan 198
scientific community: cooperation calls 255; empowerment 249; human rights activism 256; justification of actions 249; moral responsibilities 250; opposition to nuclear weapons 250, 252, 253–4, 256–7; role of 249–57; Vietnam War and 255–6
scientism 22
Scott, James C. 121–2, 149
Scowcroft, Brent 378
SEATO 37
second Cold War 67–8, 334–5, 372, 410
Second Vatican Council 259, 264, 266, 267, 268
security dilemma 8
security studies 40
self-determination 25, 93, 95, 97, 105
Seventeen Moments of Spring (film) 343
Shanghai Communiqué, the 218
Shcharansky, Anatoly 240
Shebarshin, Leonid 384
Shelepin, Alexander 315
Shlapentokh, Dmitry and Vladimir 355
Shultz, George P. 245
Siddiqi, Asif 293
Siemens 298
Sikkink, Kathryn 242
Simpson, Bradley 127, 239
Sino-American rapprochement 74, 81, 84, 183, 200, 209–18
Sino-Indian War, 1962 81
Sino-Soviet rift 13, 37–8, 74–85, 97, 178, 183, 196, 197, 210, 278; and the Afro-Asian world 81–3; causes 76–9; Chinese propaganda 326; course of 75–6; and détente 198; and India 80–1; military clashes 285; normalization 84; and nuclear weapons 280–1; and Pakistan 81; and the socialist world 79–80; and the Vietnam War 105, 106, 107; and the Western world 83–4
Smuts, Jan 19
Snyder, Sarah B. 380, 388
social engineering, state-initiated 122
Socialist messianism 7
soft power 294, 388–96
Solidarity 203, 244, 245, 269, 382, 388, 389, 390, 391, 392, 395
Solzhenitsyn, Aleksandr 225
Somalia 156, 157, 205–6
South Africa 151, 156, 158, 242, 244, 332
South and Central Asia 178–89; American policy 178, 179–80, 182–3, 187; development of Cold War in 179–80; end of the Cold War in 188–9; legacies of colonialism 178; the long 1970s 182–5; nonaligned movement (NAM) 181–2; periods 178; Soviet policy 178, 179, 180; Soviet–Afghan War 185–8

South East Asian Treaty Organization (SEATO) 181
South Korea. *see* Republic of Korea
South Vietnam. *see* Republic of Vietnam
Soviet consumerism 354–5
Soviet Jewry 379
Soviet studies 351–62; Brezhnev era 354–6; cultural consumption 352–6; development of 351–2; film and the film industry 357–8; media 356–62; and music 352, 359–62; radio 358; revisionist school 351; television 358–9; youth cultures 352, 354; Yurchak's study 352–3, 353–4
Soviet Union 343; Afghanistan policy 184–5; African interventions 155–8, 205–6; African policy 151, 152–3; aid to Afghanistan 180; alliance with China 77; American nuclear first strike fears 315–6; American strategic embargo 298; and Arab–Israeli wars 169, 170, 171; and the Berlin Crisis 64–5; breakdown of relations with America 6–9; Central Asia 180; collapse of xviii, 69, 114, 127, 143, 188–9, 382, 401, 413; conceptions of détente 197–201; consumer socialism 406–8; covert action 313; and CSCE 228–9, 230; development aid 27, 119, 408–9; development model 118; development of a second society 245; domestic reconstruction 5; economic development model 48–9; economic discrepancies 301–2; economic model 401–2, 402–3, 405, 406–8; economic reforms 411–3; economic weaknesses 373, 401, 407; extraction of reparations 24–5; film and the film industry 340, 341, 341–2, 344, 344–5, 345, 346–7, 347–8; film consumption 357–8; financial burden 199; first atomic test 12, 39; German policy 5–6, 6; hegemony 78; Helsinki Group 241; housing shortages 300; and human rights 240–1, 244–5, 256; imperialist ambitions 7; India policy 179; industrial espionage 297–8; intelligence 305, 306–7, 309, 310, 313, 315–7; invasion of Afghanistan 67–8, 84, 114, 178, 185–8, 206, 372; Jewish population 379; Kennan on 7; Latin American interventions 143; Latin American links 133; living standards 406–7; Marxist ideology 35; media studies 356–62; Middle East involvement 163, 164, 167, 168, 169, 170; Middle East policy 176, 205; military strength 3, 60; military-industrial complex 296, 373; monolithic model 351; music 353, 359–62, 407; Muslim population 187, 206; and the NAM 182; NGO influence on 388; nuclear bluff policy 278–80; nuclear strategy 40; nuclear weapons 39, 199, 251, 276–7; nuclear weapons tests 281; opposition to nuclear weapons 254; outreach program 325–6; peace offensive 278; Poland policy 389; post-war European policy 9–12; post-war objectives 5–6; post-war weakness 3–4; propaganda 323, 323–4,

333, 335–6; propaganda machine 324–6; as propaganda state 357; Public Group to Promote Fulfillment of the Helsinki Accords 241; radio 358; relations with India 183; relations with Poland 48, 51, 52–3, 53–4; and Saddam Hussein 174; satellite states 45–54; scientific dissidents 256; security interests 8; Sigint 309, 310; and Sino-American rapprochement 211; South and Central Asia policy 178, 179, 180; Soviet studies view of 351–62; Soviet–Yugoslav rift 10, 45, 47; spheres of influence 5, 45–54; support for Africa 155; support for China 77; support for GDR 60, 65; technological advancements 61; technological assistance 300–1; technological development model 295–7; technological superiority 294–5; technological transfers 298–9; Third World failure 382–3; Third World propaganda 329, 330–1, 331, 332; and the Vietnam War 108, 112, 114, 196–7; view of Nixon 197–8; Westernization of visual culture 359; withdrawal from Afghanistan 187–8, 188–9, 374; youth cultures 352, 354. *see also* Sino-Soviet rift

Sovietization 10

Sovietologists. *see* Soviet studies

space race, the 252–3, 281, 293, 294–5, 326

spheres of influence, Soviet 5, 45–54

sporting diplomacy 325

Sputnik 252, 293, 294–5

Spy, Stand Up (film) 344

Spy Who Came in from the Cold, The (film) 344

spying. *see* intelligence

Sri Lanka 188

Stalin, Iosif 5, 7, 10, 19, 24–5, 33; African policy 151; and the Berlin Blockade 34–5; and the Berlin Crisis 61; death 38, 45, 47, 48, 51–2, 167, 179, 406; economic model 402, 403; election speech 323–4; and the film industry 341; Germany proposals 58–9; Middle East policy 164; nuclear policy 276; and Poland 46; purges 325, 347

Starr, Frederick 355

Stehle, Hansjakob 260

Stevenson, Adlai 249–57

Stimson, Henry 250

Stites, Richard 351, 352, 355

Stockholm Appeal, the 265

Stoessel, Walter 211

Storey, John 352

Storm Center (film) 342

Strataegic Arms Limitation Talks 333

Strategic Arms Limitation Treaty (SALT I) 285–6

Strategic Arms Limitation Treaty (SALT II) 185, 195, 201, 206, 254, 286–7

strategic arms reduction treaty (START) 288

Strategic Defense Initiative (SDI) 257, 269, 287, 288, 373, 378

strategic situation, post World War II 3–4

Suez Crisis 98, 151, 152, 167, 167–8, 176, 279

Sukarno 38, 82

Syria 168, 170–1, 172

Szilard, Leo 250–1

Taiwan 38, 214, 216

Tajikistan 180

Tanganyika 155

Taylorism 300

technological developments 292–302; American model 295, 297; American strategic embargo 298; American superiority 293–5; borrowings 297; competition 293–5, 301–2; consumption 292; exchanges 297, 297–300; housing 300; intelligence 308, 310, 315; literature 292–3; propaganda 295; role of 293; scientific community and 249–57; Soviet model 295–7; Soviet superiority 294–5

television, Soviet 358–9

Teller, Edward 250, 251, 253, 257, 378

terrorist attacks, 9/11 189

Tesla, Nikola 341

Thatcher, Margaret 158, 245, 372, 379, 381

Third World xviii, 36–7; debt crisis 410; and détente 203–6; economic collapse 158–9; end of the Cold War in 382–3; propaganda battle 329–33

Thorez, Maurice 261

Tito, Josif 10, 46–7, 79, 127

Tooze, Adam 91–2

Torre, Haya de la 138

torture 242

Touré, Ahmed Sékou 152

transnational development 122–3

transnational movements, end of the Cold War role 379–81; Helsinki Watch 241, 379. *see also* nuclear weapons, opposition to; scientific community

Truman, Harry S. xvii, 8–9, 13, 14, 23, 24, 33, 97, 108, 250, 324; American policy 6; inaugural address 26–7, 121; Middle East policy 165; nuclear policy 276; Point Four program xviii, 119, 121; propaganda policy 328

Truman Doctrine xvii, 9, 136, 165, 324, 342

Tumarkin, Nina 355

Turkey 7, 8–9, 12, 36, 165, 166, 176

Two Plus Four Agreement 68, 379

U-2 reconnaissance plane incident 201, 254, 308, 317

Ulbricht, Walter 56–7, 57, 58–9, 59–60, 69; and the Berlin Crisis 62–3, 63–4, 65, 66; and the Berlin Wall 65–6; economic policy 406; and *Ostpolitik* 67

underdevelopment problem 119

UNESCO 23, 325, 333

Union Internationale des Architectes, congresses 298
United Arab Republic (UAR) 168
United Nations: agencies 33; aims 33; and America 33; Charter 19; and collective security 33; Commission on Human Rights 20; Commission on the Status of Women 20; creation of 19–20; decline 32; Economic and Social Council (ECOSOC) 20, 27; General Assembly resolutions 19–20; Human Rights Commission 237–8; International Year for Human Rights (IYHR) 240; and the Korean War 13–4; membership and decolonization 95–7, 98–9, 100–1; peacekeeping 33; Special Committee on Apartheid 239; Special Committee on Decolonization 239; trusteeship system 95–6, 100
United Nations International Children's Emergency Fund 23
United Nations Relief and Rehabilitation Agency (UNRRA) 23
United Nations Security Council: Chinese membership 95; permanent members 19, 32; Resolution 217 239; Resolution 242 169, 171–2; resolutions 20; veto 20
United States Information Agency (USIA) 328, 329, 329–30, 334, 336
United States International Communication Agency (USICA) 333
United States of America: Act of Chapultepec 33; in Afghanistan 189; Afghanistan policy 185; African interventions 156, 158–9; African policy 151, 152, 154, 155, 158; aid 100, 159, 179–80, 388–96; and Arab–Israeli wars 169, 171; bases 4; and the Berlin Crisis 64; breakdown of relations with Soviet Union 6–9; and Cambodian genocide 243; Catholic Church influence 264, 268–9; cinematic diplomacy 346; Cold War Consensus 111–2; and the Congo Crisis 153; containment strategy 34, 165, 206; Coordinating Committee for Multilateral Export Controls (CoCom) 298; covert action 310–2; and CSCE 228–9, 230; cultural essentialism 124; and decolonization 91, 94–7, 100–1, 107–8; defense budget 376; defense build-up 376–7; deploys nuclear weapons in FRG 61; détente policy 102; and development 120–2, 122–3, 126; development aid 118–8, 119, 408–9; development assistance 27; development model 118, 120; Doolittle Report 311; economic model 404–6; and economic security 34; end of the Cold War role 375–8, 396; film and the film industry 340, 341, 342, 343, 344, 345, 347, 348–9; GDP 4; German policy 6; global economic integration 97; global strategy 14; Good Neighbor Policy 139; hegemony 95, 102; House Committee on Un-American Activities (HUAC) 347–8; and human rights 238, 243, 243–4; humanitarianism 23–4; impact of aid program 393–6; Indian policy 179, 188; industrial innovations 300; intelligence 305, 307–8, 308–10, 310–2, 315–6; intervention in Lebanon 174–5; interventionism 133; investment in China 411; Jackson-Vanik Amendment 240, 379; Korean policy 216–7; Latin American interventions 133, 135, 139–40, 142, 143, 144; Latin American policy 139–40; Manifest Destiny 120, 125; Middle East policy 163, 164–6, 168, 171–2, 176, 204–5, 376; military strength 60; military-industrial complex 253, 279, 283; missile gap 279, 315; and the NAM 181–2; National Science Foundation 295; National Security Agency (NSA) 309; national security state 34; New Look policy 60; nuclear bluff policy 284–5; nuclear monopoly ended 12, 39, 251, 276–7; nuclear strategy 40; nuclear weapons 39, 276–7; nuclear weapons development 249–57; nuclear weapons tests 277–8; opposition to nuclear weapons 250, 252, 253–4, 256–7; and Pakistan 183, 185–6; Peace Corps 330; personal income 294; Poland policy 388–96; Polish population 395; positive image 393; post-war objectives 4–5; post-war strength 3–4; President's Science Advisory Committee (PSAC) 252–3, 254, 255, 256; propaganda 323, 324, 336; propaganda machine 327–9; psychological warfare 328–9; racism 124–5, 328, 330; return of isolationism 5; rise of global finance 409–11; and Saddam Hussein 174; scientific community 249–57; scientific tensions 255–6; security interests 8; Sigint 308–10; Sino-American rapprochement 74, 81, 84, 183, 200, 209–18, 285; and the Sino-Soviet rift 78–9; Smith-Mundt Act 328; soft power 388–96; South and Central Asia policy 178, 179–80, 182–3, 187; Soviet agents in 306–7; Soviet analysis of 7–8; and the Soviet–Afghan War 187, 187–8; State Department 123; strategic embargo 298; superiority 4; support for Africa 155; support for anti-communist freedom fighters 377; Taiwan policy 216; Technical Cooperation Administration 26–7; technological development model 295–7; technological developments propaganda 295; technological superiority 293–5; Third World propaganda 329–30, 331–3; and the UN 33; and the Vietnam War 106, 107–8, 109–11, 111–3, 113–4, 209; Vietnam War legacy 113–4; Warsaw talks 211; withdrawal from Vietnam 212, 214, 216
Universal Declaration of Human Rights (UDHR) 25–6, 33, 237, 237–8, 240
universalized development 91
Uruguay 138, 242

U.S. dollar 21, 409
USAID 389
Ussuri River incident 198, 210

Vandenberg, Arthur H. 324
Vargas, Getulio 139
Vassiliev, Alexander 314
Venezuela 141
Versailles Peace Conference 150
Vietnam War xvii, 54, 76, 101, 105–15, 110, 126, 196–7, 209, 284–5; America and 106, 107–8, 109–11, 113–4; American withdrawal 212, 214, 216; Americanization 111–3; anti-government insurgency 110; the August Revolution 106–7; division of Vietnam 108–11; domino theory 109; the French War 106, 106–8; Geneva Accords 108; historians and 106; legacies 113–4; origins 106–7; Paris Agreement on Ending the War and Restoring Peace 113; peace negotiations 112, 113–4; propaganda 330; scientific community and 255; the sect crisis 110; self-immolations 111; and the Sino-Soviet rift 80, 105, 106, 107; Soviet Union and 108; Tonkin Gulf incident 111
Voice of America 327, 328, 329, 334, 335, 359
VOKS 325
Volcker, Paul 410
Vucinich, Alexander 292

wage differentials 403
Wagnleitner, Reinhold 405
Walesa, Lech 203, 245, 392, 395
Walk East on Beacon (film) 342
Walker, Vanessa 243
Wallerstein, Immanuel 102, 154
want, freedom from 17, 21–5
War and Peace (film) 346
Warsaw Pact: Budapest Appeal 224; foundation of 12, 36; GDR joins 60; nuclear strategy 40; Poland and 54
Warsaw Treaty 203

Washington consensus 382, 410
Weigel, George 259, 267, 268
Weitz, Eric 92
Welles, Sumner 96
West Germany. *see* Federal Republic of Germany
Westad, Odd Arne 119, 126, 136, 149, 150, 295, 408
Western European Union 11–2
White, Anne 355
White, Hayden 344
Williams, William Appleman 121
Willkie, Wendell 95
Wilson, Woodrow 22, 149, 150, 151
Woodroofe, Louise P. 205–6
World Bank 21, 33, 121, 243, 404, 410
World Health Organization 23, 33
world revolution 78
World Trade Organization 33
World War I 149
World War II 3–4, 4–6, 18–9, 46, 97, 107, 139, 164, 261–2, 276, 300, 305, 323–4
WORLDNET 334
Wyszyñski, Stefan 262

Yalta Conference 46
Yom Kippur War 170–1
Youngblood, Denise 351, 355
youth cultures 352, 354
Yugoslavia 127, 226, 406; Soviet–Yugoslav rift 10, 45, 46–7, 79
Yurchak, Alexei 352–3, 353–4, 407

Zaghlul, Sa'd 151
Zaire 153
Zawieyski, Jerzy 265
Zhang Wenjin 212
Zhang Ying 213
Zhdanov, Andrei 329
Zhou, Enlai 80–1, 82–3, 97, 209–18
Zubkova, Elena 354
Zubok, Vladislav M. 7, 29n26, 354